THE PARALLAX VIEW

SHORT CIRCUITS
Slavoj Žižek, editor

THE PARALLAX VIEW

Slavoj Žižek

THE MIT PRESS   CAMBRIDGE, MASSACHUSETTS   LONDON, ENGLAND

MIT Press books may be purchased at special quantity discounts for business or sales promotional use. For information, please email special_sales@mitpress.mit.edu or write to Special Sales Department, The MIT Press, 55 Hayward Street, Cambridge, MA 02142.

This book was set in Joanna and Copperplate by Graphic Composition, Inc.
Printed and bound in the United States of America.

Library of Congress Cataloging-in-Publication Data

Žižek, Slavoj.
    The parallax view / Slavoj Žižek.
        p. cm. — (Short circuits)
    Includes bibliographical references (p.) and index.
    ISBN 0-262-24051-3 (alk. paper)
    1. Philosophy. I. Title. II. Series.

B4870.Z593P37 2006
199'.4973—dc22

                                                                    2005051704

10 9 8 7 6 5 4 3

para Analia, el axioma de mi vida

CONTENTS

A short circuit occurs when there is a faulty connection in the network—faulty, of course, from the standpoint of the network's smooth functioning. Is not the shock of short-circuiting, therefore, one of the best metaphors for a critical reading? Is not one of the most effective critical procedures to cross wires that do not usually touch: to take a major classic (text, author, notion), and read it in a short-circuiting way, through the lens of a "minor" author, text, or conceptual apparatus ("minor" should be understood here in Deleuze's sense: not "of lesser quality," but marginalized, disavowed by the hegemonic ideology, or dealing with a "lower," less dignified topic)? If the minor reference is well chosen, such a procedure can lead to insights which completely shatter and undermine our common perceptions. This is what Marx, among others, did with philosophy and religion (short-circuiting philosophical speculation through the lens of political economy, that is to say, economic speculation); this is what Freud and Nietzsche did with morality (short-circuiting the highest ethical notions through the lens of the unconscious libidinal economy). What such a reading achieves is not a simple "desublimation," a reduction of the higher intellectual content to its lower economic or libidinal cause; the aim of such an approach is, rather, the inherent decentering of the interpreted text, which brings to light its "unthought," its disavowed presuppositions and consequences.

And this is what "Short Circuits" wants to do, again and again. The underlying premise of the series is that Lacanian psychoanalysis is a privileged instrument of such an approach, whose purpose is to illuminate a standard text or ideological formation, making it readable in a totally new way—the long history of Lacanian interventions in philosophy, religion, the arts (from the visual arts to the cinema, music, and literature), ideology, and politics justifies this premise. This, then, is not a new series of books on psychoanalysis, but a series of "connections in the Freudian field"—of short Lacanian interventions in art, philosophy, theology, and ideology.

"Short Circuits" intends to revive a practice of reading which confronts a classic text, author, or notion with its own hidden presuppositions, and thus reveals its disavowed truth. The basic criterion for the texts that will be published is that they effectuate such a theoretical short circuit. After reading a book in this series, the reader should not simply have learned something new: the point is, rather, to make him or her aware of another—disturbing—side of something he or she knew all the time.

Slavoj Žižek

THE PARALLAX VIEW

INTRODUCTION

DIALECTICAL MATERIALISM AT THE GATES

Two remarkable stories were reported in the media in 2003.

A Spanish art historian uncovered the first use of modern art as a deliberate form of torture: Kandinsky and Klee, as well Buñuel and Dalí, were the inspiration behind a series of secret cells and torture centers built in Barcelona in 1938, the work of a French anarchist, Alphonse Laurenčič (a *Slovene* family name!), who invented a form of "psychotechnic" torture: he created his so-called "colored cells" as a contribution to the fight against Franco's forces.[1] The cells were as inspired by ideas of geometric abstraction and surrealism as they were by avant-garde art theories on the psychological properties of colors. Beds were placed at a 20-degree angle, making them near-impossible to sleep on, and the floors of the 6-foot-by-3-foot cells were strewn with bricks and other geometric blocks to prevent the prisoners from walking backward and forward. The only option left to them was staring at the walls, which were curved and covered with mind-altering patterns of cubes, squares, straight lines, and spirals which utilized tricks of color, perspective, and scale to cause mental confusion and distress. Lighting effects gave the impression that the dizzying patterns on the wall were moving. Laurenčič preferred to use the color green because, according to his theory of the psychological effects of various colors, it produced melancholy and sadness.

The second story: Walter Benjamin did not kill himself in a Spanish border village in 1940 out of fear that he would be returned to France, and thus to Nazi agents—he was killed there by Stalin's agents.[2] A few months before he died, Benjamin wrote "Theses on the Philosophy of History," his short but devastating analysis of the failure of Marxism; he died at a time when many former Soviet loyalists were becoming disillusioned with Moscow because of the Hitler-Stalin pact. In response, one of the "killerati" (Stalinist agents recruited from socialist intellectuals who were carrying out assassinations) killed him. The ultimate cause of his murder was that, as Benjamin fled through the mountains from France toward Spain, he was hugging a manuscript—the masterwork on which he had been working in the Bibliothèque Nationale in Paris, the elaboration of the "Theses." The briefcase containing this manuscript was entrusted to a fellow refugee who conveniently lost it on a train from Barcelona to Madrid. In short, Stalin read Benjamin's "Theses," he knew about the new book project based on the "Theses," and he wanted to prevent its publication at any cost. . . .

What these two stories share is not just the surprising link between high culture (fine art and theory) and base brutal politics (murder, torture). At this level, the link is not even as unexpected as it may appear: is it not one of the most vulgar common-sense opinions that viewing abstract art (like listening to atonal music) is torture (along the same lines, we can easily envisage a prison in which the detainees are exposed constantly to atonal music)? On the other hand, the "deeper" common sense is that Schoenberg, in his music, expressed the horrors of holocaust and mass bombings before they actually occurred. More radically, what the two stories share is that the link they establish is an *impossible short circuit* of levels which, for structural reasons, can never meet: it is simply not possible, say, for what "Stalin" stands for to move at the same level as "Benjamin," that is, to grasp the true dimensions of Benjamin's "Theses" from a Stalinist perspective. The illusion on which these two stories rely, that of putting two incompatible phenomena on the same level, is strictly analogous to what Kant called "transcendental illusion," the illusion of being able to use the same language for phenomena which are mutually untranslatable and can be grasped only in a kind of parallax view, constantly shifting perspective between two points between which no synthesis or mediation is possible. Thus there is no rapport between the two levels, no shared space—although they are closely connected, even identical in a way, they are, as it were, on the opposed sides of a Moebius strip. The encounter between Leninist politics and modernist art (exemplified in the fantasy of Lenin meeting Dadaists in the Cabaret Voltaire in Zurich) cannot structurally take place; more radically, revolutionary politics and revolutionary art move in different temporalities—although they are linked, they are *two sides* of the same phenomenon which, precisely as two sides, can never meet.[3] There is more than a historical accident in the fact that, in matters of culture, Leninists admired great classic art, while many modernists were political conservatives, proto-Fascists even. Is this not already the lesson of the link between the French Revolution and German Idealism? Although they are two sides of the same historical moment, they could not directly meet—that is to say, German Idealism could emerge only in the "backward" conditions of a Germany where no political revolution occurred.

In short, what both these anecdotes share is the occurrence of an insurmountable *parallax gap*, the confrontation of two closely linked perspectives between which no neutral common ground is possible.[4] In a first approach, such a notion of parallax gap cannot but appear as a kind of Kantian revenge over Hegel: is not "parallax" yet another name for a fundamental *antinomy* which can never be dialectically "mediated/sublated" into a higher synthesis, since there is no common language, no shared ground, between the two levels? It is the wager of this book that, far from posing an irreducible obstacle to dialectics, the notion of the parallax gap provides the key which enables us to discern its subversive core. To theorize this parallax gap properly is the necessary first step in the rehabilitation of the philosophy of *dialectical materialism*.[5] Here we encounter a basic paradox: while many of today's sciences spontaneously practice *materialist dialectic*, philosophically they oscillate between mechanical materialism and idealist obscurantism. There is no space for compromise here, no "dialogue," no search for allies in difficult times—today, in an epoch of the temporary retreat of dialectical materialism, Lenin's strategic insight is crucial: "When an army is in retreat, a hundred times more discipline is required than when the army is advancing. . . . When a Menshevik says, 'You are now retreating; I have been advocating retreat all the time; I agree with you, I am your man, let us retreat together,' we say in reply, 'For public manifestation of Menshevism our revolutionary courts must pass the death sentence, otherwise they are not our courts, but God knows what.'"[6]

Today's crisis of Marxism is not due only to the sociopolitical defeats of Marxist movements; at an inherent theoretical level, the crisis can (and *should*) also be indexed through the decline (virtual disappearance, even) of dialectical materialism as the philosophical underpinning of Marxism—dialectical materialism, *not* the much more acceptable, and much less embarrassing, "materialist dialectic": the shift from determinate reflection to reflective determination is crucial here—this is another case where a word or the position of words decides everything.[7] The shift we are dealing with here is the key dialectical shift—the one which is most difficult to grasp for a "negative dialectics" in love with explosions of negativity, with all imaginable forms of "resistance" and "subversion," but unable to overcome its own parasitizing on the preceding positive order—from the wild dance of the liberation from the (oppressive) System to (what German Idealists called) the System of Liberty. Two examples from revolutionary politics should suffice here: it is easy to fall in love with the multitude of freethinkers who blossomed in the prerevolutionary France of the late eighteenth century, from libertarians debating in the salons, enjoying the paradoxes of their own inconsistencies, to pathetic artists amusing those in power with their own protests against power; it is much more difficult fully to endorse the reversal of this unrest into the harsh new Order of the revolutionary Terror. Similarly, it is easy to fall in love with the crazy creative unrest of the first years after the October Revolution, with suprematists, futurists, constructivists, and so on, competing for primacy in revolutionary fervor; it is much more difficult to recognize in the horrors of the forced collectivization of the late 1920s the attempt to translate this revolutionary fervor into a new positive social order. There is nothing ethically more disgusting than revolutionary Beautiful Souls who refuse to recognize, in the Cross of the postrevolutionary present, the truth of their own flowering dreams about freedom.

That, philosophically speaking, Stalinist "dialectical materialism" is imbecility incarnate, is not so much beyond the point as, rather, the point itself, since my point is precisely to conceive the identity of my Hegelian-Lacanian position and the philosophy of dialectical materialism as a Hegelian infinite judgment, that is, as the speculative identity of the highest and the lowest, like the formula of phrenology "the Spirit is a bone." In what, then, does the difference between the "highest" and the "lowest" reading of dialectical materialism consist? The steely Fourth Teacher[8] committed a serious philosophical error when he ontologized the difference between dialectical and historical materialism, conceiving it as the difference between *metaphysica universalis* and *metaphysica specialis,* universal ontology and its application to the special domain of society. All we have to do here in order to pass from the "lowest" to the "highest" is to displace this difference between the universal and the particular into the particular itself: "dialectical materialism" provides another view on humanity itself, different from historical materialism . . . yes, once again, the relationship between historical and dialectical materialism is that of parallax; they are substantially the same, the shift from the one to the other is purely a shift of perspective. It introduces topics like the death drive, the "inhuman" core of the human, which reach over the horizon of the collective *praxis* of humanity; the gap is thus asserted as inherent to humanity itself, as the gap between humanity and its own inhuman excess.

There is a structural analogy between this relationship between historical and dialectical materialism and the properly psychoanalytic reply to the boring standard criticism of the application of psychoanalysis to social-ideological processes: is it "legitimate" to expand the use of notions which were originally deployed for the treatment of individuals to collective entities, and to talk about religion, for example, as a "collective compulsive neurosis"? The focus of psychoanalysis resides elsewhere: the Social, the field of social practices and socially held beliefs, is not simply on a different level from individual experience, but something to which *the individual himself has to relate*, which *the individual himself* has to experience as an order which is minimally "reified," externalized. The problem, therefore, is not "how to jump from the individual to the social level"; the problem is: *how should the external-impersonal socio-symbolic order of institutionalized practices and beliefs be structured, if the subject is to retain his "sanity," his "normal" functioning?* (Take the proverbial egotist, cynically dismissing the public system of moral norms: as a rule, such a subject can function only if this system is "out there," publicly recognized—that is to say, in order to be a private cynic, he has to presuppose the existence of naive other(s) who "really believe.") In other words, the gap between the individual and the "impersonal" social dimension is to be inscribed back within the individual himself: *this "objective" order of the social Substance exists only insofar as individuals treat it as such, relate to it as such.* And is the supreme example here not (again) that of Christ himself: in him, the difference between God and man is transposed into man himself?

With regard to the relationship between thought and being, both historical and dialectical materialism, of course, leave behind the prephilosophically naive "dialectical materialist" notion of thought as a reflection/mirroring of being (of "independent, objectively existing, reality"); however, they do so in different ways. Historical materialism overcomes this external parallelism of thought and being, of thought as a passive mirroring of "objective reality," through the notion of thought ("consciousness") as an inherent moment of the very process of (social) being, of collective *praxis*, as a process embedded in social reality (although today, after the invasion of Iraq, one is somehow ashamed to use this verb), as its active moment. Georg Lukács's discussion of this overcoming in *History and Class Consciousness* cannot be bettered: "consciousness" (becoming-conscious of one's concrete social position and its revolutionary potential) changes being itself—that is to say, it transforms the passive "working class," a stratum in the social edifice, into the "proletariat" as a revolutionary subject. Dialectical materialism, as it were, approaches the same knot from the opposite side: its problem is not how to overcome the external opposition of thought and being by deploying their practico-dialectical mediation, but *how, from within the flat order of positive being, the very gap between thought and being, the negativity of thought, emerges.* In other words, while Lukács et al. endeavor to demonstrate how thought is an active-constitutive moment of social being, the fundamental categories of dialectical materialism (like the negativity of the "death drive") aim at the "practical" aspect of the very passivity of thought: how is it possible, for a living being, to break/suspend the cycle of the reproduction of life, to *install a non-act, a withdrawal into reflexive distance from being, as the most radical intervention?* To put it in Kierkegaard's terms: the point is not to overcome the gap that separates thought from being, but to conceive it in its "becoming." Of course, the Lukácsian philosophy of *praxis* contains its own account of how the gap between thought and being emerges: the figure of the observing subject, exempt from the objective processes and intervening in them as an external manipulator, is itself *an effect of social alienation/ reification*; however, this account—which moves within the field of social *praxis* as the insurmountable horizon—leaves out of consideration the very emergence of *praxis*, its repressed "transcendental genesis." This supplement to historical materialism is crucial: without it, we either elevate society into a pseudo-Hegelian absolute Subject, or we have to leave open the space for some more encompassing general ontology.

The key problem here is that the basic "law" of dialectical materialism, the struggle of opposites, was colonized/obfuscated by the New Age notion of the polarity of opposites (*yin-yang*, and so on). The first critical move is to replace this topic of the polarity of opposites with the concept of the inherent "tension," gap, noncoincidence, of the One itself. This book is based on a strategic politico-philosophical decision to designate this gap which separates the One from itself with the term *parallax*.[9] There is an entire series of the modes of parallax in different domains of modern theory: *quantum physics* (the wave-particle duality); the parallax of *neurobiology* (the realization that, when we look behind the face into the skull, we find nothing; "there's no one at home" there, just piles of gray matter—it is difficult to tarry with this gap between meaning and the pure Real); the parallax of *ontological difference*, of the discord between the ontic and the transcendental-ontological (we cannot reduce the ontological horizon to its ontic "roots," but neither can we deduce the ontic domain from the ontological horizon; that is to say, transcendental constitution is not creation); the parallax of the *Real* (the Lacanian Real has no positive-substantial consistency, it is just the gap between the multitude of perspectives on it); the parallax nature of the gap between desire and drive (let us imagine an individual trying to perform some simple manual task—say, grab an object which repeatedly eludes him: the moment he changes his attitude, starting to find pleasure in just repeating the failed task, squeezing the object which, again and again, eludes him, he shifts from desire to drive);[10] the parallax of the *unconscious* (the lack of a common measure between the two aspects of Freud's theoretical edifice, interpretations of the formations of the unconscious [*The Interpretation of Dreams*, *The Psychopathology of Everyday Life*, *Jokes and Their Relation to the Unconscious*] and theories of drives [*Three Essays on the Theory of Sexuality*, and so on]); up to—last *and* least—the parallax of the *vagina* (the shift from the ultimate object of sexual penetration, the embodiment of the mystery of sexuality, to the very organ of maternity [birth]).

And, last *but not* least, we should assert the parallax status of philosophy as such. At its very inception (the Ionian pre-Socratics), philosophy emerged in the interstices of substantial social communities, as the thought of those who were caught in a "parallax" position, unable fully to identify with any of the positive social identities. In *On Tyranny*, Leo Strauss answered the question "In what does philosophic politics consist?" with: "In satisfying the city that the philosophers are not atheists, that they do not desecrate everything sacred to the city, that they reverence what the city reverences, that they are not subversives, in short that they are not irresponsible adventurers, but the best citizens."[11] This, of course, is a defensive survival strategy to cover up the actual subversive nature of philosophy. This crucial dimension is missing in Heidegger's account: how, from his beloved pre-Socratics onward, philosophizing involved an "impossible" position displaced with regard to any communal identity, be it "economy" (*oikos*, the household organization) or *polis* (the city-state). Like exchange according to Marx, philosophy emerges in the interstices *between* different communities, in the fragile space of exchange and circulation between them, a space which lacks any positive identity. Is this not especially clear in the case of Descartes? The grounding experience of his position of universal doubt is precisely a "multicultural" experience of how our own tradition is no better than what looks to us like the "eccentric" traditions of others:

> I had been taught, even in my College days, that there is nothing imaginable so strange or so little credible that it has not been maintained by one philosopher or other, and I further recognized in the course of my travels that all those whose sentiments are very contrary to ours are yet not necessarily barbarians or savages, but may be possessed of reason in as great or even a greater degree than ourselves. I also considered how very different the self-same man, identical in mind and spirit, may become, according as he is brought up from childhood amongst the French or Germans, or has passed his whole life amongst Chinese or cannibals. I likewise noticed how even in the fashions of one's clothing the same thing that pleased us ten years ago, and which will perhaps please us once again before ten years are passed, seems at the present time extravagant and ridiculous. I thus concluded that it is much more custom and example that persuade us than any certain knowledge, and yet in spite of this the voice of the majority does not afford a proof of any value in truths a little difficult to discover, because such truths are much more likely to have been discovered by one man than by a nation. I could not, however, put my finger on a single person whose opinions seemed preferable to those of others, and I found that I was, so to speak, constrained myself to undertake the direction of my procedure.[12]

Thus Karatani is justified in emphasizing the insubstantial character of the *cogito*: "It cannot be spoken of positively; no sooner than it is, its function is lost."[13] The *cogito* is not a substantial entity but a pure structural function, an empty place (Lacan's $) — as such, it can emerge only in the interstices of substantial communal systems. The link between the emergence of the *cogito* and the disintegration and loss of substantial communal identities is therefore inherent, and this holds even more for Spinoza than for Descartes: although Spinoza criticized the Cartesian *cogito*, he criticized it as a positive ontological entity — but he implicitly fully endorsed it as the "position of the enunciated," the one which speaks from radical self-doubting, since, even more than Descartes, Spinoza spoke from the interstices of the social space(s), neither a Jew nor a Christian.

Spinoza is, in effect, the "philosopher as such," with his subjective stance of double outcast (excommunicated even from the community of the outcasts of Western civilization); this is why we should use him as a paradigm that enables us to discover the traces of a similar displacement, a communal "out-of-joint," with regard to all other great philosophers, up to Nietzsche, who was ashamed of the Germans and proudly emphasized his alleged Polish roots. For a philosopher, ethnic roots, national identity, and so on, are simply *not a category of truth*—or, to put it in precise Kantian terms, when we reflect upon our ethnic roots, we engage in a *private use of reason*, constrained by contingent dogmatic presuppositions; that is to say, we act as "immature" individuals, not as free human beings who dwell in the dimension of the universality of reason. This, of course, does not in any way entail that we should be ashamed of our ethnic roots; we can love them, be proud of them; returning home may warm our hearts—but the fact remains that all this is ultimately irrelevant. We should act like Saint Paul who, while he was proud of his particular identity (a Jew and a Roman citizen), was nonetheless aware that, in the proper space of the Christian absolute Truth, "there is neither Jew nor Greek." . . . The struggle which truly engages him is not simply "more universal" than that of one ethnic group against another; it is a struggle which obeys an entirely different logic: no longer the logic of one self-identical substantial group fighting another group, but of an antagonism that cuts diagonally across all particular groups.

It would be easy to counterargue here that this Cartesian multiculturalist opening and relativizing of one's own position is just a first step, the abandoning of inherited opinions, which should allow us to acquire the absolutely certain philosophical knowledge—the abandoning of the false, unstable home in order to reach our true home. Did not Hegel himself compare Descartes's discovery of the *cogito* to a sailor who, after drifting around in the sea for a long time, finally catches sight of firm ground? Is this Cartesian homelessness not just a deceitful strategic move? Are we not dealing here with a Hegelian "negation of negation," the *Aufhebung* of the false traditional home in the finally discovered conceptual true home? In this sense, was Heidegger not justified in approvingly quoting Novalis's determination of philosophy as longing for the true lost home? Two things should be added here. First, Kant himself is in fact unique with regard to this topic: in his transcendental philosophy, homelessness remains irreducible; we remain forever split, condemned to a fragile position between the two dimensions, and to a "leap of faith" without any guarantee. Secondly, is the Hegelian situation really so clear? Is it not that, for Hegel, this new "home" is in a way *homelessness itself*, the very open movement of negativity?

Along these lines of the constitutive "homelessness" of philosophy, Karatani asserts—against Hegel—Kant's idea of the cosmopolitan "world-civil-society/ *Weltburgergesellschaft*," which is not simply an expansion of the citizenship of a nation-state to the citizenship of a global transnational State; it involves a shift from the principle of identification with one's "organic" ethnic substance actualized in particular tradition, to a radically different principle of identification—Karatani refers here to Deleuze's notion of universal singularity as opposed to the triad individuality-particularity-generality; this opposition is the opposition between Kant and Hegel. For Hegel, "world-civil-society" is an abstract notion without substantial content, lacking the mediation of the particular, and thus the force of full actuality—that is to say, it involves an abstract identification which does not seize the subject substantially; the only way for an individual to participate effectively in universal humanity is therefore via full identification with a particular nation-state: I am "human" only as a German, an Englishman. . . .[14] For Kant, on the contrary, "world-civil-society" designates the paradox of the universal singularity, of a singular subject who, in a kind of short circuit, bypassing the mediation of the particular, directly participates in the Universal. This identification with the Universal is not the identification with an all-encompassing global Substance ("humanity"), but the identification with a universal ethico-political principle—a universal religious collective, a scientific collective, a global revolutionary organization, all of which are in principle accessible to everyone. This is what Kant, in the famous passage of "What Is Enlightenment?", means by "public" as opposed to "private": "private" is not individual as opposed to communal ties, but the very communal-institutional order of one's particular identification; while "public" is the transnational universality of the exercise of one's Reason. The paradox is thus that one participates in the universal dimension of the "public" sphere precisely as a singular individual extracted from or even opposed to one's substantial communal identification—one is truly universal only as radically singular, in the interstices of communal identities.[15]

It would be easy to get lost in a nonsystematic deployment of the multitude of parallax gaps; my aim here is to introduce a minimum of conceptual order into this multitude by focusing on its three main modes: philosophical, scientific, and political. First, there is the *ontological difference* itself as the ultimate parallax which conditions our very access to reality; then there is the *scientific parallax*, the irreducible gap between the phenomenal experience of reality and its scientific account/explanation, which reaches its apogee in cognitivism, with its endeavor to provide a "third-person" neurobiological account of our "first-person" experience; last, but not least, there is the *political parallax*, the social antagonism which allows for no common ground between the conflicting agents (once upon a time, it was called "class struggle"), with its two main modes of existence on which the last two chapters of this book focus (the parallax gap between the public Law and its superego obscene supplement; the parallax gap between the "Bartleby" attitude of withdrawal from social engagement and collective social action). These three modes account for the tripartite structure of the book; between each part an interlude is added which applies the conceptual network to a more specific domain (Henry James's novels; the link between capitalism and anti-Semitism).

In each of the three parts, the same formal operation is discerned and deployed, each time at a different level: a gap is asserted as irreducible and insurmountable, a gap which posits a limit to the field of reality. Philosophy revolves around ontological difference, the gap between ontological horizon and "objective" ontic reality; the cognitivist brain sciences revolve around the gap between the subject's phenomenal self-relating and the biophysical reality of the brain; political struggle revolves around the gap between antagonisms proper and socioeconomic reality. This triad, of course, is that of the Universal-Particular-Singular: *universal* philosophy, *particular* science, the *singularity* of the political.[16] In all three cases, the problem is how to think this gap in a *materialist* way, which means: it is not enough merely to insist on the fact that the ontological horizon cannot be reduced to an effect of ontic occurrences; that phenomenal self-awareness cannot be reduced to an epiphenomenon of "objective" brain processes; that social antagonism ("class struggle") cannot be reduced to an effect of objective socioeconomic forces. We should take a step further and reach beneath this dualism itself, into a "minimal difference" (the noncoincidence of the One with itself) that generates it. Since I have written many pages in which I struggle with the work of Jacques Derrida, now—when the Derridean fashion is fading away—is perhaps the moment to honor his memory by pointing out the proximity of this "minimal difference" to what he called *différance*, this neologism whose very notoriety obfuscates its unprecedented materialist potential.

If anything, however, this reappraisal is intended to draw an even stronger line of demarcation from the usual gang of democracy-to-come-deconstructionist-postsecular-Levinasian-respect-for-Otherness suspects. So—to paraphrase Vladimir Nabokov's famous barbed anti-Freudian warning from his Foreword to the English translation of *King, Queen, Knave*—as usual, I would like to point out that, as usual (and, as usual, several sensitive people I like will look huffy), the democracy-to-come delegation has not been invited. If, however, a resolute democrat-to-come manages to slip in, he or she should be warned that a number of cruel traps have been set here and there throughout the book.

Our everyday academic experience provides a nice example of the Lacanian difference between the subject of the enunciated and the subject of the enunciation. When, at a conference, a speaker asks me: "Did you like my talk?", how do I politely imply that it was boring and stupid? By saying: "It was interesting. . . ." The paradox is that, if I say this directly, I say *more*: my message will be perceived as a personal attack on the very heart of the speaker's being, as an act of hatred toward him, not simply as a dismissal of his talk—in this case, the speaker will have the right to protest: "If you really just wanted to say that my talk was boring and stupid, why didn't you simply say that it was interesting?". . . If, however, I sincerely hope that readers will find the present book *interesting*, then I am nonetheless using this word in a more precise, properly dialectical, sense: the explanation of a universal concept becomes "interesting" when the particular cases evoked to exemplify it are in tension with their own universality—how?

In any large American bookstore, it is possible to purchase volumes of *Shakespeare Made Easy*, a unique series edited by John Durband and published by Barron's: a "bilingual" edition of Shakespeare's plays, with the original archaic English on the left-hand page and the translation into common contemporary English on the right-hand page. The obscene satisfaction provided by reading these volumes derives from the fact that what purports to be a mere translation into contemporary English turns out to be much more: as a rule, Durband tries to formulate directly, in everyday locution, (what he considers to be) the thought expressed in Shakespeare's metaphoric idiom—"To be or not to be, that is the question" becomes something like: "What's bothering me now is: Shall I kill myself or not?" Maybe the only way to de-jargonize a literary classic is to accept this crazy wager of "retranslating" its text into everyday colloquial speech.

One can imagine the translation of the most sublime of Hölderlin's verses into every-day German: "Wo aber Gefahr ist, wächst das Rettende auch"—"When you're in deep trouble, don't despair too quickly, look around carefully, the solution may be just around the corner." Or, in a similar procedure, one can well imagine supplementing the Heideggerian commentary on some pre-Socratic line with an obscene twist. When, in *Holzwege*, apropos of Anaximander, Heidegger deploys all the dimensions of the word *Fug*, *fügen*, of the tension between *Fug* and *Unfug*, ontological accord and discord, what about indulging in speculation about how the f . . . word itself is rooted in this cosmic *Fug*, along the lines of the pagan notion of the universe as resulting from the primordial copulation of the masculine and feminine cosmic principles (*yin* and *yang*, and so on)—so, to put it in Heideggerian terms, the essence of fucking has nothing to do with the ontic act of fuck itself; rather it, concerns the harmonious-struggling Fucking which provides the very composition of the universe.

In the documentary *Derrida*, in answer to the question of what he would ask some great classic philosopher if he were to meet him, Derrida immediately snaps back: "About his sex life." Here, perhaps, we should supplement Derrida: if we asked this question directly, we would probably get a common answer; the thing to look for, rather, would be the *theory* about sexuality at the level of each's respective philosophy. Perhaps the ultimate philosophical fantasy here would be the discovery of a manuscript in which Hegel, the systematician *par excellence*, develops a system of sexuality, of sexual practices contradicting, inverting, sublating each other, deducing all (straight and "perverse") forms from its basic deadlock.[17] As in Hegel's *Encyclopaedia*, we would first get the deduction of the main "subjective attitudes toward sex" (animal coupling, pure excessive lust, expression of human love, metaphysical passion), followed by the proper "system of sexuality," organized, as one would expect from Hegel, into a sequence of triads. The starting point here is copulation *a tergo*, the sexual act in its animal, presubjective immediacy; we then go on to its immediate (abstract) negation: masturbation, in which solo self-excitation is supplemented by fantasizing. (Jean Laplanche argued that masturbation-with-fantasy is the elementary, zero-level, form of the properly human drive as opposed to the animal instinct.) What follows is the synthesis of the two: the sexual act proper in a missionary position, in which face-to-face contact guarantees that full bodily contact (penetration) remains supplemented by fantasizing. This means that the "normal" human sexual act has the structure of double masturbation: each participant is masturbating with a real partner. However, the gap between the raw reality of copulation and its fantasmatic supplement can no longer be closed; all variations and displacements of sexual practices that follow are so many desperate attempts to restore the balance of the two.

The dialectical "progress" thus first goes through a series of variations with regard to the relationship between face, sexual organs, and other bodily parts, and the modes of their respective uses: the organ remains the phallus, but the opening to be penetrated changes (anus, mouth). Then, in a kind of "negation of negation," not only does the object to be penetrated change, but the totality of the person who is the partner passes into its opposite (homosexuality). In a further development, the goal itself is no longer orgasm (fetishism). Fist-fucking introduces into this series an impossible synthesis of hand (the organ of instrumental activity, of hard work) and vagina (the organ of "spontaneous" passive generation). The fist (focus of purposeful work, the hand as the most tightly controlled and trained part of our body) replaces the phallus (the organ out of our conscious control *par excellence*, since its erection comes and goes independently of our will), in a kind of correlate to somebody who approaches a state that should emerge "spontaneously" in a well-planned instrumental way (a poet who constructs his poems in a "rational" way, for instance, is a poetic fist-fucker). There are, of course, further variations here which call for their speculative deduction: in masculine masturbation, the vagina, the ultimate passive organ, is substituted by the hand, the ultimate active organ which passivizes the phallus itself. Furthermore, when the phallus penetrates the anus, we obtain the correct insight into the speculative identity of excrementation and insemination, the highest and the lowest. There is no room here to explore further variations to be deduced: doing it with an animal, with a machine-doll; doing it with many partners, sadism and masochism. . . . The main point is that the very "progress" from one form to another is motivated by the structural imbalance of the sexual relationship (Lacan's *il n'y a pas de rapport sexuel*), which condemns any sexual practice to eternal oscillation between the "spontaneous" pathos of self-obliteration and the logic of external ritual (following the rules). Thus the final outcome is that sexuality is the domain of "spurious infinity" whose logic, brought to an extreme, cannot but engender tasteless excesses like those of "spermathon" contests—how many men can a woman bring to orgasm in an hour, and so on . . . for a true philosopher, there are more interesting things in the world than sex.

What accounts for the weird (if not—for some, at least—tasteless) character of this exercise is not the reference to sexual practices as such, but the short circuit between two spheres which are usually perceived as incompatible, as moving at ontologically different levels: that of sublime philosophical speculation and that of the details of sexual practices. Even if there is nothing which, *a priori*, prohibits the application of the Hegelian conceptual machinery to sexual practices, it nonetheless appears that the entire exercise is somehow meaningless, a (rather bad) joke. The unpleasant, weird effect of such short circuits shows that they play a symptomal role in our symbolic universes: they bring home the implicit, tacit prohibitions on which these universes rely. One practices concrete universality by confronting a universality with its "unbearable" example. Of course, Hegelian dialectics can be used to analyze anything—nonetheless, one is tacitly summoned not to apply it to sexuality, as if this move would make the very notion of dialectical analysis ridiculous; of course, all people are equal—nonetheless, one is tacitly summoned to treat some of them as "less equal," as if asserting their full equality would undermine the very notion of equality.

This, then, is the nontrivial sense in which I hope readers will find the present book interesting: insofar as I succeed in my effort to *practice* concrete universality—to engage in what Deleuze, that great anti-Hegelian, called "expanding the concepts."

PART I

THE STELLAR PARALLAX:
THE TRAPS OF ONTOLOGICAL DIFFERENCE

CHAPTER 1

THE SUBJECT, THIS "INWARDLY CIRCUMCISED JEW"

Many times I am asked the obvious yet pertinent question about the title of my longest book (the present one excepted): "So who or what is tickling the ticklish subject?" The answer, of course, is: the object—however, which object? This, in a nutshell (or, rather, like a nut within the shell), is the topic of this book. The difference between subject and object can also be expressed as the difference between the two corresponding verbs, to subject (submit) oneself and to object (protest, oppose, create an obstacle). The subject's elementary, founding, gesture is to subject itself—voluntarily, of course: as both Wagner and Nietzsche, those two great opponents, were well aware, the highest act of freedom is the display of amor fati, the act of freely assuming what is necessary anyway. If, then, the subject's activity is, at its most fundamental, the activity of submitting oneself to the inevitable, the fundamental mode of the object's passivity, of its passive presence, is that which moves, annoys, disturbs, traumatizes us (subjects): at its most radical the object is that which objects, that which disturbs the smooth running of things.[1] Thus the paradox is that the roles are reversed (in terms of the standard notion of the active subject working on the passive object): the subject is defined by a fundamental passivity, and it is the object from which movement comes—which does the tickling. But, again, what object is this? The answer is: the parallax object.

The standard definition of parallax is: the apparent displacement of an object (the shift of its position against a background), caused by a change in observational position that provides a new line of sight. The philosophical twist to be added, of course, is that the observed difference is not simply "subjective," due to the fact that the same object which exists "out there" is seen from two different stances, or points of view. It is rather that, as Hegel would have put it, subject and object are inherently "mediated," so that an "epistemological" shift in the subject's point of view always reflects an "ontological" shift in the object itself. Or—to put it in Lacanese—the subject's gaze is always-already inscribed into the perceived object itself, in the guise of its "blind spot," that which is "in the object more than the object itself," the point from which the object itself returns the gaze. "Sure, the picture is in my eye, but I, I am also in the picture":[2] the first part of Lacan's statement designates subjectivization, the dependence of reality on its subjective constitution; while the second part provides a materialist supplement, reinscribing the subject into its own image in the guise of a stain (the objectivized splinter in its eye). Materialism is not the direct assertion of my inclusion in objective reality (such an assertion presupposes that my position of enunciation is that of an external observer who can grasp the whole of reality); rather, it resides in the reflexive twist by means of which I myself am included in the picture constituted by me—it is this reflexive short circuit, this necessary redoubling of myself as standing both outside and inside my picture, that bears witness to my "material existence." Materialism means that the reality I see is never "whole"—not because a large part of it eludes me, but because it contains a stain, a blind spot, which indicates my inclusion in it.

Nowhere is this structure clearer than in the case of Lacan's *objet petit a*, the object-cause of desire. The same object can all of a sudden be "transubstantiated" into the object of my desire: what is just an ordinary object to you is to me the focus of my libidinal investment, and this shift is caused by some unfathomable X, a *je ne sais quoi* in the object which can never be pinned down to any of its particular properties. *L'objet petit a* is therefore close to the Kantian transcendental object, since it stands for the unknown X, the noumenal core of the object beyond appearances, for what is "in you more than yourself." *L'objet petit a* can thus be defined as a pure parallax object: it is not only that its contours change with the shift of the subject; it exists—*its presence can be discerned—only when the landscape is viewed from a certain perspective*. More precisely, *objet petit a* is the very cause of the parallax gap, that unfathomable X which forever eludes the symbolic grasp, and thus causes the multiplicity of symbolic perspectives. The paradox here is a very precise one: it is at the very point at which a pure difference emerges—a difference which is no longer a difference between two positively existing objects, but a minimal difference which divides one and the same object from itself—that this difference "as such" immediately coincides with an unfathomable object: in contrast to a mere difference between objects, *the pure difference is itself an object*. Another name for the parallax gap is therefore *minimal difference*, a "pure" difference which cannot be grounded in positive substantial properties. In Henry James's "The Real Thing," the painter-narrator agrees to hire the impoverished "true" aristocrats Major and Mrs. Monarch as models for his illustrations of a *de luxe* book. However, although they are the "real thing," drawings of them look fake, so the painter has to rely more and more on a low-class couple: the vulgar Cockney model Miss Churm and the lithe Italian Oronte, whose imitation of the high-class pose works much better . . . is this not the unfathomable "minimal difference" at its purest?

A more complex literary case of this minimal difference is the editorial fate of *Tender Is the Night*, F. Scott Fitzgerald's masterpiece, the sad story of the disintegrating marriage between the rich American heiress Nicole Warren, a schizophrenic victim of incest, and Richard Diver, a brilliant young psychiatrist who treated her in Switzerland. In the first edition, the novel begins years later at the Divers' villa on the French Riviera, where the couple live a glamorous life; the story is told from the perspective of Rosemary, a young American movie actress who falls in love with Dick, fascinated by the Divers' glitzy lifestyle. Gradually, Rosemary gets hints of a dark underside of traumas and psychic breakdowns beneath the surface of this glamorous social life. At this point, the story moves back into how Dick met Nicole, how they got married in spite of her family's doubts, and so on; after this interlude the story returns to the present, continuing the description of the gradual falling apart of Nicole's and Dick's marriage (Dick's desperate affair with Rosemary, and so on, up to one of the most depressing and hopeless endings in modern literature). For the novel's second edition, however (the first printing was a failure), Fitzgerald tried to improve it by rearranging the material in chronological order: now the novel begins in 1919 Zurich, with Dick as a young doctor called by a psychiatrist friend to take over the difficult case of Nicole.[3]

Why is neither of the two versions satisfying? Obviously, the first version is the more adequate one, and not only for purely dramatic-narrative reasons (it first creates the enigma—what is the secret behind the glitzy surface of the Divers' marriage?—and then, after arousing the reader's interest, proceeds to give the answer). Rosemary's external point of view, fascinated by the ideal(ized) couple of Dick and Nicole, is not simply external. Rather, it embodies the gaze of the social "big Other," the Ego-Ideal, for which Dick enacts the life of a happy husband who tries to charm everybody around him: that is to say, this external gaze is internal to Dick, part of his immanent subjective identity—he leads his life in order to satisfy this gaze. What this implies, furthermore, is that Dick's fate cannot be accounted for in terms of the immanent deployment of a flawed character: to present Dick's sad fate in this way (in the mode of a linear narrative) is a lie, an ideological mystification that transposes the external network of social relations into inherent psychological features. I am even tempted to say that the flashback chapter on the prehistory of Dick's and Nicole's marriage, far from providing a truthful account of the reality beneath the false glitzy appearance, is a retroactive fantasy, a kind of narrative version of what, in the history of capitalism, functions as the myth of "primordial accumulation."[4] In other words, there is no direct immanent line of development from the prehistory to the glitzy story proper: the jump is irreducible here; a different dimension intervenes.

The enigma is: why was Fitzgerald not satisfied with the first version? Why did he replace it with the clearly less satisfying linear narrative? If we take a closer look, we can easily discern the limitations of the first version: the flashback after the first part sticks out—while the jump from the present (the French Riviera in 1929) to the past (Zurich in 1919) is convincing, the return to the present "doesn't work," is not fully justified artistically. The only consistent answer is therefore: because the only way to remain faithful to the artistic truth is to "bite the bullet" and admit defeat—to circumscribe the gap itself by presenting both versions.[5] In other words, the two versions are not consecutive, they should be read structurally (synchronously), like the two maps of the same village in the example from Lévi-Strauss (developed in detail below). In short, what we encounter here is the parallax function at its purest: the gap between the two versions is irreducible, it is the "truth" of both of them, the traumatic core around which they circulate; there is no way to resolve the tension, to find a "proper" solution. What at first looks like a merely formal narrative deadlock (how, in what order, to tell the story) is thus symptomatic of a more radical deadlock that pertains to the social content itself. Fitzgerald's narrative failure and his oscillation between the two versions tells us something about social reality itself, about a certain gap that is *stricto sensu* a fundamental *social fact*. The "tickling object" here is the absent Cause, the unfathomable X that undermines every narrative solution.

Since *l'objet petit a* is the object of psychoanalysis, it is no wonder that we encounter a parallax gap at the very core of psychoanalytic experience. When Jean Laplanche elaborates the impasses of the Freudian topic of seduction, he in effect reproduces the precise structure of a Kantian antinomy. On the one hand, there is the brutal empirical realism of the parental seduction: the ultimate cause of later traumas and pathologies is that children were in fact seduced and abused by adults; on the other hand, there is the (in)famous reduction of the seduction scene to the patient's fantasy. As Laplanche points out, the ultimate irony is that the dismissal of seduction as fantasy passes today for the "realistic" stance, while those who insist on the reality of seduction end up advocating all kind of abuse, up to satanic rites and extraterrestrial harassment. . . . Laplanche's solution is precisely the transcendental one: while "seduction" cannot be reduced simply to the subject's fantasy, while it does refer to a traumatic encounter with the Other's "enigmatic message," bearing witness to the Other's unconscious, it cannot be reduced to an event in the reality of the actual interaction between child and his or her adults either. Seduction is, rather, a kind of transcendental structure, the minimal *a priori* formal constellation of the child confronted with the impenetrable acts of the Other which bear witness to the Other's unconscious—and we are never dealing here with simple "facts," but always with facts located in the space of indeterminacy between "too soon" and "too late": the child is originally helpless, thrown into the world when he is unable to take care of himself—that is, his or her survival skills develop too late; at the same time, the encounter with the sexualized Other always, by a structural necessity, comes "too soon," as an unexpected shock which can never be properly symbolized, translated into the universe of meaning.[6] The fact of seduction is thus that of the Kantian transcendental X, a structurally necessary transcendental illusion.

THE KANTIAN PARALLAX

In his impressive book *Transcritique*,[7] Kojin Karatani endeavors to assert the critical potential of such a "parallax view": confronted with an antinomic stance in the precise Kantian sense of the term, we should renounce all attempts to reduce one aspect to the other (or, even more so, to enact a kind of "dialectical synthesis" of opposites); on the contrary, we should assert antinomy as irreducible, and conceive the point of radical critique not as a certain determinate position as opposed to another position, but as the irreducible gap between the positions itself, the purely structural interstice between them. Kant's stance is thus "to see things neither from his own viewpoint, nor from the viewpoint of others, but to face the reality that is exposed through difference (parallax)."[8] (Is this not Karatani's way of asserting the Lacanian Real as a pure antagonism, as an impossible difference which precedes its terms?) This is how Karatani reads the Kantian notion of the *Ding an sich* (the Thing-in-itself, beyond phenomena): this Thing is not simply a transcendental entity beyond our grasp, but something that is discernible only via the irreducibly antinomic character of our experience of reality.[9]

Let us take Kant's confrontation with the epistemological antinomy which characterized his epoch: empiricism versus rationalism. Kant's solution is neither to choose one of these terms nor to enact a kind of higher "synthesis" which would "sublate" the two as unilateral, as partial moments of a global truth (neither, of course, does he withdraw into pure skepticism); the stake of his "transcendental turn" is precisely to avoid the need to formulate one's own "positive" solution. What Kant does is to change the very terms of the debate; his solution—the transcendental turn—is unique in that it, first, rejects the ontological closure: it recognizes a certain fundamental and irreducible limitation ("finitude") of the human condition, which is why the two poles, rational and sensual, active and passive, can never be fully mediated-reconciled—the "synthesis" of the two dimensions (the fact that our Reason seems to fit the structure of external reality that affects us) always relies on a certain *salto mortale*, or "leap of faith." Far from designating a "synthesis" of the two dimensions, the Kantian "transcendental" stands, rather, for their irreducible gap "as such": the "transcendental" points to something in this gap, a new dimension which cannot be reduced to either of the two positive terms between which the gap is gaping. And Kant does the same with regard to the antinomy between the Cartesian *cogito* as *res cogitans*, the "thinking substance," a self-identical positive entity, and Hume's dissolution of the subject in the multitude of fleeting impressions: against both positions, he asserts the subject of transcendental apperception which, while displaying a self-reflective unity irreducible to the empirical multitude, nonetheless lacks any substantial positive being—that is to say, it is in no way a *res cogitans*. Here, however, we should be more precise than Karatani, who directly identifies the transcendental subject with transcendental illusion:

> yes, an ego is just an illusion, but functioning there is the transcendental apperception X. But what one knows as metaphysics is that which considers the X as something substantial. Nevertheless, one cannot really escape from the drive [*Trieb*] to take it as an empirical substance in various contexts. If so, it is possible to say that an ego is just an illusion, but a transcendental illusion.[10]

The precise status of the transcendental subject, however, is not that of what Kant calls a transcendental illusion or what Marx calls the objectively necessary form of thought. First, the transcendental I, its pure apperception, is a purely formal function which is neither noumenal nor phenomenal—it is empty, no phenomenal intuition corresponds to it, since, if it were to appear to itself, its self-appearance would be the "thing itself," that is, the direct self-transparency of a noumenon.[11] The parallel between the void of the transcendental subject ($) and the void of the transcendental object, the inaccessible X that causes our perceptions, is misleading here: the transcendental object is the void *beyond* phenomenal appearances, while the transcendental subject *already appears as a void*.[12]

Perhaps the best way to describe the Kantian break toward this new dimension is with regard to the changed status of the notion of the "inhuman." Kant introduced a key distinction between negative and indefinite judgment: the positive judgment "the soul is mortal" can be negated in two ways: when a predicate is denied to the subject ("the soul is not mortal"), and when a non-predicate is affirmed ("the soul is non-mortal")—the difference is exactly the same as the one, known to every reader of Stephen King, between "he is not dead" and "he is un-dead." The indefinite judgment opens up a third domain which undermines the underlying distinction: the "undead" are neither alive nor dead, they are precisely the monstrous "living dead."[13] And the same goes for "inhuman": "he is not human" is not the same as "he is inhuman"—"he is not human" means simply that he is external to humanity, animal or divine, while "he is inhuman" means something completely different: the fact that he is neither human nor inhuman, but marked by a terrifying excess which, although it negates what we understand as "humanity," in inherent to being-human. And, perhaps, we should risk the hypothesis that this is what changes with the Kantian revolution: in the pre-Kantian universe, humans were simply humans, beings of reason, fighting the excesses of animal lusts and divine madness, while only with Kant and German Idealism is the excess to be fought absolutely immanent, the very core of subjectivity itself (this is why, with German Idealism, the metaphor for the core of subjectivity is Night, "Night of the World," in contrast to the Enlightenment notion of the Light of Reason fighting the darkness all around).[14] So when, in the pre-Kantian universe, a hero goes mad, it means he is deprived of his humanity—that is, animal passions or divine madness have taken over—while with Kant, madness implies the unconstrained explosion of the very core of a human being. (In Kafka's *Metamorphosis*, Gregor Samsa's sister Grete calls her brother-turned-insect a monster—the German word used is "ein Untier," an inanimal, in strict symmetry to inhuman. What we get here is the opposite of inhuman: an animal which, while remaining animal, is not really animal—the excess over the animal in animal, the traumatic core of animality, which can emerge "as such" only in a human who has become an animal.)[15]

What, then, is this new dimension that emerges in the gap itself? It is that of the transcendental I itself, of its "spontaneity": the ultimate parallax, the third space between phenomena and the noumenon itself, is the subject's freedom/spontaneity, which—although, of course, it is not the property of a phenomenal entity, so that it cannot be dismissed as a false appearance which conceals the noumenal fact that we are totally caught in an inaccessible necessity—is also not simply noumenal. In a mysterious subchapter of his *Critique of Practical Reason* entitled "Of the Wise Adaptation of Man's Cognitive Faculties to His Practical Vocation," Kant endeavors to answer the question of what would happen to us if we were to gain access to the noumenal domain, to the *Ding an sich*:

> instead of the conflict which now the moral disposition has to wage with inclinations and in which, after some defeats, moral strength of mind may be gradually won, God and eternity in their awful majesty would stand unceasingly before our eyes. . . . Thus most actions conforming to the law would be done from fear, few would be done from hope, none from duty. The moral worth of actions, on which alone the worth of the person and even of the world depends in the eyes of supreme wisdom, would not exist at all. The conduct of man, so long as his nature remained as it is now, would be changed into mere mechanism, where, as in a puppet show, everything would gesticulate well but no life would be found in the figures.[16]

In short, direct access to the noumenal domain would deprive us of the very "spontaneity" which forms the kernel of transcendental freedom: it would turn us into lifeless automata—or, to put it in today's terms, into "thinking machines." The implication of this passage is much more radical and paradoxical than it may appear. If we ignore its inconsistency (how could fear and lifeless gesticulation coexist?), the inescapable conclusion is that, at the level of phenomena as well as at the noumenal level, we—humans—are "mere mechanisms" with no autonomy and no freedom: as phenomena, we are not free, we are part of nature, "mere mechanisms," totally submitted to causal links, part of the nexus of causes and effects; as noumena, we are again not free, but reduced to "mere mechanisms." (Is what Kant describes as a person who has direct knowledge of the noumenal domain not strictly analogous to the utilitarian subject whose acts are fully determined by the calculus of pleasures and pains?) *Our freedom persists only in a space in between the phenomenal and the noumenal.* It is therefore not that Kant simply limited causality to the phenomenal domain in order to be able to assert that, at the noumenal level, we are free autonomous agents: we are free only insofar as our horizon is that of the phenomenal, insofar as the noumenal domain remains inaccessible to us.

Is the way out of this predicament to assert that we are free insofar as we are noumenally autonomous, but our cognitive perspective remains restricted to the phenomenal level? In this case, we are "really free" at the noumenal level, but our freedom would be meaningless if we were also to have cognitive insight into the noumenal domain, since that insight would always determine our choices—who would choose evil, confronted with the fact that the price of doing evil will be divine punishment? However, does this imagined case not provide us with the only logical answer to the question "what would a truly free act be," a free act for a noumenal entity, an act of true *noumenal* freedom? It would be to know all the inexorable horrible consequences of choosing evil, *and nonetheless to choose it.* This would be a truly "nonpathological" act, an act of acting with no regard for one's pathological interests. . . . Kant's own formulations are misleading here, since he often identifies the transcendental subject with the noumenal I whose phenomenal appearance is the empirical "person," thus drawing back from his radical insight into how the transcendental subject is a pure formal-structural function beyond the opposition of the noumenal and the phenomenal.

The philosophical consequences of this Kantian parallax are fully explored in the notion of ontological difference, the focus of Heidegger's entire thought, which can be properly grasped only against the background of the theme of finitude. There is a double *doxa* on Heidegger's ontological difference: it is a difference between the What-ness, the essence of beings, and the mere That-ness of their being—it liberates beings from subordination to any ground/*arche*/goal; furthermore, it is a difference not merely between (different levels of) beings, of reality, but between the All of reality and something else which, with regard to reality, cannot but appear as "Nothing.". . . This *doxa* is deeply misleading.

With regard to the notion of ontological difference as the difference between what things are and the fact that they are, the *doxa* says that the mistake of metaphysics is to subordinate being to some presupposed essence (sense, goal, *arche* . . .) embodied in the highest entity, while ontological difference "de-essentializes" beings, setting them free from their enslavement to Essence, letting-them-be in their an-archic freedom—prior to any "what-for? why?", and so on, things simply *are*, they just *occur.* . . . If, however, this were Heidegger's thesis, then Sartre, in *Nausea*, would also outline ontological difference at its most radical—does he not describe there the experience of the stupid and meaningless inertia of being at its most disgusting, indifferent to all our (human) meanings and projects? For Heidegger, in contrast to Sartre, "ontological difference" is, rather, the difference between the entities' stupid being-there, their senseless reality, and their horizon of meaning.

There is a link between ontological and sexual difference (conceived in a purely formal-transcendental way, along the lines of Lacan's "formulas of sexuation," of course).[17] The male side—universality and exception—is literally "meta-physical" (the entire universe, all of reality, is grounded in its constitutive exception, the highest entity which is *epekeina tes ousias*), while the ontological difference proper is feminine: reality is non-all, but there is nothing beyond-outside it, and this Nothing is Being itself. Ontological difference is not between the Whole of beings and their Outside, as if there were a Super-Ground of the All. In this precise sense, ontological difference is linked to finitude (Heidegger's original insight and link to Kant), which means that Being is the horizon of finitude which prevents us from conceiving beings in their All. Being cuts from within beings: ontological difference is not the "mega-difference" between the All of beings and something more fundamental, it is always also that which makes the domain of beings itself "non-all." Apropos of "telling all the truth," we should again apply the Lacanian paradoxes of the non-All; that is to say, we should strictly oppose two cases. Because truth is in itself non-all, inconsistent, "antagonistic," every *telling of "all the Truth"* has to rely on an exception, on *a secret that is withheld*; the opposite case, the *telling of non-all truth*, does not imply that we keep some part of truth secret—its obverse is that *there is nothing we did not tell.*[18]

This also means that ontological difference is not "maximal," between all beings, the highest genus, and something else/more/beyond, but, rather, "minimal," the bare minimum of a difference not between beings but between the minimum of an entity and the void, nothing. Insofar as it is grounded in the finitude of humans, ontological difference is that which makes a totalization of the "All of beings" impossible—ontological difference means that the field of reality is finite. In this precise sense, ontological difference is "real/impossible": to use Ernesto Laclau's determination of antagonism, in it, *external difference overlaps with internal difference.* The difference between beings and their Being is simultaneously a difference within beings themselves; that is to say, the difference between beings/entities and their Opening, their horizon of Meaning, always also cuts into the field of beings themselves, making it incomplete/finite. Therein lies the paradox: *the difference between beings in their totality and their Being precisely "misses the difference" and reduces Being to another, "higher" Entity.* The parallel between Kant's antinomies and Heidegger's ontological difference is to be found in the fact that, in both cases, the gap (phenomenal/noumenal; ontic/ontological) is to be referred to the non-All of the phenomenal-ontic domain itself. However, the limitation of Kant was that he was not able fully to assume this paradox of finitude as constitutive of the ontological horizon: ultimately, he reduced the transcendental horizon to a way in which reality appears to a finite being (man), with all of it located in a wider encompassing realm of noumenal reality.

Thus the shift of the place of freedom from the noumenal beyond to the very gap between phenomenal and noumenal is crucial—is this shift not the very shift from Kant to Hegel, from the tension between immanence and transcendence to the minimal difference/gap in immanence itself? Hegel, therefore, is not external to Kant: the problem with Kant was that he produced the shift but was unable, for structural reasons, to formulate it explicitly—he "knew" that the place of freedom is in fact not noumenal, but the gap between phenomenal and noumenal, but he could not put it so explicitly, since, had he done so, his transcendental edifice would have collapsed. Without this implicit "knowledge," however, there would also have been no transcendental dimension, so that we are forced to conclude that, far from being a stable consistent position, the dimension of the Kantian "transcendental" can sustain itself only in a fragile balance between the said and the unsaid, through producing something the full consequences of which we refuse to articulate, to "posit as such."[19] This means that Karatani is wrong in the way he opposes Kant and Hegel: far from overcoming the parallax logic, Hegel brings it from the Kantian "in itself" to "for itself." It is only Hegel who can think the parallax in its radicality, as the priority of the inherent antagonism over the multiple/failed reflection of the transcendent/impossible Thing.

Claude Lévi-Strauss's exemplary analysis, from Structural Anthropology, of the spatial disposition of buildings in the Winnebago, one of the Great Lakes tribes, might be of some help here. The tribe is divided into two subgroups ("moieties"), "those who are from above" and "those who are from below"; when we ask an individual to draw on a piece of paper, or on sand, the ground-plan of his or her village (the spatial disposition of cottages), we obtain two quite different answers, depending on his or her belonging to one or the other subgroup. Both perceive the village as a circle; but for one subgroup there is within this circle another circle of central houses, so that we have two concentric circles, while for the other subgroup the circle is split in two by a clear dividing line. In other words, a member of the first subgroup (let us call it "conservative-corporatist") perceives the ground-plan of the village as a ring of houses more or less symmetrically disposed around the central temple, whereas a member of the second ("revolutionary-antagonistic") subgroup perceives his or her village as two distinct heaps of houses separated by an invisible frontier. . . .[20] The point Lévi-Strauss wants to make is that this example should in no way entice us into cultural relativism, according to which the perception of social space depends on the observer's group-belonging: the very splitting into the two "relative" perceptions implies a hidden reference to a constant—not the objective, "actual" disposition of buildings but a traumatic kernel, a fundamental antagonism the inhabitants of the village were unable to symbolize, to account for, to "internalize," to come to terms with, an imbalance in social relations that prevented the community from stabilizing itself into a harmonious whole. The two perceptions of the ground-plan are simply two mutually exclusive endeavors to cope with this traumatic antagonism, to heal its wound via the imposition of a balanced symbolic structure. It is here that one can see in what precise sense the Real intervenes through anamorphosis. We have first the "actual," "objective" arrangement of the houses, then its two different symbolizations which both distort the actual arrangement in an anamorphic way. However, the "Real" here is not the actual arrangement, but the traumatic core of some social antagonism which distorts the tribe members' view of the actual arrangement of the houses in their village.

The Real is thus the disavowed X on account of which our vision of reality is anamorphically distorted; it is simultaneously the Thing to which direct access is not possible and the obstacle which prevents this direct access, the Thing which eludes our grasp and the distorting screen which makes us miss the Thing. More precisely, the Real is ultimately the very shift of perspective from the first standpoint to the second. Recall Adorno's well-known analysis of the antagonistic character of the notion of society: in a first approach, the split between the two notions of society (the Anglo-Saxon individualistic-nominalistic notion and the Durkheimian organicist notion of society as a totality which preexists individuals) seems irreducible; we seem to be dealing with a true Kantian antinomy which cannot be resolved via a higher "dialectical synthesis," and elevates society into an inaccessible Thing-in-itself; in a second approach, however, we should merely take note of how this radical antinomy which seems to preclude our access to the Thing is already the Thing itself—the fundamental feature of today's society is the irreconcilable antagonism between Totality and the individual. This means that, ultimately, the status of the Real is purely parallactic and, as such, non-substantial: is has no substantial density in itself, it is just a gap between two points of perspective, perceptible only in the shift from the one to the other. The parallax Real is thus opposed to the standard (Lacanian) notion of the Real as that which "always returns to its place"—as that which remains the same in all possible (symbolic) universes: the parallax Real is, rather, that which accounts for the very multiplicity of appearances of the same underlying Real—it is not the hard core which persists as the Same, but the hard bone of contention which pulverizes the sameness into the multitude of appearances. In a first move, the Real is the impossible hard core which we cannot confront directly, but only through the lenses of a multitude of symbolic fictions, virtual formations. In a second move, this very hard core is purely virtual, actually nonexistent, an X which can be reconstructed only retroactively, from the multitude of symbolic formations which are "all that there actually is."[21]

In philosophical terms, the topic of parallax confronts us with the key question of the passage from Kant to Hegel. There are two main versions of this passage (which is still one of the great dividing lines among philosophers: those—mostly of the analytic orientation—who think that Kant is the last one who "makes sense," and that the post-Kantian turn of German Idealism is one of the greatest catastrophes, regressions into meaningless speculation, in the history of philosophy; and those for whom the post-Kantian speculative-historical approach is the highest achievement of philosophy):

1. Kant asserts the gap of finitude, transcendental schematism, negative access to the Noumenal (via the Sublime) as the only possible one, and so on, while Hegel's absolute idealism closes the Kantian gap and returns to pre-critical metaphysics;

2. It is Kant who goes only halfway in his destruction of metaphysics, still maintaining the reference to the Thing-in-itself as the external inaccessible entity; Hegel is merely a rad-icalized Kant, who takes the step from negative access to the Absolute to the Absolute itself as negativity. Or, to put it in the terms of the Hegelian shift from epistemological obstacle to positive ontological condition (our incomplete knowledge of the Thing turns into a positive feature of the Thing which is in itself incomplete, inconsistent): it is not that Hegel "ontologizes" Kant; on the contrary, it is Kant who, insofar as he con-ceives the gap as merely epistemological, continues to presuppose a fully constituted noumenal realm existing out there, and it is Hegel who "deontologizes" Kant, intro-ducing a gap into the very texture of reality.

In other words, Hegel's move is not to "overcome" the Kantian division but, rather, to assert it "as such," to drop the need for its "overcoming," for the additional "reconciliation" of opposites: to gain insight—through a purely formal parallax shift—into how posit-ing the distinction "as such" already is the looked-for "reconciliation." The limitation of Kant is not in his remaining within the confines of finite oppositions, in his inabil-ity to reach the Infinite, but, on the contrary, in his very search for a transcendent domain beyond the realm of finite oppositions: Kant is not unable to reach the Infinite—he is unable to see how he already has what he is looking for. This reversal provides the key to the infamous "Hegelian triad."

When we talk about the "Hegelian triad," the first thing to do is to forget the story about alienation, loss of the original organic unity, and the return to a "higher" medi-ated unity. To get a more appropriate idea of it, it is worth recalling the sublime rever-sal found, among others, in Charles Dickens's *Great Expectations*. When, at his birth, Pip is designated a "man of great expectations," everybody perceives this as a forecast of his worldly success; at the end, however, when he abandons London's false glamour and returns to his modest childhood community, we become aware that he did live up to the forecast that marked his life—only by finding the strength to leave the vain thrill of London's high society behind does he authenticate the notion of being a "man of great expectations." We are dealing here with a kind of Hegelian reflexivity: what changes in the course of the hero's ordeal is not only his character, but also the very ethical stan-dard by which we measure his character. And did not something of the same order happen at the opening ceremony of the 1996 Olympic Games in Atlanta, when Muham-mad Ali lit the Olympic flame with the torch held by a hand shaking violently on ac-count of his severe illness—when the journalists claimed that, in doing this, he truly was "The Greatest" (a reference to Ali's boastful self-designation decades ago, the title of the film about himself in which he starred, and of his autobiography), they, of course, wanted to emphasize that Muhammad Ali has achieved true greatness now, through his dignified endurance of his debilitating illness, not when he was enjoying the full adu-lation of popularity and smashing his opponents in the ring. . . . This is what "negation of negation" is: the shift of perspective which turns failure into true success.

The main way to assert the actuality of Hegel—that is, to save him from the accusation that his system is totally outdated metaphysical madness—is to read his thought as an attempt to establish the normative conditions or presuppositions of our cognitive and ethical claims: Hegel's logic is not a system of universal ontology, but simply a systematic deployment of all the ways available to us of making claims about what there is, and the inherent inconsistencies of these ways. In this reading, Hegel's starting point is the fact that the fundamental structure of the human mind is self-reflective: a human being does not simply act, he or she (can) act(s) upon rational freely assumed norms and motivations, which means that, in order to account for our statements and attitudes, we can never simply refer to some positive data (natural laws and processes, divine Reason, God's Will . . .)—each of these references has to be justified; its normative binding power has to be somehow accounted for. The problem with this elegant solution is that, in contrast to the robust direct metaphysical reading of Hegel as presenting the structure of the Absolute, it is too modest: it silently reduces Hegel's logic to a system of global epistemology, of all possible epistemological stances, and what gets lost to it is the intersection between the epistemological and ontological aspects, the way "reality" itself is caught in the movement of our knowing it (or, vice versa, how our knowing of reality is embedded in reality itself, like journalists embedded with the US Army units in Iraq).

THE BIRTH OF (HEGELIAN) CONCRETE UNIVERSALITY
OUT OF THE SPIRIT OF (KANTIAN) ANTINOMIES

On the southern side of the demilitarized zone in Korea, there is a unique visitors' site: a theater building with a large screenlike window in front, opening up onto the North. The spectacle people observe when they take their seats and look through the window is reality itself (or, rather, a kind of "desert of the real"): the barren demilitarized zone with walls, and so on, and, beyond, a glimpse of North Korea. (As if to comply with the fiction, North Korea has built in front of this theater a pure fake, a model village with beautiful houses; in the evening, the lights in all the houses are turned on at the same time, although nobody lives in them.) Is this not a pure case of the symbolic efficiency of the frame as such? A barren zone is given a fantasmatic status, elevated into a spectacle, solely by being enframed. Nothing substantially changes here—it is merely that, viewed through the frame, reality turns into *its own appearance*. A supreme case of such an ontological comedy occurred in December 2001 in Buenos Aires, when Argentinians took to the streets to protest against the current government, and especially against Cavallo, the economy minister. When the crowd gathered around Cavallo's building, threatening to storm it, he escaped wearing a mask of himself (sold in disguise shops so that people could mock him by wearing his mask). It thus seems that at least Cavallo did learn something from the widespread Lacanian movement in Argentina—the fact that *a thing is its own best mask*. What one encounters in tautology (the repetition of the same) is thus pure difference—not the difference between the element and other elements, but the difference of the element from itself.

The fundamental lesson of Hegel is that the key ontological problem is not that of reality, but that of appearance: not "Are we condemned to the interminable play of appearances, or can we penetrate their veil to the underlying true reality?", but "How could—in the middle of the flat, stupid reality which just is there—something like appearance emerge?" The minimal ontology of parallax is therefore that of the Moebius strip, of the curved space that is bent onto itself. That is to say, the minimal parallax constellation is that of a simple frame: all that has to intervene in the Real is an empty frame, so that the same things we saw "directly" before are now seen through the frame. A certain surplus-effect is thus generated which cannot simply be cancelled through "demystification": it is not enough to display the mechanism behind the frame, the stage effect within the frame acquires an autonomy of its own. How is this possible? There is only one conclusion which can account for this gap: there is no "neutral" reality within which gaps occur, within which frames isolate domains of appearances. Every field of "reality" (every "world") is always-already enframed, seen through an invisible frame. The parallax is not symmetrical, composed of two incompatible perspectives on the same X: there is an irreducible asymmetry between the two perspectives, a minimal reflexive twist. We do not have two perspectives, we have a perspective and what eludes it, and the other perspective fills in this void of what we could not see from the first perspective.

One of the minimal definitions of a modernist painting concerns the function of its frame. The frame of the painting in front of us is not its true frame; there is another, invisible, frame, the frame implied by the structure of the painting, the frame that enframes our perception of the painting, and these two frames by definition never overlap—an invisible gap separates them. The pivotal content of the painting is not communicated in its visible part, but located in this dis-location of the two frames, in the gap that separates them. This dimension in-between-the-two-frames is obvious in Kazimir Malevich (what is his *Black Square on White Background* if not the minimal marking of the distance between the two frames?), in Edward Hopper (recall his lone figures at night in office buildings or diners, where it seems as if the picture's frame has to be redoubled with another window frame—or, in the portraits of his wife close to an open window, exposed to the sun's rays, the opposite excess of the painted content itself with regard to what we actually see, as if we see only the fragment of the whole picture, the shot with a missing countershot), and, again, in Edvard Munch's *Madonna*—the droplets of sperm and the small fetuslike figure from *The Scream* squeezed in between the two frames. The frame is always-already redoubled: the frame within "reality" is always linked to another frame enframing "reality" itself. Once introduced, the gap between reality and appearance is thus immediately complicated, reflected-into-itself: once we get a glimpse, through the Frame, of the Other Dimension, *reality itself turns into appearance*. In other words, things do not simply appear, they *appear to appear*. This is why the negation of a negation does not bring us to a simple flat affirmation: once things (start to) appear, they not only appear as what they are not, creating an illusion; they can also appear to just appear, concealing the fact that they are what they appear to be.

It is this logic of the "minimal difference," of the constitutive noncoincidence of a thing with itself, which provides the key to the central Hegelian category of "concrete universality." Let us take a "mute" abstract universality which encompasses a set of elements all of which somehow subvert, do not fit, this universal frame—in this case, is the "true" concrete universal not this distance itself, the universalized exception? And vice versa, is not the element which directly fits the universal the true exception? Not only—as the cliché would have it—is universality based in an exception; Lacan goes a step further: universality *is* its exception, it "appears as such" in its exception. This is what Badiou et al. deployed as the logic of the "supernumerary" element: the exception (the element with no place in the structure) which immediately stands for the universal dimension. Christianity first introduced this notion: Christ, the miserable outcast, *is* man as such (*ecce homo*). Democracy—in its true grandeur, not in its postpolitical logic of administration and compromise among multiple interests—is part of the same tradition: the "part of no-part," those with no proper place within the social edifice, *are* directly the universality of "people."

Universality is not the neutral container of particular formations, their common measure, the passive (back)ground on which the particulars fight their battles, but this battle itself, the struggle leading from one particular formation to another. Take Krzysztof Kieślowski's passage from documentary to fiction cinema: we do not simply have two species of cinema, documentary and fiction; fiction emerges out of the inherent limitation of the documentary. Kieślowski's starting point was shared with all the cineastes in the Socialist countries: the conspicuous gap between the drab social reality and the bright, optimistic image which pervaded the heavily censored official media. The first reaction to the fact that, in Poland, social reality was "unrepresented," as Kieślowski put it, was, of course, the move toward a more adequate representation of real life in all its drabness and ambiguity—in short, an authentic documentary approach:

> There was a necessity, a need—which was very exciting for us—to describe the world. The Communist world had described how it should be and not how it really was. . . . If something hasn't been described, then it doesn't officially exist. So that if we start describing it, we bring it to life.[22]

I need only mention *Hospital*, Kieślowski's 1976 documentary, in which the camera follows orthopedic surgeons on a 32-hour shift. Instruments fall apart in their hands, the electric current keeps breaking, there are shortages of the most basic materials, but the doctors persevere hour after hour, and with humor. . . . Then, however, the obverse experience set in, best captured by the slogan used recently to publicize a Hollywood movie: "It's so real, it must be fiction!"—at the most radical level, one can portray the Real of subjective experience only in the guise of a fiction. Toward the end of the documentary *First Love* (1974), in which the camera follows a young unmarried couple during the girl's pregnancy, through their wedding, and the delivery of the baby, the father is shown holding the newborn baby in his arms and crying—Kieślowski reacted to the obscenity of such unwarranted probing into the other's intimacy with the "fright of real tears." His decision to move from documentaries to fiction films was thus, at its most radical, an ethical one:

> Not everything can be described. That's the documentary's great problem. It catches itself as if in its own trap. . . . If I'm making a film about love, I can't go into a bedroom if real people are making love there. . . . I noticed, when making documentaries, that the closer I wanted to get to an individual, the more objects which interested me shut themselves off.
>   That's probably why I changed to features. There's no problem there. I need a couple to make love in bed, that's fine. Of course, it might be difficult to find an actress who's willing to take off her bra, but then you just find one who is. . . . I can even buy some glycerine, put some drops in her eyes and the actress will cry. I managed to photograph some real tears several times. It's something completely different. But now I've got glycerine. I'm frightened of real tears. In fact, I don't even know whether I've got the right to photograph them. At such times I feel like somebody who's found himself in a realm which is, in fact, out of bounds. That's the main reason why I escaped from documentaries.[23]

The crucial intermediary in this passage from documentary to fiction is *Camera Buff* (1979), the portrait of a man who, because of his passion for the camera, loses his wife, child, and job—a fiction film about a documentary film-maker. So there is a domain of fantasmatic intimacy which is marked by a "No trespassers!" sign and should be approached only via fiction, if one is to avoid pornographic obscenity. This is why the French Véronique in *The Double Life of Véronique* rejects the puppeteer: he wants to penetrate her too much, which is why, toward the end, after he tells her the story of her double life, she is deeply hurt and escapes to her father.[24] "Concrete universality" is a name for this process through which fiction explodes documentary from within— for the way the emergence of fiction cinema resolves the inherent deadlock of documentary cinema. (Or, in philosophy, the point is not to conceive eternity as opposed to temporality, but eternity as it emerges from within our temporal experience—or, in an even more radical way, as Schelling did it, to conceive time itself as a subspecies of eternity, as the resolution of a deadlock of eternity.)[25]

This brings us to the very heart of the concept of concrete universality: concrete universality is not merely the universal core that animates a series of its particular forms of appearance; it persists in the very irreducible tension, noncoincidence, between these different levels. Hegel is usually perceived as an "essentialist historicist," positing the spiritual "essence" of an epoch as a universal principle which expresses itself in a specific way in each domain of social life; the modern principle of subjectivity, for example, expresses itself in religion as Protestantism, in ethics as the subject's moral autonomy, in politics as democratic equality, and so on. What such a view misses is what I am tempted to call temporal parallax: in the complex dialectic of historical phenomena, we encounter events or processes which, although they are the actualization of the same underlying "principle" at different levels, for that very reason cannot occur at the same historical moment.

Take the old topic of the relationship between Protestantism, the Kantian philosophical revolution, and the French political revolution. Rebecca Comay recently refuted the myth that Hegel's critique of the French Revolution can be reduced to a variation of the "German" idea of how the Catholic French had to perform the violent "real" political revolution because they missed the historical moment of Reformation which had already accomplished in the spiritual sphere the reconciliation between spiritual Substance and infinite subjectivity sought after in social reality by the revolutionaries. According to this standard view, the German ethico-aesthetic attitude "sublates" revolutionary violence in the inner ethical order, thus enabling the replacement of the abstract "terrorist" revolutionary freedom by the concrete freedom of the State as an aesthetic organic Whole. Already, however, the temporality of this relationship between the French political revolution and the German spiritual reformation is ambiguous: all three possible relations seem to overlap here. First, the idea of "sublation" points toward a succession: the French "immediate" unity of the Universal and the Subject is followed by its sublation, the German ethico-aesthetic mediation. Then there is the idea of a simultaneous choice (or lack thereof) which made the two nations follow a different path: the Germans opted for Reformation, while the French remained within the Catholic universe, and had thus to take the tortuous route of violent revolution. However, the empirical fact that Kant's philosophical revolution precedes the French Revolution is also not just an insignificant accident—in the spectacle of revolutionary Terror, Kantian ethics itself encounters the ultimate consequence of its own "abstract" character, so that Kant's philosophy should be read retroactively, through the prism of the French Revolution, which enables us to perceive its limitations:

> If [the Kantian moral view] presents itself as the narrative successor to the revolution, this is not because it logically fulfils or supersedes it: Kant's critical venture *phenomenologically* succeeds the revolution that it *chronologically*, of course, anticipates only insofar as his text becomes legible only retroactively through the event that in institutionalizing the incessant short circuit of freedom and cruelty puts the project of modernity to its most extreme trial. . . .The revolution itself inflicts on Kant's own text a kind of retroactive trauma.[26]

This means that the revolutionary Terror is a kind of obscene double of Kant's ethical thought: its destructive violence merely "externalizes" the terrorist potential of Kant's thought. That is why—and this is Hegel's central insight—it is hypocritical to reject the "excesses" of the French Revolution from the standpoint of the "German" moral view: all its terrifying features found their counterpart in, are contained and repeated within, the Kantian spiritual edifice (and here the term "repetition" has to be given the entire weight of Freud's *Wiederholungszwang*):

the purity of the moral will can be no antidote to the terrifying purity of revolutionary virtue. All the logical problems of absolute freedom are essentially carried over into Hegel's analysis of Kantian morality: the obsessionality, the paranoia, the suspicion, the evaporation of objectivity, within the violent hyperbole of a subjectivity bent on reproducing itself within a world it must disavow.[27]

So, insofar as we are dealing here with a historical choice (between the "French" way of remaining within Catholicism, and thus being obliged to engage in self-destructive revolutionary Terror, and the "German" way of Reformation), this choice involves exactly the same elementary dialectical paradox as the one, also from *Phenomenology of Spirit*, between the two readings of "the Spirit is a bone" which Hegel illustrates by the phallic metaphor (the phallus as the organ of insemination or the phallus as the organ of urination): Hegel's point is not that, in contrast to the vulgar empiricist mind which sees only urination, the proper speculative attitude has to choose insemination. The paradox is that the direct choice of insemination is the infallible way of missing it: it is not possible to choose the "true meaning" directly, one has to begin by making the "wrong" choice (of urination)—the true speculative meaning emerges only through the repeated reading, as the after-effect (or by-product) of the first, "wrong" reading.

The same goes for social life in which the direct choice of the "concrete universality" of a particular ethical life-world can only end in a regression to premodern organic society that denies the infinite right of subjectivity as the fundamental feature of modernity. Since the subject-citizen of a modern state can no longer accept his immersion in some particular social role that confers on him a determinate place within the organic social Whole, the only way to the rational totality of the modern State leads through revolutionary Terror: we should ruthlessly tear up the constraints of the premodern organic "concrete universality," and fully assert the infinite right of subjectivity in all its abstract negativity. In other words, the point of Hegel's analysis of the revolutionary Terror is not the rather obvious insight into how the revolutionary project involved the unilateral direct assertion of abstract Universal Reason, and was as such doomed to perish in self-destructive fury, since it was unable to organize the transposition of its revolutionary energy into a concrete stable and differentiated social order; Hegel's point is, rather, the enigma of why, despite the fact that revolutionary Terror was a historical deadlock, we have to go through it in order to arrive at the modern rational State. So—back to the choice between the Protestant "inner revolution" and the French violent political revolution—this means that Hegel is far from endorsing the self-complacent German superiority ("We made the right choice, and can thus avoid revolutionary madness"): precisely because the Germans *made the right choice at the wrong time* (too early: in the age of Reformation), they cannot gain access to the rational State that would be at the level of true political modernity.

We should take a step further here: it is not only that the universal Essence articulates itself in the discord between its particular forms of appearance; this discord is propelled by a gap that pertains to the very core of the universal Essence itself. In his book on modernity, Fredric Jameson refers to the Hegelian "concrete universality" in his concise critique of the recently fashionable theories of "alternate modernities":

> How then can the ideologues of "modernity" in its current sense manage to distinguish their product—the information revolution, and globalized, free-market modernity— from the detestable older kind, without getting themselves involved in asking the kinds of serious political and economic, systemic questions that the concept of a postmodernity makes unavoidable? The answer is simple: you talk about "alternate" or "alternative" modernities. Everyone knows the formula by now: this means that there can be a modernity for everybody which is different from the standard or hegemonic Anglo-Saxon model. Whatever you dislike about the latter, including the subaltern position it leaves you in, can be effaced by the reassuring and "cultural" notion that you can fashion your own modernity differently, so that there can be a Latin-American kind, or an Indian kind or an African kind, and so on. . . . But this is to overlook the other fundamental meaning of modernity which is that of a worldwide capitalism itself.[28]

The significance of this critique reaches far beyond the case of modernity—it concerns the fundamental limitation of nominalist historicizing. The recourse to multiplication ("there is not one modernity with a fixed essence, there are multiple modernities, each of them irreducible to others . . .") is false not because it does not recognize a unique fixed "essence" of modernity, but because multiplication functions as the disavowal of the antagonism that inheres to the notion of modernity as such: the falsity of multiplication resides in the fact that it frees the universal notion of modernity of its antagonism, of the way it is embedded in the capitalist system, by relegating this aspect to just one of its historical subspecies. (We should not forget that the first half of the twentieth century was marked by two big projects which fit this notion of "alternate modernity" perfectly: Fascism and Communism. Was not the basic idea of Fascism that of a modernity which provides an alternative to the standard Anglo-Saxon liberal-capitalist one of saving the core of capitalist modernity by casting away its "contingent" Jewish-individualist-profiteering distortion? And was not the rapid industrialization of the USSR in the late 1920s and 1930s also an attempt at a modernization different from the Western-capitalist one?) And, insofar as this inherent antagonism could be designated as a "castrative" dimension, and, furthermore, insofar as, according to Freud, the disavowal of castration is represented as the multiplication of the phallus-representatives (a multitude of phalluses signals castration, the lack of the one), it is easy to conceive such a multiplication of modernities as a form of fetishist disavowal.

Jameson's critique of the notion of alternate modernities thus provides a model of the properly *dialectical* relationship between the Universal and the Particular: the difference is not on the side of particular content (as the traditional *differentia specifica*), but on the side of the Universal. The Universal is not the encompassing container of the particular content, the peaceful medium-background of the conflict of particularities; the Universal "as such" is the site of an unbearable antagonism, self-contradiction, and (the multitude of) its particular species are ultimately nothing but so many attempts to obfuscate/reconcile/master this antagonism. In other words, the Universal names the site of a Problem-Deadlock, of a burning Question, and the Particulars are the attempted but failed Answers to this Problem. The concept of State, for instance, names a certain problem: how to contain the class antagonism of a society? All particular forms of State are so many (failed) attempts to propose a solution to this problem.

This is how one should answer the standard critique of Christian universalism: what this all-inclusive attitude (recall Saint Paul's famous "There is neither male nor female, neither Jew nor Greek") involves is a thorough exclusion of those who do not agree to be included into the Christian community. In other "particularistic" religions (and even in Islam, despite its global expansionism) there is a place for others; they are tolerated, even if they are looked upon condescendingly. The Christian motto "All men are brothers," however, also means that "Those who are not my brothers are not (even) men." Christians usually praise themselves for overcoming the Jewish exclusivist notion of the Chosen People, and encompassing the whole of humanity—the catch here is that, in their very insistence that they are the Chosen People with a privileged direct link to God, the Jews accept the humanity of other people who celebrate their false gods, while Christian universalism tendentially excludes nonbelievers from the very universality of humankind. . . .

But Christian universality is not the all-encompassing global medium where there is a place for all and everyone—it is, rather, a struggling universality, the site of a constant battle. Which battle, which division? To follow Saint Paul: not the division between Law and sin, but between, on one side, the totality of Law and sin as its supplement, and, on the other, the way of Love. Christian universality is the universality which emerges at the symptomal point of those who are "part of no-part" of the global order—this is where the accusation of exclusion gets it wrong: Christian universality, far from excluding some subjects, *is formulated from the position of those excluded*, of those for whom there is no specific place within the existing order, although they belong to it; universality is strictly codependent with this lack of specific place/determination.

Or, to put it in a different way: the accusation against Saint Paul's universalism misses the true site of universality: the universal dimension he opened up is not the "neither Greek nor Jew but all Christians," which implicitly excludes non-Christians; *it is, rather, the difference Christians/non-Christians itself which, as a difference, is universal*, that is to say, cuts across the entire social body, splitting, dividing from within every substantial ethnic, etc., identity—Greeks are divided into Christians and non-Christians, as well as Jews. The standard accusation thus, in a way, knocks on an open door: the whole point of the Pauline notion of struggling universality is that true universality and partiality do not exclude each other, but *universal Truth is accessible only from a partial engaged subjective position*.

Another name for this cut across the entire social body is, of course, antagonism; the logic of irreducible antagonism was recently developed by Ernesto Laclau in contrast to the Hegelian concrete universality which, allegedly, "sublates" (overcomes) all antagonisms in a higher mediated unity. Is this really the case, however, or, on the contrary, does the reference to Hegel enable us to discern a flaw in Laclau's theory? The philosophical/notional limitation of Laclau's coupling of two logics, that of difference and that of antagonism, is that he treats them as two externally opposed poles. When Laclau elaborates his fundamental opposition between the logic of difference and the logic of equivalence, he asserts the coincidence of opposites: the two logics are not simply opposed, but each logic, brought to its extreme, converts into its opposite.[29] That is to say, as he repeatedly points out, a system of pure differentiality (a system totally defined by the differential structure of its elements, with no antagonism and/or impossibility traversing it) would lead to a pure equivalence of all its elements—they are all equivalent with regard to the void of their Outside; and, at the other extreme, a system of radical antagonism with no structure at all, just the pure opposition of Us and Them, would coincide with a naturalized difference between Us and Them as the positively existing opposed species. . . . From a Hegelian standpoint, however, this logic continues to rely on the two externally opposed poles—the fact that each of the opposites, in its abstraction from the other (that is, brought to the extreme at which it no longer needs the other as its opposite), falls into this other, merely demonstrates their mutual reliance. What we need to do is to take a step further from this external opposition (or mutual reliance) into direct internalized overlapping, which means: not only does one pole, when abstracted from the other and thus brought to the extreme, coincide with its opposite, but *there is no "primordial" duality of poles in the first place, only the inherent gap of the One.* Equivalence is primordially not the opposite of difference; equivalence emerges only because no system of differences can ever complete itself, it "is" a structural effect of this incompleteness.[30] The tension between immanence and transcendence is thus also secondary with regard to the gap within immanence itself: "transcendence" is a kind of perspective illusion, the way we (mis)perceive the gap/discord that inheres to immanence itself. In the same way, the tension between the Same and the Other is secondary with regard to the noncoincidence of the Same with itself.

This means that the opposition of two logics, that of antagonism and that of difference, is the deployment of a logically preceding term, of the inherent "pure" difference, the minimal difference which marks the noncoincidence of the One with itself. This noncoincidence, this "pure difference," can either unravel into a multitude of entities forming a differential totality, or split into the antagonistic opposition of two terms. And this duality again follows the logic of Lacan's formulas of sexuation—contrary to expectations, the differential multitude is "masculine," while the antagonism is "feminine." The primordial gap is thus not the polar opposition of two principles (masculine and feminine, light and dark, opening and closure . . .), but the minimal gap between an element and itself, the Void of its own place of inscription. It is this gap that Schelling aims at when he distinguishes between Existence and its impenetrable Ground, and this is why he is right to reject the accusation of dualism: Schelling remains a monist: there is only One, the gap is inherent to this One itself—not as the gap between its two opposite aspects, but as the gap between One and the Void.[31]

In Lacanian terms, the space of the Laclauian logic of hegemony is that of the tension between the empty Master-Signifier and the series of "ordinary" signifiers which struggle to fill in the Master-Signifier with a particular content: the struggle for Democracy (today's Master-Signifier) is in what it will mean, which kind of democracy will hegemonize the universal notion.

So what is a Master-Signifier? Let us imagine a confused situation of social disintegration, in which the cohesive power of ideology loses its efficiency: in such a situation, the Master is the one who invents a new signifier, the famous "quilting point," which stabilizes the situation again and makes it readable; the university discourse which then elaborates the network of Knowledge which sustains this readability by definition presupposes and relies on the initial gesture of the Master. The Master adds no new positive content—he merely adds a signifier which, all of a sudden, turns disorder into order, into "new harmony," as Rimbaud would have put it. Think about anti-Semitism in 1920s Germany: people experienced themselves as disoriented, thrown into undeserved military defeat, an economic crisis which eroded away their life savings, political inefficiency, moral degeneration . . . and the Nazis provided a single agent which accounted for it all—the Jew, the Jewish plot. Therein lies the magic of a Master: although there is nothing new at the level of positive content, "nothing is quite the same" after he pronounces his Word. . . . For example, in order to illustrate *le point de capiton*, Lacan quotes the famous lines from Racine's *Athalie*: "*Je crains Dieu, cher Abner, et je n'ai point d'autre crainte.*/I fear God, my dear Abner, and have no other fears"—all fears are exchanged for one fear; that is to say, it is the very fear of God which makes me fearless in all worldly matters. The same reversal that gives rise to a new Master-Signifier is at work in ideology: in anti-Semitism, all fears (of economic crisis, of moral degradation . . .) are exchanged for the fear of the Jew—*je crains le Juif, cher citoyen, et je n'ai point d'autre crainte.* . . . And is not the same logic also discernible in a horror film like Spielberg's *Jaws?* I fear the shark, my friend, and have no other fears. . . .

So when, in his (forthcoming) *Logique des mondes*, in order to designate the moment of pure subjective decision/choice which stabilizes a world, Badiou proposes the concept of "point" as a simple decision in a situation reduced to a choice of Yes or No, he implicitly refers to Lacan's *point de capiton*, of course—and does this not imply that there is no "world" outside language, no world whose horizon of meaning is not determined by a symbolic order? The passage to truth is therefore the passage from language ("the limits of my language are the limits of my world") to *letter*, to "mathemes" which run diagonally across a multitude of worlds. Postmodern relativism is precisely the thought of the irreducible *multitude of worlds*, each of them sustained by a specific language-game, so that each world "is" the narrative its members are telling themselves about themselves, with no shared terrain, no common language between them; and the problem of truth is how to establish something that—to use terms that are popular in modal logic—remains the same in all possible worlds.

We can now see in what precise sense we are to conceive of Lacan's thesis according to which what is "primordially repressed" is the binary signifier (that of *Vorstellungs-Repräsentanz*): what the symbolic order precludes is the full harmonious presence of the couple of Master-Signifiers, S_1–S_2 as *yin-yang*, or any other two symmetrical "fundamental principles." The fact that "there is no sexual relationship" means precisely that the secondary signifier (that of the Woman) is "primordially repressed," and *what we get in the place of this repression, what fills in its gap, is the multitude of "returns of the repressed," the series of "ordinary" signifiers*. In Woody Allen's Tolstoy parody *Love and Death*, the first association that automatically crops up, of course, is: "If there is Tolstoy, where is Dostoevsky?" In the film, Dostoevsky (the "binary signifier" to Tolstoy) remains "repressed"—however, the price exacted for this is that a conversation in the middle of the film, as it were, accidentally includes the titles of all Dostoevsky's main novels: "Is that man still in the underground?" "You mean one of the Karamazov brothers?" "Yes, that idiot!" "Well, he did commit his crime and was punished for it!" "I know, he was a gambler who always risked too much!", and so on. Here we encounter the "return of the repressed," that is, the series of signifiers which fills in the gap of the repressed binary signifier "Dostoevsky."

This is why the standard deconstructionist criticism according to which Lacan's theory of sexual difference falls into the trap of "binary logic" totally misses the point: Lacan's *la femme n'existe pas* aims precisely at undermining the "binary" polar couple Masculine and Feminine—the original split is not between the One and the Other, but is strictly inherent to the One; it is the split between the One and its empty place of inscription (this is how we should read Kafka's famous statement that the Messiah will come one day after his arrival). This is also how we should conceive the link between the split inherent to the One and the explosion of the multiple: the multiple is not the primordial ontological fact; the "transcendental" genesis of the multiple resides in the lack of the binary signifier: that is, the multiple emerges as the series of attempts to fill in the gap of the missing binary signifier. The difference between S_1 and S_2 is thus not the difference of two opposed poles within the same field but, rather, the cut inherent to the one term, its noncoincidence with itself: the original couple is not that of two signifiers, but that of the signifier and its *reduplicatio*, that is to say, the minimal difference between a signifier and the place of its inscription, between one and zero.[32]

The same self-reflexivity is crucial for the status of the gaze itself: the gaze turns into an object when it passes "from inquisitiveness, from the gaze into the interior, to the gaze *ex qua*—from inside to outside. This turning constitutes a fundamental upheaval: it assumes that one goes from a kind of public gaze on intimate scenes to the entry of the gaze itself into the secret, the intimate—this would also be the ultimate moment necessary for the entry of the voyeur."[33] The homology with the figure of the Master (agent of symbolic prohibition) is significant here: just as the Father *qua* the agent of prohibition (preventing the subject's free access to libidinal objects) himself has to be prohibited (as a libidinal object), the gaze which seeks satisfaction by peering into intimate domain of private secrets has itself to turn into a secret, into something that strives to remain hidden, invisible in the public space. What this reflexivity of the symbolic order (the fact that this order involves the minimal difference between an element and its structural place) does to the ethical choice is to introduce its redoubling: the choice is never simply the one between doing my duty or following my striving for "pathological" pleasures and satisfactions; this elementary choice is always redoubled by the one between elevating my striving for pleasures itself into my supreme Duty, and doing my Duty not for the sake of Duty but because it gives me satisfaction to do it. In the first case *pleasures are my duty*: the "pathological" striving for pleasures is located into the formal space of Duty; in the second case *duty is my pleasure*: doing my duty is located in the formal space of "pathological" satisfactions. Thus Derrida is fully justified in emphasizing the self-reflexivity of the prohibition with regard to the Law—the Law not only prohibits, it is *itself* prohibited:

> The law is prohibition: this does not mean that it prohibits, but that it is itself prohibited, a prohibited place . . . one cannot reach the law, and in order to have a rapport of respect with it, one must not have a rapport with the law, one must interrupt the relation. One must enter into relation only with the law's representatives, its examples, its guardians. These are interrupters as much as messengers. One must not know who or what or where the law is.[34]

In one of his short fragments, Kafka himself pointed out how the ultimate secret of the Law is that it *does not exist*—another case of what Lacan called the nonexistence of the big Other. This nonexistence, of course, does not simply reduce the Law to an empty imaginary chimera; rather, it makes it into an impossible Real, a void which nonetheless functions, exerts influence, causes effects, curves the symbolic space. So when Derrida writes:

> the inaccessible transcendence of the law, before which and prior to which man stands fast, only appears infinitely transcendent and thus theological to the extent that, nearest to him, it depends only on him, on the performative act by which he institutes it. . . . The law is transcendent and theological, and so always to come, always promised, *because* it is immanent, finite, and thus already past,[35]

the ambiguity of this statement is crucial: does it mean that this appearance of transcendence is a necessary illusion, a structural misperception (as Deleuze also claims in his reading of Kafka)? Is it, then, possible to break out of this misreading, to fully assume that "it all depends only on me"? And does this not happen precisely in Christianity? Is this not the core of incarnation? The obverse aspect of this reflexivity is to be found in the fact that what Lacan calls "Master-Signifier" is the reflexive signifier that fills in the very lack of the signifier. Spinoza's own supreme example of "God" is crucial here: conceived as a mighty person, God merely embodies our ignorance of true causality. Examples from the history of science abound here—from phlogiston (a pseudo-concept which merely betrayed the scientist's ignorance of how light really travels) to Marx's "Asiatic mode of production" (a kind of negative container: the only true content of this concept is "all the modes of production which do not fit Marx's standard categorization of the modes of production"), not to mention today's popular "postindustrial society"—notions which, while they appear to designate a positive content, merely reveal our ignorance.

However, did we not oscillate here between two opposed versions? In the first version, the binary signifier, the symmetric counterpart of S_1, is "primordially repressed," and it is in order to supplement the void of his repression that the chain of S_2 emerges—that is to say, the original fact is the couple of S_1 and the Void at the place of its counterpart, and the chain of S_2 is secondary; in the second version, in the account of the emergence of S_1 as the "enigmatic term," the empty signifier, the primordial fact is, on the contrary, S_2, the signifying chain in its incompleteness, and it is in order to fill in the void of this incompleteness that S_1 intervenes. How are the two versions to be coordinated? Is the ultimate fact the vicious circle of their mutual implication? What if, yet again, these two versions point toward the logic of Lacan's "formulas of sexuation"? Contrary to our expectations, it is the first version—the multitude emerges in order to fill in the void of the binary signifier—which is "feminine," that is, which accounts for the explosion of the inconsistent multitude of the feminine non-All; and the second version which is "masculine," that is, which accounts for the way a multitude is totalized into an All through the exception which fills in its void.

Thus we have generated the four constituents of a discourse: S_1, S_2, $, a$; their interaction, of course, always implies a more complex web.[36] How, then, does objet petit a function in this tension between the Master-Signifier and the series of "ordinary" signifiers that struggle to hegemonize it? While Ernesto Laclau is on the right track when he emphasizes the necessary role of objet petit a in rendering an ideological edifice operative,[37] he curtails the true dimension of this role when he restricts it to the fact of hegemony (of how the void of the Master-Signifier has to be filled in with some particular content). Things are much more precise here: since objet petit a is (also) the object of fantasy, the catch lies in what I am tempted to call, with Kant, the role of "transcendental scheme" played by objet petit a—a fantasy constitutes our desire, provides its coordinates; that is to say, it literally "teaches us how to desire."

The role of fantasy is thus, in a way, analogous to that of the ill-fated pineal gland in Descartes's philosophy, this mediator between res cogitans and res extensa: fantasy mediates between the formal symbolic structure and the positivity of the objects we encounter in reality: it provides a "scheme" according to which certain positive objects in reality can function as objects of desire, filling in the empty places opened up by the formal symbolic structure. To put it in somewhat simplified terms: fantasy does not mean that, when I desire a strawberry cake and cannot get it in reality, I fantasize about eating it; the problem is, rather, how do I know that I desire a strawberry cake in the first place? This is what fantasy tells me. This role of fantasy hinges on the fact that "there is no sexual relationship," no universal formula or matrix guaranteeing a harmonious sexual relationship with one's partner: on account of the lack of this universal formula, every subject has to invent a fantasy of his own, a "private" formula for the sexual relationship—for a man, the relationship with a woman is possible only inasmuch as she fits his formula. In exactly the same way, *objet petit a* is the "sublime object of ideology": it serves as the fantasmatic support of ideological propositions—the anti-abortion struggle, for example, is "schematized" in the figure of a successful professional woman who suppresses her maternal vocation in order to pursue her career; or, as in the UK under John Major's Conservative government, the single unemployed mother was stigmatized by the media as the singular cause of all social ills (Are taxes too high? It is because the state has to support unemployed single mothers! Is there too much juvenile delinquency? It is because single mothers, lacking firm paternal authority, cannot provide proper moral education . . .).

The crucial point here is that, in this tension between a universal statement and its fantasmatic support, *the "truth" is on the side of the universality.* Consider Marx's brilliant analysis of how, in the French Revolution of 1848, the conservative-republican Party of Order functioned as the coalition of the two branches of royalism (Orleanists and Legitimists) in the "anonymous kingdom of the Republic."[38] The parliamentary deputies of the Party of Order perceived their republicanism as a mockery: in parliamentary debates, they continually generated royalist slips of the tongue, ridiculed the Republic, and so on—to let it be known that their true aim was to restore the monarchy. What they were not aware of was that they themselves were duped as to the true social significance of their rule: what they were actually doing was establishing the very conditions of bourgeois republican order that they despised so much in their heart of hearts (guaranteeing the safety of private property, etc.). So it is not that they were royalists who were just wearing a republican mask: although they experienced themselves as such, it was their very "inner" royalist conviction which was the deceptive front masking their true social role. In short, far from being the hidden truth of their public republicanism, their "sincere" royalism was the fantasmatic support of their *actual* republicanism—it was what provided their activity with "passion."[39]

Furthermore, it is not enough to say that every ideological universal functions as an empty signifier which has to be filled in with (hegemonized by) a particular content—to demonstrate how all positive content is a contingent fill-in of the void of the empty signifier; we should move beyond this gap between empty signifier and determinate content, and ask a more radical question: *how, through what violent gesture, does the very void of the empty signifier arise?* This empty space of universality arises from the radical inadequacy (noncoincidence, inherent gap) of a Particular with itself. In other words, not only has the structural lack/void of all universality to be filled in by a particular content, its stand-in; it is this empty universality itself which is a *stand-in* for the radical noncoincidence of the particular to itself, *for a missing particular*, the element whose addition would make the particular "full," coinciding with itself.

Such a convoluted topology is totally absent from Spinoza's thought. Does Spinoza not formulate the highest parallax? The substance is One, and the difference between mind and body, its two modes, is purely that of parallax: "body" or "mind" are the same Substance perceived in a different mode. There is nonetheless a key difference between Spinoza and Hegel here: for Spinoza, the parallax is symmetric (there is no point of contact or of passage between the two modes, each of them merely reveals the same network in a different mode), while for Hegel, the two levels involved in a parallax shift are radically asymmetric: one of the two levels appears to be able to stand on its own, while the other stands for the shift as such, for the gap between the two. In other words, Two are not simply One and One, since Two stands for the very move/shift from One to Two. (A simplified example: in the class struggle between bourgeoisie and proletariat, the proletariat stands for the struggle as such.) The passage from the Spinozan One *qua* the neutral medium/container of its modes and the One's inherent gap is the very passage from Substance to Subject.[40]

The standard critical procedure today is to mobilize the opposition of man and subject: the notion of subjectivity (self-consciousness, self-positing autonomy, and so on) stands for a dangerous hubris, a will to power, which obfuscates and distorts the authentic essence of man; the task is thus to think the essence of man outside the domain of subjectivity. What Lacan tries to accomplish seems to be the exact opposite of this standard procedure: in all his great literary interpretations, from *Oedipus* and *Antigone* through Sade's *Juliette* to Claudel's *The Hostage*, he is in search of a point at which we enter the dimension of the "inhuman," a point at which "humanity" disintegrates, so that all that remains is a pure subject. Sophocles' Antigone, de Sade's Juliette, Claudel's Sygne—they are all figures of such an "inhuman" subject (in contrast to their "human" counterpoint: Ismene, Justine . . .). To paraphrase Nietzsche, what we should consider problematic is what is "human, all too human" in us. We should not be afraid to apply this insight to politics as well: it is only too easy to dismiss the Nazis as inhuman and bestial—what if the problem with the Nazis was precisely that they remained "human, all too human"?[41]

One of the curious stories about Hitler reported in the (in)famous record of his "table conversations" is that, one morning in the early 1940s, he awakened terrified and then, tears streaming down his cheeks, explained the nightmare that haunted him to his doctor: "In my dream, I saw the future overman—they are so totally ruthless, without any consideration for our pains, that I found it unbearable!" The very idea of Hitler, our main candidate for the most evil person of all time, being horrified at a lack of compassion is, of course, weird—but, philosophically, the idea makes sense. Hitler was implicitly referring to the Nietzschean passage from Lion to Child: it is not yet possible for us, caught as we are in the web of the reflective attitude of nihilism, to enter the "innocence of becoming," the full life beyond justification; all we can do is engage in "self-overcoming of morality through truthfulness,"[42] that is, bring the moralistic will-to-truth to its self-cancellation, become aware of the truth about will-to-truth itself (that it is an illusion of and for the weak). We "cannot create new values," we can only be the Lion who, in an outburst of active nihilism, clears the table and thus "creates freedom for new creation";[43] it is after us that the Child will appear who will mark "a new Beginning, a sacred Yes."[44]

The field of comedy is defined by two strangely opposed features: on the one hand, comedy is usually perceived as the intrusion of the vulgar materiality of ordinary life into high pretentious dignity—it cannot but produce a comic effect when the Leader, entering a Hall to preside over a formal meeting, slips on the proverbial banana peel; on the other hand, there is a strange immortality that pertains to comic figures, analogous to the ability of Sadeian victims to survive all their misfortunes. Back to our example of the Leader slipping on a banana peel: the truly comic thing is that even after he slips, he is able to maintain his dignity and go on as if nothing has happened . . . (if he is not, then we are dealing, rather, with a sad—if not downright tragic—spectacle of a Leader deprived of his dignity). How are we to think these two features together? Alenka Zupančič[45] provides a properly Hegelian answer: it is true that the space of the comic is the space between the dignified symbolic mask and the ridiculous vulgarity of ordinary life, with its petty passions and weaknesses; the properly comic procedure, however, is not simply to undermine the dignified mask (or task or sublime passion) through the intrusion of everyday reality, but to enact a kind of structural short circuit or, rather, exchange of places between the two in which the very dignified mask/task/passion appears as a pathetic idiosyncrasy, an utterly human weakness. Think of the standard generic comic heroes (Miser, Drunkard, Seducer): it is this very attachment to some excessive task/passion which *makes them human*. This is why Chaplin was right in his *Great Dictator*: Hitler's hubris was not "inhuman," out of the range of sympathy for ordinary pleasures and weaknesses—Hitler was "human, all too human," his political hubris was an "all too human" idiosyncrasy which makes him ridiculous. In short, Hitler was a burlesque figure of Evil Dictator who belongs into the same series as Seducer, Miser, and Deceiving Servant.

What, then, is the elementary dimension of subjectivity? Rebecca Comay has drawn attention to how, in Hegel's reading, the self-destructive fury of the revolutionary Terror as the actualization of Absolute Freedom simultaneously abolishes every Beyond, while reducing death to a meaningless chopping-off of a cabbage-head, and remains haunted by an obscene spectral Beyond which returns in the guise of "undead" apparitions:

> The obsessive fantasies of survival entertained by the popular imaginary of the guillotine, and that preoccupied both literature and medical science from the 1970s, are but the inversion and confirmation of the living death to which life had seemingly been reduced—thus the proliferation of blushing heads, talking heads, suffering heads, heads that dreamed, screamed, returned the gaze, the disembodied body parts, detached writing hands, the ghosts and ghouls and zombies that would fill the pages of gothic novels throughout Europe.[46]

Does this not take us back to the famous passage from the beginning of Hegel's "Jenaer Realphilosophie" about the "night of the world"?

> The human being is this night, this empty nothing, that contains everything in its simplicity—an unending wealth of many representations, images, of which none belongs to him—or which are not present. This night, the interior of nature, that exists here—pure self—in phantasmagorical representations, is night all around it, in which here shoots a bloody head—there another white ghastly apparition, suddenly here before it, and just so disappears. One catches sight of this night when one looks human beings in the eye—into a night that becomes awful.[47]

It is thus as if the frenzy of the revolutionary upheaval brings us back to the zero-level of subjectivity in which the subject is confronted not with constituted reality but with the spectral obscene proto-reality of partial objects floating around against the background of the ontological Void.[48] This "inter-space," the gap constitutive of a human being, appears at three levels:

1. First, as the "vanishing mediator" between Nature and Culture, the "inhuman" excess of freedom which is to be disciplined through culture. This zero-degree of "humanization" can be formulated in Hegelian terms as the reflexive reversal of the human animal (*Mensch-Tier*) into the animal human (*Tier-Mensch*): the shift of the structural place of the same element from the excess to the neutral base, zero-level—that is, from the human excess which distorts animality to the zero-level of humanity.[49]
2. Then, as the Real of antagonism, the difference which paradoxically precedes what it is a difference of, the two terms being a reaction to the difference, two ways of coping with its trauma.
3. Finally, as the "minimal difference" on account of which an individual is never fully him/herself, but always only "resembles him/herself." The Marx Brothers were right: "You look like X, so no wonder you *are* X. . . ." This means, of course, that there is no positive-substantial determination of man: man is the animal which recognizes itself as man, what makes him human is this formal gesture of recognition as such, not the recognized content. Man is a lack which, in order to fill itself in, recognizes itself as something.

This triad, of course, is that of Universal-Particular-Individual: the Vanishing Mediator constitutive of the Universality of Humankind; the "particular" division into species (sexual difference, class difference) which cuts into that Universality; the minimal distance, noncoincidence-with-itself, constitutive of the Individual.

In Leonardo da Vinci's *Mona Lisa*, there is a strange discrepancy between figure and background: there is no continuity between the two, between the figure of Mona Lisa and the strangely complex, almost Gothic, background of trees, rocks, and so on. It is as if, in effect, Mona Lisa stands in front of a painted background, not in a real environment: the painted background stands for the void which is filled in with painting.[50] Does this same discrepancy not account also for the strange attraction of old Hollywood films from the 1930s and 1940s in which actors are so obviously acting in front of a projected background? Take the systematic use of this device in Hitchcock: Ingrid

Bergman skiing down a mountain slope in front of a ridiculously discrepant snowy background in *Spellbound*; Ingrid Bergman again, driving a car in a studio with the uncoordinated background of a night landscape passing by in *Notorious*; and two exemplary cases from his late films (the dining-car-table conversation between Cary Grant and Eva-Marie Saint with a Hudson Bay background in which we pass the same barn three times in *North by Northwest*; Tippi Hedren riding a horse in *Marnie*). Although it is easy to project a conscious strategy into what may simply have been Hitchcock's sloppiness, it is difficult to deny the strange psychological resonance of these shots, as if the very discord between figure and background conveys a key message about the depicted person's subjectivity. It was Orson Welles above all who perfected the expressive use of this technique: one of his standard shots is the American one of the hero too close to the camera, with a blurred background which, even if it is a "true" background, nonetheless generates the effect of something artificial, acquiring a spectral dimension, as if the hero is moving not in the real world but in a phantasmagoric virtual universe. . . . And does the same not go for modern subjectivity? Perhaps it is a crucial fact that the *Mona Lisa* was painted at the dawn of modernity: this irreducible gap between the subject and its "background," the fact that a subject never fully fits its environment, is never fully embedded in it, *defines* subjectivity.

In *Seminar XI*, Lacan denounces the "essential flaw in philosophical idealism":

> There is no subject without, somewhere, *aphanasis* of the subject, and it is in this alienation, in this fundamental division, that the dialectic of the subject is established. In order to answer the question I was asked last time concerning my adhesion to the Hegelian dialectic, is it not enough that, because of the *vel*, the sensitive point, point of balance, there is an emergence of the subject at the level of meaning only from its *aphanasis* in the Other locus, which is that of the unconscious?[51]

Is it not a telltale detail that, in order to designate the subject's fundamental division, he has to resort to the Hegelian term "dialectic"? What is the core of the Hegelian dialectic of the subject if not the very fact that, whenever a subject "posits" a meaning (a project), the truth of this gesture escapes him and persists in another locus, from which it undermines his project?

True, the Hegelian subject is "ecstatic," its mediation opens it up to otherness, shifting, loss of self-identity; however, there is a crucial step further to be accomplished here. Not only is the subject always-already dispossessed-ecstatic, and so on; this ecstasy *is* the subject—that is to say, the subject is the void $ which emerges when a substance is "dispossessed" through ecstasy. Hair-splitting as it may appear, this distinction is crucial: is the status of the subject always limited, dispossessed, exposed, *or is the subject itself a name for/of this dispossession?* From the subject's limitation, we have to move to limit itself as the name for the subject. This is why it is not enough to say that, in Hegel, there is a move of "self-castration," that the subject castrates itself—who is this Self? The problem is that this Self emerges only as the outcome, the result, of castration. This is how the key moment in a dialectical process is the "transubstantiation" of its focal point: what was at first just a predicate, a subordinate moment of the process (money in market economy), becomes (with capitalism) its central moment, retroactively degrading its presuppositions, the elements out of which it emerged, into its subordinate moments, elements of its self-propelling circulation. And this is also how we should approach Hegel's outrageously "speculative" formulations about Spirit as its own result, a product of itself: while "Spirit has its beginnings in nature in general,"

> the extreme to which spirit tends is its freedom, its infinity, its being in and for itself. These are the two aspects, but if we ask what Spirit is, the immediate answer is that it is this motion, this process of proceeding from, of freeing itself from, nature; this is the being, the substance of spirit itself.[52]

Spirit is thus radically de-substantialized: Spirit is not a positive counterforce to nature, a different substance which gradually breaks and shines through the inert natural stuff; it is *nothing but* this process of freeing-itself-from. Hegel directly disowns the notion of Spirit as some kind of positive Agent which underlies the process:

> Spirit is usually spoken of as subject, as doing something, and apart from what it does, as this motion, this process, as still something particular, its activity being more or less contingent . . . it is of the very nature of spirit to be this absolute liveliness, this process, to proceed forth from naturality, immediacy, to sublate, to quit its naturality, and to come to itself, and *to free itself*, it being itself only as it comes to itself as such a product of itself; *its actuality being merely that it has made itself into what it is.*[53]

If, then, "it is *only* as a result of itself that it is spirit,"[54] this means that the standard talk about the Hegelian Spirit which alienates itself to itself and then recognizes itself in its otherness, and thus reappropriates its content, is deeply misleading: the Self to which spirit returns is produced in the very movement of this return, or, that to which the process of return is returning is produced by the very process of returning. Take the superbly concise formulations from Hegel's *Logic* on how essence

> presupposes itself and the sublating of this presupposition is essence itself; conversely, this sublating of its presupposition is the presupposition itself. Reflection therefore *finds before* it an immediate which it transcends and from which it is the return. But this return is only the presupposing of what reflection finds before it. What it thus found only *comes to be* through being *left behind.* . . . For the presupposition of the return-into-self— that from which essence *comes*, and is only as this return—is only in the return itself.[55]

When Hegel says that a Notion is the result of itself, that it provides its own actualization, this claim which, on a first approach, cannot but appear extravagant (the Notion is not simply a thought activated by the thinking subject, but possesses a magic property of self-movement . . .), is to be approached from the opposite side, as it were; the Spirit as the spiritual substance is a substance, an In-itself, which sustains itself only through the incessant activity of the subjects engaged in it. A nation, for instance, exists only insofar as its members take themselves as members of this nation, and act accordingly; it has absolutely no content, no substantial consistency, outside this activity; and the same goes for, say, the notion of Communism—this notion "generates its own actualization" by motivating people to struggle for it.

The relation between Kant and Hegel is very precise here, and we should avoid the temptation to reduce it to the simple opposition between Kantian "ethical narcissism" and Hegelian trust in the ethical substance. It is with regard to the Kantian "leap of faith" that Adorno moves too fast in his critical rejection of Kant's so-called "ethical narcissism," the Kantian stance of following one's ethical principles independently of consequences in the real world, of rejecting consequences as the criterion of moral value as "pathological," of insisting on the purity of my Will, of my intention, as the ultimate criterion.[56] The opposite view usually attributed to Hegel—the view that the "truth" of my acts is disclosed in its actual consequences, in the way it is received by (inscribed into) the ethical substance—is also problematic insofar as it presupposes a preestablished harmony between (individual) subject and substance, the fundamentally "benevolent" status of the substance. What, however, if I cannot fully recognize myself in the social substance—not because of my narcissism, but because the social substance of myself is "evil" and, as such, inverts all my acts into the opposite of what they intended to achieve? In other words, if the intention of my act is thwarted, should all the blame be put on me? Hegel was well aware of this deadlock; this is why, in his *Philosophy of Right*, he admits that the "mob" has the right to revolt against "social substance."

It was Bernard Williams who formulated a third position, beyond the alternative "the purity of intention—actual consequences," the alternative which focuses on the irreducible contingency of our situation, on how the value of our acts relies on an irreducible contingency—a scandalous result, because, against Kant, it claims that a pathological stain is irreducible to ethics, and, against Hegel, it rejects the trust in ethical substance. Williams[57] is unique in advocating a position which questions Kantian universalist apriorism as well as utilitarianism—what these two opposed positions share is the idea of some "common currency," some universal medium which allows us to judge all moral experiences, either the moral Law or utility. While he is well aware of the limitation of utilitarianism (the reference to a "greater good" can justify injustices to individuals), Williams, in his critique of "moral self-indulgence," also perceives the basic weakness of those who reject morally distasteful acts, even if they would benefit some people (in contrast to a logical utilitarian who can find strong reasons for doing something he finds morally distasteful): there is always "the suspicion that what the agent cares about is not so much other people, as himself caring about other people."[58] His more fundamental point is directed against the partisans of "rational deliberation as directed to a *life-plan*" (notably Rawls), who insist that we are responsible to ourselves as one person over time, which is why a rational individual should always act so that he need never blame himself, no matter how things finally turn out. Williams's counterargument here is dialectical in the strict Hegelian sense—he shows how such a position ignores the fact that what one does and the sort of life one leads condition one's later desires and judgments. The standpoint of that retrospective judge who will be my later self will be the product of my earlier choices. So there is no set of preferences both fixed and relevant, relative to which the various fillings of my life-space can be compared.[59]

This means that temporality (and thereby contingency) is irreducible in moral judgments:

> The perspective of deliberative choice on one's life is constitutively *from here*. Correspondingly the perspective of assessment with greater knowledge is necessarily *from there*, and not only can I not guarantee how factually it will be then, but I cannot ultimately guarantee from what standpoint of assessment my major and most fundamental regrets will be.[60]

We should take care not to miss the point here: we cannot guarantee it precisely because we cannot account in advance for the way our present acts will affect our future retrospective view.

From this perspective, the Kantian emphasis on autonomy itself can be read not so much as an expression of "ethical narcissism," but more as an acknowledgment of our unsurpassable limitation: since I always act in a situation which is ultimately opaque, and thus cannot control the consequences of my acts, all I can do is act with sincere intentions. Thus Kant is not simply the ethical philosopher in stipulating that the purity of the inner intention is the only criterion of the moral character of my act: he is well aware that, in order for my moral activity to have any sense at all, we have to presuppose a deep affinity or harmony between our moral intentions and the objective structure of reality—that is the role of the postulates of pure practical reason. And this is where the "moral luck" apparently excluded by Kant returns with a vengeance: Kant admits that we cannot effectively practice morality while constraining ourselves to our inner intention alone, totally dismissing actual consequences—we are compelled to engage in a kind of "leap of faith," and commit ourselves to a fundamental trust in the friendly structure of reality. I cannot help recalling here the wonderful "Soave sia il vento" trio from Mozart's *Così fan tutte*, with its appeal to the "elements" (of the Real) to respond benignly to our desires:

> Gentle be the breeze,
> calm be the waves,
> and may every element
> respond benignly
> to our desires[61]

—an appeal sustained by the suspicion that there is no match between our desires and reality, that their discord is irreducible, that our desires themselves are in no way gentle, that they tend to explode in violence, and thus to provoke an even more violent answer from the Real.

If we read Kant in this way, focusing on the need to wage a *salto mortale,* then the opposition of autonomy and thrownness/unaccountability loses its edge: the subject's thrownness/unaccountability is the very condition of his autonomy. We should refer here to Lacan's logic of "non-All": the position of true autonomy is not "I am responsible for everything," but, rather, "there is nothing for which I am not responsible," the counterpart of which is "I am not responsible for All": precisely because I cannot have an overview of All, there is nothing for which I can exempt myself from responsibility. (And vice versa, of course: if I am responsible for everything, then there must be something for which I cannot be responsible.)

Another aspect of the thesis that contingency is irreducible in moral activity is the gap that forever separates *must* from *ought:* "*Ought* is related to *must* as *best* is related to *only.*"[62] We arrive at what we must do after a long and anxious consideration of alternatives, and "can have that belief while remaining uncertain about it, and still very clearly seeing the powerful merits of alternative courses."[63] This also opens up the space of manipulation, as when a bargaining partner or outright blackmailer says that, "deplorably," this leaves him with no alternative to taking an unpleasant action. The falsity of this position lies in the fact that when we "must" do something, it is not only that, within the limits that our situation sets to deliberation, we "cannot do anything but this": the character of a person is revealed not only in the fact that he does what he must do, but also "in the location of those limits, and in the very fact that one can determine, sometimes through deliberation itself, that one cannot do certain things, and must do others."[64] And I am responsible for my character, that is, for the choice of coordinates which prevent me from doing some things and impel me to do others. This brings us to the Lacanian notion of act: in an act, I precisely redefine the very coordinates of what I cannot and must do.

When Lacan asserts that ethics belongs to the Real, is it not that—to put it in Kantian terms—he is claiming that, in our fleeting temporal phenomenal reality with no ultimate ontological grounding, the ethical, the unconditional demand of duty, is our only contact with the Eternal (noumenal)? The question is thus not simply that of how Ought emerges out of Is, the positive order of Being, or how to assert the ethical as external—irreducible—to the order of Being (the Levinasian topic of "beyond Being"), but that of the place of Ought *within the very order of Being: within what ontology is the ethical dimension proper possible* without being reduced to an epiphenomenon (in the style of Spinoza, for whom Ought simply indicates the limitation of our knowledge)? In other words, it is misleading to ask how we can overcome the gap that separates Being from Ought, *Sein* from *Sollen,* facticity from the domain of norms: there is no need for an additional "synthesis" here—the question to be asked, rather, is: how does the dimension of *Sollen* emerge in the midst of Being, how does the positivity of Being engender the Ought? This explanation of how the gap emerges is already the sought-for synthesis, just as it is meaningless to supplant psychoanalysis with "psycho-synthesis"—psycho-*analysis* already is this "synthesis."

The basic Hegelian correction of Kant is thus that the three domains of reason (theoretical, practical, aesthetic) emerge through the shift in the subject's attitude, that is, through "bracketing": the object of science emerges through bracketing moral and aesthetic judgments; the moral domain emerges through bracketing cognitive-theoretical and aesthetic concerns; and the aesthetic domain emerges through bracketing theoretical and moral concerns. For example, when we bracket moral and aesthetic concerns, a human being appears as non-free, totally conditioned by the causal nexus; if, on the contrary, we bracket theoretical concerns, he or she appears as a free autonomous being. Thus antinomies should not be reified—the antinomic positions emerge through shifts in the subject's attitude.[65] Karatani's crucial breakthrough, however, consists in his application of such a parallax reading to Marx, in his reading of Marx himself as a Kantian.

"I replaced Freud's energetics with political economy," said Lacan in *Seminar XVII*—did he really mean it? When, in his "Critique of Political Economy," Marx deals with the opposition of "classical" political economy (Ricardo and his labor theory of value—the counterpart to philosophical rationalism) and the neoclassic reduction of value to a purely relational entity without substance (Bailey—the counterpart to philosophical empiricism), he resolves this opposition by repeating the Kantian breakthrough toward the "parallax" view: he treats it as a Kantian antinomy, that is to say, value has to originate outside circulation, in production, *and* in circulation. Post-Marx "Marxism"—in both its versions, Social Democratic and Communist—lost this "parallax" perspective and regressed into the unilateral elevation of production as the site of truth against the "illusory" sphere of exchange and consumption. As Karatani emphasizes, even the most sophisticated theorists of reification, those of commodity fetishism, from the young Lukács through Adorno up to Fredric Jameson, fall into this trap: the way they account for the lack of revolutionary movement is to say that the workers' consciousness is obfuscated by the seductions of consumerist society and/or manipulation by the ideological forces of cultural hegemony, which is why the focus of critical work should shift to "cultural criticism" (the so-called "cultural turn")—the disclosure of ideological (or libidinal—this is the origin of the key role of psychoanalysis in Western Marxism) mechanisms which keep the workers under the spell of bourgeois ideology.

In a close reading of Marx's analysis of the commodity-form, Karatani grounds the insurmountable persistence of the parallax gap in the *salto mortale* that a product has to accomplish in order to assert itself as a commodity:

> The price [of iron expressed in gold], while on the one hand indicating the amount of labour-time contained in the iron, namely its value, at the same time signifies the pious wish to convert the iron into gold, that is to give the labour-time contained in the iron the form of universal social labour-time. If this transformation fails to take place, then the ton of iron ceases to be not only a commodity but also a product; since it is a com-

modity only because it is not a use-value for its owner, that is to say his labour is only really labour if it is useful labour for others, and it is useful for him only if it is abstract general labour. It is therefore the task of the iron or of its owner to find that location in the world of commodities where iron attracts gold. But if the sale actually takes place, as we assume in this analysis of simple circulation, then this difficulty, the *salto mortale* of the commodity, is surmounted. As a result of this alienation—that is its transfer from the person for whom it is a non-use-value to the person for whom it is a use-value— the ton of iron proves to be in fact a use-value and its price is simultaneously realised, and merely imaginary gold is converted into real gold.[66]

This is Karatani's key Kantian/anti-Hegelian point: the jump by means of which a commodity is sold, and thus effectively constituted as commodity, is not the result of an immanent self-development of (the concept of) Value, but a *salto mortale* comparable to a Kierkegaardian leap of faith, a temporary fragile "synthesis" between use-value and exchange-value comparable to the Kantian synthesis between sensitivity and understanding: in both cases, the two irreducibly external levels are brought together.[67] For this precise reason, Marx abandoned his original project (discernible in the *Grundrisse* manuscripts) of "deducing," in a Hegelian way, the split between exchange-value and use-value from the very concept of Value: in *Capital*, the split of these two dimensions, the "dual character of a merchandise," is the starting point. The synthesis has to rely on an irreducibly external element, as in Kant, where being is not a predicate (that is, cannot be reduced to a conceptual predicate of an entity), or as in Saul Kripke's *Naming and Necessity*, in which the reference of a name to an object cannot be grounded in the content of this name, in the properties it designates.

This is why, although Marx's *Darstellung* of the self-deployment of Capital is full of Hegelian references,[68] the self-movement of Capital is far from the circular self-movement of the Hegelian Notion (or Spirit): the point of Marx is that this movement never catches up with itself, that it never recovers its credit, that its resolution is postponed forever, that the crisis is its innermost constituent (the sign that the Whole of Capital is the non-True, as Adorno would have put it), which is why the movement is one of the "spurious infinity," forever reproducing itself:

> Notwithstanding the Hegelian descriptive style . . . *Capital* distinguishes itself from Hegel's philosophy in its motivation. The end of *Capital* is never the 'absolute Spirit.' *Capital* reveals the fact that capital, though organizing the world, can never go beyond its own limit. It is a Kantian critique of the ill-contained drive of capital/reason to self-realize beyond its limit.[69]

It is interesting to note that it was Adorno who, in *Three Studies on Hegel*, critically characterized Hegel's system in the same "financial" terms as a system which lives on credit it can never pay off. And the same "financial" metaphor is often used for language itself—Brian Rotman, among others, has determined meaning as something which is always "borrowed from the future," relying on its forever-postponed fulfillment-to-come.[70] That is to say: how does shared meaning emerge? Through what Alfred

Schütz called "mutual idealization": subjects cut the impasse of the endless probing into "do we all mean the same thing by 'bird'?" by simply taking for granted, presupposing, acting as if they *do* mean the same thing. There is no language without this "leap of faith."

This presupposition, this "leap of faith," should not be conceived, in the Habermasian vein, as the normativity built into the functioning of language, as the ideal for which the speakers (should) strive: far from being an ideal, this presupposition is the fiction, the *as if* . . . , that sustains language—as such, it should be undermined again and again in the progress of knowledge. So, if anything, this presupposed *as if* . . . is profoundly *anti-normative*. To this, a Habermasian may reply that the ideal, the norm inscribed into language, is nonetheless the state in which this fiction would no longer be a fiction—in which, in a smooth communication, subjects would in fact mean the same thing. This reply, however, misses the point, which is not only and simply that such a state is inaccessible (and also undesirable), but that the "leap of faith" by means of which the subjects take it for granted that they mean the same thing not only has no normative content, but can even block further elaboration—why strive for something that we allegedly already have? In other words, what the reading of this *as if* . . . as normativity misses is that the "leap of faith" is both necessary and productive (enabling communication) precisely insofar as it is a counterfactual fiction: its "truth effect," its positive role of enabling communication, hinges precisely on the fact that it is *not* true, that it jumps ahead into fiction—its status is not normative because it cuts the debilitating deadlock of language, its ultimate lack of guarantee, by *presenting what we should strive for as already accomplished.*[71]

The tension between production and circulation processes is again that of parallax: yes, value is created in the production process; however, it is created there, as it were, only potentially, since it is actualized as value only when the produced commodity is sold, and the circle M–C–M' is thus completed. This temporal gap between the production of value and its actualization is crucial: even if value is produced in production, without the successful completion of the process of circulation, there *stricto sensu* is no value—the temporality here is that of the *futur antérieur*: value "is" not immediately, it only "will have been," it is retroactively actualized, performatively enacted. In production, value is generated "in itself," while only through the completed circulation process does it become "for itself." This is how Karatani resolves the Kantian antinomy of value which is *and* is not generated in the process of production: it is generated there only "in itself." And it is because of this gap between in- and for-itself that capitalism needs formal democracy and equality:

> What precisely distinguishes capital from the master-slave relation is that the worker confronts him as consumer and possessor of exchange values, and that in the form of the possessor of money, in the form of money he becomes a simple center of circulation—one of its infinitely many centres, in which his specificity as worker is extinguished.[72]

This means that capital, in order to complete the circle of its reproduction, has to pass through this critical point at which the roles are inverted: "surplus value is realized in principle only by workers in *totality* buying back what they produce."[73] This point is crucial for Karatani: it provides the key leverage from which to oppose the rule of capital today: is it not natural that the proletarians should focus their attack on that unique point at which they approach capital from the position of a buyer, and, consequently, at which it is capital that is forced to court them? "[I]f workers can become subjects at all, it is only as consumers."[74] This is perhaps the ultimate case of the parallax situation: the position of worker-producer and that of consumer should be sustained as irreducible in their divergence, without privileging one as the "deeper truth" of the other.[75] (And, incidentally, did not the planned economy of State Socialism pay a terrible price for privileging production at the expense of consumption precisely by failing to provide consumers with necessary goods, by producing things which nobody needed or wanted?)[76] This brings us to Karatani's key theme: we should utterly reject the (proto-Fascist, if anything) opposition of financial-speculative profiteering capital to the "substantial" economy of capitalists engaged in productive activity: in capitalism, the production process is only a detour in the speculative process of money engendering more money—that is to say, the profiteering logic is ultimately also what sustains the incessant drive to revolutionize and expand production:

> The majority of economists warn today that the speculation of global financial capital is detached from the "substantial" economy. What they overlook, however, is that the substantial economy as such is also driven by illusion, and that such is the nature of the capitalist economy.[77]

As a result, there are three basic positions apropos of money: (1) the mercantilist one: a direct naive fetishist belief in money as a "special thing"; (2) the "classical bourgeois political economy" embodied in Ricardo, which dismissed money-fetishism as a mere illusion, and perceived money as a mere sign of the quantity of socially useful labor— here value was conceived as inherent to a commodity; (3) the "neoclassical" school, which rejected the labor theory of value and also any "substantial" notion of value: the price of a commodity is simply the result of the interplay between supply and demand: of the commodity's usefulness with regard to other commodities. And Karatani is right to emphasize how, paradoxically, Marx broke out of the confines of the "classical" Ricardo labor theory of value through his reading of Bailey, the first "vulgar" economist who emphasized the purely *relational* status of value: value is not inherent to a commodity, it expresses the way this commodity relates to all other commodities. In this way Bailey opened up the path toward the structural-formal approach of Marx, which insists on the gap between an object and the structural place it occupies: just as a king is a king not because of his inherent properties, but because people treat him as one (Marx's own example), a commodity is money because it occupies the formal place of the general equivalent of all commodities, not because gold, for example, is "naturally" money. But it is crucial to take note of how both the mercantilists and their Ricardoan critics remain "substantialist": Ricardo was, of course, aware that the object which serves as money is not "naturally" money; he laughed at naive superstitions about money, and dismissed the mercantilists as primitive believers in magic properties; by reducing money to a secondary external sign of the value inherent to a commodity, however, he nonetheless again naturalized value, conceiving it as a direct "substantial" property of a commodity. It is this illusion that opened the way to the naive early-Socialist and Proudhonian practical proposal to overcome money-fetishism by introducing a direct "labor money" which would simply designate the amount each individual contributed to social labor. The strict formal analogy between Marx and Freud should be emphasized here.[78] Here are the three key passages from Marx:

> The determination of the magnitude of value by labour-time is therefore a secret, hidden under the apparent fluctuations in the relative values of commodities. Its discovery, while removing all appearance of mere accidentality from the determination of the magnitude of the values of products, yet in no way alters the mode in which that determination takes place.[79]

> Political Economy has indeed analysed, however incompletely, value and its magnitude, and has discovered what lies beneath these forms. But it has never once asked the question why labour is represented by the value of its product and labour-time by the magnitude of that value.[80]

> It is as clear as noon-day, that man, by his industry, changes the forms of the materials furnished by Nature, in such a way as to make them useful to him. The form of wood, for instance, is altered, by making a table out of it. Yet, for all that, the table continues to be that common, every-day thing, wood. But, so soon as it steps forth as a commodity, it is changed into something transcendent. It not only stands with its feet on the ground, but, in relation to all other commodities, it stands on its head, and evolves out of its wooden brain grotesque ideas, far more wonderful than "table-turning" ever was.
>
> The mystical character of commodities does not originate, therefore, in their use-value. Just as little does it proceed from the nature of the determining factors of value. For, in the first place, however varied the useful kinds of labour, or productive activities, may be, it is a physiological fact, that they are functions of the human organism, and that each such function, whatever may be its nature or form, is essentially the expenditure of human brain, nerves, muscles, etc. Secondly, with regard to that which forms the ground-work for the quantitative determination of value, namely, the duration of that expenditure, or the quantity of labour, it is quite clear that there is a palpable difference between its quantity and quality. In all states of society, the labour-time that it costs to produce the means of subsistence, must necessarily be an object of interest to mankind, though not of equal interest in different stages of development. And lastly, from the moment that men in any way work for one another, their labour assumes a social form.
>
> Whence, then, arises the enigmatical character of the product of labour, so soon as it assumes the form of commodities? Clearly from this form itself. The equality of all sorts of human labour is expressed objectively by their products all being equally values; the measure of the expenditure of labour-power by the duration of that expenditure, takes the form of the quantity of value of the products of labour; and finally the

mutual relations of the producers, within which the social character of their labour affirms itself, take the form of a social relation between the products.[81]

In Freud, the key explanation is hidden in a footnote at the very end of the key chapter of *The Interpretation of Dreams*, on "The Dream-Work":

> Formerly I found it extraordinarily difficult to accustom my readers to the distinction between the manifest dream-content and the latent dream-thoughts. Over and over again arguments and objections were adduced from the un-interpreted dream as it was retained in the memory, and the necessity of interpreting the dream was ignored. But now, when the analysts have at least become reconciled to substituting for the manifest dream its meaning as found by interpretation, many of them are guilty of another mistake, to which they adhere just as stubbornly. They look for the essence of the dream in this latent content, and thereby overlook the distinction between latent dream-thoughts and the dream-work. The dream is fundamentally nothing more than a special form of our thinking, which is made possible by the conditions of the sleeping state. It is the dream-work which produces this form, and it alone is the essence of dreaming—the only explanation of its singularity.[82]

We should therefore be extremely attentive to the gap which separates Marx from Ricardo and his Leftist followers who accomplished the move from appearance to essence—from the fascination with the domain of exchange to the site of production as its secret core; Marx's basic move is the opposite one, the move back to the secret of the form itself. The key trap is not to be blinded by form, but to reduce form to a "mere form," that is, to overlook how the secret essence *needs* this form, how the form itself is essential.

Is not the ultimate Marxian parallax, however, the one between economy and politics—between the "critique of political economy," with its logic of commodities, and the political struggle, with its logic of antagonism? Both logics are "transcendental," not merely ontico-empirical; and they are both irreducible to each other. Of course they both point toward each other (class struggle is inscribed into the very heart of economy, yet has to remain absent, nonthematized—recall how the manuscript of *Capital* volume III abruptly ends with it; and class struggle is ultimately "about" economic power relations), but this very mutual implication is twisted so that it prevents any direct contact (any direct translation of political struggle into a mere mirroring of economic "interests" is doomed to fail, as is any reduction of the sphere of economic production to a secondary "reified" sedimentation of an underlying founding political process).

The "pure politics" of Alain Badiou, Jacques Rancière, and Étienne Balibar, more Jacobin than Marxist, shares with its great opponent, Anglo-Saxon Cultural Studies and their focus on struggles for recognition, the degradation of the sphere of economy. That is to say: what all the new French (or French-oriented) theories of the Political, from Balibar through Rancière and Badiou to Laclau and Mouffe, aim at is—to put it in traditional philosophical terms—the reduction of the sphere of economy (of material production) to an "ontic" sphere deprived of "ontological" dignity. Within this horizon, there is simply no place for the Marxian "critique of political economy": the structure of the universe of commodities and capital in Marx's *Capital* is not just that of a limited empirical sphere, but a kind of socio-transcendental *a priori*, the matrix which generates the totality of social and political relations. The relationship between economy and politics is ultimately that of the well-known visual paradox of "two faces or a vase": one sees either two faces or a vase, never both—one has to make a choice. In the same way, one either focuses on the political, and the domain of economy is reduced to the empirical "servicing of goods," or one focuses on economy, and politics is reduced to a theater of appearances, to a passing phenomenon which will disappear with the arrival of the developed Communist (or technocratic) society, in which, as Engels put it, the "administration of people" will vanish in the "administration of things."

The "political" critique of Marxism (the claim that, when we reduce politics to a "formal" expression of some underlying "objective" socioeconomic process, we lose the openness and contingency constitutive of the political field proper) should thus be supplemented by its obverse: the field of economy is *in its very form* irreducible to politics—this level of the form of economy (of economy as the determining form of the social) is what French "political post-Marxists" miss when they reduce economy to one of the positive social spheres. In Badiou, the root of this notion of pure "politics," radically autonomous with regard to history, society, economy, State, even Party, is his opposition between Being and Event—it is here that Badiou remains "idealist." From the materialist standpoint, an Event emerges "out of nowhere" within a specific constellation of Being—the space of an Event is the minimal "empty" distance between two beings, the "other" dimension which shines through this gap.

Parallax means that *the bracketing itself produces its object*—"democracy" as a form emerges only when we bracket the texture of economic relations as well as the inherent logic of the political state apparatus: they both have to be abstracted from; people who are effectively embedded in economic processes and subjected to state apparatuses have to be reduced to abstract units. The same goes for the "logic of domination," the way people are controlled/manipulated by the apparatuses of subjection: in order to discern these mechanisms of power clearly, we have to abstract not only from the democratic imaginary (as Foucault does in his analyses of the micro-physics of power, but also as Lacan does in his analysis of power in *Seminar XVIII*), but also from the process of economic (re)production. Finally, the specific sphere of economic (re)production emerges only if we methodologically bracket the concrete existence of state and political ideology—no wonder critics of Marx complain that Marx's "critique of political economy" lacks a theory of power and state. And, of course, the trap to be avoided here is precisely that of trying to formulate the totality parts of which are democratic ideology, the exercise of power, and the process of economic (re)production: if we try to keep them all in view, we end up seeing nothing; the contours disappear. This bracketing is not only epistemological, it concerns what Marx called "real abstraction": the abstraction from power and economic relations is inscribed into the very actuality of the democratic process, and so on.

Karatani's account, impressive as it is, cannot but solicit a series of critical remarks. As for his advocacy of the LETS (Local Exchange Trading System) economic model, it is difficult to see how it avoids the very trap of which Karatani is well aware: the trap of money which would no longer be a fetish, but would serve just as "labor money," a transparent instrument of exchange designating each individual's contribution to the social product. Furthermore, Karatani's account of the Marxian notion of surplus-value and exploitation is strangely inadequate in that it totally ignores the key element of Marx's critique of the standard labor theory of value: workers are not exploited by not being paid their full value—their wages are in principle "just," they are paid the full value of the commodity they are selling ("labor-power"); the key is, rather, that the use-value of this commodity is unique, it produces a new value greater than its own value, and this surplus is appropriated by the capitalists. Karatani, on the contrary, reduces exploitation to just another case of a difference in price between value systems: because of incessant technological innovation, capitalists can earn more from selling the products of labor than they have to pay their workers—capitalist exploitation is thus posited as structurally the same as the activity of merchants who buy and sell at different locations, exploiting the fact that, because of differing productivity, the same product is cheaper here (where they buy it) than there (where they sell it):

> only where there is a difference in price between value systems: A (when they sell their labor power) and B (when they buy the commodities), is surplus value realized. This is so-called relative surplus value. And this is attained only by incessant technological innovation. Hence one finds that industrial capital too earns surplus value from the interstice between two different systems.[83]

Perhaps these limitations are rooted in the constraints of Karatani's Kantianism.[84] When Karatani proposes his "transcendental" solution to the antinomy of money (we need an X which will be money and will not be money); when he reapplies this solution also to power (we need some centralized power, but not fetishized into a substance which is "in itself" Power); and when he explicitly evokes the structural analogy with Duchamp (where an object becomes a work of art not because of its inherent properties, but simply by occupying a certain place in the structure); does all this not exactly fit Lefort's theorization of democracy as a political order in which the place of Power is originally empty, and is only temporary filled in by elected representatives? Along these lines, even Karatani's apparently eccentric notion of combining elections with lottery in the procedure of determining who will rule us is more traditional than it may appear (he himself mentions ancient Greece): paradoxically, it fulfills the same task as Hegel's theory of monarchy. . . .

Here Karatani takes the heroic risk of proposing a crazy-sounding definition of the difference between the dictatorship of the bourgeoisie and the dictatorship of the proletariat: "If universal suffrage by secret ballot, namely, parliamentary democracy, is the dictatorship of the bourgeoisie, the introduction of lottery should be deemed the dictatorship of the proletariat."[85] In this way, "*the center exists and does not exist at the same time*":[86]

it exists as an empty place, a transcendental X, and it does not exist as a substantial positive entity. But is this, in fact, enough to undermine the "fetishism of Power"? When an accidental individual is temporarily allowed to occupy the place of Power, the charisma of Power is bestowed on him, following the well-known logic of fetishist disavowal: "I know very well that this is an ordinary person just like me, *but nonetheless* . . . (while he is in power, he becomes an instrument of a transcendent force; Power speaks and acts through him)!" Does all this not fit the general matrix of Kant's solutions, where the metaphysical propositions (God, immortality of the soul . . .) are asserted "under erasure," as postulates? Consequently, would not the true task be precisely to get rid of the very mystique of the *place* of Power?

". . . CE SEUL OBJET DONT LE NÉANT S'HONORE"

Let us take a closer look at Marx's classical description of the passage from money to capital, with its explicit allusions to the Hegelian and Christian background. First, there is the simple act of market exchange in which I sell in order to buy—I sell the product I own or have made in order to buy another one which is of some use to me: "The simple circulation of commodities—selling in order to buy—is a means of carrying out a purpose unconnected with circulation, namely, the appropriation of use-values, the satisfaction of wants."[87] What happens with the emergence of capital is not just the simple reversal of C–M–C/Commodity–Money–Commodity/into M–C–M— that is, of investing money in some commodity in order to sell it again, and thus get back to (more) money; the key effect of this reversal is the *eternalization* of circulation: "The circulation of money as capital is, on the contrary, an end in itself, for the expansion of value takes place only within this constantly renewed movement. The circulation of capital has therefore no limits."[88] The difference between the traditional miser, hoarding his treasure in a secret hideout, and the capitalist who augments his treasure by throwing it into circulation is crucial here:

> The restless never-ending process of profit-making alone is what he aims at. This boundless greed after riches, this passionate chase after exchange-value, is common to the capitalist and the miser; but while the miser is merely a capitalist gone mad, the capitalist is a rational miser. The never-ending augmentation of exchange-value, which the miser strives after, by seeking to save his money from circulation, is attained by the more acute capitalist, by constantly throwing it afresh into circulation.[89]

This madness of the miser is nonetheless not something which simply disappears with the rise of "normal" capitalism, or its pathological deviation. It is, rather, *inherent* to it: the miser has his moment of triumph in the economic *crisis*. In a crisis, it is not—as one would expect—money which loses its value, and we have to resort to the "real" value of commodities; commodities themselves (the embodiment of "real [use-] value") become useless, because there is no one to buy them. In a crisis, money suddenly and immediately changes from its merely nominal shape, money of account, into hard cash. Profane commodities can no longer replace it. The use-value of commodities becomes value-less, and their value vanishes in the face of their own form of value. The bourgeois, drunk with prosperity and arrogantly certain of himself, has just declared that money is a purely imaginary creation. "Commodities alone are money," he said. But now the opposite cry resounds over the markets of the world: only money is a commodity. . . . In a crisis, the antithesis between commodities and their value-form, money, is raised to the level of an absolute contradiction.[90]

Does this not mean that at this moment, far from disintegrating, fetishism is fully asserted in its direct madness?[91] In a crisis, the underlying belief, disavowed and just practiced, is thus *directly* asserted. It is crucial how, in this elevation of money to the status of the only true commodity ("The capitalist knows that all commodities, however scurvy they may look, or however badly they may smell, are in faith and in truth money, inwardly circumcised Jews"),[92] Marx resorts to the precise Pauline definition of Christians as "inwardly circumcised Jews": Christians do not need external actual circumcision (that is, the abandonment of ordinary commodities with use-values, dealing only with money), since they know that each of these ordinary commodities is already "inwardly circumcised," that its true substance is money. The way Marx describes the passage from money to capital in the precise Hegelian terms of the passage from substance to subject is even more crucial:

> In truth, however, value is here [in capital] the active factor in a process, in which, while constantly assuming the form in turn of money and commodities, it at the same time changes in magnitude, differentiates itself by throwing off surplus-value from itself; the original value, in other words, expands spontaneously. For the movement, in the course of which it adds surplus-value, is its own movement, its expansion, therefore, is automatic expansion. Because it is value, it has acquired the occult quality of being able to add value to itself. It brings forth living offspring, or, at the least, lays golden eggs. . . .
>
> In simple circulation, C–M–C, the value of commodities attained at the most a form independent of their use-values, i.e., the form of money; but the same value now in the circulation M–C–M, or the circulation of capital, suddenly presents itself as an independent substance, endowed with a motion of its own, passing through a life-process of its own, in which money and commodities are mere forms which it assumes and casts off in turn. Nay, more: instead of simply representing the relations of commodities, it enters now, so to say, into private relations with itself. It differentiates itself as original value from itself as surplus-value; as the father differentiates himself from himself *qua* the son, yet both are one and of one age: for only by the surplus-value of 10 pounds does the 100 pounds originally advanced become capital, and so on as this takes place, so soon as the son, and by the son, the father is begotten, so soon does their difference vanish, and they again become one, 110 pounds.[93]

In short, capital is money which is no longer a mere substance of wealth, its universal embodiment, but value which, through its circulation, generates more value, value which mediates-posits itself, retroactively positing its own presuppositions. First, money appears as a mere means of the exchange of commodities: instead of endless bartering, one first exchanges one's product for the universal equivalent of all commodities, which can then be exchanged for any commodity one may need. Then, once the circulation of the capital is set in motion, the relationship is inverted, the means turns into an end in itself, that is to say, the very passage through the "material" domain of use-values (the production of commodities which satisfy an individual's particular needs) is posited as a moment of what is substantially the self-movement of capital itself—from this moment onward, the true aim is no longer the satisfaction of individual needs, but simply more money, the endless repeating of the circulation as such. . . . This arcane circular movement of self-positing is then equated with the central Christian tenet of the identity of God-the-Father and his Son, of the Immaculate Conception by means of which the single Father directly (without a female spouse) begets his only son, and thus forms what is arguably the ultimate single-parent family.

Is capital, then, the true Subject/Substance? Yes and no: for Marx, this self-engendering circular movement is—to put it in Freudian terms—precisely the capitalist "unconscious fantasy" which parasitizes upon the proletariat as the "pure substanceless subjectivity"; for this reason, capital's speculative self-generating dance has a limit, and it brings about the conditions of its own collapse. This insight allows us to solve the key interpretive problem of the quote above: how are we to read its first three words, "In truth, however"? First, of course, they imply that this truth has to be asserted against some false appearance or experience: the everyday experience that the ultimate goal of capital's circulation is still the satisfaction of human needs, that capital is just a means to bring this satisfaction about in a more efficient way. This "truth," however, is not the reality of capitalism: in reality, capital does not engender itself, but exploits the worker's surplus-value. There is thus a necessary third level to be added to the simple opposition of subjective experience (of capital as a simple means of efficiently satisfying people's needs) and objective social reality (of exploitation): the "objective deception," the disavowed "unconscious" fantasy (of the mysterious self-generating circular movement of capital), which is the truth (although not the reality) of the capitalist process. Again—to quote Lacan—truth has the structure of a fiction: the only way to formulate the truth of capital is to present this fiction of its "immaculate" self-generating movement. And this insight also enables us to locate the weakness of the "deconstructionist" appropriation of Marx's analysis of capitalism: although it emphasizes the endless process of deferral which characterizes this movement, as well as its fundamental inconclusiveness, its self-blockade, the "deconstructionist" retelling still describes the fantasy of capital—it describes what individuals believe, although they don't know it.

This shift from the goal-oriented stance of consumption toward the properly capitalist stance of self-propelling circulation allows us to locate desire and drive with regard to capitalism. Following Jacques-Alain Miller, a distinction has to be introduced here between lack and hole: lack is spatial, designating a void within a space, while hole is more radical, it designates the point at which this spatial order itself breaks down (as in the "black hole" in physics).[94] That is the difference between desire and drive: desire is grounded in its constitutive lack, while drive circulates around a hole, a gap in the order of being. In other words, the circular movement of drive obeys the weird logic of the curved space in which the shortest distance between the two points is not a straight line, but a curve: drive "knows" that the shortest way to attain its aim is to circulate around its goal-object. At the immediate level of addressing individuals, capitalism, of course, interpellates them as consumers, as subjects of desire, soliciting in them ever new perverse and excessive desires (for which it offers products to satisfy them); furthermore, it obviously also manipulates the "desire to desire," celebrating the very desire to desire ever new objects and modes of pleasure. However, even if it already manipulates desire in a way which takes into account the fact that the most elementary desire is the desire to reproduce itself as desire (and not to find satisfaction), at this level, we have not yet reached drive. Drive inheres to capitalism at a more fundamental, *systemic*, level: drive is that which propels the whole capitalist machinery, it is the impersonal compulsion to engage in the endless circular movement of expanded self-reproduction. We enter the mode of drive the moment the circulation of money as capital becomes "an end in itself, for the expansion of value takes place only within this constantly renewed movement. The circulation of capital has therefore no limits." (Here we should bear in mind Lacan's well-known distinction between the aim and the goal of drive: while the goal is the object around which drive circulates, its (true) aim is the endless continuation of this circulation as such.) Thus the capitalist drive belongs to no definite individual—rather, it is that those individuals who act as direct "agents" of capital (capitalists themselves, top managers) have to display it.

Miller has proposed a Benjaminian distinction between "constituted anxiety" and "constituent anxiety," which is crucial with regard to the shift from desire to drive: while the first term designates the standard notion of the terrifying and fascinating abyss of anxiety which haunts us, its infernal circle which threatens to draw us in, the second stands for the "pure" confrontation with *objet petit a* as constituted in its very loss.[95] Miller is right to emphasize here how the difference which separates constituted from constituent anxiety concerns the status of the object with regard to fantasy. In a case of constituted anxiety, the object dwells within the confines of a fantasy, while we get constituent anxiety only when the subject "traverses the fantasy" and confronts the Void, the gap, filled in by the fantasmatic object—as Mallarmé put it in the famous bracketed last two lines of his "Sonnet en -yx," *objet petit a* is *"ce seul objet dont le Néant s'honore* [this sole object with which Nothing is honored]."

Clear and convincing as it is, Miller's formula misses the true paradox or, rather, ambiguity of *objet petit a*: when he defines *objet petit a* as the object which overlaps with its loss, which emerges at the very moment of its loss (so that all its fantasmatic incarnations, from breasts to voice and gaze, are metonymic figurations of the Void, of nothing), he remains within the horizon of *desire*—the true object-cause of desire is the Void filled in by its fantasmatic incarnations. While, as Lacan emphasizes, *objet petit a* is also the object of drive, the relationship here is completely different: although the link between object and loss is crucial in both cases, in the case of *objet petit a* as the object-cause of *desire* we have an object which is originally lost, which coincides with its own loss, which emerges as lost; while in the case of *objet petit a* as the object of drive, the "object" is directly loss itself—in the shift from desire to drive, we pass from the *lost object* to *loss itself as an object*. That is to say: the weird movement called "drive" is not driven by the "impossible" quest for the lost object; it is *a push to enact "loss"—the gap, cut, distance—itself directly*. There is thus a *double* distinction to be drawn here: not only between *objet petit a* in its fantasmatic and postfantasmatic status, but also, within this postfantasmatic domain itself, between the lost object-cause of desire and the object-loss of drive.

This is why we should not confuse the death drive with the so-called "*nirvana* principle," the thrust toward destruction or self-obliteration: the Freudian death drive has nothing whatsoever to do with the craving for self-annihilation, for the return to the inorganic absence of any life-tension; it is, on the contrary, the very opposite of dying—a name for the "undead" eternal life itself, for the horrible fate of being caught in the endless repetitive cycle of wandering around in guilt and pain. The paradox of the Freudian "death drive" is therefore that it is Freud's name for its very opposite, for the way immortality appears within psychoanalysis, for an uncanny *excess* of life, for an "undead" urge which persists beyond the (biological) cycle of life and death, of generation and corruption. The ultimate lesson of psychoanalysis is that human life is never "just life": humans are not simply alive, they are possessed by the strange drive to enjoy life in excess, passionately attached to a surplus which sticks out and derails the ordinary run of things.

This means that it is wrong to claim that the "pure" death drive would have been the impossible "total" will to (self-)destruction, the ecstatic self-annihilation in which the subject would have rejoined the fullness of the maternal Thing, but that this will is not realizable, that it gets blocked, stuck to a "partial object." Such a notion retranslates the death drive into the terms of desire and its lost object: it is in desire that the positive object is a metonymic stand-in for the Void of the impossible Thing; it is in desire that the aspiration to fullness is transferred to partial objects—this is what Lacan called the metonymy of desire. We have to be very precise here if we are not to miss Lacan's point (and thereby confuse desire and drive): drive is not an infinite longing for the Thing which gets fixated onto a partial object—"drive" is this fixation itself in which resides the "death" dimension of every drive. Drive is not a universal thrust (toward the incestuous Thing) braked and broken up, it is this brake itself, a brake on instinct—its "stuckness," as Eric Santner might have put it.[96] The elementary matrix of drive is not that of transcending all particular objects toward the Void of the Thing (which is then accessible only in its metonymic stand-in), but that of our libido getting "stuck" onto a particular object, condemned to circulate around it forever.

The basic paradox here is that the specifically human dimension—drive as opposed to instinct—emerges precisely when what was originally a mere by-product is elevated into an autonomous aim: man is not more "reflexive" than an animal; on the contrary, man perceives as a direct goal what, for an animal, has no intrinsic value. In short, the zero-degree of "humanization" is not a further "mediation" of animal activity, its reinscription as a subordinated moment of a higher totality (for example, we eat and procreate in order to develop a higher spiritual potential), but the radical narrowing of focus, the elevation of a minor activity into an end in itself. We become "humans" when we get caught into a closed, self-propelling loop of repeating the same gesture and finding satisfaction in it.

We can all recall one of the archetypal scenes from cartoons: while dancing, a cat jumps up into the air and turns around its own axis; instead of falling back down toward the earth's surface in accordance with the normal laws of gravity, however, it remains for some time suspended in the air, turning around in the levitated position as if caught in a loop of time, repeating the same circular movement again and again. (We also find the same shot in some musical comedies which make use of elements of slapstick: when a dancer turns around him- or herself in the air, she or he remains up there a little bit too long, as if, for a short period of time, she or he succeeded in suspending the law of gravity. And, in fact, is such an effect not the ultimate goal of the art of dancing?) At such moments, the "normal" run of things, the "normal" process of being caught in the imbecilic inertia of material reality, is for a brief moment suspended; we enter the magical domain of a suspended animation, a kind of ethereal rotation which, as it were, sustains itself, hanging in the air like Baron Münchhausen, who raised himself from the swamp by grabbing his own hair and pulling himself up. This rotary movement, in which the linear progress of time is suspended in a repetitive loop, is drive at its most elementary. This, again, is "humanization" at its zero-level: this self-propelling loop which suspends/disrupts linear temporal enchainment. This shift from desire to drive is crucial if we are fully to grasp the crux of the "minimal difference": at its most fundamental, the minimal difference is not the unfathomable X which elevates an ordinary object into an object of desire, but, rather, the inner torsion which curves the libidinal space, and thus transforms instinct into drive.

Consequently, the concept of drive makes the alternative "either burned by the Thing or maintaining a distance towards it" false: in a drive, the "thing itself" is a circulation around the Void (or, rather, hole, not void). To put it even more pointedly: the object of drive is not related to the Thing as a filler of its void: drive is literally a countermovement to desire, it does not strive toward impossible fullness and, being forced to renounce it, gets stuck onto a partial object as its remainder—drive is quite literally *the very "drive" to break the All of continuity in which we are embedded*, to introduce a radical imbalance into it, and the difference between drive and desire is precisely that, in desire, this cut, this fixation on a partial object, is as it were "transcendentalized," transposed into a stand-in for the Void of the Thing.

This is also how we should read Lacan's thesis on the "satisfaction of drives": a drive does not bring satisfaction because its object is a stand-in for the Thing, but because a drive, as it were, turns failure into triumph—in it, the very failure to reach its goal, the repetition of this failure, the endless circulation around the object, generates a satisfaction of its own. As Lacan put it, the true aim of a drive is not to reach its goal, but to circulate endlessly around it. In the well-known vulgar joke about a fool having intercourse for the first time, the girl has to tell him exactly what to do: "See this hole between my legs? Put it in here. Now push it deep. Now pull it out. Push it in, pull it out, push it in, pull it out. . . ." "Now wait a minute," the fool interrupts her, "make up your mind! In or out?" What the fool misses is precisely the structure of a drive which gets its satisfaction from the indecision itself, from repeated oscillation.

Bruno Boostels's central Badiouian objection to this topic of death drive *qua* self-relating negativity (from his unpublished essay "Badiou without Žižek") is that, by giving priority to the Act as a negative gesture of radical (self-relating) negativity, as "death drive" in *actu*, I devalue in advance every positive project of imposing a new Order, fidelity to any positive political Cause:

> what causes are there to be kept alive from a psychoanalytical perspective, if for the latter the most radical act consists in the subject's defining gesture of pure negativity that precedes and undermines every one of the possible candidates? . . . Before any inscription of a new truth even has a chance to take place, actually blocking this process in advance by virtue of a structural necessity, the death drive always already has had to come first to wipe the slate clean.

The first thing to note here is how Boostels simply "axiomatically" opposes Lacan's and Badiou's respective notions of act, constraining Lacan to the paradigm of "tragic failure," to the primacy of negativity over any of its positivizations, while, for Badiou, all "death drive" phenomena are the result of the failure (betrayal, exhaustion) of a positive emancipatory project (do we not find here an echo of the old theological notion of Evil as a mere absence of Good, not as a positive power in itself?). Such a direct confrontation says nothing about the truth value of the two competing theories: Boostels's ultimate reproach to Lacan is tautological: he is not Badiou—of which Lacan is, for sure, guilty.

Is, however, the opposition between the primacy of negativity and the primacy of the positive Truth really as simple and symmetrical as that? Is Boostels, in order to take sides with Badiou, not compelled to conflate two notions of negativity: "pure" self-relating negativity and negativity as an ethico-practical failure, as a betrayal of a positive project? In order to approach this topic properly, one would have to focus on the crucial, but often ambiguous, role of the *Unnameable* in Badiou. To cut a long story short: while, for Badiou, the unnameable Real is the *unfathomable external background* to a process of Truth (the resisting X which can never be fully "forced" by Truth), for Lacan, the Unnameable is *absolutely inherent, it is the Act itself in its excess over its namings.* Badiou's rationalism remains at the level of the external opposition of Reason and the Unnameable (the Unnameable as the obscure background of Reason): there is no place in it for the moment of "madness" at the very core of Reason itself. A reference to German Idealism is crucial here: following Kant, Schelling deployed the notion of the primordial decision-differentiation (*Ent-Scheidung*), the unconscious atemporal deed by means of which the subject chooses his eternal character which, afterward, within his conscious-temporal life, he experiences as the inexorable necessity, as "the way he always was":

> The deed, once accomplished, sinks immediately into the unfathomable depth, thereby acquiring its lasting character. It is the same with the will which, once posited at the beginning and led into the outside, immediately has to sink into the unconscious. This is the only way the beginning, the beginning that does not cease to be one, the truly eternal beginning, is possible. For here also it holds that the beginning should not know itself. Once done, the deed is eternally done. The decision that is in any way the true beginning should not appear before consciousness, it should not be recalled to mind, since this, precisely, would amount to its recall. He who, apropos of a decision, reserves for himself the right to drag it again to light, will never accomplish the beginning.[97]

With this abyssal act of freedom, the subject breaks up the rotary movement of drives, this abyss of the Unnameable—in short, this deed is the very founding gesture of naming. Therein resides Schelling's unprecedented philosophical revolution: he does not simply oppose the dark domain of the rotary movement of preontological drives, this unnameable Real which can never be totally symbolized, to the domain of Logos, of articulated Word which can never totally "force" it (like Badiou, Schelling is insistent that there is always a remainder of the unnameable Real—the "indivisible remainder"—which eludes symbolization); at its most radical, the unnameable Unconscious is not external to Logos, it is not its obscure background, but, rather, *the very act of Naming, the very founding gesture of Logos*. The greatest contingency, the ultimate act of abyssal madness, is the very act of imposing a rational Necessity onto the prerational chaos of the Real. And, since we are dealing with German Idealism here, we should summon up the courage to propose another paradoxical identification: what if this curved structure of drive is none other than that of what Hegel meant by "self-consciousness"? The crucial mistake to be avoided is to grasp Hegelian self-consciousness as a kind of meta-Subject, a Mind, much larger than an individual human mind, aware of itself: once we do this, Hegel inevitably looks like a ridiculous spiritualist obscurantist, claiming that there is a kind of mega-Spirit controlling our history. Against this cliché, we should emphasize how Hegel is fully aware that "it is in the finite consciousness that the process of knowing spirit's essence takes place and that the divine self-consciousness thus arises. Out of the foaming ferment of finitude, spirit rises up fragrantly."[98]

However, although our awareness, the (self-)consciousness of finite humans, is the only actual site of spirit, this does not entail any kind of nominalist reduction—there is another dimension at work in "self-consciousness," the one designated by Lacan as the "big Other" and by Karl Popper as the Third World. That is to say, for Hegel, "self-consciousness" in its abstract definition stands for a purely nonpsychological self-reflexive ploy of registering (re-marking) one's own position, of reflexively "taking into account" what one is doing. That is the link between Hegel and psychoanalysis: in this precise nonpsychological sense, "self-consciousness" is in psychoanalysis an object—for example, a tic, a symptom which articulates the falsity of my position, of which I am unaware. For instance, I have done something wrong, and I consciously deluded myself that I had the right to do it; but, unbeknown to me, a compulsive act which appears mysterious and meaningless to me "registers" my guilt, it bears witness to the fact that, somewhere, my guilt is noted. Along the same lines, Ingmar Bergman once observed that, toward the end of their careers, both Fellini and Tarkovsky (whom he admired) unfortunately started to make "Fellini films" and "Tarkovsky films," and that this very feature was the cause of the failure of his own *Autumn Sonata*—it is a "Bergman film made by Bergman." This means that, in *Autumn Sonata*, Bergman lost the spontaneous attitude toward his creative substance: he started to "imitate himself," reflexively to follow his own formula—in short, *Autumn Sonata* is a "self-conscious" film, even if Bergman himself was psychologically totally unaware of it. . . . This is the function of the Lacanian "big Other" at its purest: this impersonal, nonpsychological agency (or, rather, site) of registering, of "taking note of" what takes place.

This is how we should grasp Hegel's notion of the State as the "self-consciousness" of a people: "The state is the *self-conscious* ethical substance."[99] A state is not merely a blindly running mechanism applied to regulate social life; it always also contains a series of practices, rituals, and institutions that serve to "declare" its own status, in the guise of which the state appears to its subjects as what it is—parades and public celebrations, solemn oaths, legal and educational rituals which assert (and thereby enact) the subject's belonging to the state:

> the self-consciousness of the state has nothing mental about it, if by "mental" we understand the sorts of occurrences and qualities that are relevant to *our* own minds. What self-consciousness amounts to, in the state's case, is the existence of reflective practices, such as, but not limited to, educational ones. Parades displaying the state's military strength would be practices of this kind, and so would statements of principle by the legislature, or sentences by the Supreme Court—and they would be that *even* if all individual (human) participants in a parade, all members of the legislature or of the Supreme Court were personally motivated to play whatever role they play in this affair by greed, inertia, or fear, *and* even if all such participants or members were thoroughly uninterested and bored through the whole event, and totally lacking in any understanding of its significance.[100]

So it is quite clear to Hegel that this appearing has nothing to do with conscious awareness: it does not matter what individuals' minds are preoccupied with while they are participating in a ceremony; the truth resides in the ceremony itself. Hegel made the same point apropos of the marriage ceremony, which registers the most intimate link of love: "the solemn declaration of consent to the ethical bond of marriage and its recognition and confirmation by the family and community constitute the formal *conclusion* and *actuality* of marriage," which is why it is the role of "impertinence and its ally, understanding," to see "the ceremony whereby the essence of this bond is expressed and *confirmed* . . . as an external formality," irrespective of the inwardness of passionate feeling.[101]

This, of course, is not the whole story: Hegel also emphasized that a state fully actualizes itself only via a subjective element of individual self-awareness—there has to be an actual individual "I will!" which immediately embodies the will of the state; hence Hegel's deduction of monarchy. Here, however, we are in for a surprise: the Monarch is not the privileged point at which the state is fully aware of itself, of its nature and spiritual content; the Monarch is, rather, an idiot who merely provides the purely formal aspect of "This is my will! So be it!" to a content imposed on it from outside: "In a fully organized state . . . all that is required in a monarch is someone to say 'yes' and to dot the 'I'; for the supreme office should be such that the particular character of its occupant is of no significance."[102] The state's "self-consciousness" is thus irreducibly split between its "objective" aspect (self-registration in state rituals and declarations) and its "subjective" aspect (the person of the Monarch conferring on it the form of individual will)—the two never overlap. The contrast between the Hegelian Monarch and the "totalitarian" Leader who is effectively supposed to know cannot be stronger.

In a unique case of ethical perversion, however, "totalitarianism" itself exploits this gap of reflexivity that characterizes the structure of self-consciousness. In her *Eichmann in Jerusalem*, Hannah Arendt describes the self-reflexive twist the Nazi executioners accomplished in order to be able to endure the horrific acts they performed: most of them were not simply evil, they were well aware that they were doing things which brought humiliation, suffering, and death to their victims; the way they dealt with it was to accomplish the "Himmler trick," so that, "instead of saying: What horrible things I did to people!, the murderers would be able to say: What horrible things I had to watch in the pursuance of my duties, how heavily the task weighed upon my shoulders!"[103] In this way, they were able to turn the logic of resisting temptation around: the temptation to be resisted was the temptation to succumb to the very elementary pity and sympathy in the presence of human suffering, and their "ethical" effort was directed toward the task of resisting this temptation *not* to murder, torture, and humiliate. In a kind of *recapitonnage*, my very violation of spontaneous ethical instincts of pity and compassion is thus turned into proof of my ethical grandeur: to do my duty, I am ready to assume the heavy burden of inflicting pain on others.[104] No wonder Eichmann considered himself a Kantian: in him, the Kantian contrast between the subject's spontaneous egotistic strivings and the ethical struggle to overcome them is turned around into the struggle between the spontaneous ethical strivings and the "evil" effort to overcome these barriers which make it so difficult for us to accomplish a terrible act of torturing or killing another human being, as in the short poem by Brecht apropos of a statue of a Japanese demon, in which Brecht emphasizes the immense effort it takes to be truly evil.

CHAPTER 2

Building Blocks for a Materialist Theology

In one of the most painful and troubling scenes from David Lynch's *Wild at Heart*, Willem Dafoe exerts rude pressure on Laura Dern in a lonely motel room: he touches and squeezes her, invading the space of her intimacy, and repeating, in a threatening way, "Say fuck me!"—that is, extorting from her a word that would signal her consent to a sexual act. The ugly, unpleasant scene drags on, and when, finally, the exhausted Laura Dern utters a barely audible "Fuck me!", Dafoe abruptly steps away, assumes a nice, friendly smile, and cheerfully retorts: "No, thanks, I don't have time today, I've got to go; but on another occasion I would do it gladly. . . ." The uneasiness of this scene, of course, derives from the fact that the shock of Dafoe's final rejection of Dern's forcibly extorted offer gives the final pitch to him: his unexpected rejection is his ultimate triumph and, in a way, humiliates her more than direct rape. He has attained what he really wanted: not the act itself, just her consent to it, her symbolic humiliation. What we have here is rape in fantasy which refuses its realization in reality, and thus further humiliates its victim—the fantasy is forced out, aroused, and then abandoned, thrown upon the victim. That is to say, it is clear that Laura Dern is not simply disgusted by Dafoe's (Bobby Peru's) brutal intrusion into her intimacy: just prior to her "Fuck me!", the camera focuses on her right hand, which she slowly spreads out—the sign of her acquiescence, the proof that he has stirred her fantasy.

We should read this scene in a Lévi-Straussian way, as an inversion of the classic seduction scene (in which the gentle approach is followed by the brutal sexual act, after the woman, the target of the seducer's efforts, finally says "Yes!"). Or, to put it in another way, Bobby Peru's friendly negative answer to Dern's extorted "Yes!" owes its traumatic impact to the fact that it makes public the paradoxical structure of the empty gesture as constitutive of the symbolic order: after brutally wrenching out of her the consent to the sexual act, Peru treats this "Yes!" as an empty gesture to be politely rejected, and thus brutally confronts her with her own underlying fantasmatic investment in it.

This turn to politeness, however, calls for a different reading of the scene. In his very brutality, Bobby Peru is a figure of politeness: the true aim of his brutal intrusion is to force Laura Dern to pronounce an offer which she will mean literally, and then treat it as an offer meant to be refused (since it would be impolite to act on it directly). Therein resides the libidinal investment of a polite gesture: in it, I let you know what I really desire, but do not want it to be enacted, and therefore expect you to refuse my offer. What we find here is a kind of twist on Kant's classic formula of the inexorability of ethical duty: "You can, because you have to!"—here, it is, rather: "You can, but you should not!" Of course, our first reaction is that such a way of treating a "real" offer as an offer to be refused cannot but function as an act of extreme humiliation; at the same time, however, it isolates what I desire as opposed to what I want: "I desire it, but I do not want it!" As Lacan put it, desire is mostly experienced as that which I do not want. In other words, Bobby Peru puts Laura Dern to shame, he compels her to lose face, when she cannot but helplessly observe how a part of her body (her fist, precisely) autonomizes itself and signals on its own its accord with Peru's intrusion, sexual arousal, acceptance of his brutal offer.

This is why it is crucial to remember that the scene from *Wild at Heart* goes on for half a minute: when, after his cheerful retort "No, thanks, I don't have time today . . . ," Laura Dern starts to cry, Peru consoles her with kind, soft-spoken words: "Don't cry, everything will be OK." What if, instead of dismissing this kindness as brutal cynicism, we take it literally, as a sincere act of concern, and thus risk a rehabilitation of the unique figure of Bobby Peru? What if Peru, by enacting the sudden cut, shift, in the mode of discourse, from brutal intrusion to friendly thanking, acts more as a kind of "wild analyst," compelling Dern to confront the truth of her fantasmatic core that regulates her desire? What if his non-act is trading position with the analyst? What if the ultimate result of his intervention is to awaken Dern to her (split) subjectivity? In short, what if Bobby Peru, in his (mis)treatment of Dern, provides an exemplary case of *practicing* the love of one's neighbor, of what Christians call the "work of love"?

Another way of accounting for the uncanny impact of this scene from *Wild at Heart* is to focus on the underlying *reversal* of the standard division of roles in the heterosexual process of seduction. We could take as our starting point the emphasis on Dafoe's all-too-large mouth, with its thick wet lips, spitting its saliva around, contorted in an obscene way, with ugly, twisted, discolored teeth—do they not recall the image of *vagina dentata*, displayed in a vulgar way, as if this vaginal opening itself is provoking Dern into "Fuck me!" This clear reference to Dafoe's distorted face as the proverbial "cuntface" indicates that beneath the obvious scene of the aggressive male imposing himself on a woman, another fantasmatic scenario is played out: that of a young, blond, innocent adolescent boy aggressively provoked and then rejected by a mature, overripe vulgar woman; at this level, the sexual roles are reversed, and it is Dafoe who is the woman teasing and provoking the innocent boy. Again, what is so unsettling about the Bobby Peru figure is its ultimate sexual ambiguity, oscillating between the noncastrated raw phallic power and the threatening vagina, the two facets of the presymbolic life-substance. The scene is thus to be read as the reversal of the standard Romantic theme of "death and the maiden": what we have here is "life and the maiden."

This theme of the innocent/vulnerable boy confronted by an "overripe" sexualized mature woman (like the couple of Tomek and Magda from Kieślowski's *A Short Film about Love*) has a long prehistory which goes back to the *fin-de-siècle* emergence of the (self-)destructive *femme fatale*. Of special interest here is "Language in the Poem," Heidegger's seminal essay on Georg Trakl's poetry, the only place where he approaches the topic of sexual difference:

A human cast, cast in one mold and cast away into this cast, is called a kind [*Geschlecht*]. The word refers to mankind as a whole as well as to kinship in the sense of race, tribe, family—all of these in turn cast in the duality of the sexes. The cast of man's "decomposed form" is what the poet calls the "decomposing" kind. It is the generation that has been removed from its kind of essential being, and this is why it is the "displaced" kind.

What curse has struck this humankind? The curse of the decomposing kind is that the old human kinship has been struck apart by discord of *Geschlechter*. Each of the *Geschlechter* strives to escape from that discord into the unleashed turmoil of the always isolated and sheer wildness of the wild game. Not duality as such, the discord is the curse. Out of the turmoil of blind wildness it carries each kind into an irreconcilable plot, and so casts it into unbridled isolation. The "fallen *Geschlecht*," so cleft in two, can on its own no longer find its proper cast. Its proper cast is only with that kind whose duality leaves discord behind and leads the way, as "something strange," into the gentleness of simple twofoldness following in the stranger's footsteps.[1]

This, then, is Heidegger's version of "there is no sexual relationship"—the reference and indebtedness to Plato's myth from *Symposium* is obvious here, and this unproblematic reference to metaphysics should give us cause to think: the undead pale-faced ethereal boy Elis ("Elis in wonderland," one is tempted to add) stands for gentle Sex, for the harmonious duality of the sexes, not their discord. This means that, in the ambiguous series of discords, sexual difference ("the duality of the sexes") occupies a privileged role—it is, in a way, the generating site of "decomposition": all other levels are "decomposed" insofar as they are infected by the fundamental discord of the sexual difference—by what Heidegger, later in this essay, refers to as the "degenerate kind [*entartete Geschlecht*]."[2]

The first thing to do (and this is not done by Heidegger) is to situate this figure of a presexual boy into its context, whose first point of reference is Edvard Munch's paintings: is this "unborn" fragile boy not the very terrified asexual figure of *The Scream*, or the figure squeezed between the two frames in his *Madonna*, the same fetuslike asexual figure floating among the droplets of sperm? The horror of this figure is not Heideggerian anxiety (*Angst*), but suffocating horror pure and simple. And I am tempted to insert in the same series the famous shot in the scene at the florist's early in Hitchcock's *Vertigo*, in which Scottie observes Madeleine through the crack of the half-open door close to the big mirror. Most of the screen is occupied by the mirror-image of Madeleine; on the right side of the screen, between the two vertical lines (which function as the double lines of the frame), there is Scottie looking at her, resembling the dwarf on the border of the mirror who answers the evil queen's questions in the Grimm Brothers' *Snow White*. Although we see only the image of Madeleine, while Scottie is there in reality, the effect of the shot is nonetheless that it is Madeleine who is really there, part of our common reality, while Scottie is observing her from a crack in our reality, from the same preontological shadowy realm of the hellish underworld. And what about, in Lynch's *The Lost Highway*, the boyish Pete confronted with the woman's face, contorted by the sexual ecstasy, displayed on a gigantic video screen? And should we not risk a step further here, and put in the same lineage the paradigmatic image of the war or Holocaust victim, the starved asexual boy with a terrified look? Here we should also recall the key scene from Syberberg's *Parsifal*, the transformation of the boy-Parsifal into the girl-Parsifal after Parsifal rejects Kundry's advances, all this played out against the background of the gigantic interface-Thing, the spectral contours of Wagner's head.

When the boy repudiates (his fascination with) the Woman, he at the same time loses his boyishness and turns into a blue-faced, monstrously cold young woman. The message of this is not some obscurantist hermaphroditism but, on the contrary, the violent reinscription of sexual difference into the spectral-undead boyish figure.

Perhaps the outstanding example of this confrontation between the asexual boy and the Woman are the famous shots, from the beginning of Ingmar Bergman's *Persona*, of a preadolescent boy with large glasses, examining with a perplexed gaze the giant unfocused screen-image of a feminine face; this image gradually shifts to the close-up of what seems to be another woman who closely resembles the first one—yet another exemplary case of the subject confronted with the fantasmatic interface-screen.[3] This same boy already figures in Bergman's masterpiece *Silence* (1962), whose Weiningerian background is unmistakable: of the two women, one (the mother) is Woman as such, the oversexualized seducer enjoying dirty copulation; the other, an intellectual, caught in the vicious cycle of reflection, is repressing her femininity, and thus inexorably sliding toward self-destruction.[4] The action takes place in a nondescript Eastern European country whose atmosphere of sensual decay and sexual corruption provides a perfect "objective correlative" to the malaise of modern life.

In short, what Heidegger's reading does not take into account is how the very opposition between the asexual boy and the discordant *Geschlecht* is sexualized as the opposition between a *boy* and a *woman*. The discordant *Geschlecht* is not neutral but feminine, and the very apparent gender neutrality of Elis makes him a boy. So when Heidegger claims that "the boyishness in the figure of the boy Elis does not consist in the opposite of girlishness. His boyishness is the appearance of his stiller childhood. That childhood shelters and stores within it the gentle two-fold of sex, the youth and the 'golden figure of the maiden',"[5] he misses the key fact that sexual difference does not designate the two sexes of the human stock/species, but, in this case, the very difference between the asexual and the sexual: to put it in the terms of Laclau's logic of hegemony, sexual difference is the Real of an antagonism, since, in it, the external difference (between the sexual and the asexual) is mapped onto the internal difference between the two sexes. Furthermore, what Heidegger (and Trakl) already hint at is that, precisely as presexual, this innocent "undead" child confronted with the overripe and overblown feminine body is properly monstrous, one of the figures of Evil itself:

> Spirit or ghost understood in this way has its being in the possibility of both gentleness and destructiveness. Gentleness in no way dampens the ecstasy of the inflammatory, but holds it gathered in the peace of friendship. Destructiveness comes from unbridled license, which consumes itself in its own revolt and thus is active evil. Evil is always the evil of a ghostly spirit.[6]

This innocently evil ghost of a child is, of course, what Santner called "creature" at its purest.[7] Perhaps we should insert the figure of Elis into the series of similar figures from horror stories *à la* Stephen King: the "undead," white, pale, ethereal monstrous asexual child returning to haunt the adults. At a different level, is not Patricia Highsmith's Tom Ripley also such a subject, uniting ruthless destructiveness with angelic innocence, since his subjective position is, in a way, not yet marked by sexual difference? To go to the end of this series: in Kieślowski's *Decalogue*, is not the mysterious Christ-like home-less young man who appears to the hero at decisive moments also such an asexual ghostlike presence? And is not the ultimate irony that this Trakl-Heidegger vision of the asexual angelic entity found its most recent expression in Michel Houellebecq's *Les particules élémentaires* (1998): at the end of this bestseller, which triggered a lively debate all around Europe, humanity collectively decides to replace itself with genetically mod-ified asexual humanoids in order to avoid the deadlock of sexuality?

Although one of today's main candidates for the figure of Evil is child sexual abuse, there is nonetheless something in the image of a hurt, vulnerable child which makes it unbearably touching: the figure of a child, between two and five years old, deeply wounded but retaining a defiant attitude, his face and poise remaining stubborn, al-though he is barely able to prevent an outburst of tears—is this not one of the figures of the Absolute? One thinks here about the photos of children dying from exposure to radiation after the Chernobyl accident, or—also from Ukraine—one of the photos on a child-porn website showing a really young child, no more than four years old, con-fronting a big ejaculating penis, face covered with fresh sperm. Although the shot probably plays on the link between the penis ejaculating sperm and the mother's breast full of milk, the expression on the child's face is clearly a mixture of terror and per-plexity: the child cannot make out what is going on. This horrified face must be linked to the child's defiant gaze: if ever there was an image that illustrates the Levinasian point about the wound to the face, this is it.

And should we not take the risk of also rereading from this perspective the famous love affair between the young Ben Braddock (Dustin Hoffman) and the older Mrs. Robinson (Anne Bancroft) in Mike Nichols's *The Graduate?* This affair is usually per-ceived as a relationship between a proto-hippy sensitive and honest but confused boy and a mature corrupted shallow seducer; not unlike Bobby Peru, Mrs. Robinson is bombarding the confused Ben with "Fuck me!" declarations—and, unlike Bobby Peru, she really means it. The first thing that introduces discord into this image, how-ever, is Ben's brutal self-righteousness—recall how he snaps back at Mrs. Robinson: "Do you think I'm proud that I spend my time with a broken-down alcoholic?" The scene in which Ben tries to give some human depth to their affair by getting Mrs. Robinson to talk to him presents Mrs. Robinson with more complexity than usual. When, in the middle of their abortive conversation, she orders Ben not to take her daughter out, the only reason he can guess for the command is that she thinks he isn't good enough for Elaine, and he announces angrily that he considers this liaison "sick and perverted." Bancroft's face, expressive of deeply rooted social and personal dis-content, makes it clear that this is *not* Mrs. Robinson's reason, that her reasons are much more intense and tortured than Ben suspects, that they also reach well beyond the envy of youth and the fear of being cast off for her daughter—she deserves Ben's sympathy, not his shallow moralistic outrage:

> Ben is too insensitive to see that when she seems to acknowledge that she thinks her daughter too good for him, it's only out of desperation and confusion; she has feelings more intricate and disturbed than she knows how to explain to him. His rejection of her at this moment may look moral, but given the depth and the anguish of her emotional experience, it's a pretty ugly, unfeeling response. Mrs. Robinson's answer to Ben's plea that she talk to him—"I don't think we have much to say to each other"—proves to be quite accurate, but it doesn't expose her shallowness, as Nichols seems to have intended, it exposes *Ben's*. She has so much more self-awareness than he, and so many more real problems, why *should* she talk to him?[8]

It is interesting to note how, by "minimizing Ben's participation in the affair with Mrs. Robinson, by suggesting that it's boring and unpleasant to him, and then by leaving sex out of the relationship with Elaine altogether,"[9] the film surprisingly *reproduces* Mrs. Robinson's prohibition: sex and love remain totally split—that is to say, while Ben's interest in Mrs. Robinson is presented as purely sexual, devoid of any deeper emotional entanglement, there is literally no trace of sexual attraction in his love for Elaine, her daughter.

The central enigma, then, is: why does Mrs. Robinson insist so ferociously that Ben should not date her daughter; why is she ready to put *everything* at stake, to risk her marriage and her entire social existence, just to prevent their link? What we encounter here is another case of the underlying act of censorship, of *prohibition that sustains ruthless promiscuity*: Mrs. Robinson can engage in her illicit affairs only insofar as her daughter remains "pure," outside their circuit; far from being a late intruder into the affair, Elaine is there from the very beginning, as its absent Third. Consequently, far from being a simple dissolute vulgar middle-aged housewife, Mrs. Robinson is the only true *ethical* figure in the film: her promiscuity is part of her private deal with God, similar to the final twist of Evelyn Waugh's *Brideshead Revisited*: at the end of the novel, Julia refuses to marry Ryder (although they both recently got divorced for that very reason) as part of what she ironically refers to as her "private deal" with God—although she is corrupt and promiscuous, maybe there is still a chance for her if she sacrifices what matters most to her, her love for Ryder. As Julia makes clear in her final speech to Ryder, she is fully aware that, after she has dropped him, she will have numerous insignificant affairs; however, they don't really count, they don't condemn her irrevocably in the eyes of God—what would condemn her is giving priority to her only true love over her dedication to God, since there should be no competition between supreme goods. Like Julia, Mrs. Robinson thus arrives at the conclusion that for her, a promiscuous corrupted life is the only way to retain the purity of Elaine, to save *her* from corruption. (And do we not find an obverse sacrifice in the case of Bobby Peru himself? The price he has to pay for his obscene intrusions is that they should remain polite offers meant to be rejected—this is what makes him an ethical subject.)

The crucial point, therefore, is not to reduce Mrs. Robinson's prohibition to any positive psychological explanation (her envy of her daughter's youth, and so on): here, "God" is ultimately the name for the purely negative gesture of meaningless sacrifice—in the case of Julia, the sacrifice of her happy marital life; for Mrs. Robinson, the sacrifice of any authentic emotional link. In theology proper, it was Kierkegaard who fully articulated this logic of meaningless sacrifice (his term for it is "infinite resignation")—no wonder only a thin, almost imperceptible line separates Kierkegaard from dialectical materialism proper. Such a meaningless sacrifice is one of the key ingredients of what Badiou calls "anti-philosophy"—it is not surprising that Kierkegaard laid out its most concise formula: "The fact of the matter is that we must acknowledge that in the last resort there is no theory."[10] In all great "anti-philosophers," from Kierkegaard and Nietzsche to the late work of Wittgenstein, the most radical authentic core of being-human is perceived as a *concrete practico-ethical engagement and/or choice which precedes (and grounds) every "theory,"* every theoretical account of itself, and is, in this radical sense of the term, *contingent* ("irrational")—it was Kant who laid the foundation for "anti-philosophy" when he asserted the primacy of practical over theoretical reason; Fichte simply spelled out its consequences when he wrote, apropos of the ultimate choice between Spinozism and the philosophy of subjective freedom: "What philosophy one chooses depends on what kind of man one is." Thus Kant and Fichte—unexpectedly—would have agreed with Kierkegaard: in the last resort there is no theory, just a fundamental practico-ethical decision about what kind of life one wants to commit oneself to.

This unexpected continuity between German Idealism and Kierkegaard gives us the first hint of how Kierkegaard's anti-Hegelianism (like that of Deleuze, for that matter) is much more ambiguous than it may appear: the elevation of Hegel into a straw figure of the enemy obfuscates a disavowed proximity. For Kierkegaard, Hegel is the ultimate "systematizer," reducing the uniqueness of a living subjectivity to a subordinated moment in the logical self-deployment of the universal Notion; and, since the systematizing mortification of thought is the business of the university discourse, no wonder Kierkegaard shares the threat of being swallowed up by the university discourse, the standard complaint not only of poets and artists, but of all those who perceive themselves as "creative" minds: "Alas, but I know who is going to inherit from me, that character I find so repulsive, he who will keep on inheriting all that is best just as he has done in the past—namely, the assistant professor, the professor."[11]

The professor is, of course, Hegel. Kierkegaard remarks that Hegel's speculative philosophy "has a comical presupposition occasioned by its having forgotten, in a sort of world-historical absent-mindedness, what it means to be a human being. Not, indeed, what it means to be a human being in general; for this is the sort of thing that one might even induce a speculative philosopher to agree to; but what it means that you and I and he are human beings, each one for himself."[12] In short, the comical aspect of Hegel's system cannot fail to strike us when we recall that this system of Absolute Knowing was written by a contingent individual, Hegel . . . does not Kierkegaard, yet again, miss the point here? This umbilical link between the universal System and the accidental individual obeys the very logic of what Hegel called "infinite judgment": the paradoxical conjunction of the Universal with the "lowest" singularity ("Spirit is a bone," etc.).

Kierkegaard's critique of Hegel is based on the (thoroughly Hegelian) opposition between "objective" and "subjective" thought: "objective thought translates every-thing into results, subjective thought puts everything into process and omits results—for as an existing individual he is constantly in process of coming to be."[13] For Kierkegaard, obviously, Hegel is the ultimate achievement of "objective thought": he "does not understand history from the point of view of becoming, but with the illu-sion attached to pastness understands it from the point of view of a finality that ex-cludes all becoming."[14] Here, we should be very careful not to miss Kierkegaard's point: for him, only subjective experience is in fact "in becoming," and any notion of objective reality as an open-ended process with no fixed finality still remains within the confines of being—why? Because any objective reality, "processual" as it may be, is by definition ontologically fully constituted, present as a positively existing domain of objects and their interactions; only subjectivity designates a domain which is in itself "open," marked by an inherent ontological failure:

> Whenever a particular existence has been relegated to the past, it is complete, has ac-quired finality, and is in so far subject to a systematic apprehension . . . but for whom it is so subject? Anyone who is himself an existing individual cannot gain this finality outside existence which corresponds to the eternity into which the past has entered.[15]

What, however, if Hegel actually does the exact opposite? Three thinkers as different as Nietzsche, Heidegger, and Derrida all conceive their own age as that of the critical turn-ing point of metaphysics: in their (our) time, metaphysics has exhausted its potential, and the thinker's duty is to prepare the ground for a new, postmetaphysical, think-ing. . . . More generally, the whole of Judeo-Christian history, right up to our own post-modernity, is determined by what I am tempted to call the Hölderlin paradigm which was first articulated by Saint Augustine in City of God: "Where the danger is grows also what can save us. (Wo aber Gefahr ist wächst das Rettende auch.)" The present moment appears as the lowest point in the long process of historical decadence (the flight of the gods, alienation . . .), but the danger of the catastrophic loss of the essential dimension of being-human also opens up the possibility of a reversal (Kehre)—proletarian revolution, the arrival of new gods (who, according to Heidegger's late work, are the only ones that can save us), and so forth. Are we able to imagine a "pagan" nonhistorical universe, a universe completely outside this paradigm, a universe in which (historical) time just flows, with no teleological curvature, in which the idea of a dangerous moment of de-cision (Benjamin's Jetzt-Zeit), out of which a "bright future" which will redeem the past itself can emerge, is simply meaningless?

Although this Hölderlin paradigm is usually identified with Christianity, Christianity, at its most radical, nonetheless seems to give a unique twist to it: everything that has to happen has already happened; there is nothing to wait for, we do not have to wait for the Event, for the arrival of the Messiah, the Messiah has already arrived; the Event has already taken place, we are living in its aftermath. This basic attitude of historical closure is also the message of Hegel, of his dictum that the Owl of Minerva flies at dusk—and the difficult (but crucial) thing to grasp is how this stance, far from condemning us to passive reflection, opens up the space for active intervention. And does not the same go for Kierkegaard who, despite his standard rumblings against the mass society of the "present age," also does not seem to rely on the Hölderlin paradigm of historicality (and on the hubris in the self-perception of the thinker that such a view involves): there is nothing really exceptional about our age; if anything, we live in ordinary and uninteresting times?

Two opposing passages characterize the analytic process: the one from possibility to necessity, and the one from impossibility to contingency.[16] At the level of transference, the analyst operates as the "subject supposed to know," as the illusory Other Place at which everything is always-already written, at which the (unconscious) meaning of all symptoms is always-already fixed. This figure of the analyst stands for the Unconscious in its atemporal dimension, for the Unconscious which, as Freud put it, knows of no time—his message to the subject is always a variation of "You are now repeating your interaction with your father thirty years ago . . . ," and so on. This is the passage from possibility to necessity: what at first looks like a mere possibility, an accidental occurrence which also may not have happened, is retroactively transformed into something that was predestined to happen from all eternity. . . . (This position, of course, is based on a retroactive illusion, on misrecognizing its own performative dimension: the "eternal" meaning discovered by the patient is constructed in the very process of its discovery.) This aspect of the figure of the analyst, however, has to be supplemented by its opposite: the analyst's interpretive interventions also stand for the element of surprise, of the intrusion of the Real; the passage here is from impossibility to contingency, that is, what appeared impossible, what did not belong to the domain of possibilities, all of a sudden—contingently—takes place, and thus transforms the coordinates of the entire field.

If we follow the conventional view of the opposition between Hegel and Kierkegaard, it must seem as if these two passages condense the basic operation of Hegel and Kierkegaard. Is not the Hegelian dialectical process a self-enclosed circle in which things actualize their potential and become what they always-already were? Does Hegel himself not emphasize that, in itself, the beginning of the process is already the end? And, on the other side, does not the main thrust of Kierkegaard's anti-Hegelianism reside precisely in his effort to break this Hegelian closed circle, and open up the space for contingent cuts, "jumps," intrusions, which undermine the field of what appears to be possible?

So what about this obvious contrast between Hegel and Kierkegaard: for Hegel, everything has already happened (and thought is, in its basic dimension, a recollection of what has happened); while for Kierkegaard, history is open toward the future? Here, however, we should avoid a key misunderstanding about Hegel's dialectics: its wager is not to adopt toward the present the "point of view of finality," viewing it as if it were already past, but, precisely, to *reintroduce the openness of the future into the past*, to *grasp that-which-was in its process of becoming*, to see the contingent process which generated existing necessity. Is this not why we have to conceive the Absolute "not only as Substance, but also as Subject"? This is why German Idealism explodes the coordinates of the standard Aristotelian ontology which is structured around the vector running from possibility to actuality. In contrast to the idea that every possibility strives fully to actualize itself, we should conceive of "progress" as a move of *restoring the dimension of potentiality to mere actuality*, of unearthing, at the very heart of actuality, a secret striving toward potentiality.

Take Walter Benjamin's notion of revolution as redemption-through-repetition of the past:[17] apropos of the French Revolution, the task of a true Marxist historiography is not to describe the events as they really were (and to explain how these events generated the ideological illusions that accompanied them); the task is, rather, to unearth the hidden potentialities (the utopian emancipatory potentials) which were betrayed in the actuality of revolution and in its final outcome (the rise of utilitarian market capitalism). The point of Marx is not primarily to make fun of the wild hopes of the Jacobins' revolutionary enthusiasm, to point out how their high emancipatory rhetoric was just a means used by the historical "cunning of reason" to establish vulgar commercial capitalist reality; it is to explain how these betrayed radical-emancipatory potentials continue to "insist" as historical specters and to haunt the revolutionary memory, demanding their enactment, so that the later proletarian revolution should also redeem (lay to rest) all these past ghosts. . . . And, at a different level, was not Schelling making the same point when he conceived God before Creation as the domain of pure potentialities? In human thought, this potentiality, obfuscated in nature, explodes again, is "posited as such."[18]

Does not Kierkegaard, however, posit possibility as, precisely, the fundamental category of *conceptual* "objective thought," in contrast to the proper ethical approach, which deals with an actually existing I? "The real subject is not the cognitive subject, since in knowing he moves in the sphere of the possible; the real subject is the ethically existing subject."[19] The idea is that, in a cognitive approach, every singular entity is reduced to an instance of some universality, to an arbitrary example of a universal law or rule—to a *possible* instantiation of the law; while in the ethico-existential approach, it is my actual singular existence that matters. How, then, are we to combine this with the priority of the possible over the actual that is supposed to characterize the ethical stance? The opposition to bear in mind here is the one between what is *contingent* and what is *arbitrary* or accidental, best illustrated by the example of language: the fact that I (sort of) speak English is accidental with regard to the universal fact that, as a human being, I am a "being-of-language"; however, the fact that, in speaking English, I use language as a mere means of expression and/or instrumental manipulation, or that I use it poetically, in its world-opening capacity, is contingent. In short, "accidental" stands for a secondary specific difference within the universal confines of a genus, while "contingent" points toward the more radical level of deploying the potentials of the universal dimension itself. In this precise sense, the possibility that pertains to cognitive thought is the possibility of an arbitrary instantiation of the universal law, while the possibility that pertains to the ethico-existential approach concerns the thorough contingency of the decision about what to do with my singular life.

Nonetheless, such a reading of Hegel cannot but appear counterintuitive: does not Hegel present his System as the "flight of the Owl of Minerva," which flies at dusk— a retroactive recapitulation/remembering of the path of the Absolute—thus explicitly endorsing the "point of view of finality"? Here we should invert the existentialist commonplace according to which, when we are engaged in the present historical process, we perceive it as full of possibilities and ourselves as agents free to choose among them; while from a retroactive point of view the same process appears as fully determined and necessary, with no opening for alternatives: on the contrary, it is the engaged agents who perceive themselves as caught in a Destiny, merely reacting to it, while, retroactively, from the standpoint of later observation, we can discern alternatives in the past, possibilities of events taking a different path.

That is the difference between idealism and materialism: for the idealist, we experience our situation as "open" insofar as we are engaged in it, while the same situation appears "closed" from the standpoint of finality, that is, from the eternal point of view of the omnipotent and all-knowing God who alone can perceive the world as a closed totality; for the materialist, the "openness" goes all the way down, that is, necessity is not the underlying universal law that secretly regulates the chaotic interplay of appearances—it is the "All" itself which is non-All, inconsistent, marked by an irreducible contingency. And here Kierkegaard's theology presents the extreme point of idealism: he admits the radical openness and contingency of the entire field of reality, which is why the closed Whole can appear only as a radical Beyond, in the guise of a totally transcendent God: "The incessant becoming generates the uncertainty of earthly life, where everything is uncertain,"[20] and the deity "is present as soon as the uncertainty of all things is thought infinitely."[21]

Here we encounter the key formula: Kierkegaard's God is strictly correlative to the ontological openness of reality, to our relating to reality as unfinished, "in becoming." "God" is the name for the Absolute Other against which we can measure the thorough contingency of reality—as such, it cannot be conceived as any kind of Substance, as the Supreme Thing (that would again make him part of Reality, its true Ground). This is why Kierkegaard has to insist on God's thorough "desubstantialization"—God is "beyond the order of Being," he is nothing but the mode of how we relate to him; that is to say, we do not relate to him, he is this relating:

God himself is this: how one involves himself with Him. As far as physical and external objects are concerned, the object is something else than the mode: there are many modes. In respect to God, the *how* is the what. He who does not involve himself with God in the mode of absolute devotion does not become involved with God.[22]

The Christian passage to the Holy Spirit as Love (Christ's "whenever there is love between the two of you, I will be there") is to be taken literally: God as the divine *individual* (Christ) passes into the purely *nonsubstantial link* between individuals. This absolute devotion is enacted in the gesture of total self-renunciation: "in self-renunciation one understands one is capable of nothing."[23] This renunciation bears witness to the total gap that separates man from God: the only way to assert one's commitment to the unconditional Meaning of Life is to relate *all* of our life, our entire existence, to the absolute transcendence of the divine, and since there is no common measure between our life and the divine, sacrificial renunciation cannot be part of an exchange with God—we sacrifice all (the totality of our life) *for nothing:* "The contradiction which arrests [the understanding] is that a man is required to make the greatest possible sacrifice, to dedicate his whole life as a sacrifice—and wherefore? There is indeed no wherefore."[24] This means that there is no guarantee that our sacrifice will be rewarded, that it will restore Meaning to our life—we have to make a leap of faith which, to an external observer, cannot but look like an act of madness (like Abraham's readiness to kill Isaac): "At first glance the understanding ascertains that this is madness. The understanding asks: what's in it for me? The answer is: nothing."[25] Or, to quote Michael Weston's concise formulation:

> It is true that in terms of the measure an end remains, that "eternal happiness" of which Kierkegaard speaks, for which everything must be ventured, but it is an end which can be related to only as essentially absent. As soon as one thinks about it as something that could be present, and so as a reward, one ceases to venture everything and so ceases to have a relation to it. Such an end is not the satisfaction of human capacities, since if it is to be granted all such satisfaction must be given up as a goal.[26]

The Good is thus (not unlike the Kantian Thing-in-itself) a *negatively determined concept:* when, in the movement of "infinite resignation," I turn away from all temporal goods, goals, and ideals, then—to quote Simone Weil—

> my reason for turning away from them is that I judge them to be false by comparison with the idea of the good. . . . And what is this good? I have no idea— . . . It is that whose name alone, if I attach my thought to it, gives me the certainty that the things of this world are not goods.[27]

Remember how, for Kierkegaard, God's infallibility is also a negatively determined concept: its true meaning is that *man is always wrong.* This Kierkegaardian "infinite resignation" displays the structure of what, following Freud, Lacan calls *Versagung:* the radical (self-relating) loss/renunciation of the very fantasmatic core of being: first, I sacrifice all I have for the Cause-Thing which is more to me than my life; what I then get in exchange for this sacrifice is *the loss of this Cause-Thing itself.*[28]

Lacan elaborates this concept apropos of Paul Claudel's play *The Hostage*: in order to save the Pope hiding in her house, Sygne—the heroine—agrees to marry Toussaint Ture-lure, a person she despises utterly, the son of her servant and wet nurse who has used the Revolution to promote his career (as a Jacobin local potentate, he ordered the ex-ecution of Sygne's parents in the presence of their children). She thus sacrifices every-thing that matters to her—her love, her family name and estate. Her second act is her final No! to Turelure: Turelure, standing by the bed of the fatally wounded Sygne, des-perately asks her to give a sign which would confer some meaning on her unexpected suicidal gesture of saving the life of her loathed husband—anything, even if she didn't do it for love of him but merely to save the family name from disgrace. The dying Sygne doesn't utter a sound: she merely indicates her rejection of a final reconciliation with her husband by a compulsive tic, a kind of convulsed twitching which repeatedly dis-torts her gentle face. The same goes for the great act of renunciation at the end of Henry James's *The Portrait of a Lady* (Isabel Archer decides to stay with her repulsive husband, although she is free to leave him), the ultimate proof of James's materialism: it has nothing whatsoever to do with any kind of religious transcendence; what makes this renunciation so enigmatic is that it is, on the contrary, conditioned by the very lack of any transcendence—*it can occur only as a kind of empty gesture in a Godless universe*. This detour through James enables us to discern the hidden materialist content of Kierkegaard's religious sacrifice in which we give up everything, all that really matters, for nothing.

That is to say: how should we interpret the great feminine "No!" of Isabel Archer at the end of *The Portrait of a Lady?* Why doesn't Isabel leave Osmond, although she defi-nitely doesn't love him and is fully aware of his manipulations? The reason is not the moral pressure exerted on her by the notion of what is expected of a woman in her position—Isabel has sufficiently proven that, when she wants to, she is quite willing to override conventions: "Isabel stays because of her commitment to the bond of her word, and she stays because she is unwilling to abandon what she still sees as a deci-sion made out of her sense of independence."[29] In short, as Lacan put it apropos of Sygne de Coufontaine in *The Hostage*, Isabel is also "the hostage of the word." So it is wrong to interpret this act as a sacrifice bearing witness to the proverbial "feminine masochism": although Isabel was obviously manipulated into marrying Osmond, her act was her own, and to leave Osmond would simply equal depriving herself of her autonomy.[30] While men sacrifice themselves for a Thing (country, freedom, honor), only women are able to sacrifice themselves for nothing. (Or: men are moral, while only women are properly ethical.)[31]

Recently, Dominick Hoens and Ed Pluth have proposed a perceptive reading of La-can's interpretation of *The Hostage*: in the play's climactic finale, Sygne de Coufontaine, its heroine, interposes herself between Turelure, her repugnant and corrupted hus-band, and Georges, her true love, intercepting the bullet from the pistol that Georges aims at Turelure; afterward, when Turelure asks the dying Sygne why she did it:

Sygne makes no answer, or rather, it is her body that performs an answer in the form of a tic, a sign of "no." Sygne, who sacrificed everything in order to preserve a past order of things, who broke off her engagement with her cousin in order to save the Pope, cannot and will not tolerate this last and ultimate sacrifice to Turelure. . . . Sygne gives up everything in order to bind herself to an enemy, Turelure, and ultimately saves his life from her cousin's gunshot, but, when asked to confess that she did this out of marital love, only answers with a negating trait. The place where Sygne gives up everything in order to enter into a symbolic universe that is not hers appears later on as a negation of this order. Is this not the endpoint of the symbolic order, where an ugly, obscene feature puts the whole order into question and is thus a pure negation of what the order stands for? Sygne herself ultimately becomes a sign incarnate, saying "No" to the very point where the subject's introduction to or assumption of the symbolic order begins (with a primordial sacrifice).[32]

The Ver- of Sygne's Versagung thus permits the subject "to refuse the symbolic order within the symbolic order"[33]—here Hoens and Pluth suggest a reading of Sygne's "No" as prefiguring what Lacan later called sinthome. However, the dimension of inherent refusal that pertains to Versagung, its self-negating quality, almost Aufhebung, does not enter only with the sinthome of Sygne's "No"; it is already clearly discernible in the situation after Sygne's marriage, as the final outcome of her sacrificing everything: she sacrifices everything for X, her Cause (the old order embodied in the Pope), the Thing that really matters, and, as a result, she finally loses this X itself. . . . Thus we should complicate Hoens' and Pluth's analysis: Sygne performs four acts in The Hostage:

1. Sygne's and Georges's pathetic betrothal, promise of eternal love and fidelity to preserve the traditional order—the elementary, zero-level act of asserting one's fidelity to one's ethical Substance;
2. her decision to marry Turelure, sacrificing everything for the Pope, symbol of the old order;
3. her suicidal act of intercepting the bullet Georges aimed at Turelure, thus saving Turelure's life;
4. her final "No," the refusal to inscribe this sacrificial gesture into the existing ideologico-symbolic order.

The crucial enigma here is not (4), Sygne's "No," but, rather, (3): why did Sygne intercept the bullet? Her "No" comes afterward; it indicates Sygne's insistence on the radically ethical character of her suicidal gesture (in the Lacanian sense of the term), that is, her refusal to endorse the standard ideological recuperation of (3) as a gesture done out of marital duty and love (or any other reading that would reinscribe this act into the field of "pathological" motivations in the Kantian sense of the term, like the notion that, out of her natural goodness, she automatically moved to save a threatened human life). But is her "No" really a kind of minimal resistance, the refusal of a sacrifice, in the sense of "I've gone far enough, but this I will not do . . ."? Is it not too simple to say that her "No" signals a Pascalian answer: "I went to the end in doing what is expected of a faithful wife, I sacrificed my life for my husband, but don't force me now, on my deathbed, to confess that I did it out of my belief in marital or any other ideology; leave my inner life to me"? Far from indicating that she "will not tolerate this last and ultimate sacrifice to Turelure," Sygne's "No" rather signals her insistence on the "purity" of her sacrificial suicidal gesture: Sygne did it for the sake of it, her act cannot be inscribed into any sacrificial economy, into any calculating strategy. In other words, this "No" is not a "No" to a particular content, a refusal to reveal the secret, to disclose the intimacy of our true motivation, some secret idiosyncratic content, but a *"No as such,"* *the form-of-No which is in itself the whole content,* behind which there is nothing. Such an act of pure loss is constitutive of the Symbolic itself, so that, in this respect, Hoens and Pluth are right: Sygne's gesture of separating herself from the Symbolic repeats the very form of the subject's entry into the Symbolic.

It is crucial, however, not to confound this "No" with "No" as the zero-level symbolic prohibition, as the purely formal "No" which grounds the symbolic order (what Lacan calls the "No-of-the-Father/*le Non-du-Père*" as opposed to its positive articulation in the actual "Name-of-the-Father/*le Nom-du-Père*"): Sygne's "No" names a more primordial negation, a feminine refusal/withdrawal which cannot be reduced to the paternal "No" constitutive of the symbolic order. Even at the abstract level, the difference between the two is clear: while the paternal "No" is purely formal, Sygne's "No" is, on the contrary, a "No" embodied in a little piece of the Real, the excremental remainder of a disgusting "pathological" tic that sticks out of the symbolic form. The two "No"'s are thus like the same X on the two opposed sides of a Moebius strip: if the paternal "No" is the pure form, an empty place without content, Sygne's "No" is an excessive element that lacks its "proper" place.

The term "separating" is to be taken here in its precise Lacanian sense: in the sense of the opposition between alienation and separation. The *Versagung* contained in the move from (1) to (2)—or, more precisely, the *Versagung* which occurs as the twist inherent to (2)—takes place at the level of alienation: it designates a shift from the emphatic alienation in the Cause for which the subject is ready to give everything, to the loss of this Cause itself: after I have sacrificed everything, my happiness, my honor, my wealth, for the Cause, all of a sudden I realize that I've lost the Cause itself—my alienation is thereby redoubled, reflected-into-itself. What occurs in (3) and (4), on the contrary, enacts the separation from the Symbolic: we pass from the big Other to the small other, from A to *a*, the A's "ex-timate" core/stain, from the symbolic order (the order of symbolic identifications, of assuming symbolic mandates-titles) to some tiny tic, some idiosyncratic pathological gesture, which sustains the subject's minimal consistency. Just as, when I sacrifice everything for the Cause, I end up losing (betraying) this Cause itself, when I alienate myself fully, without restraint, in the Symbolic, I end up reduced to a tiny excremental object/tic that sticks out and stains the Symbolic, like Oedipus at Colonus. . . . No wonder, then, that in the Seminar on anxiety (1962–63),[34] which elaborates the consequences of the Seminar on transference with its reading of *The Hostage,* Lacan changes his position with regard to the ultimate support of the signifying order. In his key *écrit* on the subversion of the subject and the dialectic of desire, Lacan's answer is: the phallic signifier *qua* "reflexive" signifier, the signifier of the barred Other, the signifier of the lack of signifier, the signifier without signified, the signifier which, while deprived of all determinate meaning, stands for the pure potentiality of meaning—this means that although Lacan is already clear here about the inconsistency of the big Other, about its barred character, about the fact that "there is no Other of the Other," that the symbolic order turns in a vicious circle, lacking any guarantee, he nonetheless endeavors to inscribe this very lack back into the signifying order, in the guise of a paradoxical "reflexive" signifier which marks the lack itself, and thus enables the symbolic order to function.[35] Soon afterward, Lacan provides a new answer to the question

> which is the guarantee of the function of the Other that withdraws itself in the indefinite referral of significations. In the Seminar on Anxiety, the answer discards the [previous] signifying answer, and claims: this guarantee can only consist in that, somewhere, there is *jouissance*. Then—there are more stages, I condense—one needs as a guarantee of the signifying order, of the signifying chain . . . a piece of the body, a pound of flesh, that is to say, one has to cede an organ. The subject has to separate itself from an organ, but this organ is not an organ which is thereby transformed into signifier, it is an organ-*jouissance*. Later in his teaching, Lacan will call this organ a condenser of *jouissance*, a surplus-enjoyment, that is to say, that part of *jouissance* which resists being contained by the homeostasis, by the pleasure principle.[36]

"Sygne's No" should thus not, in a pseudo-Hegelian way, be confounded with the zero-gesture of negativity which grounds the symbolic order; it is not a signifying "No" but, rather, a kind of bodily gesture of (self-)mutilation, the introduction of a minimal torsion, of the curved space of drive, of the void around which a drive circulates. Therein resides the highest Hegelian speculative identity, the "infinite judgment" that lies at the very foundation of the symbolic order: "the Spirit is a bone," that is, the ideal symbolic order, the (quasi-)autonomous universe of meaning that floats above common reality, is (linked by a kind of umbilical cord to) a repulsive tic/protuberance that sticks out from the (human) body, disfiguring its unity. . . .

The "materialist" twist to be given to this radical gesture of "infinite resignation" seems obvious—we find it in Nietzsche: what if, while accepting Kierkegaard's point about the primacy of Becoming in human life, about the impossibility for an individual of assuming the "point of view of finality" over his own life, we joyously *affirm* the non-All of Becoming, in its openness and uncertainty? In other words, what if, after ascertaining that no positive object or value or idea can provide meaning to the Whole of my life, *I renounce the very need for such a Measure?* Kierkegaard's utter despair thus turns into what Nietzsche called the "innocence of becoming/*die Unschuld des Werdens*": our life needs no transcendent Measure to confer meaning on its totality, it is a creative play of incessantly creating new meanings and values. . . . What, however, if Kierkegaard is right here? What if such a direct assertion of the primacy of Becoming over Being proceeds all too quickly? What if it *misses a gap in Becoming*, a deadlock which propels the process of Becoming? That is to say: Kierkegaardian resignation, of course, "is not the descent into a 'loss of meaning,' a 'nihilism,' which is only possible as a defeat of a desire for humanly possible significance which must therefore still be present, but a significance which life can take on as the surrendering of such desire itself."[37] A Nietzschean reply would have been: what if I go to the end and surrender not only this desire for humanly possible significance, but *the desire for significance (for the meaning of my life in its totality) as such?* Why is this reply insufficient?

What Kierkegaardian "infinite resignation" confronts us with is pure Meaning, Meaning as such, reduced to the empty form of Meaning which remains after I have renounced all humanly determined finite Meaning: pure, unconditional Meaning can appear (and it *has* to appear) only as nonsense. The content of pure Meaning can only be negative: the Void, the absence of Meaning. We are dealing here with a kind of philosophico-religious correlate to Malevich's *Black Square on White Background*: meaning is reduced to the minimal difference between the presence and absence of meaning itself—that is to say, in a strict analogy to Lévi-Strauss's reading of "mana" as the zero-signifier, the only "content" of pure Meaning is its form itself as opposed to non-Meaning. This extreme position is, perhaps, what Nietzsche does not take into account: he leaps too quickly from imposed determinate Meaning to the meaning-less (groundless) process of Becoming which generates all meaning.

THE TRAPS OF PURE SACRIFICE

Among film-makers, Andrei Tarkovsky focused on this same act of meaningless sacrifice as the ultimate guarantee of sense—his last two films, *Nostalgia* and *Sacrifice*, are deeply Kierkegaardian. The hero of *Sacrifice*, Alexander, lives with his large family in a remote cottage in the Swedish countryside (another version of the very Russian *dacha* which obsesses Tarkovsky's heroes). His birthday celebrations are marred by the terrifying news that low-flying jet planes mark the start of a nuclear war between the superpowers. In his despair, Alexander turns himself in prayer to God, offering everything that is most precious to him to have the war not happen at all. The war is "undone," and at the end of the film Alexander, in a sacrificial gesture, burns down his beloved cottage and is taken to a lunatic asylum. . . . This theme of a pure, senseless act that restores meaning to our earthly life is the focus of Tarkovsky's last two films, shot abroad; on both occasions the act is accomplished by the same actor (Erland Josephson) who, as the old fool Domenico, burns himself publicly in *Nostalgia*, and as the hero of *Sacrifice* burns down his house, his most precious possession, what is "in him more than himself." (This opens up a possible connection with Lars von Trier's *Breaking the Waves*, which also culminates in an act of sacrifice by the heroine: if she goes to the boat with the violent sailor, and lets herself be beaten up, probably to death, this sacrifice will revive her crippled husband.) Tarkovsky is well aware that a sacrifice, in order to work and to be efficient, must be in a way "meaningless," a gesture of "irrational," useless expenditure or ritual (like traversing an empty pool with a lit candle, or burning down one's own house)—the idea is that only such a gesture of just "doing it" spontaneously, a gesture not covered by any rational consideration, can restore the immediate faith that will deliver us and heal us of our modern spiritual malaise. I am even tempted here to formulate this Tarkovskyan logic of meaningless sacrifice in terms of a Heideggerian inversion: the ultimate Meaning of sacrifice is the sacrifice of Meaning itself. The crucial point here is that the object sacrificed (burned) at the end of *Sacrifice* is the very ultimate object of the Tarkovskyan fantasmatic space, the wooden *dacha* standing for the safety and authentic rural roots of Home—for this reason alone, *Sacrifice* was, appropriately, Tarkovsky's last film.[38]

Kierkegaard's position on this limit-point is extremely ambivalent—it should be minimally rectified to obtain the proper materialist theory of subjectivity. The problem is that, despite his radical antiphilosophical stance, Kierkegaard repeats the fundamental Cartesian gesture, so that we can designate his most elementary operation as a kind of "existential *cogito*." The starting point of both Descartes and Kierkegaard is radical doubt—in Descartes, a cognitive one; in Kierkegaard, an existential one, a despair concerning the meaning of one's entire life; in Descartes, this doubt is pushed to extremes in the hypothesis of the "evil spirit"; in Kierkegaard, this despair pushes us to "infinite resignation." Through this doubt, a pure *cogito* emerges in Descartes, which, in Kierkegaard, acquires the features of the singularity of the first-person I, the insurmountable presupposition of all thinking and acting. And, in both cases, doubt is resolved through reference to God: in Descartes, a God who doesn't cheat, and thus guarantees the truth of our ideas; in Kierkegaard, a God belief in whom alone can give meaning to my whole life. Thus Kierkegaard's procedure remains transcendental: his question is that of the *conditions of possibility* of leading a meaningful life, and belief emerges as the only truly viable answer.

Patricia Huntington[39] has tried to establish a proper balance, a kind of synthesis, between Kierkegaard's concrete ethical engagement and Heidegger's ontologization of ethics, which suspends this engagement by neutralizing it. On the one hand, Kierkegaard's insistence on authentic personal engagement emphasizes the need for concrete ethical responsibility, for me to behave as if I am responsible for what I am, but leaves intact the traditional ontological frame of reference which sustains the unauthentic modes of existence (Kierkegaard formulates his very subversion of the traditional Greek ontology of the closed positive universe in terms descended from it: he talks about subject, truth, dialectics . . .). On the other hand, Heidegger elaborates the opposition between authentic and unauthentic modes of *Dasein* by revolutionizing the frame of traditional ontology; the price he pays for this, however, is that this opposition is deprived of the dimension of concrete ethical engagement, translated into a kind of proto-transcendental, formal *a priori* indifference toward concrete choices (Heidegger, in a symptomatic way, repeatedly insists on how his recourse, in order to designate the unauthentic mode of *Dasein*, to terms with a distinct negative ethical connotation is to be taken as a wholly neutral ontological description.)

The problem here is that no synthesis is possible. We cannot have it both ways: we can never achieve a concrete ethical engagement based on a full critico-philosophical reflection. On the one hand, for the ethical engagement to be truly binding and unconditional, it has to rely on an accepted *doxa* (which, in this case, of course, means: on the *doxa* impregnated by the tradition of metaphysical ontology). Such an engagement cannot survive endless self-reflective probing, the full questioning of its presuppositions. On the other hand, critico-historical philosophical reflection easily reveals how the very norms on which our engagement has to rely are the ultimate source of the "regression" to the unethical, to the unauthentic mode of existence; that is, how they are never sufficient to ground a proper ethical attitude (in his own way, Kierkegaard was well aware of this when he posited the necessity of the religious suspension of universal ethical norms as the very fulfillment of the Ethical). The reference to the established set of norms is thus simultaneously the condition of possibility and the condition of impossibility of ethical engagement: we must refer to it, but, simultaneously, this normative dimension, in its determinate form, always-already somehow betrays the Otherness from which every ethical call/injunction emanates.

This means that both sides are false: Heidegger's dismissal of all choices as "ontic," as well as liberal-democratic criticism of Heidegger in the style of Habermas, which focuses on Heidegger's indifference toward the "ontic" problems of terror, abuse, democracy, justice, and disrespect for human rights. What both sides have in common is the inability to ground a concrete ethical engagement. In this sense, they are both "formalist," that is, they both refer to some universal frame of reference (the historical Destiny of the Epochs of Being; the universal, pragmatic, procedural norms of communicational ethics) that precedes and is external to ontic ethical engagement in a concrete situation. In other words, Heidegger's indifference toward problems of human rights, democracy, and so on, as ontic dilemmas unworthy of philosophical concern, is the mirror-image of Habermas's universal, pragmatic, normative presuppositions. What both positions reject is the situation of radical contingency, in which there is no guarantee for my decisions, in which the agent has to confront the abyss of freedom. Habermas mobilizes the fear of the lack of a universal normative frame of reference: for him, the moment we renounce such a universal frame, the path is wide open to proto-Fascist "irrationalist" decisionism, the project of the Enlightenment is renounced. . . . What, however, if this lack of an *a priori* universal frame—of a frame exempted from the contingencies of the political struggle—is precisely what opens up the space for the struggle (for "freedom," "democracy," and so on)? Is this not the lesson of Kierkegaard—that every translation of ethics into some positive universal frame already betrays the fundamental ethical Call, and thus necessarily gets entangled in inconsistencies? Is the only true ethical stance, therefore, acceptance of this paradox and its challenge?

Let us begin with Kierkegaard's account of the leap from innocence to sin; in the primordial state of a spirit which is still asleep and, as such, ignorant, there is peace and repose, but there is simultaneously something else that is not contention and strife, for there is indeed nothing against which to strive. What, then, is it? Nothing. But what effect does nothing have? It begets anxiety. This is the profound secret of innocence, that it is at the same time anxiety. Dreamily the spirit projects its own actuality, but this actuality is nothing, and innocence always sees this nothing outside itself.[40]

This anxiety is still within the domain of psychology: "Anxiety is a qualification of dreaming spirit, and as such it has its place in psychology."[41] We should be very precise here: the nonpsychological dimension Kierkegaard is talking about—that is, that which, for him, is of the order of the supernatural which cannot be explained by science—is strictly equivalent to what Freud called "metapsychology." The passage to the ethical domain of guilt, good and evil, involves a leap (a fall into sin) which can appear to psychology only as utter ambiguity (we love what we fear, and so on). What, according to Kierkegaard, disturbs the primordial peace and balance of the "dreaming spirit" is an intervention from outside—the divine prohibition:

When it is assumed that the prohibition awakens the desire, one acquires knowledge instead of ignorance, and in that case Adam must have had a knowledge of freedom, because the desire was to use it. The explanation is therefore subsequent. The prohibition induces in him anxiety, for the prohibition awakens in him freedom's possibility. What passed by innocence as the nothing of anxiety has now entered into Adam, and here again it is a nothing—the anxious possibility of *being able*. He has no conception of what he is able to do; otherwise—and this is what usually happens—that which comes later, the difference between good and evil, would have to be presupposed. Only the possibility of being able is present as a higher form of ignorance, as a higher expression of anxiety, . . . because in a higher sense he both loves it and flees from it.[42]

Although this prohibition comes from outside, however, its effects—the rise of the anxiety of freedom—can still be accounted for in terms of psychology; the crucial leap comes afterward:

Anxiety may be compared with dizziness. He whose eye happens to look down into the yawning abyss becomes dizzy. . . . Hence anxiety is the dizziness of freedom, which emerges when the spirit wants to posit the synthesis and freedom looks down into its own possibility, laying hold of finiteness to support itself. Freedom succumbs in this dizziness. Further than this, psychology cannot and will not go. In that very moment everything is changed, and freedom, when it again rises, sees that it is guilty. Between these two moments lies the leap, which no science has explained and which no science can explain.[43]

The precise temporality is crucial here: dizzy with the abyss of its own freedom, the spirit renounces it, searching for a support in some finite positivity (the theme which later became popular under the name of "escape from freedom"); however, this fall into finitude, conditioned by the spirit's (subject's) weakness, is not yet the Fall proper. The

Fall occurs only when, after this fall into finitude, freedom rises again, it paradoxically *coincides with this rise*—it is only now that freedom perceives itself as guilty (and— another aspect of the same leap—that sexuality and the sensuous as such appear as sinful). We enter the domain of sin and guilt only in the *second* rise of freedom—why?

To explain this properly, I should introduce a further complication here. There is something—a crucial step—missing in Kierkegaard's description: that is, his otherwise refined psychological sensibility leads him astray: the passage from primordial repose filled with the joyous anxiety of nothing to prohibition is not direct; what comes in between is what Schelling called *Zusammenziehung*, primordial self-withdrawal, primordial egotistic contraction.[44] For this reason, Kierkegaard proceeds too quickly in ironically rejecting Schelling's topic of the moods and states in God, of God's suffering, and so on, and other "creative birth pangs of the deity"[45]—for Kierkegaard, God is absolute transcendence to whom no such anthropomorphic predicate can be applied (which is why Kierkegaard mockingly observes that, when Schelling focuses on God's frustration that pushes him to creativity, he compares God to Mr. Müller . . .); however, if it does not apply to God, it certainly applies to human subjects. That is the crucial insight of Freudian metapsychology emphasized by Lacan: *the function of Prohibition is not to introduce disturbance into the previous repose of paradisiacal innocence, but, on the contrary, to resolve some terrifying deadlock.*

It is only now that we can reconstruct the full sequence: primordial repose is first disturbed by the violent act of contraction, of self-withdrawal, which provides the proper density of the subject's being; the result of this contraction is a deadlock that tears the subject apart, throwing him into the vicious cycle of sabotaging its own impetus—the experience of this deadlock is *dread* at its most terrifying. In Lacanese, this contraction creates a *sinthome*, the minimal formula of the subject's consistency— through it, the subject becomes a creature proper, and anxiety is precisely the reaction to this overproximity of one's *sinthome*. This deadlock is then resolved through Prohibition, which brings relief by externalizing the obstacle, by transposing the inherent obstacle, the bone in the subject's throat, into an external impediment. As such, Prohibition gives rise to desire proper, the desire to overcome the external impediment, which then gives rise to the anxiety of being confronted with the abyss of our freedom. Thus we have a succession of three anxieties: the joyous "*anxiety of nothing*" that accompanies the repose of primordial innocence; the deadening *anxiety/dread* of overproximity to one's *sinthome*; the *anxiety of freedom* proper, of being confronted with the abyss of possibilities, of what I "can do."[46]

We should bear Lacan's lesson in mind here: accepting guilt is a maneuver which delivers us of anxiety, and its presence indicates that the subject has compromised his desire. So when, in a move described by Kierkegaard, we withdraw from the dizziness of freedom by seeking a firm support in the order of finitude, *this withdrawal itself is the true Fall*. More precisely: this withdrawal is the very withdrawal into the constraints of the externally imposed prohibitory Law, so that the freedom which then arises is freedom to violate the Law, freedom caught up in the vicious cycle of Law and its transgression, where Law engenders the desire to "free oneself" by violating it, and "sin" is the temptation inherent to the Law—the ambiguity of attraction and repulsion which characterizes anxiety is now exerted not directly by freedom but by sin. The dialectic of Law and its transgression does not reside only in the fact that Law itself solicits its own transgression, that it generates the desire for its own violation; our obedience to the Law itself is not "natural," spontaneous, but always-already mediated by the (repression of the) desire to transgress it. When we obey the Law, we do it as part of a desperate strategy to fight against our desire to transgress it, so the more rigorously we obey the Law, the more we bear witness to the fact that, deep within ourselves, we feel the pressure of the desire to indulge in sin. The superego feeling of guilt is therefore right: the more we obey the Law, the more we are guilty, because this obedience is in effect a defense against our sinful desire.

What changes in this move is the status of the Law: we shift from psychology to the "metapsychological" symbolic order proper as an external machine that parasitizes upon the subject. Or, to put it in precise Kantian terms: "Fall" is the very renunciation of my radical ethical autonomy: it occurs when I take refuge in a heteronomous Law, in a Law which is experienced as imposed on me from the outside, that is, the finitude in which I search for a support to avoid the dizziness of freedom is the finitude of the external-heteronomous Law itself. Therein lies

THE DIFFICULTY OF BEING A KANTIAN

Every parent knows that a child's provocations, wild and "transgressive" as they may appear, ultimately conceal and express a demand, addressed to the figure of authority, to set a firm limit, to draw a line which means "This far and no further!", thus enabling the child to achieve a clear mapping of what is possible and what is not possible. (And does the same not go also for the hysteric's provocations?) This, precisely, is what the analyst refuses to do, and that is what makes him so traumatic—paradoxically, it is the setting of a firm limit which is liberating, and it is the very absence of a firm limit which is experienced as suffocating. This is why the Kantian autonomy of the subject is so difficult—its implication is precisely that there is nobody out there, no external agent of "natural authority," who can do the job for me and set me my limit, that I myself have to pose a limit to my natural "unruliness." Although Kant famously wrote that man is an animal which needs a master, this should not deceive us: what Kant aims at is not the philosophical commonplace according to which—in contrast to animals, whose behavioral patterns are grounded in their inherited instincts—man lacks such firm coordinates which, therefore, have to be imposed on him from the outside, through a cultural authority; Kant's true aim, rather, is to point out how *the very need of an external master is a deceptive lure*: man needs a master in order to conceal from himself the deadlock of his own difficult freedom and self-responsibility. In this precise sense, a truly enlightened "mature" human being is a subject who *no longer needs a master*, who can fully assume the heavy burden of defining his own limitations. This basic Kantian (and also Hegelian) lesson was put very clearly by G. K. Chesterton: "Every act of will is an act of self-limitation. To desire action is to desire limitation. In that sense every act is an act of self-sacrifice."[47] Along the same lines, a promiscuous teenager may engage in extreme orgies with group sex and drugs, but what he cannot bear is the idea that his mother could be doing something similar—his orgies rely on the supposed purity of his mother, which serves as the point of exception, the external guarantee: I can do whatever I like, since I know my mother keeps her place pure for me. . . . The most difficult thing is not to violate the prohibitions in a wild orgy of enjoyment, but to do this without relying on someone else who is presupposed not to enjoy so that I can enjoy: *to assume my own enjoyment directly, without mediation through another's supposed purity.* (The same goes for belief: the difficult thing is not to reject belief in order to shock a believing other, but *to be a nonbeliever without the need for another subject supposed to believe on my behalf.*)

Lacan's famous reply to the revolting students in 1968—"As hysterics, you want a new master. You will get one"—has to be given its entire Kantian weight: it has to be read against the background of Kant's statement that man is an animal which needs a master—in short, what this means, from the psychoanalytic standpoint, is that *man is a hystericized* (and, in this sense, subjectivized) *animal,* an animal who no longer knows what it wants, an animal who needs a Master figure of an Other to set it the limits, to tell it what it wants (through prohibitions), an animal caught in the game of provoking the Master, an animal in whom this provoking, this questioning of the Master's authority, is inextricably linked to the call for a new Master, and vice versa, in whom the desire for a Master is always accompanied by a hidden qualification ". . . a Master whom I will be able to dominate/manipulate." And this statement has to be read together with Kant's "What Is Enlightenment?", in which he calls for man's step out of immaturity: a man who (still) needs a master is "immature." However, the qualification quoted above (". . . a Master whom I will be able to dominate/manipulate") is Lacan's reply to Freud's *Was will das Weib?,* "What does woman want?"—does this mean that woman is structurally, formally, in her very definition, immature, an immature subject? Yes—but not in the simple sense that would oppose her to a "mature" man who doesn't need a Master to tell him what he wants, who can autonomously set his own limits. What this conclusion amounts to is, rather, that woman is a true subject, a subject at its most fundamental, while man is a ridiculous fake, a false pretender. Of course, Kant's (and Lacan's) wager is that this "immaturity" is not the human's inevitable lot, that one *can* reach "maturity"—but not by adopting the position of the Master: what Lacan defines as the subjective position of the Analyst is the only "autonomous" form of subjectivity, and it paradoxically overlaps with what he called "subjective destitution."

Kant's limitation, his compromise with regard to his own breakthrough, his failure to follow its consequences to the end, can best be approached through the distinction, elaborated by Bernard Williams, between *must* and *ought:*[48] in his formulations of the ethical imperative, Kant seems to confuse them, reducing, (mis)reading, the

Must (the injunction at the level of the Real, the hard "I cannot do otherwise") as an Ought (the *Sollen* at the level of the inaccessible symbolic Ideal, what you are striving for but can never accomplish). In other words, Kant misreads the Real as the impossible which *happens* (that which "I cannot not do") with the Real as the cannot-possibly-happen (that which "I can never fully accomplish"). That is to say: in Kantian ethics, the true tension is not between the subject's idea that he is acting only for the sake of duty, and the hidden fact that there was actually some pathological motivation at work (vulgar psychoanalysis); the true tension is exactly the opposite one: the free act in its abyss is unbearable, traumatic, so that when we accomplish an act out of freedom, in order to be able to bear it, we experience it as conditioned by some pathological motivation. Here I am tempted to bring in to the key Kantian concept of schematization: a free act *cannot be schematized*, integrated into our experience; so, in order to schematize it, we have to "pathologize" it. And Kant himself, as a rule, misreads the true tension (the difficulty of endorsing and assuming a free act) as the standard tension of the agent who can never be sure if his act was in fact free, not motivated by hidden pathological impetuses. So, as far as the distinction between *must* and *ought* is concerned, Kant's famous "*Du kannst, denn du sollst!*" should not be translated as "You can, because you must!", but, rather, more tautologically, as "You can, because *you cannot not do it!*" This is how we should reply Lorenzo Chiesa, who recently suggested a perceptive critical reading of the topic of "Kant with Sade":

> Kant's ethics and Sade's "anti-ethics" similarly endeavor to exacerbate and finally break with the dialectics between Law and desire *qua* inherent transgression which Saint Paul expressed in the following way: "If it had not been for the law, I would not have known sin." The lack of mediation between Law and desire in favor of one of the two should hypothetically give rise to either a pure *jouissance of the Law*, in the case of Kant, or, an—ultimately indistinguishable—pure *law of Jouissance*, in the case of Sade . . . the elimination of the gap between the Sovereign Good and the positive moral law in Kant also entails the obliteration of the space for inherent transgression which is coextensive with any morality; as Lacan repeatedly points out, without such a space . . . society is *impossible*: "We spend our time breaking the ten commandments, and that is why society is possible." (E–69) ". . . societies prosper as a result of the transgression of these maxims." (E–78)[49]

This is why a Kantian ideal society in which human beings would overcome their "radical Evil," the penchant toward Evil inscribed into human nature itself, and the moral Law would overlap with human nature, so that obeying it would no longer be experienced as painful, as a traumatic humiliation of our natural egotism, is no less "unworkable" than the thoroughly "immoral" society outlined by Sade in his "Frenchmen, yet another effort . . .". Every "actually existing society" is a compromise between the extreme of total ignorance of moral rules and the opposite extreme of absence of their violations—they are both a mortal threat to society. Symbolic norms are impossible(-to-follow), yet *necessary*.

The first thing to note here, however, is that, for Kant, radical Evil can never be abolished, so that the very notion of a new human nature harmonized with ethical demands is meaningless or, rather, an extremely dangerous angelic temptation. With regard to the problem of human nature, we should note that, for both Kant and Sade, the recourse to "nature" is a symptomatic gesture by means of which they shrink from the ultimate consequences of their theoretical edifice: "Nature is, in Sade as well as in Kant, the symptom of that which remains unthought in these two thinkers of the universal."[50] That is to say: in both cases we are dealing with a certain structurally necessary ambiguity of this term. Kant first defines nature as the Whole of phenomena, of phenomenal reality, insofar as it is held together by (and subject to) universal laws; later, however, he also talks about another, noumenal Nature as the kingdom of ethical goals, as the community of all rational ethical beings. The very excess of freedom over nature (the natural enchainment of causes and effects) is thus again naturalized. . . . Sade, on the other hand, first conceives of nature as the indifferent system of matter subject to eternal change, inexorably following its course, submitted to no external Divine Master; however, in his claim that, when we find pleasure in torturing our fellow beings and destroying them, up to the interruption of the very natural cycle of reproduction, we effectively fulfill Nature's innermost request, he secretly introduces another form of nature, no longer the usual indifferent run of things "beyond Good and Evil," but Nature which is already somehow subjectivized, turned into a transgressive/diabolic entity commanding us to pursue evil, and to find pleasure in the destruction and sacrifice of every form of morality and compassion. Is not this second nature, what Lacan referred to as the "Supreme Being of Evilness," the Sadeian counterpoint to (or reversal of) the Kantian Nature *qua* the community of suprasensible rational beings, the kingdom of ethical Goals?

This ambiguity can also be stated in the following terms: what, in fact, gives pleasure to the Sadeian hero? Is it the mere "return to the innocence of nature," the unconstrained following of the laws of nature that also demand destruction, or is pleasure nonetheless inherently linked to the moral Law it violates, so that what gives us pleasure is the very awareness that we are committing a blasphemy? This ambiguity between innocence and blasphemous corruption is irreducible.[51] So, in both cases, in Kant as well as in Sade, the "elementary" neutral notion of Nature as the indifferent mechanism that follows its course is supplemented by another, "ethical" notion of Nature (the suprasensible kingdom of ethical goals; the diabolical commandment to pursue the evil path of destruction); and, in both cases, this second notion of Nature masks a certain gesture of shrinking back, of avoiding confrontation with the ultimate paradox of one's position: the uncanny abyss of freedom without any ontological guarantee in the Order of Being.

For Lacan, the Kantian overcoming of the "dialectic" of Law and desire—as well as the concomitant "obliteration of the space for inherent transgression"—is a *point of no return* in the history of ethics: there is no way of undoing this revolution, and returning to the good old times of prohibitions whose transgression sustained us. This is why today's desperate neoconservative attempts to reassert "old values" are ultimately a failed perverse strategy of imposing prohibitions which can no longer be taken seriously. No wonder Kant is the philosopher of freedom: with him, the deadlock of freedom emerges. That is to say: with Kant, the reliance on any preestablished Prohibition against which we can assert our freedom is no longer viable, our freedom is asserted as autonomous, every limitation/constraint is completely self-posited.

This is also why we should reverse the standard reading of "Kant with Sade" according to which the Sadeian perversion is the "truth" of Kant, more "radical" than Kant; that it draws out the consequences Kant himself did not have the courage to confront. It is not in this sense that Sade is the truth of Kant; on the contrary, the Sadeian perversion emerges as the result of the Kantian compromise, of Kant's avoiding the consequences of his breakthrough. Sade is the *symptom* of Kant: while it is true that Kant retreated from drawing all the consequences of his ethical revolution, the space for the figure of Sade is opened up by this compromise of Kant, by his unwillingness to go to the end, to retain the full fidelity to his philosophical breakthrough. Far from being simply and directly "the truth of Kant," Sade is the symptom of how Kant betrayed the truth of his own discovery—the obscene Sadeian *jouisseur* is a stigma bearing witness to Kant's ethical compromise; the apparent "radicality" of this figure (the Sadeian hero's willingness to go to the end in his Will-to-Enjoy) is a mask of its exact opposite.[52]

Furthermore, far from being the seminar of Lacan, his *Ethics of Psychoanalysis* is, rather, the point of deadlock at which Lacan comes dangerously close to the standard version of the "passion for the Real." Do not the unexpected echoes between this seminar and the thought of Georges Bataille, the philosopher of the passion for the Real if ever there was one, point unambiguously in this direction? Is Lacan's ethical maxim "do not compromise your desire" (which, we should always bear in mind, he never used again in his later work) not a version of Bataille's injunction "to think everything to a point that makes people tremble,"[53] to go as far as possible—to the point at which opposites coincide, at which infinite pain turns into the joy of the highest bliss (discernible in the photograph of the Chinese submitted to the terrifying torture of being slowly cut to pieces—a photograph reproduced in Bataille's *Eroticism*), at which the intensity of erotic enjoyment encounters death, at which sainthood overlaps with extreme dissolution, at which God himself is revealed as a cruel Beast? Is the temporal coincidence of Lacan's seminar on the ethics of psychoanalysis and Bataille's *Eroticism* more than a mere coincidence? Is not Bataille's domain of the Sacred, of the "accursed part," his version of what, apropos of *Antigone*, Lacan deployed as the domain of *ate*? Does not Bataille's opposition of "homogeneity," the order of exchanges, and "heterogeneity," the order of limitless expenditure, echo Lacan's opposition of the order of symbolic exchanges and the excess of the traumatic encounter with the Real? "Heterogeneous reality is that of a force or shock."[54] And how can Bataille's elevation of the dissolute woman to the status of God fail to remind us of Lacan's claim that Woman is one of the names of God? Not to mention Bataille's term for the experience of transgression— impossible—which is Lacan's qualification of the Real. . . . It is this urge to "go to the end," to the extreme experience of the Impossible as the only way of being authentic, which makes Bataille *the* philosopher of the passion for the Real—no wonder he was obsessed with Communism and Fascism, these two excesses of life against democracy, which was "a world of appearances and of old men with their teeth falling out."[55]

Bataille was fully aware of how this transgressive "passion for the Real" *relies on pro-hibition*; this is why he was explicitly opposed to the "sexual revolution," to the rise of sexual permissiveness which began in his last years:

> In my view, sexual disorder is accursed. In this respect and in spite of appearances, I am opposed to the tendency which seems today to be sweeping it away. I am not among those who see the neglect of sexual interdictions as a solution. I even think that human potential depends on these interdictions: we could not imagine this potential without these interdictions.[56]

Thus Bataille brought to its climax the dialectical interdependence between Law and its transgression—"system is needed and so is excess," as he liked to repeat: "Often, the criminal himself wants death as the answer to the crime, in order finally to impart the sanction, without which the crime would be *possible* instead of being *what it is*, what the criminal wanted."[57] This, also, was why he ultimately opposed Communism: he was for the excess of the revolution, but feared that the revolutionary spirit of excessive expenditure would afterward be contained in a new order, even more "homogeneous" than the capitalist one: "the idea of a revolution is intoxicating, but what happens afterward? The world will remake itself and remedy what oppresses us today to take some other form tomorrow."[58]

This, perhaps, is why Bataille is strictly premodern: he remains stuck in this dialectic of the Law and its transgression, of the prohibitive Law as generating the transgressive desire, which forces him to the debilitating perverse conclusion that one has to install prohibitions in order to be able to enjoy their violation—a clearly unworkable pragmatic paradox. What Bataille is unable to perceive are simply the consequences of the Kantian philosophical revolution: the fact that *the absolute excess is that of the Law itself*—the Law intervenes in the "homogeneous" stability of our pleasure-oriented life as the shattering force of the absolute destabilizing "heterogeneity." In his *Ethics* seminar, Lacan himself clearly oscillates on this key point: in Chapter IV, he interprets the link between Law and desire along the lines of the Pauline "transgressive" model (it is the prohibition itself which engenders the desire to transgress it); while later, toward the end of the seminar, he moves toward the properly Kantian formula of the categorical imperative (the moral Law) as directly identical to pure desire.[59]

So, far from announcing a triumphant solution, Lacan's "Kant avec Sade," his assertion of Sade as the truth of Kant, rather names an embarrassing problem that Lacan failed to resolve—and did not even fully confront—in his *Ethics* seminar: how are we to distinguish the appearance of pure desire—the violent gesture of transgressing the social domain of "servicing goods" and entering the terrifying domain of *ate*, that is, the ethical stance of the subject who "does not compromise his desire"—from the fully consummated "passion for the Real," the subject's disappearance-immersion in the primordial *jouissance*? For Chiesa,[60] the solution lies in the thesis deployed by Lacan later, most clearly in *Seminar XXIII*: there is no substantial Thing-*jouissance* beyond the Symbolic, *jouissance* is as such—in Hegelese: in its very notion—*jouissance* of/in the lack of itself, a *jouissance* that arises when its movement repeatedly misses its goal, a pleasure that is generated by the repeated failure itself. And since, according to Lacan, such a repetitive circulation around the goal is what defines *drive*, it is clear that "Kant with Sade" (the indiscernibility between pure desire and immersion in the abyss of primordial *jouissance*) names a deadlock constitutive of desire as such, an impasse whose solution ("passage") is drive.

What, then, is the Fall from this Kantian perspective? Consider the first moments of a feminist awakening: it all begins not with a direct attack on patriarchy, but with experiencing one's situation as unjust and humiliating, one's passivity as a failure to act—is this very overwhelming awareness of failure not in itself a positive sign? Does it not, in a negative way, bear witness to the fact that women clearly perceive the need to assert themselves, that they perceive the lack of it as a failure? In the same way, "Fall" is the first step toward liberation—it represents the moment of knowledge, of cognizance of one's situation. Thus "fall into sin" is a purely formal change: nothing changes in reality, it is just the subject's stance toward reality that undergoes a radical change. This means that the Fall in the religious sense (the knowledge of sin) is already a reaction to the Fall proper, the retreat from the "dizziness of freedom." This is why it is crucial to realize that Kierkegaard leaps over the first contraction of finitude, the first emergence of a *sinthome* which makes the subject a creature proper, and goes directly from the primordial repose to the Prohibition. We should focus on the difference between the two withdrawals from the Void of infinity: the first one is the primordial contraction that creates the *sinthome*—it precedes Prohibition, while it is only the second one, the retreat from the "dizziness of freedom," which is the Fall proper: with it, we enter the domain of the *superego*, of the vicious cycle of the Law and its transgression.

Consequently, is the paradox of the forced choice not inscribed already in the structure of God's original gift of freedom to man? Man is given freedom—with the expectation that he will not (mis)use it to break free from the Creator, that is, to become really free.[61] The only way to use the gift of freedom without incurring guilt is not to use it at all—in short, what we find here is the very structure of the forced choice: "You are free to choose—on condition that you make the right choice. . . ." No wonder that, according to the standard Gnostic reading of the Fall, the serpent which tempts Eve in Paradise is a benevolent agent of wisdom, trying to impart knowledge to Adam and Eve imprisoned within the walls of Paradise by their evil Creator, who wants to keep them in ignorance. There is, however, a third (and rather obvious) solution, neither the orthodox reading of the Fall as the act of original sin nor the redemption of the Fall as the first step to wisdom: God himself, by explicitly forbidding Adam and Eve to eat the apple from the Tree of Knowledge, actually *wants* them to violate his prohibition, to take the step into knowing good and evil, and thus becoming aware of the shame of their nakedness. Here God himself is inconsistent, divided, saying one thing and, between the lines, giving another covert injunction. This brings us to the central enigma of Christ's sacrifice: "No one takes my life from me, but I lay it down of my own accord." So Christ dies freely, of his own accord, but we all nonetheless share the guilt for his death—why? Because he died for us, to redeem us, to pay for us? Or because, although his death could not have occurred without his accord, we *wanted* him dead? The cynical-opportunistic justification of Caiaphas, the Hebrew high priest, for delivering Christ to the Romans, is: "It is expedient for you that one man should die for the people, so that the whole nation should not perish." Did Christ not follow the same logic of scapegoating the innocent—he, the innocent, went freely to his death to give eternal life to all humanity?[62] What we find at the end of this road is atheism—not the ridiculously pathetic spectacle of a heroic defiance of God, but insight into the irrelevance of the divine, along the lines of Brecht's Herr Keuner:

> Someone asked Herr Keuner if there is a God. Herr Keuner said: I advise you to think about how your behavior would change with regard to the answer to this question. If it would not change, then we can drop the question. If it would change, then I can help you at least insofar as I can tell you: You already decided: You need a God.[63]

Brecht is right here: we are never in a position to choose directly between theism and atheism, since the choice as such is located within the field of belief. "Atheism" (in the sense of deciding not to believe in God) is a miserable pathetic stance of those who long for God but cannot find him (or who "rebel against God". . .). A true atheist does not choose atheism: for him, the question itself is irrelevant. . . . So what if the forthcoming ideological battle will be not religion versus science (or hedonism, or any other form of atheist materialism) but, cutting diagonally across this divide, the struggle against a new form of "evil" Gnostic spirituality whose forms are already discernible today in the "proto-Fascist" tendencies of Jungian psychology, some versions of Hinduism and Tibetan Buddhism, and so on?[64]

Here we come to the unique function of Judas (and Satan himself), which is to "reveal" (*apocalypsis*) Christ, to "deliver" (*paredosis*: to transmit—in the sense of tradition—and to betray) him to the Law. This coincidence of transmission and betrayal is not the same as the standard reversal/sublation of the individual's death into the universal notion-message: Christ's death and resurrection in the Holy Spirit are not the same as, say, the death of the individual Julius Caesar and his "resurrection" in the guise of the universal symbolic title "caesar." One can say that, precisely prior to his death, as a living Teacher, Christ remained all too "universal," delivering a universal message (of love, and so on) and "exemplifying" it with his behavior and acts. It is only in his death on the Cross that Christ—up to that point a man who was a divine messenger—directly became God: that is to say, in Hegelese, the gap between the universal content and its representation was closed:

Without Judas, Christ would be only a Buddha or a prophet like others. He would have communicated till his old age a sublime teaching of generosity and peace, but he would not have "revealed" in a human body and behaviour the invincible power of humble Love faced with absurdity, violence and death.[65]

This may appear simply wrong: did not great teachers like the Buddha also do exactly this—did they also not "reveal" in their very behavior the power of love and generosity? More generally, is not—in contrast to scientific discourse, in which the qualities of the person of the scientist are irrelevant (if we were to learn that Einstein was a pedophile mass murderer, it would in no way affect the status of his scientific discoveries)—the central feature of the religious Wise Man that he is obliged to testify to the truth of his teaching by exemplifying it in his life? Here psychoanalysis introduces a further variation: a true analyst is not an example to follow—when he is caught doing the opposite of what he is advising the patient to do, his answer is: "Listen to my words, do not look at what I do!" This reversal of the standard motto "What you do reveals the truth of what you say!" is by no means hypocritical—recall Henry James's "The Lesson of the Master," in which Paul Overt, a young novelist, meets Henry St. George, his great literary master, who advises him to stay single, since a wife is not an inspiration but a hindrance. When Paul asks St. George if there are no women who would "really understand—who can take part in a sacrifice," the answer he gets is: "How can they take part? They themselves are the sacrifice. They're the idol and the altar and the flame." Paul follows St. George's advice and renounces the young Marian, whom he passionately loves. After returning to London from a trip to Europe, however, Paul learns that, after the sudden death of his wife, St. George himself is about to marry Marian. When Paul accuses St. George of shameful conduct, the older man says that his advice was right: he will not write again, but Paul will achieve greatness. . . . Far from displaying cynical wisdom, St. George acts as a true analyst: as the one who is not afraid to profit from his ethical choices, that is to say, as the one who is able to break the vicious cycle of ethics and sacrifice.

How, then, does the analyst stand with regard to Christ? There is proximity and gap, but not where we would expect them. Back to great Teachers like the Buddha: they did not *reveal* their Truth in the strict Christian sense; they merely *exemplified* by their model life the universal teaching they were spreading. In this precise sense, *the Buddha was a Buddhist, even an exemplary one, while Christ was not a Christian*—he was Christ himself in his absolute singularity. Christ does not "demonstrate with his acts his fidelity to his own teaching"—there simply is no gap between his individuality and his teaching, a gap to be filled in by the fidelity of his acts to his teaching; *Christ's ultimate "teaching"—lesson— immediately is his very existence as an individual* who is, in absolute simultaneity, man and God.

Thus we obtain four positions which form a kind of Greimasian semiotic square whose elements are disposed along the two axes: the one of enacting X versus merely talking about it, and the one of being X versus having X: the scientist and the analyst speak, it is irrelevant what they "actually do or are," while the teacher and Christ have to *enact* what they claim to be; along the other axis, the Teacher and the scientist are qualified for what they are through their activity, while the analyst and Christ immediately *are* what they claim to be (Christ is not divine because of his acts, his acts are divine because he is Christ; in a—surprisingly—similar way, the analyst is not obeyed/followed by the patient because of the wisdom of his speech, his speech produces effects because of what he is, that is, because of the place he occupies in transference). This is why Lacan talked about the "presence of the analyst": like Christ, the analyst is an object. This is why Analyst does not stand for objective Wisdom, that is, his message is not "Focus on the objective truth of my words, even if I myself do not follow them. . . ." There is nonetheless an obvious difference between Christ and the analyst: the legitimization of Christ is grounded in the reality of his being, he directly *is* divine on account of his birth (being the son of God), while the analyst's being is the result of transference, that is, an individual X functions as an analyst not because he was born an analyst but because, for contingent reasons, he has come to occupy the place of the analyst.

For this immediate identity to be "revealed," Christ—in contrast to an analyst—had to die. And it is the function of the figures of the Devil (and Judas) to enable, to bring about, this "revelation." Not only is the figure of the Devil specific to Judeo-Christian tradition; insofar as *diabolos* (to separate, to tear apart the One into Two) is the opposite of *symbolos* (to gather and unify), Christ himself is the ultimate diabolic figure, insofar as he brings "the sword, not peace," disturbing the existing harmonious unity: "if anyone comes to me and does not hate his father and his mother, his wife and children, his brothers and sisters—yes even his own life—he cannot be my disciple" (Luke 14: 26). Christ himself is thus the "diabolic" founding gesture of the Holy Spirit as the properly "symbolic" community, the gathering of the believers.

To be more precise, there are two main figures of Evil in pagan religions: the personification of primordial violence and destructive fury (like Kali in Hinduism), and temptation personified, that is to say, evil spirits who tempt people to abandon the right path and chose the way of egotism, lust, and earthly pride and power; what is unthinkable in this tradition is—as all intelligent Christians, from Kierkegaard to T. S. Eliot knew—Satan as a figure of evil whose ultimate temptation is the reference to Good itself—"the highest form of treason: to do the right deed for the wrong reason," as Eliot put it. Satan's ultimate trump card is not "Give way to your lust for power, enjoy life, abandon the chimera of higher ethical values!", but "Do all the noble deeds your heart tells you to do, live the highest ethical life, and be aware that there is no need for reference to God in all this, it is your own inner nature which is your guide here, you are following the law of your heart!"

Of course, we find a kind of "diabolic" tension in pagan religions too: their main concern is to teach us how to achieve and retain inner peace amid the turbulent ways of the world. Exemplary here is *Bhagavad-Gita*, its teaching of acting through inner distance: one should fully engage oneself in worldly conflicts, fights wars, and so on, while retaining inner peace and distance, that is, not getting really involved. But is not the stance of Christianity here exactly the opposite one: in Christianity, the point is not to retain inner peace while participating-with-a-distance in worldly struggles, but to adopt in our worldly existence the passive stance of peace ("If somebody hits you on your right cheek, turn to him also your left cheek") which directly embodies its opposite, a *diabolos*, an antagonistic tension that affects the innermost core of our subjectivity.

This role of the Devil does not amount to the platitude according to which the rise of Evil is the obstacle (the temptation, the testing ground) which forces the Good to realize itself, to pass from potentiality to actuality. What, then, *is* true Evil? For Schelling, it is the actualization of that which should remain pure potentiality: the same force which, insofar as it remains in the background, provides the secure caring/protective ground for the individual's activity, turns in its actualization into the most destructive fury. Along these lines, for Richard Wagner there is nothing more horrible and disgusting than a woman who intervenes in the political life, driven by the desire for power. In contrast to male ambition, a woman wants power in order to promote her own narrow family interests or, even worse, her personal caprice, incapable as she is of perceiving the universal dimension of state politics. This is one of the readings of Schelling's claim that "the same principle carries and holds us in its ineffectiveness which would consume and destroy us in its effectiveness":[66] a power which, when it is kept in its proper place, can be benign and pacifying, turns into its radical opposite, into the most destructive fury, the moment it intervenes at a higher level, the level which is not its own—the same femininity which, within the close circle of family life, is the very power of protective love, turns into obscene frenzy when it is displayed at the level of public and state affairs. . . . At a different level, Hegel makes the same point: the abstract universality of a Ground, when it is directly actualized, turns into the destructive fury of absolute Terror which threatens to destroy all particular content. We should generalize this principle: Evil *is as such the very principle of the actualization of a Ground*.

That is the ideological interest of the *Star Wars* saga—more precisely, of its pivotal moment: the reversal of the "good" Ken Anakin into the "bad" Darth Vader. *Star Wars* draws here on the explicit parallel between individual and political levels. At the individual level, the "explanation" refers to a pop-Buddhist cliché: "He turns into Darth Vader because he gets attached to things. He can't let go of his mother; he can't let go of his girlfriend. He can't let go of things. It makes you greedy. And when you're greedy, you are on the path to the dark side, because you fear you're going to lose things."[67] The Jedi Order is thus presented as a closed male community which forbids its members to have romantic attachments—a new version of the Grail community from Wagner's *Parsifal*. But even more telling is the political parallel: "How did the Republic turn into the Empire? That's paralleled with: how did Anakin turn into Darth Vader? How does a good person go bad, and how does a democracy become a dictatorship? It isn't that the Empire conquered the Republic, it's that the Empire *is* the Republic." The Empire thus emerged out of the inherent corruption of the Republic: "One day Princess Leia and her friends woke up and said, 'This isn't the Republic anymore, it's the Empire. We are the bad guys.'" One cannot overlook the contemporary connotations of this ancient Rome reference: the shift from Nation-State to global Empire. We should therefore read the *Star Wars* problematic (from Republic to Empire) precisely against the background of Hardt and Negri's *Empire*: from the Nation-State to the global Empire.[68]

The political connotations of the *Star Wars* universe are multiple and inconsistent, and that is the key to the "mythic" power of this universe: free world versus the Evil Empire; the retreat of Nation-States which can be given a Buchanan–Le Pen Rightist connotation; the symptomatic contradiction of persons of *noble* status (Princess, members of the elite Jedi Order) defending the "democratic" republic against the Evil Empire; finally, the correct key insight into how "we are the bad guys" (the bad Empire is not out there; it emerges through the very way we, the "good guys," fight the bad Empire, the enemy out there—in today's "war on terror," the problem is what this war will turn the USA into). That is to say: a political *myth* proper is not so much a narrative with some determinate political meaning but, rather, an empty container of a multitude of inconsistent, even mutually exclusive, meanings—it is wrong to ask "But what does this political myth really mean?", since its "meaning" is precisely to serve as the container for a multitude of meanings.

Already *Star Wars I: The Phantom Menace* gives us the crucial hint to orient ourselves in this *mêlée*: the "Christological" features of the young Anakin (his mother claims that she became pregnant with him in an immaculate conception; the race which he wins clearly echoes the famous chariot race in *Ben Hur*, this "tale of Christ"); second, the fact that he is identified as the one who has the potential to "restore the balance of the Force." Since the ideological universe of *Star Wars* is the New Age pagan universe, it is quite logical that its central figure of Evil should echo Christ—within the pagan horizon, the Event of Christ is the ultimate scandal.

This brings us to *Revenge of the Sith*, the latest installment of the saga: the price it pays for sticking to these same New Age themes is its inferior narrative quality. These themes are the ultimate cause of why Anakin's reversal into Darth Vader—the pivotal moment of the entire series—lacks the proper tragic grandeur. Instead of focusing on Anakin's hubris as an overwhelming desire to intervene, to do Good, to go to the end for those he loves (Amidala) and thus to fall into Dark Side, Anakin is simply shown as an indecisive warrior who is gradually sliding into evil by giving way to the temptation of Power, falling into the prey of the evil Emperor. In other words, Lucas lacked the strength really to apply the parallel between Republic to Empire and Anakin to Darth Vader that he himself proposed: Anakin should have become a monster out of his very excessive attachment to seeing Evil everywhere and fighting it. Instead of oscillating between Good and Evil, he should have turned Evil through the very wrong mode of his attachment to the Good. For instance, when Palpatine, Chancellor of the Republic, comes clean to Anakin about his other identity as the evil Sith Master, and reveals his intention to form an empire, he plays on Anakin's fear and other weaknesses, exploiting the young Jedi's ego and arrogance, painting the Jedi as corrupt and ineffective and the cause of all Anakin's suffering.

When, toward the end of the film, Anakin learns that Padme has helped Obi-wan to find him, he lashes out at her, choking her with the force that lifts her right off her feet, unable to govern his terrible passion, then throws her against a wall, where she hits her head badly. When, later, after his duel with Obi-wan, Anakin regains awareness and asks where Padme is, and Palpatine informs him that he himself has killed her, Anakin screams, setting the force into a furious storm—the walls buckle from the assault, throwing medical droids to and fro, so that Palpatine must shield himself from the onslaught. . . . This two scenes epitomize the failure of the film: two identical outbursts of uncontrollable destructive rage, the first against Padme, the second as an acting-out of the remorse for committing the first—Anakin appears here to be simply oscillating between different positions, the "bad" one (fury at Padme) and the "good" one (remorse and love for her). The proper task would have been to show how Anakin's very excessive love for Padme, his excessive attachment to her, makes him follow the path of Evil. . . .

The final duel between Obi-wan and Anakin ends up with Anakin knocked off balance and falling into a molten pit, where he is horribly scarred and burned to a crisp. Barely alive, Anakin is rescued by Palpatine's henchmen, and brought to a medical facility, where he is kept alive, submerged in healing liquid, limbless and horrifically deformed. The imperial medical droids heal him by building him into the armored terror of the stars we all know as Darth Vader. At the end, Anakin-turned-into-Vader exits the medical facility and walks through the bridge of the star destroyer, joining his new master, Darth Sidious, emperor of the galaxy. They stare out the window at their ultimate weapon, the Death Star, which has begun construction. Vader breathes evilly, now more machine than man.

Two moments are crucial here. Just before the end of the duel, Obi-wan makes one last appeal to Anakin to return to the path of Goodness; Anakin rejects it, and although he is already seriously wounded, he summons up his last forces in a desperate attempt to strike back. I cannot resist the temptation to perceive Anakin's insistence as a properly ethical stance, similar to that of Mozart's Don Giovanni, who refuses the Stone Guest's last-minute offer of salvation. In both cases, what appears at the level of content to be the choice of Evil is, at the formal level, an act of asserting one's ethical consistency. That is to say: they are both aware that, from the standpoint of pragmatic egotist calculation, renouncing Evil is preferable; they are both at the end of their lives, aware that there is no profit in persisting in their choice of Evil—nonetheless, in an act of defiance that cannot but appear uncannily ethical, they courageously remain faithful to their choice out of principle, not on account of the promise of any material or spiritual profit.

Through this ethical consistency, through this fidelity to his existential choice, Anakin emerges as a subject—the only true subject in the entire *Star Wars* saga. Here we should confer on the term "subject" its strict philosophical status: subject as opposed to (human) person, subject as the excessive core of inhuman monstrosity at the very heart of a human being. This is why Darth Vader is not simply a mask of Anakin—

paraphrasing the good old Althusserian formula, we can say that Anakin the human individual is interpellated into the subject Darth Vader.

The privileged medium of this newly born subjectivity is voice—the strangely echoing Voice, Darth Vader's trademark in subsequent installments of the saga, the voice in which the external and the internal strangely coincide. His voice is enhanced through a machine, artificially amplified; for this very reason, however, it appears as if, on account of the closely registered breathing, the inner life itself directly reverberates in it. It is a *spectral* voice, not the organic voice of a body: not a sound which is part of everyday external reality, but the direct expression of the Real of "psychic reality."

The failure of *Star Wars* III is thus double. First, it fails on its own terms: it does not stage Anakin's turn to Evil as the outcome of his very excessive attachment to the Good. The notion that our very excessive attachment to the Good may lead to Evil, however, is a commonplace wisdom, a standard warning against the dangers of moralizing fanaticism; what we should do—and therein resides the film's second failure, its true missed opportunity—is to turn this entire constellation around, and present Anakin–Vader as a *good* figure, a figure which stands for the "diabolical" foundation of the Good. That is to say: is not the origin of our ethical commitment precisely our "excessive" care and attachment, our readiness to break the balance of the ordinary flow of life, and to put everything at stake for the Cause to which we adhere? This is what proper Christian love is about: excessive care for the beloved, a "biased" commitment which disturbs the balance of the Whole. This is why, when, at the end of the Part III of the saga, Darth Vader asks Luke, his son, to take off his mask, so that he will see his father's human face, this displaying of one's face equals the ethical regression to the dimension of what Nietzsche called the "human, all too human." In his final moments, Darth Vader desubjectivizes himself, turning into an ordinary mortal: what gets lost is Vader as subject, the one who dwells in the void behind the black metal mask (not to be confused with the human face behind the mask), the subject who resonates in the artificially resonating voice.

Today, theists no longer despise atheists—on the contrary, one of their standard rhetorical turns is to emphasize how, in leaving behind the abstract "God of philosophers," atheists are much closer to the "true" God than metaphysical theologists: "The god-less thinking which must abandon the god of philosophy . . . is . . . perhaps closer to the divine God . . . more open to Him than [metaphysics] would like to admit."[69] Even in Derrida's late work, we find a variation on this turn, when, in his reflections on prayer, he points out how not only do atheists also pray, but how, today, it is perhaps *only atheists who truly pray*. . . .[70] Against this rhetoric, we should assert the *literal* truth of Lacan's statement according to which theologists are the only true materialists.

THE COMEDY OF INCARNATION

It was without doubt Kierkegaard who pushed to extremes this divine parallax tension, best encapsulated in his notion of the "teleological suspension of the ethical."[71]

In "The Ancient Tragical Motif as Reflected in the Modern," a chapter of Volume I of *Either/Or*,[72] Kierkegaard sketches out his fantasy of what a modern Antigone would be like. The conflict is now entirely internalized: there is no longer a need for Creon. While Antigone admires and loves her father Oedipus, the public hero and savior of Thebes, she knows the truth about him (murder of the father, incestuous marriage). Her deadlock is that she is prevented from sharing this accursed knowledge (like Abraham, who also could not communicate to others the divine injunction to sacrifice his son): she cannot complain, share her pain and sorrow with others. In contrast to Sophocles' Antigone, who acts (buries her brother, and thus actively assumes her fate), she is unable to act, condemned forever to impassive suffering. This unbearable burden of her secret, of her destructive *agalma*, finally drives her to death, the only path that will lead her to the peace otherwise provided by symbolizing/sharing one's pain and sorrow. And Kierkegaard's point is that this situation is no longer properly tragic (again, in a similar way, Abraham is not a tragic figure either).[73]

Furthermore, insofar as Kierkegaard's Antigone is a paradigmatically modernist one, we should go along with his mental experiment and imagine a postmodern Antigone with, of course, a Stalinist twist to her image: in contrast to the modernist one, she should find herself in a position in which, to quote Kierkegaard, the ethical itself would be the temptation. One version would undoubtedly be for Antigone publicly to renounce, denounce, and accuse her father (or, in a different version, her brother Polynices) of his terrible sins out of her unconditional love for him. The Kierkegaardian catch is that such a public act would render Antigone even more isolated, absolutely alone: no one—with the exception of Oedipus himself, if he were still alive—would understand that her act of betrayal is the supreme act of love. . . . Antigone would thus be entirely deprived of her sublime beauty—all that would indicate the fact that she is not a pure and simple traitor to her father, but that she did it out of love for him, would be some barely perceptible repulsive tic, like the hysteric twitch of the lips of Claudel's Sygne de Coufontaine, a tic which longer belongs to the face: it is a grimace whose insistence disintegrates the unity of a face.

It is on account of the parallax nature of Kierkegaard's thought that, apropos his "triad" of the Aesthetic, the Ethical, and the Religious, we should bear in mind how the choice, the "either-or," is always between the two. The true problem is not the choice between the aesthetic and the ethical level (pleasure versus duty), but between the ethical and its religious suspension: it is easy to do one's duty against one's pleasures or egotistic interests; it is much more difficult to obey the unconditional ethico-religious call against one's very ethical substance. (This dilemma faced by Sygne is the extreme paradox of Christianity as the religion of modernity: how—as with Julia in Waugh's *Brideshead Revisited*—if one is to remain faithful to one's unconditional Duty, one should indulge in what may appear to be aesthetic regression, opportunistic betrayal.) In *Either/Or*, Kierkegaard gives no clear priority to the Ethical, he merely confronts the two choices, that of the Aesthetic and of the Ethical, in a purely parallax way, emphasizing the "jump" that separates them, the lack of any mediation between them.

The Religious is by no means the mediating "synthesis" of the two, but, on the contrary, the radical assertion of the parallax gap (the "paradox," the lack of common measure, the insurmountable abyss between the Finite and the Infinite). That is to say: what makes the Aesthetic or the Ethical problematic is not their respective positive characteristics, but their very formal nature: the fact that, in both cases, the subject wants to live a consistent mode of existence, and thus disavows the radical antagonism of the human situation. This is why Julia's choice at the end of *Brideshead Revisited* is properly religious, *although it is, in its immediate appearance, a choice of the Aesthetic* (*transient love affairs*) *against the Ethical* (*marriage*): what matters is that she confronted and fully assumed the paradox of human existence. This means that her act involves a "leap of faith": there is no guarantee that her retreat to transient love affairs is not just that—a retreat from the Ethical to the Aesthetic (in the same way, there is no guarantee that Abraham's decision to kill Isaac is not his private madness).[74] We are never safely within the Religious, doubt forever remains, the same act can be seen as religious or as aesthetic, in a parallax split which can never be abolished, since the "minimal difference" which transubstantiates (what appears to be) an aesthetic act into a religious one can never be specified, located in a determinate property.

This parallax split, however, is itself caught up in a parallax: it can be viewed as condemning us to permanent anxiety, but also as something that is inherently *comical*. This is why Kierkegaard insisted that there is a *comical* side to Christianity: is there anything more comical than Incarnation, this ridiculous overlapping of the Highest and the Lowest, the coincidence of God, creator of the universe, and a miserable man?[75] Take the elementary comical scene from a film: after the trumpets announce the King's entrance into the royal hall, the surprised public sees a miserable crippled clown who enters staggering . . . this is the logic of Incarnation.[76] The only proper *Christian* comment on Christ's death is thus: *"La commedia è finita . . ."*. And, again, the point is that the gap that separates God from man in Christ is purely one of parallax: Christ is not a person with two substances, immortal and mortal. Perhaps this would also be one way of distinguishing between Gnosticism and Christianity: the problem with Gnosticism is that it is all too serious in developing its narrative of ascent toward Wisdom, that it misses the humorous side of religious experience—Gnostics are Christians who *miss the joke* of Christianity. . . . (And, incidentally, this is why Mel Gibson's *Passion* is ultimately an anti-Christian film: it totally lacks this comic aspect.)[77]

As is often the case, Kierkegaard here is unexpectedly close to his official major opponent, Hegel, for whom the passage from tragedy to comedy concerns overcoming the limits of representation: while, in a tragedy, the individual actor represents the universal character he plays, in a comedy, he immediately *is* this character. The gap of representation is thus closed, exactly as in the case of Christ who, in contrast to previous pagan divinities, does not "represent" some universal power or principle (as in Hinduism, in which Krishna, Vishna, Shiva, and so on, all "stand for" certain spiritual principles or powers—love, hatred, reason): as this miserable human, Christ directly *is* God. Christ is not *also* human, apart from being God; he is a man precisely *insofar as he is God*; that is, the *ecce homo* is the highest mark of his divinity. There is thus an objective irony in Pontius Pilate's "*Ecce homo!*", when he presents Christ to the enraged mob: its meaning is *not* "Look at this miserable tortured creature! Do you not see in it a simple vulnerable man? Have you no compassion for it?", but, rather, "Here is God himself!"[78]

In a comedy, however, the actor does not coincide with the person he plays in the way that he plays himself on the stage, that he just "is what he really is" there. It is rather that, in a properly Hegelian way, the gap which separates the actor from his stage persona in a tragedy is transposed into the stage persona itself: a comic character is never fully identified with his role, he always retains the ability to observe himself from outside, "making fun of himself." (Remember the immortal Lucy from *I Love Lucy*, whose trademark gesture, when something surprised her, was to bend her neck slightly and cast a direct fixed gaze of surprise into the camera—this was not Lucille Ball, the actress, mockingly addressing the public, but an attitude of self-estrangement that was part of "Lucy" [as a screen persona] herself.) This is how Hegelian "reconciliation" works: not as an immediate synthesis or reconciliation of opposites, but as the redoubling of the gap or antagonism—the two opposed moments are "reconciled" when the gap that separates them is posited as inherent to one of the terms. In Christianity, the gap that separates God from man is not directly "sublated" in the figure of Christ as God-man; it is rather that, in the most tense moment of crucifixion, when Christ himself despairs ("Father, why have you forsaken me?"), the gap that separates God from man is transposed into God himself, as the gap that separates Christ from God-Father; the properly dialectical trick here is that the very feature which appeared to separate me from God turns out to unite me with God.

More generally, we should always bear in mind that, in Hegel's dialectic of appearance and essence, it is appearance which is the asymmetrical encompassing term: the difference between essence and appearance is internal to appearance, *not* to essence. When Hegel says that essence *has* to appear, that it is only as deep as it appears, this does not mean that essence is a self-mediating power which externalizes itself in its appearing and then "sublates" its otherness, positing it as a moment of its own self-movement. On the contrary, "essence appears" means that, with regard to the opposition essence/appearance, immediate "reality" is on the side of appearance: the gap between appearance and reality means that reality itself (what is immediately given to us "out there") appears as an expression of inner essence, that we no longer take reality at its "face value," that we suspect that there is in reality "more than meets the eye," that is to say, that an essence appears to subsist somewhere within reality, as its hidden core. This dialectical shift in the meaning of appearance is crucial: first, immediate reality is reduced to a "mere appearance" of an inner essence; then, this essence itself is posited as something that appears in reality as a specter of its hidden core.

And we should follow this logic to the end: the true problem is not how to reach the Real when we are confined to the interplay of the (inconsistent) multitude of appearances, but, more radically, the properly Hegelian one: *how does appearance itself emerge from the interplay of the Real?* The thesis that the Real is just the cut, the gap of inconsistency, between the two appearances has thus to be supplemented by its opposite: appearance is the cut, the gap, between the two Reals, or, more precisely, *something that emerges in the gap that separates the Real from itself*. Consider the status of Kantian spontaneity: at the phenomenal level, we are mechanisms, parts of the chain of causes and effects; at the noumenal level, we are again puppets, lifeless mechanisms; the only place of freedom is thus the gap between these two levels in which appearance as such emerges.

If, then, there is an "essence" only because appearance does not fully coincide with itself, what does this mean for the notion of God? Is it that there is God because man is not fully man (just as that there is Universal-for-itself insofar as the Particular is not fully identical with itself), so that God is the excess of the (in)human in man itself, or is it that there is man because God is not fully himself, because there is something non-divine in him (Schelling's solution)? Although we may be tempted to oppose these two positions as the materialist one and the idealist one, a truly radical materialist approach should opt for the *second* one—to put it in Hegelese, there is the Particular because the Universal is not fully itself; there is the opaque material reality because the Notion is not fully itself, because it does not fully coincide with itself. That is to say, we should not presuppose the existence of particular objects and then go on to assert how they do not fully coincide with themselves: the "primordial fact" is the noncoincidence of the Absolute with itself, the gap which traverses it from within, the inner split of the primordial Void itself.

This brings us back to comedy: for Hegel, what happens in comedy is that, in it, the Universal directly *appears*, it appears "as such," in direct contrast to the mere "abstract" universal which is the "mute" universality of the passive link (common feature) between particular moments. In other words, in a comedy, universality directly acts—how? Comedy does not rely on the undermining of our dignity with reminders of the ridiculous contingencies of our earthly existence; on the contrary, comedy is the full assertion of universality, the immediate coincidence of universality with the character's/actor's singularity. That is to say: what actually happens when, in a comedy, all the universal features of dignity are mocked and subverted? The negative force that undermines them is that of the individual, of the hero with his attitude of disrespect toward all elevated universal values, and *this negativity itself is the only true remaining universal force*. Does not the same hold for Christ? All stable-substantial universal features are undermined, relativized, by his scandalous acts, so that the only remaining universality is the one embodied in him, in his very singularity. The universals undermined by Christ are "abstract" substantial universals (presented in the guise of the Jewish Law), while "concrete" universality is the very negativity of undermining abstract universals.

This direct overlapping of the Universal and the Singular also sets a limit to the standard critique of "reification." While observing Napoleon on a horse in the streets of Jena after the battle of 1807, Hegel remarked that it was as if he saw there the World Spirit riding a horse. The Christological implications of this remark are obvious: what happened in the case of Christ is that God himself, the creator of our entire universe, was walking out there as a common individual. This mystery of incarnation is discernible at different levels, up to the parent's speculative judgment apropos of a child: "Out there our love is walking!", which stands for the Hegelian reversal of determinate reflection into reflexive determination—just as with a king, when his subject sees him walking around: "Out there our state is walking." Marx's evocation of reflexive determination (in his famous footnote in chapter 1 of *Capital*) is also inadequate here: individuals think they treat a person as a king because he is a king in himself, while in fact he is a king only because they treat him as one. The crucial point, however, is that this "reification" of a social relation in a person cannot be dismissed as a simple "fetishist misperception"; what such a dismissal itself misses is something that, perhaps, could be designated as the "Hegelian performative": of course a king is "in himself" a miserable individual, of course he is a king only insofar as his subjects treat him like one; the point, however, is that the "fetishist illusion" which sustains our veneration of a king has in itself a performative dimension—*the very unity of our state, that which the king "embodies," actualizes itself only in the person of a king.* This is why it is not enough to insist on the need to avoid the "fetishist trap," and to distinguish between the contingent person of a king and what he stands for: what the king stands for is embodied only in his person, just as a couple's love (at least within a certain traditional perspective) is embodied only in their offspring. And it is not difficult to see the extreme proximity of the sublime and the ridiculous in these cases: there is something sublime in exclaiming "Look! The world spirit itself is riding a horse there!", but also something inherently comical. . . .[79]

This limitation of the critique of fetishism, of the mantra that a fetish is just a contingent ordinary object which fills in an empty place in the structure, has crucial philosophical and political consequences: what this critique misses is the umbilical link that connects the big Other (the formal order, ultimately an empty place) to the small other (the ridiculous/excessive/excremental object, tic, that sticks out of the Other). Where the space of politics is concerned, this reveals the insufficiency of the democratic *topos* (deployed *ad infinitum* by Claude Lefort) about the empty Place of Power for the temporary occupancy of which multiple agents struggle; where philosophy is concerned, it reveals the insufficiency of the standard ontology of finitude/contingency, again based on the priority of the empty Place (of the Absolute, this time) over any element that may temporarily occupy it. Although one of the names for this finitude is supposed to be "(symbolic) castration," what this ontology of finitude/contingency misses is precisely the whole scope of the strict psychoanalytic notion of castration: "castration" designates not only the irreducible gap between the element and the (preceding) empty space this element occupies, but, first and foremost, also the fact that this empty space, which lacks any "natural" element that would occupy it, is strictly correlative to an excessive element which wanders around, lacking its "proper" place—this is *stricto sensu* the "castrated" object, the partial object which sticks out and floats around. To put it in a different way: in a philosophical perspective, we cannot accept the empty place (of the impossible Universality, the place to be filled in—"hegemonized"—by contingent particulars) as the ultimate given; we should hazard a step further and ask how—through what cut in the texture of the living body—this empty place itself emerges.

Thus comedy is the very opposite of shame: shame endeavors to maintain the veil, while comedy relies on the gesture of unveiling. More to the point, the comic effect proper occurs when, after the act of unveiling, we confront the ridicule and the nullity of the unveiled content: in contrast to the pathetic scene of encountering, behind the veil, the terrifying Thing, too traumatic for our gaze, the ultimate comical effect occurs when, after removing the mask, we confront exactly the same face as the one on the mask. This is why the Marx Brothers' "This man looks like an idiot and acts like an idiot; but this should not deceive you—he is an idiot!" is properly comical: when, instead of a hidden terrifying secret, we encounter the same thing behind the veil as in front of it, this very lack of difference between the two elements confronts us with the "pure" difference that separates an element from itself. And is this also not the ultimate definition of the divinity—God, too, has to wear a mask of himself? Perhaps "God" is the name for this supreme split between the Absolute as the noumenal Thing and the Absolute as the appearance of itself, for the fact that the two are the same, that the difference between the two is purely formal. In this precise sense, "God" names the supreme contradiction: God—the absolute unrepresentable Beyond—*has to appear as such*.

According to an anecdote from May '68, there was graffiti on a Paris wall: "God is dead. Nietzsche." Next day, more graffiti appeared below it: "Nietzsche is dead. God." What is wrong with this joke? Why is it so obviously reactionary? It is not only that the reversed statement relies on a moralistic platitude with no inherent truth; its failure goes deeper, it concerns the form of reversal itself: what makes the joke a *bad* joke is the *pure symmetry of the reversal*—the underlying claim of the first graffiti ("God is dead. Signed by [obviously living] Nietzsche") is turned around into a statement which implies: "Nietzsche is dead, while *I am still alive*. God." There is a well-known Yugoslav riddle-joke: "What is the difference between the Pope and a trumpet? The Pope is from Rome, and the trumpet is [made] from tin. And what is the difference between the Pope from Rome and the trumpet [made] from tin? The trumpet [made] from tin can be from Rome, while the Pope from Rome cannot be [made] from tin." In a similar way, we should redouble the Paris graffiti joke: "What is the difference between 'God is dead' and 'Nietzsche is dead'? It was Nietzsche who said 'God is dead,' and it was God who said 'Nietzsche is dead.' And what is the difference between Nietzsche, who said 'God is dead,' and God, who said 'Nietzsche is dead'? Nietzsche, who said 'God is dead,' was not dead, while the God who said 'Nietzsche is dead' *was himself dead*." Crucial for the proper comic effect is not a difference where we expect sameness but, rather, a sameness where we expect difference;[80] this is why, as Alenka Zupančič[81] has pointed out, the materialist (and therefore properly comic) version of the above joke would have been something like: "God is dead. And, as a matter of fact, I don't feel too well either. . . ." Is this not a comic version of Christ's complaint on the Cross? Christ will not die on the Cross in order to shuffle off his mortal coil and rejoin the divine;

he will die *because he is God*. No wonder, then, that Nietzsche in the last years of his intellectual activity, used to sign his texts and letters "Christ": the proper comic supplement to Nietzsche's "God is dead" would have been to make *Nietzsche himself* add: "And, as a matter of fact, I don't feel too well either. . . ."

From here, we can also elaborate a critique of the philosophy of finitude which predominates today. The idea is that, against the big metaphysical constructs, we should humbly accept our finitude as our ultimate horizon: there is no absolute Truth, all we can do is accept the contingency of our existence, the ineluctable character of our being-thrown into a situation, the basic lack of any absolute point of reference, the playfulness of our predicament. . . . The first thing that strikes us here, however, is the utter seriousness of this philosophy of finitude, its all-pervasive pathos which runs against the expected playfulness: the ultimate tone of the philosophy of finitude is that of ultraserious heroic confrontation with our destiny—no wonder the philosopher of finitude *par excellence*, Heidegger, is also the philosopher who is completely devoid of any sense of humor.[82] (Unfortunately, there is also a Lacanian version of the philosophy of finitude: when, in a tragic tone, we are informed that we have to renounce our impossible striving for full *jouissance* and accept "symbolic castration," the ultimate constraint of our existence—as soon as we enter the symbolic order, all *jouissance* has to pass through the mortification of the symbolic medium, every attainable object is already a displacement of the impossible-real object of desire, which is constitutively lost. . . .) We could say that Kierkegaard relied so much on humor precisely because he insisted on the relationship to the Absolute, and rejected the limitation to finitude.

So what is it that this emphasis on finitude as the ultimate horizon of our existence misses? How can we assert it in a materialist way, without any resort to spiritual transcendence? The answer is, precisely, *objet petit a* as the "undead" ("noncastrated") remainder which persists in its obscene immortality. No wonder Wagnerian heroes want so desperately to die: they want to get rid of this obscene immortal supplement which stands for libido as an organ, for drive at its most radical, that is, the death drive. In other words, the properly Freudian paradox is that what explodes the constraints of our finitude is the death drive itself. So when Badiou, in his disparaging dismissal of the philosophy of finitude, talks about "positive infinity," and, in a Platonic way, celebrates the infinity of the generic productivity opened up by fidelity to an Event, what he fails to take into account from the Freudian standpoint is the obscene insistence of the death drive as the true material(ist) support of "positive infinity."

Of course, according to the standard view of the philosophy of finitude, Greek tragedy, the tragic experience of life, signals the acceptance of gap, failure, defeat, nonclosure, as the ultimate horizon of human existence, while Christian comedy relies on the certainty that a transcendent God guarantees a happy final outcome, the "sublation" of the gap, the reversal of failure into final triumph. The excess of divine rage as the obverse of Christian love allows us to perceive what this standard view misses; the Christian comedy of love can occur only against the background of a radical loss of human dignity, of a degradation which, precisely, undermines the tragic experience:

to experience a situation as "tragic" is possible only when a victim retains a minimum of dignity. This is why it is not only wrong but also ethically obscene to designate a *Muselmann* in the concentration camp or a victim of a Stalinist show-trial as tragic— their predicament is simply too terrible to deserve this designation. "Comic" also stands for a domain which emerges when the horror of a situation outgrows the confines of the tragic. And it is at this point that properly Christian love comes in: it is not love for man as a tragic hero, but love for the miserable abject creature to which a man or woman is reduced after being exposed to an outburst of arbitrary divine rage.

ODRADEK AS A POLITICAL CATEGORY

It is this obscene infinity of the "undead" partial object that not only the philosopher of finitude but also those who follow the Levinasian "ethical turn" fail to take into consideration. The limitation of Levinas is not simply that of a Eurocentrist who relies on too narrow a definition of what is human, a definition that secretly excludes non-Europeans as "not fully human." What Levinas fails to include in the scope of "human" is, rather, the *inhuman* itself, a dimension which eludes the face-to-face relationship between humans. The same goes for Adorno: while he is well aware of the violence involved in the predominant definition of what counts as "human" (the implied exclusion of whole dimensions as "nonhuman"), he nonetheless basically conceives the "inhuman" as the repository of "alienated" humanity—ultimately, for Adorno, the "inhuman" is the power of barbarism we have to fight.[83] What he misses is the paradox that every normative determination of the "human" is possible only against an impenetrable ground of "inhuman," of something which remains opaque and resists inclusion in any narrative reconstitution of what counts as "human." In other words, although Adorno recognizes that being-human is constitutively finite, nontotalized, that the very attempt to posit the Human as "absolute subject" dehumanizes it, he does not explain how this self-limitation of the Human defines "being-human": is being-human just the limitation of human, or is there a positive notion of this limitation which constitutes being-human?

This paradox is at work in the very core of the "dialectic of Enlightenment": although Adorno (and Horkheimer) conceive(s) the catastrophes and barbarisms of the twentieth century as inherent to the very project of Enlightenment, not as a result of some remainder of preceding barbarism to be abolished by bringing "Enlightenment as an unfinished project" to its completion, they insist on fighting this excess consequence of Enlightenment by the means of Enlightenment itself.[84] So, again, if Enlightenment brought to the end equals regression into barbarism, does this mean that the only concept of Enlightenment that we possess is the one which should be constrained, made aware of its limitation, or is there another positive notion of Enlightenment which already includes this limitation? There are two basic answers to this inconsistency of Adorno's critical project: Habermas or Lacan. One either breaks the deadlock by formulating a positive normative frame of reference; or one reconceptualizes the "humanity" of the deadlock/limitation as such, that is, one provides a definition of the "human" which, beyond and above (or, rather, beneath) the previous infinite universal, accentuates the limitation as such: being-human is a specific attitude of finitude, of passivity, of vulnerable exposure. . . . This is the basic paradox: while we should, of course, condemn as "inhuman" all those situations in which our will is violated, thwarted, under pressure of an external violence, we should not draw from this the "obvious" conclusion that a positive definition of humanity is the autonomy of will: there is a kind of passive exposure to an overwhelming Otherness which is the very basis of being-human. How, then, are we to distinguish "bad" inhumanity, the violence which crushes our will, from the passivity constitutive of humanity?

What Adorno fails to thematize is the changed status of the "inhuman" in Kant's transcendental turn;[85] this dimension is also missing in Levinas:[86] in a properly dialectical paradox, what Levinas, with all his celebration of Otherness, fails to take into account is not some underlying Sameness of all humans, but the radically "inhuman" Otherness itself: the Otherness of a human being reduced to inhumanity, the Otherness exemplified by the terrifying figure of the *Muselmann*, the "living dead" in the concentration camps. This is why, although Levinas is often perceived as the thinker who endeavored to articulate the experience of the *shoah*, one thing is self-evident apropos of his questioning of one's own right to be and his emphasis on my unconditional asymmetrical responsibility: this is not how a survivor of the *shoah*, how one who actually experienced the ethical abyss of *shoah*, thinks and writes. This is how those who feel guilty for observing the catastrophe from a minimal safe distance think.[87]

Agamben posits the *Muselmann* as a kind of absolute/impossible witness: he is the only one who fully witnessed the horror of the concentration camp and, for that very reason, is not able to bear witness to it—it is as if he was "burned by the black sun" of the horror he saw. "Authentic" witnessing can thus be defined as involving the mediation of an invisible Third embodied in the *Muselmann*: it is never just me and the event I am witnessing; my relationship to this event is always mediated by someone who fully witnessed it and is, for that very reason, no longer able to report on it. That is to say: insofar as, in his description of the ethical call, Levinas reproduces the basic coordinates of ideological interpellation (I become an ethical subject when I respond with "Here I am!" to the infinite call emanating from the vulnerable face of the other), we could say that the *Muselmann* is precisely the one who is no longer able to say "Here I am!" (and in front of whom I can no longer say "Here I am!").[88] Recall the grand gesture of identification with the exemplary victim: "We are all citizens of Sarajevo!", and so on; the problem with the *Muselmann* is that, precisely, this gesture is no longer possible—it would be obscene to proclaim pathetically: "We are all *Muselmannen!*". . . Agamben should also be supplemented here by transposing the same gap into the counterpart of the witness, the receiver of its testimony, the big Other whose full acceptance of my testimony would permit me to exorcize my inner demons. In a precisely symmetrical way, I never encounter a "true" recipient who would fully authenticate my witnessing: my words of witnessing are always received by finite others who fail to authenticate them.

Is this structure not that of the so-called "Schema L" of communication from early-1950s Lacan, in which the "true communication" (the diagonal S–A) is cut across by the diagonal *a–a′* of the imaginary relationship?[89] Here S would be the *Muselmann*, the ideal-impossible witness, A his ideal-impossible recipient authenticating his words, *a* the survivors as imperfect witnesses, and *a′* the imperfect recipients of their words. The tragedy of witnessing is thus not only that the ideal witness (the *Muselmann* who would himself bear witness, report on what he went through) is impossible, but also that there is no ideal Recipient, so that, when we are aware that our testimony is safely deposited there, we get rid of our demons—*there is no big Other*.

Consequently, is not the paradox of the *Muselmann* that this figure is simultaneously life at its zero-level, a total reduction to life, *and* a name for the pure excess as such, excess deprived of its "normal" base? This is why the figure of the *Muselmann* reveals the limitation of Levinas: Primo Levi, describing it, repeatedly uses the adjective "faceless," a term which should be given its full Levinasian weight here.[90] When we are confronted with a *Muselmann*, we precisely cannot discern in his face the trace of the abyss of the Other in his or her vulnerability, addressing us with the infinite call of our responsibility—what we get is a kind of blank wall, a lack of depth. Maybe the *Muselmann* is thus the zero-level neighbor, the neighbor with whom no empathic relationship is possible. At this point, however, we again confront the key dilemma: what if it is precisely in the guise of the "faceless" face of a *Muselmann* that we encounter the Other's call at its purest and most radical? What if, facing a *Muselmann*, we are made aware of our responsibility toward the Other at its most traumatic? In short, what about bringing together Levinas's face and the topic of the "neighbor" in its strict Freudo-Lacanian sense, as the monstrous, impenetrable Thing that is the *Nebenmensch*, the Thing that hystericizes and provokes me? What if the neighbor's face stands neither for my imaginary double/*semblant* nor for the purely symbolic abstract "partner in communication," but for the Other in his or her dimension of the Real? What if, along these lines, we restore to the Levinasian "face" all its monstrosity: the face is not a harmonious Whole of the dazzling epiphany of a "human face," the face is something a glimpse of which we get when we stumble upon a grotesquely distorted face, a face in the grip of a disgusting tic or grimace, a face which, precisely, confronts us when the neighbor "loses face"? To recall a case from popular culture: the "face" is what, in Gaston Leroux's *The Phantom of the Opera*, the heroine gets a glimpse of when she sees the Phantom without his mask for the first time (and, as a reaction to the horror that confronts her, immediately loses consciousness and falls to the ground). . . .

The problem with this solution, which is acceptable in itself, is that it undermines the ethical edifice Levinas is trying to build upon it: far from standing for absolute authenticity, such a monstrous face is, rather, the ambiguity of the Real embodied, the extreme/impossible point at which opposites coincide, at which the innocence of the Other's vulnerable nakedness overlaps with pure Evil. That is to say: what we should focus on here is the precise meaning of the term "neighbor": is the "neighbor" in the Judeo-Freudian sense, the neighbor as the bearer of a monstrous Otherness, this properly inhuman neighbor, the same as the neighbor we encounter in the Levinasian experience of the Other's face? Is there not, at the very heart of the Judeo-Freudian inhuman neighbor, a monstrous dimension which is already minimally "gentrified," domesticated, once it is conceived in the Levinasian sense? What if the Levinasian face is yet another defense against this monstrous dimension of subjectivity? And what if the Jewish Law is to be conceived as strictly correlative to this inhuman neighbor? In other words, what if the ultimate function of the Law is not to enable us not to forget the neighbor, to retain our proximity to the neighbor, but, on the contrary, to keep the neighbor at a proper distance, to serve as a kind of protective wall against the monstrosity of the neighbor? The neighbor is thus the ultimate *organ without a body*—or, as Rilke put it in his *Notebooks of Malte Laurids Brigge*:

> There exists a creature that is perfectly harmless; when it passes before your eyes, you hardly notice it and immediately forget it again. But as soon as it somehow, invisibly, gets into your ears, it begins to develop, it hatches, and cases have been known where it has penetrated into the brain and flourished there devastatingly, like the pneumococci in dogs which gain entrance through the nose. . . . This creature is Your Neighbor.[91]

The temptation to be resisted here is the ethical "gentrification" of the neighbor, the reduction of the radically ambiguous monstrosity of the Neighbor-Thing into an Other as the abyssal point from which the call of ethical responsibility emanates.

This topic perturbs the very heart of Kafka's universe. Reading Kafka demands a great effort of abstraction—not of learning more (the proper interpretive horizon of understanding his work), but of *unlearning* the standard interpretive references, so that we become able to open up to the raw force of Kafka's writing. There are three such interpretive frames: theological (the anxious search for the absent God); socio-critical (Kafka's staging of the nightmarish world of modern alienated bureaucracy); psychoanalytic (Kafka's "unresolved Oedipus complex," which prevented him from engaging in a "normal" sexual relationship). All this has to be erased; a kind of childish naivety has to be regained in order for a reader to be able to feel the raw force of Kafka's universe. This is why, in Kafka's case, the first (naive) reading is often the most adequate one, and the second reading is the one which tries to "sublate" the first reading's raw impact by forcing him into the frame of a given interpretation. This is how we should approach "Odradek," one of Kafka's key achievements:

> Some say the word Odradek is of Slavonic origin, and try to account for it on that basis. Others again believe it to be of German origin, only influenced by Slavonic. The uncertainty of both interpretations allows one to assume with justice that neither is accurate, especially as neither of them provides an intelligent meaning of the word.
>
> No one, of course, would occupy himself with such studies if there were not a creature called Odradek. At first glance it looks like a flat star-shaped spool for thread, and indeed it does seem to have thread wound upon it; to be sure, they are only old, broken-off bits of thread, knotted and tangled together, of the most varied sorts and colors. But

it is not only a spool, for a small wooden crossbar sticks out of the middle of the star, and another small rod is joined to that at a right angle. By means of this latter rod on one side and one of the points of the star on the other, the whole thing can stand upright as if on two legs.

One is tempted to believe that the creature once had some sort of intelligible shape and is now only a broken-down remnant. Yet this does not seem to be the case; at least there is no sign of it; nowhere is there an unfinished or unbroken surface to suggest anything of the kind; the whole thing looks senseless enough, but in its own way perfectly finished. In any case, closer scrutiny is impossible, since Odradek is extraordinarily nimble and can never be laid hold of.

He lurks by turns in the garret, the stairway, the lobbies, the entrance hall. Often for months on end he is not to be seen; then he has presumably moved into other houses; but he always comes faithfully back to our house again. Many a time when you go out of the door and he happens just to be leaning directly beneath you against the banisters you feel inclined to speak to him. Of course, you put no difficult questions to him, you treat him—he is so diminutive that you cannot help it—rather like a child. "Well, what's your name?" you ask him. "Odradek," he says. "And where do you live?" "No fixed abode," he says and laughs; but it is only the kind of laughter that has no lungs behind it. It sounds rather like the rustling of fallen leaves. And that is usually the end of the conversation. Even these answers are not always forthcoming; often he stays mute for a long time, as wooden as his appearance.

I ask myself, to no purpose, what is likely to happen to him? Can he possibly die? Anything that dies has had some kind of aim in life, some kind of activity, which has worn out; but that does not apply to Odradek. Am I to suppose, then, that he will always be rolling down the stairs, with ends of thread trailing after him, right before the feet of my children, and my children's children? He does no harm to anyone that one can see; but the idea that he is likely to survive me I find almost painful.[92]

Odradek as an object which is transgenerational (exempt from the cycle of generations), immortal, outside finitude (because outside sexual difference), outside time, displaying no goal-oriented activity, no purpose, no utility, is *jouissance* embodied: "*Jouissance* is that which serves nothing," as Lacan put in *Seminar XX: Encore*. There are different figurations of the Thing-*jouissance*—an immortal (or, more precisely, undead) excess—in Kafka's work: the Law that somehow insists without properly existing, making us guilty without knowing what we are guilty of; the wound that won't heal and does not let us die; bureaucracy in its most "irrational" aspect; and, last but not least, "partial objects" like Odradek. They all display a kind of mock-Hegelian nightmarish "bad infinity"—there is no *Aufhebung*, no resolution proper, the thing just drags on . . . we never reach the Law, the Emperor's letter never reaches its destination, the wound never closes (or kills me). The Kafkan Thing is either transcendent, forever eluding our grasp (the Law, the Castle), or a ridiculous object into which the subject is metamorphosed, and which we can never get rid of (like Gregor Samsa, who changes into an insect). The point is to read these two features together: *jouissance* is that which we can never reach, attain, *and* that which we can never get rid of.

Kafka's genius was to eroticize bureaucracy, the nonerotic entity if ever there was one. In Chile, when a citizen wants to identify himself to the authorities, the clerk on duty demands that the poor petitioner produce proof that he was born, that he isn't a criminal, that he paid his taxes, that he registered to vote, and that he's still alive, because even if he throws a tantrum to prove that he hasn't died, he is obliged to present a "certificate of survival." The problem has reached such proportions that the government itself has created an office to combat bureaucracy. Citizens may now complain of being shabbily treated and may file charges against incompetent officials . . . on a form requiring a seal and three copies, of course.[93]

This is state bureaucracy at its most crazy. Are we aware that this is our only true contact with the divine in our secular times? What can be more "divine" than the traumatic encounter with the bureaucracy at its craziest—when, say, a bureaucrat tells me that, legally, I don't exist? It is in such encounters that we get a glimpse of another order beyond mere earthly everyday reality. Like God, bureaucracy is simultaneously all-powerful and impenetrable, capricious, omnipresent and invisible. Kafka was well aware of this deep link between bureaucracy and the divine: it is as if, in his work, Hegel's thesis on the State as the terrestrial existence of God is "buggered," given a properly obscene twist. It is only in this sense that Kafka's works stage a search for the divine in our deserted secular world—more precisely, they not only search for the divine, they find it in state bureaucracy.

There are two memorable scenes in Terry Gilliam's *Brazil* which perfectly stage the crazy excess of bureaucratic *jouissance* perpetuating itself in its auto-circulation. After the hero's plumbing breaks down, and he leaves a message asking the official repair service for urgent help, Robert de Niro enters his apartment, a mythical-mysterious criminal whose subversive activity is that he listens in on the emergency calls and then goes immediately to the customer, repairing his plumbing for free, bypassing the inefficient state repair service's paperwork. Indeed, in a bureaucracy caught in this vicious cycle of *jouissance*, the ultimate crime is simply and directly to do the job one is supposed to do—if a state repair service actually does its job, this is (at the level of its unconscious libidinal economy) considered an unfortunate by-product, since the bulk of its energy goes into inventing complicated administrative procedures that enable it to invent ever-new obstacles, and thus postpone the work indefinitely. In a second scene, we meet—in the corridors of a vast government agency—a group of people permanently running around, a leader (big-shot bureaucrat) followed by a bunch of lower-rank administrators who shout at him all the time, asking him for a specific opinion or decision, and he nervously spurts out fast "efficient" replies ("This is to be done by tomorrow latest!" "Check that report!" "No, cancel that appointment!". . .). The appearance of a nervous hyperactivity is, of course, a staged performance which masks a self-indulgent nonsensical spectacle of imitating, of playing "efficient administration." Why do they walk around all the time? The leader whom they follow is obviously not on his way from one meeting to another—the meaningless fast walk around the corridors is all he does. The hero stumbles upon this group from time to time, and the Kafkaesque answer is, of course, that this entire performance is here to attract his gaze, staged for his eyes only. They pretend to be busy, not to be bothered by the hero, but all their activity is intended to provoke the hero into addressing a demand to the group's leader, who then snaps back nervously "Can't you see how busy I am!", or, occasionally, does the reverse: greets the hero as if he has been waiting for him for a long time, mysteriously expecting his plea.

Lurking behind the misleading appearance of social critique or satire here is the *mystery of institution*. The best way to locate the line of thought from Kierkegaard to Kafka properly is to oppose it to liberal theology, which emphasizes sincere inner belief against any "merely external" social religious institution. The Kierkegaardian believer is alone not in the sense of an individual's isolation, but alone in his total exposure to the traumatic impact of the divine Thing. This is why, in his polemic against "Christendom," Kierkegaard was attacking not only the Church as a state institution, but also its inherent counterpart, "inner belief." What this opposition misses is *the traumatic "inner" impact—the libidinal status—of the institution itself*. When I greet an acquaintance: "Hello, how are you?", and we both know very well that "I don't mean it seriously," my greeting was nonetheless not a simple act of hypocrisy, because there was more truth in the external social form than in my inner intention or conviction. "Institution" at its most elementary is this minimal reification of meaning which allows me to say: "Independently of what you intended to say, your speech actually meant this!" And what if we go to the end, and conceive of the Holy Spirit itself in these terms? The Holy Spirit is in the pure performativity of the Institution, when the religious ritual is properly performed, independently of the participants' inner beliefs.

Back to Odradek: in his concise analysis of the story, Jean-Claude Milner[94] first draws attention to a peculiarity of Odradek: he has two legs, he speaks, laughs . . . in short, he displays all the features of a human being; although he is human, however, he does not resemble a human being, but clearly appears as inhuman. As such, he is the opposite of Oedipus, who (lamenting his fate at Colonus) claims that he became nonhuman when he finally acquired all the properties of an ordinary human: in line with the series of other Kafka heroes, Odradek becomes human only when he no longer resembles a human being (by metamorphosing himself into an insect, or a spool,[95] or . . .). In effect, he is a "universal singular," a stand-in for humanity by embodying its inhuman excess, by not resembling anything "human." The contrast with Aristophanes' myth (in Plato's *Symposium*) of the original spherical human being divided into two parts, eternally searching for its complementary counterpart in order to return to the lost Whole, is crucial here: although he is also a "partial object," Odradek does not look for any complementary parts, he lacks nothing. And, especially, he is not spherical: Milner deciphers "odradek" as the anagram of the Greek *dōdekaedron*, a volume of twelve faces, each of them a pentagon (in the *Timaeus* [55c], Plato himself claims that our universe is a *dōdekaedron*); it is an anagram divided by two, so Odradek is the half of a *dōdekaedron*. Thus Odradek is simply what Lacan, in *Seminar XI* and in his seminal *écrit* "Positions de l'inconscient," developed as the *lamella*, the libido as an organ, the inhuman-human "undead" organ without a body, the mythical presubjective "undead" life-substance, or, rather, the remainder of the Life-Substance which has escaped the symbolic colonization, the horrible palpitation of the "acephalic" drive which persists beyond ordinary death, outside the scope of paternal authority, nomadic, with no fixed abode. The choice underlying Kafka's story is thus Lacan's le père ou pire, "Father or worse": Odradek is "worse" as the alternative to the father.

Although they are not to be directly identified, there is a link between Odradek and the "alien" from Ridley Scott's film of the same name:

> The alien's form of life is (just, merely, simply) life, life as such: it is not so much a particular species as the essence of what it means to be a species, to be a creature, a natural being—it is Nature incarnate or sublimed, a nightmare embodiment of the natural realm understood as utterly subordinate to, utterly exhausted by, the twinned Darwinian drives to survive and reproduce.[96]

This disgust at Life is a disgust at drive at its purest. And it is interesting to note how Ridley Scott inverts the usual sexual connotations: Life is presented as inherently male, as the phallic power of brutal penetration which parasitizes on the female body, exploiting it as the carrier of its reproduction. "Beauty and the beast" here is the female subject horrified at disgusting immortal Life. There are two properly sublime moments in Jeunet's Alien Resurrection: in the first one, the cloned Ripley enters the laboratory room in which the previous seven aborted attempts to clone her are on display—here she encounters the ontologically failed, defective versions of herself, up to the almost successful version with her own face, but with some of her limbs distorted so that they resemble the limbs of the Alien Thing—this creature asks Ripley's clone to kill her, and, in an outburst of violent rage, the clone effectively destroys the horror-exhibition by torching the whole room; then there is the unique scene, perhaps the shot of the entire series, in which Ripley's clone "is drawn down into the embrace of the alien species, luxuriating in her absorption into the writhing mass of its limbs and tails—as if engulfed by the very lability of organic being being that she had earlier attempted to consume in fire."[97] Thus the link between the two scenes is clear: we are dealing with two sides of the same coin. This fascination with the monstrous alien should not, however, be allowed to obfuscate the anticapitalist edge of the Alien series: what ultimately endangers the lone group on a spaceship are not the aliens as such but the way the group is used by the anonymous earthly Corporation which wants to exploit the alien form of life. The point here is not to play the card of the superficial and simplistic "metaphorical meaning" (the vampiric alien monsters "really mean" Capital . . .), but to conceive the link at the metonymic level: how Capital parasitizes on and exploits the pure drive of Life. Pure Life is a category of capitalism. If, as Benjamin asserted,[98] capitalism is actually, at its core, a religion, then it is an obscene religion of the "undead" spectral life celebrated in the black masses of stock exchanges.

In *City Lights*, one of Chaplin's absolute masterpieces, there is a memorable scene (commented on by, among others, Levinas)[99] which directly touches upon this obscene excess of life. After the Tramp swallows a whistle by mistake, he gets an attack of hiccups, which leads to a comical effect—because of the movement of air in his stomach, each hiccup makes the whistle blow, and thus generates a weird sound of whistling from inside his body; the embarrassed Tramp desperately tries to cover up these sounds, not knowing what exactly to do . . . does not this scene stage shame at its purest? I am ashamed when I am confronted with the excess in my body, and it is significant that the source of shame in this scene is sound: a spectral sound emanating from within my body, sound as an autonomous "organ without a body," located in the very heart of my body and at the same time uncontrollable, like a kind of parasite, a foreign intruder—in short, what Lacan called the voice-object, one of the incarnations of *objet petit a*, of the *agalma*, that which is "in me more than myself."[100]

We find this object even when we would not expect to find it: if there is a novel which is the absolute classic of literary Stalinism, it is Nikolai Ostrovsky's *How the Steel Was Tempered*. Pavka, a Bolshevik fully engaged first in the Civil War and then, during the 1920s, in the construction of steel mills, ends his life in dirty rags and totally crippled, immobilized, deprived of limbs, thus reduced to an almost nonbodily existence. In such a state, he finally marries a young girl named Taya, making it clear that there will be no sex between them, just companionship, with her function being to take care of him. Here, in a way, we encounter the "truth" of the Stalinist mythology of the Happy New Man: a dirty desexualized cripple, sacrificing everything for the construction of Socialism. This fate coincides with that of Ostrovsky himself, who, in the mid-1930s, after finishing the novel, was dying crippled and blind; and, like Ostrovsky, Pavka— reduced to a living dead, a kind of living mummy—is reborn at the end through writing a novel about his life.[101] (In the last two years of his life, Ostrovsky lived in a Black Sea resort house as a "living legend," on a street named after himself, his house a site of countless pilgrimages and of great interest to foreign journalists.) This mortification of one's own treacherous body is itself embodied in a piece of shrapnel that has lodged itself in Pavka's eye, gradually blinding him; at this point, Ostrovsky's bland style suddenly explodes into a complex metaphor:

> The octopus has a bulging eye the size of a cat's head, a dull-red eye, green in the center, burning, pulsating with a phosphorescent glow. . . . The octopus moves. He can see it almost next to his eyes. The tentacles creep over his body; they are cold and they burn like nettles. The octopus shoots out its sting, and it bites into his head like a leech, and, wriggling convulsively, it sucks at his blood. He feels the blood draining out of his body into the swelling body of the octopus.[102]

To put it in Lacanian-Deleuzian terms, the octopus stands here for the "organ without a body," the partial object which invades our ordinary biological body and mortifies it; it is not a metaphor for the capitalist system squeezing and choking workers in its tentacles (the standard popular use of the metaphor between the two world wars) but, surprisingly, a "positive" metaphor for the absolute self-control that a Bolshevik revolutionary has to exert over his body (and over "pathological," potentially corrupting, bodily desires)—the octopus is a superego organ which controls us from within: when, at the low point of despair, Pavka reviews his life, Ostrovsky himself characterizes this moment of reflection as "a meeting of the Politburo with his 'I' about the treacherous behavior of his body." Yet another proof of how literary ideology can never simply lie: truth articulates itself in it through displacements. We cannot help recalling Kafka's "Country Doctor" here: is Ostrovsky's octopus not another name for the Kafkan "undead" wound which, while parasitizing upon my body, prevents me from dying?[103]

Politically, the concept of the "organ without a body" is to be opposed to the corporatist notion of the social body as an organic Whole. This is how "a subject emerges out of an individual person": when an organ—a partial object, the objectal correlative of the subject—autonomizes itself with regard to the person whose "soul" is the form of its body. Is not the first big story about the "organ without a body" Gogol's "The Nose," which relates the misadventures of a St. Petersburg official named Kovalev: his nose mysteriously disappears, only to reappear on the streets of the capital in the form of a higher-ranking official; after a number of tragicomic turns, when Kovalev has given up all hope of getting his nose back, it just as inexplicably reappears on its owner's face. Gogol concludes the story with an ironic self-referential afterword: "What is even stranger, more inexplicable than the rest—is how authors could select such subject. . . . First of all, there is absolutely no benefit to the homeland; secondly . . . and secondly there is no benefit either."[104]

This, however, is not the whole story: Lacan's formula of the fetishist object is *a* above *minus phi* (castration)—*objet petit a* fills in (and simultaneously bears witness to) the gap of castration. This is why Lacan specifies shame as *respect for castration*, as an attitude of discreetly covering up the fact of being-castrated. (No wonder women have to be covered more than men: what is concealed is their lack of a penis. . . .) While shamelessness resides in openly displaying one's castration, shame enacts a desperate attempt to keep up the appearance: although I know the truth (about castration), let us pretend that it hasn't happened. . . . This is why, when I see my crippled neighbor "shamelessly" pushing his disfigured limb toward me, it is I, not he, who is overwhelmed by shame. When a man exposes his distorted limb to his neighbor, his real target is to expose not himself, but the neighbor: to put the neighbor to shame by confronting him with his own ambivalent repulsion/fascination with the spectacle he is forced to witness. In a strictly analogous way, one is ashamed of one's ethnic origins, of the specific "torsion" of one's particular identity, of being caught in the coordinates of a life-world into which one was thrown, with which one is stuck, unable to get rid of it.

The father's/narrator's final words in Kafka's "Odradek" ("the idea that he is likely to survive me I find almost painful") echo the final words of The Trial ("as if the shame will survive him"): Odradek is, in effect, *the shame of the father of the family* (the story's narrator). Odradek is the father's *sinthome,* the "knot" onto which the father's *jouissance* is stuck. This, however, seems to complicate the link between shame and castration: for Lacan, is such a partial object, *lamella,* the "undead" organ without a body, not precisely that which escapes castration? Lacan defines the *lamella* as an asexual object, as the remainder of sexuation.[105] For a human being to be "dead while alive" is to be colonized by the "dead" symbolic order; to be "alive while dead" is to give body to the remainder of Life-Substance which has escaped the symbolic colonization (*lamella*). What we are dealing with here is thus the split between O(ther) and J(*ouissance*), between the "dead" symbolic order which mortifies the body and the nonsymbolic Life-Substance of *jouissance.* In Freud and Lacan, these two notions are not what they are in our everyday or standard scientific discourse: in psychoanalysis, they both designate a properly monstrous dimension—Life is the horrible palpitation of the *lamella,* of the nonsubjective ("acephalic") "undead" drive which persists beyond ordinary death; death is the symbolic order itself, the structure which, as a parasite, colonizes the living entity. What defines the death drive in Lacan is this double gap: not the simple opposition of life and death, but the split of life itself into "normal" life and horrifying "undead" life, and the split of the dead into "ordinary" dead and the "undead" machine. The basic opposition between Life and Death is thus supplemented by the parasitic symbolic machine (language as a dead entity which "behaves as if it possesses a life of its own") and its counterpoint, the "living dead" (the monstrous life-substance which persists in the Real outside the Symbolic)—this split which runs within the domains of Life and Death constitutes the space of the death drive.

In his reading of Kafka, Benjamin focuses on "a long series of figures with the prototype of distortion, the hunchback": "Among the images in Kafka's stories, none is more frequent than that of the man who bows his head far down on his chest: the fatigue of the court officials, the noise affecting the doormen in the hotel, the low ceiling facing the visitors in the gallery."[106] It is crucial to remember here that, in the encounter between the man from the country and the guardian of the Door of the Law, it is the guardian, the figure of authority, who is hunched, not the man from the country, who stands upright. (This point is noted by the priest in his debate with Josef K. that follows the parable on the Door of the Law in *The Trial:* the priest makes it clear that it is the guardian who is subordinated here, playing the role of a servant.) We should therefore not idealize the disfigured "creature" into a pathetic figure of the marginalized, excluded from full humanity, the object of solidarity with the victim—if anything, the creaturely hunchback is the prototype of the servant of Power. Let us not forget who are "creatures" *par excellence: woman* is more "creaturely" than man, *Christ on the Cross* is the creature—and, last but not least, the *psychoanalyst* is an inhuman creature, not a human partner (and the wager of the discourse of the analyst is precisely that one can establish a social link based directly on this creaturely excess, bypassing the Master-Signifier). Recall here Lacan's *le père ou pire,* "Father or worse": insofar as the analyst is not a father figure (a figure of paternal symbolic authority), insofar as his presence represents and enacts the suspension of this authority, is there not also in his figure something of the "primordial" (I am tempted to say *anal*) father, the One exempt from symbolic castration?

This is how we should approach the topic of the Eucharist: what exactly do we eat when we eat the body of Christ? We eat the partial object, the undead substance which redeems us and guarantees that we are raised above mortality; that, while we are still alive here on earth, we already participate in the eternal divine Life. Does this not mean that the Eucharist is like the undead substance of the indestructible eternal life that invades the human body in a horror movie? Are we not, through the Eucharist, terrorized by an alien monster which invades our body?[107] In the fall of 2003, a weird case of cannibalism was discovered in Germany: a guy ate his partner. What was so weird was the strictly consensual nature of the act: there was none of the usual secret abduction and torture; the killer put announcements on the web, asking for somebody who would be willing to be killed and eaten, and found a volunteer. The two first ate together the cooked penis of the victim; then the victim was killed, cut into pieces, and gradually eaten. If ever there was an act of Eucharistic love, this was it. . . .

Shame thus overwhelms the subject when he is confronted with what, in him, remains *noncastrated*, with the embarrassing surplus-appendix which continues to dangle out. Is Odradek not the reminder/remainder of the father's failure to accomplish his work of imposing the Law (of "castration")? Or are we dealing here, yet again, with the structure of parallax? That is to say: what if the lack and the surplus refer to the *same* phenomenon, and are simply two perspectives on it? In his "structuralist" *Logic of Sense*, Deleuze pointed out how, as soon as the symbolic order emerges, we are dealing with the minimal difference between a structural place and the element that occupies (fills out) this place: an element is always logically preceded by the place in the structure it fills out. We are dealing here with two series (or, rather, levels): the "empty" formal structure (signifier) and the series of elements filling out the empty places in the structure (signified); the paradox consists in the fact that these two series never overlap: we always encounter an entity that is simultaneously—with regard to the structure—an empty, unoccupied place and—with regard to the elements—a rapidly moving, elusive object, an occupant without a place.[108] We have thereby produced Lacan's formula of fantasy, since the matheme for the subject is $, an empty place in the structure, an elided signifier, while *objet petit a* is, by definition, an excessive object, an object that lacks its place in the structure.

Consequently, the point is not that there is simply the surplus of an element over the places available in the structure or the surplus of a place that has no element to fill it out. An empty place in the structure would still sustain the fantasy of an element that will emerge and fill out this place; an excessive element lacking its place would still sustain the fantasy of some as yet unknown place waiting for it. The point is, rather, that the empty place in the structure is strictly correlative to the errant element lacking its place: they are not two different entities, but the front and the back of one and the same entity, that is, one and the same entity inscribed onto the two surfaces of a Moebius strip. At its most formal, "castration" designates the precedence of the empty place over the contingent elements filling it; this is what accounts for the elementary structure of hysteria, of the hysterical question "Why am I what you are saying I am? Why am I at that place in the symbolic order?" Correlative to it, however, is the fact of being stuck with an object with no (symbolic) place, an object which escaped castration. We should therefore not be afraid to draw the ultimate paradoxical conclusion: castration and its disavowal are two sides of the same coin; castration has to be sustained by a noncastrated remainder, a fully realized castration cancels itself. Or, to put it more precisely: *lamella*, the "undead" object, is not a remainder of castration in the sense of a little part which somehow escaped the swipe of castration unscathed, but, literally, the *product* of the cut of castration, the *surplus* generated by it.

This link between castration and *sinthome* means that the "undead" partial object is the inscription on the body of what Eric Santner called "signifying stress": the wound, the disfiguration/distortion, inflicted upon the body when the body is colonized by the symbolic order; this is why animals are not "creatures" in this precise sense, they are not stuck onto a *sinthome*.[109] However, we should avoid the temptation to translate this feature into the terms of the traditional philosophical anthropology according to which an animal is immersed in its environs, its behavior regulated by innate instincts, while man is a "homeless" animal deprived of immediate instinctual support, which is why he needs a master to impose on him his "second nature," symbolic norms and regulations. The key difference is that the "cringe" of the *sinthome* is not a cultural device destined to impose a new balance onto the uprooted human being which threatens to explode into untamed excess, but the name of this excess itself: a human being (to come) loses its instinctual animal coordinates by getting transfixed/stuck onto an "inhuman" *sinthome*. This means that the *differentia specifica* which defines a human being is not the difference between man and animal (or any other real or imaginary species like gods), but an *inherent* difference, the difference between the human and the inhuman excess that is inherent to being-human.

Consequently, is not the "theological" dimension without which, for Benjamin, revolution cannot win, the very dimension of the excess of drive, of its "too-muchness"? In other words, is not our task—the properly *Christological* one—to change the modality of our being-stuck in a mode that allows, solicits even, the activity of sublimation?

KATE'S CHOICE, OR, THE MATERIALISM OF HENRY JAMES

It may sound surprising to call Henry James the ultimate writer of history, of the impact of history on the most intimate spheres of experience; this properly historical dimension, however, is discernible even at the level of style: the main feature of James's late style is what Seymour Chatman called "psychological nominalization," [1] the transformation of "John observed X" into "John's observation was X"; of "You are not proud enough" into "Your pride falls short." Verbs that designate psychic activity or experience are nominalized, and such a procedure puts on stage an abstract entity where previously there had been only a human actor—characters themselves (diegetic persons) tend to evolve into "anchors for abstractions": "Thoughts and perceptions in James' world are entities more than actions, things more than movements" (22). Psychological abstractions thus acquire a life of their own; they are not only the true topic of James's texts, but even their true agents which interact—in The Wings of the Dove, consciousness can "breath in a sigh," an impression can become a "witness.". . . Consequently, in several forms of ellipsis that James practiced, the human agent of an action tends to disappear completely—witness his heavy use of it. Linked to this is James's distaste for adjectives, since they seem to add a qualification to some preexisting entity; his favored way of avoiding them was to replace the standard adjective-noun form with the nominalized adjective followed by "of" and the noun: in The Wings of the Dove, we find not a charming demonstration of Kate's and Merton's need for each other, but the "charm of the demonstration" of this need; Kate displays not graceful gaiety, but the "grace of gaiety"; she does not have a free fancy, but the "freedom of fancy"— in all these cases, again, the quality itself becomes a thing.

James's widespread use of deixis points in the same direction, especially in its extreme form of what Chatman called "appositive deixis" (63), in which a pronoun is given first, anticipating the real subject which follows in apposition, as in the very first sentence of The Wings of the Dove: "She waited, Kate Croy, for her father to come in . . ."— a minimal gap is thus introduced between the nameless "she" and her determinate qualification, indicating the uncertain and vacillating character of every qualification. Deixis is not merely an ersatz for a previously introduced determinate person or thing; rather, it stands for an unnameable X (a kind of Kantian noumenal Thing—and let us not forget that "thing" is another favored James term) which eludes all its qualifications. In a strict parallel to nominalization of verbs, here again the subject is reduced to an anonymous "anchor of abstractions." The subject is not a thing to which attributes are attached, or which undergoes changes—it is a kind of empty container, a space in which things can be located.

To anyone versed in the Marxist critique of the speculative-Hegelian ideological inversions in which an abstract predicate turns into the Subject of the process, while "real individuals" are reduced to its subordinated predicates, it is difficult to resist here the temptation to (dis)qualify these stylistic procedures as indications of James's fall into "bourgeois ideological reification," especially since his shift of emphasis from nouns to their properties does not rely on the standard "dialectical" notion of the priority of the process over things caught up in this process, of "becoming" over "being."

If anything, James is a true antipode to Proust's "Bergsonism": instead of presenting the flux of Becoming as the truth of fixed Beings, as the process which generates them, he turns verbs and predicates themselves—signs of the process of becoming, of what happens to things, or of what specifies/qualifies them—into "things." At a deeper, properly Hegelian, dialectical level, however, things are much more complex: it is James's very nominalizing of predicates and verbs, their change into substantive agents, which in effect *desubstantializes the subject*, reducing it to a formal empty space in which the multitude of agents interact—somewhat like today's neo-Darwinist theories of subjectivity as the space in which memes fight their battles for survival and reproduction.

Insofar as the paradigmatic case of the Marxist critique of the reification of an ideological abstraction mentioned above is money, we should not be surprised that the ultimate topic of Henry James's work is the effect of capitalist modernization on ethical life: indeterminacy and contingency undermine old reliance on stable forms prescribing how we are to act and to evaluate our own and others' acts; there is no longer a fixed frame which enables us to find our (ethical) way. The greatness of James, however, is that, while he fully assumes this break of modernity and emphasizes the falsity of any retreat to old mores, he also avoids ethical relativism and historicism, that is, the relativization of norms and ethical values to an expression of some more fundamental underlying (economic, psychological, political) historical process. Far from throwing us back into ourselves, into our individualistic experience, this decline of the stable social-normative framework makes our radical *dependence* on others even more evident:

> this altered situation of indeterminacy and contingency might itself reveal an altered social state, one wherein [others'] claims are experienced differently, mean something new, are more directly necessary for me to lead my own life, to give it sense, to assess, and judge. The key issue in morality might not be the rational justifiability with which I treat others, but the proper acknowledgment of, and enactment of, a dependence on others without which the process of any justification (any invocation of common normative criteria at all) could not begin. . . . This uncertainty and doubt and profound ambiguity, unresolvability about meaning . . . makes possible and even requires a form of dependency, a dependency even at the level of possible consciousness itself, and some "lived out" acknowledgment of such dependency, that now makes up the new moral experience, the claims and entitlements of each on others, that [James] is interested in.[2]

This shift is, of course, properly Hegelian: the uncertainty itself, the lack of a fixed socio-ethical frame of reference, far from simply condemning us to moral relativism, opens up a new "higher" field of ethical experience, that of intersubjectivity, of the mutual dependence of subjects, of the need not only to rely on others, but also to recognize the ethical weight of others' claims on me. Ethics as a system of norms is thus not simply given, it is itself the result of the ethical *work* of "mediation," of me recognizing the legitimacy of others' claims on me. That is to say: in the Hegelian passage from Substance to Subject, the substance (for example, at the social level, the ethical substance, the mores that sustain a way of life) does not disappear, it is just that its status changes: the substance loses its substantial character, it is no longer experienced as a firm foundation given in advance but as a fragile symbolic fiction, something which exists only insofar as individuals treat it as existing, or only insofar as they relate to it as their ethical substance. There is no directly existing "ethical substance," the only "actually existing" thing is the incessant activity and interaction of individuals, and it is only this activity that keeps it alive.

There is a saying that some things can be found only if, before finding them, one gets lost—does this properly Hegelian paradox not provide the formula of the Jamesian search for the ethical position? It can be "found," formulated, only after one gets lost—only after one accepts that there is no given ethical substance which provides the fixed coordinates for our ethical judgment in advance, that such a judgment can emerge only from our own work of ethical reflection with no external guarantee. It is not that we are dealing here with the simple "Hegelian" movement into alienation (getting lost) and recuperation of oneself (finding a firm position); the point is a more precise one: *it is the very movement of "getting lost" (of losing ethical substance) that opens up the space for the ethical work of mediation which alone can generate the solution.* The loss is thus not recuperated but fully asserted as liberating, as a positive opening.[3]

This means that the space of James's novels is thoroughly secular, postreligious; paradoxically, this dimension is most obfuscated in *The Princess Casamassima*, his neglected masterpiece which deals directly with a sociopolitical topic.[4] *Casamassima*'s limitations are obvious: approaching the topic of revolutionary anarchists in the London slums of the 1880s, James engaged in a kind of intellectual test, in "an exercise in the sheer power, the grasping power, of intelligence to divine that which it did not really know."[5] This is where it differs from his masterpieces like *The Portrait of a Lady* or *The Wings of the Dove*, where he is effectively at home in his material; in *Casamassima*, James is simply unable to confront the contours of revolutionary politics directly—he does not know the inner texture of this explosive topic. That is why, in order to mask this fact, he engages in elaborate sets of impressions of the London slums, written with great sympathy for the speechless suffering poor. This failure emerges at its purest apropos of the novel's characters: James can provide brilliant descriptions of individual revolutionary types (Poupin, Schinkel, Muniment), but what is totally missing is a portrait of the collective revolutionary movement as such: "He made the mistake of supposing that the whole was equal to a sum of its parts; that if you exhausted the radicals you had gotten at radicalism."[6]

However, there is still a fundamental, often overlooked and misunderstood, lesson to be learned from *The Princess Casamassima*: to present the deadlock in all its radicality is much more pertinent than simple progressist solutions. The *doxa* on this book is that it stands for the conservative James at his purest: its message is aesthetic conservatism— great monuments of culture and the "civilized" way of life of the upper classes justify the suffering of millions. Today, this problem confronts us, if anything, in a much more aggravated way: liberal-democratic affluent societies with their culture, versus billions living in poverty in the Third World; the recourse to terrorist violence. . . . In the way it approaches this topic, however, the book is much more radical and ambiguous than it may appear; the first clue is provided by the rather superficial fact that all low-class revolutionary characters are portrayed as basically sympathetic, while the upper-class ones are clearly presented as vain and vulgar. James is thus far from endorsing a resigned conservative attitude of "Let us preserve what we can of our great cultural heritage, even if it was paid for by the suffering of the anonymous millions": all individuals who stand for this heritage are fake, following an empty ritual; their finesse is a mask of vulgarity. The deadlock is thus real, there is no easy way out; Hyacinth Robinson's suicide, with which the book concludes, indicates an unsolvable antinomy: the impossibility of choosing between the rights of the dispossessed and high culture. More pertinently, what Hyacinth cannot bring together are the two sides of a parallax view—a feature that characterized James himself, with his "power to see both sides of a question. Hyacinth also, to his destruction, can see each side of the question so well that the only action available to him is self-destruction, which is itself a symbolic statement, the only work of art available to him."[7]

The key difference between Hyacinth and James was that James was able to "work through" his inability to act, his withdrawal from participation in life, to transpose it into the art of writing. This is why, paradoxically, Hyacinth's failure to carry out the act (and murder an upper-class figure) is also a sign of his lack of creativity: "Hyacinth's refusal to destroy is also an inability to create, and reflects deeper internal conflicts in the story."[8] Thus we should reverse the well-known platitude according to which destructive rage is a sign of creative impotence: every authentic creative breakthrough starts with the negative gesture of destruction, of cleaning the slate.[9]

Far from concerning only the intricacies of intimate libidinal investments, the parallax gap is therefore of the utmost political importance—here we should think of the narrative structure of the novels of Henning Mankell, arguably today's greatest crime writer, an author with no affinity whatsoever for James's universe. Most of Mankell's police stories—set in the southern Swedish town of Ystad, with Inspector Kurt Wallander as their hero—follow the same formula: they start with a brief prologue set in a poor Third World country, then the novel proper moves to Ystad. The Other of today's World History, poor Third World countries, is thus inscribed into the universe of the Wallander novels; this big Other of World History has to remain in the background, as the distant Absent Cause. There is one novel (*The Dogs of Riga,* the second in the Wallander series) in which Mankell violates his rule and allows Wallander to intervene directly in the Other of History: in the course of investigating the murder of two Russians whose corpses were found on the coast close to Ystad, Wallander visits Latvia, where he gets involved in the *imbroglio* of the big Story of the Day, the explosion of national independence and the collapse of the Soviet Union—no wonder the novel is a complete failure, contrived and ridiculously pretentious. To add insult to injury, Wallander finds there his (temporary) love-partner, the widow of an honest Latvian police investigator whose name is Liepa Baiba ("liepa" is Slavic for "beautiful," so we get a "beautiful babe". . .).

This absent Third World Other is, however, present in Mankell's artistic universe and life in another surprising way: the "real" Mankell divides his time between Ystad and

Maputo (the capital of Mozambique), where he runs a small theater for which he writes and directs plays performed by local actors; he has also written a couple of non-detective novels set in the desperate conditions of today's Mozambique. And it is only this that brings us to Mankell's true achievement: among today's writers, he is a unique *artist of the parallax view.* That is to say, the two perspectives—that of the affluent Ystad and that of Maputo—are irretrievably "out of sync," so that there is no neutral language enabling us to translate one into the other, even less to posit one as the "truth" of the other. All we can ultimately do in today's conditions is to remain faithful to this split as such, to record it. Every exclusive focus on the First World topics of late-capitalist alienation and commodification, of ecological crisis, of the new racisms and intolerances, and so on, cannot but appear cynical in the face of raw Third World poverty, hunger, and violence; on the other hand, attempts to dismiss First World problems as trivial in comparison with "real" permanent Third World catastrophes are no less a fake—focusing on the "real problems" of the Third World is the ultimate form of escapism, of avoiding confrontation with the antagonisms of one's own society. Take Fredric Jameson's succinct description (from the 1980s) of the deadlock of the dialogue between the Western New Left and the Eastern European dissidents, the absence of any common language between them:

> To put it briefly, the East wishes to talk in terms of power and oppression; the West in terms of culture and commodification. There are really no common denominators in this initial struggle for discursive rules, and what we end up with is the inevitable comedy of each side muttering irrelevant replies in its own favorite language.[10]

Does the same not go for Mankell himself, for his work as well as his life? Aware that there is no common denominator between Ystad and Maputo, and simultaneously aware that the two stand for the two aspects of the same total constellation, he shifts between the two perspectives, trying to discern in each the echoes of its opposite. It is because of this insistence on the irreparable character of the split, on the failure of any common denominator, that Mankell's work provides an insight into the *totality* of today's world constellation.

Back to the final deadlock of James's *Casamassima*: perhaps we should introduce sexual difference here: far from indicating some kind of "feminine" indecision and passivity, Hyacinth's deadlock signals precisely his inability to perform a properly feminine act. The negative feminine gesture would be the only way to break out of this deadlock, to cut its Gordian knot, repeating *mutatis mutandis* what Isabel Archer does at the end of *The Portrait of a Lady*. It is in *The Wings of the Dove* that we find what could be called the final and supreme version of this gesture—but where? This novel offers one of the cases in which the only way of interpreting a scene or story properly is to read it in multiple ways, repeatedly, focusing each time on the perspective of one of the main characters. *The Wings of the Dove* is the novel of a moral trial—but *whose* trial?

Recall Delmer Daves's *3:10 to Yuma*, one of the great late Westerns in which the key Act is performed not by the central character who appears to be the focus of the ethical ordeal, but by the secondary character who may even be the very source of temptation. 3:10 to Yuma tells the story of a poor farmer (Van Heflin) who, for 200 dollars that he badly needs in order to save his cattle from drought, accepts the job of escorting a bandit with a high price on his head (Glenn Ford) from the hotel where he is being held to the train that will take him to prison in Yuma. What we have here, of course, is a classic story of an ethical ordeal; throughout the film, it seems that the person submitted to the ordeal is the farmer himself, exposed as he is to temptations in the style of the (undeservedly) more famous High Noon: all those who promised to help him abandon him when they discover that the hotel is surrounded by a gang sworn to save their boss; the imprisoned bandit himself alternately threatens the farmer and tries to bribe him, and so on. The last scene, however, in retrospect totally changes our perception of the film: near the train, which is already leaving the station, the bandit and the farmer find themselves face to face with the entire gang, waiting for the right moment to shoot the farmer and thus free their boss. At this tense moment, when the situation seems hopeless for the farmer, the bandit suddenly turns to him and says: "Trust me! Let's jump on the wagon together!" In short, the one actually going through the ordeal is the bandit himself, the apparent agent of temptation: at the end, he is overtaken by the farmer's integrity, and sacrifices his own freedom for him . . . and we should approach The Wings of the Dove in the same way. This question has to be unambiguously resolved; any recourse to platitudes about the allegedly "undecided," "open" character of the narrative is an excuse for weak thinking. Again, Pippin is right to emphasize how James's achievement is fully to assert as the basic defining feature of modernity the lack of any transcendent ethical Substance, while simultaneously avoiding the easy position of ethical relativism.

The most obvious candidate is Milly, the mortally ill American heiress: The Wings of the Dove can be read as the story of how Milly, after learning about the plot of which she is the object, finds a space of an autonomous act not by sabotaging it, taking revenge, but by playing along with it to the end. The novel's moments of decision occur when unwanted knowledge (even knowledge about knowledge) is imposed on people—how will this knowledge affect their acts? What will Milly do when she learns of the link between Densher and Kate, and of the plot part of which Densher's display of love for her reveals itself to be? How will Densher react when he learns that Milly knows about his and Kate's plan? The one on trial here is Milly: upon learning of the plot, she reacts with a gesture of sacrifice, leaving her fortune to Densher. This utterly altruistic gesture is, of course, manipulative in a much more profound way than Kate's plot: Milly's aim is to ruin the link between Kate and Densher through her bequest of money to Densher. She freely assumes and stages her death itself as a self-obliterating sacrifice which, together with the bequest, should enable Kate and Densher to live happily ever after . . . the best way of ruining any prospect of happiness for them. She leaves her wealth to them, at the same time making it ethically impossible for them to accept her gift.

We all know the elementary form of politeness, that of the empty symbolic gesture, a gesture—an offer—which is meant to be rejected. In John Irving's A Prayer for

Owen Meany, after the little boy Owen accidentally kills John's—his best friend's, the narrator's—mother, he is, of course, terribly upset, so, to show how sorry he is, he discreetly delivers to John a gift of the complete collection of color photos of baseball stars, his most precious possession; however, Dan, John's delicate stepfather, tells him that the proper thing to do is to return the gift. What we have here is symbolic exchange at its purest: a gesture made to be rejected; the point, the "magic" of symbolic exchange, is that, although at the end we are where we were at the beginning, the overall result of the operation is not zero but a distinct gain for both parties, the pact of solidarity. And is not something similar part of our everyday mores? When, after being engaged in a fierce competition for a job promotion with my closest friend, I win, the proper thing to do is to offer to withdraw, so that he will get the promotion, and the proper thing for him to do is to reject my offer—in this way, perhaps, our friendship can be saved. . . .

Milly's offer is the very opposite of such an elementary gesture of politeness: although it also is an offer that is meant to be rejected, what makes hers different from the symbolic empty offer is the cruel alternative it imposes on its addressee: I offer you wealth as the supreme proof of my saintly kindness, but if you accept my offer, you will be marked by an indelible stain of guilt and moral corruption; if you do the right thing and reject it, however, you will also not be simply righteous—*your very rejection will function as a retroactive admission of your guilt,* so whatever Kate and Densher do, the very choice Milly's bequest confronts them with makes them guilty. As such, Milly's "ethical" sacrifice is a fake:

> By willing death in this way, Milly in effect dies in order to "keep dreaming," to maintain the fantasy that has sustained her as a desiring subject. Milly's death thus recalls, albeit inversely, the dream Freud recounts of the father whose child cries out that he is burning. In the Freudian dream, the father wakes up, *in order to continue dreaming,* that is, in order to avoid the traumatic confrontation expressed by the child's cries. Milly, in reverse, dies to avoid waking up; she dies in order to sustain the desiring fantasy. . . . Her "hysterical" solution, then, is nothing but a cleaving to the sustaining barrier that prevents us from ever achieving the full realization of desire. Milly's death is thus, in Lacan's very precise sense, an ethical death, a death died in accordance with desire.[11]

While I agree with Jöttkandt's description of Milly's sacrificial gesture as a hysterical solution, I am tempted to propose the opposite ethical judgment. Jöttkandt relies on a simplified notion of the Lacanian ethics of desire as hysterical: as if, since desire is primarily the desire for its own unfulfillment, for its own remaining desire, the ethical act proper is the one of continuing to dream, to postpone satisfaction, to sustain the desiring fantasy . . . what about *traversing* the fantasy?

The second perspective from which the novel can be read is that of Densher. As Milly's perfect counterpoint, he falls into the trap set by her sacrificial goodness: he cannot accept happiness (money plus beloved woman). The trial here is that of Densher: by rejecting Milly's money, he displays "moral growth" . . . or does he? At the end, the envelope containing money functions as one of the Hitchcockian objects in James: not the proverbial MacGuffin, but the "dirty" Hitchcockian object which circulates among the subjects, casting a bad spell on its possessor.[12] Densher's burning of the letter, his refusal to accept Milly's gift, far from standing for an ethical gesture, is—no less than Milly's sacrifice—a fake, and Kate is right to claim that, while Densher did not really love Milly when she was alive, he loves her dead—a false love if ever there was one.[13]

This brings us to the novel's true ethical hero, Kate, who should in no way be dismissed as either a cold manipulator or a mere victim of social circumstances—hers is the "No" at the novel's end (leaving Densher), a properly Kierkegaardian moment in which *the ethical itself is the temptation*: Kate is right to dismiss Densher's "ethical" rejection of the money as a fake, she is right in guessing that the only truly ethical thing for Densher to do, even with regard to Milly, would be to accept her gift. Her ethical act—the only true one in the entire novel—is her refusal to marry Densher under the conditions dictated by his acceptance of the terms of Milly's fantasy. She gets the paradox: it is precisely by refusing Milly's money that Densher attests his fidelity to Milly's fantasy.

Alejandro Iñárritu's *21 Grams* (scenario by Guillermo Arriaga) displays a surprising formal parallel with James's *Wings*. Its three main characters find themselves "between the two deaths": Paul is living on borrowed time, he is dying because his transplanted heart is failing; Cristina is a living dead, totally devastated by the accidental death of her husband and two sons; Jack, who accidentally caused their death, is an ex-con who found his way back into family life by becoming a born-again Christian. As in *The Wings of the Dove*, each of the three has his or her perspective from which the whole story can be read; and, also as in *The Wings of the Dove*, the story focuses on the sacrificial gesture of selling the inevitable death as a free act. At the end of the film, Jack comes into the motel room in which Paul and Cristina are staying and asks them, in an outburst of desperate violence, to kill him; Cristina complies and starts beating him with a poker, almost killing him; at this moment Paul, who is helplessly watching the scene, grabs the gun and shoots *himself*:

> He's going to die because of his failed heart transplant, so if he shoots himself it will be so powerful that it will stop any further violence. If he shoots the gun into the air maybe they'll stop for a moment, I don't know. But if he shoots himself he knows that his action is so sacrificial that there will be no further violence between Cristina and Jack . . . the only method he has of taking the attention of Cristina away from killing Jack is for him to shoot himself. I think of it as an act of love.[14]

Thus *21 Grams* confronts us with the same interpretive dilemma as the one in *The Wings of the Dove*: is the suicidal sacrificial gesture a true ethical act or not? In contrast to *Wings*, the answer here is yes: there is no narcissistic staging of one's death at work when Paul shoots himself, no manipulative strategy of using one's death as a gift destined to secretly sabotage what it appears to make possible. Paul finds himself in a paradoxical predicament: the only way to change the situation, to interrupt the catastrophic flow of violence, is not to intervene in it but to turn it back on oneself, to target oneself.

Back to James's Kate: the true contours of her act can be discerned only through a close reading of the novel's final pages. Before this scene, Densher has received a thick envelope full of money from Milly's lawyers in New York—Milly's bequest of the bulk of her wealth to him; he has sent the envelope to Kate unopened. The last scene starts with Kate coming into Densher's room and ostentatiously laying on the table the envelope which has obviously been opened by her. Densher shows his disappointment in Kate who, by opening the envelope, has failed his test; he refuses to have anything to do with the money, and challenges her to marry him without it, or to lose him and have her freedom and the money—he wants to escape any acquaintance with the tainted money. She believes he is afraid, and suggests that, although he did not love Milly before her death, he does so now, after her death: he is in love with Milly's memory. He offers to marry her immediately "as we were" but she, leaving, says: "We shall never be again as we were." This swift ending is to be read as somewhat akin to the analyst's intervention which concludes the session, a sudden unexpected closure which elevates a marginal detail into the significant Cut.

Among recent films, the otherwise rather mediocre and pretentious *Before Sunset* is one of the few which displays such an art of unexpected ending. A couple (Ethan Hawke and Julie Delpy), who once spent a night together in Vienna, accidentally meet again nine years later in Paris; they have only a short time to talk, since Hawke, a successful writer, has a plane to catch in a couple of hours. Their easy conversation gradually turns serious when it becomes clear that neither has recovered from the trauma of their past encounter; when he is already on the way to the airport, Delpy invites him to drop into her apartment while his limousine waits outside. As they drink tea, their conversation lightens again; they discuss Nina Simone's songs and, in a mocking imitation of Simone's dancing style, Delpy ironically comments: "This boy is gonna miss his plane." Cut to Hawke, who nodes with a smile: "I know." Cut to darkness: the end of the film. . . .

In the same way, Kate's remark which concludes *The Wings of the Dove* is a passing remark which nonetheless, through its strategic placing at the novel's end, functions as a *point de capiton* which "quilts" its meaning. Here are the brilliant last pages of the novel, arguably James's supreme achievement,[15] starting with a direct jump *in medias res*, to the Hitchcockian object:

> She had laid on the table from the moment of her coming in the long envelope, substantially filled, which he had sent her enclosed in another of still ampler make. He had however not looked at it—his belief being that he wished never again to do so; besides which it had happened to rest with its addressed side up. So he "saw" nothing, and it was only into her eyes that her remark made him look, declining any approach to the object indicated. "It's not 'my' seal, my dear; and my intention—which my note tried to express—was all to treat it to you as not mine."

Here the object is clearly established in its "Hitchcockian" quality, as the materialization of an intersubjective libidinal investment—note the key sentence: "So he 'saw' nothing, and it was only into her eyes that her remark made him look, declining any approach to the object indicated"; this directly presents the object as the relay of an intersubjective tension. Such an object is never possessed: we do not manipulate it, it is the object itself which determines what *we* are, its possession affects us in an uncontrollable way. Note the paradigmatically Jamesian "unnatural" syntactic order (not the standard "She had laid on the table the long envelope from the moment of her coming in . . ." or, even more, "From the moment of her coming in, she had laid on the table the long envelope . . ."): in order to create a proto-Hitchcockian suspense, the object—the libidinal focal point—is named only at the end, its appearance is delayed. Furthermore, the first fast reading creates a grammatical confusion: one tends to read the sentence as "She had laid on the table [from the moment of her coming] in the long envelope," giving rise to a nonsensical quasi-surrealist scene of Kate herself wrapped up in the long envelope on the table; only after reaching the end of this passage—upon registering the nonsense of the outcome of our first reading, and rereading it—do we get the proper meaning. The elegance of this complication is that it shifts the emphasis from the person (Kate) to the object (the letter). Not only is this object Hitchcockian; we can also easily visualize this paragraph as a scene in a Hitchcock film: first the exchange of gazes; only then, slowly, does the camera approach the object, the focal point of the scene . . .

> "Do you mean that it's to that extent mine then?"
>
> "Well, let us call it, if we like, theirs—that of the good people in New York, the authors of our communication. If the seal is broken well and good; but we *might*, you know," he presently added, "have sent it back to them intact and inviolate. Only accompanied," he smiled with his heart in his mouth, "by an absolutely kind letter."

Since the object-letter is cursed, as in Poe's "The Purloined Letter," the first reaction is to escape its hold by refusing to act as its receiver, and, in this way, to avoid being caught in its circular path, to *stay out* of it.

> Kate took it with the mere brave blink with which a patient of courage signifies to the exploring medical hand that the tender place is touched. He saw on the spot that she was prepared, and with this signal sign that she was too intelligent not to be, came a flicker of possibilities. She was—merely to put it at that—intelligent enough for anything. "Is it what you're proposing we *should* do?"
>
> "Ah it's too late to do it—well, ideally. Now, with that sign that we *know*—!"
>
> "But you don't know," she said very gently.
>
> "I refer," he went on without noticing it, "to what would have been the handsome way. Its being dispatched again, with no cognizance taken but one's assurance of the highest consideration, and the proof of this in the state of the envelope—*that* would have been really satisfying."
>
> She thought an instant. "The state of the envelope proving refusal, you mean, not to be based on the insufficiency of the sum?"
>
> Densher smiled again as for the play, however whimsical, of her humor. "Well yes—something of that sort."
>
> "So that if cognizance *has* been taken—so far as I'm concerned—it spoils the beauty?"

The intersubjective status of knowledge, of "cognizance being taken," is crucial here: not simply knowledge, but *knowledge about the Other's knowledge*. Take the final reversal of Edith Wharton's *The Age of Innocence*, in which the husband who for many years has harbored an illicit passionate love for Countess Olenska is, after his wife's early death, free to join his love; however, when, on the way to her, he learns from his son that his young wife *knew* about his secret passion all the time, his union with Countess Olenska becomes impossible for him. . . . That is the enigma of knowledge: how is it possible that the whole psychic economy of a situation changes radically not when the hero directly learns something (some long-repressed secret), but when he *gets to know that the other* (whom he mistook for ignorant) *also knew it all the time*, and just pretended not to know to keep up appearances—is there anything more humiliating than the situation of a husband who, after a long secret love affair, learns all of a sudden that his wife knew about it all the time, but kept silent about it out of politeness or, even worse, out of love for him? In exactly the same way, for Densher, marrying Kate while accepting money from the dead Milly becomes impossible the moment he learns that Milly knew about his and Kate's plot. . . .

"It makes the difference that I'm disappointed in the hope—which I confess I entertained—that you'd bring the thing back to me as you had received it."

"You didn't express that hope in your letter."

"I didn't want to. I wanted to leave it to yourself. I wanted—oh yes, if that's what you wish to ask me—to see what you'd do."

"You wanted to measure the possibilities of my departure from delicacy?"

He continued steady now; a kind of ease—from the presence, as in the air, of something he couldn't yet have named—had come to him. "Well, I wanted—in so good a case—to test you."

She was struck—it showed in her face—by his expression. "It is a good case. I doubt whether a better," she said with her eyes on him, "has ever been known."

"The better the case then the better the test!"

"How do you know," she asked in reply to this, "what I'm capable of?"

"I don't, my dear! Only with the seal unbroken I should have known sooner."

"I see"—she took it in. "But I myself shouldn't have known at all. And you wouldn't have known, either, what I do know."

Here are the terms of Densher's hypocritical test: he forwarded Kate the unopened letter, expecting her *not* to open it—his hope was that, in this way, they would conclude a kind of pact of ignorance, cementing their relationship (marriage) in a refusal not only to accept the gift, but even to know what the gift was. Here we encounter a properly melodramatic moment which is a key (and often ignored) part of James's imaginary, and which we find, among others, also in the fourth episode of Krzysztof Kieślowski's *Decalogue*, in which the daughter "honors her father" in the guise of a burning incestuous desire for him. The question is again: is it better not to know certain things? At the end, father and daughter together burn the letter that answers the question if he is really her father, thereby endorsing ignorance as the basis of their relationship—not a lie, but a consensual withdrawal from truth, the attitude of "It's better not to know" the truth about the fatherhood contained in the "letter from an unknown mother" (she was unknown to the daughter, since she died days after giving birth to her). Here, in order to maintain the fragile and delicate libidinal balance of daily life, the letter should *not* reach its destination. In contrast to this solution, Kate, by opening the letter, shows her refusal to "live a lie."

"Let me tell you at once," he returned, "that if you've been moved to correct my ignorance I very particularly request you not to."

She just hesitated. "Are you afraid of the effect of the corrections? Can you only do it by doing it blindly?"

He waited a moment. "What is it that you speak of my doing?"

"Why the only thing in the world that I take you as thinking of. Not accepting—what she has done. Isn't there some regular name in such cases? Not taking up the bequest."

"There's something you forget in it," he said after a moment. "My asking you to join with me in doing so."

Her wonder but made her softer, yet at the same time didn't make her less firm. "How can I 'join' in a matter with which I've nothing to do?"

"How? By a single word."

"And what word?"

"Your consent to my giving up."

"My consent has no meaning when I can't prevent you."

"You can perfectly prevent me. Understand that well," he said.

She seemed to face a threat in it. "You mean you won't give up if I *don't* consent?"

"Yes. I do nothing."

"That, as I understand, is accepting."

Densher paused. "I do nothing formal."

"You won't, I suppose you mean, touch the memory."

"I won't touch the money."

It had a sound—though he had been coming to it—that made for gravity. "Who then in such an event *will?*"

"Any one who wants or who can."

Again a little she said nothing: she might say too much. But by the time she spoke he had covered ground. "How can I touch it but *through* you?"

"You can't. Any more," he added, "than I can renounce it except through you."

"Oh ever so much less! There's nothing," she explained, "in my power."

"I'm in your power," Merton Densher said.

"In what way?"

"In the way I show—and the way I've always shown. When have I shown," he asked as with a sudden cold impatience, "anything else? You surely must feel—so that you needn't wish to appear to spare me in it—how you 'have' me."

"It's very good of you, my dear," she nervously laughed, "to put me so thoroughly up to it!"

"I put you up to nothing. I didn't even put you up to the chance that, as I said a few moments ago, I saw for you in forwarding that thing. Your liberty is therefore in every way complete."

The stakes of the cat-and-mouse game between Kate and Densher in this passage are very precise: they concern the delicate interplay between a formal (explicit) symbolic act and an implicit act of consenting (of accepting by "doing nothing formal"). Densher wants Kate neither to accept Milly's bequest nor to reject it in a grand symbolic gesture, but passively to consent to his not touching the money—to join him in his hypocritical attempt to sell avoidance, escape, as an ethical gesture, to sell the refusal to choose as a choice. In short, Densher wants to *deceive the big Other*, to accomplish a gesture that would not be noted as such by the big Other. The ultimate irony, of course, is that Densher's concluding point—"Your liberty is therefore in every way complete"—names the exact opposite of freedom: the utter cornering of Kate, her total enslavement to the coordinates of his "test." He puts himself into her power in such a way that he totally dominates her: what, in the eyes of the big Other, will look like Kate's free choice should conceal the brutality of a forced choice imposed by him on her.

It had come to the point really that they showed each other pale faces, and that all the unspoken between them looked out of their eyes in a dim terror of their further conflict. Something even rose between them in one of their short silences—something that was like an appeal from each to the other not to be too true. Their necessity was somehow before them, but which of them must meet it first? "Thank you!" Kate said for his word about her freedom, but taking for the minute no further action on it. It was blest at least that all ironies failed them, and during another slow moment their very sense of it cleared the air.

There was an effect of this in the way he soon went on. "You must intensely feel that it's the thing for which we worked together."

She took up the remark, however, no more than if it were commonplace; she was already again occupied with a point of her own. "Is it absolutely true—for if it is, you know, it's tremendously interesting—that you haven't so much as a curiosity about what she has done for you?"

"Would you like," he asked, "my formal oath on it?"

"No—but I don't understand. It seems to me in your place—!"

"Ah," he couldn't help breaking in, "what do you know of my place? Pardon me," he at once added; "my preference is the one I express."

She had in an instant nevertheless a curious thought. "But won't the facts be published?"

"'Published'?"—he winced.

"I mean won't you see them in the papers?"

"Ah never! I shall know how to escape that."

It seemed to settle the subject, but she had the next minute another insistence. "Your desire is to escape everything?"

"Everything."

Here Densher blurts out the lie of his subjective position: his maneuver of putting Kate to the test was done in order for *him* to escape—what, precisely? Confronting the predicament Milly's bequest put him into. It was Densher himself who failed the ethical test—how?

"And do you need no more definite sense of what it is you ask me to help you to renounce?"

"My sense is sufficient without being definite. I'm willing to believe that the amount of money's not small."

"Ah there you are!" she exclaimed.

"If she was to leave me a remembrance," he quietly pursued, "it would inevitably not be meager."

Kate waited as for how to say it. "It's worthy of her. It's what she was herself—if you remember what we once said that was."

He hesitated—as if there had been many things. But he remembered one of them. "Stupendous?"

"Stupendous." A faint smile for it—ever so small—had flickered in her face, but had vanished before the omen of tears, a little less uncertain, had shown themselves in his own. His eyes filled—but that made her continue. She continued gently. "I think that what it really is must be that you're afraid. I mean," she explained, "that you're afraid of all the truth. If you're in love with her without it, what indeed can you be more? And you're afraid—it's wonderful!—to be in love with her."

"I never was in love with her," said Densher.

She took it, but after a little she met it. "I believe that now—for the time she lived. I believe it at least for the time you were there. But your change came—as it might well—the day you last saw her; she died for you then that you might understand her. From that hour you did." With which Kate slowly rose. "And I do now. She did it for us." Densher rose to face her, and she went on with her thought. "I used to call her, in my stupidity—for want of anything better—a dove. Well she stretched out her wings, and it was to that they reached. They cover us."

"They cover us," Densher said.

Here Kate spells out the truth of Densher's betrayal: he feels guilty, and refuses to profit from Milly's death, not because he doesn't love her and is for this reason unworthy of her gift, but because he does love her—not while she was alive, but from the moment she died. He fell in love with her gesture of dying for him and Kate, with how she turned her inevitable death from illness into a sacrificial gesture. Why, precisely, is this a betrayal? Because such love is a fake, a case of what Freud called "moral masochism."

"That's what I give you," Kate gravely wound up. "That's what I've done for you."

His look at her had a slow strangeness that had dried, on the moment, his tears. "Do I understand then—?"

"That I do consent?" She gravely shook her head. "No—for I see. You'll marry me without the money; you won't marry me with it. If I don't consent you don't."

"You lose me?" He showed, though naming it frankly, a sort of awe of her high grasp. "Well, you lose nothing else. I make over to you every penny."

Prompt was his own clearness, but she had no smile this time to spare. "Precisely—so that I must choose."

"You must choose."

Now we finally reach the (ethical) crux of the matter, the terms of the choice Densher with which confronts Kate: not "Here I am, without money; choose me or not!", but

"Me *or* money!"—you can have Milly's money (without me) or me (without money), that is, if you do *not* choose me, you get the money. Kate, however, rejects these terms and imposes her own choice, more radical than that of Sophie: "I want either Densher with money or no Densher no money," which does not mean that she "really wants money"—she wants neither "Densher without money" *nor money without Densher*. For this precise reason, *she* is the only ethical figure in the novel: she chooses losing Densher and money. This choice is possible only within an atheist perspective, it is the sign of a properly atheist ethics.

> Strange it was for him then that she stood in his own rooms doing it, while, with an intensity now beyond any that had ever made his breath come slow, he waited for her act. "There's but one thing that can save you from my choice."
>
> "From your choice of my surrender to you?"
>
> "Yes"—and she gave a nod at the long envelope on the table—"your surrender of that."
>
> "What is it then?"
>
> "Your word of honor that you're not in love with her memory."
>
> "Oh—her memory!"
>
> "Ah"—she made a high gesture—"don't speak of it as if you couldn't be. I could in your place; and you're one for whom it will do. Her memory's your love. You *want* no other."
>
> He heard her out in stillness, watching her face but not moving. Then he only said: "I'll marry you, mind you, in an hour."
>
> "As we were?"
>
> "As we were."
>
> But she turned to the door, and her headshake was now the end. "We shall never be again as we were!"

Why not? Again, because of their shared *knowledge*: they can pretend that nothing happened, but they "shall never be again as [we] were" because the big Other knows it.

James's last novel, *The Golden Bowl*, a true counterpoint to *Wings*, focuses on this strange status of knowledge. If there was ever a work for which the commonplace that, in order to understand it in all its complexity, one has to read it repeatedly, at least twice, does not hold, it is *The Golden Bowl*: it should be read once only. Even if one returns to the novel repeatedly, one should trust the first "confusing" impressions of it— repeated reading tends to cover up its cracks. Here is the summary of the story: Adam Verver, an extremely rich widowed businessman from a nondescript American city, and his daughter Maggie are enjoying an extended stay in Europe, where he is building up a massive art collection which will become the basis of a fine arts museum in his city. Through the matchmaking efforts of Fanny, their American friend living in Europe, Maggie meets and marries Prince Amerigo, an impoverished Italian nobleman. Maggie invites to her wedding Charlotte Stant, an old school friend, also without means; she is unaware that Charlotte and Amerigo were once lovers. Charlotte and Amerigo keep silent about their past affair (in order not to hurt Maggie, or to protect their secret bond?). A day before the wedding, Charlotte secretly meets Amerigo so that they can buy a present for Maggie; she selects a beautiful golden bowl, but Amerigo immediately notices that it is cracked.

After the marriage, Charlotte enters Maggie's household and comes to the attention of Adam; Maggie encourages her father to propose to Charlotte, and they also marry. Even after the arrival of Maggie's child, however, father and daughter remain inseparable. Thrown back upon themselves, Amerigo and Charlotte succumb to their old feelings and, at Charlotte's instigation, renew their affair. Here, the golden bowl reenters the story: by accident, Maggie visits the same store and buys it as a gift for her father. When the shopkeeper, stricken with a bad conscience, pays a call to inform her that the bowl is flawed, has a crack, he notices photographs of Charlotte and Amerigo in her apartment, and tells Maggie about their previous visit to his store. Becoming aware of the secret link between Charlotte and her husband, Maggie does not expose the couple; instead, she maneuvers to keep things under control and steer them her way. She first tells the story of the bowl to Fanny, who, in a gesture of rage, throws the bowl to the floor, wanting to destroy the object which bears witness to such falsity; Maggie admonishes her not to tell her father anything, so that he will not worry. Amerigo, who has overheard Maggie telling the story of the bowl to Fanny, and sees the broken bowl, is confronted by Maggie: he assures her that he loves only her, and wants to live with her. Later, he lies to Charlotte, denying that Maggie knows about their affair. Charlotte suspects a change in Maggie's attitude, and asks her if she holds anything against her; in response, Maggie flatly lies to her, telling her that she holds no grudge against her, and warmly embraces her—at this point, she experiences a strange solidarity with her lying husband.

In order to cut this growing web of protective lies, Maggie and her father, in a paradigmatically Jamesian conversation in which unspoken implications have more weight than direct statements, make a silent pact that he will take Charlotte away to America to save his daughter's marriage: although Adam makes the move of proposing his and Charlotte's departure to Maggie, he is merely conniving with her subtle maneuvering. After learning about this decision, Charlotte lies to Maggie, presenting it as her own: she tells Maggie that it was she who convinced Adam to leave because Maggie opposed their marriage, since father and daughter are in love. To make things easier for her friend, Maggie self-sacrificially lies, falsely admitting the truth of Charlotte's version: she did oppose her father's marriage, but she failed to prevent it. The story thus ends with two broken couples: Adam returns home to what he considers a life in hell, never to see his daughter again; Charlotte is totally devastated, losing her lover forever. Maggie has won: appearances are saved, although there is an emotional desert all around. . . . Maggie, of course, is the hard-willed version of the innocent wife from Wharton's *Age of Innocence*: beneath her fragile, naive and innocent appearance of being in need of protection, there is a steely will to take care of herself and pursue her own goals. This is James's vision of American innocence as opposed to European decadence: it is the European corruption which is weak and all too naive, while American innocence is sustained by a ruthless determination.

In *The Golden Bowl*, we have four main characters who form two times two couples (plus Fanny, who stands for common-sense wisdom, for the "big Other" protective of appearances): there are the two "official" public couples (Amerigo and Maggie, Adam and Charlotte) and the two "unofficial" couples linked by true passion (Amerigo and Charlotte, Adam and Maggie). This constellation opens up the utopian prospect of the four of them—an incestuous couple and a licentious couple—living happily together, accepting their illicit passions. Why is this solution not feasible? Because of the bowl. The bowl of the novel's title is not a symbol à la Grail, a sublime elusive object of lost perfection: it is, rather, again a Hitchcockian object, a little piece of reality which circulates around, the focus of intense libidinal investments. For some readers, the cracked bowl is emblematic of "the relations between the lovers and their legal mates": to all appearances, the world of the two couples is a flawless rare crystal, all of a piece, beautifully gilded with American money, but beneath this appearance there are deep cracks. The cracked bowl is thus what Lacan called the signifier of the barred Other, the embodiment of the falsity of intersubjective relations condensed in it; consequently, we should not treat it primarily as a metaphor but as an agent in and of intersubjective relations: its possession, destruction, the knowledge about its possession, and so on, structure the libidinal landscape.

The first thing to note about this landscape is, of course, that the proverbial Jamesian elliptical procedure, reliance on silences, and so on, is brought to an extreme here. What, however, if this *finesse*, this sticking to politeness at all costs, this game of innuendoes in which the key decisions are often marked merely by a heavy silence, mask— keep at bay—an underlying extreme brutality and violence? The person who stands for extreme consideration, desperately trying not to hurt anyone, ready to do anything to protect his daughter, whom he perceives as fragile, is Adam—this proverbial American "robber baron," a character like a Morgan or a Carnegie, who could be said to have created his wealth in an extremely brutal way, through cheating, bribing, exploiting, and murdering? The reason he feels a need to "give something back" is to cover up for his dark past (not to mention the fact that his attitude toward the works of art he collects is that of possession, not of true sensitivity to their beauty).[16]

We should venture a step further here, and introduce another quintessentially American early-twentieth-century theme: that of incest between a daughter and her rich father. Traces of it are discernible right up to F. Scott Fitzgerald's *Tender Is the Night* and Roman Polanski's film *Chinatown*: the brutal robber baron father exerts his unimpeded right also in the sexual domain, enjoying his precious daughter and ruining her life. It is as if this excess of sexual exploitation is a coded inscription of a wider ruthless economic exploitation—these are "men of power who can do anything they like." And it is significant that the work of Edith Wharton, a feminine counterpart to Henry James if there ever was one, is deeply marked by this topic: among her unpublished texts is "Beatrice Palmato," a short story which describes father-daughter incest in a most explicit hardcore way, with all the details of fellatio, cunnilingus, and so on.[17] Is this not the hidden reference of *The Golden Bowl?* What if, then, the father's protective attitude masks (and thereby symbolizes) the reality of brutal capitalist exploitation and family rape? What if the ultimate protector is a rapist? In *The Golden Bowl*, the incest is not "real"; however, it is as if its intensity is felt in the incestuous proximity of language itself: Maggie and Adam communicate almost telepathically, with no need to formulate their thoughts fully, immediately sensing what the other is aiming at.

The ultimate agent of protection is Adam, ready to do anything to protect the innocence of his daughter—the paradox, however, is that he, the agent of their incestuous passion, is simultaneously the greatest threat to her innocence. Incest is both the ultimate protection (the child remains safe from the traps of social circulation) and the ultimate threat—so it is absolutely logical that the highest sacrifice falls to Adam: the most radical act of protection is for Adam to withdraw his protective shield, to erase himself from the picture, to let his daughter go into the real world, with all its dangers.

When the truth about the bowl comes out, a network of protective lies explodes: all the four characters become ensnared in a web of lies, or of pretending not to know what they know in order not to hurt the other. The two lovers pretend not to know to protect Charlotte and her father; Amerigo lies to Charlotte that Maggie doesn't suspect them in order to save her from guilt; Adam pretends he doesn't suspect anything to make it easier for his daughter; Maggie pretends to oppose Charlotte's marriage to allow her an honorable exit, and so on. Who, then, is protecting whom from what? And who manipulates whom? It may appear that Charlotte and Amerigo manipulate the Ververs in order to continue their illicit affair; what, however, if both Adam and Maggie get married as a cover to go on with their incestuous relationship? Here, the shopkeeper is wrong when he says to Charlotte, who cannot see the crack in the bowl, but suspects it because of its low price: "But if it's something you can't find out, isn't it as good as if it were nothing?" Applied to the libidinal tensions of the novel, this obviously means: if you don't know about the illicit affair, that is as good as there being no affair. But which affair are we talking about here? Adultery or incest? What is ordinary adultery compared with incest? And *who* is the one for whom it holds that if he or she doesn't know, it is "as good as if it were nothing"? This is where things go wrong with all the protective lies: it doesn't matter if he or she knows, what matters is that *others do not know that he or she knows*—if his or her knowledge is not known, it allows him or her to *pretend* not to know, and thus to *keep up appearances*. Ultimately, it is thus the "big Other," the order of social appearances, that should be kept in ignorance: if the big Other doesn't know, it is "as good as if it were nothing." . . .

The parallel with *The Wings of the Dove* is obvious here, and has often been noted: in both stories, the two lovers decide to keep their link secret in order not to hurt the innocent and rich American heiress; in contrast to Kate, however, Charlotte is decidedly not ethical. Neither is she egotistically calculating—she is simply not controlling the situation, being thrown around by her passions. Is it Maggie, then, whose maneuvering is ethical? Is she a new version of Isabel Archer in *The Portrait of a Lady?* Does her act repeat Isabel's decision to remain in a loveless marriage? Here, also, the ethical difference is insurmountable: Maggie in fact does what Isabel is sometimes falsely accused of—get involved in maneuvering in order to maintain social appearances. Robert Pippin is therefore right again: *The Golden Bowl* ends "in a great moral crash."[18] The final dénouement of *The Golden Bowl* offers no solution proper, no act that would tear the web of lies apart, or, in Lacanian terms, would disclose the big Other's nonexistence.

Maggie's act endorses a false ethics of the unspoken whose perfect deployment we find in one of James's truly great short stories, "The Great Condition" (1899): Bertram, who is in love with Mrs. Damerel, is bothered by rumors of her obscure scandalous past. He proposes to her, declaring his readiness to marry her on condition that she tells him all about her past; she accepts, but with a condition of her own—she will tell him the truth about her past six months after their marriage. When the shocked Bertram withdraws, his friend Henry, who is also in love with Mrs. Damerel, proposes to her unconditionally, and they marry. Later, Bertram returns to visit Mrs. Damerel, telling her that he has explored her past and discovered that there are no dark secrets in it. Mrs. Damerel admits that her past is devoid of scandal, but asks him not to tell Henry about it: Henry will never ask her about her past, he considers himself noble for it, so telling him about it would deprive him of his *noblesse.* . . . This logic of refusing to disclose the whole truth, of keeping the secret as a means of maintaining integrity, is profoundly ambivalent: it can be read as indicating Mrs. Damerel's insistence on trust; but it can also be read as manipulation with a feminine secret, as her awareness that the shadow of an illicit mystery enhances the attraction a woman exerts on men. This logic of "feminine mystery" is totally foreign to Kate from *Wings*—no wonder some misdirected feminists dismiss Kate as caught in the masculine logic of exploitative domination, opposing her to Milly's authentically "feminine" attitude of unconstrained giving, of self-sacrificial goodness, of course! Against such deviations, we should insist that Milly is a figure of *male* fantasy, in accordance with Lacan's key thesis according to which "female masochism," far from pertaining to "feminine nature" or to "femininity," is a *male fantasy.*

This is also why Kate cannot accept Densher's "being in love with a memory": it would imply her acceptance of the logic of "to each his or her own small private secret." Take the cliché (which, like all clichés, contains a grain of truth) of the different answers one gets from men or women to the question: "What would you prefer your partner to do? To have sex with another person and, while doing it, fantasize about you, or to have sex only with you and, while doing it, fantasize about other partners?" The majority of men prefer the second option; the majority of women the first. In the same way, Kate is ready to swallow the first option (Densher can sleep with Milly, he should think only about her . . .), she even pushes Densher into it, and rejects the second option (the two of them married, with Densher thinking about Milly) which, for her, the marriage with Densher would have been.

The novel's title which refers to the 55th Psalm ("Oh that I had wings like a dove! For then I would fly away and be at rest") can thus again be read in three ways. The first obvious dove, explicitly referred to as such in the text, is, of course, Milly herself, who flew away and found rest in death. The second dove is Densher, whose desire is "to escape everything"; the true dove, however, is disclosed in the novel's very last line: Kate who, throughout the story, stretched out her wings, covering Milly and Densher with her plot, and then, when Densher or money was at her disposal, turned to the door and left—refusing the choice, she leaves both behind, and flies away forever.

PART II

THE SOLAR PARALLAX:
THE UNBEARABLE LIGHTNESS OF BEING NO ONE

CHAPTER 3

THE UNBEARABLE HEAVINESS OF BEING DIVINE SHIT

At the top of Gellert Hill in the Buda part of Budapest, there is a monument to the liberation of the city by the Red Army in 1945: the gigantic statue of a woman waving an outstretched flag. This statue, usually perceived as an exemplary case of socialist-realist baroque kitsch, was actually made in 1943 on the orders of the Fascist dictator Admiral Horthy to honor his son, who fell on the Russian front fighting the Red Army; in 1945, when Marshal Kliment Voroshilov, the Soviet commander, was shown the statue, he thought it could serve as the monument of liberation . . . does this anecdote not say a lot about the openness of the "message" of a work of art? This plasticity of the alleged meaning of works of art is almost infinite: in the opposite direction to that of the Budapest monument to liberation, the very Shostakovich symphony (Fifth or Seventh) which, at its first performance, was celebrated as the perfect example of the Stalinist Socialist Realism is now interpreted as containing a hidden "dissident" message of mocking and subverting Communist ideology—the gradual progress of the mechanical rhythm of the marching music *à la Bolero* from the first movement of the Seventh Symphony, which was usually interpreted as depicting the cold advance of the German Army into Russia, is now read as the depiction of the mechanically cruel progress of Communism.

Something changes radically here, however, with the advent of modern art. Within the horizon of traditional metaphysics, art is about (beautiful) appearances with elusive and confused meanings, while science is about the reality beneath appearances. In a strange reversal, today's sciences focus more and more on the weird domain of autonomized appearances, of phenomenal processes deprived of any substantial support; no wonder, then, that, in a symmetrical countermovement, modern art is focused more and more on the Real Thing. Is not the most succinct definition of modern art that it is art "beyond the pleasure principle"? We are supposed to enjoy traditional art, it is expected to generate aesthetic pleasure, in contrast to modern art, which causes displeasure—modern art, by definition, *hurts*. In this precise sense, modern art is sublime: it causes pleasure-in-pain, it produces its effect through its own failure, insofar as it refers to the impossible Things.[1] In contrast, beauty, harmonious balance, seems more and more the domain of the sciences: Einstein's theory of relativity, that paradigm of modern science, was praised for its simple elegance—no wonder the title of Brian Greene's bestselling introduction to string theory is *The Elegant Universe*.

The traditional Platonic frame of reference is thus turned around: the sciences deal with phenomena, events, appearances; while the arts deal with the hard Real—this "Real Thing," the struggle to portray it, is the proper "object" of art. In his memoirs, Dmitri Shostakovich dismissed Sergei Prokofiev, his great competitor, as refusing to take historical horrors seriously, always playing a "wise guy." To name just one supreme example, however, Prokofiev's first violin sonata (opus 80) clearly demonstrates the obverse of his (in)famous "irony":

Throughout its four movements . . . one senses a powerful undertow of struggle. Yet it is not the struggle of a work against something outside itself, but rather the struggle of something within the work, unmanifested, trying desperately to break out, and constantly finding its emergence "blocked" by the existing, outward form and language of the piece. This blocking of "something within" . . . has to do with the frustration of a desire for cathartic release into some supremely positive state of being, where meaning—musical and supra-musical—is transparent, un-ironizable: in short, a domain of spiritual "purity."[2]

This is where Prokofiev pays the price for his ironic stance, and it is such passages that bear witness to his artistic integrity: far from representing any kind of vain intellectual superiority, this ironic stance is just the falsely bright obverse of the *failure of Prokofiev's constant struggle to bring the "Thing from Inner Space"* (the *"something within"*) *out*. The superficial "playfulness" of some of his works (like his popular first symphony) merely reveals, in a negative way, the fact that Prokofiev is the ultimate anti-Mozart, a kind of Beethoven whose "titanic struggle" ended in disaster: if Mozart was *the* supreme musical genius, perhaps the last composer with whom the musical Thing transposed itself into a spontaneous flow of notes, and if in Beethoven a piece achieved its definitive Form only after a long heroic struggle with the musical material, Prokofiev's greatest pieces are monuments to the defeat of this struggle.[3]

Is, then, this "Thing from inner space" my inner "genius" (what is in me more than myself, the impersonal force that drives me)?[4] The relationship between this "genius" and my "ego," the core of my being, belongs to a field which has nothing to do with the Freudian unconscious proper or, even more, with the strict philosophical notion of subjectivity. Its proper place is, rather, in the *Lebensphilosophie* and Jungian problematic: man's ego does not cover all of our subjectivity, it is something that can emerge only through a long process of individuation out of and against the background of a vast impersonal field of my "psychic substance," the id in a more Jungian than proper Freudian sense. That is to say: the Freudian Unconscious has nothing to do with the id of *Lebensphilosophie* (and, consequently, the subject of the unconscious has nothing to do with the ego). So what is the subject of the unconscious (or, simply, the subject proper)? Here we should recall Kierkegaard's wonderful short text "On the Difference between Genius and Apostle," where he defines the genius as the individual who is able to express/articulate "that which is in him more than himself," his spiritual substance, in contrast to the apostle who, "in himself," does not matter at all: the apostle is a purely formal function of the one who has dedicated his life to bearing witness to an impersonal Truth that transcends him. He is a messenger who was chosen (by grace): he possesses no inner features that would qualify him for his role. Lacan cites a diplomat who serves as a representative of his country: his idiosyncrasies are irrelevant; whatever he does is read as a message from his country to the country in which he is posted—if, at a big diplomatic conference, he coughs, this is interpreted as softly indicating his state's doubt about the measures debated at the conference, and so on. And Lacan's paradoxical conclusion is that the Freudian "subject of the unconscious" (or what Lacan calls "subject of the signifier") has the structure of the Kierkegaardian apostle: he is the witness of an "impersonal" Truth.

Is not what we encounter in hysteria precisely a "body of truth": in the physical symptoms that result from the hysterical "conversion," the immediate organic body is invaded, kidnapped, by a Truth, transformed into a bearer of truth, into a space/surface onto which the Truths (of the unconscious) are inscribed—hysteria is the ultimate case of Lacan's *c'est moi, la vérité, qui parle*. In short, the structure here is that of a Kierkegaardian apostle: the body is cancelled/suspended as indifferent in its immediate reality, it is taken over as the medium of Truth. And we should not be afraid to draw the line from here to Stalin's notorious words at Lenin's funeral: "We, communists, are not like other people. We are made of a special stuff"—this "special stuff" is precisely the body transubstantiated into the body of truth. In his famous short poem "The Solution" (1953, published in 1956), Brecht mocks the arrogance of the Communist *nomenklatura* faced with the workers' revolt:

> After the uprising of the 17th June
> The Secretary of the Writers' Union
> Had leaflets distributed in the *Stalinallee*
> Stating that the people
> Had forfeited the confidence of the government
> And could win it back only
> By redoubled efforts.
> Would it not be easier
> In that case for the government
> To dissolve the people
> And elect another?[5]

This poem, however, is not only politically opportunistic, the obverse of his letter of solidarity with the East German Communist regime published in *Neues Deutschland* (to put it brutally, Brecht wanted to cover both his flanks, to profess his support for the regime and to hint at his solidarity with the workers, so that whoever won, he would be on the winning side), but also simply *wrong* in the theoretico-political sense: we should bravely admit that it is in fact a duty—even *the* duty—of a revolutionary party to "dissolve the people and elect another," that is, to bring about the transubstantiation of the "old" opportunistic people (the inert "crowd") into a revolutionary body aware of its historical task, to transform the body of the empirical people into a body of Truth. Far from being an easy task, to "dissolve the people and elect another" is the most difficult of all.

Thus we have two couples of opposites which should be strictly distinguished: the axis *ego-id* and the axis *subject-Truth*. The subject has nothing to do with ego as the expression and organizing agency of a reservoir of psychic forces and drives: he is rather, in an almost bureaucratic sense, a functionary of anonymous Truth. When, at the very end of Shakespeare's *The Tempest*, after setting Ariel, his genius, free, Prospero stands alone

("Now my charms are all overthrown, / And what strength I have is mine own"), does he not thereby leave behind not only his genius but also his ego? Does he not enter a different field, that of subjectivity proper? The subject is the one who can say: "What strength I have is mine own." The subject proper is empty, a kind of formal function, a void which remains after I sacrifice my ego (the wealth that constitutes my "person"). The shift from ego to subject, from the axis *ego-id* to the axis *subject-Truth*, is synonymous with the emergence of the ethical dimension proper: I change from an individual, a person, into a subject the moment I turn into the agent of an impersonal Truth, the moment I accept as my task the endless work of bearing witness to this truth.[6] As such, I am nothing in myself: my entire authority is that of Truth—or, as Kierkegaard put it apropos of Christ: with regard to their content, Christ's positive statements are no more profound than the statements of an average student of theology; what accounts for the abyss that separates them is that one was the ultimate apostle of Truth, while the other was not. Here the structure is extremely "dogmatic": what matters is who said it, not what he said.

This may appear to contradict my previous point that what matters is Truth, not the subject propagating it; that, however, is the paradox of the authority of Truth: Truth is characterized not by the inherent features of true propositions, but by the mere formal fact that these propositions were spoken from the *position* of Truth. Consequently, in an exact parallel to the fact that the subject is a pure messenger, an apostle of Truth, irrespective of his inherent properties, Truth itself is not a property of statements, but *that which makes them true*. Truth is like ready-made art: an *urinoir* is a work of art when it occupies the place of a work of art—no material property distinguishes Duchamp's *urinoir* from the *urinoir* in a nearby public lavatory.

What, then, is this "thing from inner space," insofar as it stands for Truth as *agency*? The famous "stolen boat" episode from Wordsworth's *Prelude* provides the precise coordinates of its emergence:

> One summer evening (led by her [Nature]) I found
> A little boat tied to a willow tree
> Within a rocky cave, its usual home.
> Straight I unloosed her chain, and stepping in
> Pushed from the shore. It was an act of stealth
> And troubled pleasure, nor without the voice
> Of mountain-echoes did my boat move on;
> Leaving behind her still, on either side,
> Small circles glittering idly in the moon,
> until they melted all into one track
> Of sparkling light. But now, like one who rows,
> Proud of his skill, to reach a chosen point
> With an unswerving line, I fixed my view
> Upon the summit of a craggy ridge,
> The horizon's utmost boundary; far above
> Was nothing but the stars and the grey sky.

She was an elfin pinnace; lustily
I dipped my oars into the silent lake,
And, as I rose upon the stroke, my boat
Went heaving through the water like a swan;
When, from behind that craggy steep till then
The horizon's bound, a huge peak, black and huge,
As if with voluntary power instinct,
Upreared its head. I struck and struck again,
And growing still in stature the grim shape
Towered up between me and the stars, and still,
For so it seemed, with purpose of its own
And measured motion like a living thing,
Strode after me. With trembling oars I turned,
And through the silent water stole my way
Back to the covert of the willow tree;
There in her mooring-place I left my bark,
And through the meadows homeward went, in grave
And serious mood; but after I had seen
That spectacle, for many days, my brain
Worked with a dim and undetermined sense
Of unknown modes of being; o'er my thoughts
There hung a darkness, call it solitude
Or blank desertion. No familiar shapes
Remained, no pleasant images of trees,
Of sea or sky, no colours of green fields;
But huge and mighty forms, that do not live
Like living men, moved slowly through the mind
By day, and were a trouble to my dreams.

It is clear what "actually happens" in this episode: the young boy was the victim of an optical illusion:

> When he rowed away from the cave the boy had fixed his gaze upon the top of a ridge, behind which there initially seemed to be nothing but the sky. As he rowed further out on to the lake, however, a more distant peak, behind the ridge, came into view. The further he is from the shore (and his first instinct is to row faster: "I struck, and struck again") the more he can see of the mountain; it therefore seemed to be "growing still in stature." There is, then, an extremely rational explanation for what the boy sees. His imagination, however, transforms the mountain into a "living thing" which "strode after me."[7]

This is how a "thing from the inner space" emerges. All the ingredients of a fantasy-staging are here—the noumenal "shines through" in what is "in fact" just an optical illusion. That is to say: far from being a simple descendant of the Kantian Thing-in-itself, the Freudian "Thing from the Inner Space" is its inherent opposite: what appears to be the excess of some transcendent force over "normal" external reality is the very place of the direct inscription of my subjectivity into this reality. In other words, what I get back in the guise of the horrifying-irrepresentable Thing is the objectivization, the objectal correlate, of my own gaze—as Wordsworth put it, the Thing is the "sober colouring" reality gets from the eye observing it:

> The Clouds that gather round the setting sun
> Do take a sober colouring from an eye
> That hath kept watch o'er man's mortality.[8]

From this perspective of the Thing as Evil, one should perhaps turn around the well-known Augustinian notion of Evil as having no positive substance or force of its own, but being merely the absence of Good: *Good itself is the absence of Evil*, the distance toward the Evil Thing. To put it in transcendental terms: Good is the mode of appearance of Evil, "schematized" Evil. The difference between Good and Evil is thus a parallax.

We can observe a similar phenomenon—that of an unfathomable, almost imperceptible, *je ne sais quoi* which accounts for a big difference—in contemporary painting. What characterizes some of Gerhard Richter's paintings is the sudden passage from (slightly transposed/blurred, true) photographic realism to a pure abstraction of color stains, or the opposite passage from an utterly object-less texture of stains to realist representation—as if, all of a sudden, we found ourselves on the opposite side of a Moebius strip. Richter focuses on that mysterious moment when a picture emerges out of chaos (or, again, the opposite moment: when a clear mirror-image gets blurred into meaningless stains). And this brings us to Lacan's *objet petit a*, which is precisely that imponderable X that makes a consistent pictural representation out of a texture of stains, as in the famous scene toward the end of 2001, *a Space Odyssey*, when the surreal play of intense abstract visual movements turns into a hyperrealist representation of fantasy-space. Here Richter inverts the normal relationship: in his paintings, photographic realism strikes us as artificial, constructed, while there is much more "natural life" in the interplay of "abstract" forms and stains. It is as if the confused intensity of nonrepresentative shapes is the last remainder of reality, so that when we pass from it to clearly identifiable representation, we enter the aetheric fantasy-space in which reality is irretrievably lost. The shift is purely parallactic: not so much a shift in the object as a shift in our attitude toward the viewed object.

For this reason, Richter is not simply a postmodern artist; his work is, rather, a kind of meta-commentary on the very split between (or passage from) modernism and (to) postmodernism. Or, to put it another way: consider the two works which stand for the inaugural gesture of the modernist break in the visual arts: Marcel Duchamp's ready-made display of a bicycle and Kazimir Malevich's black square on a white background; these two extremes are related in a way that recalls the Hegelian speculative identity of opposites. And does Richter not endeavor precisely to capture the very *passage* between these two extremes—in his case from photographic realism to the abstraction of the purely formal minimal distinction?[9]

This is where modern art meets ancient epic. *Kalevala*, the epic poem that put into words the very core of Finnish identity, is composed in so-called "Kalevala meter": its most characteristic features are unrhymed, nonstrophic trochaic tetrameters, with alliteration of lines and "echo" lines. This is called parallelism: the technique of re-phrasing the previous line in the current line, with a different accent or perspective— to quote the very beginning of the poem (in the old translation by W. F. Kirby):

> I am driven by my longing,
> And my understanding urges,
> That I should commence my singing,
> And begin my recitation,
> I will sing the people's legends,
> And the ballads of the nation.
> To my mouth the words are flowing,
> And the words are gently falling . . .
> Dearest friend, and much-loved brother,
> Best beloved of all companions,
> Come and let us sing together,
> Let us now begin our converse,
> Since at length we meet together,
> From two widely sundered regions,
> Rarely can we meet together,
> Rarely one can meet the other,
> In these dismal Northern regions,
> In the dreary land of Pohja.
> Let us clasp our hands together,
> Let us interlock our fingers;
> Let us sing a cheerful measure,
> Let us use our best endeavors,
> While our dear ones hearken to us,
> And our loved ones are instructed,
> While the young are standing round us,
> Of the rising generation,
> Let them learn the words of magic,
> And recall our songs and legends. . . .

The second and third strophes of this introductory canto provide the material staging of how *Kalevala* was recited at public gatherings; this staging literally enacts the paral-lelism of the text: two singers sat on a bench and held hands; one of them sang a line with eight syllables, then the other took over and sang the same thing, but with dif-ferent words in his eight syllables, while their bodies waved rhythmically in a poetic trance—does this strange staging not present parallax at its purest, the endeavor to en-circle/discern the unfathomable gap of the Difference by repeatedly formulating both perspectives? When, later in the poem, we read: "Might I say something / Would I be allowed to ask / What kind of man you may be / What sort of fellow?", the Thing is the very X that occurs between "Might I say" and "Would I be allowed to ask," between "What kind of man" and "What sort of fellow."

If ever there was a writer of minimal difference, it is Juan José Saer. The "action" of his *Nobody Nothing Never* (*Nadie nada nunca*, 1980), a masterpiece of pure parallax, is minimal, practically nonexistent: during a stifling Argentinian summer, Cat Garay, heir to a once prosperous, now decaying family, and his lover Elisa try to protect their horse from a horse-killer on the loose; their intense affair and the hunt for the killer on the banks of the Paraná river take place in an atmosphere of political anxiety and disintegration. The story progresses so that every event is told twice, first in the voice of an "objective" narrator, then in Cat's voice—with the same phrases often repeated verbatim. Is this not like Malevich's *Black Square on White Background*, the marking of a purely formal minimal difference, gap, against the background of the "nothing" of narrated content? We are dealing here not with a substantial difference between two particular contents but with a "pure" difference that separates an object from itself and that, as such, marks the point at which the subject's gaze is inscribed into the perceived object. The same minimal difference is the point around which the poems of Alejandra Pizarnik, another superb Argentinian writer, turn. Three short poems from her supreme achievement, *Arbol de Diana* / *Tree of Diana* (1962), which display to the full her succinct, almost Zen-like precision—

like a poem buried in [*enterrado del*: by]
the silence of things
you speak to ignore me [*para no verme*: in order not to see me][10]

far beyond any forbidden zone
is a mirror for our sad reflections [*transparencia*][11]

This song of regret [*arrepentido*], alert, behind my poems:
This song denies me, chokes my voice.[12]

—are interconnected in a way which becomes discernible if we add a line from "Signs," a poem from a later collection, *El infierno musical* / *The Musical Hell* (1971): "Everything makes love with silence."[13]

Pizarnik is arguably the poet of subtraction, of minimal difference: the difference between nothing and something, between silence and a fragmented voice. The primordial fact is not Silence (waiting to be broken by the divine Word) but Noise, the confused murmur of the Real in which there is not yet any distinction between figure and background. The first creative act is therefore to *create silence*—it is not that silence is broken, but that silence itself breaks, interrupts, the continuous murmur of the Real, thus opening up a clearing in which words can be spoken. There is no speech proper without this background of silence: as Heidegger knew, all speech answers the "sound of silence." Hard work is needed to create silence, to encircle its place in the way a vase creates its central void. This is how the death drive and sublimation are strictly correlative: the death drive has first to erase the murmur of the Real, and thus open up the space for sublime formations. With regard to poetry, this difference is not between poems, but between poem(s) and the song which, of course, has to remain unsung, unspoken, since it is the song of silence.

This is where the visual dimension comes in; remember Nietzsche's complaint: "Must one smash their ears before they learn to listen with their eyes?" (*Thus Spake Zarathustra*, Prologue, 5.) Is not this complaint about the difficulty of teaching people how to listen ambiguous? Does it mean that it is difficult to learn to *listen with one's eyes*, or that it is simply difficult to learn to *truly listen*? In other words, if we follow Wagner's Tristan (who, while dying, shouts: "I see her [Isolde's] voice!") and accept, as one of the definitions of modern art, that one has to listen to it with one's eyes, does this mean that we can truly hear (hear the silence, the silent Message-Thing covered up by the chatter of words) only with our eyes? consequently, is modern painting (as suggested by Munch's *Scream*) not a "sound of silence," the visual rendering of the point at which words break down? Incidentally, this is also how the critique of ideology (whose Platonic origins we should frankly admit) functions: it endeavors to smash our ears (hypnotized by ideology's siren song) so that we can start to hear with our eyes (in the mode of *theoria*).

Back to Pizarnik: avoiding fake obscurantism, we should not be afraid to read these four fragments "logically," as parts of a complex *argument*, providing clues for each other. So let us begin with the last line, "Everything makes love with silence": this, of course, does not mean that there is a sexual relationship between Something and Nothing, but, precisely, its failure: this lovemaking is failed. That is to say: the voice of silence, that of "a poem buried in the silence of things," is not a silent support, protective and caring of the poet's words, but that which speaks "to ignore" the poet, a brutal malevolently neutral entity which "alert, behind my poems . . . denies me, chokes my voice." So when Pizarnik refers to this song of silence as a "mirror for our sad reflections," located "far beyond any forbidden zone," this, again, makes it an inaccessible threatening entity, in Kantian terms: a song which dwells in the terrifying noumenal domain of the Real in which a kind of "objective" truth (or, rather, a totally objectifying knowledge) about me is inscribed.

In order to clarify this key point, let us recall a wonderful scene in *The Matrix*, where Cipher, the traitor, the agent of the Matrix among the rebels, who is located in reality, kills one rebel after another (they are immersed in the VR of the Matrix) simply by unplugging them from the connection to the machine. While the rebels are experiencing themselves as fully immersed in ordinary reality, they are in fact in the "desert of the Real," immobilized on the chair on which they are connected to the Matrix: Cipher has a direct physical approach to them as they "really are," helpless creatures just sitting on the chair as if under anesthetic at the dentist's, who can be mishandled in any way the torturer wants. Cipher is communicating with them via the phone which serves as the communicating link between virtual reality and the "desert of the Real," and the horror of the situation is that, while the rebels feel like normal human beings freely walking around in reality, they know that, at the Other Scene of the "desert of the Real," a simple unplugging of the cable will cause then to drop dead in both universes, virtual and real. This situation, while it is parallel to that of all humans who are plugged into the Matrix, is worse insofar as here, humans are fully aware not only of their true situation, but also of the threat posed in reality by the evil agent who intends to kill them soon. It is as if the subjects obtain here the impossible direct link with the Real of their situation, the Real in all its threatening dimensions. This Other Scene is "a mirror for our sad reflections . . . far beyond any forbidden zone."

This, of course, brings us back to Plato's cave: how can we survive a direct confrontation with the Sun, the ultimate Real, without getting burned by the rays of its heat? Among poets, it was Hölderlin who focused on the risks of this confrontation, paying for it the highest price of madness. And we are in a domain in which the fall into madness has a clear political connotation. Georg Lukács should be consulted here—take "Hölderlin's *Hyperion*," his weird but crucial, short essay (1935), in which Lukács praises Hegel's endorsement of the Napoleonic Thermidor against Hölderlin's intransigent fidelity to the heroic revolutionary utopia:

> Hegel comes to terms with the post-Thermidorian epoch and the close of the revolutionary period of bourgeois development, and he builds up his philosophy precisely on an understanding of this new turning-point in world history. Hölderlin makes no compromise with the post-Thermidorian reality; he remains faithful to the old revolutionary ideal of renovating "polis" democracy and is broken by a reality which has no place for his ideals, not even on the level of poetry and thought.[14]

Here Lukács is referring to Marx's notion that the heroic period of the French Revolution was the necessary enthusiastic breakthrough followed by the unheroic phase of market relations: the true social function of the Revolution was to establish the conditions for the prosaic reign of bourgeois economy, and true heroism consists not in blindly clinging to the early revolutionary enthusiasm, but in recognizing "the rose in the cross of the present," as Hegel liked to paraphrase Luther—that is, in abandoning the position of the Beautiful Soul and fully accepting the present as the only possible domain of actual freedom. It is thus this "compromise" with social reality which enabled Hegel's crucial philosophical step forward, that of overcoming the proto-Fascist notion of "organic" community in his *System der Sittlichkeit* manuscript, and engaging in the dialectical analysis of the antagonisms of bourgeois civil society. (That is the properly dialectical paradox of the proto-Fascist endeavor to return to a premodern "organic" community: far from being simply "reactionary," Fascist "feudal Socialism" is a kind of compromise solution, an ersatz attempt to build socialism within the constraints of capitalism itself.)

It is obvious that this analysis by Lukács is deeply allegorical: it was written a couple of months after Trotsky launched his thesis of Stalinism as the Thermidor of the October Revolution. Lukács's text has thus to be read as an answer to Trotsky: he accepts Trotsky's characterization of Stalin's regime as "Thermidorian," giving it a positive twist—instead of bemoaning the loss of utopian energy, we should, in a heroically resigned way, accept its consequences as the only actual space of social progress. . . . For Marx, of course, the sobering "day after" which follows the revolutionary intoxication marks the original limitation of the "bourgeois" revolutionary project, the falsity of its promise of universal freedom: the "truth" is that universal human rights are the rights of commerce and private property. If we read Lukács's endorsement of the Stalinist Thermidor, it implies (arguably against his conscious intention) an utterly anti-Marxist pessimistic perspective: the proletarian revolution itself is also characterized by the gap between its illusory universal assertion of freedom and the ensuing awakening in the new relations of domination and exploitation, which means that the Communist project of realizing "actual freedom" failed.

Hölderlin's starting point is the same as Hegel's: how are we to overcome the gap between (the impossible return to) traditional organic unity and modern reflective freedom? His answer is what he calls the "eccentric path": the insight into how the very endless oscillation between the two poles, the very impossibility of and repeated failure to reach final peace, is already the thing itself, that is, this eternal way is man's fate. Hölderlin fails, however, to accomplish the next properly Hegelian step into the true speculative unity of the two poles: his limitation is best epitomized by the title of his philosophical fragment, "Being and Judgment (Ur-Teil, primordial division)." Being is for Hölderlin the always-already lost prereflexive Ground to which we eternally long to return—what he does not do is conclude that this very presupposed Ground is already retroactively posited and, as such, already (a name for) *pure difference*. In short, what eludes Hölderlin is the true nature of Hegelian Universality as the site of the structural deadlock, of an impasse which particular formations endeavor to resolve. It is for this reason that, toward 1800, he definitely turns to poetry as the most appropriate way to express the "eccentric path" of man—so, in his case at least, the turn to poetry is an escape, an index of the failure to accomplish the work of thought.

The solution of *Hyperion* is that of a narrative: what cannot be reconciled in reality is reconciled afterward, through its narrative reconstruction. (The interesting and crucial feature of *Hyperion*, this novel composed of letters, is that all the letters are written after the "actual" events.) Is it then adequate to read this solution as *Hegelian*: to claim that, in a clear parallel to Hegel's *Phenomenology of Spirit*, Hölderlin sees the solution in a narrative which retroactively reconstructs the very "eccentric path" of permanent oscillation between the loss of the Center and the repeated failed attempts to regain the immediacy of the Center as the process of maturation, of spiritual education? Read in this way, Hölderlin's later shift can easily be interpreted as a farewell to the metaphysics of subjectivity, as breaking out of the metaphysical closure and assuming an irreducible gap covered by metaphysics. The model for such a reading is Eric Santner's book on Hölderlin: for Santner, the break of Hölderlin's later work occurs when this narrative synthesis and *Aufhebung* of the tension is threatened, even abandoned, by the "sober" acceptance of an irreducible multitude which can no longer be reconciled in an overall narrative scheme. And, as Santner points out, this abandonment of the encompassing narrative frame leads not to an abandonment of links between fragments but to a discovery of new level of interconnectedness, a "paratactic" field of secret links, of echoes and reverberations between monadic elements—something, I am tempted to claim, not unlike the inner links of Plato's *chora* which precede the grid of Ideas.[15]

Here we should introduce a triple, not just a bipolar, structure: the narrative procedure is neither the direct exposure to "fire from heaven" (the ecstatic throwing-oneself into the lethal bliss of the divine Thing) nor the deadly sobriety of icy everyday life, with its meaningless multiplicity, but a mediation of the multiplicity itself. In other words, while Santner locates the "narrative vigilance" on the side of the "fire from heaven," treating it exclusively as a defense against the dispersed multitude of sober and icy ordinary life, would it not be even more appropriate to treat it as a defense against the ecstatic dissolution of all structure in the "fire from heaven," as an attempt to retain a minimal structure of life? Is narrative not ultimately a narrative about what Hölderlin called the "law of succession," the paternal symbolic order which keeps the chaotic abyss of the Sacred at a proper distance?[16] Furthermore, are not paratactic coexistence and a mystical experience of Oneness on the same side, both opposed to narrative organization? Is not the ecstatic experience of Oneness something which emerges only when we step outside the grid of a narrative and confront absolutely particular monadic entities?

The shift in Hölderlin, deployed by Santner, from "narrative vigilance"—from subordinating everything to the grand narrative of the westward movement of gods and laying the foundations for the arrival of new gods—to "sobriety," to the marking of the signs of daily life, can be perfectly accounted for in the Heideggerian terms of the shift from onto-theology, from an all-encompassing metaphysical narrative, to the postmetaphysical attitude of *Gelassenheit*, of "letting things be" outside any frame of metaphysical justification, like Angelus Silesius's rose, which is "ohne Warum."[17] The irony here, however, is double. First, Santner himself develops this shift in a book which totally ignores Heidegger (and to write a book on Hölderlin ignoring Heidegger is an achievement in itself). Secondly, Heidegger himself, in his detailed readings of Hölderlin, also ignores this "Heideggerian" aspect of the texture of Hölderlin's poetry—the paratactic disintegration of narrative unity—and focuses precisely on the grand narrative of the withdrawal and possible arrival of new gods.

What if we read Hölderlin's shift as a shift from desire to drive? "Vigilance" is the vigilance for partial objects around which drives circulate. Such a reading has a precise sociopolitical background: we should approach Hölderlin's openness toward the signs of everyday life through the perspective of one of the key features of capitalism, namely, the permanent production of piles of waste. The obverse of the incessant capitalist drive to produce new and newer objects is thus the growing piles of useless waste, piled-up mountains of used cars, computers, and so on, like the famous airplane "resting place" in the Mojave desert—in these ever-growing piles of inert, disfunctional "stuff," whose useless, inert presence cannot fail to strike us, we can, as it were, perceive the capitalist drive at rest. Here we should think of Benjamin's insight into how we encounter historicity proper precisely when we observe cultural artifacts in decay, in the process of being reclaimed by nature.

In November 2003, after a visit to Poland where he participated in the Camerimage festival and opened an exhibition of his own paintings and sculptures in Łódź, David Lynch was absolutely fascinated by this truly "postindustrial" city: the big industrial center, with most of the steel works and other factories in decay, full of crumbling gray concrete housing developments, with extremely polluted air and water. . . . Lynch wants to invest money to create his own cinema studio there, and help to transform Łódź into a thriving center of cultural creativity (Peter Weir and Roland Joffe are also linked to this project). Lynch emphasized that he "feels very much at home in Poland"—not in the Romantic Poland of Chopin and Solidarność, but precisely in this ecologically ruined Poland of industrial wasteland. This news confirms once more Lynch's extraordinary sensitivity on account of which we should be ready to forget his reactionary political statements, as well as his ridiculous support for the megalomaniac New Age project of a mega-center for meditation. The postindustrial wasteland of the Second World is in effect the privileged "evental site," the symptomal point out of which one can undermine the totality of today's global capitalism. We should love this world, even its gray decaying buildings and its sulfurous smell—all this stands for history, threatened with erasure between the posthistorical First World and prehistorical Third World.

Halldor Laxness's World Light[18] is, in effect, a kind of twenty-first-century counterpart to Hölderlin's Hyperion: its hero, a poor second-rate local poet, but utterly dedicated to his art, is also "burned by the sun," ending his life (and the novel) with a suicidal march toward the icy Sun of the Glacier, this Nordic Thing. In the tradition of "Leftist Hölderlin," the novel focuses on the tension between the two fascinations by the Thing: the poetic Thing, which culminates in its deadly embrace; and the political Thing, the growing sense of injustice generating the need for a revolutionary outburst. Laxness was (for most of his life) a committed Communist and deeply marked by the experience of poetico-mystical withdrawal from external reality into the inner "Night of the World." What distinguishes his work is the refined entanglement of the two processes: in contrast to the rich exploiters involved in cheap spiritualist experiments, the authentic poetico-mystical experience emerges out of abject material poverty, when the hero is reduced to less than bare survival, and his utter pain and starvation, as well as social exclusion and humiliation, push him to withdraw from reality into the domain of preontological hallucinatory freedom.[19]

The greatness of Laxness's two key novels, World Light and the earlier Independent People, unquestionably his masterpiece, is that they resist the temptation to cover up the gap that forever separates these two dimensions. Laxness avoids both traps: the standard opposition of the two dimensions ("dreaming poets versus revolutionaries") and their utopian unification ("Lenin with Dadaists"). While the two can never meet, there is nonetheless a deep solidarity in tension here, a true love-relationship of the Twosome—in short, another case of parallax where the two elements can never meet precisely because they are one and the same element in two different spaces. This parallax tension is the truth of the pro-democratic "Lacanian" argument which starts with the (highly problematic) homology between the ideal of a fully emancipated self-transparent

Society and the fullness of the maternal Thing—the old story of how revolutionaries who endeavor to establish a perfect society want to return to the safety of the incestuous maternal Thing. From this illegitimate short circuit, it is then easy to go on to the further parallel between the Lacanian symbolic Law prohibiting direct access to the Thing and the "democratic invention" (Claude Lefort) in which the central place of Power is also empty: in both cases, the Thing is prohibited, its place is empty, and the same danger lurks: that of direct contact with the Thing (libidinal incest, political totalitarianism). . . .

Against this external homology, parallelism, between the two ways to relate to the Thing, one should go on to their metonymic enchainment: the true question is not that of the *parallel* between libidinal incest and political totalitarianism, but that of in what exact conditions a political process has to mobilize the libidinal economy of ecstatic direct relating to the Thing ("the Thing-Cause itself acts through us"). Here, it is again crucial to bear in mind the noncontemporaneity of these two levels: just as Germany in the late eighteenth century was able to produce the philosophical revolution-counterpart to the French Revolution precisely because the political revolution did not take place there, politics itself acquires the features of a direct ecstatic relating to the Thing precisely when such a relating does *not* take place at the individual-mystical level (and vice versa, as the case of the monstrous Père Joseph, Cardinal Richelieu's foreign policy executioner, demonstrates: intense personal-mystical relating to the Thing is fully compatible with the most ruthless political manipulation and calculation).

Laxness's late masterpiece *Under the Glacier* (from 1968) gives a different twist to this topic of the proximity to the Thing embodied in the glacier (anyone who visits Vatna-jökull in the southeast of Iceland cannot escape the impression that he is in the proximity of the Thing: giant ribs of white-brown thousands-of-years-old ice laid bare due to the gradual melting of the surface snow are just like the carcass of a primordial Animal of biblical proportions). "Embi," a young priest from Reykjavik, is sent to a small town under the glacier to investigate reports about the strange things going on in the local parish: a kind of alternative community has arisen, ignoring all traditional Christian rules, creating its own utopian space of liberated, noninstitutionalized spirituality, "a freakish enchanted kingdom with an alternative normality."[20] Even if a sympathetic introduction to its English translation was the last piece Susan Sontag finished only days before her death, we should reject the notion that *Under the Glacier* is a regression to New Age neopaganism. Pastor Jon abdicated his authority by ceasing to perform the duties of a minister and choosing instead to be a mechanic, but he has actually sought access to a much larger authority—mystical, cosmic, galactic. No wonder, then, that, in this alternative kingdom, not even the benevolent Matriarch is absent: Ua, who

gives her age as 52, which makes her twice as old as Embi (the young priest-reporter)—the same difference of age, she points out, as Saint Theresa and San Juan de la Cruz when they first met—but in fact she is a shape-shifter, immortal. Eternity in the form of a woman. Ua has been pastor Jon's wife (although she is a Roman Catholic), the madam of a brothel in Buenos Aires, a nun, and countless other identities. She appears to speak all the principal languages. She knits incessantly: mittens, she explains, for the fisher-men of Peru. Perhaps most peculiarly, she has been dead, conjured into a fish and pre-served up on the glacier until a few days earlier, has now been resurrected by pastor Jon, and is about to become Embi's lover.[21]

PICK UP YOUR CAVE!

The Platonic reference to the Sun in Hölderlin and Laxness should not deceive us: the overproximity of the Sun undermines the very coordinates of Plato's ontology. Where do we stand today with regard to Plato? Here is the basic outline of Plato's allegory of the cave (*Republic*, 514a–520a). Imagine prisoners chained since childhood deep inside a cave: not only are their limbs immobilized by the chains, their heads are as well, so that their eyes are fixed on a wall. Behind the prisoners is an enormous fire, and be-tween the fire and the prisoners there is a raised way, along which men carry shapes of various animals, plants, and other things. The shapes cast shadows on the wall, which occupy the prisoners' attention. Also, when one of the shape-carriers speaks, an echo against the wall causes the prisoners to believe that the words come from the shadows. The prisoners engage in what appears to us to be a game: naming the shapes as they come by. This, however, is the only reality they know, even though they are see-ing mere shadows of shapes. Suppose a prisoner is released, and compelled to stand up and turn around. His eyes will be blinded by the firelight, and the passing shapes will appear less real than their shadows. Similarly, if he is dragged up out of the cave into the sunlight, his eyes will be so blinded that he will not be able to see anything; at first, he will be able to see darker shapes such as shadows, and only later brighter and brighter objects. The last object he would be able to see is the sun, which, in time, he would learn to perceive as the cause of all the things he has seen. Once thus en-lightened, the freed prisoner would no doubt want to return to the cave to free his fel-low bondsmen; the problem, however, is that they would not want to be freed: descending back into the cave would require that the freed prisoner's eyes adjust again, and for a time he would be inferior at the ludicrous process of identifying shapes on the wall. This would make his fellow prisoners murderous toward anyone who at-tempted to free them.

As is always the case with allegories, the literal texture of Plato's narrative threatens to overflow its later interpretations, so that we are constantly forced to make choices: how literally are we to take the literal texture? What are features to be interpreted, and what mere details of imagination? For example, are the puppeteers who deal with the shapes political manipulators, so that Plato is also proposing an implicit theory of ide-ological manipulation, or are we, cavemen, directly deluding ourselves? There is a deeper problem here, however, which could be best put in Hegel's terms. We can, of course, start with the naive notion of people perceiving true reality from a limited/distorted perspective, and thus constructing in their imagination false idols which they mistake for the real thing; the problem with this naive notion is that it reserves for us the external position of a neutral observer who can, from his safe place, compare true reality with its distorted mis(perception). What gets lost here is that all of us *are* these people in the cave—so how can we, immersed in the cave's spectacle, step onto our own shoulder, as it were, and gain insight into true reality? Is it that we should look for small inconsistencies in the realm of the shadows, which provide a hint that what we take for reality is an artificial spectacle (as in a scene from *The Matrix*, in which a cat runs across a threshold twice, drawing attention to a glitch in the functioning of the Matrix)? Whatever the case, we, the cavemen, have to work hard to arrive at some idea of the "true reality" outside the cave—the true substance, the *presupposition*, of our world is in this sense *always-already posited*, it is the result of a long process of distilling, extracting, the core of reality from the flurry of deceiving shadows.

Perhaps, however, we should risk a different approach, and read Plato's parable as a myth in Lévi-Straussian sense, so that we have to look for its meaning not through direct interpretation but, rather, by locating it in a series of variations: that is, by comparing it with other variations on the same story. The elementary frame of so-called "postmodernism" can in fact be conceived as a network of three modes of inversion of Plato's allegory. First, there is the inversion of the meaning of the central source of light (sun): what if this center is a kind of Black Sun, a terrifying monstrous Evil Thing, and for this reason impossible to sustain? Second, what if (along the lines of Peter Sloterdijk's *Spheres*) we invert the meaning of the cave: it is cold and windy out in the open, on the earth's surface, too dangerous to survive there, so people themselves decided to dig out the cave to find a shelter/home/sphere? In this way, the cave appears as the first model of building a home, a safe isolated place of dwelling—building one's cave is what distinguishes us from the beasts, it is the first act of civilization. . . . Finally, there is the standard postmodern variation: the true myth is precisely the notion that, outside the theater of shadows, there is some "true reality" or a central Sun—all there is are different theaters of shadows and their endless interplay. The properly Lacanian twist to the story would have been that for us, within the cave, the Real outside can appear only as a *shadow of a shadow*, as a gap between different modes or domains of shadows. It is thus not simply that substantial reality disappears in the interplay of appearances; what happens in this shift, rather, is that the very irreducibility of the appearance to its substantial support, its "autonomy" with regard to it, engenders a Thing of its own, the true "real Thing."

In his *Being No One*, Thomas Metzinger[22] proposes a further brain-sciences variation: Plato was right—with the proviso that *there is no one (no observing subject) in the cave*. The cave, rather, projects *itself* (its entire machinery) onto the screen: the theater of shadows works as the self-representation (self-model) of the cave. In other words, the observing subject itself is also a shadow, the result of the mechanism of representation: the "Self" stands for the way a human organism experiences itself, appears to itself, and there is no one behind the veil of self-appearance, no substantial reality:

> The illusion is irresistible. Behind every face there is a self. We see the signal of consciousness in a gleaming eye and imagine some ethereal space beneath the vault of the

skull, lit by shifting patterns of feeling and thought, charged with intention. An *essence*. But what do we find in that space behind the face, when we look?

The brute fact is there is nothing but material substance: flesh and blood and bone and brain. . . . You look down into an open head, watching the brain pulsate, watching the surgeon tug and probe, and you understand with absolute conviction that there is nothing more to it. There's no one there.[23]

Is this not the ultimate parallax—this absolute gap between the experience of encountering somebody and the "nothing behind" of the open skull? It seems that, with this cognitivist naturalization of the human mind, the process described by Freud as the progressive humiliations of man in modern sciences reached its apogee.

COPERNICUS, DARWIN, FREUD . . . AND MANY OTHERS

The story of the three successive humiliations of man, the three "narcissistic illnesses" ("Copernicus-Darwin-Freud"), is more complex than it may appear. The first thing to note is that the latest scientific breakthroughs seem to add a whole series of further "humiliations" which radicalize the first three, so that, as Peter Sloterdijk has perspicuously noted, with regard to today's "brain sciences," psychoanalysis seems, rather, to belong to the traditional "humanist" field threatened by the latest humiliations. Is the proof not the predominant reaction of psychoanalysts to the latest advances in brain sciences? Their defense of psychoanalysis often reads as just another variation of the standard philosophico-transcendental gesture of pointing out how a positive science can never encompass and account for the very horizon of meaning within which it is operative. . . . There are, however, some complications to this image.

The first one: from the very beginning of modernity, humiliation, "narcissistic illness," seems to generate a sense of superiority, paradoxically grounded in the very awareness of the miserable character of our existence. As Pascal put it in his inimitable way, man is a mere insignificant speck of dust in the infinite universe, but he knows about his nullity, and that makes all the difference. This notion of greatness not simply as opposed to misery, but as a misery aware of itself, is paradigmatically modern.

The second one concerns the precise status of this knowledge: it is not only knowledge about our own vanity, but also its inherent obverse, technological *savoir-faire*, knowledge which is power. Strictly correlative to the "humiliation" of man is the exponential growth of humankind's technological domination over nature in modernity. This *savoir-faire* implies the collapse of the difference between a principle and its application: the principle immediately is the logic of its application, just as, for Wittgenstein, the meaning of a word is its use. The key aspect of Wittgenstein's notion of rule is that a rule is its application: if you are unable to apply a rule correctly, you do not "get" this rule itself. For instance, with regard to the philosophical (pseudo-) problem of how we can be sure that the meaning of words refers to objects and processes in reality, this question is in itself meaningless, since the meaning of a phrase is the way it refers and relates to the reality of its user's life-world. The same goes for love;

this is why, when a woman grudgingly concedes to her lover: "If sex is the condition for our love-relationship, then I'll endure it, although I would prefer not to do it" (thereby implying that the lover who wants sex as part of their love-relationship is blackmailing her), she is showing that she doesn't love him: sex is not a vulgar expression-application of love, it is part of the definition of love, of "practicing" (literally: making) love.

These features combined give us the basic paradox of the modern philosophy of subjectivity: the couplet of the humiliation of empirical man and the elevation of transcendental subject. Descartes, who asserted the *cogito* as the starting point of philosophy, simultaneously reduced all reality, life included, to *res extensa*, the field of matter obeying mechanical laws. In this precise sense, the thought of modern subjectivity is not a "humanism" but, from the very outset, "antihumanist": humanism characterizes Renaissance thought, which celebrated man as the crown of creation, the highest term in the chain of created beings, while modernity proper occurs only when man loses his privileged place and is reduced to just another element of reality—and correlative to this loss of privilege is the emergence of the subject as the pure immaterial void, not as a substantial part of reality. The Kantian sublime itself is grounded in this gap: it is the very experience of the impotence and nullity of man (as a part of nature) when he is exposed to a powerful display of natural forces that evokes, in a negative way, his greatness as a noumenal ethical subject. This is what is so unbearable about Darwin's discovery: not that man emerged out of a natural evolution, but the very *character* of this evolution—chaotic, nonteleological, mocking any "attunement of mind to world":

> Where Lamarck had made much of the reasonableness and truthfulness of nature, Darwin savored its eccentricities and quirks, even occasionally its silliness. He looked for the marginal, the out-of-kilter, to bolster his argument for natural selection. . . . One might say that nature has taken delight in accumulating contradictions in order to remove all foundation from the theory of a preexisting harmony between the external and internal worlds. Here we have the quintessence of Darwinism. No special creation, no perfect adaptation, no given attunement of mind to world. It was precisely the disharmonies that caught Darwin's fancy.[24]

Yet another paradox to take note of is the link between modern science and a certain theological tradition. The paradox of the scientific discourse is that it is not simply the universe of knowledge with no need for the "empty" Master-Signifier; and this necessity of a Master-Signifier is also not grounded in the elementary fact that scientific discourse remains embedded in our life-world and, as such, has to rely on everyday language as its ultimate metalanguage. That is to say: while the illusory perception of scientific discourse is that it is a discourse of pure description of facticity, the paradox resides in the coincidence of bare facticity and radical voluntarism: facticity can be sustained as meaningless, as something that "just is as it is," only if it is secretly sustained by an arbitrary divine will. This is why Descartes is the founding figure of modern science: precisely because he made even the most elementary mathematical facts like $2 + 2 = 4$ dependent on the arbitrary divine will. Two and two are four because God willed it so, with no hidden obscure chain of reasons behind it. Even in mathematics, this unconditional voluntarism is discernible in its axiomatic character: one begins by arbitrarily positing a series of axioms, out of which everything else is then supposed to follow.

These complications, however, are part of the standard narrative of modernity; what, in effect, disturbs the received image of modern science is the fact that the twentieth-century "humiliations" are much more ambiguous than they may seem—and, retroactively, reveal the ambiguity of the classic humiliations themselves. That is to say, in a first approach, Marx, Nietzsche, and Freud all share the same "desublimating" hermeneutics of suspicion: a "higher" capacity (ideology and politics, morality, consciousness) is unmasked as a shadow-theater which is actually run by the conflict of forces that takes place on another, "lower" stage (economic process, conflict of unconscious desires). And today, things have gone much further: in cognitivism, human thinking itself is conceived as modeled after the functioning of a computer, so that the very gap between understanding (the experience of meaning, of the openness of a world) and the "mute" functioning of a machine potentially disappears; in neo-Darwinism, human individuals are conceived as mere instruments—or, rather, vehicles—of the reproduction of "their" genes, and, analogously, human culture, the cultural activity of mankind, as a vehicle for the proliferation of "memes."

I am tempted to say, however, that, insofar as nineteenth-century "demystification" is a reduction of the noble appearance to some "lower" reality (Marx-Nietzsche-Freud), then the twentieth century adds another turn of the screw by *rehabilitating* (a weird, previously unheard-of) *appearance itself*. This began with Husserlian *phenomenology*, the first true event of twentieth-century philosophy, with its attitude of "reduction" which aims at observing phenomena "as such," in their autonomy, not as attributes/expressions/effects of some underlying "real entities"—a line is opened up here which leads to figures as different as Bergson, Deleuze, and Wittgenstein, and to theories like quantum physics, all of them focusing on the autonomy of the pure flux-event of becoming with regard to real entities ("things").

In short, is not the shift from substantial Reality to (different forms of) Event one of the defining features of modern sciences? Quantum physics posits as the ultimate reality not some primordial elements but, rather, a kind of string of "vibrations," entities which can only be described as desubstantialized processes; cognitivism and system theory focus on the mystery of "emerging properties" which also designate purely processual self-organizations, and so on. No wonder, then, that the three contemporary philosophers—Heidegger, Deleuze, Badiou—deploy three thoughts of the Event: in Heidegger, it is the Event as the epochal disclosure of a configuration of Being; in Deleuze, it is the Event as the desubstantialized pure becoming of Sense; in Badiou, it is the Event reference to which grounds a Truth-process. For all three, Event is irreducible to the order of being (in the sense of positive reality), to the set of its material (pre)conditions. For Heidegger, Event is the ultimate horizon of thought, and it is meaningless to try to think "behind" it and to thematize the process that generated it—such an attempt equals an ontic account of the ontological horizon; for

Deleuze, one cannot reduce the emergence of a new artistic form (film noir, Italian neo-realism, and so on) to its historical circumstances, or account for it in these terms; for Badiou, a Truth-Event is totally heterogeneous with regard to the order of Being (positive reality).

Although, in all three cases, Event stands for historicity proper (the explosion of the New) versus historicism, the differences between the three philosophers are, of course, crucial. For Heidegger, Event has nothing to do with ontic processes; it designates the "event" of a new epochal disclosure of Being, the emergence of a new "world" (as the horizon of meaning within which all entities appear). Deleuze is a vitalist insisting on the absolute immanence of the Event to the order of Being, conceiving Event as the One-All of the proliferating differences of Life. Badiou, on the contrary, asserts the radical "dualism" between Event and the order of being. It is here, in this terrain, that we should locate today's struggle between idealism and materialism: idealism posits an ideal Event which cannot be accounted for in terms of its material (pre)conditions, while the materialist wager is that we *can* get "behind" the event and explore how Event explodes out of the gap in/of the order of Being. The first to formulate this task was Schelling, who, in his *Weltalter* fragments, outlined the dark territory of the "prehistory of Logos," of what had to occur in preontological proto-reality so that the openness of Logos and temporality could take place. With regard to Heidegger, we should risk a step behind the Event, naming/outlining the cut, the terrifying seizure/contraction, which enables any ontological disclosure.[25] The problem with Heidegger is not only (as John Caputo argues)[26] that he dismisses ontic pain with regard to ontological essence, but that he dismisses the proper (pre)ontological pain of the Real ("symbolic castration").

In contrast to Heidegger, both Deleuze and Badiou perform the same paradoxical philosophical gesture of defending, as materialists, the autonomy of the "immaterial" order of the Event. As a materialist, and in order to be thoroughly materialist, Badiou focuses on the idealist *topos par excellence:* How can a human animal forsake its animality and put its life in the service of a transcendent Truth? How can the "transubstantiation" from the pleasure-oriented life of an *individual* to the life of a *subject* dedicated to a Cause occur? In other words, how is a free act possible? How can we break (out of) the network of the causal connections of positive reality, and conceive an act that begins by and in itself? In short, Badiou *repeats within the materialist frame the elementary gesture of idealist anti-reductionism:* human Reason cannot be reduced to the result of evolutionary adaptation; art is not just a heightened procedure of providing sensual pleasures, but a medium of Truth; and so on. Additionally, against the false appearance that this gesture is also aimed at psychoanalysis (is not the point of the notion of "sublimation" that the allegedly "higher" human activities are just a roundabout, "sublimated" way of realizing a "lower" goal?), this is in fact the crucial achievement of psychoanalysis: its claim is that sexuality itself, sexual drives pertaining to the human animal, cannot be accounted for in evolutionary terms.[27] This makes the true stakes of Badiou's gesture clear: in order for materialism truly to win over idealism, it is not enough to succeed in the "reductionist" approach and demonstrate how mind, consciousness, and so on, can nonetheless somehow be accounted for within the evolutionary-positivist frame of materialism. On the contrary, the materialist claim should be much stronger: it is only materialism that can accurately explain the phenomena of mind, consciousness, and so on; conversely, it is idealism that is "vulgar," that always-already "reifies" these phenomena.

When Badiou emphasizes the undecidability of the Real of an Event, his position here is radically different from the standard deconstructionist notion of undecidability. For Badiou, undecidability means that there are no neutral "objective" criteria for an Event: an Event appears as such only to those who recognize themselves in its call, or, as Badiou puts it, an Event is self-relating, it includes itself—its own nomination—among its components.[28] While this does mean that we have to decide about an Event, such an ultimately groundless decision is not "undecidable" in the standard sense; it is, rather, uncannily similar to the Hegelian dialectical process in which, as Hegel made clear in the Introduction to his *Phenomenology*, a "figure of consciousness" is measured not by any external standard of truth but in an absolutely immanent way, through the gap between itself and its own exemplification/staging. An Event is thus "non-All" in the precise Lacanian sense of the term: it is never fully verified precisely because it is infinite/illimited—because there is no external limit to it. And the conclusion to be drawn here is that, for the very same reason, the Hegelian "totality" is also "non-All." In other (Badiou's) terms, an Event is *nothing but* its own inscription into the order of Being, a cut/rupture in the order of Being on account of which Being can never form a consistent All. Of course, Badiou—as a materialist—is aware of the idealist danger that lurks here:

> We must point out that in what concerns its material the event is not a miracle. What I mean is that what composes an event is always extracted from a situation, always related back to a singular multiplicity, to its state, to the language that is connected to it, etc. In fact, so as not to succumb to an obscurantist theory of creation *ex nihilo*, we must accept that an event is nothing but a part of a given situation, nothing but a *fragment of being*.[29]

Here, however, we should go a step further than Badiou is ready to go: there is no Beyond of Being which inscribes itself into the order of Being—there is nothing but the order of Being. Recall the central ontological paradox of Einstein's general theory of relativity, in which matter does not curve space, but is an effect of space's curvature: an Event does not curve the space of Being through its inscription in it—on the contrary, an Event is *nothing but* this curvature of the space of Being. "All there is" is the interstice, the non-self-coincidence, of Being, that is, the ontological nonclosure of the order of Being.[30] The "minimal difference" which sustains the parallax gap is thus the difference on account of which the "same" series of real occurrences which, in the eyes of a neutral observer, are just part of ordinary reality are, in the eyes of an engaged participant, inscriptions of fidelity to an Event. For example, the "same" occurrences (fights on the streets of St. Petersburg) which are to a neutral historian just violent twists and turns in Russian history are, for an engaged revolutionary, parts of the epochal Event of the October Revolution. This means that, from the Lacanian perspective, the notions of parallax gap and of "minimal difference" obey the logic of the non-All.[31]

So when David Chalmers proposes that the basis of consciousness will have to be found in a new, additional, fundamental—primordial and irreducible—force of nature, like gravity or electromagnetism, something like an elementary (self-)sentience or awareness,[32] does he not thereby provide a new proof of how idealism coincides with vulgar materialism? Does he not precisely miss the pure ideality of (self-)awareness? This is where the topic of finitude in the strict Heideggerian sense should be mobilized: if we try to conceive of consciousness within an ontologically fully realized field of reality, it can only appear as an additional positive moment; but what about linking consciousness to the very finitude, ontological incompleteness, of the human being, to its being originally out-of-joint, thrown-into, exposed to, an overwhelming constellation?

It is here that, in order to specify the meaning of materialism, we should apply Lacan's formulas of sexuation: there is a fundamental difference between the assertion "everything is matter" (which relies on its constitutive exception—in the case of Lenin who, in *Materialism and Empiriocriticism*, falls into this trap, the very position of enunciation of the subject whose mind "reflects" matter) and the assertion "there is nothing which is not matter" (which, with its other side, "not-All is matter," opens up the space for the account of immaterial phenomena). This means that a truly radical materialism is by definition nonreductionist: far from claiming that "everything is matter," it confers upon "immaterial" phenomena a specific positive nonbeing.

When, in his argument against the reductive explanation of consciousness, Chalmers writes: "[e]ven if we knew every last detail about the physics of the universe—the configuration, causation, and evolution among all the fields and particles in the spatiotemporal manifold—that information would not lead us to postulate the existence of conscious experience,"[33] he makes the classic Kantian mistake: such a total knowledge is strictly nonsensical, both epistemologically and ontologically. It is the obverse of the vulgar determinist notion articulated, in Marxism, by Nikolai Bukharin, when he wrote that if we knew the whole of physical reality we would also be able to predict precisely the emergence of a revolution. This line of reasoning—consciousness as an excess, surplus, over physical totality—is misleading, since it has to evoke a meaningless hyperbole: when we imagine the Whole of reality, there is no longer any place for consciousness (and subjectivity). There are two options here: either subjectivity is an illusion, or reality is in itself (not only epistemologically) not-All.[34]

With regard to Deleuze, is not the ontology of cartoons that of pure becoming in Deleuze's precise sense of the term? Cartoons take place in a universe of radical plasticity, in which entities are deprived of all substance and reduced to pure surface: they literally possess no depth, there is nothing beneath their surface skin, no meat, bones and blood inside, which is why they all act and react like balloons—they can be blown up; when they are pricked by a needle, they lose air and shrink like a burst balloon, and so on. Think of the nightmarish fantasy of accidentally triggering a trickle which then never stops: in *Alice inWonderland*, when Alice starts to cry, her tears gradually flood the entire room; Freud relates in his *Interpretation of Dreams* the scene of a small child who starts to urinate on the edge of a street; his flow grows into a river and then into an ocean, with a big ship passing by on it; and, closer to our ordinary daily experience, when we witness torrential rain, who among us does not get the "irrational" fear that the rain will simply never stop? What happens in such moments of anxiety is that the flow of becoming acquires autonomy, loses its mooring in substantial reality.

In *TheWhip Hand* (William Cameron Menzies, 1951), a rainstorm soaks a vacationing fisherman in northern Minnesota, close to the Canadian border, who takes refuge in a local town and asks for help in getting treatment for a head injury he sustained when he fell against a rock. The townsfolk refuse to be more than perfunctorily friendly (with the exception of a superficially outgoing and jokey innkeeper, superbly played by Raymond Burr), and are continually contradicting one another. It seems that there are strange goings-on in a lodge across the lake; there are nocturnal visits to the lodge by the doctor, who doesn't want to talk about it. As things turn out, Communists have already taken over the town and turned it into a center for the study of germ warfare. . . . The interest of this rather ridiculous Howard Hughes production is that it should be read as a reflexive inversion of the standard thesis according to which the "invasion-of-the-aliens" formula of the early 1950s (the ordinary American who, by chance, finds himself in a small American town gradually discovers that the town is already controlled by aliens) is an allegory for the Communist "takeover" ("aliens" stand for Communists): here, the allegory is translated back into its "true meaning," with the easily predicted result that *the Communist plotters themselves are haunted by the aura of "aliens."* This is why the meaning of a metaphor cannot be reduced to its "true" referent: it is not enough to point out the *reality* to which a metaphor refers; once the metaphorical substitution is accomplished, this reality itself is forever haunted by the spectral *real* of the metaphorical content.

Ingmar Bergman's *The Mirror*, one of his lesser-known films, involves the encounter between a scientist (representative of state power), a positivist rationalist who firmly believes that there is a rational explanation for all phenomena, and the director-actor of a small, marginal traveling theater, whose job is to create magical, sometimes terrifying, illusions. In their key confrontation one stormy night, the actor stages a nightmarish spectacle of haunting shadows which causes the rationalist's momentary breakdown—although the rationalist later regains his composure, he is fully aware that he was defeated, that he succumbed to the horror of cheap magic tricks. The message of *The Mirror* is not that of cheap obscurantism: Bergman is one of the great materialists of the twentieth century, and not only among cinema directors; he wrote simply but fascinatingly about the liberating power of the awareness that absolutely nothing awaits us after death, no "deeper" spiritual realm. The true stakes of *The Mirror* concern what Lacan, after Freud, would have called the Real of illusions. There is nonetheless something naive and outdated in the central confrontation of *The Mirror*—why? Because contemporary sciences no longer aim at a simple and direct reduction of deceiving appearance to raw material reality: their central topic is, rather, that of the paradoxical pseudo-autonomy and efficiency of the "illusion," of illusory appearance, itself.[35]

TOWARD A NEW SCIENCE OF APPEARANCES

What is even more crucial is that this insight into the autonomy of phenomena enables us to approach the classic "demystifiers" themselves in a new way. What we find in Marx is not only the "reduction" of ideology to an economic base and, within this base, of exchange to production, but a much more ambiguous and mysterious phenomenon of "commodity fetishism," which designates a kind of proto-"ideology" inherent to the reality of the "economic base" itself. Freud accomplishes a strictly analogous breakthrough with regard to the paradoxical status of fantasy: the ontological paradox, even scandal, of the notion of fantasy lies in the fact that it subverts the standard opposition of "subjective" and "objective": of course fantasy is by definition not "objective" (in the naive sense of "existing independently of the subject's perceptions"); however, it is not "subjective" (in the sense of being reducible to the subject's consciously experienced intuitions either). Fantasy, rather, belongs to the "bizarre category of the objectively subjective—the way things actually, objectively seem to you even if they don't seem that way to you" (as Dennett put it in his acerbic critical remark against the notion of qualia [direct immediate sensations]). When, for example, we claim that someone who is consciously well disposed toward Jews nonetheless harbors profound anti-Semitic prejudices of which he is not consciously aware, are we not claiming that (insofar as these prejudices do not reflect the way Jews really are, but the way they appear to him) he is not aware of how Jews really seem to him? Or, to put the same paradox in a different way, the fundamental fantasy is constitutive of (our approach to) reality ("everything we are allowed to approach by way of reality remains rooted in fantasy"),[36] yet, for that very reason, its direct assuming or actualization cannot fail to give rise to catastrophic consequences: "If what [subjects] long for the most intensely in their phantasies is presented to them in reality, they none the less flee from it."[37] As the common wisdom puts it: a nightmare is a dream come true.

Apropos of commodity fetishism, Marx himself uses the term "objectively necessary appearance." This difference between the two appearances (the way things really appears to us versus the way they appear to appear to us) is linked to the structure of the well-known Freudian joke about a Jew who complains to his friend: "Why are you telling me you are going to Lemberg when you are really going to Lemberg?": for instance, in the case of commodity fetishism, when I immediately perceive money as just a knot of social relations, not any kind of magical object, and I treat it like a fetish only in my practice, so that the site of fetishism is my actual social practice, I could in effect be upbraided: "Why are you saying that money is just a knot of social relations, when money really *is* just a knot of social relations?"

Jean Laplanche wrote about the hysteric's "primordial lie" which articulates the original fantasy: "the term '*proton pseudos*' aims at something different from a subjective lie; it describes a kind of passage from the subjective to the founding—even, one could say, to the transcendental; in any case, a kind of objective lie, inscribed into the facts."[38] Is this not also the status of Marxian commodity fetishism?—not simply a subjective illusion, but an "objective" illusion, an illusion inscribed into facts (social reality) themselves. Let us read carefully the famous opening sentences of Chapter 1 of *Capital*: "A commodity appears, *at first sight*, a very trivial thing, and easily understood. Its analysis shows that it is, *in reality*, a very queer thing, abounding in metaphysical subtleties and theological niceties."[39] Kojin Karatani[40] is right to link this passage to the starting point of the Marxian critique, the famous lines from 1843 about how "the criticism of religion is the premise of all criticism":[41] with it, the circle is, in a way, closed upon itself, that is to say, at the very bottom of the critique of actual life (of the economic process), we again encounter the theological dimension inscribed in social reality itself. Karatani is referring here to the Freudian notion of drive (*Trieb*) as opposed to the multitude of human desires: capitalism is grounded in the Real of a certain quasi-theological impersonal "drive," the drive to reproduce and grow, to expand and accumulate profit.[42]

This is also one way of specifying the meaning of Lacan's assertion of the subject's constitutive "decenterment": its point is not that my subjective experience is regulated by objective unconscious mechanisms which are "decentered" with regard to my self-experience and, as such, beyond my control (a point asserted by every materialist), but, rather, something much more unsettling—I am deprived of even my most intimate "subjective" experience, the way things "really seem to me," that of the fundamental fantasy that constitutes and guarantees the core of my being, since I can never consciously experience it and assume it. . . . According to the standard view, the dimension that is constitutive of subjectivity is that of phenomenal (self-)experience—I am a subject the moment I can say to myself: "No matter what unknown mechanism governs my acts, perceptions, and thoughts, nobody can take from me what I see and feel now." For example, when I am passionately in love, and a biochemist informs me that all my intense sentiments are merely the result of biochemical processes in my body, I can answer him by clinging to the appearance: "All that you're saying may be true; nonetheless, nothing can take from me the intensity of the passion I am now experiencing. . . ." Lacan's point, however, is that the psychoanalyst is the one who, precisely, *can* take this from the subject—that is to say, his ultimate aim is to deprive the subject of the very fundamental fantasy that regulates the universe of his (self-)experience.

The Freudian "subject of the Unconscious" emerges only when a key aspect of the subject's phenomenal (self-)experience (his "fundamental fantasy") becomes inaccessible to him, that is, is "primordially repressed." At its most radical, the Unconscious is the inaccessible phenomenon, not the objective mechanism that regulates my phenomenal experience. So, in contrast to the commonplace that we are dealing with a subject the moment an entity displays signs of "inner life," that is, of a fantasmatic self-experience that cannot be reduced to external behavior, we should claim that what characterizes human subjectivity proper is, rather, the gap that separates the two: the fact that fantasy, at its most elementary, becomes inaccessible to the subject; it is this inaccessibility that makes the subject "empty." We thus obtain a relationship that to- tally subverts the standard notion of the subject who directly experiences himself, his "inner states": an "impossible" relationship between the empty, nonphenomenal sub- ject and the phenomena that remain inaccessible to the subject. When David Chalmers opposes phenomenal and psychological concepts of the mind (conscious aware- ness/experience, and what the mind actually does), he cites the Freudian Unconscious as the quintessential case of psychological mind external to phenomenal mind: what Freud describes as the work of the Unconscious is a complex network of mental causality and behavioral control which takes place "on the other scene," without be- ing experienced.[43] However, is it really like that? Is not the status of the unconscious fantasy nonetheless, in an unprecedented sense, phenomenal? Is not this the ultimate paradox of the Freudian Unconscious—that it designates the way things "really ap- pear" to us, beyond their conscious appearance? Far from being superseded by the later brain-sciences decenterment, Freudian decenterment is thus much more un- settling and radical than the later one, which remains within the confines of a simple naturalization: it opens up a new domain of weird "asubjective phenomena," of ap- pearances with no subject to whom they can appear: it is only here that the subject is "no longer a master in his own house"—in the house of his (self-)appearances themselves.

The twentieth-century evolution of "hard" sciences generated the same paradox: in quantum physics, the "appearance" (perception) of a particle determines its real- ity. The very emergence of "hard reality" out of the quantum fluctuation through the collapse of the wave function is the outcome of observation, that is, of the interven- tion of consciousness. Thus consciousness is not the domain of potentiality, multiple options, and so on, opposed to hard singular reality—reality previous to its percep- tion is fluid-multiple-open, and conscious perception reduces this spectral, preonto- logical multiplicity to one ontologically fully constituted reality. This gives us the way quantum physics conceives of the relationship between particles and their interac- tions: in an initial moment, it appears as if first (ontologically, at least) there are par- ticles interacting in the mode of waves, oscillations, and so forth; then, in a second moment, we are forced to enact a radical shift of perspective—the primordial onto- logical facts are the waves themselves (trajectories, oscillations), and particles are nothing but the nodal points at which different waves intersect.

Consequently, quantum physics confronts us with the gap between the Real and re- ality at its most radical: what we get in it is the mathematized Real of formulas which cannot be translated into ontologically consistent reality—or, to put it in Kantian terms, they remain pure concepts which cannot be "schematized," translated/transposed into objects of experience. This is also how, after the crisis of the 1920s, quantum physics in practice resolved the crisis of its ontological interpretation: by renouncing the very effort to provide such an interpretation—quantum physics is scientific formalization at its most radical, formalization without interpretation. Is it then not accurate to say that quantum physics involves a kind of reversal of Kantian transcendental ontology?[44] In Kant, we have access to ordinary experiential reality, while the moment we try to apply our transcendental categories to the noumenal Real itself, we get involved in contradictions; in quantum physics, it is the noumenal Real which can be grasped and formulated in a consistent theory, while the moment we try to translate this theory into the terms of our experience of phenomenal reality, we get involved in senseless contradictions (time runs backward, the same object is in two places at once, an entity is a particle and a wave, and so on). (It can still be claimed, however, that these contradictions emerge only when we try to transpose into our experiential reality the "Real" of the quantum processes—in itself, this reality remains the same as before, a consistent realm with which we are well acquainted.)

So not only is appearance inherent to reality; what we get beyond this is a weird split in appearance itself, an unheard-of mode designating "the way things really appear to us" as opposed to both their reality and their (direct) appearance to us. This shift from the split between appearance and reality to the split, inherent to appearance itself, between "true" and "false" appearance is to be linked to its obverse: to a split inherent to reality itself. If, then, there is appearance (as distinct from reality) because there is a (logically) prior split inherent to reality itself, is it also that "reality" itself is ultimately nothing but a (self-)split of appearance? But how does this *topos* differ from the boring old *Rashomon* theme of an irreducible multiplicity of subjective perspectives on reality, with no way (no exempted position from which) to establish the one truth represented in a distorted way by these multiple perspectives? What better way to clarify this point than to refer to the very film (and the short story on which the film is based) whose title was elevated into a notion, Akira Kurosawa's *Rashomon?*

According to the legend, it was through *Rashomon*, its European triumph in the early 1950s, that the Western public discovered the "Oriental spirit" in the cinema; the little-known obverse of this legend is that this same film was a failure in Japan itself, where it was perceived as much too "Western"—and it is easy to see why. When the same tragic event (in a lonely forest, a notorious bandit rapes the samurai's beautiful wife and kills the samurai) is retold by four witnesses-participants, the effect (pertaining to the very Western realism of the cinematic image) is simply that we are shown four different subjective perspectives. What, in effect, distinguishes the so-called "Oriental spirit" from the Western attitude, however, is that, precisely, ambiguity and undecidability are not "subjectivized": they should not be reduced to different "subjective perspectives" on some reality beyond reach—rather, they pertain to this "reality" itself, and it is this ontological ambiguity-fragility of the "thing itself" that is difficult to express through the realism of the cinematic medium. This means that the authentic *Rashomon* has nothing to do with pseudo-Nietzschean perspectivism, with the notion that there is no objective truth, just an irreducible multitude of subjectively distorted-biased narratives.

The first thing to do apropos of *Rashomon* is to avoid the formalist trap: what I am tempted to call the film's formal-ontological thesis (the impossibility of reaching the truth from multiple narratives of the same event) should not be abstracted from the particular nature of this event—the feminine challenge to male authority, the explosion of feminine desire. The four witness reports are to be conceived as four versions of the same myth (in the Lévi-Straussian sense of the term), as a complete matrix of variations: in the first (bandit's) version, he rapes the wife and then, in an honest duel, kills her husband; in the second (surviving wife's) version, in the course of the rape she gets caught up in the passion of the bandit's forceful lovemaking and, at the end, tells him that she cannot live in shame with both men knowing about her disgrace—one of them must die, and it is then that the duel ensues; in the third version (told by the ghost of the dead husband himself), after the husband is set free by the bandit, he stabs and kills himself out of shame; in the last version (told by the woodcutter who observed the events hidden in a nearby bush), when, after the rape, the bandit cuts the rope binding the husband, and the husband furiously rejects his wife as a dishonored whore, the ecstatically furious wife explodes against both men, accusing them of weakness and challenging them to fight for her. The succession of the four versions is thus not neutral, they do not by any means move at the same level: in the course of their progression, male authority is weakened step by step, and feminine desire is asserted. So when we privilege the last (woodcutter's) report, the point is not that it tells us what "really happened" but that, within the immanent structure that links the four version, it functions as the traumatic point with regard to which the other three versions are to be conceived as defenses, defense-formations.

The "official" message of the film is clear enough: at the very beginning, in the conversation that provides the frame for the flashbacks, the monk points out that the lesson of the events recounted is more terrifying than the hunger, war, and chaos that pervaded society at that time—in what does this horror consist? In the disintegration of the social link: there was no "big Other" on which people could rely, no basic symbolic pact guaranteeing trust and sustaining obligations. Thus the film is not engaged in ontological games about how there is no ultimate unambiguous reality behind the multitude of narratives; rather, it is concerned with the socio-ethical consequences of the disintegration of the basic symbolic pact that holds the social fabric together. However, the story—the incident retold from different perspectives—tells more: it locates the threat to the big Other, the ultimate Cause that destabilizes the male pact and blurs the clarity of the male vision, in a woman, in *feminine desire*. As Nietzsche put it: in its very inconsistency and lack of any ultimate point of reference beneath multiple veils, truth is feminine.

RESISTANCES TO DISENCHANTMENT

Today we encounter a series of attitudes toward subjectivity which can be vaguely systematized into three couples of opposites: each of the three main "antihumanist" and/or "antisubjectivist" positions (cognitivist-biologist reductionism: the dismissal of subjective self-experience itself as a mere "user illusion"; the Heideggerian position:

the essence of man is not reducible to subjectivity, there is a more primordial dimension of being-human; the deconstructionist "decentering" of the Subject: the subject emerges out of presubjective textual processes) is accompanied by an assertion of subjectivity (those cognitivists, from Nagel to Chalmers, who argue for the irreducible/inexplicable character of experience; the [revival of the] standard transcendental-philosophical defense of the irreducibility of [self-]consciousness through the critique of its reflexive model: there is a dimension of self-acquaintance which precedes reflexive self-recognition in the other [Dieter Henrich and his school]; the Freudian subject as rethought by Lacan: the nonsubstantial *cogito* is the subject of the unconscious).

The paradoxical short circuit within this space which cannot be explained away as a result of simple misunderstanding is that of cognitivist Heideggerians (Hubert Dreyfus, Auge Haugeland). That is to say: from a Heideggerian standpoint, cognitivist psychology is the extreme of "danger," of the forgetting of the essence of man: man's mind itself is reduced to a particular object of scientific exploration and manipulation—with it, philosophy "turns into the empirical science of man, of all of what can become for man the experiential object of his technology."[45] Nonetheless, there are cognitivists who, in order to resolve the deadlocks of their approach, turn to Heidegger, thereby ironically confirming Heidegger's favorite quote from Hölderlin: "But where there is danger, the saving force [*das Rettende*] also grows."[46]

As for the link between the brain sciences and psychoanalysis, it will never be established through a direct complementing of the two approaches within a shared conceptual field; rather, we should develop one approach to its extreme, radically abstracting from the other—develop the logic of brain science, for instance, at its purest. At this point, we encounter a gap which opens up the space for the other approach. Today's achievements in brain sciences seem to fulfill the prospect envisaged by Freud of sciences supplanting psychoanalysis: once the biological mechanisms of pain, pleasure, trauma, repression, and so on, are known, psychoanalysis will no longer be needed, since, instead of intervening at the level of interpretation, we will be able to regulate the biological processes that generate pathological psychic phenomena. Hitherto, psychoanalysts replied to this challenge in two ways:

- They had recourse to the usual philosophico-transcendental gesture of pointing out how a positive science can never encompass and account for the very horizon of meaning within which it is operative ("Even if the brain sciences do succeed in totally objectivizing a symptom, formulating its bioneuronal equivalent, the patient will still have to adopt a subjective stance toward this objectivity . . ."). Even Jacques-Alain Miller, in his public appearances, often adopts this move: even when science has fully objectified our thought, achieving the goal of translating mental processes into their neuronal counterparts, the subject will still have to subjectivize this fact, assume it, integrate it into his or her universe of meaning—and this excess of symbolic integration, what this discovery will "mean to us and for us," eludes science. . . . This self-complacent answer, however, is much too short: the success of the brain sciences, if they were really subjectively assumed, would undermine our very status as subjects of meaning. (Its *mauvaise foi* is clear already from the oscillation of critics of brain sciences between two extremes: as a rule they combine the quick "transcendental" answer ["science *a priori* cannot objectivize our subjective attitude toward objectivity"] with empirical arguments against—and rejoicing at—the specific failures of scientific accounts of the brain: this very form of specific argumentation is meaningful only against the background of possible success.)

Along these lines, the standard neo-Kantian reproach to cognitivists who question the existence of free will in humans is that of committing a "category mistake": in an illegitimate operation, they reduce the normative level of reasons (motivations) for an act to its positive causes (how this act fits into the texture of physical reality part of which it is). My saying "Yes!" at a wedding ceremony can be described as a physical act enchained in a causal texture of material (neuronal, biological, and so on) reality, but this does not account for the reasons why I said "Yes!" There is a normative dimension in humans (quests for truth, for the good, for the beautiful, for the sake of it, not as parts of a survival strategy) which operates at a level which ontologically differs from factual reality, and cannot be reduced to it. . . . This kind of reply misses the point of the brain sciences' approach: when they claim that, in principle, all our choices can be explained in terms of neuronal processes, they present a claim which, if it is true, effectively undermines our freedom, reducing it to an illusory lived experience which misrecognizes the biological process that really runs the show. In other words, they do not deny the gap between the normative level that sustains our subjective experience of freedom and ourselves as biological mechanisms; what they claim is that this gap is the gap between reality and its illusory subjective experience.[47]

In May 2002, it was reported that scientists at New York University had attached a computer chip able to receive signals directly to a rat's brain, so that the rat could be controlled (the direction in which it would run could be determined) by means of a steering mechanism (in the same way as a remote-controlled toy car). For the first time, the "will" of a living animal agent, its "spontaneous" decisions about the movements it would make, were taken over by an external machine. Of course, the big philosophical question here is: how did the unfortunate rat "experience" its movement, which was effectively determined from outside? Did it continue to "experience" it as something spontaneous (that is to say, was it totally unaware that its movements were being steered?), or was it aware that "something was wrong": that another, external power was determining its movements? It is even more crucial to apply the same reasoning to an identical experiment performed on humans (which, ethical questions notwithstanding, should not be much more complicated, technically speaking, than in the case of the rat). In the case of the rat, we can argue that one should not apply to it the human category of "experience," while in the case of a human being, we should ask this question. So, again, will a steered human being continue to "experience" his movements as spontaneous? Will he remain totally unaware that his movements are steered, or will he become aware that "something is wrong": that another, external power is determining his movements? And, how, precisely, will this "external power" appear—as something "inside me," an unstoppable inner drive, or as a simple external coercion? If the subject remains totally unaware that their spontaneous behavior is steered from outside, can we really go on pretending that this has no consequences for our notion of free will?

· Psychoanalysts cling desperately to the parallels or structural analogies between psychoanalysis and the brain sciences ("See, we were right: there is a neuronal process that corresponds to repression"). In this last stance there is more then a trace of the desperate strategy of "If you can't beat them, join them": cognitivism is expected to give scientific legitimacy to psychoanalysis.

Do we not encounter here yet again the notorious argument about the broken kettle (the listing of arguments which exclude each other)? First, cognitivism is factually wrong. Second, even if it is factually accurate, it is limited by its very scientific horizon. Third, cognitivism confirms what psychoanalysis predicted long ago about the functioning of the human mind. . . . Both these approaches—which complement each other in their two respective excesses, the first one with its abstract arrogance, the second one with its subservient modesty—are inadequate as an answer to the challenge of the brain sciences: the only proper reply to this challenge is to meet the brain sciences' neuronal Real with another Real, not simply to ground the Freudian *semblant* within the neuronal Real. In other words, if psychoanalysis is to survive and retain its key status, *we have to find a place for it within the brain sciences themselves, starting from their inherent silences and impossibilities*. Different versions of the emergence of consciousness, from Dennett to Damasio,[48] all seem to "get stuck" at the same paradox: that of a certain self-propelling mechanism, of a closed loop of self-relating, which is constitutive of consciousness: they all pinpoint this paradox, trying to describe it as precisely as possible, yet they seem to miss its proper formulation, and thus get lost in vague metaphors or outright inconsistencies. The wager of Chapter 4 of this book, the hypothesis it endeavors to substantiate, is that this missing concept—a kind of absent Cause of cognitivist accounts—is none other than what German Idealism called self-relating negativity and Freud called "the death drive."

The first impression we get of cognitive sciences, however, is of a variety of incompatible accounts of the emergence of consciousness—whither consciousness? The surprising thing is how "everything goes," all possible answers coexist, from dismissing the question as meaningless through evolutionist accounts of it up to declaring it an unsolvable mystery and proposing that consciousness has no (evolutionary) function at all, that it is a by-product—not a central phenomenon, but an epiphenomenon. What strikes us is how evolutionist or cognitivist accounts always seem to stumble over the same deadlock: after we have constructed an artificial intelligence machine which can solve even very complex problems, the questions crops up: "But if it can do it precisely as a machine, as a blind operating entity, why does it need (self-)awareness to do it?" So the more consciousness is demonstrated to be marginal, unnecessary, nonfunctional, the more it becomes enigmatic—here it is consciousness itself which is the Real of an indivisible remainder.

Generally, this multitude can be reduced to four main positions:

1. Radical/reductive materialism (Patricia and Paul Churchland): there simply are no qualia, there is no "consciousness," these things exist only as a kind of "naturalized" cognitive mistake. The anti-intuitional beauty of this position is that it turns around subjectivist phenomenalism (we are aware only of phenomena, there is no absolute certainty that anything beyond them exists)—here, it is pure phenomenality itself which does not exist!
2. Antimaterialism (David Chalmers): consciousness-awareness cannot be accounted for in terms of other natural processes; it has to be conceived as a primordial dimension of nature, like gravity or magnetism.

3. The position of "cognitive closure" which asserts the inherent unknowability of consciousness (Colin McGinn, even Steven Pinker): although consciousness emerged out of material reality, it is necessarily unknowable.
4. Nonreductive materialism (Daniel Dennett): consciousness exists, but it is the result of natural processes, and has a clear evolutionary function.

These four positions obviously form a Greimasian semiotic square: the main opposition is the one between 2 and 4, idealism and materialism; 1 and 3 both give materialism or idealism a cognitive twist. That is to say, both 2 and 4 believe in the possibility of the scientific explanation of consciousness: there is an object ("consciousness") and its explanation, either accounting for it in the terms of nonconscious natural processes (materialism) or conceiving it as an irreducible dimension of its own (idealism). For 1, however, the scientific explanation of consciousness leads to the result that the object-to-be-explained itself does not exist, that it is an epistemological mistake, like the old notion of phlogiston; 3 inverts this position: what disappears here is not the object but explanation itself (although materialism is true, it cannot *a priori* explain consciousness).

Perhaps the problem of consciousness should be formulated in Badiou's terms: what if the emergence of *thought* is the ultimate Event? Does not the zombie problem (how to differentiate a zombie who acts like a human from a "real" human with inner life?) directly indicate the *indiscernibility* of the emergence of consciousness—there are no "objective" criteria that enable us to differentiate a zombie from a "real" human, that is to say, this difference can be perceived only from within, from the standpoint of a conscious subject? In Kierkegaard's terms, the problem here is to grasp "mind-in-becoming": not the already-constituted mind opposed to bodily reality, but the way mind is "for the body," that is, the break (the vanishing mediator) as such.

It is a standard philosophical observation that we should distinguish between knowing a phenomenon and acknowledging it, accepting it, treating it as existing—we do not "really know" if other people around us have minds, or are just robots programmed to act blindly. This observation, however, misses the point: if I were to "really know" the mind of my interlocutor, intersubjectivity proper would disappear; he would lose his subjective status and turn—for me—into a transparent machine. In other words, not-being-knowable to others is a crucial feature of subjectivity, of what we mean when we impute to our interlocutors a "mind": you "truly have a mind" only insofar as this is opaque to me. Perhaps we should nonetheless rehabilitate the good old Hegelian-Marxist topic of the thoroughly *intersubjective* character of my innermost subjective experience. What makes the zombie hypothesis wrong is that, if all other people are zombies (more precisely: if I perceive them as zombies), I cannot perceive *myself* as having full phenomenal consciousness either.

The moment we introduce the paradoxical dialectics of identity and similarity best exemplified by a series of Marx Brothers' jokes ("No wonder you look like X, since you *are* X!"; "This man looks like an idiot and acts like an idiot, but this should not deceive you—he is an idiot!"), the uncanniness of cloning becomes clear. Let us take the well-known case of a beloved only child who dies, and the parents then decide to clone him and so get him back: is it not more than clear that the result is monstrous? The new child has all the properties of the dead one, but *this very similarity makes the difference all the more palpable*—although he looks exactly the same, he is not the same person, so he is a cruel joke, a terrifying impostor—not the lost son, but a blasphemous copy whose presence cannot fail to remind us of the old joke from the Marx Brothers' *Night at the Opera*: "Everything about you reminds me of you—your eyes, your ears, your mouth, your lips, your arms and legs . . . everything *but yourself!*"[49]

These cognitivist impasses bear witness to the fact that today's sciences shatter the basic presuppositions of our everyday life-world notion of reality. There are three main attitudes we can adopt toward this breakthrough. The first one is simply to insist on radical naturalism: heroically to pursue the logic of the scientific "disenchantment of reality" whatever the cost, even if the very fundamental coordinates of our horizon of meaningful experience are shattered. (In brain sciences, Patricia and Paul Churchland have most radically opted for this attitude.) The second one is the attempt at some kind of New Age "synthesis" between scientific Truth and the premodern world of Meaning: the claim is that new scientific results themselves (for example, quantum physics) compel us to abandon materialism and point toward some new (Gnostic or Eastern) spirituality—here is a standard version of this theme: "The central event of the twentieth century is the overthrow of matter. In technology, economics, and the politics of nations, wealth in the form of physical resources is steadily declining in value and significance. The powers of mind are everywhere ascendant over the brute force of things."[50] This line of reasoning represents ideology at its worst: what the reinscription of a proper scientific problematic (the role of waves and oscillations in quantum physics, and so on) into the ideological field of "mind versus brute things" obfuscates is the true paradoxical result of the notorious "disappearance of matter" in modern physics: how the "immaterial" processes themselves lose their spiritual character and become a legitimate topic of natural sciences. The third option is that of a neo-Kantian state philosophy whose exemplary case today is Habermas. It is a rather sad spectacle to see Habermas trying to control the explosive results of biogenetics, to curtail the philosophical consequences of biogenetics—his entire effort betrays his fear that something will actually happen, that a new dimension of the "human" will emerge, that the old image of human dignity and autonomy will not survive unscathed. Such excessive reactions are symptomatic here, like the ridiculous overreaction to Sloterdijk's Elmau speech on biogenetics and Heidegger,[51] discerning echoes of Nazi eugenics in the (quite reasonable) suggestion that biogenetics compels us to formulate new rules of ethics. This attitude toward scientific progress amounts to a kind of "temptation of (resisting) temptation": the temptation to be resisted is precisely the pseudo-ethical attitude of presenting scientific exploration as a temptation which can lead us into "going too far"—entering the forbidden territory (of biogenetic manipulations, and so on), and thus endangering the very core of our humanity.

The latest ethical "crisis" apropos of biogenetics has in effect created the need for what one is fully justified in calling a "state philosophy": a philosophy that would, on the one hand, condone scientific research and technical process, and, on the other hand, contain its full socio-symbolic impact: prevent it from posing a threat to the existing theologico-ethical constellation. No wonder those who come closest to meeting these demands are neo-Kantians: Kant himself focused on the problem of how, while fully taking into account Newtonian science, one can guarantee that there is a space of ethical responsibility exempt from the reach of science; as Kant himself put it, he limited the scope of knowledge to create the space for faith and morality. And are not today's state philosophers facing the same task? Is their effort not focused on how, through different versions of transcendental reflection, to restrict science to its preordained horizon of meaning, and thus to denounce as "illegitimate" its consequences for the ethico-religious sphere?

It is interesting to note how, although Sloterdijk was the target of a violent Habermasian attack, his proposed solution, a "humanist" synthesis of the new scientific Truth and the old horizon of Meaning, although much more refined and ironically skeptical than Habermasian "state philosophy," is ultimately separated from it by an almost invisible line (more precisely, it seems to persist in the ambiguity between the Habermasian compromise and the New Age obscurantist synthesis). According to Sloterdijk, "humanism" always involves such a reconciliation, a bridge between the New and the Old: when scientific results undermine the old universe of Meaning, we should find a way to reintegrate them into the universe of Meaning, or, rather, metaphorically to expand the old universe of Meaning so that it can "cover" new scientific propositions. If we fail in this mediating task, we remain stuck in a brutal dilemma: either a reactionary refusal to accept scientific results, or the shattering loss of the very domain of Meaning. Today, we are confronting the same challenge: "Mathematicians will have to become poets, cyberneticists philosophers of religion, [medical] doctors composers, information-workers shamans."[52] Is not this solution, however, that of *obscurantism* in the precise sense of an attempt to keep meaning and truth harnessed together?

> . . . the simplest definition of God and of religion lies in the idea that truth and meaning are one and the same thing. The death of God is the end of the idea that posits truth and meaning as the same thing. And I would add that the death of Communism also implies the separation between meaning and truth as far as history is concerned. "The meaning of history" has two meanings: on the one hand "orientation," history goes somewhere; and then history has a meaning, which is the history of human emancipation by way of the proletariat, etc. In fact, the entire age of Communism was a period where the conviction that it was possible to take rightful political decisions existed; we were, at that moment, driven by the meaning of history. . . . Then the death of Communism becomes the second death of God but in the territory of history. There is a connection between the two events and the consequence is, so to speak, that we should be aware that to produce truthful effects that are primarily local (be they psychoana-

lytical, scientific, etc.) is always an effect of local truth, never of global truth. . . . Today we may call "obscurantism" the intention of keeping them harnessed together—meaning and truth.[53]

Badiou is right here to emphasize the gap between meaning and truth—that is, the nonhermeneutic status of truth—as the minimal difference that separates religious idealism from materialism. This is also the difference between Freud and Jung: while Jung remains within the horizon of meaning, Freudian interpretation aims at articulating a truth which is no longer grounded in meaning. Badiou is also right to formulate the ultimate alternative that confronts us today, when the impossibility of the conjunction of meaning and truth is imposed on us: either we endorse the "postmodern" stance and renounce the dimension of truth altogether, restricting ourselves to the interplay of multiple meanings, or we engage in an effort to discern a dimension of truth outside meaning—that is, in short, the dimension of truth as *real*.

What rings false, however, is the parallel between the death of God and the death of Communism, implicitly referring back to the boring old anti-Communist cliché that Communism was a "secular religion"; also linked to this falsity is the all-too-quick acceptance of the "postmodern" notion that, in today's politics, we are limited to "local" truths since, without a grounding in global meaning, it is no longer possible to formulate an all-encompassing truth. The fact which makes this conclusion problematic is the very fact of capitalist globalization—what is capitalist globalization? Capitalism is the first socioeconomic order which *de-totalizes meaning*: it is not global at the level of meaning (there is no global "capitalist world-view," no "capitalist civilization" proper—the fundamental lesson of globalization is precisely that capitalism can accommodate itself to all civilizations, from Christian to Hindu and Buddhist); its global dimension can be formulated only at the level of truth-without-meaning, as the "Real" of the global market mechanism. Consequently, insofar as capitalism already enacts the rupture between meaning and truth, it can be opposed at two levels: either at the level of meaning (conservative reactions to re-enframe capitalism into some social field of meaning, to contain its self-propelling movement within the confines of a system of shared "values" which cement a "community" in its "organic unity"), or by questioning the Real of capitalism with regard to its truth-outside-meaning (basically, what Marx did). Of course, the predominant religious strategy today is that of trying to contain the scientific Real within the confines of meaning—it is as an answer to the scientific Real (materialized in biogenetic threats) that religion is finding its new *raison d'être*:

Far from being effaced by science, religion, and even the syndicate of religions, in the process of formation, is progressing every day. Lacan said that ecumenism was for the poor of spirit. There is a marvelous agreement on these questions between the secular and all the religious authorities, in which they tell themselves they should agree somewhere in order to make echoes equally marvelous, even saying that finally the secular is a religion like the others. We see this because it is revealed in effect that the discourse of science has partly connected with the death drive. Religion is planted in the position of unconditional defense of the living, of life in mankind, as guardian of life, making life an absolute. And that extends to the protection of human nature. . . . This is . . . what gives a future to religion through meaning, namely by erecting barriers—to cloning, to the exploitation of human cells—and to inscribe science in a tempered progress. We see a marvelous effort, a new youthful vigor of religion in its effort to flood the real with meaning.[54]

So when the late Pope John Paul II opposed the Christian "culture of Life" to the modern "culture of Death," he was not merely exploiting different attitudes toward abortion in a hyperbolic way. His statements are to be taken much more literally and, at the same time, universally: it is not only that the Church harbors "good news," trust in our future, the Hope that guarantees the Meaning of Life; the couple culture of Life/culture of Death must be related to the Freudian opposition of life and death drives. "Life" stands for the rule of the "pleasure principle," for the homeostatic stability of pleasures protected from the stressful shocks of excessive *jouissance*, so that Pope John Paul II's wager was that, paradoxically, not only is religious spirituality not opposed to earthly pleasures, but it is only this spirituality that can provide the frame for a full and satisfying pleasurable life. "Death," on the contrary, stands for the domain "beyond the pleasure principle," for all the excesses through which the Real disturbs the homeostasis of life, from excessive sexual *jouissance* up to the scientific Real which generates artificial monsters. . . . Miller's simple but salient diagnosis ends up in a surprising paraphrase of Heidegger, defining the analyst as the "shepherd of the Real." However, it leaves some key questions open. Is the death drive for which science stands, which it mobilizes in its activity, not simultaneously an excess of obscene life, of life as real, exempt from and external to meaning (life that we find embodied in Kafka's "Odradek" as well as in the "alien" from the film of the same name)? We should not forget that the death drive is a Freudian name for immortality, for a pressure, a compulsion, which persists beyond death (and let us also not forget that immortality is also implicitly promised by science). We should therefore also assert a gap between life and meaning, analogous to the gap between truth and meaning—life and meaning do not in any way fully overlap.[55]

WHEN THE GOD COMES AROUND

The key question about religion today is: can all religious experiences and practices in fact be contained within this dimension of the conjunction of truth and meaning? Does not Judaism, with its imposition of a traumatic Law, adumbrate a dimension of truth outside meaning (which is why Judaism is the mortal enemy of any Gnostic obscurantism)? And, at a different level, does not the same go for Saint Paul himself?

The best starting point for such a line of inquiry is the point at which religion itself faces a trauma, a shock which dissolves the link between truth and meaning, a truth so traumatic that it resists integration into the universe of Meaning. Every theologian sooner or later faces the problem of how to reconcile the existence of God with the fact of *shoah* or similar excessive evil: how are we to reconcile the existence of an omnipotent and good God with the terrifying suffering of millions of innocents, like the children killed in the gas chambers? Surprisingly (or not), the theological answers build a strange succession of Hegelian triads.

First, those who want to leave divine sovereignty unimpaired, and thus have to attribute to God full responsibility for *shoah*, start with (1) the "legalistic" sin-and-punishment theory (*shoah* has to be a punishment for the past sins of humanity—or Jews themselves); then they go on to (2) the "moralistic" character-education theory (*shoah* is to be understood along the lines of the story of Job, as the most radical test of our faith in God—if we survive this ordeal, our character will stand firm . . .); finally, they take refuge in a kind of "infinite judgment" which should save the day after all common measure between *shoah* and its meaning breaks down: (3) the divine mystery theory (facts like *shoah* bear witness to the unfathomable abyss of divine will). In accordance with the Hegelian motto of a redoubled mystery (the mystery God is for us has also to be a mystery for God himself), the truth of this "infinite judgment" can only be to deny God's full sovereignty and omnipotence. The next triad is thus composed of those who, unable to combine *shoah* with God's omnipotence (how could he have allowed it to happen?), opt for some form of divine limitation: (1) first, God is directly posited as finite or, at least, contained, not omnipotent, not all-encompassing: he finds himself overwhelmed by the dense inertia of his own creation; (2) then, this limitation is reflected back into God himself as his free act: God is self-limited, He voluntarily constrained his power in order to leave the space open for human freedom, so it is we humans who are fully responsible for the evil in the world—in short, phenomena like *shoah* are the ultimate price we have to pay for the divine gift of freedom; (3) finally, self-limitation is externalized, the two moments are posited as autonomous—God is embattled, there is a counterforce or principle of demoniac Evil active in the world (the dualistic solution). Only here, however, do we encounter the core of the problem of the origin of Evil.

The standard metaphysical-religious notion of Evil is that of doubling, gaining a distance, abandoning the reference to the big Other, our Origin and Goal, turning away from the original divine One, getting caught up in the self-referential egotistical loop, thus introducing a gap into the global balance and harmony of the One-All. The easy, all-too-slick, postmodern solution to this is to retort that the way out of this self-incurred impasse consists in abandoning the very presupposition of the primordial One from which we turned away: to accept that our primordial state is one of finding ourselves in a complex situation, one within a multitude of foreign elements— only the theologico-metaphysical presupposition of the original One compels us to perceive the alien as the outcome of (our) alienation.[56] From this perspective, Evil is not the redoubling of the primordial One, turning away from it, but the very imposition of an all-encompassing One onto the primordial dispersal. What if the true task of thought, however, is to think the self-division of the One, to think the One itself as split within itself, as involving an inherent gap?

The very gap between Gnosticism and monotheism can thus be accounted for in terms of the origin of Evil: while Gnosticism locates the primordial duality of Good and Evil in God himself (the material universe into which we are fallen is the creation of an evil and/or stupid divinity, and what gives us hope is the good divinity which keeps alive the promise of another reality, our true home), monotheism saves the unity (one-ness) of God by locating the origin of Evil in our freedom (Evil is either finitude as such, the inertia of material reality, or the spiritual act of willfully turning away from God). It is easy to bring the two together by claiming that the Gnostic duality of God is merely a "reflexive determination" of our own changed attitude toward God: what we perceive as two Gods is in fact the split in our own nature, in our own relating to God. The real task, however, is to locate the source of the split between Good and Evil in God himself *while remaining within the field of monotheism*—the task which German mystics (Jakob Böhme) and later philosophers who pursued their logic (Schelling, Hegel) tried to accomplish. In other words, the task is to transpose the human "external reflection" which enacts the split between Good and Evil back into the One God himself.

Think of the embarrassing situation in which a person of authority can find himself when, although he would love to do it, he is unable to accomplish a good deed he promised to his subject—in such a predicament, the only way to save the appearance of his full power is to pretend that he did not really want to do it—either because the subject does not deserve it, or because he is not as good as he seemed, but has an evil side to him. Appearing "evil" can thus conceal a desperate strategy to save the appearance of one's full power—does the same not hold for God himself?

Back to the topic of *shoah*: this brings us to the third position above and beyond the first two (the sovereign God, the finite God), that of a *suffering God*: not a triumphalist God who always wins in the end, although "his ways are mysterious," since he secretly pulls all the strings; not a God who dispenses cold justice, since he is by definition always right; but a God who—like the suffering Christ on the Cross—is agonized, assumes the burden of suffering, in solidarity with human misery.[57] It was Schelling who wrote: "God is a life, not merely a being. But all life has a fate and is subject to suffering and becoming. . . . *Without the concept of a humanly suffering God . . . all of history remains incomprehensible.*"[58] Why? Because God's suffering implies that he is involved in history, affected by it, not just a transcendent Master pulling the strings from above: God's suffering means that human history is not just a theater of shadows but the place of real struggle, the struggle in which the Absolute itself is involved, and its fate is decided. This is the philosophical background of Dietrich Bonhoeffer's profound insight that, after *shoah*, "only a suffering God can help us now"[59]—a proper supplement to Heidegger's "Only a God can still save us!" from his last interview.[60] We should therefore take the statement that "the unspeakable suffering of the six million is also the voice of the suffering of God"[61] quite literally: the very excess of this suffering over any "normal" human measure makes it divine.

This paradox has been succinctly formulated by Jürgen Habermas: "Secular languages which only eliminate the substance once intended leave irritations. When sin was converted to culpability, and the breaking of divine commands to an offense against human laws, something was lost."[62] This is why the secular-humanist reaction to phenomena like shoah or Gulag (and others) is experienced as inadequate: in order to be at the level of such phenomena, something much stronger is needed, something akin to the old religious topic of a cosmic perversion or catastrophe in which the world itself is "out of joint"—when we confront a phenomenon like shoah, the only appropriate reaction is the perplexed question "Why did the heavens not darken?" (the title of Arno Mayor's famous book on shoah). That is the paradox of the theological significance of shoah: although it is usually conceived as the ultimate challenge to theology (if there is a God, and if he is good, how could he have allowed such a horror to take place?), at the same time it is only theology which can provide the frame that enables us somehow to approach the scope of this catastrophe—the fiasco of God is still the fiasco of God.

Remember the second of Walter Benjamin's "Theses on the Philosophy of History": "The past carries with it a temporal index by which it is referred to redemption. There is a secret agreement between past generations and the present one."[63] Can this "weak messianic power" still be asserted in the face of shoah? How does shoah adumbrate redemption-to-come? Is not the suffering of the victims of shoah a kind of absolute expenditure which can never be retroactively accounted for, redeemed, rendered meaningful? It is at this very point that God's suffering comes in: what it signals is the failure of any Aufhebung of the raw fact of suffering. What resounds here is, more than the Jewish tradition, the basic Protestant lesson: there is no direct access to freedom/ autonomy; between the master-slave exchange relationship of man and God and the full assertion of human freedom, an intermediary stage of absolute humiliation has to intervene in which man is reduced to a pure object of the unfathomable divine caprice.

Do not the three main versions of Christianity form yet another Hegelian triad? In the succession of Orthodoxy, Catholicism, and Protestantism, each new term is a subdivision, split off a previous unity. This triad of Universal-Particular-Singular can be designated by three representative founding figures (John, Peter, Paul), as well as by three races (Slavic, Latin, German). In Eastern Orthodoxy, we have the substantial unity of the text and the corpus of believers, which is why the believers are allowed to interpret the sacred Text, the Text goes on and lives in them, it is not outside living history as its exempted standard and model—the substance of religious life is the Christian community itself. Catholicism stands for radical alienation: the entity which mediates between the founding sacred Text and the corpus of believers, the Church, the religious Institution, regains its full autonomy. The highest authority resides in the Church, which is why the Church has the right to interpret the Text; the Text is read during the Mass in Latin, a language which is not understood by ordinary believers, and it is even considered a sin for an ordinary believer to read the Text directly, bypassing the priest's guidance. For Protestantism, finally, the only authority is the Text itself, and the wager is on every believer's direct contact with the Word of God as it was delivered in the

Text; the mediator (the Particular) thus disappears, withdraws into insignificance, enabling the believer to adopt the position of a "universal Singular," the individual in direct contact with the divine Universality, bypassing the mediating role of the particular Institution.[64] This reconciliation, however, becomes possible only after alienation is brought to an extreme: in contrast to the Catholic notion of a caring and loving God with whom we can communicate, even negotiate, Protestantism starts with the notion of God deprived of any "common measure" shared with man, of God as an impenetrable Beyond who distributes grace in a totally contingent way.[65] We can discern traces of this full acceptance of God's unconditional and capricious authority in the last song Johnny Cash recorded just before his death, "The Man Comes Around," an exemplary articulation of the anxieties contained in Southern Baptist Christianity:

There's a man going around taking names and he decides
Who to free and who to blame everybody won't be treated
Quite the same there will be a golden ladder reaching down
When the man comes around

The hairs on your arm will stand up at the terror in each
Sip and each sup will you partake of that last offered cup
Or disappear into the potter's ground
When the man comes around

Hear the trumpets hear the pipers one hundred million angels singing
Multitudes are marching to a big kettledrum
Voices calling and voices crying
Some are born and some are dying
Its alpha and omegas kingdom come
And the whirlwind is in the thorn trees
The virgins are all trimming their wicks
The whirlwind is in the thorn trees
It's hard for thee to kick against the pricks
Till Armageddon no shalam no shalom

Then the father hen will call his chickens home
The wise man will bow down before the thorn and at his feet
They will cast the golden crowns
When the man comes around

Whoever is unjust let him be unjust still
Whoever is righteous let him be righteous still
Whoever is filthy let him be filthy still

This song is about Armageddon, the End of Days when God will appear and perform the Last Judgment, and this event is presented as pure and arbitrary terror: God almost appears as Evil personified, as a kind of political informer, a man who "comes around" and provokes consternation by "taking names," by deciding who is saved and who is lost. If anything, Cash's description evokes the well-known scene of people lined up for a brutal interrogation, and the informer pointing out those selected for torture:

there is no mercy, no forgiveness of sins, no jubilation; we are all fixed in our roles: the just remain just and the filthy remain filthy. Even worse, in this divine proclamation, we are not simply judged in a just way; we are informed from outside, as if learning about an arbitrary decision, that we were righteous or sinners, that we are saved or condemned—this decision has nothing to do with our inner qualities.[66] And, again, this dark excess of ruthless divine sadism—excess over the image of a severe, but nonetheless just, God—is a necessary negative, an underside, of the excess of Christian love over the Jewish Law: love which suspends the Law is necessarily accompanied by the arbitrary cruelty which also suspends the Law.

When, in his seminar on *The Ethics of Psychoanalysis*, Lacan claims that the "sovereign Good is *das Ding*,"[67] this identification of the highest Good with the evil Thing can be properly understood only as involving a parallax shift: the very thing which, viewed from a proper distance, looks like the supreme Good changes into repulsive Evil the moment we come too near it. This is also why it is wrong to oppose the Christian God of Love to the Jewish God of cruel justice: excessive cruelty is the necessary obverse of Christian Love, and, again, the relationship between these two is one of parallax: there is no "substantial" difference between the God of Love and the God of excessive-arbitrary cruelty, lo 'mperador del doloroso regno, it is one and the same God who appears in a different light only due to a parallax shift of our perspective.[68]

Martin Luther directly proposed an excremental identity of man: man is like divine shit, he fell out of God's anus. We can, of course, pursue the question of the deep crises that pushed Luther toward his new theology; he was caught in a violent debilitating superego cycle: the more he acted, repented, punished, and tortured himself, did good deeds, and so on, the more he felt guilty. This convinced him that good deeds are calculated, dirty, selfish: far from pleasing God, they provoke God's wrath and lead to damnation. Salvation comes from faith: it is our faith alone, faith in Jesus as savior, which allows us to break out of the superego impasse.[69] This "anal" definition of man, however, cannot be reduced to a result of this superego pressure which pushed Luther toward self-abasement—there is more to it: only within this Protestant logic of man's excremental identity can the true meaning of the Incarnation be formulated. In Orthodoxy, Christ ultimately loses his exceptional status: his very idealization, elevation to a noble model, reduces him to an ideal *image*, a figure to be *imitated* (all men should strive to become God)—*imitatio Christi* is more an Orthodox than a Catholic formula. In Catholicism, the predominant logic is that of a *symbolic exchange*: Catholic theologians enjoy long scholastic juridical arguments about how Christ paid the price for our sins, and so on—no wonder Luther reacted to the most contemptible outcome of this logic, the reduction of redemption to something that can be bought from the Church. Protestantism, finally, posits the relationship as *real*, conceiving Christ as a God who, in his act of Incarnation, freely *identified himself with his own shit*, with the excremental Real that is man—and it is only at this level that the properly Christian notion of divine love can be apprehended, as love for the miserable excremental entity called "man."

This excremental identification of man, the key element of the Protestant revolution, opened the way for two tendencies whose impact is fully felt only today, in our late modernity. First, in a rather obvious way, the full scientific-technological naturalization of man: the divine shit can in effect be treated as just another phenomenon of natural evolution. Then—less obviously, but perhaps with even greater consequences—the elevation of enjoyment into a central ethico-political category: the divine shit is deprived of any "higher" vocation, it is ultimately reduced to a machine oscillating between the search for a homeostatic balance of pleasures and the fatal attraction exerted by some excessive *jouissance* which threatens to disturb this homeostatic balance.

The problem with today's superego injunction to enjoy is that, in contrast to previous modes of ideological interpellation, it opens up no "world" proper—it simply refers to an obscure Unnameable. In this sense—and in this sense only—we in effect live in a "postideological universe": what addresses us is a direct "desublimated" call of *jouissance*, no longer masked in an ideological narrative proper.[70] In what, more precisely, does this "worldlessness" consist? As Lacan points out in *Seminar XX: Encore*, *jouissance* involves a logic that is strictly homologous to that of the ontological proof of the existence of God. In the classic version of this proof, my awareness of myself as a finite, limited being immediately gives birth to the notion of an infinite, perfect being, and since this being is perfect, its very notion contains its existence; in the same way, our experience of *jouissance* accessible to us as finite, located, partial, "castrated," immediately gives birth to the notion of a full, achieved, unlimited *jouissance* whose existence is necessarily presupposed by the subject who imputes it to another subject, his or her "subject supposed to enjoy."[71]

Our first reaction here, of course, is that this absolute *jouissance* is a myth, that it never actually existed, that its status is purely differential: that it exists only as a negative point of reference with regard to which every actually experienced *jouissance* falls short ("pleasurable as this is, it is not *that!*"). The recent advances in brain studies, however, open up another approach: we can (no longer only) imagine a situation in which pain (or pleasure) is generated not through sensory perceptions but through a direct excitation of the appropriate neuronal centers (by means of drugs or electrical impulses)—what the subject will experience in this case will be "pure" pain, pain "as such," the Real of pain—or, to put it in precise Kantian terms, nonschematized pain, pain which is not yet rooted in the experience of reality constituted by transcendental categories.[72]

In order to grasp what takes place here properly, we must take a detour through what Lacan called *la jouissance de l'Autre*—what is this mysterious *jouissance*? Imagine (a real clinical case) two love-partners who excite one another by verbalizing, telling one another their innermost sexual fantasies to such a degree that they reach full orgasm without touching, just as the effect of "mere talking." The result of such an excess of intimacy is not difficult to guess: after such a radical mutual exposure, they will no longer be able to maintain their amorous link—too much was being said, or, rather, the spoken word, the big Other, was too directly flooded by *jouissance*, so the two are embarrassed by one another's presence and slowly drift apart, they start to avoid one another's presence. This, not a full perverse orgy, is the true excess: not "putting your innermost fantasies into practice instead of just talking about them," but, precisely, talking about them, allowing them to invade the medium of the big Other to such an extent that one can literally "fuck with words," that the elementary, constitutive, barrier between language and *jouissance* breaks down. Measured by this standard, the most extreme "real orgy" is a poor substitute.

The presentation of the sexual act in Adrian Lyne's *Unfaithful* is a perfect instance of the logic of the feminine *jouissance de l'Autre*: after the couple (the married Diane Lane and the young Frenchman) embrace in his apartment, there is a direct cut to Diane Lane returning home on the suburban train, sitting alone and reminiscing. Her remembering (portrayed through a wonderful display of embarrassed smiles, tears, gestures of incredulity at what happened, and so on) is intercepted by short fragmented flashbacks of the couple making love—thus we see the love act only, as it were, in *futur antérieur*, as it is recollected. The direct sexual *jouissance* is immediately "sublated" in the *jouissance* of the Other; the two magically overlap. The lesson is that the "true" *jouissance* is neither in the act itself nor in the thrill of the expectation of pleasures to come, but in the melancholic remembrance of it. And the enigma is: is it possible to imagine a sexual act in which the participants, while "really doing it," already adopt the imagined position of remembering it, from which they *now* enjoy it? Furthermore, can we say that this melancholic position of *futur antérieur* is feminine, while the *jouissance* engendered by the thrill of pleasures to come is masculine? Recall the famous scene, in Bergman's *Persona*, of Bibi Andersson telling the story of a beach orgy and passionate lovemaking in which she participated: we see no flashback pictures; nonetheless the scene is one of the most erotic in the entire history of cinema—the excitement is in how she tells it, and this excitement which resides in speech itself is *jouissance féminine*. . . .

In *Nathalie* (Anne Fontaine, 1999), Fanny Ardant and Gérard Depardieu are Catherine and Bernard, a longtime married couple. When Catherine stumbles by chance upon a phone message which suggests that Bernard is having an affair, Bernard shrugs it off with "It's too banal to talk about." But Catherine is deeply disturbed, and she becomes desperate for the causes and details of Bernard's liaisons. Being a gynecologist, she proceeds as a clinician, hiring a prostitute, Marlène (Emmanuelle Béart), to act as "Nathalie," a woman who will seduce Bernard and then tell her, in detail, the story of her love encounters with him. The film sticks obstinately to Catherine's perspective: except in Marlène's initial approach to Bernard, when she asks him for a light in a café, it does not show us Marlène's interactions with Bernard, choosing instead to focus on Catherine and her state of mind, which grows increasingly unsettled as she learns the details of more and more passionate sexual encounters. Gradually it becomes obvious that Catherine and Marlène are drawn to each other—and not just because Marlène happens to be the woman Catherine has chosen to perform an unusual task. Soon it is Catherine who makes excuses to get away from Bernard to visit Marlène, even inviting her to spend an evening with her mother, and Bernard who wonders why his wife has become so distant, rather than the other way round. Although Marlène seems to be more distant and "professional," her attachment to Catherine is, if anything, even more profound.

Then something (not really) unexpected happens: when Catherine organizes a meeting between Marlène and Bernard in her presence (making a date in a café with both of them at the same time), the surprised Bernard does not even recognize Marlène, who turns around and runs away in a panic. Later, she confesses to Catherine that Bernard rejected her advances: she was inventing all the reports of their love trysts . . . why? Was it only for money—that is to say, did Marlène merely guess and fabricate what Catherine wanted? The film hints at a deeper link between the two women: it is not about Catherine and Bernard, or about Marlène and Bernard; in fact, Bernard turns out to be only tangentially relevant to the development of the film's central relationship, between Catherine and Marlène. The trap to avoid here, however, is to read this intense relationship between the two women as (implicitly) lesbian: it is crucial that the narrative they share is heterosexual, and it is no less crucial that all they share is a narrative. There is no "frustration" in it, no sacrificial renunciation of consummating their relationship "in the flesh," their conversation is not a foreplay endlessly postponing full satisfaction. All the speculation about the lesbian subtext, about the feminine bond excluding the man, and so on, is superfluous here—it merely distracts us from perceiving the crucial role of the fact that the two women realize their link at the level of "mere words," that their *jouissance* is the *jouissance* of the Other through and through.

And it is this dimension of the *jouissance* of the Other that is threatened by the prospect of "pure" *jouissance*. Is such a short circuit not the basic and most disturbing feature of consuming drugs to generate the experience of enjoyment? What drugs promise is a purely autistic *jouissance*, a *jouissance* accessible without a detour through the Other (of the symbolic order)—*jouissance* generated not by fantasmatic representations but by directly attacking our neuronal pleasure centers. It is in this precise sense that drugs involve the suspension of symbolic castration, whose most elementary meaning is precisely that *jouissance* is accessible only through the medium of (as mediated by) symbolic representation. This brutal Real of *jouissance* is the obverse of the infinite plasticity of imagining, no longer constrained by the rules of reality. Significantly, the experience of drugs encompasses both these extremes: on the one hand, the Real of noumenal (nonschematized) *jouissance* which bypasses representations; on the other, the wild proliferation of fantasizing (think of the proverbial reports on how, after taking a drug, you imagine scenes you never thought you were able to access—new dimensions of shapes, colors, smells . . .).

Some of us remember the tamagochi phenomenon from a decade or so ago: the virtual pet with whom one interacts only through the screen of a small electronic toy, exchanging signs with it. The mass media informed us that, in March 2005, tamagochi finally matured: for those who were tired of the time, effort, and expense demanded by a real-life girlfriend, the Hong Kong software company Artificial Life put on the market Vivienne, a virtual girlfriend. This product of computerized voice synthesis, streaming video and text messages, is meant to be a lure for the new, higher-tech, third-generation (or 3G) cell phones.[73] Vivienne likes to be taken to movies and bars, to be given virtual flowers and chocolates, but she never undresses and draws the line at anything beyond blowing kisses; however, Artificial Life has already been contacted by companies interested in a racier, even pornographic, version. Vivienne, who is scheduled to become available in Western Europe by late spring 2005, and possibly in a few American cities by the end of the year, may soon be joined by a virtual boyfriend for women and, after that, a virtual boyfriend for gay men and a virtual girlfriend for lesbians. At Artificial Life, they emphasize that Vivienne is not a substitute for a flesh-and-blood girlfriend: she is more a practice round before the real one—or is she? On a first approach, Vivienne cannot but look like the next logical step in the development of our interhuman contacts: we complain that our relations to "real people" are more and more mediated by screens—so why not simply drop the flesh-and-blood person altogether? Surprisingly, this brings us back to the original human intelligence test proposed by Alan Turing: a machine possesses human intelligence if, after a long conversation with it, a human interlocutor cannot decide if he is dealing with a human or a machine.

Of course, Vivienne plays upon the fantasmatic structure of the "ghost in the machine" that I myself experience every time I have to use the automated coffee machine at an airport or a train station: I cannot get rid of the crazy idea that there is a dwarf hidden within the machine who, after a customer presses the buttons and puts in the coins, quickly pours the coffee and puts the cup into the appropriate opening. . . . The efficacy of Vivienne—although users are well aware that "she doesn't really exist"—brings us back to what Lacan had in mind with his *il n'y a pas de rapport sexuel*: not only is masturbation sex with an imagined partner (one does it to oneself, arousing oneself with imagined activity with partners); in a strictly symmetrical way, "real sex" has the structure of *masturbation with a real partner*—in effect, I use the flesh-and-blood partner as a masturbatory prop for enacting my fantasies. In other words, what makes the notion of Vivienne so traumatic for those attached to "real communication with real people" is not that the link to a flesh-and-blood person is severed, but that we are forced to realize how sex always-already was "virtual," with flesh-and-blood persons used as masturbatory props for dwelling in our fantasies.

How, then, does this thorough virtualization of sexual interplay, this severing of the links with a "real person," relate to the Real of *jouissance?* Here again the key is provided by the Hegelian "infinite judgment" in which extreme opposites coincide: the "passion for the Real" and the "passion for semblance" are two sides of the same phenomenon, that is, the reality of the "flesh-and-blood partner" excluded in the complete virtualization of sex returns with a vengeance in the Real, as a drive to experience the Real of pleasure/pain in its most extreme forms.

We should therefore learn to discern the lesson of recent biotechnological break-throughs. In 2003, Japanese telecom companies came up with the world's first mobile phone that enables users to listen to calls inside their heads—by conducting sound through bone. The phone is equipped with a "Sonic Speaker" which transmits sounds through vibrations that move from the skull to the cochlea in the inner ear, instead of relying on the usual method of sound hitting the outer eardrum. With the new hand-set, the key to better hearing in a noisy situation is thus to plug your ears to prevent outside noise from drowning out bone-conducted sounds. Here we encounter the Lacanian distinction between reality and the Real: this spectral voice which we hear in our interior reality, although it has no place in external reality, is the Real at its purest.

In a step further, in 2003, at the Center for Neuroengineering at Duke University, monkeys with brain implants were trained to move a robot arm with their thoughts: a series of electrodes containing tiny wires was implanted into the brains of two mon-keys; a computer then recorded signals produced by the monkeys' brains as they ma-nipulated a joystick controlling the robotic arm in exchange for a reward—sips of juice. The joystick was later unplugged and the arm, which was in a separate room, was controlled directly by the brain signals coming from the implants. The monkeys eventually stopped using the joystick, as if they knew their brains were controlling the robot arm. The Duke researchers have now moved on to researching similar implants in humans: in summer 2004 it was reported that they had succeeded in temporarily implanting electrodes into the brains of volunteers; the volunteers then played video games while the electrodes recorded their brain signals—the scientists trained a com-puter to recognize the brain activity corresponding to the different movements of the joystick. This procedure of "eavesdropping" on the brain's digital crackle with elec-trodes (where computers use zeros and ones, neurons encode our thoughts in all-or-nothing electrical impulses) and transmitting the signals to a computer that can read the brain's code and then use the signals to control as machine already has an official name: brain-machine interface. Further prospects include not only more complex tasks (for instance, implanting the electrodes into the language centers of the brain, and thus transmitting a person's inner voice to a machine via wireless, so that one can speak "directly," bypassing voice or writing), but also sending the brain signals to a machine thousands of miles away, and thus directing it from a distance. And what about sending the signals to somebody standing nearby with electrodes implanted in his hearing centers, so that he can "telepathically" listen to my inner voice?[74] The Or-wellian notion of "thought control" will thus acquire a much more literal meaning.

Even Stephen Hawking's proverbial little finger—the minimal link between his mind and outside reality, the only part of his paralyzed body that Hawking can move—will thus no longer be necessary: with my mind, I can directly cause objects to move; that is to say, it is the brain itself which will serve as the remote-control machine. In the terms of German Idealism, this means that what Kant called "intellectual intuition [intellektuelle Anschauung]"—the closing of the gap between mind and reality, a mind-process which, in a causal way, directly influences reality, this capacity that Kant attributed only to the infinite mind of God—is now potentially available to all of us, that is to say, we are potentially deprived of one of the basic features of our finitude. And since, as we learned from Kant as well as from Freud, this gap of finitude is at the same time the resource of our creativity (the distance between "mere thought" and causal intervention in external reality enables us to test the hypotheses in our mind and, as Karl Popper put it, let them die instead of ourselves), the direct short circuit between mind and reality implies the prospect of a radical closure.

In his *Ethics* seminar, Lacan invokes the "point of the apocalypse,"[75] the impossible saturation of the Symbolic by the Real of *jouissance*, its full immersion in massive *jouissance*. When, in a Heideggerian way, he asks: "Have we crossed the line . . . in the world in which we live?",[76] he is alluding to the fact that "the possibility of the death of the Symbolic has become a tangible reality."[77] Lacan mentions the threat of atomic holocaust; today, however, we are in a position to offer other versions of this death of the Symbolic, principal among them the full scientific naturalization of the human mind.[78]

The same point can be made in Nietzschean terms—what, in effect, is Nietzsche's eternal return of the same? Does it stand for the factual repetition, for the repetition of the past which should be willed as it was, or for a Benjaminian repetition, a return-reactualization of that which was lost in the past occurrence, of its virtual excess, of its redemptive potential? There are good reasons to read it as the heroic stance of endorsing factual repetition: recall how Nietzsche emphatically points out that, faced with every event in my life, even the most painful one, I should summon up the strength to joyfully will it to return eternally. If we read the thought of eternal return in this way, then Agamben's evocation of the Holocaust as the conclusive argument against the eternal return retains its full weight: who can will it to return eternally? What, however, if we reject the notion of the eternal return of the same as the repetition of the reality of the past, insofar as it relies on an all-too-primitive notion of the past, on the reduction of the past to the one-dimensional reality of "what really happened," which erases the virtual dimension of the past? If we read the eternal return of the same as the redemptive repetition of the past virtuality? In this case, applied to the nightmare of the Holocaust, the Nietzschean eternal return of the same means precisely that one should will the repetition of the potential which was lost through the reality of the Holocaust, the potential whose nonactualization opened up the space for the Holocaust to occur.

There is, however, another problem with the eternal return of the same. What would the digital virtualization of our lives, the shift of our identity from hardware to software, our change from finite mortals to "undead" virtual entities able to persist indefinitely, migrating from one material support to another—in short: the passage from human to posthuman—mean in Nietzschean terms? Is this posthumanity a version of the eternal return? Is the digital posthuman subject a version (a historical actualization) of the Nietzschean "overman"? Or is this digital version of posthumanity a version of what Nietzsche called the Last Man? What if it is, rather, the point of indistinction of the two, and, as such, a signal of the limitation of Nietzsche's thought?

In other words, is the eternal return rooted in human finitude (since the gap between virtuality and actuality persists only from the horizon of finitude), or does it stand for our uncoupling from finitude?

When today's subjectivity is celebrated as rootless, migratory, nomadic, hybrid, and so on, does not digitalization provide the ultimate horizon of this migration, that of the fateful shift of hardware into software: of severing the link that attaches a mind to its fixed material embodiment (a single individual's brain), and downloading the entire content of a mind into a computer, with the possibility of the mind turning into software that can migrate indefinitely from one material embodiment to another, and thus acquire a kind of undeadness? Metempsychosis, the migration of souls, thus becomes a question of technology. The idea is that "we are entering a regime as radically different from our human past as we humans are from the lower animals":[79] by uploading yourself into a computer, you become "anything you like. You can be big or small; you can be lighter than air; you can walk through walls."[80] In good old Freudian terms, we thus get rid of the minimum of resistance that defines (our experience of) reality, and enter the domain in which the pleasure principle reigns unconstrained, with no concessions to the reality principle—or, as David Pearce put it in his most appropriately titled book *The Hedonistic Imperative*: "nanotechnology and genetic engineering will eliminate aversive experience from the living world. Over the next thousand years or so, the biological substrates of suffering will be eradicated completely," since we shall achieve "the neuro-chemical precision engineering of happiness for every sentient organism on the planet."[81] (Note the Buddhist overtones of this passage!) And, of course, since one definition of being-human is that disposing of shit is a problem, part of this new posthumanity will also entail that dirt and shit will disappear:

> a superman must be cleaner than a man. In the future, our plumbing (of the thawed as well as the newborn) will be more hygienic and seemly. Those who choose to will consume only zero-residue foods, with excess water all evaporating via the pores. Alternatively, modified organs may occasionally expel small, dry compact residues.[82]

Next comes the confused functioning of our orifices: is the multipurpose mouth not "awkward and primitive"? "An alien would find it most remarkable that we had an organ combining the requirements of breathing, ingesting, tasting, chewing, biting, and on occasion fighting, helping to thread needles, yelling, whistling, lecturing, and grimacing"[83]—not to mention kissing, licking, and sucking. Is not the ultimate target here the penis itself, with its embarrassing overlapping of the highest (insemination) with the lowest (urination)?

DANGER? WHAT DANGER?

Today, with the prospect of the biogenetic manipulation of human physical and psychic features, the notion of "danger" inscribed into modern technology, elaborated by Heidegger, has become common currency. Heidegger emphasizes how the true danger is not the physical self-destruction of humanity, the threat that something will go terribly wrong with biogenetic interventions, but, precisely, that *nothing will go wrong*, that genetic manipulations will function smoothly—at this point, the circle will, in a way, be closed, and the specific openness that characterizes being-human abolished. That is to say: is not the Heideggerian danger (*Gefahr*) precisely the danger that the on-tic will "swallow" the ontological (with the reduction of man, the *Da* [here] of Being, to just another object of science)? Do we not encounter here again the formula of fear-ing the impossible: what we fear is that what cannot happen (since the ontological di-mension is irreducible to the ontic) will nonetheless happen. . . . And the same point is made in more common terms by cultural critics from Fukuyama and Habermas to McKibben, worried about how the latest techno-scientific developments (which po-tentially have made the human species able to redesign and redefine itself) will affect our being-human—the call we hear is best encapsulated by the title of Bill McKibben's book: "Enough."

Humanity as a collective subject has to set a limit, and freely renounce further "progress" in this direction. McKibben endeavors to specify this limit empirically: so-matic genetic therapy is still this side of the enough point, we can practice it without leaving behind the world as we have known it, since we simply intervene in a body formed in the old "natural" way; germline manipulations lie on the other side, in the world beyond meaning.[84] When we manipulate psychic and bodily properties of individuals before they are even conceived, we cross the threshold into full-fledged planning, turning individuals into products, preventing them from experiencing themselves as responsible agents who have to educate/form themselves by the effort of focusing their will, thus obtaining the satisfaction of achievement—such individ-uals no longer relate to themselves as responsible agents. . . .

This reasoning is doubly inadequate. First, as Heidegger would have put it, the sur-vival of the being-human of humans cannot depend on an ontic decision by humans. Even if we try to define the limit of the permissible in this way, *the true catastrophe has al-ready taken place*: we already experience ourselves as in principle manipulable, we just freely renounce the full deployment of this potential. But the crucial point is that, not only will our universe of meaning disappear with biogenetic planning—not only are utopian descriptions of the digital paradise wrong, since they imply that meaning will persist; the opposite, negative descriptions of the "meaningless" universe of techno-logical self-manipulation are also the victim of a perspective fallacy, they also measure the future according to inadequate present standards. That is to say: the future of tech-nological self-manipulation appears to be "deprived of meaning" only if it is mea-sured by (or, rather, from within the horizon of) the traditional notion of what a meaningful universe is. Who knows what this "posthuman" universe will reveal itself to be "in itself"? What if there is no singular and simple answer, what if contempo-rary trends (digitalization, biogenetic self-manipulation) open themselves up to a mul-titude of possible symbolizations? What if both the utopia—the perverted dream of the passage from hardware to software of a subjectivity floating freely between different embodiments—and the dystopia—the nightmare of humans voluntarily transforming themselves into programmed beings—are just the positive and the negative of the same ideological fantasy? What if it is only and precisely this technological prospect that fully confronts us with the most radical dimension of our finitude?

Today you can buy laptops with a keyboard that artificially imitates the resistance to the fingers of the old typewriter, as well as the typewriter sound of the letter hitting the paper—what better example of the recent need for pseudo-concreteness? Today, when not only social relations but also technology are getting more and more nontransparent (who can visualize what is going on inside a PC?), there is a great need to re-create an artificial concreteness in order to enable individuals to relate to their complex environs as to a meaningful life-world. In computer programming, this was the step accomplished by Apple: the pseudo-concreteness of icons. Guy Debord's old formula about the "society of spectacle" is thus getting a new twist: images are created in order to fill in the gap that separates the new artificial universe from our old life-world surroundings: that is, to "domesticate" this new universe.

Throughout the twentieth century, the art of cinema—its emblematic art—was defined as the site of the irreducible tension between the mechanical passivity of the registering camera and the active imposition of the director's will through staging the registered scene and its subsequent (re)combination in the process of cutting: no matter how manipulated the scene, there always remained an element of irreducible passivity, of "it really had to happen." (This is why, as Rancière rightly observed, what we call "documentary film" is no less—perhaps even more—"fictional" than narrative film.) This tension seems to undergo a radical shift with the recent advent of digitalization: when, say, in *The Gladiator*, the public in the arena observing the fights was generated and added digitally, or when, in the last *Star Wars* installments and some other sci-fi films, whole characters are just digital creations—not even to mention the (realistic) prospect of digitally bringing to life dead stars, so that we will soon be able to watch new films with Marilyn Monroe or Humphrey Bogart, something changes radically. The cinematic stuff loses its passivity, its minimum of the Real, and turns into a purely plastic medium in which our inventive capacity is given free rein.[85]

"Neurotheologians" can identify the brain processes which accompany intense religious experiences: when, for instance, a subject experiences himself as timeless and infinite, part of the cosmic All, released from the confines of his Self, the region of his brain which processes information about space, time, and the orientation of the body in space "goes dark"; in the blocking of sensory inputs which occurs during intense meditative concentration, the brain has no choice but to perceive the self as endless and intimately interwoven with everyone and everything. The same goes for visions: they clearly correspond to abnormal bursts of electrical activity in the temporal lobes ("temporal-lobe epilepsy"). The counter-argument here is: while, of course, everything we experience also exists as a neurological activity, this does not in any way resolve the question of causality. When we eat an apple, we also experience the satisfaction of its good taste as a neuronal activity, but this does not in any way affect the fact that the apple was really out there, and caused our activity. In the same way, it is totally undecided whether our brain wiring creates (our experience of) God, or whether God created our brain wiring. . . . Is, however, the question of causality not easily resolved? If we (the experimenting doctor) directly intervene in the appropriate parts of the brain, causing the brain activity in question, and if, during this activity of ours, the subject "experiences the divine dimension," does this not provide a conclusive answer?

The next question is: how will the subject who is aware of all this *subjectivize* his religious experience? Will he continue to experience it as "religious" in the appropriate ecstatic sense of the term? The extreme solution here is that of a US religious sect which claims that God, who observes us all the time, and took note of the lack of authentic religious experiences among his believers, organized the discovery of drugs which can generate such experiences. . . . Further experiments show that when individuals are able to stimulate their neuronal pleasure centers directly, they do not get caught up in a blind compulsive drive toward excessive pleasure, but provide themselves pleasure only when they judge that they have "deserved" it (on account of their everyday acts)—however, do many of us not do the same with pleasures provided in a "normal" way? What all this indicates is that people who experience directly generated pleasures do not suffer a breakdown of their symbolic universe, but integrate these pleasure experiences smoothly into it, or even rely on them to enhance their experience of sacred meaning. Again, however, the question is: what disavowals do such integrations involve; can I really accept that the industrially fabricated pill I hold in my hand puts me in contact with God?

Consciousness is "phenomenal" in contrast to "real" brain processes, but therein lies the true (Hegelian) problem: not how to get from phenomenal experience to reality, but how and why phenomenal experience emerges/explodes in the midst of "blind"/wordless reality. There must be a non-All, a gap, a hole, in reality itself, filled in by phenomenal experience. What happens to this gap, and to the "phenomenal" level, when computers communicate among themselves? How will we represent this communication to ourselves? When two stock exchange agents let their computers conclude a deal, the machines, of course, *stricto sensu* do not communicate, they just exchange signals which acquire meaning at both extremes—*there is no "interface" when computers interact*. Communication will thus be reduced to a pure presupposition—and this is intuitively difficult to accept. Take the final scene of *The Matrix Revolutions*, where the meeting of the couple who make the deal, the (feminine) Oracle and the (masculine) Architect, takes place *within the virtual reality of the Matrix*—why? They are both mere computer programs, and the virtual interface is there only for the human gaze—computers themselves do not communicate through the screen of the virtual imaginary, they directly exchange digital bytes. . . . For which gaze, then, is this scene staged?

In the development of the technology of communication, what was at first meant to serve as a means turns all of a sudden into the "thing itself." Computers were first used in desktop publishing as an instrument for more efficient printing—that is to say, the "real thing" was still the printed final product; then people started to conceive the virtual text in the computer as already the "thing itself" which, later, can be printed on paper or not. And what if the same goes for "thinking" computers? They were constructed as a means of facilitating human thinking, but, at a certain point, will they do the "thing itself," and will the humans using them be reduced to an aesthetic supplement, like the printed book in a digital era?

The prospect of radical self-objectivization brought about by cognitivism cannot fail to cause anxiety—why? Here we should follow Lacan, who inverted Freud's two main theses on anxiety: (1) in contrast to fear, which is focused on determinate objects or situations, anxiety has no object; (2) anxiety is caused by an experience of the threat of a loss (castration, weaning). Lacan turns the two theses around (or, rather, tries to demonstrate that, without knowing it, Freud himself did so): it is fear which blurs its object, while anxiety has a precise object—*objet petit a*; anxiety emerges not when this object is lost, but when we get too close to it. The same goes for the relationship between anxiety and (free) act. On a first approach, anxiety emerges when we are totally determined, objectivized, forced to assume that there is no freedom, that we are just neuronal puppets, self-deluded zombies; at a more radical level, however, anxiety arises when we are compelled to confront our freedom. (It is the same in Kant: when we are able to identify a pathological cause of an act of ours, this cannot but be a relief from the anxiety of freedom; or, as Kierkegaard would have put it, the true horror is to discover that we are *immortal*, that we have a higher Duty and responsibility— how much easier would it be to be a mere natural mechanism. . . .) Consequently, cognitivist self-objectivization causes anxiety because—although, in terms of its enunciated content, it "objectivizes" us—it has the opposite effect in terms of the implied position of enunciation: it confronts us with the abyss of our freedom, and, simultaneously, with the radical contingency of the emergence of consciousness:

> Consciousness is a product of our brain, which in turn is a product of evolution. But the features of the human brain are emergent, are the result of a series of random acquisitions . . . that may have been encouraged by natural selection only *after* the brain was formed.[86]

This means that the human brain did not develop "in view of" its future uses (because it is indispensable for some specific biological function); it suddenly exploded in the course of a process in which "a new combination of characteristics randomly produces an entirely unforeseen result."[87] There is a more refined dialectical reasoning than it may seem at work here. That is to say: at first sight, it may seem that there is no big difference between this notion of "ex-aptation" and the standard "hard" Darwinian notion: Dennett himself refers approvingly to the Nietzschean idea of how nature functions as a *bricoleur*, reusing organs which originally evolved for a particular function for another function. The "hard" Darwinians are thus fully aware of how evolutionary adaptation only uses (chooses from) multiple variations which emerge in a contingent aleatory way, with no purpose. The difference that separates the "hard"

Darwinians from dialecticians proper like Stephen Jay Gould, however, is double. First, the dialectical approach proper is *structural*: the New emerges not as an element, but as a structure. In an aleatory way, all of a sudden, a new Order, new harmony, emerges out of Chaos. Although we can (retroactively) ascertain a long gestation period, one last element triggers the swift shift from Chaos to new Order—"hard" Darwinists do not talk in terms of such a structural "totality." Second difference: this new Order cannot be accounted for in terms of "adaptation"—it is not only that a univocal *ad quem* is missing here (adaptation to what?), one also cannot presuppose a univocal agent of it (adaptation of what?). A vicious cycle is inescapable here: we cannot explain the very emergence of an organism in the terms of a strategy of adaptation. If an organism is to adapt in order to survive, it must be there in the first place. An organism evolves to survive, but it cannot emerge in order to survive: it is meaningless to say that I live *in order* to adapt myself. In short, a newly emerging Order "creates" ("posits") its environs—in relating to its other, it relates to itself:

> Regardless of the moment and the place where it happened, the evolution of consciousness was not a gradual process. Some philosophers, refusing to acknowledge great discontinuities in nature, suggested that consciousness had emerged slowly and by degrees, from "less" conscious animals to other "more" conscious ones and so on. . . . Actually, consciousness could not have arisen unless and until the activity of the retroaction loops had reached the level of reverberating activity, and a property of feedback loops is "all or nothing": either reverberating activity is supported by a significant life span or it dies at birth. . . . a threshold was reached beyond which consciousness appeared out of the blue, just like there is a threshold beyond which we go from sleeping to being awake.[88]

Why, then, does the New emerge? Ultimately, there are only two consistent explanations: either an (open or hidden) teleology, or what Varela called "feminine ontology":

> Because, among all these possibilities, there was the possibility to emerge. It is an effect of the situation. It could just as well have happened as not. There is a very aleatory dimension in the world, connected with the notion of "gentle evolution" or "drifting". . . . It is as though the ontology of the world were very feminine, an ontology of permissivity, an ontology of possibility. As long as it is possible, it is possible. I do not need to seek a justification in an ideal optimality. In the midst of it all, life attempts the possible, life is a bricolage.[89]

This notion of "feminine ontology," far from relying on a vague metaphor, fits perfectly the coordinates of the Lacanian logic of non-All: necessity is "not all," yet nothing escapes it.

CHAPTER 4

THE LOOP OF FREEDOM

The universe of cartoons obeys two opposing rules, both of which violate the logic of our ordinary reality. First, a cat is walking above the precipice, with no ground beneath its feet, but it falls down only when it looks down and realizes that there is no firm ground beneath its feet. Second, a character witnesses an act which goes against his interests (someone is driving along in his stolen car, and so on); he smiles benignly, even waves at the passerby, becoming aware only when it is already too late that the car is his own—at that point only, the smile changes into consternation. . . . What these two opposing gags share is the temporal delay: the body falls down only when it becomes aware of its lack of ground; the character notices too late that the process going on in front of him affects him. . . . The role of awareness, however, is inverted: the first case is similar to the one of quantum physics, since taking note of it, registration, being-aware-of-it, is the condition of the event's actualization—it actually happens only when one becomes aware of one's situation; in the second case, awareness comes too late, after the thing has already taken place—not behind the subject's back, but in full view—and the comic effect occurs when we see the subject clearly seeing what is going on in front of him (someone driving his own car) without being aware of what this means, of how it affects him, of how he is involved in it. Although the two procedures seem surreal, even ridiculous, in both of them a real-life situation reverberates.

Is it not true that when a political system is in deep crisis, it *drags on only because it doesn't notice that it is already dead*—the moment when those in power (as we usually put it) "lose faith in themselves," stop believing in themselves, admit that the game is up, is crucial. And there is always a temporal gap between this awareness that "the game is up" and the actual loss of power—those in power can prolong their desperate hold on it; battles can go on, with lots of blood and corpses, even if the game is already up. This same political process of disintegration of a power structure also provides the case of the second process in which consciousness is out of sync with the actual state of things: those in power are not aware that their time is over, that the process they are watching is their own funeral, so they smile and wave like the idiot who waves at the guy driving away his own car. . . .

The two opposing procedures can thus be united in a single process: a catastrophic X occurs, but the affected agent remains unaware of it and goes on with life as usual; only when it registers/perceives its state is the catastrophe actualized, does it strike with full force.[1] Is this not also the ultimate lesson of Benjamin Libet's famous experiment (on which more below)?[2] Consciousness is in itself deprived of any substantial role, merely registering a process that goes on independently of it—yet this registration is crucial if the "objective" process is to actualize itself.

Toward the end of Spielberg's *Minority Report*,[3] there is a moment which stages something like an ethical act proper. John Anderton (Tom Cruise) finally confronts the man who, six years before, was supposed to have raped and killed his little son;[4] when he is on the verge of shooting the killer (as he was predetermined to do, according to the vision of the three "precognitives"), he stops, blocking the execution of his decision, arresting his gesture—does he not thereby confirm Libet's "Hegelian" insight into how the elementary act of freedom, the manifestation of free will, is that of saying no, of stopping the execution of a decision? At its most elementary, freedom is not the freedom to do as you like (that is, to follow your inclinations without any externally imposed constraints), but to do what you do not want to do, to thwart the "spontaneous" realization of an impetus. This is the link between freedom and the Freudian "death drive," which is also a drive to sabotage one's inclination toward pleasure. And is this not why Freud was so fascinated by Michelangelo's *Moses*? He read the statue as depicting the moment when, full of rage and intending to smash the tablets containing the Decalogue, Moses summons up the strength to stop his act in the midst of its execution. So when Daniel Wegner,[5] in a very Kantian way, claims that "[a] voluntary action is something a person can do when asked," the implication is precisely that we thus obey an order which goes *against* our spontaneous inclination. Here, Badiou is wrong: the elementary ethical gesture is a negative one, the one of blocking one's direct inclination.

This free act fundamentally changes the coordinates of the entire situation: Anderton breaks the closure of future/past *possibility*. The idea that the emergence of a radically New retroactively changes the past—not the actual past, of course (we are not in science fiction), but past possibilities, or, to put it in more formal terms, the truth value of the modal propositions about the past—was first explored by Henri Bergson. In "Two Sources of Morality and Religion," Bergson describes the strange sensations he experienced on August 4, 1914, when war was declared between France and Germany: "In spite of my turmoil, and although a war, even a victorious one, appeared to me as a catastrophe, I experienced what [William] James spoke about, a feeling of admiration for the facility of the passage from the abstract to the concrete: who would have thought that such a formidable event can emerge in reality with so little fuss?"[6] The modality of the break between before and after is crucial here: before its outbreak, the war appeared to Bergson "*simultaneously probable and impossible*: a complex and contradictory notion which persisted to the end";[7] afterward, all of a sudden it become real *and* possible, and the paradox resides in this retroactive appearance of probability:

> I never pretended that one can insert reality into the past and thus work backwards in time. However, one can without any doubt insert there the possible, or, rather, at every moment, the possible inserts itself there. Insofar as unpredictable and new reality creates itself, its image reflects itself behind itself in the indefinite past: this new reality finds itself all the time having been possible; but it is only at the precise moment of its actual emergence that it *begins to always have been*, and this is why I say that its possibility, which does not precede its reality, will have preceded it once this reality emerges.[8]

Such experiences show the limitation of the ordinary "historical" notion of time: at each moment of time, there are multiple possibilities waiting to be realized; once one of them actualizes itself, the others are cancelled. The supreme case of such an agent of historical time is the Leibnizian God, who created the best possible world: before creation, he had in his mind the entire panoply of possible worlds, and his decision consisted in choosing the best one among these options. Here, possibility precedes choice: the choice is a choice among possibilities. What is unthinkable within this horizon of linear historical evolution is the notion of *a choice/act which retroactively opens up its own possibility.*[9] This is exactly what Anderton does with his negative act: he breaks the closed circle of determinism which legitimizes preemptive arrests, and introduces the moment of ontological openness.[10] It does not simply "change the future"; it changes the future by changing the past itself (in the Bergsonian sense of inserting a new possibility into it).

As intelligent participants in the ongoing "freedom versus brain sciences" debate have noted, the problem should not be reduced to the dilemma "is the (deterministic) natural causal link complete, or is there a gap in it which allows an opening for a free act?", as it often is by those philosophers who think that, once one "proves"— through a vague reference to quantum physics, as a rule—that there is a genuine indeterminacy/contingency in nature, freedom is thereby possible, its space "ontologically guaranteed." It was Daniel Dennett who pointed out, against this line of reasoning, that one can easily imagine a universe in which genuine chance has its place, but there is no freedom: even if my decision to do something or not (say, to stop writing at this moment) is genuinely not fully covered by the preceding causal networks, it is not a "free act" if it means only that a purely mechanical contingency (like tossing a coin) tipped my decision in one direction or another.[11] "Freedom" is not simply the opposite of deterministic causal necessity: as Kant knew, it means a specific mode of causality, the agent's self-determination. There is in fact a kind of Kantian antinomy of freedom: if an act is fully determined by preceding causes, it is, of course, not free; if, however, it depends on the pure contingency which momentarily severs the full causal chain, it is also not free. The only way to resolve this antinomy is to introduce a second-level reflexive causality: I am determined by causes (be it direct brute natural causes or motivations), and the space of freedom is not a magic gap in this first-level causal chain but my ability retroactively to choose/determine which causes will determine me. "Ethics," at its most elementary, stands for the courage to accept this responsibility.

If, in the story of modern literature, there was ever a person who exemplifies ethical defeat, it is Ted Hughes. The true Other Woman, the focus of the Hughes-Plath saga ignored by both camps, is Assia Wevill, a dark-haired Jewish beauty, a Holocaust survivor, Ted's mistress on account of whom he left Sylvia. So this was like leaving a wife and marrying the madwoman in the attic—however, how did she get mad in the first place? In 1969, she killed herself in the same way as Sylvia (by gassing herself), but killing along with her also Shura, her daughter by Ted. Why? What drove her into this uncanny repetition? This was Ted's true ethical betrayal, not Sylvia—here, his *Birthday Letters*, with their fake mythologizing, turn into an ethically repulsive text, putting the blame on the dark forces of Fate which run our lives, casting Assia as the dark seductress: "You are the dark force. You are the dark destructive force that destroyed Sylvia."[12]

(The psychoanalytic notion of the Unconscious is the very opposite of this instinctual irrational Fate onto which we can transpose our responsibility.) Recall the line from Oscar Wilde's *The Importance of Being Ernest*: "To lose one parent may be regarded as a misfortune; to lose both looks like carelessness"—does not the same go for Ted Hughes? "To lose one wife through suicide may be regarded as a misfortune; to lose two wives looks like carelessness. . . ." Hughes's version is one long variation on Valmont's *"ce n'est pas ma faute"* from *Les liaisons dangereuses*: it wasn't me, it was Fate—as he put it, responsibility is "a figment valid only in a world of lawyers as moralists."[13] All his babble about Feminine Goddess, Fate, astrology, and so forth, is ethically worthless; this is how sexual difference was connoted here: *she* was hysterical, probing, authentic, self-destructive; while *he* was mythologizing and putting the blame on the Other.[14]

In Kant's terms, as we have seen, I am determined by causes, but I (can) retroactively determine which causes will determine me: we, subjects, are passively affected by pathological objects and motivations; but, in a reflexive way, we ourselves have the minimal power to accept (or reject) being affected in this way—that is to say, we retroactively determine the causes allowed to determine us, or, at least, the mode of this linear determination. "Freedom" is thus inherently retroactive: at its most elementary, it is not simply a free act which, out of nowhere, starts a new causal link, but a retroactive act of endorsing which link/sequence of necessities will determine me. Here, we should add a Hegelian twist to Spinoza: freedom is not simply "recognized/known necessity," but recognized/assumed necessity, the necessity constituted/actualized through this recognition. This excess of the effect over its causes thus also means that the effect is retroactively the cause of its cause—this temporal loop is the minimal structure of life. At the level of reality, there are only bodies interacting; "life proper" emerges at the minimally "ideal" level, as an immaterial event which provides the form of unity of the living body as the "same" in the incessant changing of its material components. The basic problem of evolutionary cognitivism—that of the emergence of the ideal life-pattern—is none other than the old metaphysical enigma of the relationship between chaos and order, between the Multiple and the One, between parts and their whole. How can we get "order for free," that is, how can order emerge out of initial disorder? How can we account for a whole that is larger than the mere sum of its parts? How can a One with a distinct self-identity emerge out of the interaction of its multiple constituents? A series of contemporary researchers, from Lynn Margulis to Francisco Varela, assert that the real problem is not how an organism and its environs interact or connect but, rather, the opposite one: how does a distinct self-identical organism emerge out of its environs? How does a cell form the membrane which separates its inside from its outside? Thus the real problem is not how an organism adapts to its environs, but how it is that there is something, a distinct entity, which must adapt itself in the first place. And it is here, at this crucial point, that today's biologists' language starts to resemble, quite uncannily, the language of Hegel. When Varela, for example, explains his notion of *autopoiesis*, he repeats, almost verbatim, the Hegelian notion of life as a teleological, self-organizing entity. His central notion, that of a loop or bootstrap, is reminiscent of the Hegelian *Setzung der Voraussetzungen* (positing the presuppositions):

> Autopoiesis attempts to define the uniqueness of the emergence that produces life in its fundamental cellular form. It's specific to the cellular level. There's a circular or network process that engenders a paradox: a self-organizing network of biochemical reactions produces molecules, which do something specific and unique: they create a boundary, a membrane, which constrains the network that has produced the constituents of the membrane. This is a logical bootstrap, a loop: a network produces entities that create a boundary, which constrains the network that produces the boundary. This bootstrap is precisely what's unique about cells. A self-distinguishing entity exists when the bootstrap is completed. This entity has produced its own boundary. It doesn't require an external agent to notice it, or to say, "I'm here." It is, by itself, a self-distinction. It bootstraps itself out of a soup of chemistry and physics.[15]

The conclusion to be drawn, therefore, is that the only way to account for the emergence of the distinction between "inside" and "outside" constitutive of a living organism is to posit a kind of self-reflexive reversal by means of which—to put it in Hegelese—the One of an organism as a Whole retroactively "posits" as its result, as that which it dominates and regulates, the set of its own causes (that is, the very multiple process out of which it emerged). In this way—and only in this way—an organism is no longer limited by external conditions, but is fundamentally self-limited—again, as Hegel would have put it, life emerges when external limitation (of an entity by its environs) turns into self-limitation.[16] This brings us back to the problem of infinity: for Hegel, true infinity stands not for limitless expansion but for active self-limitation (self-determination), in contrast to being-determined-by-the-other. In this precise sense, life (even at its most elementary: as a living cell) is the basic form of true infinity, since it already involves the minimal loop by means of which a process is no longer simply determined by the Outside of its environs, but is itself able to (over)determine the mode of this determination, and thus "posits its presuppositions." Infinity acquires its first actual existence the moment a cell's membrane starts to function as a self-boundary. So, when Hegel includes minerals in the category of "life," as the lowest form of organism, does he not anticipate Lynn Margulis, who also insists on forms of life preceding vegetable and animal life? The further key fact is that we thus obtain a minimum of ideality. A property emerges which is purely virtual and relational, with no substantial identity:

> My sense of self exists because it gives me an interface with the world. I'm "me" for interactions, but my "I" doesn't substantially exist, in the sense that it can't be localized anywhere. . . . An emergent property, which is produced by an underlying network, is a coherent condition that allows the system in which it exists to interface at that level— that is, with other selves or identities of the same kind. You can never say, "This property

is here; it's in this component." In the case of autopoiesis, you can't say that life—the condition of being self-produced—is in this molecule, or in the DNA, or in the cellular membrane, or in the protein. Life is in the configuration and in the dynamical pattern, which is what embodies it as an emergent property.[17]

Here we encounter the minimum of "idealism" which defines the notion of Self: a Self is precisely an entity without any substantial density, without any hard kernel that would guarantee its consistency. If we penetrate the surface of an organism, and look deeper and deeper into it, we never encounter some central controlling element that would be its Self, secretly pulling the strings of its organs. The consistency of the Self is thus purely virtual; it is as if it were an Inside which appears only when viewed from the Outside, on the interface-screen—the moment we penetrate the interface and endeavor to grasp the Self "substantially," as it is "in itself," it disappears like sand between our fingers. Thus materialist reductionists who claim that "there really is no self" are right, but they nonetheless miss the point. At the level of material reality (inclusive of the psychological reality of "inner experience"), there is in effect no Self: the Self is not the "inner kernel" of an organism, but a surface-effect. A "true" human Self functions, in a sense, like a computer screen: what is "behind" it is nothing but a network of "selfless" neuronal machinery. Hegel's thesis that "subject is not a substance" has thus to be taken quite literally: in the opposition between the corporeal-material process and the pure "sterile" appearance, subject is appearance itself, brought to its self-reflection; it is *something that exists only insofar as it appears to itself.* This is why it is wrong to search behind the appearance for the "true core" of subjectivity: behind it there is, precisely, nothing, just a meaningless natural mechanism with no "depth" to it.

When Heidegger emphasizes that the authentic *Dasein* decides freely, that it enacts authentic freedom, in contrast to those who merely follow the "one," his notion of freedom involves the same paradoxical overlapping of free choice/decision and assuming a predestined necessity which we encounter from Protestant theology through Nietzsche and Wagner (the highest freedom is freely to assume and enact one's fate, what inexorably has to happen): what is in fact set free in an authentic decision is not *Dasein* as such but, rather, its destiny itself—the "power of destiny becomes free." To put it succinctly, what makes my decision free is not primarily that I myself choose freely, but that my decision frees the power of Destiny itself. . . . Is it not legitimate to detect here a link with the Hegelian notion of "positing the presuppositions"? This link, however, harbors a fundamental ambiguity: is it that the subject literally and simply assumes a preceding necessity, or is it, rather, that his decision is "performative" in the sense that it retroactively *posits* the assumed necessity? The question "How is a free act possible? Is there a causality of freedom?" thus equals the question: *How can appearance exert a causality of its own?*

The 2001 Darwin award for the most stupid act was posthumously conferred on an unfortunate woman from the Romanian countryside who woke up in the midst of her own funeral procession; after crawling out of her coffin, and realizing what was going on, she blindly ran away in terror, was hit by a truck on a nearby road, and died instantly. . . . Is this not the ultimate example of what we call fate? The question of freedom is, at its most radical, the question of how this closed circle of fate can be broken. The answer, of course, is that it can be broken not because "it is not truly closed," because there are cracks in its texture, but, on the contrary, because it is overclosed, that is, because the subject's very endeavor to break out of it is included in it in advance. That is to say: since our attempts to assert our freedom and escape fate are themselves instruments of fate, the only real way to escape fate is to *renounce* these attempts, to accept fate as inexorable. (Oedipus' fate—killing his father, marrying his mother—was realized through his parents' very attempt to avoid it: without this attempt to avoid fate, fate cannot realize itself.) Recall the anecdote, retold by W. Somerset Maugham, about the appointment in Samarra: a servant on an errand in the busy market of Baghdad meets Death; terrified by its gaze, he runs home to his master and asks him to give him a horse, so that he can ride all day and reach Samarra, where Death will not find him, in the evening. The good master not only provides the servant with a horse, but goes to the market himself, looks for Death, and reproaches it for scaring his faithful servant. Death replies: "But I didn't want to scare your servant. I was just surprised. What was he doing here, when I have an appointment with him in Samarra tonight? . . ."

What if the message of this story is not that our demise is impossible to avoid, that trying to twist free of it will only tighten its grip, but the exact opposite: accept fate as inevitable, and you will break its grasp on you—how, exactly? Here again, *Minority Report* provides a useful hint: the title refers to a discord between visions of the future by the three "precogs"—sometimes, we learn, one of them has a different vision of the future. And, insofar as the three "precogs" are a direct medium of the "big Other," their discord is not simply subjective, an erroneous cognition of the future, but a direct expression of the inconsistency of, inherent cracks in, the "big Other" itself. Philip K. Dick's story provides a more salient reason why the "unanimity of all three precogs is a hoped-for but seldom-achieved phenomenon":

> It is much more common to obtain a collaborative majority report of two precogs, plus a minority report of some slight variation, usually with reference to time and place, from the third mutant. This is explained by the theory of *multiple-futures*. If only one time-path existed, precognitive information would be of no importance, since no possibility would exist, in possessing this information, of altering the future.[18]

The final account of how the story's hero, Anderton, is accused of a future murder is even more precise: it relies on the temporality of symbolization. That is to say: each of the three precogs, Donna, Jerry, and Mike, made their report (their insight into the future) at a different moment in time, and what happened in between was that the killer-to-be (Anderton) learned about the first report, and changed his future plans: in his report, the next precog took this knowledge into account, that is, his report already included the first report and its consequences as a fact. First, this is how Jerry's "minority report" is accounted for:

"Jerry's" vision was misphased. Because of the erratic nature of precognition, he was examining a time-area slightly different from that of his companions. For him, the report that Anderton would commit a murder was an event to be integrated along with everything else. That assertion—and Anderton's reaction—was one more piece of datum.

Obviously, "Jerry's" report superseded the majority report. Having been informed that he would commit a murder, Anderton would change his mind and not do so. The preview of the murder had cancelled out the murder; the prophylaxis had occurred simply in his being informed. Already, a new time path had been created.[19]

And in Anderton's final account, we learn that there was no majority report—all we had were three minority reports:

"Mike" was the last of the three, yes. Faced with the knowledge of the first report, I had decided not to kill Kaplan. That produced report two. But faced with that report, I changed my mind back. . . . The third report invalidated the second one in the same way the second one invalidated the first.[20]

But why, then, did the computer which reads the precogs' visions produce a "majority report" in the first place, concluding, from the fact that two out of three precogs agreed that Anderton would kill Kaplan, that he should be arrested for a future murder?

Each report was different. Each was unique. But two of them agreed on one point. If left free, I would kill Kaplan. That created the illusion of a majority report. Actually, that's all it was—an illusion. "Donna" and "Mike" previewed the same event—but in two totally different time paths, occurring under totally different situations. "Donna" and "Jerry," the so-called minority report and half of the majority report, were incorrect. Of the three, "Mike" was correct—since no report came after his, to invalidate him.[21]

Thus "multiple futures" are not a direct outcome of some radical indeterminacy or "ontological openness" inscribed in the fabric of reality; the ontological "fork," the alternate path of future reality, is, rather, generated when the agent whose future acts are foretold gets to know about them; that is to say, its source is the self-referentiality of knowledge.[22]

A Cognitivist Hegel?

Where, then, do we find traces of Hegelian themes in the new brain sciences? The three approaches to human intelligence—digital, computer-modeled; the neurobiological study of brain; the evolutionary approach—seem to form a kind of Hegelian triad: in the model of the human mind as a computing (data-processing) machine we get a purely formal symbolic machine; the biological brain studies proper focus on the "piece of meat," the immediate material support of human intelligence, the organ in which "thought resides"; finally, the evolutionary approach analyzes the rise of human intelligence as part of a complex socio-biological process of interaction between humans and their environment within a shared life-world. Surprisingly, the most "reductionist" approach, that of the brain sciences, is the most dialectical, emphasizing the infinite plasticity of the brain—that is the point of Catherine Malabou's provocative Hegelian reading of the brain sciences,[23] which starts by applying to the brain Marx's well-known dictum about history: *people make their own brain, but they do not know it.* What she has in mind is something very precise and well-grounded in scientific results: the radical *plasticity* of the human brain. This plasticity is displayed in three main modes: plasticity of development, of modulation, and of reparation. Our brain is a historical product, it develops in interaction with the environment, through human praxis. This development is not prescribed in advance by our genes; what genes do is precisely the opposite: they account for the structure of the brain, which is open to plasticity, so that some parts of it develop more if they are used more; if they are disabled, other parts can take over their function, and so on. What we are dealing with here is not only differentiation but trans-differentiation, "changing the difference." Learning and memory play a key role in reinforcing or suspending synaptic links: neurons "remember" their stimulations, actively structure them, and so forth. Vulgar materialism and idealism join forces against this plasticity: idealism, to prove that the brain is just matter, a relay machine which has to be animated from the outside, not the site of activity; materialism, to sustain its mechanical determinist vision of reality. This explains the strange belief which, although it is now empirically refuted, persists: the brain, in contrast to other organs, does not grow and regenerate; its cells just gradually die out. This view ignores the fact that our mind does not only reflect the world, it is part of a transformative exchange with the world, it "reflects" the possibilities of transformation, it sees the world through possible "projects," and this transformation is also self-transformation, this exchange also modifies the brain as the biological "site" of the mind.

Only after we accept this insight, however, do we confront the key question: *what* plasticity? Here, Malabou deploys the parallel between the model of the brain in the brain sciences and the predominant ideological models of society.[24] There are clear echoes between today's cognitivism and "postmodern" capitalism: when, for example, Dennett advocates a shift from the Cartesian notion of Self as a central controlling agency of psychic life to an autopoietic interaction of competing multiple agents, does this not echo the shift from central bureaucratic control and planning to connectionism, to complex interactions of multiple local agents out of which a "Self" arises as a spontaneous "emergent property"? It is thus not only that our brain is socialized, society itself is naturalized in the brain;[25] this is why Malabou is right to emphasize the need to address the key question: "how to ensure that the image of the way the brain functions will not coincide directly and simply with the spirit of capitalism?" Or, in the terms of plasticity: do we mean by this merely a capacity for infinite accommodation to the needs and conditions given in advance by our environs—in which case we get the infinitely adaptable "protean self"—or do we mean a Self capable of "negativity," of resisting and subverting the pressure of its environs, of breaking out of the "self-maintenance" whose ideal is to maintain one's homeostasis.

Among contemporary brain scientists, it was Damasio who developed in detail the notion of "proto-Self" as the agent which regulates the homeostasis of our body—what Freud called Lust-Ich, the self-organizing agent which maintains the body within the limits of stability and self-reproduction. This, however, is not yet the domain of the "mental" proper: "proto-Self" is followed by the emergence of self-awareness, the singular "I," and, finally, the "autobiographical Self," the organization of the narrative history of "what I am."[26]

The properly dialectical tension between the singular Self and narrative is crucial here: the singular Self stands for the moment of explosive, destructive, self-referential negativity, of a withdrawal from immediate reality, and thus a violent rupture of organic homeostasis; while "autobiography" designates the formation of a new, culturally created homeostasis which imposes itself as our "second nature." This disturbance can be conceived in two ways: either as an intrusion of external accidents which disturb my inner homeostasis—in this case, an organism is in a permanent search for equilibrium between the maintenance of a constant (or the "autobiographical Self") and the exposure of this constant to accidents, to contingent encounters, to otherness; we become "aware" of ourselves through external shocks which threaten homeostasis, and our intentional action is ultimately the effort to include such disturbances in a new homeostasis. This is the basic problem of system theory: how can an organism or a system maintain its balanced functioning by integrating external disturbances? The second way is to locate the source of disturbance in the very heart of the Self—Hegel made this point long ago, when he described this double movement of, first, radical self-withdrawal into the "Night of the World," the abyss of pure subjectivity, and then the rise of the new order through the capacity of naming: symbolic order and its homeostasis is the human substitute for the loss of natural homeostasis. A free Self not only integrates disturbances, it *creates* them, it explodes any given form or stasis. This is the zero-level of the "mental" which Freud called the "death drive": the ultimate traumatic Thing the Self encounters is the Self itself.

The basic Hegelian point to be made here, however, is that we cannot simply oppose these two extremes and posit an eternal interaction between the two (our lives oscillate between explosive outbursts of—either external or internal—negativity which disturb the given balance, and the imposition of a new homeostatic order which stabilizes our situation). The standard "dialectic" between homeostasis and shocks (traumatic encounters) is not enough—in a properly Hegelian perspective, we should bring this opposition to its self-relating: *the ultimate shock is that of the violent imposition of the homeostatic order itself, the drawing of the limit between Inside and Outside.*

There are two key points to be made here. First, self-constitution is not simply the adaptation to a (biologically or culturally) given form: one "forms" oneself only through *resisting* given forms (what Hegel called *Bildung*). Secondly, the "mental" itself explodes within the neuronal through a kind of "ontological explosion":[27] it is not enough to talk about the parallel between neuronal and mental, about how mental is grounded in neuronal, about how every mental process has to have its neuronal counterpart, and so forth; the real question, rather, is the "metonymic" one: how does the emergence/explosion of the mental *occur at the level of the neuronal itself?* In Hegelese, we must conceive the identity of the two ("the mental is the neuronal") as an "infinite judgment" which indicates a radical (self-)contradiction: "the mental is the neuronal" does not mean "the mental can be reduced to neuronal processes," but "the mental explodes out of a neuronal deadlock." This "spontaneous Hegelianism" found its clearest expression in John Taylor's model of consciousness as a *relational* phenomenon (well supported by detailed studies of the activities in our cortex regions).[28] According to Taylor, conscious content arises by "using the past to fill in the present":

> consciousness involves memory structures or representations of the past of episodic, autobiographic, semantic, preprocessing, and emotional character. These structures are used to give conscious content to the input in a manner that endows that experience with meaning related to the past. Thus consciousness arises from the intermingling of recorded past experiences with incoming present activity; as such the process is dynamic.[29]

Consequently, consciousness is a strictly *relational* phenomenon: it arises from the interaction between different sets of brain activities (between the present input and the stored memories of relevant past experiences); it is this relationality that endows mental processes with a "seeming insubstantiality" (122):

> such filling out of input gives a sense of insubstantiality to the resulting total neural activity. . . . An input has triggered a whole host of related activity. The triggering process lifts the original input into what seems like a self-supporting and totally new arena. It is as if a skater has launched himself out onto the ice and glides effortlessly around, compared with earlier clumsiness as he tried to walk toward the rink in his skates. The initial clumsy walking is that of preprocessing, still hidebound to the input that caused it; only as the ice is reached—consciousness emerges—is some degree of autonomy achieved to elevate the neural activity to move as if released from the friction of clinging Earth. Such triggering of neural activity—the launching onto the ice—I suggest as being at the basis of the features of qualia, ineffability, transparency, intrinsicality, and so on. (123)

Each new sensorial input triggers the activity of "working memory," which sets out to fill in its gaps; in this preprocessing module, many different interpretations of the input are activated in a parallel way: "Competition exists in a given working memory among neural activities representing different interpretations of the inputs in the preceding second or so" (249), and the winner of this local competition gains access to consciousness, that is, it emerges as a conscious "content": "A lot of machinery has to whir away behind the scenes before consciousness can emerge full-blown the way it does" (157). This gap between the complexity of the preprocessing work of mediation and the apparent "simplicity" of the result accounts for the "immediate," "raw" character of qualia, which

> cannot be probed further from inside the system. This feature arises when a rather sharp and irreversible processing step is involved in the ultimate emergence of consciousness. A lot of to-ing and fro-ing happen to inputs to the brain before they emerge into phenomenal awareness with closed loops of neural activity converging to all sorts of final activity. Yet the final step into consciousness appears to be short, sharp, and final. It does not seem possible to go back and linger over the manner in which such emergence occurred. (275)

The neural condition (material support) of this collapse of the complex preprocessing activity into the apparent immediacy of the result is the "formation of bubbles of activity in local cortical regions owing to the recurrence of feedback of neural activity":

> Once a neuron has been activated by an input, it feeds back activity to itself and its neighbors so as to keep them all active. The bubbles are triggered by a small input, so they function as an amplifier of that input. To keep them going, excitatory feedback has to occur from one neuron to its near neighbors; to prevent the bubble from spreading out and dissipating itself across the whole of the cortex there also has to be longer-range inhibition. (276)

This brings us to the crux of the matter, which (as is often the case with perceptive cognitivists) can be formulated only in quasi-Hegelian terms. Consciousness emerges as the result of a unique short circuit between present (input) and past (working memory): in contrast to the standard *après-coup*, in which the present working-through retroactively constitutes the meaning of past memory traces, here it is via the detour through the past that our present experience itself is constituted. This interaction between present and past has to reach a point of self-relating in which past and present do not simply interact, relate to each other, but interpenetrate more intimately: in relating to the past, the present experience *relates to itself*, becomes what it is. This is where the "bubbles" metaphor comes in, as well as the beautiful skating metaphor: once the short circuit of self-relating occurs, neural activity "ceases to be slavishly attached to the input producing it but glides off onto the ice rink to perform gyrations miraculously released from the ties that previously shackled it. This process becomes freed from input by means of bubbles of activity in the upper layers of the cortex" (345). The threshold is crossed when the magic leap into the "autonomy" of the neural self-relating occurs, that is, when the neural activity starts to "glide around as if out of the control of solid earth" (335)—in Hegelese, as if it were to *posit retroactively its own presuppositions*; and it is this short circuit which generates the effect of "immediacy" proper to qualia: in it, the complex dynamic network of neural mediations is "sublated /*aufgehoben*" in the simple immediacy of direct perception. The "raw" character of our immediate experience is thus the result of a complex effort of mediation; its inertia is sustained by its very opposite, the lightness of the "free thought" freely gliding in the air.

This is also why (to put it in Kantian terms) there is no consciousness proper without self-consciousness: not only does the "I" emerge as the self-relating interaction between the present and my own past; what we call "Self" is the elementary form of escaping the "control of solid earth" through self-relating. As such, it underlies all other forms: the self-relating of the agent of perception/awareness, as it were, creates (opens up) the scene on which "conscious content" can appear; it provides the universal form of this content, the stage on which the preprocessing work of mediation can collapse into the immediate "raw" givenness of its product. The magic trick of self-relating lies in the way my very "decenterment"—the impossibility of the I's immediate self-presence, the necessity of what Derrida would have called neural différance, of the minimal detour through the past mnesic traces—is turned into the mechanism which makes direct "raw" self-awareness possible.

We should distinguish here between subject and object. Neural self-relating designates the magic moment when neural activity no longer circulates around the input that triggered it, but generates its own "object," the focal point around which its activity circulates. A new quasi-object thus emerges with neural self-relating, a paradoxical insubstantial object that merely gives body to this relating "as such"—a neural "attractor": the final states of "attractor nets" can be regarded as "attracting initial activity to become similar to their own" (79). This attractor is thus formally homologous to the Lacanian objet petit a: like a magnetic field, it is the focus of activity, the point around which neural activity circulates, yet it is in itself entirely insubstantial, since it is created-posited, generated, by the very process which reacts to it and deals with it. This is like the old joke about the conscript who pleaded insanity in order to avoid military service; his "symptom" was compulsively to examine every document within his reach, and exclaim: "That's not it!"; when he was examined by the military psychiatrists, he did the same, so the psychiatrists finally gave him a document confirming that he was released from military service. The conscript reached for it, examined it, and exclaimed: "That's it!" Here also, the search generates its own object. . . .

If, then, self-relating means here that there is no "subject" previous to activity ("that which" acts is "self-posited," the result of its own activity), in what, precisely, does the difference between the subject and the insubstantial "object" that is the attractor consist? It is crucial to bear in mind that this difference is purely topological: "subject" and "object" are not two entities which interact at the same level, but one and the same X on the opposite sides of a Moebius strip—to put it in Hegelian-Kierkegaardian terms, "subject" and "object" designate one and the same X, conceived either in the mode of "being" (object) or in the mode of "becoming" (subject), either in the mode of the self-identical (immediate) consistency of the result or in the mode of the dynamic of a generative process. Objet petit a is the paradoxical object which directly "is" the subject.

This is how the brain sciences open up the space for freedom: far from being opposed to genetic programming, and violating it, the space for freedom is itself "programmed." We now know, for instance, that the neurons specialized in language atrophy if they are not stimulated by the maternal voice: genes lay the ground for the unpredictable intersubjective interaction.

THE FALSE OPACITY

The standard formula of the ultimate goal of the debate between the humanities and cognitivism is that of "bridging the gap"—namely, the gap between nature and culture, between "blind" biological (chemical, neuronal . . .) processes and the experience of awareness and sense—what, however, if this is the wrong task? What if the actual problem is not to bridge the gap but, rather, to *formulate* it as such, to conceive it properly? Here, more than anywhere else, the proper formulation of the gap is the solution to the problem—why? Because it is in the nature of consciousness that it *misperceives* the gap which separates it from "raw nature": the Self *is* its own appearance, since it is a model which cannot perceive itself as a model, and thus exists only insofar as it does not perceive itself as a model—or, to quote Thomas Metzinger's concise formulation: "what in philosophy of mind is called the 'phenomenal self' and what in scientific or folk-psychological contexts frequently is simply referred to as 'the self' is the content of a *phenomenally transparent self-model*."[30] Metzinger defines "transparency" very precisely: "For any phenomenal state, the degree of phenomenal transparency is inversely proportional to the introspective degree of attentional availability of earlier processing stages" (165). Transparency is thus, paradoxically, "a special form of darkness" (169): we are not able to see something because it is transparent, because we see through it. Metzinger's basic thesis is that such transparency is formative of our consciousness at two levels—first, generally, we "do not experience the reality surrounding us as the content of a representational process nor do we represent its components as internal placeholders . . . of another, external level of reality. We simply experience it as *the world in which we live our lives*" (169). Then, the same holds for our conscious Self itself, for the immediacy of our self-awareness, which is a representation in our mind, and thus also relies on such an illusion, on an epistemically illegitimate short circuit of perceiving what is in effect a mere representation, a model our organism formed of itself, as "the thing itself": "We do not experience the contents of our self-consciousness as the contents of a representational process, and we do not experience them as some sort of causally active internal placeholder of the system in the system's all-inclusive model of reality, but simply as *ourselves, living in the world right now*" (331).

The basic mechanism of "transparency" is well known from the Hegelian-Marxian tradition of the critique of fetishist illusion: the agent's own "reflexive determination" is misperceived as a property of the (perceived) object itself. What Metzinger does is to bring the logic of this illusion to its extreme, *applying it to the perceiving agent itself*: the logic of object-formation, of (mis)perceiving our phenomenal experience as directly referring to "objects out there," is applied to the *subject itself*. I myself do not "really exist"; I appear only as the result of a homologous fetishist illusion. There can never be a subject (Self) that is fully "opaque" to itself in the sense of perceiving its own generative mechanism—every such cognition is limited, embedded in a global transparent context: "cognitive self-reference always takes place against the background of transparent, preconceptual self-modeling" (333). So, although cognition proper can occur only when the subject becomes aware of the gap that separates appearance from reality—of how the content of its phenomenal experience is not the "thing itself" but a mere representation which can be illusory—"the transparent process of self-modeling is a necessary condition of possibility for the higher-order, cognitive forms of self-modeling" (338).

In this precise sense, Metzinger talks about the human mind's "autoepistemic closure": "conscious experience severely limits the possibilities we have to gain knowledge about ourselves. Subjective experience has not been developed in pursuing the old philosophical ideal of self-knowledge" (175). There is nothing mysterious about this "closure"—it can be clearly accounted for as an evolutionary advantage: it enables the system to focus on the result of its activity, and not to get lost in the introspective exploration of the steps that led to it. And the same goes for the specific object which is the Self itself: "the phenomenon of *transparent* self-modeling developed as an evolutionary viable strategy because it constituted a reliable way of making system-related information available without entangling the system in endless internal loops of higher-order self-modeling" (338). Thus Metzinger's conclusion is clear and radical:

> Phenomenal selfhood results from autoepistemic closure in a self-representing system; it is a lack of information. The prereflexive, preattentive experience of *being someone* results directly from the contents of the currently active self-model being transparent . . . no such things as selves exist in the world. Under the general principle of ontological parsimony, it is not necessary (or rational) to assume the existence of selves, because as theoretical entities they fulfill no indispensable explanatory function. What exists are information-processing systems engaged in the transparent process of phenomenal self-modeling. (337)

We are given to ourselves only through PSM (the phenomenal self-model): our phenomenal immediacy "is not referential immediacy" (578): that is to say, when I experience myself "directly" as a Self, I by definition enact an epistemically illegitimate short circuit, misperceiving a representational phenomenon for "reality." As Lacan put it, with regard to the ego, every cognition is misrecognition, since the ego is an object (our self-model) with whom we identify in the transparency of our self-experience: "I am that!"—or, again, in Metzinger's words: "The phenomenal property of selfhood as such is a representational construct; it truly is a *phenomenal* property in terms of being an appearance only. For all scientific and philosophical purposes, the notion of a self—as a theoretical entity—can be safely eliminated" (563).

In the first of his "Theses on History," Walter Benjamin mentions the famous chess automaton constructed in 1769 by Baron von Kempelen, and later improved by Johann Nepomuk Maelzel: an obviously mechanical swami figure sits at a suspiciously enclosed cabinet, the doors and drawers of which are sequentially opened, permitting the audience to "see for themselves" that there is nothing but machinery inside. The swami figure then begins to play a game of chess on the board of the cabinet against a human opponent, usually winning. The solution (guessed by Edgar Allan Poe in his perceptive analysis of the case) is that there is in fact a little man, a chess-player, hidden in the cabinet, who makes the moves—a system of mirrors generates the illusion that there is only machinery there. Poe reached the right conclusion from the wrong Cartesian premise: rational reasoning cannot be done by a blind machine, it presupposes Spirit. Against Poe, cognitivists who support the idea of artificial intelligence use this chess automaton as a metaphor for how our brain really works: we are, in effect, like the swami figure puppets, while the work of reasoning is done by the "impersonal" neuronal automata of which our brain consists. . . . Benjamin refers to the same automaton to account for the relationship between historical materialism and theology: historical materialism (Marxism) is the puppet which always wins only because, deep inside its cabinet, there is a hidden puppet which stands for theology (the Messianic theme of redemption). The question is, of course: what happens if we accept that there is *no* hidden puppet, only a blind automaton?

Some New-Age-tinted cognitivists make a place for "genius" in the opposition between "Me" and "I" (ego): "Me" is the "substance" of the I, it stands for all the wealth of content which constitutes me as a person.[31] The most convincing argument of the advocates of "Me" concerns the moments when we "act spontaneously," without conscious planning and nonetheless with extreme precision, displaying an immense amount of reasoning, like the soccer player who just plays, without thinking about it, but nonetheless makes moves which involve incredibly complex and quick strategic decisions. Do these phenomena not prove that there is in me something more than my conscious reflective "I," an agency which knows much more, albeit in an intuitive, spontaneous way? Is it not a fact that we experience such activity as the paradoxical overlapping of pure spontaneous freedom and passive "letting oneself go," letting myself being driven by my inner Me? From a strictly cognitivist standpoint, however, this move from I to Me is deeply problematic: after conceding that there is no freedom of the (conscious) will (since, a split second *before* we "freely" decide on an act, a change in the electrical current in our neuronal network unmistakably signals that the decision has already been made), one is tempted, in order to save freedom, to displace the free agent from "I" to "Me." With this all too easy New Age way out, a new entity emerges—"Me" as a *psychic* agent—for whom there is absolutely no place within the strictly cognitivist framework. The New Age solution thus retreats from the radicality of cognitivist consequences: all that the cognitivist stance obliges us to presuppose is that our conscious decisions are predetermined by neurophysiological asubjective (objective) processes—to impute to these processes another, "deeper" Me is a totally unwarranted step which ultimately projects into the "blindness" of neurophysiology a psychic substance. Is not the *frisson* of cognitivism precisely in its radical notion that consciousness is in effect a "user illusion" behind which (just as behind a PC screen) there are just blind asubjective neuronal processes, and, consequently, that there is absolutely no theoretical need to posit some psychic global Entity, something "in me more than me" which is the true agent of my acts? Paradoxically, it is thus precisely as true Freudians that we should reject the notion of "Me" as the substantial background of the ego.

With regard to the topic of "cognitive closure," the solution may appear to lie in the strict distinction between *experiential* closure and a truly *cognitive* closure: it is one thing to say that, in our "lived" self-experience, we necessarily (mis)perceive ourselves as acting freely; it is quite another to make the much stronger claim that it is cognitively impossible for us fully to get to know the bio-neuronal functioning of our mind. The first case is analogous to the fact that, even after we have learned from astronomy that the Sun is much bigger than our Earth, we continue to perceive it as a small ball—this in no way impedes our knowledge (which also accounts for this misleading perception); in the second case—and it is this case which is of real philosophical interest, of course—such knowledge is in itself deemed unattainable. What disturbs this easy solution, however, is the exceptional status of our phenomenal self-experience: not only is this experience the irreducible ultimate horizon of our knowledge; moreover our Self itself exists only as a phenomenon: there is no "true substance" of the Self beneath its self-appearance (parallel to the "real" Sun out there as opposed to the way the Sun appears to us as a yellow ball in the sky), the Self "is" its own appearing-to-itself.

What we encounter here is the old paradox of an entity which exists only insofar as it remains unknown, in the case of a strange reversal of the classic solipsist formula *esse = percipi*: here, something *is* only insofar as it is *not* perceived-experienced as what it is. Is this also the way to understand Lacan's thesis of the ego as symptom? The Freudian symptom, in contrast to the standard medical meaning of the term, is also something which exists (or, rather, insists) only insofar as its causality is unknown, something which is literally embodied ignorance. Here Metzinger is opposed to Colin McGinn,[32] who posits the cognitive closure of the self in the sense of a principled unavailability of theoretical self-knowledge: his "autoepistemic closure" is strictly phenomenal, a necessary illusion of experience, not an *a priori* limitation of our knowledge. One can cognitively know the PSM theory of subjectivity, but one cannot "really believe" in it—here we are back at the idea of fetishist disavowal, of *je sais bien, mais quand même* . . . :

> You cannot believe in it . . . the SMT is a theory of which *you cannot be convinced*, in principle . . . this fact is the true essence and the deepest core of what we *actually* mean when speaking about the "puzzle"—or sometimes even about the "mystery"—of consciousness. . . . If the current story is true, there is no way in which it could be intuitively true. (627)

In a strict analogy with the Marxian theory of commodity fetishism, theoretical knowledge does not abolish practical fetishism. Is there nonetheless, beyond the theoretical effort of thinking the unthinkable (a self-less world), also a possibility of *living* it, of living as "being no one"? There is one *caveat* that Metzinger allows: Buddhist enlightenment, in which the Self directly-experientially assumes his own non-being, that is, recognizes himself as a "simulated self," a representational fiction—such a situation, in which the phenomenal dream becomes *lucid to itself*, "directly corresponds to a classical philosophical notion, well-developed in Asian philosophy at least 2500 years ago, namely, the Buddhist conception of 'enlightenment'" (566). Such an enlightened awareness is no longer self-awareness: it is no longer I who experience myself as the agent of my thoughts; "my" awareness is the direct awareness of a self-less system, a self-less knowledge.

Metzinger's position is most clearly articulated in his rereading/radicalization of the three standard metaphors of the human mind: Plato's cave; the representationalist metaphor; the metaphor of a total flight simulator. As for Plato's cave, Metzinger—as we have already seen—endorses its basic premises: we misperceive a phenomenal "theater of shadows" (our immediate experience of reality) for reality; we are constrained by this illusion in a necessarily "automatic" way, and we should struggle to achieve true self-knowledge. He differs on one very precise point: there is no self who is tied down in the depths of the cave, and can then leave the cave in search of the true light of the sun:

> There are low-dimensional phenomenal shadows of external perceptual objects dancing on the neural user surface of the caveman's brain. So much is true. There certainly is a phenomenal *self*-shadow as well. But what is this shadow the low-dimensional projection *of*? . . . It is a shadow not of a captive person, but of the cave as a whole. . . . There is no true subject and no homunculus in the cave that could confuse itself with anything. It is the cave as a whole, which episodically, during phases of waking and dreaming, projects a shadow of itself onto one of its many internal walls. The cave shadow is there. The cave is empty. (550)

This brings us to the second—representationalist—metaphor: our phenomenal experience is a dynamic multidimensional map of the world—but with a twist: "like only very few of the *external* maps used by human beings, it also has a little red arrow . . . the phenomenal self is the little red arrow in your conscious map of reality" (551). Metzinger is referring to city, airport, or shopping mall maps in which a little red arrow marks the observer's location within the mapped space ("You are here!"):

> Mental self-models are the little red arrows that help a phenomenal geographer to navigate her own complex mental map of reality. . . . The most important difference between the little red arrow on the subway map and the little red arrow in our neurophenomenological troglodyte's brain is that the external arrow is *opaque*. It is always clear that it is only a representation—a placeholder for something else. . . . The conscious self-model in the caveman's brain itself, however, is in large portions transparent: . . . it is a phenomenal self characterized not only by full-blown prereflexive embodiment but by the comprehensive, all-encompassing subjective experience of *being situated*. (552)

This "red arrow," of course, is what Lacan called the signifier which represents the subject for other signifiers; and our total immersion in the map brings us to the third metaphor, that of a *total flight simulator*:

> The brain differs from the flight simulator in not being used by a student pilot, who episodically "enters" it. . . . A total flight simulator is a self-modeling airplane that has always flown without a pilot and has generated a complex internal image of itself within its *own* internal flight simulator. The image is transparent. The information that it is an internally generated image is not yet available to the system as a whole. . . . Like the neurophenomenological caveman, "the pilot" is born into a virtual reality right from the beginning—without a chance to ever discover this fact. (557)

There is, however, a vicious cycle in this version of the Cave argument (a cave projects itself onto the cave wall, and *it generates-simulates the observer itself*): while the cave can simulate the substantial identity/content of the observer, it cannot simulate the *function* of the observer, since in this case we would have a fiction observing itself, like a Magrittean hand drawing the hand that, in its turn, draws the first hand. In other words, while what the observer immediately identifies with in the experience of self-awareness is a fiction, something with no positive ontological status, *his very activity of observing is a positive ontological fact*.

In his detailed analysis of the Cartesian "I am certain that I exist" (398–403), Metzinger introduces a distinction that is very close to Lacan's distinction between the "subject of the enunciation" and the "subject of the enunciated." Crucial for Metzinger is the distinct status of the two "I"s in "I am certain that I exist": while the second "I" simply designates the content of the *transparent* self-model—Lacan's "subject of the enunciated," the ego as an *object*—the first "I" stands for the *opaque* component of the very thinker that thinks (that is, generates) this thought—Lacan's "subject of the enunciation." The Cartesian confusion is that the self-transparent thinking substance which directly experiences itself is generated by the illegitimate identification of the two I's, where the second one is embedded in the first: the opaque component "has already been *embedded* in the continuously active background of the transparent self-model" (401). In other words, although the second "I" (the X that thinks this very thought) undoubtedly refers to *something*, to a system that generates this thought, "[w]hat is not clear is if this system is actually a *self*" (405). Was Kant not much more precise here, when he emphasized a thoroughly nonsubstantial character of the subject, and defined its noumenal substratum as the "I or he or it that thinks," implying in effect that the ignorance of one's own noumenal nature is a positive condition of thinking subjectivity?

It is crucial to note how this imprecision of Metzinger (in Lacanese, his failure to distinguish between the "subject of the enunciation" and the "subject of the enunciated") is closely linked to his other imprecision, his failure to distinguish between the "external" opacity of the generating system and the "inherent" opacity of meaning.

This distinction imposes itself most directly apropos of the process of social (re)cognition: as Lacan emphasized, the Other is for me by definition an abyss, he is "opaque," that is to say, I am always aware that what I experience is a phenomenal surface which can deceive:

> You are my wife—after all, what do you know about it? You are my master—in reality, are you so sure of that? What creates the founding value of those words is that what is aimed at in the message, as well as what is manifest in the pretense, is that the other is there *qua* absolute Other. Absolute, that is to say he is recognized, but is not known. In the same way, what constitutes pretense is that, in the end, you don't know whether it's a pretense or not. Essentially it is this unknown element in the alterity of the other which characterizes the speech relation on the level on which it is spoken to the other.[33]

Only when we are confronted with such an opaque Other does the topic of *recognition* arise: where there is full cognition, recognition is meaningless. This impenetrability of the Other, however, is not the obverse of the Other's imaginary misrecognition: it is not a reflexive insight into the process which generates what appears to us as a Self. Here Metzinger fails to distinguish the two different modes of opacity: the opacity of the generative medium (the biophysical brain processes which sustain the experience of meaning, on which the experience of meaning locally supervenes) and *the opacity which is inherent to phenomenal experience as such*, the opacity of a mask or of a sign promising that there is something behind. When someone wears a mask, what imposes itself as the secret behind the mask is not what "really is behind," the physical reality of the person's face, but another opaque threatening dimension. The same thing happens when we look deep into a person's eyes: the opaque abyss of the Other that we experience is not this person's neuronal reality—recall the passage from Broks quoted above in Chapter 3: "Behind every face there is a self. We see the signal of consciousness in a gleaming eye and imagine some ethereal space beneath the vault of the skull, lit by shifting patterns of feeling and thought, charged with intention." From the cognitivist point of view, this appearance of "depth" is an illusion—what Metzinger fails to convey, however, is how this illusion is not directly the illusion of transparency, but the very illusion of opacity: if, in the illusion of transparency, we misrecognize the generative process that sustains what is immediately given to us, then, in the illusion of opacity, we *falsely surmise a "depth" where there is none*. These two illusions are not symmetrical: the second illusion, that of opacity, is properly *symbolic*, because it is a reflexive, self-related illusion, an *illusion of illusion itself*, an illusion which, precisely, lures us into thinking that what we see directly is just an illusory surface concealing some opaque depth. The link between Metzinger's two imprecisions is clear: the second opacity, the opacity inherent to phenomenal experience as such, is, at its most radical, the very opacity of the "subject of the enunciation."

Correlative to these two types of opacity are the two different types of transparency: it is a condition of the experience of (linguistic) meaning that the (language) medium should be transparent (this transparency collapses when we suddenly become aware

of the obscene material presence of the sound of words): in order to experience meaning, we have to "see through" words. This transparency, however, is not the same as the
"fetishist" transparency of the generative process eclipsed by its product: meaning
is by definition impenetrable, it generates a new opacity of its own. Think of the big
shift in the early development of personal computers, the so-called Apple revolution:
the shift from programming to simulated environment, from "knowing the rules" to
"immersion" in the digital space. Today, we experience cyberspace as a new transparent artificial life-world whose icons simulate our everyday reality—and this new environment is by definition uncontrollable, it displays an opacity of its own, we never
master it, we perceive it as a fragment of a larger universe; our proper attitude toward
it is therefore not a programmatic mastery but a bricolage, improvising, finding our
way through its impenetrable density. The trick here is that, far from standing for a
"real" transcendence, for an awareness of the real generative process of the virtual environs, this opacity is *illusion itself*, illusion at its purest, the illusion of an endless universe sustaining our fragmented environs, as in the case of writing a long text on a PC,
when we automatically perceive the lines we see as the fragment of a continuous text
which exists somewhere behind the screen, and "scrolls down.". . .

Metzinger concludes on an optimistic note: the very fact that there is no Self opens
up a new possibility of awareness. When we claim that there is no Self—that, our experience of being Selves, we "confuse" ourselves with our phenomenal self-model—
this formulation is still misleading, since it implies that there is something *whose*
illusion this is—here are the very last lines in the book:

> There is no one *whose* illusion the conscious self could be, no one *who* is confusing her-
> self with anything. As soon as the basic point has been grasped . . . a new dimension
> opens. At least in principle, one can wake up from one's biological history. One can
> grow up, define one's own goals, and become autonomous. And one can start talking
> back to Mother Nature, elevating her self-conversation to a new level. (634)

Surprisingly, we thus encounter, at the very high point of a naturalistic reductionism
of human subjectivity, a triumphant return of the Enlightenment theme of a mature
autonomous . . . what? Certainly not Self. This triumph, however, is a mixed bless-
ing—while Metzinger considers artificial subjectivity possible, especially in the direction of hybrid bio-robotics, and, consequently, an "empirical, not philosophical"
(620) issue, he emphasizes its ethically problematic character: "it is not at all clear if
the biological form of consciousness, as so far brought about by evolution on our
planet, is a *desirable* form of experience, an actual *good in itself*" (620). This problematic
feature concerns conscious pain and suffering: evolution "has created an expanding
ocean of suffering and confusion where there previously was none. As not only the
simple number of individual conscious subjects but also the dimensionality of their
phenomenal state spaces is continuously increasing, this ocean is also deepening"
(621). And it is reasonable to expect that new artificially generated forms of awareness

will create new "deeper" forms of suffering. . . . We should be careful to note how (or, as Metzinger himself would have put it: "Please note how . . ."[34]) this ethical thesis is not an idiosyncrasy of Metzinger as a private person, but a consistent implication of his theoretical framework: the moment we endorse the full naturalization of human subjectivity, the avoidance of pain and suffering cannot but appear as the ultimate ethical point of reference.

EMOTIONS LIE, OR, WHERE DAMASIO IS WRONG

The common thread of Metzinger's complex elaborations is the insight into the parallax gap between the "inside" experience of meaning and the "outside" view of a flat, meaningless organism, this piece of meat that sustains our experience:

> There is no way the subject, from the "inside," can become aware of his own neurons, from the "inside." They can be known only objectively, from the "outside." There is no inner eye watching the brain itself, perceiving neurons and glia. The brain is "transparent" from the standpoint of the subject, but not from the standpoint of an outside observer.[35]

The opposition between the endogenic and the exogenic view, between "being inside" and "being outside" a system, is operative throughout scientific thought, from relativity theory (Einstein's breakthrough could be summed up by a question he asked: how would things appear to you if you were on a light beam instead of merely watching it flash past?) and the inevitable Gödel's Incompleteness Theorem (which, let us not forget, claims that within any consistent system of logic, statements can be made which cannot be proved or disproved using the rules of this system—if we look at this system from outside, it can be completed!) to genetics and environmental biology.[36] However, although our subjective experience (what it means to "be" X, to "inhabit" its point of view, to experience it from inside) seems to provide the ultimate example of it, it involves a strange complication: here, *"inside" is in a way "outside."* That is to say: our immediate *inner* conscious (self-)experience is by definition a process that takes place on a *surface*, at the level of appearance, and when we try to account for it in neurobiological terms, we do it by constructing, from an *outside* view, a neuronal process that can generate such an experience—think of the proverbial look into the open skull: when we see the raw meat of a human brain, we cannot fail to be shocked: "Is this it? Does this chunk of meat generate our thought?" The difference between simulation and model is crucial here. A simulation aims at imitating (reproducing) the external result through a different generative mechanism, while a model aims at grasping the internal structure of a phenomenon, its "inner working," without any similarity to the result (to "how the thing appears" in its immediacy). In the case of a human being, however, simulation gets redoubled: we can build either a robot that would simulate human activity (that would—to an external observer—act like a human, engage in conversation, and so on), or a robot whose "inner experience" would simulate that of a human (which would possess awareness, emotions, and so forth).

The conclusion to be drawn from this is the one drawn long ago by Francisco Varela: consciousness (awareness) is a matter not of inside, but of the "interface," of the surface-contact between inside and outside.[37] It is this convoluted relation between Inside and Outside that, in effect, undermines the standard notion of the Cartesian subject as a *res cogitans* (thinking substance): it brings home the fact that the subject, precisely, is *not* a substance. How does this anti-Cartesian turn relate to the other big cognitivist rejection of the Cartesian subject, that of Antonio Damasio? The surprising fact is that Damasio's critique moves in the opposite direction: if anything, he puts even more emphasis on the subject's "substantial" nature, his embeddedness in the biological reality of the body.

Against the Cartesian notion of consciousness as a pure disinterested activity of reflection which only secondarily gets stained by emotions (emotions as the price our mind pays for the curse that it is empirically rooted in a biological body, a fact which blurs our clarity of thought), Damasio[38] asserts the constitutive, necessary link between emotion and consciousness: consciousness is an "emotional reaction"—to what? Consciousness, at its most elementary, is the awareness of a *disturbance* of the organism's homeostasis caused by an encounter with an external (or internal) object which serves as its "occasion" (171). This is why consciousness is inherently "emotional": it enacts the organism's biased, "interested" reaction to a disturbance. . . . Anyone who is even vaguely acquainted with German Idealism must be struck by the parallel with J. G. Fichte, for whom also the transcendental I, (self-)consciousness, emerges as a reaction to an irreducible external *Anstoss* (a German word with a wonderfully appropriate double meaning: "obstacle" upon which one stumbles, and "instigation"). This is why, for Fichte, subject is not substance: the subject (of consciousness) is not the organism whose homeostasis precedes every disturbance, and who strives to reestablish this homeostasis after every disturbance; the subject emerges through the disturbance of the organism's homeostasis, it "is" the very activity of dealing with disturbances.

As we have already seen, Damasio distinguishes three kinds of Self (174–175). First, there is the non-conscious, still purely organic-neural, *Proto-Self*: the interconnected and coherent collection of neural patterns which, moment by moment, represent the internal state of the organism, that is, the neural "map" the organism forms of itself in order to be able to regulate and maintain its homeostasis, which is continuously disturbed by intruding objects. Then, the conscious *Core Self* emerges, the "second-order nonverbal account that occurs whenever an object modifies the proto-self" (174). The zero-level form of consciousness is thus what Damasio calls "core consciousness," "the very thought of you—the very feeling of you—as an individual being involved in the process of knowing of your own existence and of the existence of others" (127)—what philosophers like David Chalmers identify as the "hard" problem to explain: "The first basis of the conscious you is a feeling which arises in the representation of the *nonconscious proto-self in the process of being modified* within an account which establishes the cause of the modification" (172). This "thick consciousness" is irreducibly consciousness of death: we can play (as Dennett does) the boring game of "consciousness is a virtual program which is in a way immortal, able to survive the passage from one hardware to another," but "thick" consciousness is "absolutely mine." No wonder, then, that, today, we can discern echoes of the ontological proof in the cognitivist debates about "thick consciousness": is not pure passive self-awareness with no cognitive/causal function, that which cannot be accounted for in evolutionist terms, exactly the same as the pure excess of being, pure *Dass-sein*, which cannot be accounted for in conceptual terms (Kant: "being" is not a predicate)? Is this not also analogous to "sensual certainty," the first figure of consciousness in Hegel's *Phenomenology*? Hegel can set the dialectical movement in motion only by presupposing that the structure is already conceptual.[39]

Finally, this Core Self is supplemented by the *autobiographical Self*, relying on the "implicit memories of multiple instances of individual experience of the past and of the anticipated future" (174). Core consciousness is the foundation and condition of the autobiographical Self: the latter is made of the virtual set of memories and projects which can be instantiated/actualized only in the living self-awareness of the Core Self. The Core Self explodes as the "swift, second-order nonverbal account narrates a story: that of the organism caught in the act of representing its own changed state as it goes about representing something else. But the astonishing fact is that the knowable entity of the catcher has just been created in the narrative of the catching process" (170). This, again, is a fundamental Fichtean theme: the I is not an agent who acts, but an agent who has no substantial identity outside its acting, who "is" its acting, who fully coincides with its activity. The I knows itself, but this "itself" fully overlaps with the very process of knowing: the I knows itself as knowing. Or, insofar as the organism's reaction to the intrusion forms a minimal narrative (the organism's homeostasis is disturbed by the encounter with an object; the organism is affected by it, transformed, and reacts to it in order to maintain and/or restore its homeostasis), the subject/consciousness is the storyteller who, paradoxically, emerges through telling the story, who exists only within his own storytelling:

> The story contained in the images of core consciousness is not told by some clever homunculus. Nor is the story really told by *you* as a self because the core *you* is only born as the story is told, *within the story itself*. You exist as a mental being when primordial stories are being told, and only then; as long as primordial stories are being told, and only then. You are the music while the music lasts. (191)

How can this self-generation of the narrator himself through the story he narrates take place? Damasio's starting point is that an organism as a unit is constantly mapped in the organism's brain; when the organism encounters (is affected by) an object, this object is also mapped within the brain; both organism and object are mapped in neural patterns, in first-order maps:

As the brain forms images of an object—such as a face, a melody, a toothache, the memory of an event—and as the images of the object affect the state of the organism, yet another level of brain structure creates a swift nonverbal account of the events that are taking place in the varied brain regions activated as a consequence of the object-organism interaction. (170)

The maps pertaining to the object cause changes in the maps pertaining to the organism, and these changes can be represented in yet other maps (second-order maps) which thus represent the relationship of object and organism—this account of the causal relationship between object and organism can be captured only in second-order neural maps. This second-order mapping gives rise to a minimum of self-reflexivity: I not only know, I feel that I know (that it is I who knows); I not only perceive an object, I am aware of myself perceiving it; I not only act, I feel that it is I who acts. I *do not relate to (interact with) only an object: I relate to this relating "as such."* This is why consciousness is always also self-consciousness: when I know, I simultaneously know ("feel") that it is I who knows, because I am nothing outside this knowledge—I am my knowledge of myself.

The paradox of the subject as the "catcher created in the narrative of the catching process" is supplemented by its almost symmetrical opposite: not only (1) does the subject emerge as the result of the quest for it, it is its own process, not substance; but, simultaneously, (2) the subject's awareness is an answer before the question, given before it is looked for—the subject is the "answer of the Real," as Lacan would have put it: "The answers had to come first, . . . the organism had to construct first the kind of knowledge that looks like answers. The organism had to be able to produce that primordial knowledge, unsolicited, so that a process of knowing could be founded" (189).

On a first approach, the two sides cannot but appear to be mutually exclusive: first, we have a process of searching which itself generates the object it is searching for, that is, a process which—like Baron Münchhausen pulling himself out of the swamp by his own hair—turns around in its vicious circle without any substantial external support; then we have a sudden result, an answer, something given, something popping up without there being any quest for it. The link between these two paradoxes, however, is crucial: if I exist only within the story I am telling/experiencing, if I have no substantial identity/content outside it, then, when I experience myself, the story is always-already there, there is no subject preceding it who would formulate the quest, the question answered by the story—the primordial narrative that forms the Core Self is an "explanation presented prior to any request for it":

Who *does?* Who *knows?* When the answer first arrives, the sense of self emerges, and to us now, creatures endowed with rich knowledge and an autobiographical self, . . . it does appear as if the question was posed, and that the self is a knower who knows. . . . No question then asked. There is no need to interrogate the core self about the situation and the core self does not interpret anything. Knowing is generously offered free of charge. (191–192)

Thus the two illusions have to be thought together, as the face and the obverse of the same coin: the illusion that the subject is looking for something which is already there, waiting to be discovered—that is to say, the illusion that I am an agent-narrator who precedes the narrative ("somebody must be telling the story, the story cannot tell itself, it is the same nonsense as the story about the painter who drew a perfect picture and then entered it himself and disappeared in it"), and the illusion that knowledge is an answer to a previously posed question. What we are dealing with here is a paradoxical single entity that is "doubly inscribed," that is simultaneously surplus and lack—the paradox delineated long ago by Deleuze in his *Logic of Sense*: as soon as the symbolic order emerges, we always encounter an entity that is simultaneously—with regard to the structure—an empty, unoccupied place and—with regard to the elements—an excessive occupant without a place.[40]

This twisted structure gives us a clue to what is wrong with Damasio's idea of consciousness as relying on second-order mapping, a mapping which registers the very causal relationship between the two entities (organism and object) whose interaction is registered by first-order mapping: obviously, this all-too-simple complication will not do the job of generating (producing awareness of) the very agent of mapping. If second-order mapping registers first-order mapping, all we get is a two-level mapping of mapping, not *a process of mapping that includes itself in the mapped process*. For this to occur (for the agent itself to be included in the process it animates), some kind of self-relating has to occur, some kind of short circuit between the two levels of representation (mapping)—and Lacan's formula of the signifier ("a signifier represents the subject for another signifier") evokes precisely such a self-relating two-level mapping: the signifier which represents the subject is the second-order "reflexive" signifier, acting as the subject's stand-in in the first-order series of signifiers. This reflexivity is the disavowed Hegelian moment in Damasio's account. Let me clarify this point with a morbid joke: a patient in a large hospital ward with many beds complains to the doctor about the constant noise and crying from the other patients, which are driving him crazy. When the doctor replies that nothing can be done if the patients are like that, one cannot forbid them to express their despair, since they all know they are dying, the patient goes on: "Why don't you put them in a separate room for the dying then?" The doctor replies calmly: "But this *is* a room for the dying. . . ." Why does everyone who knows a little about Hegel immediately discern a "Hegelian" flavor in this morbid joke? Because of the final twist in which the patient's subjective position is undermined: he finds himself included in the series from which he wanted to maintain a distance.[41]

From here, we can also discern why Damasio's solution to the old enigma of the two sides of Self (Self qua the continuously changing stream of consciousness versus Self qua the permanent stable core of our subjectivity) misses the mark: "the seemingly changing self and the seemingly permanent self, although closely related, are not one entity but two" (217)—the first being the Core Self, the second the autobiographical Self. There is no place here, however, for what we as speaking beings experience (or, rather, presuppose) as the empty core of our subjectivity: what am I? I am neither my body (I have a body, I never "am" my body directly, in spite of all the subtle phenomenological descriptions à la Merleau-Ponty that try to convince me to the contrary), nor the stable core of my autobiographical narratives that form my symbolic identity; what "I am" is the pure One of an empty Self which remains the same One throughout the constant change of autobiographical narratives. This One is engendered by language: it is neither the Core Self nor the autobiographical Self, but what the Core Self is transubstantiated (or, rather, desubstantialized) into when it is transposed into language. This is what Kant has in mind when he distinguishes between the "person" (the wealth of autobiographical content that provides substantial content to my Self) and the pure subject of transcendental apperception which is just an empty point of self-relating.

Damasio's fundamental "Althusserian" thesis is that "there is no central feeling state before the respective emotion occurs, that expression (emotion) precedes feeling" (283). I am tempted to link this emotion which precedes feeling to the empty pure subject ($). emotions are already the subject's, but before subjectivization, before their transposition into the subjective experience of feeling. $ is thus the subjective correlative to emotions prior to feeling: it is only through feelings that I become the "full" subject of lived self-experience. And it is this "pure" subject which can no longer be contained within the frame of life-homeostasis, that is, whose functioning is no longer constrained by the biological machinery of life-regulation. When Damasio writes:

> the power of consciousness comes from the effective connection it establishes between the biological machinery of individual life regulation and the biological machinery of thought. That connection is the basis for the creation of an individual concern which permeates all aspects of thought processing, focuses all problem-solving activities, and inspires the ensuing solutions (304)

he thereby leaves out of consideration the proper empty core of subjectivity ($) which, insofar as it explodes the frame of life-regulating homeostasis, coincides with what Freud called the death drive. The chain of equivalences thus imposes itself between the "empty" cogito (the Cartesian subject, Kant's transcendental subject), the Hegelian topic of self-relating negativity, and the Freudian topic of the death drive. Is this "pure" subject deprived of emotions? It is not as simple as that: its very detachment from immediate immersion in life-experience gives rise to new (not emotions or feelings, but, rather) affects: anxiety and horror. Anxiety as correlative to confronting the Void that forms the core of the subject; horror as the experience of disgusting life at its purest, "undead" life.[42]

In *Synaptic Self*, Joseph LeDoux confronts the same problem. Principle 6 in the list of the seven basic principles of brain functioning which concludes the book is: "*Emotional states monopolize brain resources.*" When an organism is attacked by a threatening stimulus, the emotional response which immediately arises sends direct feedback by way of neural connections to sensory areas of the cortex, encouraging these areas to stay focused on those aspects of the stimulus world that are critical. [This] feedback also reaches other cortical areas engaged in thinking and explicit memory formation, encouraging them to think certain thoughts and to form certain memories about the current situation.[43]

In addition, of course, other emotional responses are inhibited: when one is dead scared, one does not think about sex or food. . . . Far from serving merely as an obstacle to "balanced" rational thought, such a unilateral focus provides the very impetus of our cognitive and behavioral activity: when we are under emotional pressure we think and act much faster, mobilizing all our resources. Consequently, when we say that an emotion "colors" our thoughts and acts, this is to be taken (*cum grano salis*) in Laclau's sense of "hegemony": a specific feature which confers a specific flavor on the whole. Its source is the imbalance that the emergence of language introduced between man's cognitive abilities and his emotional/motivational abilities:

> Language both required additional cognitive capacities and made new ones possible, and these changes took space and connections to achieve. The space problem was solved . . . by moving some things around in existing cortical space, and also by adding more space. But the connection problem was only partially solved. The part that was solved, connectivity with cortical processing networks, made the enhanced cognitive capacities of the hominid brain possible. But the part that hasn't been fully solved is connectivity between cognitive systems and other parts of the mental trilogy—emotional and motivational systems.[44]

Along these lines, it would be interesting to conceive the very specificity of "being-human" as grounded in this gap between cognitive and emotional abilities: a human being in whom emotions were to catch up with cognitive abilities would no longer be human, but a cold monster deprived of human emotions. . . . Here we should supplement LeDoux with a more structural approach: it is not simply that our emotions lag behind our cognitive abilities, stuck at the primitive animal level; *this very gap itself functions as an "emotional" fact, giving rise to new, specifically human, emotions,* from anxiety (as opposed to mere fear) to (human) love and melancholy. Is it that LeDoux (and Damasio, on whom LeDoux relies here) misses this feature because of the fundamental weakness (or, rather, ambiguity) of the proto-Althusserian distinction between emotions and feelings? This distinction has a clear Pascalian twist (and it is a mystery that, in his extensive critique of "Descartes' error,"[45] Damasio does not evoke Pascal, Descartes's major critic): physical emotions do not display inner feelings but, on the contrary, generate them. However, there is something missing here: a gap between emotions *qua* biological-organic bodily gestures and emotions *qua* learned symbolic gestures following rules (like Pascal's kneeling and praying). Specifically "human" emotions (like anxiety) arise only when a human animal loses its emotional mooring in biological instincts, and this loss is supplemented by the symbolically regulated emotions *qua* man's "second nature."

Nowhere is the gap that separates the brain sciences' unconscious from the Freudian Unconscious more clearly discernible than apropos of the status of emotions. For Damasio, the unconscious is emotional: emotions display the "spontaneous" reaction of an organism to an encounter with an object which disturbs the organism's homeostatic balance, so that even when a human being is cognitively not aware of its true attitude toward the object, his emotional response betrays this attitude. A standard example is racism: I may be sincerely convinced that the Jews are people just like other people, but when I encounter one, unbeknownst to me, my bodily gestures display an emotional reaction which bears witness to my unconscious anti-Semitic stance. The "unconscious" here is the thick impenetrable background of the emotional texture, in clear contrast to Freud. When Lacan deploys Freud's thesis that anxiety is the affect which does not lie (which is why anxiety indicates the proximity of the Real), the implication is that anxiety is the exception: all other emotions do lie, they lie in principle. In his *Interpretation of Dreams*, Freud mentions a dream in which a woman simply repeats the preceding day's event, the funeral of a beloved friend, in an atmosphere of intense sadness: Freud's explanation of the dream is that, at the funeral, the dreamer encountered again a man whom she passionately loved years ago and for whom she still harbored sexual desires. The point is not only that the meaning of a dream is to be sought in some detail unconnected with its totality (interpretation en détail versus the hermeneutic interpretation en masse), but that the accompanying emotion experienced as the feeling of intense sadness lies: it serves as a mask, a protective screen whose function is to conceal joy at encountering the beloved figure—as such, it has nothing to do with the unconscious.

Nowhere is this deceiving nature of affects clearer than in music. With the rise of Romanticism, a fundamental change occurs in the very ontological status of music: no longer reduced to a mere accompaniment of the message delivered in speech, it starts to contain/transmit a message of its own, "deeper" than the one delivered in words. It was Rousseau who first clearly articulated this expressive potential of music as such, when he claimed that music, instead of merely imitating the affective features of verbal speech, should be given the right to "speak for itself"—in contrast to deceiving verbal speech, in music it is (to paraphrase Lacan) the truth itself which speaks. As Schopenhauer put it, music directly enacts/expresses the noumenal Will, while speech remains limited to the level of phenomenal representation. Music is the substance which portrays the true heart of the subject, which is what Hegel called the "Night of the World," the abyss of radical negativity: music becomes the bearer of the true message beyond words with the shift from the Enlightenment subject of rational Logos to the Romantic subject of the "Night of the World," that is, the shift of the metaphor for the kernel of the subject from Day to Night. Here we encounter the Uncanny: no longer the external transcendence but, following Kant's transcendental turn, the excess of the Night at the very heart of the subject (the dimension of the Undead), what Tomlinson called the "internal otherworldliness that marks the Kantian subject."[46] What music expresses is no longer the "semantics of the soul" but the underlying "noumenal" flux of *jouissance* beyond linguistic meaningfulness. This noumenal dimension is radically different from the pre-Kantian transcendent divine Truth: it is the inaccessible excess which forms the very core of the subject.

If we take a closer look, however, we cannot avoid the conclusion that music itself—in its very substantial "passionate" rendering of emotions, celebrated by Schopenhauer—not only can also lie but *lies in a fundamental way as to its own formal status.* Let us take the supreme example of music as the direct rendering of the subject's immersion in the excessive enjoyment of the "Night of the World," Wagner's *Tristan,* in which the music itself seems to perform what words can only helplessly indicate: the way the amorous couple is inexorably drawn toward the fulfillment of their passion, the "highest joy/*höchste Lust*" of their ecstatic self-annihilation—is this, however, the metaphysical "truth" of the opera, its true ineffable message? Why, then, is this inexorable sliding toward the abyss of annihilation interrupted again and again by (often ridiculous) intrusions of fragments of ordinary daily life? Let us take the most obvious case, that of the finale itself: just prior to Brangäne's arrival, the music could have moved straight into the final Transfiguration, two lovers dying entwined—why, then, the rather ridiculous arrival of the second ship, which accelerates the slow pace of the action in an almost comic way—in a mere couple of minutes, more events happen than in all the preceding scenes (the fight in which Melot and Kurwenal die, and so on)—similar to Verdi's *Il Trovatore,* in which a whole package of things happen in the last two minutes. Is this simply Wagner's dramatic weakness? Here we should bear in mind that this sudden hectic action does not serve merely as a temporary postponement of the slow but inevitable drift toward orgasmic self-extinction; this hectic action follows an immanent necessity, it *has* to occur as a brief "intrusion of reality," permitting Tristan to stage the final self-obliterating act of Isolde.[47] Without this unexpected intrusion of reality, Tristan's agony of the impossibility of dying would drag on indefinitely. The "truth" lies not in the passionate drift toward self-annihilation, the opera's fundamental affect, but in the ridiculous narrative accidents/intrusions which interrupt it—again, the big metaphysical affect *lies.*

Damasio uses "the single word homeostasis"[48] as the best shorthand for the elementary self-regulation of an organism, and he describes its central component in the very Freudian terms of the "pleasure principle," where pain and pleasure are not in themselves goals of activity but, rather, indicate that the organism's homeostasis is threatened or sustained: pleasure and pain behaviors and emotions "are aimed, in one way or another, directly or indirectly, at regulating the life process and promoting survival" (35). The big question that follows is: how do we get from here to what Freud called "beyond the pleasure principle"? Is it not that, for this to occur, pleasure and pain have to detach themselves from their instrumental function of serving as signals, and turn into goals-in-themselves? Here the role of pain is more elementary than that of pleasure: the elementary formula of the "autonomization" of pain and pleasure from their instrumental functions is that of *finding pleasure in pain itself.* Instead of reacting to pain in the normal survivalist way (avoiding it), I stick to it, deriving satisfaction from it. And what if the very gap between emotion and feeling, on which Damasio insists, can occur only through such a de-instrumentalization of emotion? What if the primordial, zero, level of feeling is not a simple "transposition" of a physical emotion of pain into a feeling of pain, but the feeling of pleasure at the emotion of pain (or the other way round)? The limitation of Damasio's approach is most evident in his attempt to account for racist emotional outbursts as a misapplication of an emotional reaction which, in its original functioning, was absolutely appropriate:

> reactions that lead to racial and cultural prejudices are based in part on the automatic deployment of social emotions evolutionarily meant to detect *differences* in others because difference may signal risk or danger, and promote withdrawal or aggression. That sort of reaction probably achieved useful goals in a tribal society but is no longer useful, let alone appropriate, to ours. We can be wise to the fact that our brain still carries the machinery to react in the way it did in a very different context ages ago. And we can learn to disregard such reactions and persuade others to do the same. (40)

The problem with this explanation is that it does not account for two key components of racist "disgust" at the different Other: the way this disgust arises (its mechanism is resuscitated) as a displacement from another traumatic experience which is thereby "repressed" (for example, in our hatred of the racial Other we aggressively "act out" and cover up our social impotence, our lack of social "cognitive mapping"); and the way, in a racist emotional reaction to the presence of the ethnic Other, disgust is obviously combined with forms of perverted pleasure, fascination, and envy.

In order to account for these complications, we should bear in mind the basic anti-Darwinian lesson of psychoanalysis repeatedly emphasized by Lacan: man's radical and fundamental dis-adaptation, mal-adaptation, to his environs. At its most radical, "being-human" consists in an "uncoupling" from immersion in one's environs, in following a certain automatism which ignores the demands of adaptation—this is what the "death drive" ultimately amounts to. Psychoanalysis is not "deterministic" ("What I do is determined by unconscious processes"): the "death drive" as a self-sabotaging structure represents the minimum of freedom, of a behavior uncoupled from the utilitarian-survivalist attitude. The "death drive" means that the organism is no longer fully determined by its environs, that it "explodes/implodes" into a cycle of autonomous behavior. That is the crucial gap: between utilitarianism as the radical "ontic" denial of freedom (those who control the conditions which determine my behavior control me) and the Kantian (and, let us not forget, Sadeian) assertion of unconditional autonomy (of the moral law, of the caprice to enjoy)—in both cases, there is a rupture in the chain of being.

HEGEL, MARX, DENNETT

There is a third, even more influential, cognitivist rejection of the Cartesian *cogito*: Daniel Dennett's extended polemic against the so-called "Cartesian Theater," the idea that there is in the human mind a central point of perception-decision at which all incoming information is gathered, appreciated, and then turned into orders for (re)action. It is one of the subtle ironies of the modern history of ideas that the first to propose such a notion of the human mind as a decentered "pandemonium" was none other than Leo Tolstoy. Tolstoy is usually perceived as a much less interesting author than Dostoevsky—a hopelessly outdated realist for whom there is basically no place in modernity, in contrast to Dostoevsky's existential anguish. Perhaps, however, the time has come to fully rehabilitate Tolstoy, his unique theory of art and man in general, in which we find echoes of Spinoza's notion of *imitatio afecti* or Dawkins's notion of memes. "A person is a hominid with an infected brain, host to millions of cultural symbionts, and the chief enablers of these are the symbiont systems known as languages"[49]—is not this passage from Dennett pure Tolstoy? The basic category of Tolstoy's anthropology is *infection*: a human subject is a passive empty medium infected by affect-laden cultural elements which, like contagious bacilli, spread from one individual to another. And Tolstoy goes right to the end: he does not oppose to this spreading of affective infections a true spiritual autonomy, he does not propose a heroic vision of educating oneself into becoming a mature autonomous ethical subject by getting rid of the infectious bacilli. The only struggle is the struggle between good and bad infections: Christianity itself is an infection, albeit a good one. It is the ultimate irony that the Christian Tolstoy is more logical and radical than Dawkins here: while Dawkins emphasizes that memes are "viruses of the mind," parasitic entities which "colonize" human energy, using it as a means of multiplying themselves, he nonetheless insists that all memes are not just viruses:

> Good, useful programs spread because people evaluate them, recommend them and pass them on. Computer viruses spread solely because they embody the coded instructions: "Spread me." Scientific ideas, like all memes, are subject to a kind of natural selection, and this might look superficially virus-like. But the selective forces that scrutinize scientific ideas are not arbitrary or capricious. . . . The rapid spread of a good idea through the scientific community may even look like a description of a measles epidemic. But when you examine the underlying reasons you find that they are good ones, satisfying the demanding standards of scientific method. In the history of the spread of faith you will find little else but epidemiology, and causal epidemiology at that. . . . For scientific belief, epidemiology merely comes along afterwards and describes the history of its acceptance. For religious belief, epidemiology is the root cause.[50]

Dennett was quite right to answer this passage with a critical comment in his usual acerbic style:

> When you examine the reasons for the spread of scientific memes, Dawkins assures us, "you find they are good ones." This, the standard, official position of science, is undeniable in its own terms, but question-begging to the mullah and the nun—and Rorty, who would quite appropriately ask Dawkins: "Where is your demonstration that these 'virtues' are *good* virtues? You note that people evaluate these memes and pass them on—but if Dennett is right, people . . . are themselves in large measure the creation of memes. . . . How clever of some memes to team together to create meme-evaluators

that favor *them!* Where, then, is the Archimedan point from which you can deliver your benediction on science?"[51]

From a Hegelian standpoint, Dennett's key achievement is to demonstrate how we literally "see" concepts and judgments. When, for example, I see "a room full of red chairs," I do not quickly scan them all; rather, I make a couple of test glances and then "conclude" that all the chairs are red—and I immediately *see* this result. Dennett's thesis is even more radical than Kant's idea of the transcendental constitution of reality: it is not only that the visual input is "perlaborated" through transcendental categories, but the very content that we see—inclusive of its direct physical properties—is the result of the previous judgment. This is also how we should properly understand Dennett's paradoxical radical reply to the classic phenomenalist reproach to materialist reductionism: "What about qualia, the unique direct experience of sweetness, thirst, and so on?"—*There are no qualia.* This means that there is no direct contact with reality, no direct experience, which is then, on a second occasion, elaborated by our mind—what we experience as "reality" is already the result of this elaboration.

The main result of Dennett's criticism of the notion of qualia is thus that the immediacy of qualia is mediated, the result of a bricolage of fragmented perceptions, links, judgments. (There are no "fillings" of the gaps, because there are no gaps to be filled to constitute a smooth-continuous perception.) Here, Dennett confronts the problem of reflected appearances, of how something "appears to appear": "qualia" designate the illusion of immediate experience/appearance, and if there are no qualia this means that things do not appear to us as they seem to appear. It *seems* that we immediately experience qualia, while, in effect, this immediacy is retroactively constructed. Dennett wants to erase this second-level "appearance of appearance," and keep only the fragmentary bricolage of what actually goes on in our mind: on the one hand there are fragments of perceptions, associations, and so on; on the other hand there is the blind Real of neuronal processes—with nothing in between.[52]

In the terms of "continental" philosophy, what Dennett is describing is the insurmountable opposition between phenomenology and dialectic. The gap between the two can be best illustrated apropos of the topic of symbolic "alienation" in language clichés: for phenomenology, such "dead metaphors" are always "sedimentations" or "ossifications" of what was once a direct lived experience. When I say "Glad to see you!", I do not, of course, mean it literally, it is just a polite form of talking; according to phenomenology, however, this polite form has to be grounded in a past primordial experience when such a form was "really meant"—what is unthinkable for phenomenology is that something *directly emerges as a "cliché,"* that it was *never* meant seriously. In his reading of Morgan, Engels makes a similar mistake apropos of the so-called "punalua" family from Hawaiian tribes (the two tribes are interrelated, so that all the brothers of one tribe are married to all the sisters of the other tribe, and vice versa): while, today, the two tribes practice monogamy, all the men from the first tribe address all the women from the other tribe as "wife"—following Morgan, Engels interprets this fact as the linguistic trace-remainder of the past "punalua" family.[53] He is wrong, of course: anthropology demonstrated that there never was a "punalua" organization of family life: the use of the term "wife" for all women of the opposite tribe was a "metaphor" *from the very beginning.*

Here, Engels fell victim to the "phenomenological common sense" according to which the zero-level of language has to be its direct embeddedness in a concrete life-world constellation, where statements refer directly to their social context; the rise of "dead" clichés is a secondary phenomenon of alienation, of the gradual autonomization of the form with regard to its content. For dialectics proper, on the contrary, *form has precedence over content*: the first signifier is empty, a zero-signifier, pure "form," an empty promise of a meaning-to-come; it is only on a second occasion that the frame of this process is gradually filled in with content. So although, according to the standard notion of dialectics, the dialectical process goes from immediate unity through alienation to final synthesis, this scheme holds for phenomenology, not for dialectics: the dialectical process proper *begins with alienation*, its first gesture of "positing" is that of alienation.

This alienation provides the key to Hegel's famous formula "the secrets of the ancient Egyptians were also secrets for the Egyptians themselves": when I am confronted with a mysterious religious ritual from some "primitive" culture, my first experience is that of a mystery which is impossible to penetrate ("If only I possessed enough information to unravel the secret meaning of what I am now observing!"); what, however, if the "meaning" of this ritual is also a mystery for its participants themselves? *What if the primordial form of meaning is such an alienated meaning—"it must mean something, although I do not know what"?* What if this resistant core of frustrating non-sense is what transforms mere meaning (simple denotative reference of a statement or a practice) into a deeper Sense? This excess over transparent meaning can also appear in the opposite form, that of ironic distance toward the meaning of one's speech. In *Journey into Fear*, Eric Ambler's classic spy thriller, one of the heroes starts to advocate Socialism at dinner parties simply to embarrass and annoy his rich wife; little by little, however, he is taken in by his own Socialist arguments, so he ends up an authentic Socialist . . . what if this is the paradigm of how ideology works?

We do not only begin with an authentic articulation of a life-world experience which is then reappropriated by those in power to serve their particular interests and/or imposed on their subjects to make them docile cogs in the social machine; much more interesting is the opposite process in which something that was originally an ideological edifice imposed by colonizers is taken over all of a sudden by their subjects as a means of articulating their "authentic" grievances. Take the classic case of Virgen de Guadalupe in early colonized Mexico: with her appearance, Christianity (which until then served as the imposed ideology of the Spanish colonizers) was appropriated by the indigenous population itself as a means of symbolizing their terrible plight. Along similar lines, Dennett quotes Lincoln's famous line "You can fool all the people some of the time, and some of the people all the time, but you cannot fool all the people all of the time," drawing attention to its logical ambiguity: does it mean that there are some people who can always be fooled, or that on every occasion, someone or other is bound to be fooled? Dennett's point[54] is that it is wrong to ask "What did Lincoln really mean?"—probably, Lincoln himself was not aware of the ambiguity. He simply wanted to make a witty point, and the phrase "imposed itself on him" because "it sounded good." Here we have an exemplary case of how, when the subject has a vague intention-to-signify, and is "looking for the right expression" (as we usually put it), the influence goes both ways: it is not only that, among the multitude of contenders, the best expression wins, but some expression might impose itself which changes more or less considerably the very intention-to-signify . . . is this not what Lacan meant by the "efficiency of the signifier"?

At a different level of social life, we can discern the same logic in what Marx, in *Capital*, called the "formal subsumption (of the productive forces) under capital": in the early stages of capitalist development, the precapitalist (artisan) means of production were formally subsumed under capitalist relations (for example, weavers who previously sold their product directly to the market were now paid and given raw material by the capitalist); only after this formal subsumption did the material subsumption take place, that is to say, new means of production (large machinery, and so on) were developed which could function only within capitalist factory organization. In other words, with formal subsumption,

> there is no change as yet in the mode of production itself. *Technologically speaking*, the *labour process* goes on as before, with the proviso that it is now *subordinated* to capital. Within the production process, however . . . two developments emerge: (1) an *economic* relationship of supremacy and subordination, since the consumption of labour-power by the capitalist is naturally supervised and directed by him; (2) labour becomes far more continuous and intensive.[55]

With the ensuing real subsumption of labor under capital,

> a complete (and constantly repeated) revolution takes place in the mode of production, in the productivity of the workers and in the relations between workers and capitalists. With the real subsumption of labour under capital, all the changes in the labour process . . . now become reality . . . *capitalist production* now establishes itself as a mode of production *sui generis* and brings into being a new mode of material production.[56]

In short, we move from an organizing principle which, through exploitation and subordination, is grafted onto the logic of semi-autonomous worlds, to a principle that actively structures the very material reality of production, exchange, and circulation. In contrast to the vulgar-evolutionary Marxist *doxa* about the changes in the relations of production following revolutions in the productive forces, it was thus after the formal subsumption that productive forces materially changed to fit capitalist process. As for the development of machinery itself, we should also bear in mind that, in the first epoch of the explosive development of automata and other machines (the seventeenth century), automata were built as useless artifices, toys to amuse the Master's gaze (like the moving mechanical statues in Louis XIV's gardens); only later, in the eighteenth century, was this knowledge used to build machines for production (steam and weaving machines).

In his interpretation of *Antigone* in *Phenomenology of Spirit*, Hegel posits such an empty, purely formal, gesture as the most elementary form of symbolization itself: the first act of symbolization is sepulchral, the ritual of burying, by means of which death itself, the ultimate case of a "blind" natural process out of our control, is taken over, repeated as a cultural process—in short: "formally subsumed" under the symbolic regime. Nothing changes in reality, all that happens is that an empty form is added to an inevitable natural process. The same goes for the building of concepts: when Hegel mocks the scientific explanation which only adds a "scientific" term to the process-to-be-explained (people behave destructively when they are under the spell of the death drive—and what is the death drive? A name for such self-destructive behavior ... or—an example from recent medical practice—when a patient resists a stay in hospital, he is diagnosed with "hospitalitis": which means that the patient resists a stay in hospital), the real irony is easily missed. Hegel's point is that such an empty act of naming has to be the first move: it opens up the space to be filled later with new content.

Is not this priority of the form, however, in clear contrast to another fundamental Hegelian model, that of the "silent weaving of the Spirit," where the formal change is the final act of taking note of what has already taken place? Like the cartoon-figure suspended in the air which falls down only when it looks down and notices that it is suspended in the air, we have only to remind the dead form that it is dead, and it disintegrates—in *Phenomenology*, again, Hegel quotes the famous passage from Diderot's *Rameau's Nephew* about the "silent, ceaseless weaving of the Spirit in the simple inwardness of its substance":

> it infiltrates the noble parts through and through and soon has taken complete possession of all the vitals and members of the unconscious idol; then "one fine morning it gives its comrade a shove with the elbow, and bang! crash! the idol lies on the floor." On "one fine morning" whose noon is bloodless if the infection has penetrated to every organ of spiritual life.[57]

This, however, is not Hegel's last word: he goes on, pointing out that this "Spirit concealing its action from itself, is only one side of the realization of pure insight": at the same time, being a conscious act, this Spirit "must give its moments a definite manifest existence and must appear on the scene as a sheer uproar and a violent struggle with its anti-thesis."[58] In the transition to the New, there is a passionate struggle going on, which is over once the opposing force notices how its very opposition is already impregnated with the opponent's logic (when, say, the reactionary counter-Enlightenment argument itself secretly relies on the ideological premises of the Enlightenment—as is the case from Robert Filmer's polemics against John Locke up to today's televangelists, whose very delivery of their message undermines it—in their performance, they display the very features they criticize so ferociously in their liberal opponents, from narcissistic self-indulgence to the commercialized mediatic spectacle). This, then, is how we are to read the two apparently opposed features (the priority of the form; the "silent weaving of the Spirit") together: the "silent weaving of the Spirit" concerns not content, but the form itself—again, in the case of a televangelist preacher, this "silent weaving" undermines his message at the level of its own form (the way he delivers the message subverts its content).

From Physics to Design?

There is, however, a series of problems with Dennett's account. First, we should note how, with all his insistence on finitude, contingency, evolution as bricolage, and so on, Dennett has to introduce a proto-Platonic element: the notion of the Library of Mendel (based on Borges's notion of the Library of Babel), the logical space of all possible genome combinations; evolution takes place in the space between this vast synchronous "eternal" logical matrix of all possible combinations, and the vanishing empirical space of feasible combinations, combinations which are actually accessible.[59] So we have the old gap between the eternal logical *combinatoire* and us being constrained to a particular contingent situation.[60]

The second point concerns the dualistic ontology on which Dennett relies in his passage from "physics" to "design" (36–40)—the two basic levels of reality are the deterministic physical level and the "higher" level of design. Here is his own simple and clear example: a two-dimensional grid of pixels, each of which can be *on* or *off* (full or empty, black or white). Each pixel has eight neighbors, the four adjacent pixels and the four diagonals. This "universe" changes between each tick of the clock according to the following rule: for each cell in the grid, count how many of its eight neighbors are *on*; if the answer is three, the cell is *on* in the next instant whatever its current state; under all other conditions, the cell is *off* in the next instant. With the succession of instants, nothing "moves" here, individual cells are just going *on* and *off* in a totally deterministic way. The moment we step back and consider larger patterns, however, surprising things happen. We discover that some forms (three pixels vertically or horizontally *on*) behave like "flashers," flip-flopping back and forth from horizontal to vertical position; some other forms, like a square of four pixels, just remain the way they are; other forms, like some five-pixel configurations, behave like "gliders," swimming, amoebalike, across the plane. What, however, happens when another configuration encroaches upon the first one? We get "eaters" (forms which swallow another form), "puffer trains," some forms vanish, and so on. Another ontological level thus emerges which, although grounded in physical reality, obeys its own rules:

> At the physical level there is no motion, only *on* and *off*, and the only individual things that exist, pixels, are defined by their fixed spatial location. . . . At the design level we

suddenly have the motion of persisting objects; it is one and the same glider (though composed each generation of different pixels) that has moved southeast . . . , changing its shape as it moves; and there is one less glider in the world after the eater has eaten it. . . . Whereas the individual atoms—the pixels—flash in and out of existence, *on* and *off*, without any possibility of accumulating any changes, any history that could affect their later history, larger constructions can suffer damage, a revision of structure, a loss or gain of material that can make a difference in the future. (40)

This dualism evokes many other, similar ones in modern philosophy: Wittgenstein's opposition between things (objects) and what happens to them (what is the case, *"was der Fall ist"*) in *Tractatus*; Deleuze's opposition of being and the flux of becoming; Alexis Meinong's opposition of objective reality and objects which correspond to different intentional attitudes (desiderata, and so on). It is easy to imagine other similar examples, like the running message on an electronic publicity board, where the message seems to "run across," the same letter or word moving from left to right, although, in physical reality, only fixed light-points are going *on* and *off*; or the proverbial "movement" of the "same" shape of a sand-mountain during a storm in a desert (the shape seems to move, although individual grains of sand merely change their positions within a very short space of time). What we can do is thus to study the rules which predict the behavior of these larger configurations at the design level, without bothering to compute the physical level: how a glider should be structured to avoid being "eaten" by another, and so on. When we let the game develop in more complex ways, forms of behavior appear which, from our human perspective, we cannot but describe as "intentional": some gliders seem to "avoid" being eaten or annihilated, and so forth:

Speaking of these smallest avoiders as if they "knew" anything at all involves a large dose of poetic license . . . but it is still a useful way of keeping track of the design work that has gone into them. . . . Enriching the design stance by speaking of configurations as if they "know" or "believe" something, and "want" to accomplish some end or other, is moving up from the simple *design stance* to what I call the intentional stance . . . this permits us to think about them at a still higher level of abstraction, ignoring the details of just how they manage to store the information they "believe" and how they manage to "figure out" what to do, based on what they "believe" and "want." We just assume that however they do it, they do it rationally—they draw the right conclusions about what to do next from the information they have, given what they want. It makes life blessedly easier for the high-level designer, just the way it makes life easier for us all to conceptualize our friends and neighbors (and enemies) as intentional systems. (43)

The model of this "as if" approach is, of course, Darwinian evolution, where organisms act "as if" they are striving for survival, "as if" they are intentionally trying to choose and develop the best organs and survival strategies, although, "in itself," the process is purely mechanic and senseless. (Does not the notion of "memes" also imply intentional stance in the precise Dennettian sense of the term? When we talk about how memes use us, humans, in order to reproduce themselves, this is not a true ground-level naturalistic explanation of culture, but an explanation that offers itself when we observe the development of culture in the "as if" attitude of intentionality.) Does not "intentional stance," then, function as a kind of Kantian "regulative idea"? Does it not imply that we do not describe reality directly as it is, but in an "as if" mode, imputing to it a teleology which can never be fully proven? No wonder Damasio resorts directly to the formula of fetishist disavowal—we know, but nonetheless . . . :

> Long before living beings had anything like a creative intelligence, even before they had brains, it is as if nature decided that life was both very precious and very precarious. We know that nature does not operate by design and does not decide in the way artists and engineers do, but this image gets the point across.[61]

Darwinism is the anti-teleological thought, so the enigma remains: why do Darwinists, to get their point across, need the image of the very ideology they oppose? We are in fact dealing here with *supposed* knowledge, with a version of what Lacan called the "subject supposed to know." The greatness of Darwinism, however, is that it provides a precise account of *how* the appearance of purposeful behavior can emerge from a senseless mechanistic process, while this dimension is neglected in Dennett, and this failure is not without ironic consequences: when Dennett points out how we can perceive the "intentional stance"[62] that inheres to a natural process—say, the avoidance of a threat—only if we speed up the slow natural movement ("Along the way there was much avoidance and prevention, but at a pace much too slow to appreciate unless we artificially speed it up in imagination" [51]), he thereby celebrates the same manipulation that the notorious Catholic anti-abortion movie *The Silent Scream* resorted to, that of a fetus being cut and dragged out in an abortion procedure: by reproducing the event in a fast-forward mode, the movie creates the impression that the fetus is acting with a purpose, desperately trying to avoid the knife. . . .

The problem with Dennett's dual ontology is: does it really reach "all the way down"? Is the level of totally deterministic behavior of elements really the zero-level? What about the lesson of quantum physics, according to which there is, beneath solid material reality, the level of quantum waves, where determinism breaks down? Is the "teleological" causality of motivation (I did something because I aimed to achieve some goal), then, just an epiphenomenon, a mental translation of a process which can (also) be fully described at a purely physical level of natural determinism, or does such a "teleological" causation in fact possess a power of its own, and fill the gap in direct physical causality?

Dennett's notion that consciousness is simply a "cerebral celebrity"—the victory of the idea(s) which impose themselves as central over the pandemonium of other ideas—involves two problems: (1) on which *stage* does the celebrity appear? (2) is consciousness really linked to importance, to the capacity to impose oneself? What about the fact that some animals are (probably) aware of themselves, while computers (or human brains) can perform complex operations without being aware of them? And even if we accept his point, we cannot avoid the impression that Dennett's *Consciousness Explained* relies on a fundamental sleight of hand. After developing the evolutionary necessity for a series of mental and physical capacities *without mentioning consciousness*, he suddenly concludes: "can all these capacities really be operative without consciousness?" The *petitio principii* of his argument cannot fail to strike us: of course they cannot, but the problem is precisely that he himself develops their evolutionary emergence without any reference to consciousness. . . .[63]

"Mental contents become conscious not by entering some special chamber in the brain, not by being transduced into some privileged and mysterious medium, but by winning the competitions against other mental contents for domination in the control of behavior, and hence for achieving long-lasting effects—or as we misleadingly say, 'entering into memory'" (254). But what about *unconscious* contents which can control our behavior, and thus play a stronger role than conscious motivations? And what about Freud's thesis that consciousness and memory are fundamentally antagonistic (we remember things which we do not become conscious of)?

When "Conrad," Dennett's imagined straw-man adversary, asks how winning the competitions makes a content conscious, that is, in what, precisely, "becoming conscious" qualitatively consists, Dennett's reply is: "Such a question betrays a deep confusion, for it presupposes that what *you are* is something *else*, some Cartesian *res cogitans* in addition to all this brain-and-body activity. What you are, Conrad, just *is* this organization of all the competitive activity between a host of competences that your body has developed" (254). However, he thereby avoids the true question: what, precisely, is the place—or the quality, or the process—all these activities compete to access? Dennett's major point is that mental work is irreducibly distributed in time and space: there is no central place or stage, the core of the Self, which coordinates all the activity: "the Cartesian Theater, the imaginary place in the center of the brain 'where it all comes together' for consciousness. *There is no such place.* . . . All the work done by the imaginary homunculus in the Cartesian Theater must be distributed *in time and space* in the brain" (123).

Along these lines, Dennett proposes a very precise critique of Libet's famous experiment:[64] the physiological process appears to "precede" our conscious decision only if we presuppose a singular central place of Consciousness which perceives all the data and gives out orders. However, there is another lesson to be learned from Libet: the function of *blocking* as the elementary function of consciousness. This negative function is discernible at two main levels: first, at the level of "theoretical reason," the very strength of consciousness resides in what may appear to be its weakness: in its limitation, in its power of abstraction, of *leaving out* the wealth of (subliminal) sensory data. In this sense, what we perceive as the most immediate sensual reality is already the result of complex elaboration and judgment, a hypothesis which results from the combination of sensual signals and the matrix of expectations. Secondly, at the level of "practical reason," consciousness, while in no way able to instigate a spontaneous act, can "freely" impede its actualization: it can veto it, say "No!" to a spontaneously emerging tendency. This is where Hegel comes in, with his praise of the infinite negative power of abstraction that pertains to understanding: consciousness is possible only through this loss, this delay with regard to the fullness of immediate experience—a "direct consciousness" would be a kind of claustrophobic horror, like being buried alive with no breathing space. Only through this delay/limitation does the "world" open itself to us: without it, we would be totally suffocated by billions of data with, in a way, no empty breathing space around us, directly part of the world.[65]

THE UNCONSCIOUS ACT OF FREEDOM

So what does all this mean for Dennett's model of (self-)consciousness as a *pandemonium* of parallel networks whose interaction is not dominated by any central controller? It is the predominant *doxa* today that the microcosm of interacting agents spontaneously gives rise to a global pattern which sets the context of interaction without being embodied in any particular agent (the subject's "true Self"): cognitive scientists repeat again and again how our mind does not possess a centralized control structure which runs top-down, executing designs in a linear way; how it is, rather, a bricolage of multiple agents who collaborate bottom-up, that is, whose organization is shifting, "opportunistic," robust, adaptive, flexible. However, how do we get from here to (self-)consciousness? That is to say: (self-)consciousness is not the pattern which "spontaneously" emerges from the interaction of multiple agents but, rather, its exact obverse, or a kind of negative: it is, in its primordial dimension, the experience of some malfunctioning, of some perturbation, in this spontaneous pattern or organization. (Self-)consciousness (the "thick moment" of consciousness, the awareness that I am now-here-alive)[66] is originally passive: in clear contrast to the notion according to which self-awareness originates in the subject's active relationship toward its environs, and is the constitutive moment of our activity of realizing a determinate goal, what I am originally "aware of" is that I am not in control, that my design has misfired, that things are just drifting by. For that very reason a computer which merely executes its program in a top-down way, "does not think," is not conscious of itself.

I am therefore tempted to apply here the dialectical reversal of epistemological obstacle into positive ontological condition: what if the "enigma of consciousness," its inexplicable character, contains its own solution? What if all we have to do is to transpose the gap which makes consciousness (as the object of our study) "inexplicable" into consciousness itself? Remember how, for Kant, direct access to the noumenal domain would deprive us of the very "spontaneity" which forms the kernel of transcendental freedom: it would turn us into lifeless automata or, to put it in today's terms, into computers, into "thinking machines." However, is this conclusion really unavoidable? Are we free only insofar as we misrecognize the causes which determine us? The mistake of the identification of (self-)consciousness with misrecognition, with an epistemological obstacle, is that it stealthily (re)introduces the standard, premodern, "cosmological" notion of reality as a positive order of being: in such a fully constituted positive "chain of being" there is, of course, no place for the subject, so the dimension of subjectivity can be conceived of only as something which is strictly co-dependent with the epistemological misrecognition of the positive order of being. Consequently, the only way effectively to account for the status of (self-)consciousness is to assert the ontological incompleteness of "reality" itself: there is "reality" only insofar as there is an ontological gap, a crack, in its very heart, that is to say, a traumatic excess, a foreign body which cannot be integrated into it. This brings us back to the notion of the "Night of the World": in this momentary suspension of the positive order of reality, we confront the ontological gap on account of which "reality" is never a complete, self-enclosed, positive order of being. It is only this experience of psychotic withdrawal from reality, of absolute self-contraction, which accounts for the mysterious "fact" of transcendental freedom: for a (self-)consciousness which is in effect "spontaneous," whose spontaneity is not an effect of misrecognition of some "objective" process.

This brings us back to Dennett who, in his precise critique of Robert Kane's defense of free will,[67] also shows how any attempt to provide a precise spatio-temporal location of the moment of free decision/choice has to fail. What we should do here, however, is to translate this argumentation into the terms of the dualist ontology of physical reality and design level: what Dennett's critique of Kane amounts to is the claim that, if we limit our view to physical reality, we search in vain there for a "Self," for a material element (or process or quality) alongside other elements that would directly "be" the Self. "Self" exists only at what Dennett calls the "design" level, as an "ideal" entity; the same goes for Dennett's acerbic evocation of the nonsense paradox of the "primal mammal": every mammal has a mammal for a mother, so there can be no mammals, because the first mammal couldn't have a mammal mother. . . . The analogy is that the same goes for the free act: when Kane argues that, if we are to be held responsible for our acts, there has to be a "regress-stopper," a founding free act which grounds the series of our decisions, he falls into the same trap: "If an infinite regress is to be avoided, there must be actions somewhere in the agent's life history for which the agent's predominant motives and the will on which the agent acts were *not already set one way.*"[68]

Here Kane himself evokes Martin Luther—his famous claim, when he posted his theses against the Pope and thus triggered the Protestant break, that he could not have done otherwise: "Here I stand. I can do no other." Was this act of Luther, then, free or not? It was a free act only if his crucial earlier choices (on which his defiant gesture was grounded) were such that *he could have done otherwise* with respect to them. But we look in vain in the past for such nodal points, such path-breaking Free Acts which magically interrupt causal chains that otherwise determine our behavior:

> Events in the *distant* past were indeed not "up to me," but my choice now to Go or Stay is up to me because its "parents"—some events in the *recent* past, such as the choices I have recently made—were up to me (because *their* "parents" were up to me), and so on, not to infinity, not far enough back to give my *self* enough spread in space and time so that there is a *me* for my decisions to be up to![69]

Again, this argument proves only that the "grounding" free act is not to be found at the level of physical reality, among other empirical decisions. Let us go back to Luther: in order for his posting of the anti-papal theses to count as a free act, we do not have to presuppose some previous "purely free" acts, acts which were "really" experienced in the mode of "now I can do otherwise"; it is enough to claim that *the subject (of free choice) is responsible for the very constellation within which his particular act appears to him as inevitable, in the mode of "I cannot do otherwise."*

Bernard Williams can again be of some help here, with his distinction between *must* and *ought*, which relate as the Real and the Symbolic: the Real of a drive whose injunction cannot be avoided (which is why Lacan says that the status of a drive is ethical); the Ought as a symbolic ideal caught in the dialectic of desire (if you ought not do something, this very prohibition generates the desire to do it). When you "must" do something, it means you have no choice but to do it, even if is terrible: in Wagner's *Die Walküre*, Wotan is cornered by Fricka, and "must" ("cannot but") allow the murder of Siegmund, although his heart bleeds for him; he "must" ("cannot but") punish Brünnhilde, his dearest child, the embodiment of his own innermost striving. And, incidentally, the same goes for *Tristan und Isolde*, the Bayreuth staging of which was Müller's last great theatrical achievement: they *must*, they *cannot but*, indulge in their passion, even if this goes against their *Sollen*, their social obligations. The whole point, of course, is that even when I "cannot but" do something, this in no way absolves me from full responsibility for it.

This notion's resemblance to Kant's "incorporation thesis" is evident: just as we "freely choose" the causal link that will determine us, at a metalevel we "freely choose" the ethical necessity whose pressure we experience as unconditional, giving us no choice. No wonder a further reference to Kant imposes itself here: his notion (later developed by Schelling) of a primordial, atemporal, transcendental act by means of which we choose our "eternal character," the elementary contours of our ethical identity. And the link with Freud's notion of an *unconscious* decision is clear: this absolute beginning is never made in the present, that is to say, its status is that of a pure presupposition, of something which has always-already taken place.[70] In other words, it is the paradox of a *passive decision*, of passively assuming the Decision that grounds our being as the supreme act of freedom—the paradox of the highest free choice which consists in assuming that one is chosen.

In his *Adieu à Emmanuel Lévinas*, Derrida tries to dissociate the decision from its usual metaphysical predicates (autonomy, consciousness, activity, sovereignty . . .) and think it as the "other's decision in me": "The passive decision, condition of the event, is always, structurally, another's decision in me, a rending decision as the decision of the other. Of the absolutely other in me, of the other as the absolute who decides of me in me."[71] In psychoanalytic terms, this choice is that of the "fundamental fantasy," of the basic frame/matrix which provides the coordinates of the subject's entire universe of meaning: although I am never outside it, although this fantasy is always-already there, and I am always-already thrown into it, I have to *presuppose* myself as the one who *posited* it. In Dennett's terms: although this act never took place in spatio-temporal reality, it exerts its efficiency at the "design" level. So, in a way, Dennett is right: there is no empirical founding act of freedom; it is rather that, in a complex and gradual process, the subject all of a sudden—not so much becomes "free" and "responsible," but—retroactively becomes aware that he *already was* "responsible." The paradox here is the same as that of the proverbial grain of sand which makes a heap out of a collection of dispersed grains: we can never single out a grain which "makes the difference"; all we can do is point out a grain and say: "At some point, *at least one* grain before this one was added, the grains already formed a heap. . . ." What we should add to Dennett is "only" (and the entire weight of the Hegelian "positing of presuppositions" resides in this "only") that this "retroactivity" makes the presupposition of a "Primary Mammal" necessary: although, in physical reality, there is no "first" mammal, we *have* to refer to it at a "design" level. There is thus no need to posit a magic "downward" causality, the ability of "higher" ideal (Dennett: "design") processes to causally determine the "lower" mechanical processes, to break their causal chain: the causality of freedom is purely reflexive-transitive, it is a causality which determines which causality will determine us.

Kantian Self-Consciousness is thus more than my fragmentary and shifting awareness of the states of my mind, and less than a direct insight into "what I am myself," into my substantial identity: it is a logical fiction, a nonsubstantial point of reference, which has to be added in order to stand for "that which" has an attitude, desires, makes judgments, and so on. To put it in Dennett's terms: for Kant, Self-Consciousness is not only not hindered by the absence of the Cartesian Theater—quite the contrary, it emerges as an empty logical function because there is no Cartesian Theater, no direct phenomenal self-acquaintance of the subject. There is subject qua $ insofar as (and because) there is no direct *Selbst-Vertrautheit*, insofar as (and because) the subject is not directly accessible to himself, because (as Kant put it) I can never know what I am in my noumenal dimension, as the "Thing which thinks." I am thus tempted to revert the standard Manfred Frank gesture of concluding (from the failure of reflection, of the self-reflective grounding of the subject's identity in the recognition of "himself" in his other) that there must be a previous direct self-acquaintance: what if failure comes first, what if the "subject" is nothing but the void, the gap, opened up by the failure of reflection? What if all the figures of positive self-acquaintance are just so many secondary "fillers" of this primordial gap? Every recognition of the subject in an image or a signifying trait (in short: every identification) already betrays its core; every jubilant "That's me!" already contains the seed of "That's not me!" However, what if, far from consisting in some substantial kernel of identity, inaccessible to reflective recuperation, the subject (as distinct from substance) emerges in this very moment of the failure of identification?

The point here is that we should take Lacan's term "subject of the signifier" literally: there is, of course, no substantial signified content which guarantees the unity of the I; at this level, the subject is multiple, dispersed, and so forth—its unity is guaranteed only by the self-referential symbolic act, that is, "I" is a purely performative entity, it is the one who says "I." This is the mystery of the subject's "self-positing," explored by Fichte: of course, when I say "I," I do not create any new content, I merely designate myself, the person who is uttering the phrase. This self-designation nonetheless gives rise to ("posits") an X which is not the "real" flesh-and-blood person uttering it, but, precisely and merely, the pure Void of self-referential designation (the Lacanian "subject of the enunciation"): "I" am not directly my body, or even the content of my mind; "I" am, rather, that X which has all these features as its properties. The Lacanian subject is thus the "subject of the signifier"—not in the sense of being reducible to one of the signifiers in the signifying chain ("I" is not directly the signifier I, since, in this case, a computer or another machine writing "I" would be a subject), but in a much more precise sense: when I say "I"—when I designate "myself" as "I"—this very act of signifying adds something to the "real flesh-and-blood entity" (inclusive of the content of its mental states, desires, attitudes) thus designated, and the subject is that X which is added to the designated content by means of the act of its self-referential designation. It is therefore misleading to say that the unity of the I is "a mere fiction" beneath which there is the multitude of inconsistent mental processes: the point is that this fiction gives rise to "effects in the Real," that is to say, it acts as a necessary presupposition to a series of "real" acts.

It is significant how, in his brief account of the evolutionary emergence of self-consciousness, Dennett basically relies on G. H. Mead's famous account on how Self emerges from social interaction (from acts of imagining how I appear to another subject, and from "internalizing" the other's view: in my "conscience," I perform imaginatively, in "silent inner speech," the possible reproaches that others may voice against my acts, and so on). Here, however, we should again invoke the difference between subject and person: Dieter Henrich was quite justified in pointing out how this dialectic of self-reflection as internalized social interaction can account only for my Self or "personhood", for the features which constitute my "self-image" (my imaginary and/or symbolic identifications), not for the emergence of the subject itself qua $.

To recapitulate: Kantian Self-Consciousness is a purely logical function which implies only that every content of my consciousness is already minimally mediated/reflected: when I desire X, I can never say "I'm just like that, I can't help desiring X, it's part of my nature," since I always desire to desire X, that is, I reflectively accept my desire for X—all reasons which motivate me to act exert their causal power only insofar as I "posit" or accept them as reasons. . . . Unexpectedly, this already brings us close to the psychoanalytic problematic; that is to say, one would think that "implicit reflexivity" is limited to conscious activity and is, as such, precisely that which our unconscious acts lack—when I act unconsciously, I act as if I am following a blind compulsion, as if I am submitted to a pseudo-natural causality. According to Lacan, however, "implicit reflexivity" is not only "also" discernible in the unconscious, it is precisely that which, at its most radical, is the unconscious. Take the typical attitude of a hysterical subject who complains how he is exploited, manipulated, victimized by others, reduced to an object of exchange—Lacan's answer to this is that this subjective position of a passive victim of circumstances is never simply imposed on the subject from outside, but has to be at least minimally endorsed by him. The subject, of course, is not aware of his active participation in his own victimization—this, precisely, is the "unconscious" truth of the subject's conscious experience of being a mere passive victim of circumstances. We can now see the precise psychoanalytic context of Lacan's apparently nonsensical thesis according to which the Cartesian *cogito* (or, rather, Kantian Self-Consciousness) is the very subject of the unconscious: for Lacan, the "subject of the unconscious," the subject to be attributed to the Freudian Unconscious, is precisely this empty point of self-relating, not a subject bursting with a wealth of libidinal forces and fantasies.

This paradoxical identity of Self-Consciousness (in the precise sense that this term acquires in German Idealism) with the subject of the Unconscious becomes clear in the problematic of radical Evil, from Kant to Schelling: faced with the enigma of how it is that we hold an evil person responsible for his deeds (although it is clear to us that the propensity for Evil is part of this person's "nature," that is to say, he cannot but "follow his nature" and accomplish his deeds with an absolute necessity), Kant and Schelling postulate a nonphenomenal transcendental, atemporal act of primordial choice by means of which each of us, prior to his temporal bodily existence, chooses his eternal character.[72] Within our temporal phenomenal existence, this act of choice is experienced as an imposed necessity, which means that the subject, in his phenomenal self-awareness, is not conscious of the free choice which grounds his character (his ethical "nature")—that is to say, this act is radically unconscious (the conclusion explicitly drawn by Schelling). Here again we encounter the subject as the Void of pure reflectivity, as that X to which we can attribute (as his free decision) what, in our phenomenal self-awareness, we experience as part of our inherited or otherwise imposed nature. The conclusion to be drawn is thus, again, that Self-Consciousness itself is radically unconscious.[73]

THE LANGUAGE OF SEDUCTION, THE SEDUCTION OF LANGUAGE

How, then, did this retroactive loop of freedom materialize? Was it a purely contingent drift, something which simply emerged "because, among all these possibilities, there was the possibility to emerge" (as Varela put it), or can we risk a more precise evolutionary account of its prehistory? Some cognitivists have proposed a solution which is strangely reminiscent of Lacan's topic of sexuality and language. Among others, Geoffrey Miller[74] has argued that the ultimate impetus for the breathtaking explosion of human intelligence was not directly the issue of survival (with all its usual suspects: struggle for food, defense against enemies, collaboration in the work process, and so on) but, more indirectly, the competition in sexual choice, that is, the effort to convince the mate to select me as a sexual partner. The features which give me an advantage in sexual competition are not directly my properties which demonstrate my priority over others, but *indicators* of such properties—the so-called "fitness indicators":

> A fitness indicator is a biological trait that evolved specifically to advertise an animal's fitness. . . . This is not a function like hunting, toolmaking, or socializing that contributes directly to fitness by promoting survival and reproduction. Instead, fitness indicators serve as a sort of meta-function. They sit on top of other adaptations, proclaiming their virtues. . . . They live in the semiotic space of symbolism and strategic deal-making, not in the gritty world of factory production. (103–105)

The first question that arises here is, of course: since fitness indicators are signs, why should an animal not cheat (lie) by producing signs which present it as stronger, etc., than it really is? How can the prospective partner discern the truth? The answer is the so-called "handicap principle," which

> suggests that prodigious waste is a necessary feature of sexual courtship. Peacocks as a species would be much better if they didn't have to waste so much energy growing big tails. But as individual males and females, they have irresistible incentives to grow the biggest tails they can afford, or to choose sexual partners with the biggest tails they can attract. In nature, showy waste is the only guarantee of truth in advertising. (125)

It is the same in human seduction: if a girl gets a big diamond ring from her lover, this is not just a signal of his wealth but, simultaneously, a proof of it—he has to be rich in order to be able to afford it. . . . No wonder Miller cannot resist formulating the shift he proposes in fashionable antiproductivist terms: "I am proposing a kind of marketing revolution in biology. Survival is like production, and courtship is like marketing. Organisms are like products, and the sexual preferences of the opposite sex are like consumer preferences" (174). And, according to Miller, mental abilities unique to humans are primarily psychological fitness indicators:

> This is where we find puzzling abilities like creative intelligence and complex language that show these great individual differences, these ridiculously high heritabilities, and these absurd wastes of time, energy, and effort. . . . If we view the human brain as a set of sexually selected fitness indicators, its high costs are no accident. They are the whole point. The brain's costs are what make it a good fitness indicator. Sexual selection made our brains wasteful, if not wasted: it transformed a small, efficient ape-style brain into a huge, energy-hungry handicap spewing out luxury behaviors like conversation, music, and art. (133–134)

We should therefore upend the standard view according to which the aesthetic (or symbolic) dimension is a secondary supplement to the utility-value of a product: it is, rather, the utility-value that is a "secondary profit" of a useless object whose production cost a lot of energy in order to serve as a fitness indicator. Even such elementary tools as prehistoric stone handaxes "were produced by males as sexual displays," since the excessive and costly perfection of their form (symmetry, and so on) served no direct use-value:

> So, we have an object that looks like a practical survival tool at first glance, but that has been modified in important ways to function as a costly fitness indicator. . . . handaxes may have been the first art-objects produced by our ancestors, and the best examples of sexual selection favoring the capacity for art. In one neat package, the handaxe combines instinct and learning, strength and skill, blood and flint, sex and survival, art and craft, familiarity and mystery. One might even view all of recorded art history as a footnote to the handaxe, which reigned a hundred times as long. (291)

So it is not enough to make the rather common point that the dimension of nonfunctional "aesthetic" display always supplements the basic functional utility of an instrument; it is, rather, the other way round: the nonfunctional "aesthetic" display of the produced object is primordial, and its potential utility comes second, that is, it has the status of a by-product, of something that parasitizes on the basic function. And, of course, the paradigmatic case here is that of language itself, the mental fitness indicator *par excellence*, with its excessive display of useless rhetoric:

> Human language is the only signaling system that conveys any other sort of information in courtship. It is still a fitness indicator, but it is much more as well. . . . Language evolved as much to display our fitness as to communicate useful information. To many language researchers and philosophers, this is a scandalous idea. They regard altruistic communication as the norm, from which our self-serving fantasies might sometimes deviate. But to biologists, fitness advertisement is the norm, and language is an exceptional form of it. We are the only species in the evolutionary history of our planet to have discovered a system of fitness indicators and sexual ornaments that also happens to transmit ideas from one head to another with telepathy's efficiency, Cyrano's panache, and Scheherezade's delight. (388–391)

What Miller leaves out of consideration, however, is the fundamental shift in the relationship between the sexes that characterizes the human animal: while, in the animal kingdom, it is as a rule the male who has to grow attractive features and perform complicated rituals (dances, songs) of seduction, in the human species it is women who are expected to dress and act provocatively in order to attract male attention—whence this reversal? Miller, of course, notices the difference ("biologically, the Woodabe [a tribe in Nigeria] are behaving perfectly normally, with males displaying and female choosing. The Miss America contests are the unusual ones" [277]), but gives no account of it.

If we take a closer look, of course, the standard courtship interaction is more complex: it involves a kind of division of labor. If, in the case of animals, the male displays his fitness and the female makes the choice, in the case of humans the female displays herself, offering herself to the male gaze; then the male proceeds to active seduction, to which the female consents (or not). The function of seduction unified in the case of animals is thus split into two: the female takes over the passive display of beauty attributes, and the male the active display of seduction practices (talking, singing . . .).

Perhaps the key to this shift is to be found in another shift: only in humans is what originally served as an instrument or indicator elevated into an end in itself. In art, for instance, the display of attributes turns into an activity which brings satisfaction in itself. Along these lines, when Steven Pinker discusses art, he proposes the basic formula of this "misapplication":

> Some parts of the mind register the attainment of increments of fitness by giving us a sensation of pleasure. Other parts use a knowledge of cause and effect to bring about goals. Put them together and you get a mind that rises to a biologically pointless challenge: figuring out how to get at the pleasure circuits of the brain and deliver the little jolts of enjoyment without the inconvenience of wringing bona fide fitness increments from the harsh world.[75]

No wonder Pinker's first example of this short circuit is a rat caught in the vicious cycle of lethal enjoyment: "When a rat has access to a lever that sends electrical impulses to an electrode implanted in its medial forebrain bundle, it presses the lever furiously until it drops of exhaustion, forgoing opportunities to eat, drink, and have sex."[76] In short, the poor rat literally got her brain fucked out. This is how drugs work: by directly affecting our brain—what we get here is a "pure" aphrodisiac, not a means of stimulating our senses as themselves instruments for providing pleasure to our brain, but the direct stimulation of the pleasure centers in the brain itself. The next, more mediated step is to access the pleasure circuits "via the senses, which stimulate the circuits when they are in an environment that would have led to fitness in past generations."[77] In past generations, when the animal recognized a pattern in its environs that enhanced its chance of survival (to get food, avoid danger, and so on), this recognition was marked/accompanied by the experience of pleasure; now, the organism directly produces such patterns simply in order to obtain pleasure. This matrix accounts for food, drink, and sexual pleasures—and even for art: the foundation of the aesthetic experience is the recognition of (symmetrical, clear, etc.) sensual patterns that, originally, enabled us to orient ourselves in our environs.

Of course, the enigma here is: *how does this short circuit come about?* How can the pleasure experience, which was originally a mere by-product of goal-oriented activity aiming at our survival (that is to say, a signal that this goal was achieved), turn into an aim in itself? The exemplary case here, of course, is that of sexuality: sexual pleasure, which originally indicated that the goal of procreation was achieved, becomes an aim in itself, so that the human animal spends large amounts of time pursuing this aim, planning it in all its details, even directly blocking the original goal (through contraception). It is the Catholic attitude of allowing sex only for the goal of procreation that debases it to animal coupling.

Miller's ultimate properly Freudian lesson is thus that the explosion of human symbolic capacities does not merely expand the metaphorical scope of sexuality (activities that are in themselves thoroughly asexual can get "sexualized," everything can be "eroticized" and start to "mean that"), but that, much more importantly, this explosion *sexualizes sexuality itself*: the specific quality of human sexuality has nothing to do with the immediate, rather stupid reality of copulation, including the preparatory mating rituals; only when animal coupling gets caught in the self-referential vicious circle of drive, in the protracted repetition of its failure to reach the impossible Thing, do we get what we call sexuality, that is, sexual activity itself gets sexualized. In other words, the fact that sexuality can spill over and function as a metaphorical content of every (other) human activity is not a sign of its power but, on the contrary, a sign of its impotence, failure, inherent blockage.

And perhaps it is from here that we should return to fitness indicators: does not the uniqueness of humankind consist in how these indicators—the pleasure we take in dealing with them—turn into an end in themselves, so that, ultimately, biological survival itself is reduced to a mere means, to the foundation for the development of "higher activities"?

OBJET PETIT A IN SOCIAL LINKS, OR,
THE IMPASSES OF ANTI-ANTI-SEMITISM

What happens to *objet petit a* when we pass to the other side of modernity, from capitalist dynamics to modern state power? Jean-Claude Milner has attempted to elaborate on this; his starting point[1] is that democracy is based on a short circuit between majority and the All: the winner takes all, has all the power, even if his majority is merely a couple of hundred votes among millions, as was the case in the 2000 US elections in Florida: "the majority counts as all." In *The History of the VKP(b)*, the Stalinist bible, there is a unique paradox when Stalin (who ghost-wrote the book) describes the outcome of the voting at a Party congress in the late 1920s: "With *a large majority,* the delegates *unanimously* approved the resolution proposed by the Central Committee"—if the vote was unanimous, *where did the minority disappear to?* Far from betraying some perverse "totalitarian" twist, this identification is constitutive of democracy as such.

This paradoxical status of the minority as "something that counts as nothing" enables us to discern in what precise sense the *demos* to which democracy refers "incessantly oscillates between the all and the *nonall/pastout*": "either the language of the limited Alls encounters a figure of the unlimited, or the unlimited encounters a figure of limit."[2] That is to say: a structural ambiguity is inscribed in the very notion of *demos*: it designates either the non-All of an unlimited set (everyone is included in it, there are no exceptions, just an inconsistent multitude) or the One of the People which has to be delimited from its enemies. *Grosso modo,* the predominance of one or the other aspect defines the opposition between American and European democracy: "In the democracy in America, majority exists, but it does not speak (the silent majority) and if it speaks, it becomes a particular form of minority."[3] In the USA, democracy is perceived as the field of the interplay of multiple agents, none of which embodies the All—that is to say, which are all "minoritarian"; in Europe, democracy traditionally referred to the rule of the One-People. However, Milner draws from this an elegant conclusion as to what is going on today: in contrast to the USA, which is predominantly "non-All" as a society—in its economy, culture, ideology—Europe is now going much further toward constituting itself as an unlimited *political* (non-)All through the process of European unification, in which there is room for everyone regardless of geography or culture, right up to Cyprus and Turkey. Such a unified Europe, however, can constitute itself only on condition of the progressive erasure of all divisive historical traditions and legitimizations: consequently, the unified Europe is based on the erasure of history, of historical memory.[4]

Recent phenomena like Holocaust revisionism, the moral equalization of all victims of the Second World War (the Germans suffered under the Allied bombardments no less than the Russians and the English; the fate of the Nazi collaborators liquidated by the Russians after the war is comparable to that of the victims of the Nazi genocide, and so on), are the logical outcome of this tendency: all specified limits are potentially erased on behalf of abstract suffering and victimization. And—this is what Milner is aiming at all along—this Europe, in its very advocacy of unlimited openness and multicultural tolerance, again needs the figure of the "Jew" as a structural obstacle to this drive toward unlimited unification; today's anti-Semitism, however, is no longer the old ethnic anti-Semitism; its focus is displaced from the Jews as an ethnic group to the State of Israel: "in the program of the Europe of the twenty-first century, the State of Israel occupies exactly the position that the name 'Jew' occupied in the Europe before the cut of 39–45."[5] In this way, today's anti-Semitism can present itself as anti-anti-Semitism, full of solidarity with the victims of the Holocaust; the reproach is just that, in our era of the gradual dissolution of all limits, of the fluidization of all traditions, the Jews wanted to built their own clearly delimited Nation-State.

Thus the paradoxes of the non-All provide the coordinates for the vicissitudes of modern anti-Semitism: in early modern anti-Semitism (exemplified by the name of Fichte), the Jews were denounced for their limitation, for sticking to their particular way of life, for their refusal to dissolve their identity in the unlimited field of modern secular citizenship. With late-nineteenth-century chauvinist imperialism, the logic was inverted: the Jews were perceived as cosmopolitan, as the embodiment of an unlimited, "deracinated" existence which, like a cancerous intruder, threatens to dissolve the identity of every particular-limited ethnic community. Today, however, with the move toward the post-Nation-State globalization whose political expression is an unlimited Empire, the Jews are again cast in the role of being stuck onto a Limit, a particular identity—they are increasingly perceived as the obstacle on the path toward unification (not only of Europe, but also of Europe and the Arab world).

Milner thus locates the notion of "Jews" in the European ideological imaginary as the moment which prevents unification-peace, which has to be annihilated for Europe to unite; this is why the Jews are always a "problem" that demands a "solution"—Hitler was merely the most radical point of this tradition. No wonder that, today, the European Union is getting more and more anti-Semitic, in its blatantly biased criticism of Israel: the very concept of Europe is tainted with anti-Semitism, which is why the first duty of Jews is to "get rid of Europe"—not by ignoring it (only the USA can afford to do that), but by bringing to light the dark underside of European Enlightenment and democracy. . . . So why were the Jews elevated to this role of the obstacle? What does the Jew stand for? Milner's answer here is radical: much more than the form of existence delimited by tradition, much more than stubborn attachment to a Nation-State—the Fourfold/*quadruplicite* of masculine/feminine/parents/children, of the exchange of generations as a symbolic passage sustained by the Law.[6] The ultimate horizon of the ongoing postmodern overcoming of Limits is no longer that of Christianity, but, rather, the neopagan New Age dream of overcoming sexual difference as the index of our link to a singular body, of immortality through cloning, of our transformation from hardware into software, from human into posthuman, into virtual entities that can migrate from one temporary embodiment to another—here are the very last lines of Milner's book:

> If modernity is defined by the belief in an unlimited realization of dreams, our future is fully outlined. It leads through the absolute theoretical and practical anti-Judaism. To follow Lacan beyond what he explicitly stated, the foundations of a new religion are thus posited: anti-Judaism will be the natural religion of humanity-to-come.[7]

The figure of the "Jew" is thus elevated into the index of a properly ontological limit: it stands for human finitude itself, for symbolic tradition, language, paternal Law, and, in Milner's "Lacanian" account of anti-Semitism, as inscribed into the very identity of Europe. "Europe" stands for the (Greek and Christian) dream of *parousia*, of a full *jouissance* beyond the Law, unencumbered by any obstacles or prohibitions. Modernity itself is propelled by a desire to move beyond Laws, to a self-regulated transparent social body; the last installment of this saga, today's postmodern neopagan Gnosticism, perceives reality as fully malleable, enabling us, humans, to transform ourselves into a migrating entity floating between a multitude of realities, sustained only by infinite Love. Against this tradition, the Jews, in a radically anti-millenarian way, persist in their fidelity to the Law; they insist on the insurmountable finitude of humanity and, in consequence, on the need for a minimum of "alienation," which is why they are perceived as an obstacle by everyone bent on a "final solution.". . .

Insofar as the Jews insist on the unsurpassable horizon of the Law and resist the Christian sublation (*Aufhebung*) of the Law in Love, they are the embodiment of the irreducible finitude of the human condition: they are not just an empirical obstacle to full incestuous *jouissance*, but the obstacle "as such," the very principle of impediment, the perturbing excess that can never be integrated. Jews are thus elevated to the *objet petit a* ("*notre objet a*," the title of François Regnault's booklet on the Jews),[8] the object-cause of (our Western) desire, the obstacle which effectively sustains desire, and in the absence of which our desire itself would vanish. They are our object of desire not in the sense of that which we desire, but in the strict Lacanian sense of that which sustains our desire, the metaphysical obstacle to full self-presence or full *jouissance*, that which has to be eliminated to make way for the arrival of the full *jouissance*; and, since this non-barred *jouissance* is structurally impossible, that which returns with increasing strength as a spectral threat the more Jews are annihilated.

The weakness of Milner's version of anti-Semitism can be specified at a whole series of interconnected levels. First, is all we find beyond the Law really only the dream of a full *jouissance*, so that Lacan looks like the ultimate defender of the paternal Law? Is not the fundamental insight of Lacan's late work precisely that an inherent obstacle to full *jouissance* is already operative in the drive which functions beyond the Law: the inherent "obstacle" on account of which a drive involves a curved space, that is, gets caught in a repetitive movement around its object, is not yet "symbolic castration." In Lacan's late work, on the contrary, the Prohibition—far from standing for a traumatic cut—enters precisely in order to pacify the situation, to rid us of the inherent impossibility inscribed into the functioning of a drive. Second problem: is not one of the key sources of European modernity the tradition of secularized Judaism? Is not what could be called the ultimate formulation of a "full *jouissance* beyond the Law" found in Spinoza, in his notion of the third, highest, level of knowing? Is not the very idea of modern "total" political revolution rooted in Jewish Messianism, as Walter Benjamin, among others, made clear? The very tendency toward the unlimited which needs the Jews as its obstacle is thus grounded in Judaism. The third problematic feature concerns Milner's political premises: "The birth of the State of Israel proved that victory and justice can go hand in hand."[9] What this statement obliterates is the way the constitution of the State of Israel was, from the standpoint of Europe, the realized "final solution" of the Jewish problem (getting rid of the Jews) entertained by the Nazis themselves. That is to say: was the State of Israel not, to turn Clausewitz around, the continuation of the war against the Jews with other (political) means? Is this not the "stain of injustice" that pertains to the State of Israel?

September 26, 1937 is a date anyone who is interested in the history of anti-Semitism should remember: on that day, Adolf Eichmann and his assistant boarded a train in Berlin in order to visit Palestine: Heydrich himself gave Eichmann permission to accept an invitation from Feivel Polkes, a senior member of Hagana (the Zionist secret organization), to visit Tel Aviv and discuss the coordination of German and Jewish organizations to facilitate the Jews' emigration to Palestine. Both the Germans and the Zionists wanted as many Jews as possible to move to Palestine: the Germans wanted them out of Western Europe, and the Zionists themselves wanted the Jews in Palestine to outnumber the Arabs as quickly as possible. (The visit failed because, due to some violent unrest, the British blocked access to Palestine; but Eichmann and Polkes did meet days later in Cairo, and discussed the coordination of German and Zionist activities.)[10] Is not this weird incident the supreme case of how Nazis and radical Zionists shared a common interest—in both cases, the purpose was a kind of "ethnic cleansing," that is, to change fundamentally the ratio of ethnic groups in the population? Today is it not, rather, the Palestinians, these "Jews among the Arabs," who are a kind of *objet petit a*, the intersection of the two sets of Israelis and Arabs, the obstacle to peace?

There is one main enigmatic, albeit obvious, fact about the neocons, one question that has to be asked: *why are they not anti-Semitic?* That is to say, on the basis of their ideological coordinates, they *should be* anti-Semitic. The only consistent reply is: because today's Zionism itself, as embodied in the State of Israel's predominant politics, is already "anti-Semitic," that is to say, it relies on anti-Semitic ideological mapping. Remember the typical newspaper caricature of Yassir Arafat: the rounded face with its big nose and thick lips, on a small rounded clumsy body . . . looks familiar? No wonder: it is the old cliché drawing of the corrupt Jew from the 1930s! Another confirmation of the fact that *Zionism is a species of anti-Semitism.* It is thus not simply that religious fundamentalist neocons support Israel because, in their vision of Armageddon, the final battle will take place after the State of Israel has emerged again—the reasons go deeper.[11] What we should assert against the Zionists is the truly Jewish cosmopolitan spirit clearly discernible in Freud's address to the Vienna Branch of B'ni Brith on his seventieth birthday, when he articulated his basic mistrust of the pathetic experience of national identification: "Whenever I felt an inclination to national enthusiasm, I strove to suppress it as being harmful and wrong. . . ." And, to avoid a misunderstanding, his mistrust also included the Jewish identity—in a letter to Arnold Zweig in 1932, Freud made an uncannily prescient observation: "I can claim no sympathy at all for the misdirected piety which transforms a piece of a Herodian wall into a national relic, thus offending the feelings of the natives."

The irony missed by Milner is that today it is the Muslims, not the Jews, who are perceived as a threat and an obstacle to globalization: it is a journalistic commonplace to point out that all the great world religions have found a way to live with capitalist modernization with the exception of Islam, which is why the present conflict is often described as the one between the democratic West and "Islamic Fascism." The crucial weakness of Milner's analysis, however, is the (rather surprising) complete absence of the market economy and money in the rise of anti-Semitism: what about "Jew" as the figure in which social antagonism is reified? As the figure which stands for financial ("nonproductive") capital and profit in the sphere of exchange, and thus enables us to elude the exploitation inscribed into the very process of production, and to sustain the myth of the harmonious relationship between Labor and Capital, once we get rid of the parasitic Jewish intruder? This is where Lacan's logic of *pastout* finds its proper function: significantly, although Milner points out that the thesis "everything is political" belongs to *pastout* (a remainder of his Maoist youth?), he deploys the social dimension of the *pastout* only in the guise of inconsistent/unlimited All, not in the guise of the antagonism that cuts across the entire social body ("class struggle"). The anti-Semitic figure of the Jew enables us to obfuscate the non-All of the constitutive social antagonism, transposing it into the conflict between the social All (the corporate notion of society) and its external Limit, the Jewish intruder who brings into it imbalance and degeneration.

And this allows us to cast a new light on Milner's notion of "Jews" as the obstacle to a unified Europe: what if the persistence of the anti-Semitic logic, far from being the necessary obverse of the non-All Europe, is, on the contrary, an indication of the tendency to conceive Europe as a limited All with the need for a constitutive exception? The task should thus be to fight for a non-All Europe as a truly new political form slowly emerging through the impasses of "unification"—this non-All Europe will no longer need the "Jew" as its limit-obstacle, as its constitutive exception. What if such a Europe is a Europe of exceptions, a Europe in which every unit will be an exception? In short, what if this is the "solution to the Jewish problem"—that we all turn into "Jews," into *objets petit a*, into exceptions? That is to say: is it not that, in the "postmodern" global empire, what was hitherto the "Jewish exception" is increasingly becoming the standard rule: a particular ethnic group which participates fully in the global economy while simultaneously maintaining its identity at the level of Milner's Fourfold, that is to say, through its founding cultural myths and rituals, which are transmitted from generation to generation? Milner misses this key point insofar as he fails to grasp the actual functioning of the emerging global *pastout* empire: in it, all particular identities are *not* simply "liquefied," rendered fluid, but maintained—Empire thrives on the multiplicity of particular (ethnic, religious, sexual, lifestyle . . .) identities which form the structural obverse of the unified field of Capital.

This is the deepest irony that escapes Milner: he fails to notice the radical ambiguity of his thesis about the Jewish exception as resisting modern universality. When Milner posits the Jews as insisting on the Quadruple of the familial tradition, against the dissolution of this tradition in the non-All of modernity, he thereby repeats the standard anti-Semitic cliché according to which the Jews themselves are always in the first ranks of the struggle for universal mingling, multi-culti, racial confusion, liquefaction of all identities, nomadic, plural, shifting subjectivity—with the exception of their own ethnic identity. The passionate appeal of Jewish intellectuals to universalist ideologies is tied to the implicit understanding that Jewish particularism will be exempt, as if the Jewish identity cannot survive when Jews live side by side with other people who also insist on their ethnic identity—as if, in some kind of parallax shift, the contours of their identity can become clear only when the identity of others is blurred. The alliance between the USA and the State of Israel is thus a strange cohabitation of two opposed principles: if Israel *qua* ethnic state *par excellence* stands for the Quadruple (tradition), the USA—much more than Europe—stands for the non-All of society, the dissolution of all fixed traditional links. The State of Israel thus, in effect, functions as the small *a* of the US big A, the ex-timate core of tradition that serves as the mythic point of reference of the chaotic non-All of the USA.

Radical as it may appear, Milner's idea perfectly fits one of the two clichés that pervade the European public space with regard to the Israeli-Palestinian conflict. At one extreme, the Muslims continue to function as Europe's constitutive Other: the main opposition of today's ideologico-political struggle is the one between a tolerant multicultural liberal Europe and a fundamentalist militant Islam. Any political or even cultural organization of Muslims is immediately dismissed as a fundamentalist threat to our secular values. A good example is Oriana Fallacci, with her thesis that Europe has already spiritually capitulated: it already treats itself as a province of Islam, afraid of asserting its cultural and political identity.[12] From this perspective, the distinction between anti-Semitism and anti-Zionism is a fake: every critique of Israeli politics is a mask (and a new form of appearance) of anti-Semitism. European advocacy of peace in the Middle East and its solidarity with the Palestinians is perceived as the continuation of the old anti-Semitism with other means. . . . At the other extreme, there are those for whom the West Bank occupation is simply the last case of European colonialism, and the evocation of the Holocaust is thoroughly politically instrumentalized in order to legitimize this colonial expansion; the same ethico-political standards should apply to all, the Israelis included. From this standpoint, the fact that Arab Muslims continue to function as Europe's constitutive Other is precisely what we must submit to a critical analysis which should "deconstruct" the image of the Islamic fundamentalist threat. . . .

The truly enigmatic feature is how (again, in a kind of parallax gap) these two completely opposed views can coexist in our public space: it is possible to claim, at one and the same time, that anti-Semitism is still all-pervasive even in its "postmodern" version, *and* that the Muslims continue to function as the figure of the cultural-racial Other. Where, in this opposition, is the truth? Definitely not in any kind of middle ground, of avoiding the two extremes. Rather, we should assert the truth of both extremes, conceiving each of the two as the symptom of its opposite. Does not the idea of the Jews forming a Nation-State imply the *end* of Judaism—no wonder the Nazis supported this plan! The Jews stood for the "Fourfold" precisely in order to maintain their identity without a Nation-State. The only consistent position (theoretically and ethically) is to reject such alternatives, and recognize both dangers: "The critique of anti-Semitism or the critique of Zionist politics? Yes, please!"—far from being exclusive opposites, the two are connected by a secret link. There really is anti-Semitism in much of the contemporary Left, for instance, in the direct equating of what the State of Israel is doing in the occupied territories with the Nazi Holocaust, with the implied reasoning: "The Jews are now doing to others what was done to them, so they no longer have any right to complain about the Holocaust!" And there actually is a paradox in that the very Jews who preach the universal "melting-pot" are all the more insistent on their own ethnic identity. There is also an unfortunate tendency among some Zionists to transform *shoah* into *holocaust*, the sacrificial offering which guarantees the Jewish special status. The exemplary figure here is Elie Wiesel, who sees the Holocaust as equal to the revelation at Sinai in its religious significance: attempts to "desanctify" or "demystify" the Holocaust are a subtle form of anti-Semitism. In this type of discourse, the Holocaust is in effect elevated into a unique *agalma*, hidden treasure, *objet petit a* of the Jews—they are ready to give up everything *except the Holocaust*. . . . Recently, after I was attacked by a Jewish Lacanian for being a covert anti-Semite, I asked a mutual friend why this extreme reaction. His reply: "You should understand the guy—he does not want the Jews to be deprived of the Holocaust, the focal point of their lives. . . ."

No wonder Jacques-Alain Miller is shoulder to shoulder with Milner here: recently, the two even coauthored a booklet opposing the predominant procedure of evaluation. This book marks their final full integration into the space of parliamentary liberal democracy—Miller recently wrote that it is the duty of the psychoanalyst to participate in the debates of the city, especially when the field of mental health is involved: psychoanalysts should aspire to become recognized talking partners in the dialogue and the decisions to be taken by politicians and administrators that will determine the future of analytic practice. "The evaluation operation makes one being go from his or her unique state of being into the one-among-the-others state . . . he agrees to be compared, he becomes comparable, he accesses a statistical state . . . but in psychoanalysis we are attached to the unique, we do not compare . . . we receive each subject as if it was the first time, as incomparable."[13] Psychoanalysts deal with the subject, and each subject is unique: the subject cannot be reduced to a common diagnosis, or a list of symptoms or problems. The need for an empirical approach and accountability is intended to discredit fringe therapies or those that promise instant healing—but is this not precisely what insurance companies are requesting, demanding to see results after eight sessions? Psychoanalysts need to be out there, and to be accountable for what they do to relieve the contemporary discontents and sufferings and ways of *jouissance*; they need to be swift and efficient, but without surrendering their principles—the challenge is to go from the private language, what is said in the privacy of an office and among professional peers, to the public language and public debate.[14] In one of his "participations in the debates of the city," Miller further elaborated this point:

> It is very difficult . . . to find the just measure of how to warn the public against problems but most of all, most of all, not to create panic. . . . Analysts, psychoanalysts today, should be capable of conveying to the Nation, to its representatives . . . , a certain amount of knowledge they possess and that can indeed take care of these panic waves that burst out periodically.[15]

The theoretical background of this line of thought is made clear in Miller's public letter to Bernard Accoyer, the French *député* with responsibility for the new legal regulation of the status of psychoanalysts:

> It is a fact that the demand for the listening practices of the psys has not stopped rising over the last ten years; consultations for children are multiplying; the psy is now being expected to substitute himself for the forebear to assure the transmission of values and continuity between the generations. The listening ear of the psy, qualified or not, constitutes the compassionate cushion necessary to the "society of risk": the trust given obligatorily to abstract and anonymous systems gives rise dialectically to the need for personalized attention: "I've got my psy," "I've got my coach". . . . Everything is indicating that mental health is a political stake for the future. Detraditionalization, loss of bearings, disarray of identifications, dehumanization of desire, violence in the community, suicide among the young, *passages à l'acte* of the mentally ill insufficiently monitored due to the state of shortage that psychiatry has to endure: the "Human Bomb" in Neuilly, the killings in Nanterre, the attacks against the President and the Mayor of Paris. All this is unfortunately just the beginning (cf. the USA). . . . But it is also a strategic knot. Psychoanalysis is much more than psychoanalysis: it is constitutive, or reconstitutive, of the social bond, which is going through a period of restructuring probably without precedent since the Industrial Revolution.[16]

The intellectual misery of these reflections cannot fail to strike us: first the standard pop-sociological platitudes about today's dehumanized "risk society," with its anonymous abstract and nontransparent systems ruling over individuals; then the pseudo-personalized role of the psychiatrist as providing the "compassionate cushion," that is, as (re)constituting the social bond—or, rather, the semblance of such a bond, since, as is clear from Miller's own description, the lives of individuals continue to be run by anonymous opaque systems; nothing can be done about this, it is the fate of our late modernity (sounds familiar?).

In Brecht's learning play *The Measure Taken*, the young humanist comrade is shocked by the suffering workers employed to pull the boats up river, their bare feet getting hurt on sharp stones; so he takes some flat stones, runs alongside the workers, and places the stones in their path to prevent their feet getting hurt—to the applause of the observing rich merchants employing the workers, who comment approvingly: "Good! You see, this is true compassion! This is how one should help the suffering workers!" Is not Miller proposing a similar role for psychoanalysts—to place soft cushions beneath their patients to prevent their suffering? Of course, to ask if, perhaps, something can be done to *change* the undisputed rule of the anonymous opaque systems is a question that is not even prohibited, but simply absent, "out of the question.". . . In Miller's own description, psychoanalysts are thus described as profiting from today's "disarray of identifications": the more serious this crisis, the more business there is for them! This, not any socio-critical dimension, is the true content behind the mass protest of the psychoanalysts in France—their demand to the State is: "Why don't you let us profit from the crisis?"

So, from Lacan's notion of analysis as subversive of identifications, we are obtaining analysts who function as a kind of mental repair service, providing ersatz identifications . . . a model of how *not* to proceed, an exemplary case of conceding the terrain in advance to the enemy against whom one struggles. Analysts should participate in the debates of the city—why, exactly? In order to become "recognized talking partners in the dialogue and the decisions to be taken by politicians and administrators"? Analysts should be accountable for what they do to "relieve the contemporary discontents and sufferings and ways of *jouissance*"—really? And the theoretical coordinates within which one formulates one's position? The most boring old hermeneutic insistence on the uniqueness of the individual who should not be turned into a statistical unit, reduced to one-in-the-series-with-others. . . . Where are the days when it was clear to every critical intellectual that this insistence on the uniqueness of the subject is merely the obverse of "quantification," the two being the opposite sides of the same (ideological) coin? That one should not simply accept the task of collaborating with politicians and administrators to relieve contemporary discontents and sufferings, but, rather, ask how such subjective discontents are generated by the very social order whose smooth functioning they disturb: how a subjective discontent in civilization is a discontent that is cosubstantial with civilization itself? There is a cruel irony in the fact that Lacanian orientation lost its sociopolitical critical edge at the very moment when its representatives decided to intervene in public political debates—how much more subversive was Lacan's old arrogant "elitism"! There are situations in which the duty of the analysts is *not* to participate in debates, insofar as such participation, even if it pretends to be critical, means that one accepts the basic coordinates of the way the ruling ideology formulates the problem.

Thus Milner's failure brings us back to capitalist dynamics proper, neglected in his work. Let us explore this apropos of Michael Hardt and Antonio Negri's *Empire* and *Multitude*, which could be called the ultimate exercises in Deleuzian politics. What makes these two books such refreshing reading is the fact that they refer to and function as the moment of theoretical reflection of—I am almost tempted to say: are embedded in—an actual global movement of anticapitalist resistance: we can sense, behind the written lines, the smells and sounds of Seattle, Genoa, and the Zapatistas. So their limitation is simultaneously the limitation of the actual movement.

Hardt and Negri's (HN's) basic move, an act which is by no means ideologically neutral (and, incidentally, is totally foreign to their philosophical paradigm, Deleuze!),

is to identify (name) "democracy" as the common denominator of all today's emancipatory movements: "The common currency that runs throughout so many struggles
and movements for liberation across the world today—at local, regional, and global
levels—is the desire for democracy."[17] Far from standing for a utopian dream, democracy is "the only answer to the vexing questions of our day, . . . the only way out of our
state of perpetual conflict and war" (xviii). Not only is democracy inscribed in the
present antagonisms as an immanent *telos* of their resolution; even more, today, the rise
of the multitude at the heart of capitalism "makes democracy possible for the first
time" (340). Hitherto, democracy was constrained by the form of the One, of sovereign state Power; "absolute democracy" ("the rule of everyone by everyone, a democracy without qualifiers, without ifs or buts" [237]) becomes possible only when "the
multitude is finally able to rule itself" (340).

For Marx, highly organized corporate capitalism was already "socialism within
capitalism" (a kind of socialization of capitalism, with the absent owners becoming
more and more superfluous), so that one needs only to cut the nominal head off and
we get socialism. For HN, however, the limitation of Marx was that he was historically
restricted to centralized and hierarchically organized mechanical automatized industrial labor; this is why his vision of "general intellect" was that of a central planning
agency; only today, with the rise of "immaterial labor" to the hegemonic role, does the
revolutionary reversal become "objectively possible." This immaterial labor extends
between the two poles of intellectual (symbolic) labor (production of ideas, codes,
texts, programs, figures: writers, programmers . . .) and affective labor (those who
deal with our physical affects: from doctors to babysitters and flight attendants). Today,
immaterial labor is "hegemonic" in the precise sense in which Marx proclaimed that,
in nineteenth-century capitalism, large industrial production is hegemonic as the
specific color giving its tone to the totality—not quantitatively, but playing the key, emblematic structural role: "What the multitude produces is not just goods or services;
the multitude also and most importantly produces cooperation, communication,
forms of life, and social relationships" (339). What thereby emerges is a new vast domain, the "common": shared knowledge, forms of cooperation and communication,
and so on, which can no longer be contained by the form of private property. This,
then, far from posing a mortal threat to democracy (as conservative cultural critics
would have us believe), opens up a unique chance of "absolute democracy"—why?

In immaterial production, the products are no longer material objects, but new social (interpersonal) relations themselves—in short, immaterial production is directly
biopolitical, the production of social life. It was Marx who emphasized how material
production is always also the (re)production of the social relations within which it occurs; with today's capitalism, however, the production of social relations is the immediate end/goal of production: "Such new forms of labor . . . present new possibilities
for economic self-management, since the mechanisms of cooperation necessary for
production are contained in the labor itself" (336). The wager of Hardt and Negri is
that this directly socialized, immaterial production not only renders owners progres-

sively superfluous (who needs them when production is directly social, formally and as to its content?); the producers also master the regulation of social space, since social relations (politics) is the stuff of their work: economic production directly becomes political production, the production of society itself. The way is thus open for "absolute democracy," for the producers directly regulating their social relations without even the detour of democratic representation.

This vision gives rise to a whole series of concrete questions.[18] Much more pertinent, however, is another critical point which concerns HN's neglect of the form in the strict dialectical sense of the term. HN continuously oscillate between their fascination with global capitalism's "deterritorializing" power, and the rhetoric of the struggle of the multitude against the One of capitalist power. Financial capital, with its wild speculations detached from the reality of material labor, this standard *bête noire* of the traditional Left, is celebrated as the germ of the future, capitalism's most dynamic and nomadic aspect. The organizational forms of today's capitalism—decentralization of decision-making, radical mobility and flexibility, interaction of multiple agents—are perceived as pointing toward the oncoming reign of the multitude. It is as if everything is already here, in "postmodern" capitalism—all that is needed is an act of purely formal conversion, or, in Hegelese, the passage from In-itself to For-itself, like the one developed by Hegel apropos of the struggle between Enlightenment and Faith, where he describes the "silent, ceaseless weaving of the Spirit."

Even the fashionable parallel with the new cognitivist notion of human psyche is present here: in the same way, the brain sciences teach us how there is no central Self in the brain, how our decisions emerge out of the interaction of a pandemonium of local agents, how our psychic life is an "autopoietic" process which, without any imposed centralizing agency (a model which, incidentally, is explicitly based on the parallel with today's "decentralized" capitalism). So the new society of the multitude which rules itself will be like today's cognitivist notion of the ego as a pandemonium of interacting agents with no central deciding Self running the show. . . . However, although HN see today's capitalism as the main site of the proliferating multitudes, they continue to rely on the rhetoric of the One, the sovereign Power, against the multitude; the way they bring these two aspects together is clear: while capitalism generates multitudes, it contains them in the capitalist form, thereby unleashing a demon it is unable to control. The question to be asked here is, nonetheless, whether HN are making a mistake very similar to that of Marx: is not their notion of the pure multitude ruling itself the ultimate *capitalist* fantasy, the fantasy of capitalism's self-revolutionizing perpetual motion exploding freely when its inherent obstacle is removed? In other words, is not the capitalist *form* (the form of the appropriation of surplus-value) the necessary form, formal frame/condition, of the self-propelling productive movement?

Consequently, when HN repeatedly emphasize how "this is a philosophical book," and warn the reader: "do not expect our book to answer the question, What is to be done? or propose a concrete program of action" (xvi), this constraint is not as neutral as it may seem: it indicates a fundamental theoretical flaw. After describing multiple forms of resistance to the Empire, Multitude ends with a Messianic note adumbrating the great Rupture, the moment of Decision when the movement of multitudes will be transubstantiated in the sudden birth of a new world: "After this long season of violence and contradictions, global civil war, corruption of imperial biopower, and infinite toil of the biopolitical multitudes, the extraordinary accumulations of grievances and reform proposals must at some point be transformed by a strong event, a radical insurrectional demand" (358). At this point, however, just as we expect a minimum theoretical determination of this rupture, what we get is again withdrawal into philosophy: "A philosophical book like this, however, is not the place for us to evaluate whether the time for revolutionary political decision is imminent" (357). Here HN perform an all-too-quick jump: of course we cannot ask them to provide a detailed empirical description of the Decision, of the passage to the globalized "absolute democracy," to the multitude that rules itself; what, however, if this justified refusal to engage in pseudo-concrete futuristic predictions masks an inherent notional deadlock/impossibility? That is to say: what we do and should expect is a description of the notional structure of this qualitative jump, of the passage from the multitudes resisting the One of sovereign Power to the multitudes directly ruling themselves. Leaving the notional structure of this passage in a darkness elucidated only by vague analogies and examples from resistance movements cannot but arouse the anxious suspicion that this self-transparent direct rule of everyone over everyone, this democracy tout court, will coincide with its opposite.[19]

HN are right to raise the problem of the classic Leftist revolutionary notion of "taking power": such a strategy accepts the formal frame of the power structure, and aims merely at replacing one bearer of power ("them") with another ("us"). As Lenin shows clearly in State and Revolution, the true revolutionary aim is not to "take power," but to undermine, disintegrate, the very apparatuses of state power. That is the ambiguity of "postmodern" Leftist calls to abandon the program of "taking power": do they imply that we should ignore the existing power structure or, rather, limit ourselves to resisting it by constructing alternative spaces outside the state power network (the Zapatista strategy in Mexico); or do they imply that we should dismantle, pull away the ground of, state power, so that state power will simply collapse, implode? In the second case, poetic formulas about the multitude immediately ruling itself are inadequate.

Here HN form a kind of triad whose other two terms are Ernesto Laclau and Giorgio Agamben. The ultimate difference between Laclau and Agamben involves the structural inconsistency of power: while they both insist on this inconsistency, their positions toward it are precisely opposed. Agamben's focus on the vicious circle of the link between legal power (the rule of Law) and violence is sustained by the utopian Messianic hope that it is possible radically to break this circle and step out of it (in an act of Benjaminian "divine violence"). In Coming Community, he refers to Saint Thomas's answer to the difficult theological question: What happens to the souls of unbaptized babies who have died in ignorance of both sin and God? They have committed no sin, so their punishment cannot be an afflictive punishment, like that of hell, but only a punishment of privation that consists in the perpetual lack of the vision of God. The inhabitants of limbo, in contrast to the damned, do not feel pain from this lack: . . . they do not know that they are deprived of the supreme good. . . . The greatest punishment—the lack of the vision of God—thus turns into a natural joy: irremediably lost, they persist without pain in divine abandon.[20]

For Agamben, their fate is the model of redemption: they "have left the world of guilt and justice behind them: the light that rains down on them is that irreparable light of the dawn following the *novissima dies* of judgment. But the life that begins on earth after the last day is simply human life."[21] (I cannot help recalling here the crowd of humans who remain on stage at the end of Wagner's *Twilight of the Gods*, silently witnessing the self-destruction of the gods—what if they are the happy ones?) And, *mutatis mutandis*, the same goes for HN, who perceive resistance to power as preparing the ground for a miraculous Leap into "absolute democracy" in which the multitude will directly rule itself—at this point, tensions will be resolved, freedom will explode into eternal self-proliferation. The difference between Agamben and HN may be best apprehended by means of the good old Hegelian distinction between abstract and determinate negation: although HN are even more anti-Hegelian than Agamben, their revolutionary Leap remains an act of "determinate negation," the gesture of formal reversal, of merely freeing the potentials developed in global capitalism, which already is a kind of "Communism-in-itself"; in contrast to them, Agamben—and, again, paradoxically, in spite of his animosity to Adorno—outlines the contours of something which is much closer to the utopian longing for the *ganz Andere* (wholly Other) in the late work of Adorno, Horkheimer, and Marcuse, to a redemptive leap into a nonmediated Otherness.

Laclau and Mouffe, on the contrary, propose a new version of Édouard Bernstein's arch-revisionist motto "goal is nothing, movement is all": the real danger, the temptation to be resisted, is the very notion of a radical cut by means of which the basic social antagonism will be dissolved and the new era of a self-transparent nonalienated society will arrive. For Laclau and Mouffe, such a notion disavows not only the Political as such, the space of antagonism and struggle for hegemony, but the fundamental ontological finitude of the human condition as such—this is why any attempt to actualize such a leap must end in a totalitarian disaster. This means that the only way to elaborate and practice livable particular political solutions is to admit the global *a priori* deadlock: we can solve particular problems only against the background of the irreducible global deadlock. Of course, this does not in any way entail that political agents should limit themselves to solving particular problems, abandoning the topic of universality: for Laclau and Mouffe, universality is impossible and at the same time necessary, that is, there is no direct "true" universality, every universality is always-already caught up in the hegemonic struggle, it is an empty form hegemonized (filled in) by some particular content which, at a given moment and in a given conjuncture, functions as its stand-in.[22]

Are these two approaches, however, really as radically opposed as they seem to be? Does not Laclau and Mouffe's edifice also imply its own utopian point: the point at which political battles would be fought without remainders of "essentialism," all sides fully accepting the radically contingent character of their endeavors and the irreducible character of social antagonisms? On the other hand, Agamben's position is also not without its secret advantages: since, with today's biopolitics, the space of political struggle is closed, and any democratic-emancipatory movements are meaningless, we cannot do anything but wait complacently for the miraculous explosion of the "divine violence." As for HN, they bring us back to the Marxist confidence that "history is on our side," that historical development is already generating the form of the Communist future.

If anything, the problem with HN is therefore that they are *too* Marxist, taking over the underlying Marxist scheme of historical progress: like Marx, they celebrate the "deterritorializing" revolutionary potential of capitalism; like Marx, they locate the contradiction within capitalism: in the gap between this potential and the form of capital, of the private-property appropriation of the surplus. In short, they rehabilitate the old Marxist notion of the tension between productive forces and the relations of production: capitalism already generates the "germs of the future new form of life," it incessantly produces the new "common," so that, in a revolutionary explosion, this New should just be liberated from the old social form. However, precisely as Marxists, in keeping with our fidelity to Marx's work, we should point out Marx's mistake: he perceived how capitalism unleashed the breathtaking dynamic of self-enhancing productivity—see his fascinated descriptions of how, in capitalism, "everything solid melts into air," of how capitalism is the greatest revolutionizer in the entire history of humanity; on the other hand, he also clearly perceived how this capitalist dynamic is propelled by its own inner obstacle or antagonism—the ultimate limit of capitalism (of capitalist self-propelling productivity) is Capital itself, that is to say, the incessant capitalist development and revolutionizing of its own material conditions, the mad dance of its unconditional spiral of productivity, is ultimately nothing but a desperate flight forward to escape its own debilitating inherent contradiction. . . . Marx's fundamental mistake was to conclude, from these insights, that a new, higher social order (Communism) is possible, an order that would not only maintain but even raise to a higher level, and effectively fully release the potential of, the self-increasing spiral of productivity which, in capitalism, on account of its inherent obstacle ("contradiction"), is again and again thwarted by socially destructive economic crises. In short, what Marx overlooked is that—to put it in classic Derridean terms—this inherent obstacle/antagonism, as the "condition of impossibility" of the full deployment of the productive forces, is simultaneously its "condition of possibility": if we abolish the obstacle, the inherent contradiction of capitalism, we do not get the fully unleashed drive to productivity finally delivered of its impediment, we lose precisely this productivity that seemed to be generated and simultaneously thwarted by capitalism—if we take away the obstacle, the very potential thwarted by this obstacle dissipates. That is Lacan's fundamental reproach to Marx, which focuses on the ambiguous overlapping between surplus-value and surplus-enjoyment.[23]

All this, of course, does not in any way entail that we should abandon the search for the political "evental sites," places within our global societies which harbor a revolutionary potential. A century ago, Vilfredo Pareto was the first to describe the so-called 80/20 rule of (not only) social life: 80 percent of land is owned by 20 percent of the people, 80 percent of profits are produced by 20 percent of the employees, 80 percent of decisions are made during 20 percent of meeting time, 80 percent of the links on the Web point to less than 20 percent of Web-pages, 80 percent of peas are produced by 20 percent of peapods. . . . As some social analysts and economists have suggested, today's explosion of economic productivity confronts us with the ultimate case of this rule: the coming global economy tends toward a state in which only 20 percent of the workforce can do all the necessary job, so that 80 percent of the population are basically irrelevant and of no use, potentially unemployed.

This 80/20 rule follows from what is called "scale-free networks" in which a small number of nodes with the greatest number of links is followed by an ever larger number of nodes with an ever smaller number of links. For example, in any group of people, a small number know (have links to) a large number of other people, while the majority of people know only a small number of people—social networks spontaneously form "nodes," people with a large number of links to other people. In such a scale-free network, competition remains: while the overall distribution remains the same, the identity of the top nodes changes all the time, a latecomer replacing the earlier winners. Some of the networks, however, can pass the critical threshold beyond which competition breaks down and the winner takes all: one node grabs all the links, leaving none for the rest—this is what basically happened with Microsoft, which emerged as the privileged node: it grabbed all the links, that is, we have to relate to it in order to communicate with other entities. The big structural question is, of course: what defines the threshold, which networks tend to pass the threshold, above which competition breaks down and the winner takes all?[24]

If, then, today's "postindustrial" society needs fewer and fewer workers to reproduce itself (20 percent of the workforce, on some accounts), then *it is not workers who are in excess, but Capital itself.* The unemployed, however, constitute only one among the many candidates for today's "universal individual," for a particular group whose fate stands for the injustice of today's world: Palestinians, Guantánamo prisoners. . . . Today Palestine is the site of a potential event precisely because all the standard "pragmatic" solutions to the "Middle East crisis" repeatedly fail, so that a utopian invention of a new space is the only "realistic" choice. Furthermore, the Palestinians make a good candidate on account of their paradoxical position of being *the victims of the ultimate Victims themselves* (*the Jews*), which, of course, puts them in an extremely difficult position: when they resist, their resistance can immediately be denounced as a prolongation of anti-Semitism, as a secret solidarity with the Nazi "final solution." Indeed, if—as Lacanian Zionists like to claim—Jews are the *objet petit a* among nations, the troubling excess of

Western history, how can we resist them with impunity? Is it possible to be the *objet petit a* of *objet petit a* itself? It is precisely this ethical blackmail that we should reject.

There is, however, a privileged site in this series: what if the new proletarian position is that of the inhabitants of slums in the new megalopolises? The explosive growth of slums in recent decades, especially in Third World megalopolises from Mexico City and other Latin American capitals through Africa (Lagos, Chad) to India, China, the Philippines, and Indonesia, is perhaps the crucial geopolitical event of our times.[25] The case of Lagos, the biggest node in the shantytown corridor of 70 million people that stretches from Abidjan to Ibadan, is illustrative here: according to the official sources themselves, about two-thirds of the total Lagos State landmass of 3.577 square kilometers could be classified as shantytowns or slums; no one even knows the size of its population—officially it is 6 million, but most experts estimate it at 10 million. Since, sometime very soon (or maybe, given the imprecision of Third World censuses, it has already happened), the urban population of the earth will outnumber the rural population, and since slum-dwellers will make up the majority of the urban population, we are by no means dealing with a marginal phenomenon. We are thus witnessing the rapid growth of a population outside state control, living in conditions half outside the law, in dire need of minimal forms of self-organization. Although this population is composed of marginalized laborers, redundant civil servants, and ex-peasants, they are not simply a redundant surplus: they are incorporated into the global economy in numerous ways, many of them as informal wage-workers or self-employed entrepreneurs, with no adequate health or social security cover. (The main reason for their rise is the inclusion of Third World countries in the global economy, with cheap food imports from First World countries ruining local agriculture.) They are the true "symptom" of slogans like "Development," "Modernization," and "World Market": not an unfortunate accident, but a necessary product of the innermost logic of global capitalism.[26]

No wonder the hegemonic form of ideology in slums is Pentecostal Christianity, with its mixture of charismatic miracles-and-spectacles-oriented fundamentalism and social programs like community kitchens and taking care of children and the elderly. While we should of course resist the easy temptation to elevate and idealize the slum-dwellers into a new revolutionary class, we should nonetheless, in Badiou's terms, perceive slums as one of the few authentic "evental sites" in today's society—the slum-dwellers are literally a collection of those who are the "part of no-part," the "supernumerary" element of society, excluded from the benefits of citizenship; the uprooted and the dispossessed, those who, in effect "have nothing to lose but their chains." It is in fact surprising how many features of the slum-dwellers fit the good old Marxist description of the proletarian revolutionary subject: they are "free" in the double meaning of the word even more than the classic proletariat ("freed" from all substantial ties; dwelling in a free space, outside state police regulation); they are a large collective, forcibly thrown together, "thrown" into a situation where they have to invent some mode of being-together, and simultaneously deprived of any support in traditional ways of life, in inherited religious or ethnic life-forms.

Of course, there is a crucial break between the slum-dwellers and the classic Marxist working class: while the latter is defined in the precise terms of economic "exploitation" (the appropriation of surplus-value generated by the situation of having to sell one's own labor-power as a commodity on the market), the defining feature of the slum-dwellers is sociopolitical; it concerns their (non-)integration into the legal space of citizenship with (most of) its incumbent rights—to put it in somewhat simplified terms: a slum-dweller, much more than a refugee, is Homo sacer, the systemically generated "living dead" of global capitalism. He is a kind of negative of the refugee: a refugee from his own community, the one whom the power is not trying to control through concentration, where (to repeat the unforgettable pun from Ernst Lubitsch's To Be or Not to Be) those in power do the concentrating while the refugees do the camping, but pushed into the space of the out-of-control; in contrast to the Foucauldian micro-practices of discipline, a slum-dweller is the one with regard to whom the Power renounces its right to exert full control and discipline, finding it more appropriate to let him dwell in the twilight zone of slums.[27]

What we find in "really existing slums" is, of course, a mixture of improvised modes of social life, from religious "fundamentalist" groups held together by a charismatic leader and criminal gangs up to seeds of new "socialist" solidarity. The slum-dwellers are the counterclass to the other newly emerging class, the so-called "symbolic class" (managers, journalists and PR people, academics, artists, and so on) which is also uprooted and perceives itself as directly universal (a New York academic has more in common with a Slovene academic than with blacks in Harlem half a mile from his campus). Is this the new axis of class struggle, or is the "symbolic class" inherently split, so that we can make the emancipatory wager on the coalition between the slum-dwellers and the "progressive" part of the symbolic class? What we should be looking for are the signs of the new forms of social awareness that will emerge from the slum collectives: they will be the seeds of the future.

PART III

THE LUNAR PARALLAX:
TOWARD A POLITICS OF SUBTRACTION

CHAPTER 5

FROM SURPLUS-VALUE TO SURPLUS-POWER

It is all too easy to gloat over Heidegger's ridiculous attachment to his local roots, his "Why do I have to remain in the provinces?" theme—what if we conceive it as a kind of defensive strategy that enabled him to cope with the traumatic radicality of his thought? That is to say: what if we see in it a strategy comparable to that of Kierkegaard, who also showed up every evening at the theater, and so on? It is impossible to endure the extreme effort of thought all the time—we have to have an easy place to escape to.[1]

Heidegger was arguably the philosopher of the twentieth century (just as Hegel was the philosopher of the nineteenth): all subsequent philosophers (starting with Rudolf Carnap) have had to define themselves by drawing a line of demarcation, a critical distance toward him. The majority do not simply reject him; rather, they maintain an ambivalent relationship with him, acknowledging his breakthrough but claiming that he was not able to follow it to the end, since he remained stuck in some metaphysical presuppositions. For Marxists, for example, Heidegger was right, in Being and Time, to perform the turn from the exempted subject observing the world toward man as a being always-already thrown into the world, engaged in it; however, he was not able to locate human beings within the historical totality of their social practice; mutatis mutandis, the same goes for Levinas, Derrida, Rorty, some Wittgensteinians (Dreyfus), even Badiou.

Heidegger's greatest single achievement is the full elaboration of finitude as a positive constituent of being-human—in this way, he accomplished the Kantian philosophical revolution, making it clear that finitude is the key to the transcendental dimension. A human being is always on the way toward itself, in becoming, thwarted, thrown-into a situation, primordially "passive," receptive, attuned, exposed to an overwhelming Thing; far from limiting him, this exposure is the very ground of the emergence of the universe of meaning, of the "worldliness" of man. It is only from within this finitude that entities appear to us as "intelligible," as forming part of a world, as included within a horizon of meaning—in short, that we take them "as" something, that they appear as something (that they appear tout court). To put it in Kantian terms: it is because of this finitude that "intellectual intuition" is impossible, that a human being can grasp things only within a gap between their mere being-there and the mode, the "as such," of their appearance; in short, that every understanding is a contingent "projecting" of a link over a gap, not a direct apprehension. The transcendental "condition of possibility" is thus the obverse of the condition of impossibility: the very impossibility for a human being to directly intuit reality, the very failure, falling-short of the goal, is what constitutes the openness of the world, of its horizon.

Being-God is not simply all-powerfulness but, at the same time, a claustrophobic closure. And not only that: the very notion of God is the result of a kind of perspective-illusion, a "projection" of an impossible point of closure that can emerge only within the horizon of our finitude. God has no existence "in itself," it is an appearance that has its place within the human universe of meaning. In other words, we should turn Descartes (and the logic of the ontological proof of God's existence) around: infinity can emerge only within the horizon of finitude; it is a category of finitude. And, in effect, what Heidegger aims at in his assertion of finitude as the unsurpassable horizon of our existence can best be illustrated through the contrast to Descartes—here is the famous beginning of Chapter 3 of Descartes's *Discourse on Method*, in which he outlines the necessity and content of the "provisory code of morals" that he adopted while engaged in the search for a new unconditional foundation:

> as it is not enough, before commencing to rebuild the house in which we live, that it be pulled down, and materials and builders provided, . . . but as it is likewise necessary that we be furnished with some other house in which we may live commodiously during the operations, so that I might not remain irresolute in my actions, while my reason compelled me to suspend my judgment, and that I might not be prevented from living thenceforward in the greatest possible felicity, I formed a provisory code of morals, composed of three or four maxims, with which I am desirous to make you acquainted.
>
> The first was to obey the laws and customs of my country, adhering firmly to the faith in which, by the grace of God, I had been educated from my childhood and regulating my conduct in every other matter according to the most moderate opinions. . . .
>
> My second maxim was to be as firm and resolute in my actions as I was able, and not to adhere less steadfastly to the most doubtful opinions, when once adopted, than if they had been highly certain; imitating in this the example of travelers who, when they have lost their way in a forest, ought not to wander from side to side, far less remain in one place, but proceed constantly towards the same side in as straight a line as possible, without changing their direction for slight reasons, although perhaps it might be chance alone which at first determined the selection.[2]

Do not these first two maxims find an echo in two fundamental premises of Heidegger's ontology of finitude: the notion of our being-thrown into a contingent but unsurpassable historical horizon, and the concomitant notion of an abyssal decision to which we should unconditionally stick, although it cannot be fully grounded in reasons (what critics usually reject as Heidegger's "irrational formalist decisionism": "it doesn't matter *what* you decided, what ultimately matters is the form of an unconditional decision, your fidelity to your choice, your assuming of your choice as fully yours")? In other words, could we not say that we find ourselves in Heidegger the moment we fully assume and think to the end the fact that there is no transhistorical absolute knowledge, that every morality we adopt is "provisory"? Is not Heidegger's hermeneutics of historical being a kind of "ontology of provisory existence"? This is why the topic of finitude is inextricably linked to that of failure. Perhaps the ultimate definition of modernity proper concerns the status of failure: we enter modernity when failure is no longer perceived as opposed to success, since success itself can consist only in heroically assuming the full dimension of failure itself, "repeating" failure as "one's own." So Sloterdijk was right when he observed: "Those who miss in all this an indication of Heidegger's modernity, should only recall the fact that, according to Heidegger, the decisive and destinal manifests itself also and above all as an assumed failure."[3]

When Heidegger repeatedly insisted in his later work that those who dwell in on-tological truth necessarily err at the ontic level, did he not thereby acknowledge the irreducible parallax gap between the ontological and the ontic? Accordingly, is not the great Heideggerian *political* temptation to forget this gap and endeavor to impose an ontic order that would be adequate to the ontological truth? In his Schelling course of 1936, Heidegger wrote:

> It is in fact evident that the two men who have initiated counter-movements [to ni-hilism] in Europe for the political formation of their nation as well as their people, that both Mussolini and Hitler, are essentially determined by Nietzsche, again in differ-ent ways, and this without the authentic metaphysical domain of Nietzschean thought having an immediate impact in the process.[4]

The true problem of this passage lies not where it appears to lie (in Heidegger's all-too-mild critique of Hitler and Mussolini, which suggests a fundamentally positive attitude toward them) but, rather, in the question: what would a politics exposed to the "authentic metaphysical domain of Nietzschean thought" be? Is such a politics feasible at all? Similarly, the error of Heidegger's early work (until 1934, most directly discernible in his rectoral address) was that he believed it is possible to have sciences (the academic machinery) which will be aware of their ontological foundation, and act at the level of this foundation—this was the goal of Heidegger's plan to renew the university, according to which philosophy would directly take over the guidance of particular sciences. After 1934, Heidegger acknowledged that the gap is irreducible: "sciences don't think," and, far from being their limitation, this is their strength, the reason why they are so productive.

The ultimate version of Heidegger's rhetorical inversion ("the essence of X is the X-ing of the essence itself") is to be found in his wartime course on Hölderlin's hymn "Ister" (1944), where, in his comment after and on the Stalingrad defeat, he argues—ostensibly against "vulgar" Nazi propaganda—that "the essence of victory is the vic-tory of the essence itself," so that what really matters are not "ontic" military victories, but the strength and ability of the German people to confront and endure the "struggle" at the heart of the essence of Being itself, the antagonism of concealment and uncon-cealment. . . . The ambiguity of such a stance was identified by Balibar apropos of Fichte:[5] does this mean that, in order really ("ontologically") to win, we have to lose "ontically," or that it is only the ontological resoluteness which will give us the true strength to persevere in ontic warfare? Along the same lines, we can also generate the "Heideggerian" statement that the essence of war has nothing to do with empirical warfare: rather, it concerns the warring (Heraclitus' *polemos*) of the essence itself, the dis-cord, internal strife, of the very Essence of Being. But would Heidegger endorse the same reversal also apropos of the *human* essence? "The essence of man has nothing to do with man as an ontic being; the essence of man is, rather, the 'humaning' of the essence itself; the fact that the Essence of Being itself *needs* humans as the site of its

Being-There, of its Disclosure." And would he also accept, apropos of phenomena like *shoah*, that "the essence of suffering is the suffering of the essence itself"?[6]

One of the standard Heideggerian defenses of Heidegger is to claim that in his later work he developed the thought which only enables us truly to grasp the roots of the Nazi terror in the will to power of modern subjectivity; Heidegger shows why the humanist rejection of Nazism is not strong enough, because Nazism is nothing but the extreme result of the very philosophy of subjectivity that sustains humanist ethics. . . . This move, extraordinary in its rhetorical daring (people who risked their lives fighting Fascism on behalf of humanist values are, in a deeper sense, solidary with its horrors and, as such, more guilty than Heidegger, who was an active Nazi), is suspect in its ambiguity. How come that if Heidegger enables us to gain a deeper insight into the roots of Nazism, he himself was not able to resist its lure? The standard answer is: precisely because he "was there," experiencing the extreme of modern subjectivity, he can formulate its truth. Does this mean that, in order to gain insight into the truth of modern subjectivity, one has to go through a Nazi (or similar extreme) experience? Where exactly did things go wrong, then, where did they take a fateful turn, in *Being and Time*? It is generally agreed that the focal point is the passage from individual to communal fate:

> But if fateful *Dasein*, as being-in-the-world, exists essentially in being-with-Others, its historical happening is a co-historical happening and is determinative for it as *communal fate*. This is how we designate the historical happening of a community, of a people. Destiny is not something that puts itself together out of individual fates, any more than being-with-one-another can be conceived as the occurring together of several subjects. Our fates have already been guided in advance, in our being-with-one-another in the same world and in our resoluteness for definite possibilities. Only in communication and in struggle does the power of destiny become free. *Dasein's* fateful destiny in and with its "generation" goes to make up the full, proper historical happening of *Dasein*.[7]

What follows is the famous passage on how, in its being-thrown-into-the-world which confronts it with a concrete past, *Dasein* can choose a (past) hero and repeat his acts in a communally assumed fate. . . .

As Miguel de Beistegui has pointed out, this passage involves a whole series of displacements which are, in Heidegger's own terms of a strict phenomenological analysis, illegitimate.[8] The passage is based on the analogy between individual being-toward-death as the resolute assuming of one's innermost (im)possibility in absolute loneliness (only I can die for myself), and the community displaying the same attitude—but how can this be done if "authentic" death is uniquely my own, not shared? In what sense can communities also display the attitude of resolutely assuming one's fate in confronting death? How is the death of a community to be thought here? Simply as the entire community risking its destruction in violent confrontation with other communities? From the standpoint of the individual *Dasein*, such a death is radically different from the way Heidegger previously described being-toward-death: we are now dealing with the sacrificial death which cements a community. When, in "The Origin of the Work of Art," Heidegger lists among the modes of putting-into-work of the truth, in addition to thinking, poetry, and state-founding, also "the essential sacrifice," we should read this strange entry together with the passage from his lectures on Hölderlin from the same period which specifies this "sacrifice" as the "comradeship amongst soldiers at the front": "its most profound and only reason is that the proximity of death as sacrifice brought everyone to the same annulment, which became the source of an unconditional belonging to the others."[9] The tension between this notion of death as sacrifice and the analysis of being-toward-death in Being and Time, where, in death, I am thrown back to myself, totally alone in my uniqueness, is unmistakable.

As Beistegui points out, Heidegger's approach to social life is determined by an unthematized dominance of the notion of "domestic" economy, the "closed" economy of the "home." When Heidegger talks about technology, he systematically ignores the whole sphere of modern "political" economy, although modern technology is not only empirically, but in its very concept, rooted in the market dynamics of generating surplus-value. The underlying principle which impels the unrelenting drive of modern productivity is not technological, but economic: it is the market and commodity principle of surplus-value which condemns capitalism to the crazy dynamics of permanent self-revolutionizing. Consequently, it is not possible to grasp the dynamics of modernity properly without what Marx called the "critique of political economy." And this ignorance of the "alienated" political economy is by no means politically innocent: as, again, Beistegui points out, Heidegger shares this ignorance with Fascism, whose ultimate dream is precisely that one can "domesticate" modern technology and industry, that one can reinscribe them into the frame of a new "home economy" of the organic state-community. And what if Heidegger also overlooks the fact that the emergence of the Greek *polis* itself, this open space in which the community gathers to debate and decide shared issues together, is already the outcome of such a displacement, of *oikos* being reduced to an element of a larger encompassing order? The properly historical irony here is that Heidegger, in his focus on authentically assuming a communal fate, overlooks precisely the way in which the reign of anonymous market forces is experienced as the new version of the ancient Fate: as Marx and Hegel repeatedly claimed, in modernity, Fate looks more and more like the impenetrable and capricious socioeconomic process—the collective result of people's activity confronts them as a foreign Fate.

Is it legitimate, then, to imagine a Being and Time without this fateful turn? A Being and Time which would simply remain "individualistic," dismissing every collective experience as in-authentic, as the Fall, and allowing only the individual's resolute being-toward-death as the authentic act? Or a Being and Time which would elaborate a different, more "progressive" notion of authentic collective existence, somewhat along the lines of, say, Walter Benjamin, who also spoke of revolution as the authentic repetition of the past? In 1937–38, Heidegger wrote:

What is conservative remains bogged down in the historiographical; only what is revolutionary attains the depth of history. Revolution does not mean here mere subversion and destruction but an upheaval and re-creating of the customary so that the beginning might be restructured. And because the original belongs to the beginning, the restructuring of the beginning is never the poor imitation of what was earlier; it is entirely other and nevertheless the same.[10]

In itself, is this not a wholly pertinent description of the revolution along Benjamin's lines? Should we then propose, as a mode of authentic community, that of the revolutionary collective, or a Pauline collective of believers, which in fact served as the model both for Heidegger's early work and for Benjamin? Is not such a collective precisely something which escapes the dyad of the closed *oikos* and the mechanical anonymous *das Man*, of community and society? It is all too easy to succumb to this temptation of rewriting a "good" *Being and Time*—a temptation which should nonetheless be resisted.

The passage from individual *Dasein's* authentic decision grounded in assuming one's being-toward-death to communal decision grounded in accepting one's destiny (in *Being and Time's* (in)famous Section 74) is not as arbitrary as it may appear, since it responds to a very precise necessity: as Heidegger himself put it, resoluteness is a purely formal concept; it refers not to what you do, but to how you do it, and, as he laconically adds, (the content of) authentic existential possibilities are "not to be gathered from death"[11]—where, then, are they to be gathered from? This is where the reference to communal tradition comes in: they are to be drawn from the communal heritage in which *Dasein's* existence is caught up. In other words, it is precisely in order to avoid the standard criticism of "decisionistic formalism" that Heidegger has to pass from the individual to the communal.

GELASSENHEIT? NO, THANKS!

The interesting thing about the mysterious phase in Heidegger's thought between 1928 and 1936 (even 1938) is that it blurs the "official" dividing line between the "decisionism" of Phase 1 (heroically assuming one's fate) and the "passive receptiveness" of Phase 2 (humbly listening to the destinal voice of being)—even in *Beiträge zur Philosophie.Vom Ereignis* (1936–38), which is supposed to mark the first full formulation of Phase 2, Heidegger symptomatically uses the odd oxymoronic coinage "*Wille zum Ereignis,*" the will-to-event/appropriation, bringing together what, precisely, should be mutually exclusive: the Will as the fundamental feature of modern subjectivity, and the attitude of *Gelassenheit,* the "openness" which indicates that we have left the imposing violence of subjective self-assertion behind. Far from dismissing such formulations as "examples that mix the discourses of an activist metaphysics of spirit and the crisis ontology of the being of *Da-sein,*"[12] we should, rather, conceive them as the symptomal "point of torsion," the "impossible" intersection of the two "officially" opposed discourses which brings home their deep complicity. In his *Introduction to Metaphysics,* the key text of this period of transition, Heidegger writes:

But the essence of open resoluteness lies in the unconcealedness of human *Dasein* for the clearing of being and by no means in the reserving of strength or energy for "activity.". . . But the relation to being is letting. That all willing should be grounded in letting is a thought that is offensive to common sense.[13]

Heidegger's name for this overlapping of active resoluteness, the extreme effort of Willing, and of the passive attunement to the word of being, is *spirit*. Derrida was right to point out the exceptional role of the signifier "spirit" as the undeconstructed remainder in Heidegger's text, representing the Unthought of Heidegger's very "destruction of metaphysics."[14] Is not the supreme example of this coincidence of opposites Zen Buddhism which, while preaching utter self-renunciation and passivity, served as the legitimization of the most radical self-disciplined warrior ethics?[15]

This, incidentally, is also why we should not, as is usually done, dismiss Heidegger's reading of *Antigone* in *Introduction to Metaphysics* as still marked by the modern metaphysics of subjectivity. The heroic tone of man as the uncanniest force-doer who, in violent confrontation with the impenetrable darkness of being, enforces order and clearing, and can impose or ground a new law only by excepting himself from the rule of law, by resorting to a law-imposing violence, but whose heroic struggle is ultimately doomed to fail, so that true greatness always involves a tragic defeat,[16] this celebration of the violent nature of man's greatness (man "knows no kindness and conciliation (in the ordinary sense), no appeasement and mollification by success and prestige and by their confirmation")[17] should in no way be opposed to the attitude of *Gelassenheit*, of letting-things-be, of the "release" toward being, articulated in poetic remembrance, which dominates his (re)reading of *Antigone* in 1942, in his seminar on Hölderlin's hymn "Ister."[18] We emphatically do not have first a Heidegger who asserts the essence of man as heroically fighting a lost battle against the overpowering All of being by violently trying to impose on it a projected order, and then a Heidegger who sees the essence of man as a humble place-holder of the truth of being, serving as the medium, the "here," of being's disclosure. If anything, the first "late" Heidegger (of 1935) is preferable to the second one (post-1938).[19] The stance of *Gelassenheit* sustains the utmost violence of ontic engagements.

In his reading of Heraclitus' fragment 53 DK about war as the "father and king of everything," Heidegger starts by opposing warfare proper (*polemos*) to *agon*, a competitive struggle: in contrast to *agon*, in which two friendly opponents compete, "things are serious" in a *polemos* in which "the opponent is not a partner, but an enemy." He then goes on to specify what an enemy is (we should bear in mind that these lines were written in 1933–34, when the media were full of texts pointing out very clearly who this enemy was, and when Heidegger was politically engaged in this struggle):

Enemy is the one and anyone from whom an essential threat to the being [*Dasein*] of a people [*Volk*] and its individuals emanates. The enemy doesn't have to be external, and the external enemy is not the most dangerous by a long way. It can also look as if there is no enemy out there. In this case, the fundamental need is to find the enemy, to bring him out into the light or even first to create him, so that we can thereby assume a stance against the enemy and avoid the obtuseness of our being. The enemy can install himself in the innermost root of the being of a people, oppose himself to the latter's proper essence, and act against it. In such a case, the struggle is all the more severe and hard and difficult, since this struggle consists only minimally in striking against the enemy; often it is much more difficult and long-lasting to track down the enemy as such, to bring him to disclose himself as such, to get rid of the illusions about him, to remain ready to attack him, to cultivate and increase the constant readiness and to prepare the attack in a broad prospect with the goal of his complete annihilation [mit dem Ziel der völligen Vernichtung].[20]

Everything is to be interpreted here, right down to the precise metaphor of the enemy who "install[s] himself in the innermost root" of a people—in short, who is *parasitic* upon the people. The question here seems to be: how are we to combine (to read together) such an assertion of heroic combativeness (typical rhetoric for the Heidegger of the mid-1930s) with the predominant tone of the Heidegger from after the Second World War, which is that of *Gelassenheit*, of letting-be, of humble subordination to and listening to the voice of Being? Against the standard version, according to which this shift marks Heidegger's withdrawal from and disappointment with his political engagement, we should insist on the strict *codependence* of these two features, which are two sides of the same coin. What makes Heidegger advocate "*Vernichtung*" of the enemy is the very fact that he is afraid fully to assert the struggle as primordial and constitutive—that he subordinates struggle to the all-encompassing One which gathers the opposed forces together (and does he not treat sexual difference in the same way in his reading of Trakl?).[21] It is the same as with Judaism: the pacifying God of Love is not the opposite of the vengeful Jehovah, but his other face.

This late work of Heidegger is to be opposed to Nietzsche: what can be more incompatible with *Gelassenheit* than the Nietzschean celebration of war and ruthless struggle as the only path toward the greatness of man? As many perceptive readers have noticed, however, these "militaristic" injunctions—so numerous and well known that it is superfluous to quote them—are accompanied by a continuous line of "pacifistic" statements, most famous among them the call for a unilateral "breaking the sword"— the call for an act, if ever there was one:

And perhaps the great day will come when a people, distinguished by wars and victories and by the highest development of a military order and intelligence, and accustomed to make the heaviest sacrifices for these things, will exclaim of its own free will, "We break the sword," and will smash its entire military establishment down to its lowest foundations. Rendering oneself unarmed when one had been the best-armed, out of intense emotion—that is the means to real peace, which must always rest on peace of mind; whereas so-called armed peace, as it now exists in all countries, is the absence of peace of mind. One trusts neither oneself nor one's neighbor and, half from hatred, half from fear, does not lay down arms. Rather perish than hate and fear, and twice rather perish than make oneself hated and feared—this must someday become the highest maxim for every single commonwealth too.[22]

This line culminates in a note from 1883: "To dominate? To impose my type onto others? Disgusting! Does my luck not reside precisely in contemplating many others?"[23] The point is not simply to "overcome" or interpret away this "contradiction"; what if we conceive it, rather, as Nietzsche's *ethico-political* antinomy, the counterpart to his *epistemological* antinomy? In one and the same text (*Beyond Good and Evil*), Nietzsche seems to advocate two opposed epistemological stances:[24] on the one side, the notion of truth as the unbearable Real Thing, as dangerous, even lethal, like the direct gaze into Plato's sun, so that the problem is how much truth a man can endure without diluting or falsifying it; on the other side, the "postmodern" notion that appearance is more valuable than stupid reality—that, ultimately, there is no last Reality, just the interplay of multiple appearances, so that we should abandon the very opposition between reality and appearance—man's greatness is that he is able to give priority to brilliant aesthetic appearance over gray reality. So, in Alain Badiou's terms, the passion for the Real versus the passion of semblance. How are we to read these two opposed stances together? Is Nietzsche simply inconsistent here, oscillating between two mutually exclusive views? Or is there a "third way"? That is to say: what if the two opposed options (passion for the Real/passion for the semblance) reveal Nietzsche's struggle, his failure to articulate the "right" position whose formulation eluded him?

Back to our example from Lévi-Strauss (in Chapter 1 above); it should now be clear what this position is: everything is not just the interplay of appearances, there is a Real—this Real, however, is not the inaccessible Thing, but the *gap* which prevents our access to it, the "rock" of the antagonism which distorts our view of the perceived object through a partial perspective. And, again, the "truth" is not the "real" state of things, that is, the "direct" view of the object without perspectival distortion, but the very Real of the antagonism which causes perspectival distortion. The site of truth is not the way "things really are in themselves," beyond their perspectival distortions, but the very gap, passage, which separates one perspective from another, the gap (in this case: social antagonism) which makes the two perspectives radically *incommensurable*. The "Real as impossible" is the cause of the impossibility of ever attaining the "neutral" non-perspectival view of the object. There *is* a truth, everything is not relative—but this truth is the truth of the perspectival distortion *as such*, not the truth distorted by the partial view from a one-sided perspective.

And the solution of the ethico-political antinomy is exactly the same: the two opposed options (celebration of the militaristic spirit of growth through struggle and combat; the vision of peace through a self-imposed act of disarming, the renunciation of the need to dominate others) do reveal Nietzsche's struggle, his failure to articulate the "right" position whose formulation eluded him. This position, of course, is the one of *coming to peace with incommensurability itself*—however, what incommensurability? The solution that seems to impose itself here is the "Oriental" one: that, precisely, of *Gelassenheit*—we should remain active, engaged in the world; we should merely do it with an inner distance, without full attachment, maintaining intact throughout this engagement the core of our being—all the mystical rubbish about how, through the very incessant agility of its parts, the Whole is at peace with itself. Within this attitude, the warrior no longer acts as a person, he is completely desubjectivized—or, as D. T. Suzuki himself put it: "it is really not he but the sword itself that does the killing. He had no desire to do harm to anybody, but the enemy appears and makes himself a victim. It is as though the sword performs automatically its function of justice, which is the function of mercy."[25] What, then, is the difference between this "warrior Zen" legitimization of violence and the long Western tradition, from Christ to Che Guevara, which also extolls violence as a "work of love," as in the famous lines from Che Guevara's diary?:

> Let me say, with the risk of appearing ridiculous, that the true revolutionary is guided by strong feelings of love. It is impossible to think of an authentic revolutionary without this quality. This is perhaps one of the greatest dramas of a leader; he must combine an impassioned spirit with a cold mind and make painful decisions without flinching one muscle.[26]

Christ's "scandalous" words from Luke's gospel ("if anyone comes to me and does not hate his father and his mother, his wife and children, his brothers and sisters—yes, even his own life—he cannot be my disciple" [14: 26]) tend in exactly the same direction as Che's famous quote: "You may have to be tough, but do not lose your tenderness. You may have to cut the flowers, but it will not stop the spring."[27]

So, again, if Lenin's acts of revolutionary violence were "works of love" in the strictest Kierkegaardian sense of the term, in what does the difference from "warrior Zen" consist? There is only one logical answer: it is not that, in contrast to Japanese military aggression, revolutionary violence "really" aims at establishing a nonviolent harmony; on the contrary, authentic revolutionary liberation is much more directly identified with violence—it is violence as such (the violent gesture of discarding, of establishing a difference, of drawing a line of separation) which liberates. Freedom is not a blissfully neutral state of harmony and balance, but the very violent act which disturbs this balance. Buddhist (or Hindu, for that matter) all-encompassing Compassion must be opposed to Christian intolerant, violent Love. The Buddhist stance is ultimately one of Indifference, of quenching all passions which strive to establish differences; while Christian love is a violent passion to introduce a Difference, a gap in the order of Being, to privilege and elevate some object at the expense of others. This, then, is the solution of Nietzsche's antinomy, whose contrast to the "Oriental" one can also be put in the terms of Lacan's distinction between the subject of the enunciated and the subject of the enunciation: if, in the "Oriental" solution, my engagement leaves intact the inner peace of the very position (of enunciation) from which I act, then the proper Nietzschean solution renounces any striving for "inner peace"—insofar as I fully endorse the gap, tension, at the very heart of my being, I no longer have to engage in "external" violence, in aggression against others.

It is interesting to note how, in his interpretation of the same fragment 53 ("Conflict [polemos] is the father of all things and king of all. Some he shows to be gods and others men; some he makes slaves and others free") in his *Introduction to Metaphysics*, Heidegger—in contrast to those who accuse him of leaving out of consideration the "cruel" aspects of ancient Greek life (slavery, and so on)—openly draws attention to how "rank and dominance" are directly grounded in a disclosure of being, thereby providing a direct ontological grounding to social relations of domination:

> If people today from time to time are going to busy themselves rather too eagerly with the polis of the Greeks, they should not suppress this side of it; otherwise the concept of the polis easily becomes innocuous and sentimental. What is higher in rank is what is stronger. Thus Being, logos, as the gathered harmony, is not easily available for every man at the same price, but is concealed, as opposed to that harmony which is always mere equalizing, the elimination of tension, leveling.[28]

There are clearly three different attitudes discernible in the way Heidegger referred to the German militarization and the war effort in the 1930s and early 1940s. First, there was a direct endorsement of the aggressive military attitude on behalf of the defense of the Fatherland.[29] Second, there was a sympathetic neutrality: of course the total military mobilization was an expression of the radical nihilism of modern subjectivity; however, the *Überwindung* of metaphysics does not lead through nostalgically sticking to traditional ways of life; this is why Heidegger cannot conceal his fascination with technological efficiency: "From the perspective of bourgeois culture and spirituality one may wish to consider total 'motorization' of the army from top to bottom as manifestation of unlimited technicization and materialism. In reality this is a metaphysical act."[30] No wonder, then, that, when, in spring 1940, the German Army invaded Norway, Heidegger's comments deploy a kind of metaphysical justification of what today we call "embedded reporting":

> When today, on the occasion of the boldest military operations by the airborne landing troops, an aircraft also participates which films the jump of the paratroops, this has nothing to do with sensationalism or curiosity; the diffusion, after a few days, of the consciousness and vision of these activities is itself an element of the global activity and a factor of the armament. Such "filmed reporting" is a metaphysical procedure and will not be judged by everyday representations.[31]

This is also why Hubert Dreyfus's notion that the way to be prepared for the upcoming *Kehre*, for the arrival of new gods, is to participate in practices which function as sites of resistance to total technological mobilization is inadequate:

> Heidegger explores a kind of gathering that would enable us to resist postmodern technological practices . . . he turns from the cultural gathering he explored in "The Origin of the Work of Art" (that sets up shared meaningful differences and thereby unifies an entire culture) to local gatherings that set up local worlds. Such local worlds occur around some everyday thing that temporarily brings into their own both the thing itself and those involved in the typical activity concerning the use of the thing. Heidegger calls this event a *thing thinging* and the tendency in the practices to bring things and

people into their own, *appropriation*. . . . Heidegger's examples of things that focus such local gathering are a wine jug and an old stone bridge. Such things gather Black Forest peasant practices, . . . the family meal acts as a focal thing when it draws on the culinary and social skills of family members and solicits fathers, mothers, husbands, wives, children, familiar warmth, good humor, and loyalty to come to the fore in their excellence, or in, as Heidegger would say, their ownmost.[32]

From a strict Heideggerian position, such practices can—and, as a rule, do—function as the very opposite of resistance, as something that is included in advance in the smooth functioning of technological mobilization (like courses in transcendental meditation which make you more efficient in your job); this is why the path to salvation leads only through full engagement in technological mobilization. And, finally, the third attitude is one of *Gelassenheit*, of withdrawing from engagement, from "public" circulation, silently laying the ground for the possible arrival of gods. Consequently, Heidegger's infamous reference to the "inner greatness" of National Socialism (specified, in an insertion added after the Second World War, as consisting in the encounter between modern man and technology) can and should be read precisely in these three meanings:

1. The Nazi project already provides the proper metaphysical answer to technology (in the terms of *Being and Time*): it counteracts the "*das Man*" of modern society with the authentic act of heroically assuming one's destiny, that is, it assumes technology as a metaphysical challenge, a project, and thus undermines its nihilism, its dimension of "*das Man*," from within;
2. Nazism should be read along the lines of what Heidegger says in an interview published after his death (that he is not convinced that democracy is the most appropriate political form for the essence of today's technology): the Nazi total mobilization is more appropriate to the essence of technology than to a liberal democracy;
3. Nazism is, in its essence, modern nihilism at its most destructive and demoniac.

The shift from (1) to (2) is crucial: this is the shift that Heidegger masks—the fact of how he first thought that Nazism was already the *answer* to the technological nihilism of "*das Man*." When, in *Introduction to Metaphysics*, Heidegger makes his famous remark about the "inner greatness of the Nazi movement" betrayed by its ideologists, he covers up a shift in his understanding of this "greatness": until about 1935, he thought that Nazism did provide a unique solution of how, on the one hand, thoroughly to embrace modern technology, work, and mobilization, while simultaneously including them in an "authentic" political act of a people choosing its fate, acting on a decision, and so on. So we have technology, not aseptic traditionalism, but combined with roots, *Volk*, authentic decision, not *das Man*—in contrast to the Russian and American versions, which, each in its own way, betrays this authentic dimension (either in liberal individualism or in mass mobilization). After 1935, he no longer gave Nazism this "transcendental" cover, while still appreciating it as the most radical version to enable modern man to confront technology.[33] In 1944, Heidegger wrote: "The Greeks appear in most 'research reports' as pure National Socialists. In their zeal the scholars seem unaware that such 'results' do no service to National Socialism and its historical uniqueness and that National Socialism is not in need of them."[34] Again the same ambiguity: it deprives National Socialism of its legitimization as the successor to ancient Greece, while nonetheless implying its greatness.

As, yet again, Beistegui has pointed out,[35] the problem is not so much "Heidegger's silence" about the Holocaust, but the fact that his silence was *not* complete, that he broke it twice in a way which qualifies it. Both times, he reduced the Holocaust to an example of a larger, general, historical tendency: in a letter to Marcuse (1946), he claimed that exactly the same thing that happened to Jews under Nazism was now happening to Germans thrown out of Eastern Europe, the only difference being that now we all know about it, while the Germans did not know what the Nazis were doing to the Jews; in the essay "Das Gestell" (1950), he listed the "manufacturing of corpses in the camps" together with mechanized agriculture and the manufacturing of hydrogen bombs as the articulation of the same stance of technological "enframing." The Nazis did to the Jews what the Soviets did to all humans, reducing them to a "work force," a technologically disposable material which could be ruthlessly used and then disposed of. (The Holocaust precisely *cannot* be thought in this way: from the economic or technological standpoint of total mobilization of resources, it was clearly "irrational"—representatives of industry and the Army protested to the SS all the time that the Holocaust was a gigantic waste of precious human, economic, and military resources—among other things, precisely annihilating millions of members of the work force who could have been used much more productively!) In general we should be very careful with Heidegger's generalizations and hidden exceptions: when he specifies the "inner greatness" of Nazism as modern man's confrontation with the essence of technology, we should remember that he never attributes the same "inner greatness" to American capitalism or to Soviet Communism. It is my thesis that *he should have done so*: that, in contrast to Nazism and American capitalism, it was only Soviet Communism which, despite the catastrophe it stands for, *did* possess true inner greatness.

Recently, in Slovenia and Croatia, top ski champions and their trainers have been vying with each other to produce the strongest endorsement of Hitler: Hitler was, of course, a bad guy, responsible for the death of millions—but he definitely had balls, he pursued what he wanted with an iron will. . . .[36] It is crucial not to concede even this seemingly "obvious" point: no, Hitler did *not* "have the balls" really to change things; he did not really act, all his actions were fundamentally reactions—that is to say, he acted so that nothing would really change. If we really want to name an act which was truly daring, for which one truly had to "have the balls" to try the impossible, but which was simultaneously a horrible act, an act causing suffering beyond comprehension, it was Stalin's forced collectivization in the Soviet Union at the end of the 1920s.

Here we should follow Badiou,[37] who claims that, despite the horrors committed on its behalf (or, rather, on behalf of the specific form of these horrors), Stalinist

Communism was inherently related to a Truth-Event (of the October Revolution), while Fascism was a pseudo-event, a lie in the guise of authenticity. Badiou refers here to the difference between *désastre* (the Stalinist "ontologization" of the Truth-Event into a positive structure of Being) and *désêtre* (the Fascist imitation/staging of a pseudo-event called "Fascist Revolution"): *mieux vaut un désastre qu'un désêtre*, since *désastre* nonetheless remains inherently related to the Truth-Event whose disastrous consequence it is, while *désêtre* merely imitates the Event as an aesthetic spectacle deprived of the substance of Truth. For this very reason, the purges under Stalinism were so ferocious and, in a way, much more "irrational" than the Fascist violence: in Fascism, even in Nazi Germany, it was possible to survive, to maintain the appearance of a "normal" everyday life, if one did not involve oneself in any oppositional political activity (and, of course, if one were not of Jewish origin . . .), while in the Stalinism of the late 1930s, nobody was safe; *everyone* could be unexpectedly denounced, arrested, and shot as a traitor. In other words, the "irrationality" of Nazism was "condensed" in anti-Semitism, in its belief in the Jewish plot; while Stalinist "irrationality" pervaded the entire social body. For that reason, Nazi police investigators were still looking for proofs and traces of actual activity against the regime, while Stalinist investigators were engaged in clear and unambiguous fabrications (invented plots and sabotage, and so on). This violence inflicted by the Communist Power on its own members bears witness to the radical self-contradiction of the regime, to the inherent tension between its Communist project and the *désastre* of its realization: to the fact that, at the origins of the regime, there was an "authentic" revolutionary project—incessant purges were necessary not only to erase the traces of the regime's own origins, but also as a kind of "return of the repressed," a reminder of the radical negativity at the heart of the regime.

This point is made perfectly by Nikita Mikhalkov's film *Burned by the Sun* (1994), the story of the last day of freedom of Colonel Kotov, a high-ranking member of the *nomenklatura*, a famous hero of the Revolution, happily married to a beautiful young wife. In the summer of 1936, Kotov is enjoying an idyllic Sunday at his dacha with his beautiful young wife and daughter. Dimitri, a former lover of Kotov's wife, pays them an unexpected visit: what begins as a pleasant gathering of playing games, singing, and rekindling old memories turns into a nightmare—while Dimitri flirts with Kotov's wife, and charms his daughter with stories and music, it soon becomes clear to Kotov that Dimitri is an NKVD agent who has come to arrest him as a traitor at the end of the day. . . . Crucial here is the complete arbitrariness and nonsense of Dimitri's violent intrusion which disturbs the peace of the idyllic summer day: this idyll is to be read as emblematic of the new order in which the *nomenklatura* has stabilized its rule, so that the intervention of the NKVD agent who disturbs the idyll, in its very traumatic arbitrariness—or, in Hegelese, "abstract negativity"—bears witness to the fundamental falsity of this idyll: to the fact that the new order is founded on the betrayal of the Revolution.

The Stalinist purges of high Party echelons relied on this fundamental betrayal: the accused were in effect guilty insofar as they, as members of the new *nomenklatura*, had betrayed the Revolution. The Stalinist terror was thus not simply the betrayal of the Revolution, that is, an attempt to erase all traces of the authentic revolutionary past; rather, it bore witness to a kind of "imp of perversity" which compelled the postrevolutionary new order to (re)inscribe its betrayal of the Revolution within itself, to "reflect" it or "remark" it in the guise of arbitrary arrests and killings which threatened all members of the nomenklatura—as in psychoanalysis, the Stalinist confession of guilt conceals the true guilt. (As is well known, Stalin wisely recruited into the NKVD people of lower social origins who were thus able to act out their hatred of the nomenklatura by arresting and torturing senior apparatchiks.)

This inherent tension between the stability of the rule of the new nomenklatura and the perverted "return of the repressed" in the guise of repeated purges of the ranks of the old nomenklatura is at the very heart of the Stalinist phenomenon: purges are the very form in which the betrayed revolutionary heritage survives and haunts the regime. The dream of Gennadi Zyuganov, the Communist presidential candidate in 1996 (things would have turned out all right in the Soviet Union if only Stalin had lived at least five years longer, and accomplished his final project of having done with cosmopolitanism and bringing about a reconciliation between the Russian state and the Orthodox Church—in other words, if only Stalin had realized his anti-Semitic purge . . .), aims precisely at the point of pacification at which the revolutionary regime would finally get rid of its inherent tension and stabilize itself—the paradox, of course, is that in order to reach this stability, Stalin's last purge, the planned "mother of all purges" which was to take place in the summer of 1953 and was prevented by his death, would have had to succeed.

Sheila Fitzpatrick has argued that the collectivization and rapid industrialization of the late 1920s was part of the inherent dynamic of the October Revolution, so that the revolutionary sequence proper ended only in 1937—the true "Thermidor" occurred only when the big purges were cut short to prevent what Getty and Naumov have called the complete "suicide of the party,"[38] and the Party nomenklatura stabilized itself into a "new class." And, in effect, it was only during the terrible events of 1928–33 that the very body of Russian society actually underwent a radical transformation: in the difficult but enthusiastic years 1917 to 1921, the whole of society was in a state of emergency; the period of New Economic Policy (NEP) marked a step backward, a consolidation of Soviet state power leaving the texture of the social body (the great majority of peasants, artisans, intellectuals, and so on) basically intact. It was only the thrust of 1928 that directly and brutally aimed at transforming the very composition of the social body, liquidating peasants as a class of individual owners, replacing the old intelligentsia (teachers, doctors, scientists, engineers, and technicians) with a new one. As Sheila Fitzpatrick puts it in vivid terms: if an emigrant who left Moscow in 1914 had returned in 1924, he would still have recognized it as the same city, with the same array of shops, offices, theaters, and, in most cases, the same people in charge; if, however, he had returned another ten years later, in 1934, he would no longer have recognized the city, so different was the entire texture of social life.[39] The difficult thing to grasp about the terrible years after 1929, the years of the great push forward, was that, in all the horrors beyond recognition, we can discern a ruthless but sincere and enthusiastic will toward a total revolutionary upheaval of the social body, to create a new state, intelligentsia, legal system. . . .

Toward the Theory of the Stalinist Musical

The fate of Jože Jurančič, an old Slovene Communist revolutionary, stands out as a perfect metaphor for the twists of Stalinism.[40] In 1943, when Italy capitulated, Jurančič led a rebellion by Yugoslav prisoners in a concentration camp on the Adriatic island of Rab: under his leadership, 2,000 starving prisoners single-handedly disarmed 2,200 Italian soldiers. After the war, he was arrested and imprisoned on a nearby *Goli otok* ("naked island"), a notorious Communist concentration camp. While he was there, he was mobilized in 1953, together with other prisoners, to build a monument to celebrate the tenth anniversary of the 1943 rebellion on Rab—in short, as a prisoner of the Communists, Jurančič was building a monument *to himself*, to the rebellion led by him. . . . If poetic (not justice but, rather) injustice means anything, this was it: is not the fate of this revolutionary the fate of the entire population under the Stalinist dictatorship—of the millions who first heroically overthrew the *ancient régime* in the Revolution and then, enslaved to the new rules, are forced to build monuments to their own revolutionary past? This revolutionary is thus in effect a "universal singular," an individual whose fate stands for the fate of all.[41]

What makes the position of this revolutionary more than simply tragic is a kind of convoluted, second-level, "reflexive" betrayal: first you sacrifice everything for the (Communist) cause, then you are rejected by (the bearers of) this Cause itself, finding yourself in a kind of empty space with nothing, no point of identification, to hold on to.[42] Is there not something similar in today's position of those who, a decade and a half ago, when the USA was fully behind Saddam Hussein in his war against Iran, were drawing attention to Saddam's use of weapons of mass destruction and his other horrors, and were ignored by the US state apparatus—and who now have to listen to the mantra of Saddam-a-brutal-criminal-dictator turned against themselves? The problem with the claim about Saddam being a war criminal is not that it is false, but that the US administration has no right to utter it without admitting its own responsibility for Saddam's hold on power—the surprising belated discovery that Saddam is a brutal dictator sounds like Stalin's surprised discovery, in late 1930, that Yezhov, the head of the NKVD who organized the terror, was responsible for the death of thousands of innocent Communists. . . .

The ultimate dimension of the irony of such a convoluted situation—that of being reduced to a prisoner building monuments to oneself—is nonetheless something that is inherent to Stalinism, in contrast to Fascism: only in Stalinism are people enslaved on behalf of the ideology which claims that all the power is theirs. The first thing that strikes us about Stalinist discourse is its contagious nature: the way (almost) everyone likes to mockingly imitate it, use its terms in different political contexts, and so on, in clear contrast to Fascism. And that is not all: over the last decade, we have witnessed in most post-Communist countries a process of inventing the Communist tradition. The Communist past is re-created as a cultural and lifestyle phenomenon; products which, decades ago, were perceived as a miserable copy of the Western "real thing" (Eastern versions of cola drinks, hand lotion, low-quality refrigerators and washing machines, popular muisic . . .) are not only fondly remembered, even displayed in museums—sometimes they are even successfully put on the market again (like Florena hand lotion in the former GDR). The political aspect of the Communist past—both its good and its bad aspects, from the emancipatory dream to the Stalinist terror—is erased, replaced by everyday objects which evoke the vision of a simple and modest, but for this very reason happier, more contented, more satisfying life than the stressful dynamics of capitalism.

The process of the creation of new Nation-States out of the disintegration of Communist "empires" thus follows the logic of what, with regard to the rise of capitalism, Marx described as the priority of formal subsumption of the forces of production under capital over material subsumption: a society was first formally subsumed under the Nation-State, then its ideological content was elaborated (fabricating the tradition that grounds this Nation-State).[43] In short, Stalinism is not prohibited in the same way as Nazism: even if we are fully aware of its monstrous aspects, we find Ostalgie acceptable: "Goodbye Lenin" is tolerated, "Goodbye Hitler" is not—why? Or, another example: in today's Germany, there are many CDs on the market featuring old GDR revolutionary and Party songs, from "Stalin, Freund, Genosse" to "Die Partei hat immer Recht"—but we look in vain for a CD featuring Nazi Party songs. . . .

Already at the anecdotal level, the difference between the Fascist and the Stalinist universe is obvious; in Stalinist show trials, for example, the accused has to confess his crimes publicly and give an account of how he came to commit them—in stark contrast to Nazism, in which it would be meaningless to demand from a Jew a confession that he was involved in a Jewish plot against the German nation. This difference is symptomatic of different attitudes toward the Enlightenment: Stalinism still conceived itself as part of the Enlightenment tradition, within which truth is accessible to any rational man, no matter how depraved he is, which is why he is subjectively responsible for his crimes,[44] in contrast to the Nazis, for whom the guilt of the Jews is a direct fact of their very biological constitution; one does not have to prove that they are guilty, they are guilty solely by virtue of being Jews—why?

The key is provided by the sudden rise, in the Western ideological imaginary, of the figure of the wandering "eternal Jew" in the age of Romanticism, that is to say, precisely when, in real life, with the explosion of capitalism, features attributed to the Jews were extended over the whole of society (since commodity exchange became hegemonic). It was thus at the very moment when the Jews were deprived of their specific properties which made it easy to distinguish them from the rest of the population, and when the "Jewish question" was "resolved" at the political level by the formal emancipation of the Jews—by giving the Jews the same rights as all other "normal" Christian citizens—that their "curse" was inscribed into their very being—they were no longer ridiculous misers and usurers, but demoniac heroes of eternal damnation, haunted by an unspecified and unspeakable guilt, condemned to wander around and longing to find redemption in death. So it was precisely when the specific figure of the Jew disappeared that the *absolute* Jew emerged, and this transformation dictated the shift of anti-Semitism from theology to race: their damnation was their race, they were guilty not for what they did (exploit Christians, murder their children, rape their women, or, ultimately, betray and murder Christ), but for what they *were*—is it necessary to add that this shift laid the foundations for the Holocaust, for the physical annihilation of the Jews as the only appropriate final solution of their "problem"? Insofar as the Jews were identified by a series of their properties, the goal was to convert them, to turn them into Christians; but from the moment Jewishness pertained to their very being, only annihilation could solve the "Jewish question."[45]

It was none other than Nietzsche who suggested the correct materialist intervention destined to "traverse the [anti-Semitic] fantasy": in No. 251 of *Beyond Good and Evil*, he proposed, as a way to "breed a new caste that would rule over Europe," the mixing of the German and the Jewish race, which would combine the German ability of "giving orders and obeying" with the Jewish genius of "money and patience."[46] The ingenuity of this solution is that it combines two fantasies which are *a priori* incompatible, which cannot meet each other in the same symbolic space, as in the English television advertisement for a beer from a couple of years ago. The first part stages the well-known fairy-tale anecdote: a girl walks along the banks of a stream, sees a frog, takes it gently into her lap, kisses it, and, of course, the ugly frog turns miraculously into a beautiful young man. However, the story isn't over yet: the young man casts a covetous glance at the girls, draws her toward himself, kisses her—and she turns into a bottle of beer, which the man holds triumphantly in his hand. . . . We can have either a woman with a frog or a man with a bottle of beer; what we can never obtain is the "natural" couple of the beautiful woman and man—why not? Because the fantasmatic support of this "ideal couple" would have been the inconsistent figure of *a frog embracing a bottle of beer*. This, then, opens up the possibility of undermining the hold a fantasy exerts over us through the very overidentification with it: by *embracing simultaneously, within the same space, the multitude of inconsistent fantasmatic elements*. That is to say: each of the two subjects is involved in his or her own subjective fantasizing—the girl fantasizes about the frog who is really a young man, the man about the girl who is really a bottle of beer. What modern art and writing oppose to this is not objective reality but the "objectively subjective" underlying fantasy which the two subjects are never able to assume, rather along the lines of a Magrittesque painting of a frog embracing a bottle of beer, with the title "A man and a woman," or "The ideal couple." And is this not exactly what Nietzsche does in his suggestion? Is not his formula of the new race mixed from Germans and Jews his "frog with a bottle of beer"?

It is precisely on account of the legacy of Enlightenment that, as Jean-Claude Milner put it, comparing Rousseau to the Stalinist show trials, "in the matter of confessions, Geneva does not necessarily win over Moscow."[47] In the Stalinist ideological imaginary, universal Reason is objectivized in the guise of the inexorable laws of historical progress, and we are all its servants, the leader included—which is why, after a Nazi leader delivers a speech and the crowd applauds, he just stands and silently accepts the applause, positing himself as its addressee; while in Stalinism, when the obligatory applause explodes at the end of the leader's speech, the leader stands up and joins the others in applauding.[48] Remember the wonderful detail from the beginning of Lubitsch's *To Be or Not to Be*: when Hitler comes into a room, all the Nazi officers in the room raise their hands into a Nazi salute and shout "Heil Hitler!"; in reply, Hitler himself raises his hand and say: "Heil myself!"—in Hitler's case, this is pure humor, a thing which could not happen in reality; while Stalin actually could (and *did*) "hail himself" when he joined others in applauding himself. For this same reason, on Stalin's birthday, prisoners sent him telegrams wishing him all the best and the success of Socialism, even from the darkest Gulags like Norilsk or Vorkuta, while one cannot even imagine Jews from Auschwitz sending Hitler a telegram for his birthday. . . . Crazy and tasteless as this may sound, this last distinction illustrates the fact that the opposition between Stalinism and Nazism was the opposition between civilization and barbarism: Stalinism did not sever the last thread that linked it to civilization. The lowest Gulag inmate still participated in the universal Reason: he had access to the Truth of History.

The ultimate paradoxical argument in favor of the comparative advantage of Stalinism is the very standard argument of rabid anti-Communists against it: the ex-GDR, with its ten million inhabitants, had 100,000 full-time secret police agents to control its population, while the Gestapo covered the *whole* of Germany with about 10,000 full-time agents. . . . What this argument demonstrates, however, is rather the opposite of what it intends to demonstrate: it reveals the degree of participation of "ordinary" Germans in the political terror—there is no need for a larger number of agents, the massive network of denunciations functioned by itself, since the Gestapo could rely on the cooperation of the wider circles of civil society. In other words: yes, true, the population's support of the regime was more "spontaneous" in Nazism—but what this tells us is precisely that massive moral corruption was much more widespread in Nazism than in Communism. It is not simply that the Communist dictatorship was more directly the rule of a special caste over the majority of the population: what we should bear in mind is that the noncorruption of the large majority of the people, their resistance to spontaneously denouncing their colleagues, and so on, was not the sign of the "sane moral sense" surviving Communist indoctrination, but was sustained precisely by Communist ideology itself, which preached the ordinary people's solidarity.

This is why the biggest war of the twentieth century, the Second World War, was the war in which Stalinist Communist and capitalist democracies fought together against Fascism. This is also why we do not find in Nazism anything that could be compared to the "humanist" dissident Communists, those who went even to the point of risking their own physical survival in fighting what they perceived as the "bureaucratic deformation" of Socialism in the USSR and its empire: in Nazi Germany, there were no figures who advocated "Nazism with a human face.". . . Although, in terms of their positive content, the Communist regimes were a dismal failure, generating terror and misery, at the same time they opened up a certain space, the space of utopian expectations which, among other things, enabled us to measure the failure of really existing Socialism itself. What the anti-Communist dissidents tend as a rule to overlook is that the very space from which they themselves criticized and denounced the daily terror and misery was opened and sustained by the Communist breakthrough, by its attempt to escape the logic of Capital. In short, when dissidents like Havel denounced the existing Communist regime on behalf of authentic human solidarity, they (unknowingly, for the most part) spoke from the place opened up by Communism itself—which is why they tend to be so disappointed when "really existing capitalism" does not meet the high expectations of their anti-Communist struggle. Perhaps Václav Klaus, Havel's pragmatic double, was right when he dismissed Havel as a "socialist.". . . At a recent reception in Poland, a nouveau riche capitalist congratulated Adam Michnik for being a doubly successful capitalist (he helped to destroy socialism, and he heads a highly profitable publishing empire); deeply embarrassed, Michnik replied: "I am not a capitalist; I am a socialist who is unable to forgive socialism for the fact that it did not work."[49]

That is the flaw (and the secret bias) of all attempts à la Nolte[50] to adopt a neutral position of "objectively comparing Fascism and Stalinism," that is, of the line of argumentation which asks: "If we condemn the Nazis for illegally killing millions, why do we not apply the same standards to Communism? If Heidegger cannot be pardoned for his brief Nazi engagement, why can Lukács and Brecht and others be pardoned their much longer Stalinist engagement?" In today's constellation, such a position automatically means privileging Fascism over Communism: that is, more concretely, reducing Nazism to a reaction to—and repetition of—the practices already found in Bolshevism (struggle to the death against the political enemy, terror and concentration camps), so that the "original sin" is that of Communism.

The proper task is thus to think the tragedy of the October Revolution: to perceive its greatness, its unique emancipatory potential, and, simultaneously, the historical necessity of its Stalinist outcome. We should oppose both temptations: the Trotskyite notion that Stalinism was ultimately a contingent deviation, as well as the notion that the Communist project is, at its very core, totalitarian. In the third volume of his supreme biography of Trotsky, Isaac Deutscher makes a perceptive observation about the forced collectivization of the late 1920s:

> having failed to work outwards and to expand and being compressed within the Soviet Union, that dynamic force turned inwards and began once again to reshape violently

the structure of Soviet society. Forcible industrialization and collectivization were now substitutes for the spread of revolution, and the liquidation of the Russian kulaks was the Ersatz for the overthrow of the bourgeois rule abroad.[51]

Apropos of Napoleon, Marx once wrote that the Napoleonic Wars were a kind of export of revolutionary activity: since, with Thermidor, the revolutionary agitation was quenched, the only way to give it an outlet was to displace it toward the outside, to rechannel it into war against other states. Is not the collectivization of the late 1920s the same gesture turned around? When the Russian Revolution (which, with Lenin, explicitly conceived itself as the first step of a pan-European revolution, as a process which can survive and accomplish itself only through an all-European revolutionary explosion) remained alone, confined to one country, the energy had to be released in a thrust inward. . . . It is in this direction that we should qualify the standard Trotskyite designation of Stalinism as the Napoleonic Thermidor of the October Revolution: the "Napoleonic" moment was, rather, the attempt, at the end of the civil war in 1920, to export revolution by military means, the attempt which failed with the defeat of the Red Army in Poland; it was Tukhachevsky, if anyone, who was in fact a potential Bolshevik Napoleon.

The twists of contemporary politics exemplify a kind of Hegelian dialectical law: a fundamental historical task that "naturally" expresses the orientation of one political bloc can be accomplished only by the opposing bloc. In Argentina a decade ago, it was Menem, elected on a populist platform, who pursued tight monetary politics and the IMF agenda of privatizations much more radically than his "liberal" market-oriented opponents. In France in 1960, it was the conservative De Gaulle (not the Socialists) who broke the Gordian knot by giving full independence to Algeria. It was the conservative Nixon who established diplomatic relations between the USA and China. It was the "hawkish" Begin who concluded the Camp David treaty with Egypt. Or, further back in Argentinian history, in the 1830s and 1840s, the heyday of the struggle between "barbarian" Federalists (representatives of provincial cattle-owners) and "civilized" Unitarians (merchants, etc., from Buenos Aires interested in a strong central state), it was Juan Manuel Rosas, the Federalist populist dictator, who established a centralist system of government, much stronger than Unitarians dared to dream of.

The same logic was at work in the crisis of the Soviet Union in the second half of the 1920s: in 1927, the ruling coalition of Stalinists and Bukharinists, pursuing a policy of appeasement of the private farmers, was ferociously attacking the Left united Opposition of Trotskyists and Zinovievists who called for accelerated industrialization and the fight against rich peasants (higher taxes, collectivization). We can imagine the surprise of the Left Opposition when, in 1928, Stalin enforced a sudden "Leftist" turn, imposing a policy of rapid industrialization and a brutal collectivization of land—not only stealing their program, but realizing it much more brutally than they had dared to imagine. All of a sudden, their criticism of Stalin as a "Thermidorian" right-winger became meaningless. No wonder many Trotskyites recanted and joined the Stalinists who, at the very moment of the ruthless extermination of the Trotskyist faction, realized their program. Communist parties knew how to apply "the rule which permitted the Roman Church to endure for two thousand years: condemn those whose politics one takes over, canonize those from whom one does not take anything."[52] And, incidentally, there was the same tragicomic misunderstanding in Yugoslavia in the early 1970s: after the big student demonstrations, where, along with calls for democracy, accusations that the ruling Communists were pursuing policies which favored the new "rich" technocrats were heard, the Communist counterattack that stifled all opposition was legitimized, among others, by the idea that the Communists had heard the message of the student protests, and were meeting their demands. . . . That is the tragedy of the Leftist Communist opposition which pursued the oxymoron of antimarket "radical" economic policies combined with calls for direct and true democracy.

In *Ivan the Terrible*, Eisenstein portrayed the libidinal economy of the Stalinist "Thermidor." In the second part of the film, the only reel in color (the penultimate one) is limited to the hall in which the carnivalesque orgy takes place. It stands for the Bakhtinian fantasmatic space in which "normal" power relations are turned around, in which the Tsar is the slave of the idiot whom he proclaims a new Tsar; Ivan provides the imbecile Vladimir with all the imperial insignias, then humbly prostrates himself in front of him and kisses his hand. The scene in the hall begins with the obscene chorus and dance of the Oprichniki (Ivan's private army), staged in an entirely "unrealistic" way: a weird mixture of Hollywood and Japanese theater, a musical number whose words tell a weird story (they celebrate the ax which cuts off the heads of Ivan's enemies). The song first describes a group of boyars enjoying a lavish meal: "*Down the middle . . . the golden goblets pass . . . from hand to hand.*" The Chorus then asks, with pleasurable nervous expectation: "*Come along. Come along. What happens next? Come on, tell us more!*" And the solo Oprichnik, bending forward and whistling, shouts the answer: "*Strike with the axes!*" Here we are at the obscene site where musical enjoyment meets political liquidation. And, taking into account the fact that the film was shot in 1944, does this not confirm the carnivalesque character of the Stalinist purges? We encounter a similar nocturnal orgy in the third part of *Ivan* (which was not shot—see the scenario), where the sacrilegious obscenity is explicit: Ivan and his Oprichniks perform their nightly drinking feast as a black Mass, with black monastic robes over their normal clothing. That is the true greatness of Eisenstein: that he detected (and depicted) the fundamental shift in the status of political violence, from the "Leninist" liberating outburst of destructive energy to the "Stalinist" obscene underside of the Law.

If, then, Eisenstein stages the obscene underside of the Stalinist universe, what would have been its public face, the Stalinist genre *par excellence*? Not heroic wartime, historic, or revolutionary epics, but *musicals*, the unique genre of so-called "kolkhoz musicals" which thrived from the mid-1930s to the early 1950s, with Liubov Orlova their greatest star, a kind of Soviet counterpart to Ginger Rogers. Representative films here are: *The Merry Children* (a.k.a. *The Shepherd Kostja*), *Volga, Volga* (Stalin's favorite film), and *The Cossacks of the Kuban District*, the swan song of the genre. There are no traitors in these

films, life is fundamentally happy in them: the "bad" characters are merely oppor-
tunists or lazy frivolous seducers, who are, at the end, reeducated and gladly take their
place in society. In this harmonious universe, even animals—pigs, cows, and chicken—
dance happily with humans.

And this is where the circle of codependence with Hollywood closes: not only were
these films part of an attempt to build a Soviet version of the Hollywood production
system; surprisingly, their influence was also felt the other way around. Not only is the
legendary shot of King Kong at the top of the Empire State Building a direct echo of
a constructivist project for the Palace of Soviets with a gigantic Lenin statue on top; in
1942, Hollywood itself produced its own version of the kolkhoz musical, *The North Star*,
one of the three directly pro-Stalinist movies which were, of course, part of wartime
propaganda. The image of kolkhoz life that we get here certainly does not fall short of
its Soviet model: scenario by Lillian Hellman, words by Ira Gershwin, music by Aaron
Copland. Does this strange film not bear witness to the inner complicity between
Stalinist cinema and Hollywood?

Pluto's Judgment Day, a Disney classic from 1935, stages a mocking show-trial of Pluto
who, after falling asleep near a fire, endures a nightmarish dream about being dragged
to a cats' court, where he is designated a Public Enemy, accused by a series of witnesses
of anti-feline behavior, then condemned to public burning. When Pluto starts to burn,
of course, he wakes up: the dream scene of burning incorporated the real-life fact that
a fire was getting nearer and nearer to his tail. What makes this dream so interesting is
not merely the obvious political references (not only was 1935 the first big year of
Moscow trials; in the USA itself, the orchestrated campaign against gangster Public
Enemies was part of the PR of Hoover's FBI), but, even more, the way the cartoon stages
the show-trial as a musical number, with a series of ironic references to popular songs,
right up to "Three Little Maids from School" from Gilbert and Sullivan's *The Mikado*.
Ten years before Eisenstein, the link between musical and a political show-trial is
established.

THE BIOPOLITICAL PARALLAX

So where are we today? The first insight that suggests itself is that, in contrast to Fascism and Stalinism, two "totalitarian" systems preaching the sacrificial mobilization
of the entire social body, a kind of permanent state of exception, our late capitalism is
characterized by an unprecedented permissiveness. One of the standard *topoi* of today's
conservative cultural critique is that, in our permissive era, children lack firm limits,
prohibitions—this lack frustrates them, driving them from one excess to another.
Only a firm limit set by some symbolic authority can guarantee not only stability, but
even satisfaction itself—satisfaction brought about by violating the prohibition, transgressing the limit. . . . Would not today's analysand's reaction be the opposite of the
one reported by Freud? "Whoever this woman in my dream was, I am sure it has something to do with my mother!" What this *topos* misses, however, is the true paradox at

work here: far from frustrating us because it simply sets no limit, *the absence of explicit lim-itation confronts us with the Limit as such, the inherent obstacle to satisfaction;* the true function of the explicit limitation is thus to sustain the illusion that, through transgressing it, we can attain the limitless.

Today's subjectivity is characterized by a shift from desire to demand: demand, in-sisting on a demand, is the opposite of desire, which thrives in the gaps of a demand, in what is in a demand more than a demand—a child's demand for food, for instance, can articulate a desire for love, so the mother can sometimes meet the demand simply by giving the child a warm hug. Furthermore, desire involves Law and its transgres-sion, the place of desire is sustained by the Law; while demand is addressed to an omnipotent Other outside Law, which is why satisfying demands suffocates desire (as in spoiled children). (This is also what is false in the logic of financial compensation, which transposes a justified grievance into a demand for restitution.)

This shift to a post-Oedipal constellation can also be discerned with regard to the predominant figure of a political leader. If there is an Oliver Stone masterpiece, it is *Nixon,* a film which reaches far beyond the standard liberal Nixonophobia: Stone's ingenious idea is to present Nixon as the last truly Oedipal politician, the one who, in his final catastrophe, has to admit guilt and assume responsibility for acts he was not fully aware of committing. (Here we should recall that if we measure "Leftism" by the percentage of national product allotted to education, health, social care, and so on, then Nixon was the most Leftist of all US presidents—Carter was compelled to start the process of dismantling the welfare state; moreover, in the view of anti-Communists, Nixon committed the ultimate sin of recognizing the People's Republic of China. . . .) In contrast to Nixon, Reagan was in effect the first "post-Oedipal" president, moving in a different symbolic space, ignoring the very dimension of guilt and symbolic debt.

Unfortunately, some Lacanians refer to this shift in order to sustain a conservative agenda: in a conservative cultural criticism mode, one deplores the logic of demand and argues for a return/reinvention of desire through reimposing some sort of pro-hibition—"Come back Oedipus, all is forgiven!" While it is true, however, that insist-ing on demand is the very mode of betraying desire, there is no way back once the prohibition loses its obligatory character. What one should focus on, rather, is demand as a way to drive; that is to say, what one needs is *a demand no longer addressed to the Other.* Both desire and demand rely on the Other—either a full (omnipotent) Other of de-mand or a "castrated" Other of the Law; the task, therefore, is fully to assume the *non-existence* of the Other—even and also of the *dead* Other (as Lacan put it: God did not die, he always-already *was* dead, and this death is the very foundation of religion).

There is great irony in these desperate calls for re-Oedipalization: psychoanalysis, once perceived as *the* tool against "sexual oppression," reminding us of the traumatic price we have to pay for our culture, now advocates a return to this very culture. . . . This call is one of the three main ways in which the psychoanalytic establishment is reacting to the tectonic changes in our ideological predicament:[53]

1. In a disavowal similar to that of the few remaining "orthodox" Marxists, it continues to act as if nothing has really changed: the fundamental structure of the Unconscious and its formations as formulated by Freud still reigns supreme, the changes are merely superficial, so one should resist the temptation of the fashionable calls for a "new paradigm."
2. While recognizing the shift, the move toward a "post-Oedipal society," it perceives this as a dangerous development, as a loss of our very fundamental ethico-symbolic coordinates; as a result, it advocates some kind of return to the symbolic authority of the paternal Law as the only way to halt our slide toward the global chaos of autistic closure and violence.
3. It desperately tries to "keep up with the times," and thus acquire a new legitimacy: either by searching for proofs that the new neurosciences confirm its hypotheses, or by redefining its therapeutic role against the "new anxieties" of our "postmodern" epoch (for instance, focusing on "pathological Narcissism").

Which of these three ways is the right one? The fourth one, of course: that of asserting that, on the contrary, it is only today that we encounter in our daily lives the basic libidinal deadlock around which psychoanalysis circulates. So again, where are we today? It can easily be demonstrated that the two features of today's ideologico-political constellation—the rise of biopolitical control and regulation; the excessive narcissistic fear of harassment—are in effect two sides of the same coin. On the one hand, the very development of the narcissistic personality bent on "self-realization" leads to growing self-control (jogging, a focus on safe sex and healthy food, and so on), that is, subjects treating themselves as objects of biopolitics; on the other, the overt goal of state biopolitics is individual happiness and a pleasurable life, the abolition of any traumatic shocks that could prevent self-realization—happiness is "a commodity that was imported from America in the Fifties," as the actress Francesca Annis once put it.

However, this Janus-faced biopolitical logic of domination is itself only one of the two aspects of the University discourse as the hegemonic discourse of modernity.[54] This discourse (social link) has two forms of existence in which its inner tension ("contradiction") is externalized: the biopolitical logic of domination (which social theory conceptualized in different guises: as bureaucratic "totalitarianism," as the rule of technology, of instrumental reason, of biopolitics, as the "administered world"...) and the capitalist matrix of a system whose dynamic is propelled by the incessant production and (re)appropriation of an excess ("surplus-value"): that is, a system which reproduces itself through constant self-revolutionizing. Capitalism is not just a historical epoch among others—in a way, the once fashionable and today forgotten Francis Fukuyama was right, global capitalism is "the end of history." A certain excess which was, as it were, kept under check in previous history, perceived as a local perversion, a limited deviation, is in capitalism elevated into the very principle of social life, in the speculative movement of money begetting more money, of a system which can survive only by constantly revolutionizing its own conditions—that is to say, in which the thing can survive only as its own excess, constantly exceeding its own "normal" constraints.[55]

How, precisely, in what mode of parallax, do these two aspects relate to each other? We should not succumb to the temptation of reducing capitalism to a mere form of appearance of the more fundamental ontological attitude of technological domination; the two levels, precisely insofar as they are two sides of the same coin, are ultimately incompatible: there is no meta-language that enables us to translate the logic of domination back into the capitalist reproduction-through-excess, or vice versa. The key question thus concerns the relationship between these two excesses: the "economic" excess/surplus which is integrated into the capitalist machine as the force which drives it into permanent self-revolutionizing; the "political" excess of power inherent to its exercise (the constitutive excess of representation over the represented).

THE HISTORICITY OF THE FOUR DISCOURSES

This is where we should take note of the historicity inscribed into Lacan's matrix of the four discourses, the historicity of modern European development.[56] The Master's discourse stands—not for the premodern master, but—for the absolute monarchy, this first figure of modernity that effectively undermined the distinct network of feudal relations and interdependences, transforming fidelity to flattery, and so on: it is the "Sun King" Louis XIV, with his "l'état, c'est moi," who is the Master par excellence. Hysterical discourse and the discourse of the University then deploy two outcomes of the vacillation of the direct reign of the Master: the expert rule of bureaucracy that culminates in contemporary biopolitics, which ends up reducing the population to a collection of Homo sacer (what Heidegger called "enframing," Adorno "the administered world," Foucault the society of "discipline and punish"); the explosion of the hysterical capitalist subjectivity that reproduces itself through permanent self-revolutionizing, through the integration of the excess into the "normal" functioning of the social link (the true "permanent revolution" is already capitalism itself). Thus Lacan's formula of the four discourses enables us to deploy the two faces of modernity (total administration; capitalist-individualist dynamics) as the two ways of undermining the Master's discourse: doubt as to the efficiency of the Master-figure (what Eric Santner called the "crisis of investiture")[57] can be supplemented by the direct rule of experts legitimized by their knowledge; or the excess of doubt, of permanent questioning, can be directly integrated into social reproduction as its innermost driving force. And, finally, the Analyst's discourse stands for the emergence of revolutionary-emancipatory subjectivity that resolves the split into university and hysteria: in it, the revolutionary agent (a) addresses the subject from the position of knowledge which occupies the place of truth (that is, which intervenes at the "symptomal torsion" of the subject's constellation), and the goal is to isolate, get rid of, the Master-Signifier which structured the subject's (ideologico-political) unconscious.

Or does it? Jacques-Alain Miller[58] has suggested that, today, the discourse of the Master is no longer the "obverse" of the discourse of the Analyst; today, on the contrary, our "civilization" itself (its hegemonic symbolic matrix, as it were) fits the formula of the discourse of the Analyst: the "agent" of the social link today is *a*, surplus-enjoyment, the superego injunction to enjoy that permeates our discourse; this injunction addresses $ (the divided subject), who is put to work in order to live up to this injunction. If ever there was a superego injunction, it is the famous Oriental wisdom: "Don't think, just *do it!*" The "truth" of this social link is S_2, scientific-expert knowledge in its different guises, and the goal is to generate S_1, the self-mastery of the subject—that is, to enable the subject to "cope with" the stress of the call to enjoyment (through self-help manuals, and so on). . . . Provocative as this notion is, it raises a series of questions. If it is true, where, then, lies the difference in the discursive functioning of "civilization" as such and of the psychoanalytic social link? Here Miller resorts to a rather suspect solution: in our "civilization," the four terms are kept apart, isolated, each operates on its own, while only in psychoanalysis are they brought together into a coherent link: "in civilization, each of the four terms remains disjoined . . . it is only in psychoanalysis, in pure psychoanalysis, that these elements are arranged into a discourse."[59]

Is it not, however, that the fundamental operation of psychoanalytic treatment is not synthesis, bringing elements into a link, but, precisely, analysis, separating what, in a social link, appears to belong together? This path, opposed to that of Miller, is indicated by Agamben who, in the last pages of *The State of Exception*,[60] imagines two utopian options on how to break out of the vicious cycle of Law and violence, of the rule of Law sustained by violence. One is the Benjaminian vision of "pure" revolutionary violence with no relationship to the Law; the other is the relationship to the Law without regard to its (violent) enforcement—what Jewish scholars are doing in their endless (re)interpretation of the Law. Agamben starts from the correct insight that the task today is not synthesis but separation, distinction: not bringing Law and violence together (so that right will have might and the exercise of might will be fully legitimized), but thoroughly separating them, untying their knot. Although Agamben confers on this formulation an anti-Hegelian twist, a more correct reading of Hegel makes it clear that such a gesture of separation is what Hegelian "synthesis" is actually about: in it, the opposites are not reconciled in a "higher synthesis"—rather, *their difference is posited "as such."* The example of Saint Paul may help us to clarify this logic of Hegelian "reconciliation": the radical gap that he posits between "life" and "death," between life in Christ and life in sin, has no need of a further "synthesis"; it is itself the resolution of the "absolute contradiction" of Law and sin, of the vicious cycle of their mutual implication. In other words, once the distinction is drawn, once the subject becomes aware of the very existence of this other dimension beyond the vicious cycle of Law and its transgression, *the battle is formally already won.*

Is this vision not again, however, a case of our late-capitalist reality going further than our dreams? Are we not already encountering in our social reality what Agamben envisages as a utopian vision? Is not the Hegelian lesson that the global reflexivization-mediatization of our lives generates its own brutal immediacy, which was best captured by Étienne Balibar's notion of excessive, nonfunctional cruelty as a feature of contemporary life, a cruelty whose figures range from "fundamentalist" racist and/or religious slaughter to "senseless" outbursts of violence by adolescents and the homeless in our megalopolises, a violence I am tempted to call Id-Evil, a violence not grounded in any utilitarian or ideological reasons? All the talk about foreigners stealing work from us, or about the threat they represent to our Western values, should not deceive us: on closer examination, it soon becomes clear that this talk provides a rather superficial secondary rationalization. The answer we ultimately obtain from a skinhead is that it makes him feel good to beat up foreigners, that their presence disturbs him. . . . What we encounter here is indeed Id-Evil, that is, Evil structured and motivated by the most elementary imbalance in the relationship between the Ego and *jouissance*, by the tension between pleasure and the foreign body of *jouissance* at its very heart. Thus Id-Evil stages the most elementary "short circuit" in the subject's relationship to the primordially missing object-cause of his desire: what "bothers" us in the "other" (Jew, Japanese, African, Turk) is that he appears to entertain a privileged relationship to the object—the other either possesses the object-treasure, having snatched it away from us (which is why we don't have it), or he poses a threat to our possession of the object.

What we should propose here is the Hegelian "infinite judgment" asserting the speculative identity of these "useless" and "excessive" outbursts of violent immediacy, which display nothing but a pure and naked ("nonsublimated") hatred of the Otherness, with the global reflexivization of society; perhaps the ultimate example of this coincidence is the fate of psychoanalytic interpretation. Today, the formations of the Unconscious (from dreams to hysterical symptoms) have definitely lost their innocence, and are thoroughly reflexivized: the "free associations" of a typical educated analysand consist for the most part of attempts to provide a psychoanalytic explanation of their disturbances, so that one is quite justified in saying that we have not only Jungian, Kleinian, Lacanian . . . interpretations of the symptoms, but symptoms themselves which are Jungian, Kleinian, Lacanian . . . , that is to say, whose reality involves implicit reference to some psychoanalytic theory. The unfortunate result of this global reflexivization of interpretation (everything becomes interpretation, the Unconscious interprets itself) is that the analyst's interpretation itself loses its performative "symbolic efficiency," and leaves the symptom intact in the immediacy of its idiotic *jouissance*.

What happens in psychoanalytic treatment is strictly analogous to the response of the neo-Nazi skinhead who, when he is really pressed for the reasons for his violence, suddenly starts to talk like social workers, sociologists, and social psychologists, quoting diminished social mobility, rising insecurity, the disintegration of paternal authority, the lack of maternal love in his early childhood—the unity of practice and its inherent ideological legitimization disintegrates into raw violence and its impotent, inefficient interpretation. This impotence of interpretation is the necessary obverse of the universalized reflexivity hailed by risk-society theorists: it is as if our reflexive power can flourish only insofar as it draws its strength from and relies on some minimal "pre-reflexive" substantial support which eludes its grasp, so that its universalization comes at the price of its inefficiency, that is, via the paradoxical reemergence of the brute Real of "irrational" violence, impermeable and insensitive to reflexive interpretation.

The more today's social theory proclaims the end of Nature and/or Tradition and the rise of the "risk society," the more the implicit reference to "nature" pervades our daily discourse: even when we do not talk about the "end of history," do we not put forward the same message when we claim that we are entering a "postideological" pragmatic era, which is another way of claiming that we are entering a postpolitical order in which the only legitimate conflicts are ethnic/cultural conflicts? Typically, in today's critical and political discourse, the term "worker" has disappeared, substituted and/or obliterated by "immigrants [immigrant workers: Algerians in France, Turks in Germany, Mexicans in the USA]"—in this way, the class problematic of workers' exploitation is transformed into the multiculturalist problematic of the "intolerance of Otherness," and so on, and multiculturalist liberals' excessive investment in protecting immigrants' ethnic rights clearly draws its energy from the "repressed" class dimension. Although Francis Fukuyama's thesis on the "end of history" quickly fell into disrepute, we still silently presume that the liberal-democratic capitalist global order is somehow the finally found "natural" social regime; we still implicitly conceive conflicts in Third World countries as a subspecies of natural catastrophes, as outbursts of quasi-natural violent passions, or as conflicts based on fanatical identification with one's ethnic roots (and what is "the ethnic" here if not again a codeword for nature?). And, again, the key point is that this all-pervasive renaturalization is strictly correlative to the global reflexivization of our daily lives.

A similar process is taking place in intellectual life itself, with the rise of a new ideological barbarism, for which the Frankfurt School appeared on the scene at a precise historical moment: when the failure of the socioeconomic Marxist revolutions became apparent, the conclusion drawn was that this failure was caused by underestimating the depth of Western Christian spiritual foundations, so the emphasis of subversive activity shifted from politico-economic struggle to "Cultural Revolution," to the patient intellectual-cultural work of undermining national pride, family, religion, and spiritual commitments—the spirit of sacrifice for one's country was dismissed as involving the "authoritarian personality"; marital fidelity was supposed to express pathological sexual repression; following Benjamin's motto on how every document of culture is a document of barbarism, the highest achievements of Western culture were denounced for concealing the practices of racism and genocide. . . .

The main academic proponent of this new barbarism is Kevin MacDonald who, in *The Culture of Critique*, argues that certain twentieth-century intellectual movements led by Jews have changed European societies in fundamental ways, and destroyed the confidence of Western man; these movements were designed, consciously or unconsciously, to advance Jewish interests, even though they were presented to non-Jews as universalistic and even utopian.[61] One of the most consistent ways in which the Jews have advanced their interests has been to promote pluralism and diversity—but only for others. Ever since the nineteenth century, they have led movements that tried to discredit the traditional foundations of Gentile society: patriotism, racial loyalty, the Christian basis for morality, social homogeneity, and sexual restraint. MacDonald devotes several pages to *The Authoritarian Personality* (1950), a collective project coordinated by Adorno, the purpose of which was, for MacDonald, to make every group affiliation sound as if it were a sign of mental disorder: everything, from patriotism to religion to family—and race—loyalty, is disqualified as a sign of a dangerous and defective "authoritarian personality." Because drawing distinctions between different groups is illegitimate, all group loyalties—even close family ties—are "prejudice." Here Mac-Donald quotes approvingly Christopher Lasch's remark that *The Authoritarian Personality* leads to the conclusion that prejudice "could be eradicated only by subjecting the American people to what amounted to collective psychotherapy—by treating them as inmates of an insane asylum." It is precisely the kind of group loyalty, respect for tradition, and consciousness of differences central to Jewish identity, however, that Horkheimer and Adorno described as mental illness in Gentiles. These writers adopted what eventually became a favorite Soviet tactic against dissidents: anyone whose political views differed from theirs was insane.

For these Jewish intellectuals, anti-Semitism was also a sign of mental illness: Christian self-denial, and especially sexual repression, caused hatred of the Jews. The Frankfurt School was enthusiastic about psychoanalysis, according to which "Oedipal ambivalence toward the father and anal-sadistic relations in early childhood are the anti-Semite's irrevocable inheritance." In addition to ridiculing patriotism and racial identity, the Frankfurt School glorified promiscuity and Bohemian poverty: "Certainly many of the central attitudes of the largely successful 1960s countercultural revolution find expression in *The Authoritarian Personality*, including idealizing rebellion against parents, low-investment sexual relationships, and scorn for upward social mobility, social status, family pride, the Christian religion, and patriotism." Although he came later, the "French-Jewish deconstructionist Jacques Derrida" followed the same tradition when he wrote:

> The idea behind deconstruction is to deconstruct the workings of strong nation-states with powerful immigration policies, to deconstruct the rhetoric of nationalism, the politics of place, the metaphysics of native land and native tongue. . . . The idea is to disarm the bombs . . . of identity that nation-states build to defend themselves against the stranger, against Jews and Arabs and immigrants. . . .[62]

As MacDonald puts it: "Viewed at its most abstract level, a fundamental agenda is thus to influence the European-derived peoples of the United States to view concern about their own demographic and cultural eclipse as irrational and as an indication of psychopathology." This project has been successful: anyone opposed to the displacement of whites is routinely treated as a mentally unhinged "hatemonger," and whenever whites defend their group interests they are described as psychologically inadequate—with, of course, the silent exception of the Jews themselves: "the ideology that ethnocentrism was a form of psychopathology was promulgated by a group that over its long history had arguably been the most ethnocentric group among all the cultures of the world. . . ." We should have no illusions here: in terms of the standards of the great Enlightenment tradition, we are in effect dealing with something for which the best designation is the old orthodox Marxist term for "bourgeois irrationalists": *the self-destruction of Reason*. The only thing to bear in mind is that this new barbarism is a strictly postmodern phenomenon, the obverse of the highly reflexive self-ironical attitude—no wonder that, reading authors like MacDonald, one often cannot decide if one is reading a satire or a "serious" line of argument.

What this means with regard to Agamben's utopian vision of untying the knot of the Law and violence is that, in our postpolitical societies, *this knot is already untied*: we encounter, on the one side, the globalized interpretation whose globalization is paid for by its impotence, its failure to enforce itself, to generate effects in the Real; and, on the other, explosions of the raw Real of a violence which cannot be affected by its symbolic interpretation. Where, then, is the solution here, between the claim that, in today's hegemonic constellation, the elements of the social link are separated and, as such, to be brought together by psychoanalysis (Miller), and the knot between Law and violence to be untied, their separation to be enacted (Agamben)? What is these two separations are not symmetrical? What if the gap between the Symbolic and the raw Real epitomized by the figure of the skinhead is a false one, since this Real of the outbursts of "irrational" violence is generated by the globalization of the Symbolic?

When, exactly, does the *objet petit a* function as the superego injunction to enjoy? When it occupies the place of the Master-Signifier—that is to say, as Lacan formulated it in the last pages of *Seminar XI*, when the short circuit between S_1 and a occurs.[63] The key move to be accomplished in order to break the vicious cycle of the superego injunction is thus to enact the separation between S_1 and a. Consequently, would it not be more productive to follow a different path: to start with the different *modus operandi* of *objet petit a* which in psychoanalysis no longer functions as the agent of the superego injunction—as it does in the discourse of *perversion?*[64] This is how Miller's claim of the identity of the Analyst's discourse and the discourse of today's civilization should be read: as an indication that this latter discourse (social link) is that of perversion. That is to say: the fact that the upper level of Lacan's formula of the discourse of the Analyst is the same as his formula of perversion (a–$\mathcal{S}$) opens up a possibility of reading the entire formula of the discourse of the Analyst also as a formula of the *perverse social link*: its agent, the masochist pervert (the pervert *pas excellence*), occupies the position of the object-instrument of the other's desire, and, in this way, through serving his (feminine) victim, he posits her as the hystericized/divided subject who "doesn't know what she wants"[65]—the pervert knows it for her, that is, he pretends to speak from the position of knowledge (about the other's desire) which enables him to serve the other; and, finally, the product of this social link is the Master-Signifier, that is, the hysterical subject elevated in the role of the master (*dominatrix*) whom the pervert masochist serves.

Unlike the hysteric, the pervert knows perfectly what he is for the Other: a knowledge supports his position as the object of his Other's (divided subject's) *jouissance*. For that reason, the formula of the discourse of perversion is the same as that of the analyst's discourse: Lacan defines perversion as the inverted fantasy, that is, his formula of perversion is a–$\mathcal{S}$, which is precisely the upper level of the Analyst's discourse. The difference between the social link of perversion and that of analysis is grounded in the radical ambiguity of *objet petit a* in Lacan, which stands simultaneously for the imaginary fantasmatic lure/screen and for that which this lure is obfuscating, for the Void behind the lure. Consequently, when we pass from perversion to the analytic social link, the agent (analyst) reduces himself to the Void which provokes the subject into confronting the truth of his desire. Knowledge in the position of "truth" below the bar under the "agent," of course, refers to the supposed knowledge of the analyst, and, simultaneously, indicates that the knowledge gained here will not be the neutral "objective" knowledge of scientific adequacy, but the knowledge which concerns the subject (analysand) in the truth of his subjective position.

Recall, again, Lacan's outrageous statement that even if what a jealous husband claims about his wife (that she sleeps around with other men) is all true, his jealousy is still pathological; along the same lines, we could say that even if most of the Nazi claims about the Jews were true (they exploit the Germans, they seduce German girls . . .), their anti-Semitism would still be (and was) pathological—because it represses the true reason why the Nazis needed anti-Semitism in order to sustain their ideological position. So, in the case of anti-Semitism, knowledge about what the Jews "really are" is a fake, irrelevant, while the only knowledge at the place of truth is the knowledge about why a Nazi needs a figure of the Jew to sustain his ideological edifice. In this precise sense, what the discourse of the analyst "produces" is the Master-Signifier, the "swerve" of the patient's knowledge, the surplus-element which situates the patient's knowledge at the level of truth: after the Master-Signifier is produced, even if nothing changes at the level of knowledge, the "same" knowledge starts to function in a different mode. The Master-Signifier is the unconscious *sinthome*, the cipher of enjoyment, to which the subject was unknowingly subjected.[66]

Traditionally, psychoanalysis was expected to allow the patient to overcome the obstacles which denied him or her access to "normal" sexual enjoyment; today, however, when we are bombarded from all sides by different versions of the superego injunction "Enjoy!", from direct enjoyment of sexual performance to enjoyment of professional achievement or spiritual awakening, we should move to a more radical level: today, psychoanalysis is the only discourse in which you are allowed *not* to enjoy (as opposed to "not allowed to enjoy"). And, from this vantage point, it becomes retroactively clear how the traditional prohibition on enjoyment was already sustained by the implicit opposite injunction. The desire that no longer needs to be sustained by the superego injunction is what Lacan calls the "desire of the analyst"; this appeared before psychoanalysis proper—Lacan discerns it in different historical figures, from Socrates to Hegel. It answers a key question, and it best encapsulates the anti-Buddhist spirit of psychoanalysis: is desire only an illusion? Is it possible to sustain desire even after one gains full insight into the vanity of human desire? Or is the only choice, at that radical point, the one between serene Wisdom and melancholic resignation?

The link between the analyst and the patient is not only speech, words, but also money: one has to pay a price which hurts. The link is thus not only symbolic, at the level of the signifier, but also real, at the level of the object—this point is crucial, especially today. Is the analyst a contemporary miser? Yes and no. The link between psychoanalysis and capitalism is perhaps best exemplified by one of the great literary figures of the nineteenth-century novel, the Jewish moneylender, a shadowy figure to whom all the big figures of society come to borrow money, pleading with him and telling him all their dirty secrets and passions (think of Gobseck from Balzac's *La comédie humaine*)—this figure is a disillusioned wise man, well aware of the vanity of all human endeavor, hidden from the public gaze, with no visible power, but nonetheless the secret master who pulls all the strings of social life. This figure, cruelly indifferent, deprived of all compassion and empathy, is much closer to the analyst than the Church confessor or the wise old trustee. Against Foucault's *History of Sexuality*, the thesis of which is "the birth of psychoanalysis out of the spirit of [Christian] confession," we should, rather, assert "the birth of psychoanalysis out of the spirit of thrift." A fine line separates the analyst from the miser. For Lacan, it is the miser rather than the heroic transgressor who goes to the end, violating all moral constraints, who is the exemplary figure of desire: if we want to discern the mystery of desire, we should focus not on the lover or murderer in thrall to their passion, ready to stake anything and everything for it, but on the miser's attitude toward his chest, the secret place where he keeps and hoards his possessions. The mystery, of course, is that, in the figure of the miser, excess coincides with lack, power with impotence, avaricious hoarding with the elevation of the object into the prohibited/untouchable Thing one can only observe, never fully enjoy. The key to this mystery of the miser is provided by the basic paradox of perversion: when Lacan shows how the capitalist discourse epitomizes perversion insofar as it pretends to count/accumulate *jouissance*,[67] he demonstrates how a pervert acts as if one can accumulate zero(s) or lack(s), as if a zero plus a zero plus . . . is more than a mere zero.

The further dilemma to which this one is linked is that of the collective: when Lacan introduces the term "desire of the analyst," it is in order to undermine the notion that the climax of the analytic treatment is a momentous insight into the abyss of the Real, the "traversing of the fantasy," from which, the morning after, we have to return to sober social reality, resuming our usual social roles—psychoanalysis is *not* an insight which can be shared only in the precious initiatic moments. Lacan's aim is to establish the possibility of a collective of analysts, of discerning the contours of a possible social link between analysts (which is why, in his schema of four discourses, he talks about the discourse of the Analyst as the "obverse" of the Master's discourse). The stakes here are high: is every community based on the figure of a Master (Freud's version in *Totem and Taboo*), or its derivative, the figure of Knowledge (the modern capitalist version)?

Or is there a chance of a different link?[68] Of course, the outcome of this struggle was a dismal failure in the entire history of psychoanalysis, from Freud to Lacan's later work and his *École*—but the fight is worth pursuing. This is the properly Leninist moment of Lacan—recall how, in his late writings, he is endlessly struggling with the organizational questions of the School. The psychoanalytic collective is, of course, a collective of (and in) an emergency state. When Saint Paul defines the Messianic state of emergency as a state in which the end of time is near, in which we have only the time which remains, and are thus obliged to suspend our full commitment to earthly links ("possess things as if you do not possess them," and so on), does the same not go also for the patient, who, while in analysis, also has to suspend his social links?

Lorenzo Chiesa[69] has raised a key question of Lacanian political theory: should we stick to the revolutionary dream of a society which would leave behind the tension between the public Law and its fantasmatic support (obscene superego supplement), or is this tension irreducible? If it is irreducible, how are we to avoid the resigned conservative conclusion that every revolutionary upheaval has to end up in a new version of the positive order which reproduces itself through its obscene inherent transgression? The lesson of history seems to confirm the inevitability of this relapse. On only a couple of occasions have political regimes tried to mitigate this tension, most notably in the Spartan state, which represented a uniquely pure realization of a certain model of societal organization. Its three-caste pyramid of social hierarchy (the ruling warrior *homoi* [the "equals"], the artisans and merchants below them, and the mass of helots at the bottom who were just slaves exploited for physical labor) condensed with crystal clarity the historical succession of serfdom, capitalism, and egalitarian communism; in a way, Sparta was all three at the same time: feudalism for the lowest class, capitalism for the middle class, and communism for the ruling class.

The ethico-ideological predicament of the rulers is of special interest here: despite the absolute power they enjoyed, they had to live not only in a permanent state of emergency, at war with their own subjects, but also as if their own position were obscene and illegal. While in military training, for example, adolescents were given insufficient food on purpose, so they had to steal it; if, however, they were caught, they were severely punished—not for stealing, but for *getting caught*, thus being pushed into learning the art of secret stealing. Or, with regard to marriage: the married soldier continued to live with his comrades in military barracks; he could visit his wife only secretly during the night, as if committing a clandestine act of transgression. The most acute case of this twisted logic was the key ordeal of young trainees: in order to earn their acceptance into masculine society, they had secretly to murder one of the unsuspecting helots—in the ruling class, the transgression and the law thus directly coincided. Is this not a kind of perverse realization of Hegel's notion of the three estates of a rational state (the "substantial" peasants living in the universe of immediate mores, the dynamic artisans and industrialists ruled by their egotistic individual interest, the state bureaucracy as the universal class), with a curious twist: the universality of the "universal class" of *homoi* is self-negating, in outright conflict with itself—instead of dwelling in a peaceful universality, they lived in permanent unrest and a state of emergency. We find such a paradoxical model in which authority treats itself as an illegal obscenity in other extreme "totalitarian" regimes, most notably in the Khmer Rouge regime in Kampuchea (1975–79), where inquiring into the structure of state power was considered a crime: the leaders were referred to anonymously as "Brother No. 1" (Pol Pot, of course), "Brother No. 2," and so on.

The important lesson to be drawn from this extreme is that, *in it, the "truth" about power as such comes to light: that it is an obscene excess* (over the social body). That is to say: it would be wrong to oppose this reduction of power to the obscene excess to "pure" power which would function without any obscene support: the point is, rather, that the attempt to establish a "pure" power necessarily reverts to its opposite, a power which has to relate to itself as to an obscene excess. (And, at a different level, we encounter the same paradox in Western democratic societies in which the disappearance of the figure of the Master, far from abolishing domination, is sustained by unprecedented forms of disavowed control and domination.) Should we then, as Chiesa proposes, take seriously (not merely as cynical wisdom) Lacan's claim that the discourse of the Analyst prepares the way for a new Master, and heroically assume the need to pass from the negative gesture of "traversing the fantasy" to the formation of a New Order, including a new Master and its obscene superego underside? Was Lacan himself, in his very last seminars, not pointing in this direction with his theme "toward a new signifier/ *vers un signifiant nouveau*"? The question, however, remains: how, *structurally*, does this new Master differ from the previous, overthrown one (and its new fantasmatic support from the old one)? If there is no *structural* difference, then we are back with the resigned conservative wisdom about (a political) revolution as a revolution in the astronomic sense of the circular movement which brings us back to the starting point.

Here Chiesa touches a similar nerve center in both Badiou's and Miller's theoretical edifices. We already saw how Miller emphasizes that today's hegemonic discourse is no longer that of the Master, but that of the Analyst, with *a* (the superego injunction to enjoy) occupying the place of the agent—in what, then, does the job of the analyst consist? He resorts to a dubious difference between the four elements of the discourse operating unconnected, side by side (as in the predominant social link), and bringing them together into a structure (which happens only in analysis). What, however, if this diagnosis, if it is accurate, compels us to draw a much more radical and unexpected conclusion? Miller himself also repeatedly points out that the Unconscious has the structure of the discourse of the Master (S_1, its agent, being the Master-Signifier, the unconscious "quilting point" of the subject's space of meaning)—so what if, in the constellation in which the Unconscious itself, in its strict Freudian sense, is disappearing, the task of the analyst should no longer be to undermine the hold of the Master-Signifier, but, on the contrary, to construct/propose/install *new* Master-Signifiers? Is this not how we should (or, at least, can) read Lacan's "*vers un signifiant nouveau*"? As a call to counteract the disintegration of any consistent World in the crazy symbolic dynamics of late capitalism, and to propose new "quilting points," *new Master-Signifiers*, that would provide consistency to our experience of meaning? And, in a strictly analogous way, is this also not Badiou's predicament, after he is forced to take into account the "de-territorializing" dynamics of today's capitalism? After defining the task of emancipatory politics as undermining the state of representation from the standpoint of its constitutive excess (zero-element), and after taking note of how such a permanent undermining of every state is already the central feature of capitalist dynamics (which is why capitalism is properly "worldless"), he suddenly discovers the new task of forming a new world, of proposing signifiers that would allow a new Naming of our situation.

It is only here that we encounter the real problem: that of a *sociopolitical transformation that would entail the restructuring of the entire field of the relations between the public Law and its obscene supplement*. In other words, what about the prospect of a radical social transformation which would not involve the boring scarecrow of utopian-totalitarian "complete fullness and transparency of the social"? Why should every project for a radical social revolution automatically fall into the trap of aiming at the impossible dream of "total transparency"? Or—to go on with the celestial metaphor—does it not happen, from time to time, that a shift occurs in the very circular path of planetary revolutions, a break which redefines its coordinates and establishes a new balance, or, rather, a new measure of balance?

JOUISSANCE AS A POLITICAL CATEGORY

Esteban Echeverría's *El matadero/The Slaughterhouse*, one of the founding texts of Argentinian literature written in the early 1840s and unpublished during the author's lifetime, a ferocious polemics against the dictatorship of Juan Manuel Rosas, is perhaps the most revealing display of the obscene *jouissance* that underlies the fantasmatic bias of liberal political imagination.[70] More than half of this story, a mere thirty pages long, describes the atmosphere and events in a big Buenos Aires slaughterhouse, with a brutally open contempt and disgust for the poor (mostly black) people who live there, their barbaric habits (the cruel way they kill the animals, the vulgar way they dispose of the booty, fighting for the entrails of the slaughtered bull in the mud), their cruel jokes, and so forth. The existential disgust goes so far that the "realistic" depiction of the filth and mire of the slaughterhouse, brought to its extreme, turns into its surrealist opposite—as when the severed head of a child suddenly falls into this filth, while its trunk, propped on a forked pole of the corral, spouts blood from innumerable jets. People from the slaughterhouse were the bastion of support for Rosas, the core membership of his *mazorca*, a half-secret lower-class private army deployed to terrorize his enemies. The final part then tells the story of a proud young "Unitarian" (nicely dressed upper-class gentleman, an opponent of Rosas) who passes the slaughterhouse; the barbarous slaughterhouse workers snatch him and ritually humiliate him, undressing him. Rather than survive this humiliation, the gentleman dies in a furious attack of rage—and again his death is related with a hint of surrealism: the undaunted

Unitarian, congested with anger, bursts open like a ripe fruit. . . . The vision of tyranny here is not simply that of a brutal police and ideological force imposed on society; the key message of the story is the underground link between the tyrant and the lowest lumpenproletarian strata of society, the scum wallowing in their dirt. Consequently, the "victim of tyranny" *par excellence* is not the poor, but the respectable educated gentleman of noble dress and manners, proud and dignified. Liberalism and the "mob rule" of the lower classes are clearly opposed, and the unintended achievement of El *matadero* is that it reveals the fantasmatic background of this "hatred of tyranny": disgust at life itself in its sweat, pain, and blood. What sensitive liberals want is a decaffeinated revolution, a revolution which will not smell—in the terms of the French Revolution, a 1789 without 1793.

Today, this ideological manipulation of obscene *jouissance* has entered a new stage: our politics is more and more directly the politics of *jouissance*, concerned with ways of soliciting, or controlling and regulating, *jouissance*. Is not the entire opposition between the liberal/tolerant West and fundamentalist Islam condensed in the opposition between, on the one hand, a woman's right to free sexuality, including the freedom to display/expose herself and provoke/disturb men, and, on the other, desperate male attempts to eradicate this threat or, at least, keep it under control? (Remember the ridiculous Taliban prohibition of metal heels for women—as if, even if women were entirely covered, the ringing sound of their heels would still arouse men?) Both sides, of course, ideologically/morally mystify their position: for the liberal West, the right to expose oneself provocatively to male desire is legitimized as the right to dispose of one's body freely and to enjoy it as one wishes; while for Islam, the control of feminine sexuality is, of course, legitimized as the defense of woman's dignity against the threat of being reduced to an object of male sexual exploitation.[71] So while, when the French state forbade girls to wear the hijab to school, it could be claimed that, in this way, girls were enabled to control their own bodies, it could also be argued that the true traumatic point for critics of Muslim "fundamentalism" was that there were girls who did not participate in the game of making their bodies available for sexual seduction, for the social circulation/exchange involved in it. In one way or another, all other issues are related to this one: gay marriage and a gay couple's right to adopt children; divorce; abortion. . . .

In some "radical" circles in the USA, a proposal to "rethink" the rights of necrophiliacs (those who desire to have sex with dead bodies) has recently started to circulate—why should they be deprived? So the idea was formulated that, just as people sign a form giving permission for their organs to be used for medical purposes in the event of their sudden death, one should also allow them to sign a form for their bodies to be given to necrophiliacs to play with. . . . Is not this proposal the perfect illustration of how the PC stance realizes Kierkegaard's insight into how the only good neighbor is a dead neighbor? A dead neighbor—a corpse—is the ideal sexual partner for a "tolerant" subject trying to avoid harassment: by definition, a corpse cannot be harassed; at the same time, a dead body does not enjoy, so the disturbing threat of excess enjoyment for the subject playing with the corpse is also eliminated. . . . What the two opposite attitudes share is thus the extreme *disciplinary* approach, which is differently directed in each case: "fundamentalists" regulate feminine self-presentation in detail to prevent sexual provocation; PC feminist liberals impose a no less severe regulation of behavior aimed at containing different forms of harassment.

We should, however, add a qualification here. What we have today is not so much the politics of *jouissance* but, more precisely, the regulation (administration) of *jouissance* which is *stricto sensu* postpolitical. *Jouissance* is in itself limitless, the obscure excess of the unnameable, and the task is to regulate this excess. The clearest sign of the reign of biopolitics is the obsession with the topic of "stress": how to avoid stressful situations, how to "cope" with them. "Stress" is our name for the excessive dimension of life, for the "too-muchness" that must be kept under control. (For this reason, today, more than ever, the gap that separates psychoanalysis from therapy imposes itself in all its brutality: if you want therapeutic improvement, you will in fact get help much more quickly and efficiently from a combination of behavioral-cognitivist therapies and chemical treatment [pills].)

How, then, are we to draw the line of distinction between the two excesses: the excess of the Fascist spectacle, of its passion, with regard to "normal" bourgeois life, or, today, the excess that pertains to "normal" capitalist reproduction itself, its constant self-revolutionizing; and the excess of Life itself?[72] Perhaps the way to distinguish the constitutive ontological excess from the obscene excess supplement is, again, by means of the logic of non-All, that is, with regard to its relationship to presupposed "normality": the obscene excess is the excess of exception which sustains "normality," while the radical ontological excess is a "pure" excess, excess to nothing, the paradox of an excess "as such," of something which is in itself excessive, with no presupposed normality.

The superego imperative to enjoy thus functions as the reversal of Kant's "*Du kannst, denn du sollst!*" (You can, because you must!)—it relies on a "You must, because you can!" That is to say: the superego aspect of today's "nonrepressive" hedonism (the constant provocation to which we are exposed, enjoining us to go right to the end, and explore all modes of *jouissance*) resides in the way permitted *jouissance* necessarily turns into obligatory *jouissance*. The question here, however, is: does the capitalist injunction to enjoy in fact aim at soliciting *jouissance* in its excessive character, or are we ultimately, rather, dealing with a kind of universalized *pleasure principle*, with a life dedicated to pleasures? In other words, are not injunctions to have a good time, to acquire self-realization and self-fulfillment, and so on, precisely injunctions to *avoid* excessive *jouissance*, to find a kind of homeostatic balance? Is not the Dalai Lama's advice the advice on how to maintain a balanced "proper measure," and avoid disturbing extremes? The situation here is more complex: the problem is that, although the immediate and explicit injunction calls for the rule of a pleasure principle that would maintain homeostasis, the actual functioning of the injunction explodes these constraints into a striving toward excessive enjoyment.

Here one is tempted to oppose the post-'68 Leftist drive to *jouissance* (to reaching the extreme of forms of sexual pleasure that would dissolve all social links and allow me to find a climax in the solipsism of absolute *jouissance*) to the consummation of commodified products promising *jouissance*: the first still stands for a radical, even "authentic," subjective position; while the second implies a defeat, a surrender to market forces. However, is this opposition really so clear? Is it not all too easy to denounce *jouissance* offered on the market as "false," as providing only an empty package-promise with no substance? Is not the hole, the Void, at the very heart of our pleasures the structure of every *jouissance*? Furthermore, do not the commodified provocations to enjoy which bombard us all the time push us toward, precisely, an autistic-masturbatory, "asocial" *jouissance* whose supreme case is drug addiction? Are drugs not at the same time the means for the most radical autistic experience of *jouissance* and a commodity *par excellence?*

The drive to pure autistic *jouissance* (through drugs or other trance-inducing means) arose at a precise political moment: when the emancipatory sequence of 1968 had exhausted its potential. At this critical point (the mid-1970s), the only option left was a direct, brutal *passage à l'acte*, push-toward-the-Real, which took three main forms: a search for extreme forms of sexual *jouissance*; Leftist political terrorism (the RAF [Rote Armee Fraktion] in Germany, the Red Brigades in Italy, and so on) whose wager was that, in an epoch in which the masses are totally immersed in a capitalist ideological sleep, the standard critique of ideology is no longer operative, so that only a resort to the raw Real of direct violence—*l'action directe*—can awaken the masses); and, finally, the turn toward the Real of an inner experience (Oriental mysticism). What all three share is a withdrawal from concrete sociopolitical engagement into a direct contact with the Real.

Freud's "naive" reflections on how the artist expresses embarrassing, even disgusting, intimate fantasizing in a social context by wrapping it up in a socially acceptable form—by "sublimating" it, offering the pleasure of the beautiful artistic form as a lure which seduces us into accepting the otherwise repulsive excessive pleasure of intimate fantasizing—acquire a new relevance in today's era of permissiveness, when performance and other artists are under pressure to stage the most intimate private fantasies in all their desublimated nakedness. Such "transgressive" art confronts us directly with *jouissance* at its most solipsistic, with masturbatory phallic *jouissance*. And, far from being individualist, such *jouissance* precisely characterizes individuals insofar as they are caught up in a "crowd": what Freud called "crowd/*Masse*" is precisely *not* a distinct communal network but a *conglomerate of solipsistic individuals*—as the saying goes, one is by definition lonely in a crowd. Thus the paradox is that a crowd is a fundamentally *antisocial* phenomenon.

We should appreciate the strict symmetry between ideological fundamentalism and liberal hedonism: they both focus on the Real; the difference being that, while liberal hedonism elevates into its Cause the extra-symbolic Real of *jouissance* (which compels it to adopt a cynical attitude of reducing language, the symbolic medium, to a mere secondary irrelevant *semblant*, instrument of manipulation or seduction, the only "real thing" being *jouissance* itself), "fundamentalism" enacts a short circuit between the Symbolic and the Real—that is to say, in it, some symbolic fragment (for instance, the sacred text, the Bible in the case of Christian fundamentalists) is *itself posited as real* (to be read "literally," not to be played with, in short: exempted from all dialectic of reading).

Nowhere is this constellation staged in a clearer way than in the Matrix trilogy. The *Matrix* movies should be read not as a work sustained by a consistent philosophical discourse, but as a work whose very inconsistencies epitomize the antagonisms of our ideological and social predicament. What, then, is the Matrix? Simply what Lacan called the "big Other," the virtual symbolic order, the network that structures reality for us. This dimension of the "big Other" is that of the constitutive *alienation* of the subject in the symbolic order: the big Other pulls the strings; the subject doesn't speak, he "is spoken" by the symbolic structure. The paradox, the "infinite judgment," of *The Matrix* is the codependence of the two aspects: the total artificiality (the constructed nature) of reality, and the triumphant return of the body in the sense of the balletic quality of its fights, with their slow motion and defiance of the laws of ordinary physical reality. (Surprisingly, *The Matrix* is much more precise than we would expect with regard to the distinction between the Real and reality: Morpheus' famous "Welcome to the desert of the Real!" refers not to the real world outside the Matrix, but to the purely formal digital universe of the Matrix itself. When Morpheus confronts Neo with the image of the ruins of Chicago, he simply says: "This is the real world!", that is, what remains of our reality outside the Matrix after the catastrophe, while the "desert of the Real" refers to the grayness of the purely formal digital universe which generates the false "wealth of experience" of humans caught in the Matrix.)

Take another memorable scene in which Neo has to choose between the red pill and the blue pill; his choice is between Truth and Pleasure: either the traumatic awakening into the Real, or persistence in the illusion regulated by the Matrix. He chooses Truth, in contrast to the most despicable character in the movie, the informer-agent of the Matrix among the rebels, who, in the memorable scene of the dialogue with Smith, the agent of the Matrix, picks up a juicy red bit of steak with his fork and says: "I know it's just a virtual illusion, but I don't care, since it tastes real." In short, he follows the pleasure principle which tells him that it is preferable to stay within the illusion, even if one is aware it's only an illusion. The choice of *The Matrix*, however, is not as simple as that: what, exactly, does Neo offer humanity at the end? Not a direct awakening into the "desert of the Real," but a free floating between the multitude of virtual universes: instead of simply being enslaved by the Matrix, we can liberate ourselves by learning to bend its rules—we can change the rules of our physical universe, and thus learn to fly freely, and violate other physical laws. In short, the choice is not between bitter truth and pleasurable illusion but, rather, between the two modes of illusion: the traitor is bound to the illusion of our "reality," dominated and manipulated by the Matrix; while Neo offers humanity the experience of the universe as the playground in which we can play a multitude of games, passing freely from one to another, reshaping the rules which fix our experience of reality.

In an Adornian way, we should claim that these inconsistencies are the film's moment of truth: they exemplify the antagonisms of our late-capitalist social experience, antagonisms concerning basic ontological couples like reality and pain (reality as that which disturbs the reign of the pleasure principle), freedom and system (freedom is possible only within the system that hinders its full deployment). The ultimate strength of the film, however, is nonetheless to be located at a different level. Its unique impact is due not so much to its central thesis (what we experience as reality is an artificial virtual reality generated by the "Matrix," the mega-computer directly attached to all our minds) as to its central image of the millions of human beings leading a claustrophobic life in water-filled cradles, kept alive in order to generate energy (electricity) for the Matrix. So when (some of the) people "awaken" from their immersion in Matrix-controlled virtual reality, this awakening is not an opening into the wide space of external reality, but first the horrible realization of this enclosure, where each of us is in effect merely a fetuslike organism, immersed in the amniotic fluid. . . . This utter passivity is the foreclosed fantasy that sustains our conscious experience as active, self-positing subjects—it is the ultimate *perverse* fantasy, the notion that we are ultimately *instruments* of the Other's (Matrix's) *jouissance*, sucked out of our life-substance like batteries.

This brings us to the central libidinal enigma: why does the Matrix *need* human energy? A solution purely in terms of energy is, of course, meaningless: the Matrix could easily have found another, more reliable source of energy which would have not demanded the extremely complex arrangement of a virtual reality coordinated for millions of human units. The only consistent answer is: the Matrix feeds on human *jouissance*—so here we are back to the fundamental Lacanian thesis that the big Other itself, far from being an anonymous machine, needs a constant influx of *jouissance*. This is the correct insight of *The Matrix*: the juxtaposition of the two aspects of perversion—on the one hand, the reduction of reality to a virtual domain regulated by arbitrary rules that can be suspended; on the other, the concealed truth of this freedom, the reduction of the subject to an utterly instrumentalized passivity. And the ultimate proof of the decline in quality of subsequent installments of the *Matrix* trilogy is that this central aspect is left totally unexploited: a true revolution would have been a change in the way humans and the Matrix itself relate to *jouissance* and its appropriation. What about, for example, individuals sabotaging the Matrix by refusing to secrete *jouissance*?

As every reasonable and cultured person knows, the true greatness and historical legacy of Italian cinema, its world-historical contribution to the European and global culture of the twentieth century, is not neo-Realism, or some other quirk which appeals only to degenerate intellectuals, but three unique genres: spaghetti Westerns, erotic comedies from the 1970s, and—the greatest of them all, without a doubt—historical costume spectacles (*Hercules contra Macista*, and so on). One of the great achievements of the second genre is the charmingly vulgar *Conviene far bene l'amore* (1974, directed by Pasquale Festa Campanile), whose fundamental premise is that when, in the near future, the world runs out of energy, Doctor Nobile, a brilliant young Italian scientist, remembers Wilhelm Reich, and discovers that a tremendous amount of energy is released by a human body during the sexual act—on condition that the couple are not in love. So, in the interests of humanity's survival, the Church is persuaded to reverse its stance: love is sinful, and sex is all right only if no love is involved. So we get people confessing to their priest: "Sorry, Father, I have sinned: I have fallen in love with my wife!" To generate energy, couples are ordered to make love twice a week in large collective halls, controlled by a supervisor who admonishes them: "The couple in the second row to the left—move faster!". . . The similarity with *The Matrix* is unmistakable. The truth of both films is today's predominance of the politics of *jouissance*.

The Matrix Reloaded proposes—or, rather, plays with—a series of ways to overcome the inconsistencies of its prequel. But in so doing, it gets entangled in new inconsistencies of its own. The end is open and undecided not only narratively, but also with regard to its underlying vision of the universe. The basic tone is that of additional complications and suspicions which belie the simple and clear ideology of liberation from the Matrix that underpins Part 1. The communal ecstatic ritual of the people in the underground city of Zion cannot fail to remind us a fundamentalist religious gathering. Doubts are cast upon the two key prophetic figures. Are Morpheus' visions true, or is he a paranoid madman ruthlessly imposing his hallucinations? Neo does not know if he can trust the Oracle, a woman who foresees the future: is she also manipulating him with her prophecies? Or is she a representant of the *good* aspect of the Matrix—unlike agent Smith who, in Part 2, turns into an excess of the Matrix, a virus run amok, trying to avoid being deleted by multiplying itself? And what about the cryptic pronouncements from the Architect of the Matrix, its software writer, its God? He informs Neo that he is actually living in the sixth upgraded version of the Matrix: in each version a savior figure has arisen, but his attempt to liberate humanity ended in a large-scale catastrophe. Is Neo's rebellion, then, far from being a unique event, just part of a longer cycle of the disturbance and restitution of the Order? By the end of *The Matrix Reloaded*, everything is thus cast in doubt: the question is not only whether any revolutions against the Matrix can accomplish what they claim, or whether they have to end in an orgy of destruction, but whether they are not taken into account, even planned, by the Matrix. Are even those who are liberated from the Matrix, then, free to make a choice at all? Is the solution nonetheless to risk outright rebellion, to resign oneself to playing local games of "resistance" while remaining within the Matrix, or even to engage in a trans-class collaboration with the "good" forces in the Matrix? This is where *The Matrix Reloaded* ends: in a failure of "cognitive mapping" which perfectly mirrors the sad predicament of today's Left and its struggle against the System.

A supplementary twist is provided by the very end of the movie, when Neo magically stops the bad squidlike machines attacking the humans by merely raising his hand—how is he able to accomplish this in "real reality" and not within the Matrix, where, of course, he can do wonders: freeze the flow of time, defy the laws of gravity, and so on? Does this unexplained inconsistency lead toward the solution that "all there is is generated by the Matrix," that there is no ultimate reality? Although such a "post-modern" temptation to find an easy way out of the confusion by proclaiming that all there is is an infinite series of virtual realities mirroring themselves in each other should be rejected, there is an accurate insight in this complication of the simple and straight division between "real reality" and the Matrix-generated universe: even if the struggle takes place in "real reality," the key fight is to be won in the Matrix; this is why one should (re)enter its virtual fictional universe. If the struggle had taken place solely in the "desert of the Real," we would have had another boring dystopia about the remnants of humanity fighting evil machines.

To put it in terms of the good old Marxist couple *infrastructure/superstructure*: we should take into account the irreducible duality of, on the one hand, the "objective" material socioeconomic processes taking place in reality as well as, on the other, the politico-ideological process proper. What if the domain of politics is inherently "sterile," a theater of shadows, but nonetheless crucial in transforming reality? So, although economy is the real site and politics is a theater of shadows, the main fight is to be fought in politics and ideology. Take the disintegration of Communist power in the last years of 1980s: although the main event was the actual loss of state power by the Communists, the crucial break occurred at a different level—in those magic moments when, although formally the Communists were still in power, people suddenly lost their fear, and no longer took the threat seriously; so, even if "real" battles with the police continued, everyone somehow knew that "the game was up.". . .The title *The Matrix Reloaded* therefore is quite appropriate: if Part 1 was dominated by the impetus to exit the Matrix, to liberate oneself from its hold, Part 2 makes it clear that the battle has to be won within the Matrix, that one has to return to it.

In *The Matrix Reloaded*, the Wachowski brothers thus consciously raised the stakes, confronting us with all the complications and confusions of the process of liberation. In this way, they put themselves in a difficult spot: they now confront an almost impossible task. If *The Matrix Revolutions* were to succeed, it would have to produce nothing less than the appropriate answer to the dilemmas of revolutionary politics today, a blueprint for the political act the Left is desperately looking for. No wonder, then, that it failed miserably—and this failure provides a nice case for a Marxist analysis: the narrative failure, the impossibility of constructing a "good story," which indicates a more fundamental social failure.

The first sign of this failure is the broken contract with us, the spectators. The ontological premise of *The Matrix* (Part 1) is a straightforward realistic one: there is the "real reality" and the virtual universe of the Matrix which can be explained entirely in terms of what went on in reality. *The Matrix Revolutions* breaks these rules: the "magic" powers of Neo and Smith extend into "real reality" itself (Neo can stop bullets there also, and so on). Is this not like a detective novel in which, after a series of complex clues, the proposed solution would be that the murderer has magic powers, and was able to commit his crime by violating the laws of our reality? The reader would feel cheated—as in *The Matrix Revolutions*, where the predominant tone is the one of faith, not knowledge.

The second failure is more a narrative one: the simplicity of the proposed solution. Things are not really explained, so that the final solution is more like the proverbial cutting of the Gordian knot. This is especially deplorable when we consider the many interesting dark hints in *The Matrix Reloaded* (Morpheus as a dangerous paranoiac, the corruption of the ruling elite of Zion City) which are left unexplored in *Revolutions*. The only interesting new aspect of *Revolutions*—the focus on an interworld, neither Matrix nor reality—is also underdeveloped.

The key feature of the entire *Matrix* series is the progressive need to elevate Smith into the principal negative hero, a threat to the universe, a kind of negative of Neo. Who is Smith really? A kind of allegory of Fascist forces: a bad program gone wild, autonomized, threatening the Matrix. So the lesson of the film is, at its best, that of an anti-Fascist struggle: the brutal Fascist thugs developed by Capital to control workers (by the Matrix to control humans) run out of control, and the Matrix has to enlist the help of humans to crush them, just as liberal capital had to enlist the help of Communism, its mortal enemy, to defeat Fascism. . . . (Perhaps, from today's political perspective, a more appropriate model would have been to imagine Israel on the verge of destroying the PLO, then making a deal with them for a truce if the PLO destroys Hamas, who are running out of control. . . .) *Revolutions*, however, colors this anti-Fascist logic with potentially Fascist elements: although the (feminine) Oracle and the (masculine) Architect are both just programs, their difference is sexualized, so that the end is inscribed into the logic of the balance between feminine and masculine "principles."

When, at the end of *The Matrix Reloaded*, a miracle occurs in reality itself, only two ways out remain open: postmodern Gnosticism or Christianity. That is to say: either we shall learn, in Part 3, that "real reality" itself is just another Matrix-generated spectacle, there being no last "real" reality, or we enter the domain of divine magic. In *The Matrix Revolutions*, however, does Neo really turn into a Christ figure? It may seem so: at the very end of his duel with Smith, he turns into (another) Smith, so that when he dies, Smith (all the Smiths) is (are) also destroyed. . . . If we look more closely, however, a key difference emerges: Smith is a proto-Jewish figure, an obscene intruder who multiplies like a rat, runs amok and disturbs the harmony of Humans and Matrix-Machines, so that his destruction makes possible a (temporary) class truce. What dies with Neo is this Jewish intruder who brings conflict and imbalance; in Christ, on the contrary, God himself becomes man so that, *with the death of Christ, this man (ecce homo), God (of beyond) himself also dies*. The true "Christological" version of the *Matrix* trilogy would thus entail a radically different scenario: Neo should have been a Matrix program made human, a direct human embodiment of the Matrix, so that, when he dies, the Matrix destroys itself.

The ridiculous aspect of the final pact cannot fail to strike us: the Architect has to promise the Oracle not only that the machines will no longer fight men who are outside the Matrix, but that those humans who want to be set free from the Matrix will have their wish granted—but how will they be given the choice? So, in the end, nothing is really resolved: the Matrix is still there, continuing to exploit humans, with no guarantee that another Smith will not emerge; the majority of humans will continue in their slavery. What leads to this deadlock is that, in a typical ideological short circuit, the Matrix functions as a double allegory: for Capital (machines sucking energy out of us) and for the Other, the symbolic order as such.

Perhaps, however—and this would be the only way (partially, at least) to redeem *Revolutions*—there is a sobering message in this very failure of the conclusion of the *Matrix* series: there is no final solution on the horizon today; Capital is here to stay; all we can hope for is a temporary truce. That is to say: undoubtedly worse than this deadlock would have been a pseudo-Deleuzian celebration of the successful revolt of the multitude.

Do We Still Live in a World?

How is this predominance of *jouissance* linked to (even grounded in) global capitalism? What the superego injunction to enjoy and capitalism share is their properly *worldless* character.

There is a nice Hitchcockian detail in *Finding Nemo*: when the dentist's monstrous daughter comes into her father's office, where there is an aquarium, the music is that of the murder scene from *Psycho*. The link is more refined than the idea that the girl is a horror to small helpless animals: at the end of the scene, Nemo escapes by being thrown into the washbasin plughole—this is his passage from the world of humans to his own life-world (he ends up in the sea, close to the dentist's office, where he rejoins his father), and we all know the key role of the theme of the hole into which water disappears in *Psycho* (the fade-out of the water disappearing down the plughole to Marion's dead eye, and so on). The plughole in the washbasin thus functions as a secret passageway between two totally disparate universes, the human one and the one of the fishes—this is true multiculturalism, this acknowledgment that the only way to pass to the Other's world is through what, in our world, looks like a shit-exit, a hole leading into a dark domain, excluded from our everyday reality, into which excrement disappears. The radical disparity of the two worlds is noted in a series of details— when, for example, the father-dentist catches little Nemo in his net, he thinks he has saved him from certain death, failing to perceive that what made Nemo so terrified that he appeared to be on the brink of death was *his own* presence. . . . The wager of the notion of Truth, however, is that this obscene-unnameable link, secret channel, between worlds is not enough: there is a genuine "universal" Truth that cuts across the multitude of worlds.

Why did Badiou start to elaborate this topic of world, the "logic of worlds"? What if the impetus came from his deeper insight into capitalism? What if the concept of world was necessitated by the need to think the unique status of the capitalist universe as worldless? Badiou has claimed that our time is *devoid of world*[73]—how are we to grasp this strange thesis? Even Nazi anti-Semitism opened up a world: by describing the present critical situation, naming the enemy ("the Jewish conspiracy"), the goal, and the means to achieve it, Nazism disclosed reality in a way which allowed its subjects to acquire a global "cognitive mapping," inclusive of the space for their meaningful engagement. Perhaps this is where we should locate the "danger" of capitalism: although it is global, encompassing all worlds, it sustains a *stricto sensu* "worldless" ideological constellation, depriving the great majority of people of any meaningful "cognitive mapping." The universality of capitalism resides in the fact that capitalism is not a name for a "civilization," for a specific cultural-symbolic world, but the name for a neutral economico-symbolic machine which operates with Asian values as well as with others, so that Europe's worldwide triumph is its defeat, self-obliteration, the cutting of the umbilical link to Europe. Critics of "Eurocentrism" who endeavor to unearth the secret European bias of capitalism do not go far enough here: the problem with capitalism is not its secret Eurocentric bias, but the fact that it really is universal, a neutral matrix of social relations. Badiou, of course, is referring here to Marx's well-known passage from *The Communist Manifesto* about the "de-territorializing" force of capitalism, which dissolves all fixed social forms:

> The passage where Marx speaks of the desacralization of all sacred bonds in the icy waters of capitalism has an enthusiastic tone; it is Marx's enthusiasm for the dissolving power of Capital. The fact that Capital revealed itself to be the material power capable of disencumbering us of the "superego" figures of the One and the sacred bonds that accompany it effectively represents its positively progressive character, and it is something that continues to unfold to the present day. Having said that, the generalized atomism, the recurrent individualism and, finally, the abasement of thought into mere practices of administration, of the government of things or of technical manipulation, could never satisfy me as a philosopher. I simply think that it is in the very element of desacralization that we must reconnect to the vocation of thinking.[74]

Thus Badiou recognizes the exceptional *ontological* status of capitalism, whose dynamics undermines every stable frame of representation: what is usually a task to be performed by critico-political activity (namely, the task of undermining the representational frame of the State) is already performed by capitalism itself—and, this poses a problem for Badiou's notion of "evental" politics.[75] In precapitalist formations, every state, every representational totalization, implies a founding exclusion, a point of "symptomal torsion," a "part of no-part," an element which, although part of the system, does not have a proper place within it—and emancipatory politics had to intervene from this excessive ("supernumerary") element which, although part of the situation, cannot be *accounted for* in its terms. What happens, however, when the system no longer excludes the excess, but directly posits it as its driving force—as is the case in capitalism, which can reproduce itself only through its constant self-revolutionizing, through the constant overcoming of its own limit? To put it in simplified terms: if a political event, a revolutionary emancipatory intervention into a determinate historical world, is always linked to the excessive point of its "symptomal torsion," if it by definition undermines the contours of this world, how, then, are we to define the emancipatory political intervention into a universe which is already in itself worldless—which, for its reproduction, no longer needs to be contained by the constraints of a "world"? As Alberto Toscano noted in his perceptive analysis, here Badiou gets caught in an inconsistency: he draws the "logical" conclusion that, in a "worldless" universe (which is today's universe of global capitalism), the aim of emancipatory politics should be the precise opposite of its "traditional" *modus operandi*—the task today is to form a new world, to propose new Master-Signifiers that would provide "cognitive mapping":

> whilst in Badiou's theoretical writings on the appearance of worlds he cogently argues that events engender the *dysfunction* of worlds and their transcendental regimes, in his "ontology of the present" Badiou advocates the necessity, in our "intervallic" or world-less times, of *constructing* a world, such that those now excluded can come to invent new names, names capable of sustaining new truth procedures. As he writes, "I hold that we are at a very special moment, a moment *at which there is not any world.*". . . As a result: "Philosophy has no other legitimate aim except to help find the new names that will bring into existence the unknown world that is only waiting for us because we are waiting for it." In a peculiar inversion of some of the key traits of his doctrine, it seems that Badiou is here advocating, to some extent, an "ordering" task, one that will inevitably, if perhaps mistakenly, resonate for some with the now ubiquitous slogan "Another World is Possible."[76]

The same problem arises apropos of truth: if, for Badiou, the Truth-Event is always local, the truth of a determinate historical world, how are we to formulate the truth of a worldless universe? Is this, as Toscano seems to indicate, why, despite of his acknowledgement of the "ontological" break introduced by capitalism, Badiou avoids the topic of anticapitalist struggle, even ridiculing its main form today (the antiglobalization movement), and continues to define the emancipatory struggle in strictly political terms, as the struggle against (liberal) democracy, today's predominant ideologico-political form? "Today the enemy is not called Empire or Capital. It's called Democracy."[77] Toscano's critique of Badiou at this point is nonetheless inadequate:

> In this respect, we disagree with Badiou's strong claim. . . . This is emphatically not because we think that Badiou's attack on the fetishism of democracy is problematic, but rather because we contend that—despite chattering battalions of smug idolaters and renegade ideologues—Badiou overestimates the inhibiting force, as an "ideological, or subjective, formalization," of the liberal-democratic notion of equality. It is not the principle of democratic representation that hampers the political emancipation of subjects, but rather the deep-seated conviction that there is no alternative to the rule of profit. The cynicism of today's "democratic" subjects, who know full well that they play a negligible role in the management of the commons and are entirely aware of the sham

nature of the apparatuses of representation, is founded on the perceived inevitability of capitalism, not *vice versa*.[78]

Here I should add, in defense of Badiou, that it is not directly "the deep-seated conviction that there is no alternative to the rule of profit" which "hampers the political emancipation of subjects": what prevents the radical questioning of capitalism itself is precisely *belief in the democratic form of the struggle against capitalism*. Lenin's stance against "economism" as well as against "pure" politics is crucial today, apropos of the split attitude toward the economy in (what remains of) the Left: on the one hand, the "pure politicians" who abandon the economy as the site of struggle and intervention; on the other the "economists," fascinated by the functioning of today's global economy, who preclude any possibility of a political intervention proper. With regard to this split, today, more than ever, we should return to Lenin: yes, the economy is the key domain, the battle will be decided there, we have to break the spell of global capitalism—but the intervention should be properly *political*, not economic. Today, when everyone is "anticapitalist," right up to Hollywood "socio-critical" conspiracy movies (from *Enemy of the State* to *The Insider*) in which the enemy is the big corporations with their ruthless pursuit of profit, the signifier "anticapitalism" has lost its subversive sting. What we should problematize is the self-evident opposite of this "anticapitalism": trust in the democratic substance of honest Americans to break up the conspiracy. This is the hard kernel of today's global capitalist universe, its true Master-Signifier: democracy. And are not Michael Hardt and Antonio Negri's latest statements a kind of unexpected confirmation of Badiou's insight? Following a paradoxical necessity, their very (focusing on) anticapitalism has led them to acknowledge the revolutionary force of capitalism, so that, as they put it, one no longer needs to fight capitalism, because capitalism is already in itself generating communist potentials—the "becoming-communist of capitalism," to put it in Deleuzian terms. . . .[79]

What we are dealing with here is another version of the Lacanian "*il n'y a pas de rapport* . . .": if, for Lacan, there is no sexual relationship, then, for Marxism proper, there is *no relationship between economy and politics*, no "meta-language" enabling us to grasp the two levels from the same neutral standpoint, although—or, rather, *because*—these two levels are inextricably intertwined. The "political" class struggle takes place in the midst of the economy (recall that the very last paragraph of *Capital*, Volume 3, where the texts abruptly stops, tackles the class struggle), while, at the same time, the domain of economy serves as the key that enables us to decode political struggles. No wonder the structure of this impossible relationship is that of the Moebius strip: first, we have to progress from the political spectacle to its economic infrastructure; then, in the second step, we have to confront the irreducible dimension of the political struggle at the very heart of the economy.

It is this parallax gap that also accounts for the two irreducible dimensions of modernity: the "political" is the logic of domination, of regulative control ("biopolitics," "administered world"); the "economic" is the logic of the incessant integration of the surplus, of constant "de-territorialization." The resistance to the political domination refers to the "supernumerary" element which cannot be accounted for in terms of the political order—but how are we to formulate resistance to the economic logic of reproduction-through-excess? (And—let us not forget—this excess is strictly correlative to the excess of power itself over its "official" representative function.) The Leftist dream throughout the twentieth century was: through the subordination of the economic to the political (state control of the production process). In their latest works, Hardt and Negri seem to succumb to the opposite temptation, shifting the focus to economic struggle, in which one can rely on the state.

The same ambiguity seems to haunt Peter Hallward's outstanding "The Politics of Prescription" (unpublished text), the most perceptive conceptualization of "Badiouian politics." Hallward starts with an accurate diagnosis of our ideologico-political predicament: after the exhaustion of the emancipatory politics which culminated in 1989, (whatever remained of) the Left was split between "cautious reformism and post-revolutionary despair." We have, on the one side, the diversity of pragmatic-realist liberals in pursuit of "a reasonable chance of peaceful coexistence and mutual respect," talking about dialogue, communication, recognition of otherness, and so on—the whole gang of usual suspects, from Habermas to Rorty—and, on the other side, those who still cling to some notion of radical Change, but whose Messianism is caught up in the self-defeating vicious circle of self-postponing, of a permanent "to-come," which displays a "fundamental obscurity or paralysis—thought confronted by situations in which it is impossible to react (Deleuze), by demands that cannot be met (Levinas), needs that can never be reconciled (Lyotard), promises that can never be kept (Derrida)." Today, however, the end of this deadlock is on the horizon—the end of the end of utopias: one can discern

> a new "principal contradiction"—the convergence, most obviously in Iraq and Haiti, of ever more draconian policies of neo-liberal adjustment with newly aggressive forms of imperial intervention, in the face of newly resilient forms of resistance and critique.
>
> Political philosophy is confronted today by only one consequential decision: either to anticipate this end of an end, and to develop its implications, or else to ignore or deny it, and to reflect on its deferral.

Two strange things strike us here. First, the scarcity and ambiguity of the cases of this "end of the end" enumerated by Hallward: Haiti—OK; but what about Iraq? Is the conflict between the US occupiers and the armed resistance really a clear-cut struggle which, "in view of a specific simplification, falls . . . under the decisive logic of a 'last' or final judgement"? Second, Hallward fails to mention the main obvious candidate for this "end of an end," the antiglobalization movement—is it, for him, the last breath of the Old, or the first wind of the New? The background to this silence is easy to guess: while the antiglobalization movement does not fit either of the two terms of the alternative of the Old (liberal pragmatism, self-postponing Messianism), Badiou, Hallward's main point of reference, (for good reasons!) dismisses it as highly problematic, and unambiguously excludes it from the authentic emancipatory politics which Hall-ward tries to elaborate in Badiou's footsteps, the politics of prescription whose basic premise was most clearly stated by Jacques Rancière apropos of equality: "equality is not a goal to be attained but a point of departure, a supposition to be maintained in all circumstances." Thus the act of prescription posits an axiom as a starting point and de-mands its direct installation as the guiding principle of our actions, not as a distant goal we should approach gradually, strategically weighing the circumstances: "Prescription is direct because its element is the urgency of the here and now. Prescription ignores de-ferral, it operates in a present illuminated through anticipation of its future." So there is a kind of circular-retroactive temporality at work here: we endeavor gradually to re-alize the prescribed axiom by treating it as already realized: "Prescription is first and foremost an anticipation of its subsequent power, a commitment to its consequences, a wager on its eventual strength." The gap between this direct prescriptive logic (which enjoins us to, for instance, accept equality as a direct axiom of our social life) and the "moderate" liberal-gradualist approach of creating conditions for future equality is irreducible here. Hallward summarizes the gist of this "axiomatic" procedure with a reference to Sartre (one of Badiou's acknowledged teachers):

> Sartre explained this perfectly well: first you decide, then you justify the decision by providing it with defensible motives or reasons. First you commit, then you explore the limits of what this commitment allows you to do. The progressive-regressive method: first you act and then, in the new light of this action, you reconstruct the circumstances that led you to act.

This, of course, does not entail any kind of "irrationalist decisionism" (for which Ba-diou is often wrongly criticized);[80] what it amounts to can best be put in the theo-logical terms of the "perspective of the Last Judgment": rejecting the pragmatic rhetoric of the complexity of the present situation, and of the need for its gradual change through compromise and piecemeal reform, one directly judges it (and acts upon this judgment) by the "absolute" standard:

> the political is always that aspect of public life that, in view of a specific simplification, falls for a certain time under the decisive logic of a "last" or final judgement. The refusal to recognise the implacable dualism of a prescription is itself an *orthodox* ideological reaction; an insistence on compromise, on negotiation, on piecemeal "democratic" re-form, has long been the privileged vehicle for the reproduction and reinforcement of the status quo.

As such, the logic of prescription unites two features which our liberal logic of com-promise cannot but perceive as mutually exclusive: prescription is *divisive* (it brutally imposes on the complex social texture a line that opposes "us" and "them"), and si-multaneously *universal* (the division results from the direct application of a universal axiom). I should mention at least two important consequences of this notion of the politics of prescription. First, it allows us to draw the true line of separation between radical emancipatory politics and the predominant status quo politics: it is not the difference between two different positive visions, sets of axioms, but, rather, the difference between a politics based on a set of universal axioms and a politics which renounces the very constitutive dimension of the political, since it resorts to fear as its ultimate mobilizing principle: fear of immigrants, fear of crime, fear of Godless sexual depravity, fear of the excessive State itself (with too-high taxation), fear of ecological catastrophies—such a (post-)politics "always relies on the manipulation of a paranoid *ochlos*—the 'frightening rallying of frightened men'." Second, it entails a crucial and wonderfully irreverent anti-anti-essentialist conclusion:

> We must depoliticise (and dehistoricise) the conditions of possibility of politics. . . . It is no accident, notwithstanding dramatic differences in outlook and orientation, that the most forceful proponents of a prescriptive politics tend to ground its conditions of possibility in autonomous, "auto-poetic" and extra-political faculties or capacities— Chomsky in a mental-cognitive faculty, Gandhi in a spiritual faculty, Sartre in a faculty of imagination or negation, Rancière in a discursive capacity, Badiou in a capacity for unabashedly "immortal" truth.

This diagnosis puts "anti-essentialism" where it belongs: in the liberal-democratic repertoire of those whose automatic reaction is to denounce any axiomatic commitment as "totalitarian.". . . So far, so good: we can see how useful the notion of prescription is not only for today's politics, but also for passing judgment on past emancipatory struggles. Remember the early stages of the struggle against slavery in the USA, which, even prior to the Civil War, culminated in armed conflict between the gradualism of compassionate liberals and the unique figure of John Brown, the practitioner of the politics of prescription—here is a quote well worth repeating:

> African Americans were caricatures of people, they were characterized as buffoons and minstrels, they were the butt-end of jokes in American society. And even the abolitionists, as antislavery as they were, the majority of them did not see African Americans as equals. The majority of them, and this was something that African Americans complained about all the time, were willing to work for the end of slavery in the South but they were not willing to work to end discrimination in the North. . . . John Brown wasn't like that. For him, practicing egalitarianism was a first step toward ending slavery. And African Americans who came in contact with him knew this immediately. He made it very clear that he saw no difference, and he didn't make this clear by saying it, he made it clear by what he did.[81]

From time to time, distant echoes of the politics of prescription are to be heard even in the midst of today's Third Way Left: one of the first measures of José Luis Rodríguez Zapatero, the Spanish Prime Minister, after the Socialist victory in 2004, was directly to install the political equality of women as an axiom: he did not posit it as a goal to be approached gradually through the political education of women, and so on, he simply did it (appointing women to half the posts in his Cabinet, and so forth). . . . Problems with the "politics of prescription" arise elsewhere. While Hallward is fully justified in his uncompromising opposition to the gradualist approach, it is not clear how he stands on the elements in Badiou's own theoretical edifice which come dangerously close to the "anti-totalitarian" logic of endless "to-come." What I have in mind here are two interconnected features of Badiou's conceptual edifice: his elementary couple presentation/state-of-representation, and the concomitant notion of the "unnameable" that cannot be "enforced."

The key to Badiou's opposition of Being and Event is the preceding split, within the order of Being itself, between the pure multitude of the presence of beings (accessible to mathematical ontology) and their representation in some determinate State of Being: all of the multitude of Being can never be adequately represented in a State of Being, and an Event always occurs at the site of this surplus/remainder which eludes the grasp of the State. The question is therefore that of the exact status of this gap between the pure multitude of presence and its representation in State(s). Again, the hidden Kantian reference is crucial here: the gap which separates the pure multiplicity of the Real from the appearing of a "world" whose coordinates are given in a set of categories which predetermine its horizon is the very gap which, in Kant, separates the Thing-in-itself from our phenomenal reality, that is, from the way things appear to us as objects of our experience. The basic problem remains unsolved by Kant as well as by Badiou: how does the gap between the pure multiplicity of being and its appearance in the multitude of worlds arise? How does being appear to itself? Because of the "spurious infinity" logic of representation versus presence, Badiou is ultimately left with only two options: either to remain faithful to the destructive ethics of purification, or to take refuge in the Kantian distinction between a normative regulative Ideal and the constituted order of reality—to claim, for instance, that the Stalinist *désastre* occurs, that the (self-)destructive violence explodes, when the gap which forever separates the Event from the Order of Being is closed, when the Truth-Event is posited as fully realized in the Order of Being.

Along these lines, Badiou has proposed,[82] as (one of) the definition(s) of Evil, the total *forcing of the Unnameable*, the accomplished naming of it, the dream of total Nomination ("everything can be named within the field of the given generic truth-procedure")— the fiction (the Kantian regulative Idea?) of the accomplished truth-procedure is taken for reality (it starts to function as constitutive). According to Badiou, what such forcing obliterates is the inherent limitation of the generic truth-procedure (its undecidability, indiscernibility . . .): the accomplished truth destroys itself; the accomplished political truth turns into totalitarianism. The ethics of Truth is thus the ethics of respect for the unnameable Real that cannot be forced.[83] The problem here, however, is how to avoid the Kantian reading of this limitation. Although Badiou rejects the ontological-transcendental status of finitude as the ultimate horizon of our existence, is not his limitation of truth-procedure ultimately grounded in the fact that it is finite? Significantly, Badiou, the great critic of the notion of totalitarianism, resorts here to this notion in a way very similar to Kantian liberal critics of the "Hegelian totalitarianism":

the subject is the operator of the infinite truth-procedure who, in an act of pure decision/choice, proclaims the Event as the starting point of reference of a truth-procedure (statements like "I love you," "Christ has risen from the dead"). So, although Badiou subordinates subjectivity to the infinite truth-procedure, the place of this procedure is silently constrained by the subject's finitude. And does not Badiou, the anti-Levinas, with this topic of respect for the unnameable, come dangerously close precisely to the Levinasian topic of respect for Otherness that is, against all appearances, totally inoperative at the political level?

Consequently, does the notion of forçage, of "forcing" an Event onto the order of Being, not betray Badiou's Fichteanism (mediated by the figure of Sartre, one of Badiou's masters)—reality (Being) continues to be perceived as an unfathomable multiplicity of the Real which cannot ever be fully "forced" by the subject's project? (Furthermore and unexpectedly, do we not find one of the most poignant articulations of forçage in its link to human finitude in the Heidegger of the mid-1930s, exemplarily in his reading of Antigone in The Introduction to Metaphysics, apropos which he deploys his grandiose vision of the ancient Greek man as a heroic-tragic figure whose violent imposition of a project [Entwurf] of collective destiny onto Being ultimately ends in defeat?) Badiou is right to emphasize that this excess of the Unnameable should not be "essentialized," elevated into an unfathomable mysterious "heart of the maelstrom," the abyss of a central Thing—the excess of the Unnameable ultimately refers to the sheer stupidity of the Real, to the irrelevant and indifferent excess of multiplicities; but, nonetheless, the Real remains opposed to the subject who endeavors to "enforce" it through its fidelity to a Truth-procedure.

The notion of "forcing" is linked to another key notion of Badiou, that of the "passion of the real," of directly imposing an eventalTruth onto reality, which amounts to ruthlessly destroying reality that resists this "terrorist" imposition. No wonder that Badiou himself, in order to avoid the catastrophe of forcing, has to evoke the Unnameable as that which forever prevents the full actualization of the eventalTruth: the (paradigmatically "postmodern") withdrawal from full forcing, the insistence that the Truth (or Democracy or Justice or . . .) should remain "to-come," a possibility higher than any actualization, a spectral, not ontological, entity: the forcing and the refusal of actualization are stricto sensu two sides of the same coin, two aspects of the same constellation.

This conceptual deadlock brings us to the second questionable feature of the "politics of prescription," its problematic reliance on the axiom of equality: no wonder Badiou often de facto bypasses Marx, insisting on a direct line from the Jacobins to Lenin—Marx's fundamental insight concerns the "bourgeois" limitation of the logic of equality. Just as capitalism already asserts the primacy of presentation over the State of representation, it also already asserts the principle of equality: its inequalities ("exploitations") are not the "unprincipled violations of the principle of equality," but are absolutely inherent to the logic of equality; they are the paradoxical result of its logical realization. What I have in mind here is not only the boring old theme of how market exchange presupposes formally/legally equal subjects who meet and interact on the market; the crucial moment of Marx's critique of "bourgeois" socialists is that capitalist exploitation does not involve any kind of "unequal" exchange between the worker and the capitalist—this exchange is fully equal and "just"; ideally (in principle), the worker gets paid the full value of the commodity he is selling (his labor-power). Of course, radical bourgeois revolutionaries are aware of this limitation; the way they try to compensate for it, however, is through a direct "terrorist" imposition of more and more *de facto* equality (equal salaries, an equal health service . . .), which can be imposed only through new forms of formal inequality (various sorts of preferential treatment for the underprivileged). In short, the axiom of "equality" means either not enough (it remains the abstract form of actual inequality) or too much (enforced "terrorist" equality)—it is a formalist notion in a strict dialectical sense, that is, its limitation is precisely that its form is not concrete enough, but a mere neutral container of some content that eludes this form.

And, to make things clear here: our problem is not terror as such—if anything, Badiou's provocative idea that one should reinvent emancipatory terror today is one of his most profound insights. The problem lies elsewhere: egalitarian political "extremism" or "excessive radicalism" should always be read as a phenomenon of ideologico-political *displacement*: as an index of its opposite, of a limitation, of a refusal actually to "go to the end." What was the Jacobins' recourse to radical "terror" if not a kind of hysterical acting-out bearing witness to their inability to disturb the very fundamentals of economic order (private property, and so on)? And does the same not go even for the so-called "excesses" of Political Correctness? Do they also not display a retreat from disturbing the systemic (economic, etc.) causes of racism and sexism? Perhaps, then, the time has come to problematize the standard *topos*, shared by practically all "postmodern" Leftists, according to which political "totalitarianism" somehow results from the predominance of material production and technology over intersubjective communication and/or symbolic practice, as if the root of political terror lies in the fact that the "principle" of instrumental reason, of the technological exploitation of nature, is extended also to society, so that people are treated as raw material to be transformed into New Men. What if it is the exact *opposite* which holds? What if political "terror" indicates precisely that the sphere of (material) production is *denied* in its autonomy and *subordinated* to political logic? Is it not that all political "terror," from the Jacobins to the Maoist Cultural Revolution, presupposes the foreclosure of production proper, its reduction to the terrain of political battle?

Recall Badiou's exalted defense of Terror in the French Revolution, in which he quotes the justification of the guillotine for Lavoisier: "*La république n'a pas besoin de savants.* / The Republic has no need for scientists." Badiou's thesis is that the truth of this statement emerges if we cut it short, depriving it of its caveat: "*La république n'a pas besoins.* / The Republic has no needs." The Republic gives body to the purely political logic of equality and freedom, which should follow its path with no consideration for the "servicing of goods" destined to satisfy the needs of individuals.[84] In the revolutionary process proper, freedom becomes and end in itself, caught in its own paroxysm—this suspension of the importance of the sphere of the economy, of (material) production, brings Badiou close to Hannah Arendt, for whom—in a strict analogy to Badiou—freedom is opposed to the domain of the provision of goods and services, of the maintenance of households and the exercise of administration, which do not belong to politics proper: the only place for freedom is the communal political space. In this precise sense, Badiou's (and Sylvain Lazarus's)[85] plea for a reappraisal of Lenin is more ambiguous than it may appear: in effect, it amounts to nothing less than the abandonment of Marx's key insight into how the political struggle is a spectacle which, in order to be deciphered, has to be referred to the sphere of economics ("if Marxism had any analytical value for *political* theory, was it not in the insistence that the problem of freedom was contained in the social relations implicitly declared 'unpolitical'—that is, naturalized—in liberal discourse?").[86] No wonder that the Lenin Badiou and Lazarus prefer is the Lenin of *What Is to Be Done?*, the Lenin who (in his thesis that the socialist-revolutionary consciousness has to be brought to the working class from outside) breaks with Marx's alleged "economism" and asserts the autonomy of the Political, not the Lenin of *The State and Revolution*, fascinated by modern centralized industry, imagining (depoliticized) ways of reorganizing the economy and the state apparatus.

Bruno Bosteels addresses these issues in "The Speculative Left" (unpublished manuscript), where he defends Badiou against the criticism that he is a "Communist without being a Marxist," advocate of an abstract anti-Statist rebellion: for Badiou, Marxism and communism "rely on each other in a paradoxical history of eternity—that is, the historical unfolding of eternal revolt. To paraphrase a well-known dictum: Marxism without communism is empty, but communism without Marxism is blind." However, there is a series of problems with this declarative assertion: the theoretical core of Marxism is Marx's "critique of political economy," which is simply *wholly absent from Badiou's work*—no doubt a consequence of Badiou's refusal to admit "economy" as the potential site of Event. As if to emphasize this point, Badiou himself refers principally to the line of revolutionary explosions (Jacobins–Paris Commune–October Revolution–Maoism), bypassing Marx. And, quite logically, even in his reception of Lenin, Badiou follows Sylvain Lazarus in dismissing Leninism once the Bolsheviks took power and tried to build a new state: what interests them is the "sequence" which *ends* in October 1917. So it is interesting to contrast Boostels' critique of the merely negative character of the Lacanian Act (as a gesture of assuming the nonexistence of the big Other, of traversing the fantasy, of the pure negativity of the death drive, to which he opposes Badiou's positive notion of the patient work which enacts fidelity to the Event) with Badiou's haughty dismissal of the concrete (post-)revolutionary patient labor of building a new social order as belonging to the level of Statist police/policing.

The highest irony here is that Badiou himself, who adamantly opposes the notion of the act as negative, locates the historical significance of the Maoist Cultural Revolution precisely in signaling "the end of the party-State as the central production of revolutionary political activity. More generally, the Cultural Revolution showed that it was no longer possible to assign either the revolutionary mass actions or the organizational phenomena to the strict logic of class representation. That is why it remains a political episode of the highest importance." These lines are from Badiou's "The Cultural Revolution: The Last Revolution?",[87] which, at the end, emphatically reiterates the same point:

> In the end, the Cultural Revolution, even in its very impasse, bears witness to the impossibility truly and globally to free politics from the framework of the party-State that imprisons it. It marks an irreplaceable experience of saturation, because a violent will to find a new political path, to relaunch the revolution, and to find new forms of the workers' struggle under the formal conditions of socialism, ended up in failure when confronted with the necessary maintenance, for reasons of public order and the refusal of civil war, of the general frame of the party-State.

The key importance of the last truly great revolutionary explosion of the twentieth century is thus *negative*, it resides in its very failure, which marks the exhaustion of the party/Statist logic of the revolutionary process. What, however, if we should take a step further here, and conceive both poles, presentation ("direct" extra-Statist self-organization of the revolutionary masses) and representation, as the two interdependent poles, so that, in a truly Hegelian paradox, the end of the party-State form of revolutionary activity guided by the *telos* of "taking over state power" is simultaneously also the end of all forms of "direct" (nonrepresentational) self-organization (councils and other forms of "direct democracy")? Everybody (almost) in the West loved councils, right up to liberals like Hannah Arendt, who perceived in them the echo of the ancient Greek life of the *polis*. Throughout the age of Really Existing Socialism, the secret hope of "democratic socialists" was the direct democracy of the "soviets," local councils as the people's form of self-organization; and it is deeply symptomatic how, with the decline of Really Existing Socialism, this emancipatory shadow which haunted it all the time also disappeared—is this not the ultimate confirmation of the fact that the council version of "democratic socialism" was just a spectral double of the "bureaucratic" Really Existing Socialism, its inherent transgression with no substantial positive content of its own, that is, unable to serve as the permanent basic organizing principle of a society?

This brings us to the deadlock of Badiou's politics, after he proclaimed the end of the Jacobinian revolutionary paradigm: while he is aware that the anti-Statist revolutionary Party politics which aimed at taking over and demolishing the State apparatus is exhausted, he refuses to explore the revolutionary potential of the "economic" sphere (since, for him, this sphere belongs to the order of Being, and does not contain potential "evental sites"); for this reason, the only way left is that of a "pure" political organization which operates outside the confines of the State and, basically, limits itself to mobilizatory declarations. . . . The only way out of this deadlock is *to restore to the "economic" domain the dignity of Truth, the potential for Events.*

CHAPTER 6

THE OBSCENE KNOT OF IDEOLOGY, AND HOW TO UNTIE IT

In Amish communities there is a practice called *rumspringa* (from the German *herum-springen*, to jump around): at seventeen, their children (until then subjected to strict family discipline) are set free, allowed, even encouraged, to go out and learn and experience the ways of the "English" world around them—they drive cars, listen to pop music, watch TV, get involved in drinking, drugs, wild sex. . . . After a couple of years, they are expected to decide: will they become members of the Amish community, or leave it and turn into ordinary American citizens? Far from being permissive and allowing the youngsters a truly free choice—that is to say, giving them a chance to decide on the basis of a full knowledge and experience of both sides—such a solution is biased in a most brutal way, a fake choice if ever there was one. When, after long years of discipline and fantasizing about the transgressive illicit pleasures of the outside "English" world, the adolescent Amish are thrown into it all of a sudden and without preparation, they, of course, cannot but indulge in extreme transgressive behavior, "test it all," throw themselves fully into a life of sex, drugs, and drinking. And since, in such a life, they lack any inherent limitation or regulation, this permissive situation inexorably backfires and generates unbearable anxiety—thus it is a safe bet that, after a couple of years, they will return to the seclusion of their community. No wonder 90 percent of the children do exactly that.

This is a perfect case of the difficulties that always accompany the idea of a "free choice": while the Amish adolescents are formally given a free choice, the conditions in which they find themselves while they are making the choice make the choice unfree. In order for them to have a genuinely free choice, they would have to be properly informed about all their options, educated in them—the only way to do this, however, would be to extricate them from their embeddedness in the Amish community, that is, in effect, to make them "English." This also clearly demonstrates the limitations of the standard liberal attitude toward Muslim women wearing the veil: they can do it if it is their free choice, not an option imposed on them by their husbands or family. The moment women wear the veil as a result of their free individual choice (say, in order to express their own spirituality), however, the meaning of wearing the veil changes completely: it is no longer a sign of their belonging to the Muslim community, but an expression of their idiosyncratic individuality; the difference is the same as the one between a Chinese farmer eating Chinese food because his village has done so since time immemorial, and a citizen of a Western megalopolis deciding to go and eat at a local Chinese restaurant. The lesson of all this is that a choice is always a meta-choice, a choice of the modality of the choice itself: only the woman who does not choose to wear the veil is really making a choice. This is why, in our secular societies of choice, people who maintain a substantial religious belonging are in a subordinate position: even if they are allowed to practice their belief, this belief is "tolerated" as their idiosyncratic personal choice/opinion; the moment they present it publicly as what it is for them (a matter of substantial belonging), they are accused of "fundamentalism." This means that the "subject of free choice" (in the Western "tolerant" multicultural sense) can emerge only as the result of an extremely *violent* process of being torn out of one's particular life-world, being cut off from one's roots.

And is this not how our academic freedoms function? (This does not *a priori* render them meaningless or "co-opted"—we should simply be aware of it.) Nothing is more conducive to proper integration into the hegemonic ideologico-political community than a "radical" past in which one lived out one's wildest dreams. The latest protagonists in this saga are today's US neocons, a surprising number of whom were Trotskyites in their youth.[1] As we can now claim, retroactively, was not even the glorious Parisian May '68 such a collective *rumspringa* which, in the long term, contributed to the reproductive capacity of the system? In "The Problem of Hegemony," Simon Critchley[2] provides a consistent justification of such a critical *rumspringa*:

> We inhabit states. . . . Now, it is arguable that the state is a limitation on human existence and we would be better off without it. Such is perhaps the eternal temptation of anarchism, and we will come back to anarchism. However, it seems to me that we cannot hope, at this point in history, to attain a withering away of the state either through anarcho-syndicalism or revolutionary proletarian praxis, or through the agency of the party for example . . . if class positions are not simplifying, but on the contrary becoming more complex through processes of dislocation, if the revolution is no longer conceivable in Marx's manner, then that means that, for good or ill, let's say for ill, we are stuck with the state, just as we are stuck with capitalism. The question becomes: what should our political strategy be with regard to the state, to the state that we're in? . . . In a period when the revolutionary subject has decidedly broken down, and the political project of a disappearance of the state is not coherent other than as a beautifully seductive fantasy, politics has to be conceived at a distance from the state. Or, better, politics is the praxis of taking up distance with regard to the state, working independently of the state, working in a situation. Politics is praxis in a situation and the work of politics is the construction of new political subjectivities, new political aggregation in specific localities, new political sequences.
>
> Perhaps it is at this intensely situational, indeed local level that the atomising force of capitalist globalisation is to be met, contested and resisted. That is, it is not to be resisted by constructing a global anti-globalisation movement that, at its worst, is little more than a highly-colourful critical echo of the globalisation it contests. It is rather to be resisted by occupying and controlling the terrain upon which one stands, where one lives, works, acts and thinks. This needn't involve millions of people. It needn't even involve thousands. It could involve just a few at first. It could be what Julia Kristeva has recently called the domain of "intimate revolt." That is, politics begins right here, locally, practically and specifically, around a concrete issue and not by running off to protest at some meeting of the G8. You shouldn't meet your enemy on their ground, but on your own, on the ground that you have made your own. Also, think of the money and time you save on travel!

True democracy is "enacted or even simply acted—practically, locally, situationally—at a distance from the state. . . . It calls the state into question, it calls the established order to account, not in order to do away with the state, desirable though that might well be in some utopian sense, but in order to better it or attenuate its malicious effects."The main ambiguity of this position resides in a strange *non sequitur*: if the state is here to stay, if it is impossible to abolish the state (and capitalism), why act with a distance toward the state? Why not *with(in) the state?* Why not accept the basic premise of the New Left's Third Way? Perhaps it is time to take Stalin's obsessive critique of "bureaucracy" seriously, and to appreciate in a new (Hegelian) way the necessary work done by the state bureaucracy. In other words, is not Critchley's position one of relying on the fact that *someone else* will take on the task of running the state machinery, enabling us to engage in critical distance toward the state? Furthermore, if the space of democracy is defined by a distance toward the state, is Critchley not abandoning the field (of the state) all too easily to the enemy? Is it not crucial what form the state power has? Does not Critchley's position lead to the reduction of this crucial question to a secondary place: whatever state we have, it is inherently nondemocratic?

This brings us to the second ambiguity: is the fact that state "is here to stay" a temporary withdrawal, a specific claim about today's historico-political situation, or a transcendental limitation conditioned by human finitude? That is to say: when Critchley defines today's constellation as one in which the state is here to stay, and in which we are caught in multiple displacements, and so on, this thesis is radically (and necessarily) ambiguous: (1) is it—as some of his formulations seem to imply ("In a period when the revolutionary subject has decidedly broken down, and the political project of a disappearance of the state is not coherent other than as a beautifully seductive fantasy . . .")—that this is merely today's historical constellation, in which progressive political forces are in retreat; or is it that this is a general "truth" to which we were blinded when we believed in essentialist utopian political ideologies? Again, the ambiguity here is necessary.

> The revolution is not going to be generated out of systemic or structural laws. We are on our own and what we do we have to do for ourselves. Politics requires subjective invention. No ontology or eschatological philosophy of history is going to do it for us. Working at a distance from the state, a distance that I have tried to describe as democratic, we need to construct political subjectivities in specific situations, subjectivities that are not arbitrary or relativistic, but which are articulations of an ethical demand whose scope is universal and whose evidence is faced in a situation. This is dirty, detailed, local, practical and largely unthrilling work. It is time we made a start.

Is this dilemma not all too *coarse?* Is it not, in effect, a case of "binary opposition"? That is to say: even if the emancipatory progress cannot be directly grounded in an "objective" social necessity, even if it is true that "what we do we have to do for ourselves" (a thesis with which, incidentally, the Lukács of *History and Class Consciousness*, the ultimate straw man of the critics of "teleological" Hegelian Marxism, would fully agree—he provided the most convincing version of it), it presupposes a certain specific historical site: what Alain Badiou called "the eventual site." Does not Critchley's position, then, function as a kind of ideal supplement to the Third Way Left: a "revolt" which poses no effective threat, since it endorses in advance the logic of hysterical provocation, bombarding the Power with "impossible" demands, demands which are not meant to be met? Critchley is therefore logical in his assertion of the primacy of the Ethical over the Political: the ultimate motivating force of the type of political interventions he advocates is the experience of injustice, of the ethical unacceptability of the state of things.

Against Critchley's call for modest local "practical" action, I am therefore tempted to cite Badiou's provocative thesis: "It is better to do nothing than to contribute to the invention of formal ways of rendering visible that which Empire already recognizes as existent."[3] Better to do nothing than to engage in localized acts whose ultimate function is to make the system run more smoothly (acts like providing space for the multitude of new subjectivities, and so on). The threat today is not passivity but pseudo-activity, the urge to "be active," to "participate," to mask the Nothingness of what goes on. People intervene all the time, "do something"; academics participate in meaningless "debates," and so forth, and the truly difficult thing is to step back, to withdraw from all this. Those in power often prefer even a "critical" participation, a dialogue, to silence—just to engage us in a "dialogue," to make sure our ominous passivity is broken.

The anxious expectation that nothing will happen, that capitalism will go on indefinitely, the desperate demand to do something, to revolutionize capitalism, is a fake. The will to revolutionary change emerges as an urge, as an "I cannot do otherwise," or it is worthless. In the terms of Bernard Williams's distinction between *ought* and *must*,[4] an authentic revolution is by definition performed as a Must—it is not something we "ought to do," as an ideal for which we are striving, but something we cannot but do, since we cannot do otherwise. This is why today's Leftist worry that revolution will not occur, that global capitalism will just go on indefinitely, is false insofar as it turns revolution into a moral obligation, into something we ought to do while we fight the inertia of the capitalist present.

The deadlock of "resistance" brings us back to the topic of parallax: all is needed is a slight shift in our perspective, and all the activity of "resistance," of bombarding those in power with impossible "subversive" (ecological, feminist, antiracist, antiglobalist . . .) demands, looks like an internal process of feeding the machine of power, providing the material to keep it in motion. The logic of this shift should be universalized: the split between the public Law and its obscene superego supplement confronts us with the very core of the *politico-ideological parallax*: the public Law and its superego supplement are not two different parts of the legal edifice, they are one and the same "content"—with a slight shift in perspective, the dignified and impersonal Law looks like an obscene machine of *jouissance*. Another slight shift, and the legal regulations prescribing our duties and guaranteeing our rights look like the expression of a ruthless power whose message to us, its subjects, is: "I can do whatever I want with you!" Kafka, of course, was the inimitable master of this parallax shift with regard to the edifice of legal power: "Kafka" is not so much a unique style of writing as a weird innocent new gaze upon the edifice of the Law which practices a parallax shift of perceiving a gigantic machinery of obscene *jouissance* in what previously looked like a dignified edifice of the legal Order.

It was Marx himself who clearly formulated this parallax nature of the excess of power, of power as "in excess" in its very nature. In his analyses of the French Revolution of 1848 (in *The Eighteenth Brumaire* and *The Class Struggles in France*), he "complicated," in a properly dialectical way, the logic of social representation (political agents representing economic classes and forces), going much further than the usual notion of these "complications," according to which political representation never directly mirrors social structure (a single political agent can represent different social groups; a class can renounce its direct representation and leave to another class the job of securing the politico-juridical conditions of its rule, as the English capitalist class did by leaving to the aristocracy the exercise of political power; and so on). Marx's analyses adumbrate what, more than a century later, Lacan defined as the "logic of the signifier." Apropos of the Party of Order which took power when the revolutionary *élan* was over, Marx wrote that the secret of its existence was

> the coalition of Orléanists and Legitimists into one party, disclosed. The bourgeois class fell apart into two big factions which alternately—the big landed proprietors under the restored monarchy and the finance aristocracy and the industrial bourgeoisie under the July Monarchy—had maintained a monopoly of power. Bourbon was the royal name for the predominant influence of the interests of the one faction, Orléans the royal name for the predominant influence of the interests of the other faction—the nameless realm of the republic was the only one in which both factions could maintain with equal power the common class interest without giving up their mutual rivalry.[5]

This, then, is the first complication: when we are dealing with two or more socioeconomic groups, their common interest can be represented only in the guise of the negation of their shared premise—the common denominator of the two royalist factions is not royalism, but republicanism. (And, in the same way, today, the only political agent that could logically be said to represent the interests of capital as such, in its universality, above its particular factions, is Third Way Social Democracy . . . .). Then, in *The Eighteenth Brumaire*, Marx deployed the anatomy of the "Society of December 10," Napoleon's private army of thugs:

> Alongside decayed roués with dubious means of subsistence and of dubious origin, alongside ruined and adventurous offshoots of the bourgeoisie, were vagabonds, discharged soldiers, discharged jailbirds, escaped galley slaves, swindlers, mountebanks, *lazzaroni*, pickpockets, tricksters, gamblers, *maquereaux* [pimps], brothel keepers, porters, literati, organ grinders, ragpickers, knife grinders, tinkers, beggars—in short, the whole indefinite, disintegrated mass, thrown hither and thither, which the French call *la bohème*; from this kindred element Bonaparte formed the core of the Society of December 10. . . . This Bonaparte, who constitutes himself chief of the lumpen proletariat, who here alone rediscovers in mass form the interests which he personally pursues,

who recognizes in this scum, offal, refuse of all classes the only class upon which he can base himself unconditionally, is the real Bonaparte, the Bonaparte *sans phrase*.[6]

The logic of the Party of Order is brought to its radical conclusion here: just as the only common denominator of all royalist factions is republicanism, the only common denominator of all classes is the excremental excess, the refuse/remainder of all classes. That is to say: insofar as Napoleon III perceived himself as standing above class interests, for the reconciliation of all classes, his immediate class base can only be the excremental remainder of all classes, the rejected nonclass of/in each class. And, as Marx goes on to say in another passage, it is this support in the "social abject" which enables Napoleon to run around, permanently shifting his position, representing each class against all the others in turn:

> As the executive authority which has made itself independent, Bonaparte feels it to be his task to safeguard "bourgeois order." But the strength of this bourgeois order lies in the middle class. He poses, therefore, as the representative of the middle class and issues decrees in this sense. Nevertheless, he is somebody solely because he has broken the power of that middle class, and keeps on breaking it daily. He poses, therefore, as the opponent of the political and literary power of the middle class.[7]

Even this, however, is not all. In order for this system to function—in order for Napoleon to stand above classes, and not to act as a direct representative of any one class—he also has to act as the representative of one particular class: of the class which, precisely, is not constituted enough to act as a united agent demanding active representation. This class of people who cannot represent themselves and can thus only be represented is, of course, the class of small-holding peasants:

> The small-holding peasants form an enormous mass whose members live in similar conditions but without entering into manifold relations with each other. Their mode of production isolates them from one another instead of bringing them into mutual intercourse. . . . They are therefore incapable of asserting their class interest in their own name, whether through a parliament or a convention. They cannot represent themselves, they must be represented. Their representative must at the same time appear as their master, as an authority over them, an unlimited governmental power which protects them from the other classes and sends them rain and sunshine from above. The political influence of the small-holding peasants, therefore, finds its final expression in the executive power which subordinates society to itself.[8]

Only these three features together form the paradoxical structure of populist-Bonapartist representation: *standing above* all classes, *shifting among* them, involves a direct reliance on the *abject/remainder of all classes*, plus the ultimate reference to the class of those who are *unable to act as a collective agent demanding political representation*. This paradox is grounded in the constitutive excess of representation over represented. At the level of the Law, state Power merely represents the interests, and so on, of its subjects; it serves them, is answerable to them, and is itself subject to their control; at the level of the superego underside, however, the public message of responsibility, and so forth, is supplemented by the obscene message of the unconditional exercise of Power: "laws do not really bind me, I can do whatever I like to you, I can treat you as guilty if I decide to do so, I can destroy you if I want to. . . ." This obscene excess is a *necessary* constituent of the notion of sovereignty (whose signifier is the Master-Signifier)—the asymmetry here is structural, that is, the law can sustain its authority only if the subjects hear in it the echo of the obscene unconditional self-assertion.

HUMAN RIGHTS VERSUS THE RIGHTS OF THE INHUMAN

This excess brings us to the ultimate *rumspringa* argument against "big" political interventions aimed at global transformation: the terrifying experience of the catastrophes of the twentieth century, of course, the catastrophes which unleashed unprecedented expressions of violence. There are three main versions of theorizing these catastrophes:

1. the one epitomized by the name of Habermas: Enlightenment is in itself a positive emancipatory process with no inherent "totalitarian" potential; these catastrophes are merely an indicator that it remained an unfinished project, so our task should be to bring this project to completion;
2. the one associated with Adorno's and Horkheimer's "dialectic of Enlightenment," as well as, today, with Agamben: the "totalitarian" potential of the Enlightenment is inherent and crucial, the "administered world" is the truth of Enlightenment, the twentieth-century concentration camps and genocides were a kind of negative-teleological endpoint of the entire history of the West;
3. the third one, developed in the works of Étienne Balibar, among others: modernity opens up a field of new freedoms, but at the same time of new dangers, and there is no ultimate teleological guarantee of the outcome; the battle is open, undecided.

The starting point of Balibar's remarkable entry on "Violence"[9] is the inadequacy of the classic Hegelian-Marxist notion of "converting" violence into an instrument of historical Reason, a force which begets a new social formation: the "irrational" brutality of violence is thus *aufgehoben*, "sublated" in the strict Hegelian sense, reduced to a particular stain that contributes to the overall harmony of the historical progress. The twentieth century confronted us with catastrophes, some directed against Marxist political forces and some generated by Marxist political engagement itself, which cannot be "rationalized" in this way: their instrumentalization into tools of the Cunning of Reason is not only ethically unacceptable, but also theoretically wrong, *ideological* in the strongest sense of the term. In his close reading of Marx, Balibar nonetheless discerns in his texts an oscillation between this teleological "conversion" theory of violence and a much more interesting notion of history as an open-undecided process of antagonistic struggles whose final "positive" outcome is not guaranteed by any encompassing historical Necessity (the society of the future will be communism or barbarism, and so on).

Balibar argues that, for necessary structural reasons, Marxism is unable to think the excess of violence that cannot be integrated into the narrative of historical Progress—more specifically, that it cannot provide an adequate theory of Fascism and Stalinism and their "extreme" outcomes, shoah and Gulag. Our task is therefore double: to develop a theory of historical violence as something which cannot be mastered/instrumentalized by any political agent, which threatens to engulf this agent itself into a self-destructive vicious cycle, and—the other side of the same task—to pose the question of "civilizing" revolutions, of how to make the revolutionary process itself a "civilizing" force. Remember the infamous Saint Bartholomew's Day Massacre—what went wrong there? Catherine de Medici's goal was limited and precise: hers was a Macchiavellian plot to have Admiral de Coligny, a powerful Protestant pushing for war with Spain in the Netherlands, assassinated, and let the blame fall on the overpowerful Catholic Guise family. In this way, Catherine hoped that the final outcome would be the fall of both houses that posed a menace to the unity of the French state. This ingenious plan to play her enemies off against each other degenerated into an uncontrolled frenzy of blood: in her ruthless pragmatism, Catherine was blind to the passion with which people clung to their beliefs.

Hannah Arendt's insights are also crucial here: she has emphasized the distinction between political power and the mere exercise of (social) violence: organizations run by direct nonpolitical authority—by an order of command that is not politically grounded authority (Army, Church, school)—represent examples of violence (Gewalt), not of political Power in the strict sense of the term.[10] Here, however, it would be useful to introduce the distinction between the public symbolic Law and its obscene supplement: the notion of the obscene superego double-supplement of Power implies that there is no Power without violence. Power always has to rely on an obscene stain of violence; political space is never "pure," but always involves some kind of reliance on "prepolitical" violence. Of course, the relationship between political power and prepolitical violence is one of mutual implication: not only is violence the necessary supplement of power, (political) power itself is always-already at the root of every apparently "nonpolitical" relationship of violence. The accepted violence and direct relationship of subordination in the Army, the Church, the family, and other "nonpolitical" social forms is in itself the "reification" of a certain ethico-political struggle and decision—what a critical analysis should do is to discern the hidden political process that sustains all these "non-" or "prepolitical" relationships. In human society, the political is the encompassing structuring principle, so that every neutralization of some partial content as "nonpolitical" is a political gesture par excellence.

The excessive-violence argument nonetheless retains its power: often, we cannot but be shocked by excessive indifference toward suffering, even and especially when this suffering is widely reported in the media and condemned, as if it is the very outrage at suffering which turns us into its immobilized fascinated spectators. Remember, in the early 1990s, the three-year siege of Sarajevo, with the population starving, exposed to permanent shelling and sniper fire. The big enigma here is: although all the media were full of pictures and reports, why did not the UN forces, NATO, or the USA accomplish just one small act of *breaking the siege of Sarajevo*, of imposing a corridor through which people and provisions could circulate freely? It would have cost nothing: with a little serious pressure on the Serb forces, the prolonged spectacle of encircled Sarajevo exposed to ridiculous terror would have been over. There is only one answer to this enigma, the one proposed by Rony Brauman who, on behalf of the Red Cross, coordinated the help to Sarajevo: the very presentation of the crisis of Sarajevo as "humanitarian," the very recasting of the political-military conflict into humanitarian terms, was sustained by an eminently *political* choice: that of, basically, taking the Serb side in the conflict. Especially ominous and manipulative here was the role of François Mitterrand:

> The celebration of "humanitarian intervention" in Yugoslavia took the place of a political discourse, disqualifying in advance all conflicting debate. . . . It was apparently not possible, for François Mitterrand, to express his analysis of the war in Yugoslavia. With the strictly humanitarian response, he discovered an unexpected source of communication or, more precisely, of cosmetics, which is a little bit the same thing. . . . Mitterrand remained in favor of the maintenance of Yugoslavia within its borders and was persuaded that only a strong Serbian power was in the position to guarantee a certain stability in this explosive region. This position rapidly became unacceptable in the eyes of the French people. All the bustling activity and the humanitarian discourse permitted him to reaffirm the unfailing commitment of France to the Rights of Man in the end, and to mimic an opposition to Greater Serbian fascism, all in giving it free rein. [11]

From this specific insight, we should move on to the general level and consider the problem of the very depoliticized humanitarian politics of "Human Rights" as the ideology of military interventionism serving specific economic-political purposes. As Wendy Brown argues apropos of Michael Ignatieff, such humanitarianism "presents itself as something of an antipolitics—a pure defense of the innocent and the powerless against power, a pure defense of the individual against immense and potentially cruel or despotic machineries of culture, state, war, ethnic conflict, tribalism, patriarchy, and other mobilizations or instantiations of collective power against individuals." [12] The question, however, is: "what kind of politicization [those who intervene on behalf of human rights] set in motion against the powers they oppose. Do they stand for a different formulation of justice or do they stand in opposition to collective justice projects?" [13] It is clear, for example, that the US overthrow of Saddam Hussein, legitimized in terms of ending the suffering of the Iraqi people, was not only motivated by other political-economic interests (oil), but also based on a specific idea of the political and economic conditions that should open up the perspective of freedom to the Iraqi people (Western liberal democracy, guarantee of private property, inclusion in the global market economy, and so on). Thus the purely humanitarian antipolitical politics of merely preventing suffering amounts in effect to the implicit prohibition of elaborating a positive collective project of sociopolitical transformation.

At an even more general level, we should problematize the very opposition between universal (prepolitical) Human Rights which belong to every human being "as such," and specific political rights of a citizen, a member of a particular political community; in this sense, Balibar argues for the "*reversal of the historical and theoretical relationship between 'man' and 'citizen'*" which proceeds by "explaining how *man is made by citizenship* and not citizenship by man."[14] Here Balibar cites Hannah Arendt's insight apropos of the twentieth-century phenomenon of refugees: "The conception of human rights based upon the assumed existence of a human being as such broke down at the very moment when those who professed to believe in it were for the first time confronted with people who had indeed lost all other qualities and specific relationships—except that they were still human."[15] This line, of course, leads straight to Agamben's notion of *Homo sacer* as a human being reduced to "bare life":[16] in a properly Hegelian paradoxical dialectics of universal and particular, it is precisely when a human being is deprived of his particular sociopolitical identity, the basis of his specific citizenship, that he, in one and the same move, is no longer recognized and/or treated as human. In short, the paradox is that one is deprived of human rights precisely when one is in effect, in one's social reality, reduced to a human being "in general," without citizenship, profession, and so on—that is to say, *precisely when one in effect becomes the ideal bearer of "universal human rights"* (which belong to me "independently of" my profession, sex, citizenship, religion, ethnic identity . . .).

So we arrive at a classic "postmodern," "anti-essentialist" position, a kind of political version of Foucault's notion of sex as generated by a multitude of the practices of sexuality: "man," the bearer of Human Rights, is generated by a set of political practices which materialize citizenship—however, is this enough? Jacques Rancière[17] has proposed a very elegant and precise solution of the antinomy between Human Rights (belonging to "man as such") and the politicization of citizens: while Human Rights cannot be posited as an unhistorical "essentialist" Beyond in contrast to the contingent sphere of political struggles, as universal "natural rights of man" exempted from history, neither should they be dismissed as a reified fetish which is a product of concrete historical processes of the politicization of citizens. Thus the gap between the universality of Human Rights and the political rights of citizens is not a gap between the universality of man and a specific political sphere; rather, it "separates the whole of the community from itself," as Rancière put it, in a precise Hegelian way.[18] Far from being prepolitical, "universal Human Rights" designate the precise space of politicization proper: what they amount to is *the right to universality as such*, the right of a political agent to assert its radical noncoincidence with itself (in its particular identity), that is, to posit itself—precisely insofar as it is the "supernumerary" one, the "part of no-part," the one without a proper place in the social edifice—as an agent of universality of the Social as such. The paradox is therefore a very precise one, and symmetrical to the paradox of universal human rights as the rights of those reduced to inhumanity: *at the very moment when we try to conceive political rights of citizens without reference to universal "meta-political" Human Rights, we lose politics itself*: we reduce politics to a "postpolitical" play of negotiation of particular interests.

What happens to Human Rights, then, when they are reduced to the rights of *Homo sacer*, of those excluded from the political community, reduced to "bare life"—that is to say, when they become useless since they are the rights of those who, precisely, have no rights, are treated as inhuman? Here Rancière suggests a very striking dialectical reversal:

when they are of no use, you do the same as charitable persons do with their old clothes. You give them to the poor. Those rights that appear to be useless in their place are sent abroad, along with medicine and clothes, to people deprived of medicine, clothes, and rights. It is in this way, as the result of this process, that the Rights of Man become the rights of those who have no rights, the rights of bare human beings subjected to inhuman repression and inhuman conditions of existence. They become humanitarian rights, the rights of those who cannot enact them, the victims of the absolute denial of right. For all this, they are not void. Political names and political places never become merely void. The void is filled by somebody or something else. . . . If those who suffer inhuman repression are unable to enact Human Rights that are their last recourse, then somebody else has to inherit their rights in order to enact them in their place. This is what is called the "right to humanitarian interference"—a right that some nations assume to the supposed benefit of victimized populations, and very often against the advice of the humanitarian organizations themselves. The "right to humanitarian interference" might be described as a sort of "return to sender": the disused rights that had been send to the rightless are sent back to the senders.[19]

So, to put it in Leninist terms: what the "Human Rights of suffering Third World victims" *actually means* today, in the predominant Western discourse, is the right of Western powers themselves to intervene—politically, economically, culturally, militarily—in Third World countries of their choice on behalf of the defense of Human Rights. A reference to Lacan's formula of communication (in which the sender gets back from the receiver–addressee his own message in its inverted—that is, true—form) is absolutely relevant: in the reigning discourse of humanitarian interventionism, the developed West is, in effect, getting back from the victimized Third World its own message in its true form. And the moment Human Rights are depoliticized in this way, the discourse about them has to resort to ethics: reference to the prepolitical opposition of Good and Evil has to be mobilized. Today's "new reign of Ethics,"[20] clearly discernible in, for example, Michael Ignatieff's work, thus relies on a violent gesture of depoliticization, of denying the victimized other any political subjectivization. And, as Rancière pointed out, liberal humanitarianism à *la* Ignatieff unexpectedly meets the "radical" position of Foucault or Agamben on this depoliticization: the Foucauldian-Agambenian notion of "biopolitics" as the culmination of the whole of Western thought ends up getting caught in a kind of "ontological trap" in which concentration camps appear as a kind of "ontological destiny: each of us would be in the situation of the refugee in a camp. Any difference grows faint between democracy and totalitarianism and any political practice proves to be already ensnared in the biopolitical trap."[21]

When, in a shift from Foucault, Agamben identifies sovereign power and biopolitics (in today's generalized state of exception, the two overlap), he thus precludes the very possibility of the emergence of political subjectivity. The rise of political subjectivity, however, takes place against the background of a certain limit of the "inhuman," so that we should continue to endorse the paradox of the inhumanity of human being deprived of citizenship, and posit the "inhuman" pure man as a necessary excess of humanity over itself, its "indivisible remainder," a kind of Kantian limit-concept of the phenomenal notion of humanity. So, just as, in Kant's philosophy, the sublime Noumenal, when we come too close to it, appears as pure horror, man "as such," deprived of all phenomenal qualifications, appears as an inhuman monster, something like Kafka's Odradek. The problem with human rights humanism is that it covers up this monstrosity of the "human as such," presenting it as a sublime human essence.

How, then, do we find a way out of this deadlock? Balibar ends with an ambiguous reference to Mahatma Gandhi. It is true that Gandhi's formula "Be yourself the change you would like to see in the world" encapsulates perfectly the basic attitude of emancipatory change: do not wait for the "objective process" to generate the expected/desired change, since if you just wait for it, it will never come; instead, throw yourself into it, be this change, take the risk of enacting it directly upon yourself. Is not the ultimate limitation of Gandhi's strategy, however, that it works only against a liberal-democratic regime which abides by certain minimal ethico-political standards—in which, to put it in emotive terms, those in power still "have a conscience"? Recall Gandhi's reply, in the late 1930s, to the question of what the Jews in Germany should do against Hitler: they should commit mass suicide, and thus arouse the conscience of the world. . . . We can easily imagine the Nazi reaction to this: OK, we'll help you—where do you want the poison delivered to?

There is another way, however, in which Balibar's plea for renouncing violence can be given a specific twist—that of what I am tempted to call Bartleby politics. Recall the two symmetrically opposed modes of the "living dead," of finding oneself in the uncanny place "between the two deaths": one is either biologically dead while symbolically alive (surviving one's biological death as a spectral apparition or symbolic authority of the Name), or symbolically dead while biologically alive (those who are excluded from the sociosymbolic order, from Antigone to today's *Homo sacer*). And what if we apply the same logic to the opposition of violence and nonviolence, identifying two modes of their intersection?[22] We all know the pop-psychological notion of "passive-aggressive behavior," usually applied to a housewife who, instead of actively opposing her husband, passively sabotages him. And this brings us back to where we began: perhaps we should assert this attitude of passive aggression as a proper radical political gesture, in contrast to aggressive passivity, the standard "interpassive" mode of our participation in socio-ideological life in which we are active all the time in order to make sure that nothing will happen, that nothing will really change. In such a constellation, the first truly critical ("aggressive," violent) step is to withdraw into passivity, to refuse to participate—Bartleby's "I would prefer not to" is the necessary first step which, as it were, clears the ground, opens up the place, for true activity, for an act that will actually change the coordinates of the constellation.

How does the counterpoint to Bartleby politics, the impotent *passage à l'acte*, look today? A classic Hollywood action film is always a good illustration. Toward the end of Andrew Davis's *The Fugitive*, the innocent-persecuted doctor (Harrison Ford) confronts at a large medical convention his colleague (Jeroem Kraabe), accusing him of falsifying medical data on behalf of a large pharmaceutical company. At this precise point, when we would expect a shift to the company—corporate capital—as the real culprit, Kraabe interrupts his talk, invites Ford to step aside, and then, outside the convention hall, they engage in a passionate violent fight, beating one another until their faces are streaming with blood. The openly ridiculous character of this scene is revealing—it is as if, in order to get out of the ideological mess of playing with anticapitalism, one has to make a move which directly opens up the cracks in the narrative for all to see. Another aspect here is the transformation of the bad guy into a vicious, sneering, pathological character, as if psychological depravity (which accompanies the dazzling spectacle of the fight) should replace the anonymous nonpsychological drive of capital: the much more appropriate gesture would have been to present the corrupt colleague as a psychologically sincere and privately honest doctor who, because of the financial difficulties of the hospital in which he works, was lured into swallowing the pharmaceutical company's bait.

Thus *The Fugitive* provides a clear instance of the violent *passage à l'acte* serving as a lure, a vehicle of ideological displacement. A step further from this zero-level of violence is taken in Paul Schrader's and Martin Scorsese's *Taxi Driver*, in the final outburst of Travis (Robert de Niro) against the pimps who control the young girl he wants to save (Jodie Foster). The implicitly suicidal dimension of this *passage à l'acte* is crucial: when Travis prepares for his attack, he practices drawing the gun in front of a mirror; in what became the best-known scene in the film, he addresses his own image in the mirror with the aggressive-condescending "You talkin' to me?" In a textbook illustration of Lacan's notion of the "mirror stage," the aggression here is clearly aimed at oneself, at one's own mirror-image. This suicidal dimension reemerges at the end of the slaughter scene when Travis, heavily wounded and leaning against the wall, mimics with the forefinger of his right hand a gun aimed at his bloodstained forehead and mockingly triggers it, as if saying: "The real aim of my outburst was myself." The paradox of Travis is that he perceives *himself* as part of the degenerate dirt of the city life he wants to eradicate, so that—as Brecht put it apropos of revolutionary violence in *The Measure Taken*—he wants to be the last piece of dirt with whose removal the room will be clean.

Far from indicating an imperialist arrogance, such "irrational" outbursts of violence—one of the key topics of American culture and ideology—stand, rather, for an implicit admission of impotence: their very violence, display of destructive power, is to be conceived as the mode of appearance of its very opposite—if anything, they are exemplary cases of the impotent *passage à l'acte*. As such, these outbursts enable us to discern the hidden obverse of the much-praised American individualism and self-reliance: the secret awareness that we are all helplessly thrown around by forces out of our control. There is a wonderful early short story by Patricia Highsmith, "Button," about a middle-class New Yorker who lives with his nine-year-old Down's syndrome son, who babbles meaningless sounds all the time and smiles, saliva running out of his open mouth; late one evening, unable to endure the situation any longer, he decides to take a walk on the lonely Manhattan streets. Here he stumbles upon a destitute homeless beggar, who pleadingly extends his hand toward him; in an act of inexplicable fury, the hero beats the beggar to death and tears a button off his jacket. Afterward, he returns home a changed man, enduring his family nightmare without any traumas, even capable of a kind smile at his handicapped son; he keeps the button in the pocket of his trousers all the time—a remainder that, once at least, he did strike back against his miserable destiny.

Highsmith is at her best when even such a violent outburst fails, as in what could be considered her single greatest achievement, *Those Who Walk Away*: in this book she took crime fiction, the most "narrative" genre of them all, and imbued it with the inertia of the Real, the lack of resolution, the dragging-on of "empty time," which characterize the stupid factuality of life. In Rome, Ed Coleman tries to murder Ray Garrett, a failed painter and gallery-owner in his late twenties, his son-in-law, whom he blames for the recent suicide of his only child, Peggy, Ray's wife. Rather than flee, Ray follows Ed to Venice, where Ed is wintering with Inez, his girlfriend. What follows is Highsmith's paradigmatic agony of the symbiotic relationship between two men who are inextricably linked to one another in their very hatred. Ray himself is haunted by a sense of guilt for his wife's death, so he exposes himself to Ed's violent intentions. Echoing his death wish, he accepts from Ed a lift in a motorboat; in the middle of the lagoon, Ed pushes Ray overboard. Ray pretends he is actually dead, and assumes a false name and another identity, thus experiencing both exhilarating freedom and overwhelming emptiness. He is roaming like a living dead through the cold streets of wintry Venice when. . . . Here we have a crime novel with no murder, just failed attempts at it: there is no clear resolution at the end—except, perhaps, the resigned acceptance of both Ray and Ed that they are condemned to haunt one another to the end.

Today, with the global American ideological offensive, the fundamental insight of movies like John Ford's *Searchers* and *Taxi Driver* is more relevant than ever: we witness the resurgence of the figure of the "quiet American," a naive benevolent agent who sincerely wants to bring democracy and Western freedom to the Vietnamese—it is just that his intentions totally misfire, or, as Graham Greene put it: "I never knew a man who had better motives for all the trouble he caused." So Freud was right in his prescient analysis of Woodrow Wilson, the US President who exemplifies the American humanitarian interventionist attitude: the underlying dimension of aggression could not escape him.

The key event of John O'Hara's *Appointment in Samarra* (1934) occurs at a Christmas dinner party at the Lantenengo Country Club, where the novel's tragic hero, twenty-nine-year-old Julian English, a wealthy and popular car-dealership owner, throws a drink in the face of Harry Reilly, the richest man in town. Because of this, he becomes embroiled in a serious social scandal, and it seems that nothing will right it—the novel ends with Julian's pitiful suicide in a car. As Julian claims in the ensuing conflict over the drink-throwing, he did not do it because Harry was the richest man in town, nor because he was a social climber, and certainly not because was Catholic—yet all these reasons do play a part in his violent *passage à l'acte*. In the ensuing flashback, Julian remembers the times when his youth gang would play Ku Klux Klan after seeing *Birth of a Nation*, their distrust of Jews, and so on. In the Hollywood of the last two decades, there are numerous examples of such impotent "strikings out," from Russell Banks's *Affliction* to John Sayles's *Lone Star*.

Lone Star provides a unique insight into the twists of the "Oedipal" dynamics. In a small Texas border town, a long-dead body is discovered: that of Wade, a cruel and utterly corrupt sheriff who mysteriously disappeared decades ago. The present sheriff who pursues the investigation is the son of the sheriff who replaced Wade, and was fêted by the city as a hero who brought order and prosperity to it; however, since Wade disappeared just after a public conflict with the sheriff who replaced him, all the signs seem to indicate that Wade was killed by his successor. Driven by a properly Oedipal hatred, the present sheriff thus tries to undermine the myth of his father by demonstrating that his rule was based on murder. We are dealing with three, not two, generations. Wade (superbly played by Kris Kristofferson) is a kind of Freudian "primordial father," an obscene and cruel master of the city who violates every law, simply shooting people who do not pay him; the hero's father's crime should thus be a law-founding crime, the excess—the illegal killing of a corrupt master—which enabled the rule of law. At the end of the film, however, we learn that the crime was not committed by the hero's father: while he is innocent of the murder of Wade, he brought corruption to a more "civilized" level, replacing the outright brutal corruption of his "larger-than-life" predecessor with a corruption entwined with business interests (just "fixing" things here and there, and so on). And it is in this replacement of the big "ethical" founding crime with minor corruption that the finesse of the film lies: the hero who wanted to unearth the big secret of his father's founding crime learns that, far from being a heroic figure whose illegal violence grounded the rule of law, his father was just a successful opportunist like all the others. . . . Consequently, the final message of the film is "Forget the Alamo!" (the last words of dialogue): let us abandon the search for big founding events, and let bygones be bygones. The key to the film's underlying libidinal economy is to be found in the duality between the hero's father (the law-and-order figure) and Wade, the obscene primordial father, the libidinal focus of the film, the figure of excessive enjoyment whose murder is the central event—and does not the hero's obsession with unmasking his father's guilt betray his deep solidarity with the obscene figure of Wade?

Clint Eastwood's *Mystic River* stands out here because of the unique twist it gives to such violent *passages à l'acte*. When they were kids growing up together in a rough area of Boston, Jimmy Markum (Sean Penn), Dave Boyle (Tim Robbins), and Sean Devine (Kevin Bacon) spent their days playing stickball on the street. Nothing much out of the ordinary ever happened, until a spur-of-the-moment decision drastically altered the course of each of their lives forever. This primordial, "founding," act of violence that sets the cycle in motion is the kidnapping and serial raping of the adolescent Dave, performed by the local policeman on behalf of a priest—two people standing for the two key state apparatuses, police and Church, the repressive one and the ideological one, "the Army and the Church" mentioned by Freud in *Crowd Psychology and the Analysis of the Ego*. Today, twenty-five years later, the three find themselves thrust back together by another tragic event: the murder of Jimmy's nineteen-year-old daughter. Now a cop, Sean is assigned to the case, while, in the wake of the sudden and terrible loss of his child, Jimmy's mind becomes consumed with revenge. Caught up in the maelstrom is Dave, now a lost and broken man fighting to keep his demons at bay. As the investigation creeps closer to home, Dave's wife Celeste becomes consumed by suspicion and fear, and finally tells Jimmy about it. Two murders then occur as the frustrated acting-out: Dave kills a man engaged in homosexual activity with a boy in a car; Jimmy kills Dave, convinced that he murdered his daughter. Immediately afterward, Jimmy is informed by Sean that the police have found the real killer—he has killed the wrong man, his close friend.

The movie ends with a weird scene of family redemption: Jimmy's wife, Annabeth, draws her family tightly together in order to weather the storm. In a long emotional speech, she restores Jimmy's self-confidence by praising him as the strong and reliable head of the family, always ready to do the necessary tough things to protect the family haven. Although this symbolic reconciliation, this *Aufhebung* of the catastrophe of killing the wrong man, superficially succeeds (the last scene shows Penn's family watching the Irish parade, restored as a "normal" family), it could be said to be the strongest indictment of the redemptive power of family ties: the lesson of the film is not that "family ties heal all wounds," that the family is a safe haven enabling us to survive the most horrendous traumas, but—quite the opposite—that the family is a monstrous ideological machine that makes us blind to the most horrendous crimes we commit. Far from bringing any catharsis, the ending is thus an absolute anti-catharsis, leaving us, the spectators, with the bitter realization that nothing is really resolved, that we are witnessing an obscene travesty of the ethical core of the family.[23] (The only similar scene that comes to mind is the finale of John Ford's *Fort Apache*, in which John Wayne praises in front of the assembled journalists the noble heroism of Henry Fonda, a cruel general who died in a meaningless attack on the Indians.) And perhaps this is all we can do today, in our dark era: reveal the failure of all attempts at redemption, the obscene travesty of every gesture of reconciling us with the violence we are forced to commit. Perhaps Job is the proper hero today: the one who refuses to find any deeper meaning in the suffering he encounters.

THE IGNORANCE OF THE CHICKEN

These vicissitudes of violence (violent outbursts as symptomatic of a fundamental passivity; withdrawal into inactivity as the most radical violent gesture) are reminiscent

of the diagnosis of the twentieth century put forward long ago by the archconserva-
tive William Butler Yeats:

The blood-dimmed tide is loosed, and everywhere
The ceremony of innocence is drowned;
The best lack all conviction, while the worst
Are full of passionate intensity. ("The Second Coming," 1920)

The key to this diagnosis is contained in the phrase "ceremony of innocence," which
is to be taken in the precise sense of Edith Wharton's "age of innocence": Newton's
wife, the "innocent" to whom the title refers, was not a naive believer in her husband's
fidelity—she knew very well that he was passionately in love with Countess Olenska,
she just politely ignored it, and staged her belief in his fidelity. . . .

In one of the Marx Brothers' films, Groucho Marx, caught out in a lie, answers angrily: "Whom do you believe, your eyes or my words?" This apparently absurd logic
perfectly expresses the functioning of the symbolic order, in which the symbolic
mask-mandate maters more than the direct reality of the individual who wears this
mask and/or assumes this mandate. This functioning involves the structure of fetishist
disavowal: "I know very well that things are the way I see them [that this person is a
corrupt weakling], but nonetheless I treat him with respect, since he wears the in-
signia of a judge, so that when he speaks, it is the Law itself which speaks through
him."[24] So, in a way, I actually believe his words, not my eyes: I believe in Another Space
(the domain of pure symbolic authority) which matters more than the reality of its
spokesmen. Thus the cynical reduction to reality is inadequate: when a judge speaks,
there is in a way more truth in his words (the words of the Institution of Law) than
there is in the direct reality of the person of the judge—if one limits oneself to what
one sees, one simply misses the point. This paradox is what Lacan aims at with his
"les non-dupes errent": those who do not let themselves be caught in symbolic deception/
fiction, and continue to believe their eyes, are the ones who err most. What a cynic
who "believes only his eyes" misses is the efficiency of the symbolic fiction, the way
this fiction structures our experience of reality. The same gap is at work in our most
intimate relationship to our neighbors: we behave as if we do not know that they also
smell bad, secrete excrement, and so on—a minimum of idealization, of fetishizing
disavowal, is the basis of our coexistence.

And does not the same disavowal account for the sublime beauty of the idealizing
gesture discernible from Anne Frank to American Communists who believed in the
Soviet Union? Although we know that Stalinist Communism was an appalling thing,
we nonetheless admire the victims of the McCarthy witch-hunt who heroically persisted in their belief in Communism and support for the Soviet Union. The logic here
is the same as that of Anne Frank who, in her diaries, expresses belief in the ultimate
goodness of man despite of the horrors perpetrated against Jews in the Second World
War: what makes such an assertion of belief (in the essential goodness of Man; in the
truly human character of the Soviet regime) sublime is the very gap between it and

the overwhelming factual evidence against it, that is, the active will to disavow the actual state of things. Perhaps this is the most elementary metaphysical gesture: this refusal to accept the Real in all its idiocy, to disavow it and to search for Another World behind it. Thus the big Other is the order of the lie, of lying sincerely. And it is in this sense that "the best lack all conviction, while the worst are full of passionate intensity": even the best are no longer able to sustain their symbolic innocence, their full engagement in the symbolic ritual, while "the worst," the mob, engage in (racist, religious, sexist . . .) fanaticism. Is this opposition not a good description of today's split between tolerant but anemic liberals, and fundamentalists full of "passionate intensity"?

This brings us to the formula of fundamentalism: what is foreclosed from the symbolic (belief) returns in the Real (of a direct knowledge). A fundamentalist does not believe, he knows directly. To put it in another way: both liberal-skeptical cynicism and fundamentalism thus share a basic underlying feature: the loss of the ability to believe in the proper sense of the term. For both of them, religious statements are quasi-empirical statements of direct knowledge: fundamentalists accept them as such, while skeptical cynics mock them. What is unthinkable for them is the "absurd" act of decision which installs every authentic belief, a decision which cannot be grounded in the chain of "reasons," in positive knowledge: the "sincere hypocrisy" of somebody like Anne Frank who, as we have seen, in the face of the terrifying depravity of the Nazis, in a true act of credo quia absurdum asserted her belief in the fundamental goodness of all humans. No wonder religious fundamentalists are among the most passionate digital hackers, and always prone to combine their religion with the latest scientific results: for them, religious statements and scientific statements belong to the same modality of positive knowledge. (In this sense, the status of "universal human rights" is also that of a pure belief: they cannot be grounded in our knowledge of human nature, they are an axiom posited by our decision.) We are thus compelled to draw the paradoxical conclusion: in the opposition between traditional secular humanists and religious fundamentalists, it is the humanists who stand for belief, while the fundamentalists stand for knowledge—in short, the true danger of fundamentalism lies not in the fact that it poses a threat to secular scientific knowledge, but in the fact that it poses a threat to authentic belief itself.

The first lesson here is that the choice imposed by the ruling ideology ("fundamentalism versus liberalism") is not a real one: we always have to look for a tertium datur. One of the topoi of the theories of second modernity or reflexive "risk society" is that today, we are all exposed to too many choices: we are subjected to a true tyranny of choices, best exemplified by what we often experience when we book a hotel room—our reservation is confirmed only after we have answered a barrage of questions, and made a series of choices: "Smoking or non-smoking? Newspaper in the morning? Room-service breakfast? Soft or hard pillow? . . ." This appearance of choice, however, should not deceive us: it is the mode of appearance of its very opposite: of the absence of any real choice with regard to the fundamental structure of society. (In the case of a hotel reservation, one has to find a hotel. . . .)[25] So when, today, we are confronted with an ethical dilemma like the famous one evoked by Sartre in his example of a young man in Vichy France, torn between the obligation to take care of his sick old mother and the desire to join the Resistance, we are tempted to offer the following spontaneous reaction: "I will tell my mother that I have to leave her and go fight for the Resistance, and I will tell my Resistance contact that I have to take care of my mother and thus cannot join them, while I stay at home and duck out of the war!" The ruling ideology imposes a forced choice on us: we are free to choose only if we make the right choice ("democracy or terror"—who would choose terror?); the choice of the radical political act, however, is no less forced—we "are chosen to choose," we are no less *obliged* to do what we do, so that the choice today is between two forced choices. As they put it in a recent Hollywood court drama (*Confession*, David Jones 1999): it is not difficult to do the right thing, but to find out what the right thing is—once I know what the right thing is, it is difficult *not* to do it.

Consequently, the first rule of properly dialectical sociopolitical analysis is that *the Two (the basic antagonism) as a rule always has to appear as three*: the way a given sociopolitical field is explicitly structured, the open struggle which defines its dynamics, is never the "true" underlying antagonism—if we are to unearth the force which is the only stand-in for this antagonism, we have to look for a *third* agent. This rule has held from ancient China to today's late capitalism. The ideological constellation in ancient China was dominated by the opposition between Confucianism (reliance on traditional customs, authority, and education) and Taoism (spontaneous self-enlightenment)—with the uncanny *third* position of "legalists" rehabilitated by Mao Zedong, partisans of egalitarian revolutionary terror. In our perception, today's ideological constellation is determined by the opposition between neoconservative fundamentalist populism and liberal multiculturalism—both parasitizing on each other, both precluding any alternative to the system as such. And this enables us to propose the correct formal concept of a "revolutionary situation": a situation in which, exceptionally and momentarily, the antagonism *appears* as such, is directly "experienced"; in which the masks of the official ideological struggle fall off, the official opponents discover their "deeper solidarity" and start to share their concerns, and the situation is reduced to its true underlying antagonism—there are no longer conservatives and progressives, totalitarians and democrats, legalists and populists, fundamentalists and liberals, and all other false oppositions—there are only Us and Them.[26]

The second lesson to be learned from Yeats concerns the status of symbolic fictions. Recall the United Nations murder scene from Hitchcock's *North by Northwest*: at the very moment when Cary Grant is engaged in a conversation with the senior UN diplomat, the murderer, hidden behind the two of them in a corridor, throws a knife into the diplomat's back; the diplomat stops in the midst of a lively conversation, his eyes bulge out, and he falls forward into Grant's lap; Grant automatically grabs the knife from his back, and at that very moment a photographer who happens to be nearby takes a shot of him. This photo soon appears on the front pages of all the newspapers, a "proof" of guilt, depicting the murderer holding the weapon in his hand immediately after the killing. . . . This scene does not only tell us a lot about the falsity of photographic documents; like all cases of deceptive appearances, its very falsity contains a grain of (libidinal) truth—in this case, the truth of the parricide.

"The truth has the structure of a fiction"—is there a better exemplification of this thesis than cartoons in which the truth about the existing social order is depicted in a direct way which would never be allowed in narrative cinema with "real" actors? Think of the image of society we get from aggressive cartoons in which animals fight: ruthless struggle for survival, brutal traps and attacks, exploiting others as suckers . . . if the same story were to be told in a feature film with "real" actors, it would undoubtedly be either censored or dismissed as ridiculously overpessimistic.[27] Is not the ultimate confirmation of this paradox that of the Nazi concentration camps? The accepted notion is that we escape into fiction when a direct confrontation with reality is too traumatic to be borne—however, does not the fate of artistic depictions of the Holocaust support the opposite view? Horrible as they are, we are able to watch documentaries about the Holocaust, to look at documents about this catastrophe, while there is something fake in all attempts to provide a "realistic" narrative fiction of events in the extermination camps. This fact is more mysterious than it may appear: how it is that it is easier to watch a documentary about Auschwitz than to produce a convincing fictional portrait of what went on there? Why are all the best films about *shoah* comedies? Here we should correct Adorno: it is not poetry but, rather, *prose* which is impossible after Auschwitz. Documentary realism is therefore for those who cannot bear fiction—the excess of fantasy operative in every narrative fiction. It is the realistic prose which fails, while the poetic evocation of the unbearable atmosphere in a camp is much more to the point. That is to say: when Adorno declares poetry impossible after Auschwitz, this impossibility is an enabling impossibility: poetry is always, by definition, "about" something that cannot be addressed directly, only alluded to. And we should not be afraid to go a step further here and refer to the old saying that music enters when words fail: what if there is some truth in the common wisdom that, in a kind of historical premonition, the music of Schoenberg articulated the anxieties and nightmares of Auschwitz before the event took place?[28]

"Fundamentalism" thus concerns neither belief as such nor its content; what distinguishes a "fundamentalist" is the way he relates to his beliefs; its most elementary definition should focus on the *formal status of belief*. In "Faith and Knowledge,"[29] Derrida explores the inherent link between these two terms: knowledge always relies on a preceding elementary act of faith (in the symbolic order, in the basic rationality of the universe), while religion itself relies increasingly on scientific knowledge, although it disavows this reliance (the use of modern media for the propagation of religions, religious exploitation of the newest scientific advances, and so on). Perhaps this link reaches its apogee in New Age cyber-Gnosticism, that is, spirituality grounded in the digitalization and virtualization of our life-world. What if we add another twist to this link—what if neo-obscurantist faith in all its versions, from conspiracy theories to irrational mysticism, emerges when faith itself, basic reliance on the big Other, the symbolic order, fails? Is this not the case today?[30]

For decades, a classic joke has been circulating among Lacanians to exemplify the key role of the Other's knowledge: a man who believes himself to be a grain of seed is taken to a mental institution where the doctors do their best to convince him that he is not a grain of seed but a man; however, when he is cured (convinced that he is not a grain of seed but a man) and allowed to leave the hospital, he immediately comes back, trembling and very scared—there is a chicken outside the door, and he is afraid it will eat him. "My dear fellow," says his doctor, "you know very well that you are not a grain of seed but a man." "Of course I know," replies the patient, "but does the chicken?" That is the true stake of psychoanalytic treatment: it is not enough to convince the patient of the unconscious truth of his symptoms; the Unconscious itself must be induced to accept this truth. This is where Hannibal Lecter himself, that proto-Lacanian, was wrong: it is not the silence of the lambs but the ignorance of the chicken that is the subject's true traumatic core. . . .

Does not exactly the same hold for Marxian commodity fetishism? Here are again the first lines of subdivision 4 of chapter 1 of *Capital*, on "The Fetishism of the Commodity and its Secret": "A commodity appears at first sight an extremely obvious, trivial thing. But its analysis brings out that it is a very strange thing, abounding in metaphysical subtleties and theological niceties."[31] These lines should surprise us, since they invert the standard procedure of demystifying a theological myth, reducing it to its earthly base: Marx does not claim, in the usual way of Enlightenment critique, that critical analysis should demonstrate how what appears to be a mysterious theological entity emerged out of the "ordinary" real-life process; he claims, on the contrary, that the task of critical analysis is to unearth the "metaphysical subtleties and theological niceties" in what appears at first sight to be just an ordinary object. In other words, when a critical Marxist encounters a bourgeois subject immersed in commodity fetishism, the Marxist's reproach to him is not "The commodity may seem to you to be a magical object endowed with special powers, but it is really just a reified expression of relations between people." The real Marxist's reproach is, rather, "You may think that the commodity appears to you as a simple embodiment of social relations (that money, for example, is just a kind of voucher entitling you to a part of the social product), but this is not how things really seem to you—in your social reality, by means of your participation in social exchange, you bear witness to the uncanny fact that a commodity really appears to you as a magical object endowed with special powers." In other words, we can imagine a bourgeois subject taking a course in Marxism where he is taught about commodity fetishism; after the course is finished, however, he comes back to his teacher, complaining that he is still a victim of commodity fetishism. The teacher tells him: "But you know now how things are, that commodities are only expressions of social relations, that there is nothing magical about them!", to which the pupil replies: "Of course I know all that, but the commodities

I am dealing with don't seem to!" This situation is literally evoked by Marx in his famous fiction of commodities that start to speak to each other:

> If commodities could speak, they would say this: our use-value may interest men, but it does not belong to us as objects. What does belong to us as objects, however, is our value. Our own intercourse as commodities proves it. We relate to each other merely as exchange-values.[32]

So, again, the real task is to convince not the subject, but the chicken-commodities: not to change the way we talk about commodities, but *to change the way commodities talk among themselves.* . . . Alenka Zupančič goes to the end here, and imagines a brilliant example that involves God himself:

> In the enlightened society of, say, revolutionary terror, a man is put in prison because he believes in God. With different measures, but above all by means of an enlightened explanation, he is brought to the knowledge that God does not exist. When dismissed, the man comes running back, and explains how scared he is of being punished by God. Of course he knows that God does not exist, but does God also know that?[33]

And, of course, this is exactly what happened (only) in Christianity, when Christ, dying on the Cross, uttered his "Father, Father, why have you forsaken me?"—here, for a brief moment, *God himself does not believe in himself*—or, as G. K. Chesterton put it in emphatic terms:

> When the world shook and the sun was wiped out of heaven, it was not at the crucifixion, but at the cry from the cross: the cry which confessed that God was forsaken of God. And now let the revolutionists choose a creed from all the creeds and a god from all the gods of the world, carefully weighing all the gods of inevitable recurrence and of unalterable power. They will not find another god who has himself been in revolt. Nay (the matter grows too difficult for human speech), but let the atheists themselves choose a god. They will find only one divinity who ever uttered their isolation; only one religion in which God seemed for an instant to be an atheist.[34]

It is in this precise sense that today's era is perhaps less atheist than any prior one: we are all ready to indulge in utter skepticism, cynical distance, exploitation of others "without any illusions," violations of all ethical constraints, extreme sexual practices, and so on—protected by the silent awareness that the big Other is ignorant of it:

> the subject is ready to do quite a lot, change radically, if only she can remain unchanged in the Other (in the symbolic as the external world in which, to put it in Hegel's terms, the subject's consciousness of himself is embodied, materialized as something that still does not know itself as consciousness). In this case, the belief in the Other (in the modern form of believing that the Other does not know) is precisely what helps to maintain the same state of things, regardless of all subjective mutations and permutations.

The subject's universe would really change only at the moment when she were to arrive at the knowledge that the Other knows (that it doesn't exist).[35]

Of course, an obvious counterargument suggests itself here: but the Other, in effect, doesn't exist, all that exists is our activity—or, in more direct and simple terms: commodities do not talk among themselves, it is only we who impute to them this magic property; God doesn't exist and, consequently, cannot know or not know that he is dead. . . . True, but that is the point: as Hegel would have put it, the big Other (the social-spiritual Substance) has no existence in itself, it exists only as a point of reference animated by the chaotic activity and interaction of numerous individuals. That is why the split we are taking about—the split between the subject's knowledge and the Other's knowledge—is inherent to the subject itself: it is the split between what the subject knows and what the subject presupposes/imputes to the Other to know (which is why it has such a shattering impact on the subject when he learns that the Other knows what it was supposed not to know).

Niels Bohr, who gave the right answer to Einstein's "God doesn't play dice" ("Don't tell God what to do!"), also provided the perfect example of how a fetishist disavowal of belief works in ideology: seeing a horseshoe on his door, a surprised visitor said that he didn't believe in the superstition that it brings good luck, to which Bohr snapped back: "I don't believe in it either; I have it there because I was told that it works even if one doesn't believe in it!" What this paradox makes clear is the way a belief is a reflexive attitude: it is never a case of simply believing—one has to believe in belief itself. That is why Kierkegaard was right to claim that we do not really believe (in Christ), we just believe to believe—and Bohr simply confronts us with the logical negative of this reflexivity (one can also *not* believe one's beliefs . . .).[36]

At some point, Alcoholics Anonymous meets Pascal: "Fake it until you make it." This causality of the habit, however, is more complex than it may seem: far from offering an explanation of how beliefs emerge, it calls for an explanation. The first thing to specify is that Pascal's "Kneel down and you will believe!" has to be understood as involving a kind of self-referential causality: "Kneel down and you will believe *that you knelt down because you believed!*" The second thing is that, in the "normal" cynical functioning of ideology, belief is displaced onto another, onto a "subject supposed to believe," so that the true logic is: "Kneel down and you will thereby *make someone else believe!*" We have to take this literally, and even risk a kind of inversion of Pascal's formula: "Do you believe too much, too directly? Do you find your belief too oppressive in its raw immediacy? Then kneel down, act as if you believe, and *you will get rid of your belief*—you will no longer have to believe yourself, your belief will already ex-sist objectified in your act of praying!" That is to say: what if one kneels down and prays not so much to regain one's own belief but, quite the contrary, to *get rid* of one's belief, of its overproximity; to acquire the breathing space of a minimal distance from it? To believe—to believe "directly," without the externalizing mediation of a ritual—is a heavy, oppressive, traumatic burden which, by practicing a ritual, one has a chance of transferring onto an Other.[37]

If there is a Freudian ethical injunction, it is that one should have *the courage of one's own convictions*: one should dare fully to assume one's identifications.[38] And exactly the same goes for marriage: the implicit presupposition (or, rather, injunction) of the standard ideology of marriage is that, precisely, there should be no love in it. The Pascalian formula of marriage is therefore not "You don't love your partner? Then marry him or her, go through the ritual of shared life, and love will emerge by itself!", but, on the contrary: "Are you too much in love with somebody? Then get married, ritualize your love-relationship, in order to cure yourself of this excessive passionate attachment, to replace it with boring daily routine—and if you can't resist passion's temptation, there are always extramarital affairs. . . ."

When Alain Badiou[39] emphasizes that double negation is not the same as affirmation, he thereby merely confirms the old Hegelian motto *les non-dupes errent*. Les us take the affirmation "I believe." Its negation is: "I do not really believe, I just pretend to believe." Its properly Hegelian negation of negation, however, is not the return to direct belief, but the self-relating pretense "I pretend to pretend to believe," which means: "I really believe without being aware of it." Is not irony, then, the ultimate form of the critique of ideology today—irony in the precise *Mozartian* sense of taking statements more seriously than the subjects who utter them themselves? Or, as Descartes put it at the beginning of Chapter 3 of his *Discourse on Method*: "Very many are not aware of what it is that they really believe; for, as the act of mind by which a thing is believed is different from that by which we know that we believe it, the one act is often found without the other."[40]

WHO'S AFRAID OF THE BIG BAD FUNDAMENTALISM?

In the case of so-called "fundamentalists," this "normal" functioning of ideology in which the ideological belief is transposed onto the Other is disturbed by the violent return of the immediate belief—they "really believe it." The first consequence of this is that the fundamentalist becomes the *dupe of his fantasy* (as Lacan put it apropos of the Marquis de Sade), immediately identifying himself with it. From my own youth, I remember a fantasy concerning the origin of children: after I learned how children are made, I still had no precise idea of insemination, so I thought one had to make love every day for the whole nine months: in the woman's womb, the child is gradually built up through sperm—each ejaculation is like adding an additional brick. . . . One plays with such fantasies, not "taking them seriously," and this is the way they fulfill their function—and the fundamentalist lacks this minimal distance toward his fantasy.

Let me clarify this point apropos of Elfriede Jelinek's *The Piano Teacher*, which can also be read as the story of a psychotic who lacks the coordinates of the fantasy which would allow her to organize her desire: when, in the middle of the film, she goes to a video cabin and watches hardcore porn, she does it simply in order to learn what to do, how to engage in sex, and, in her letter to her prospective lover, she basically puts on paper what she saw there. . . . (Her psychosis and lack of fantasmatic coordinates are evident in her strange relationship with her mother—when, in the middle of the night, she embraces her and starts to kiss her, this displays her total lack of the desiring coordinates that would direct her toward a determinate object—as well as in her self-cutting of her vagina with a razor, an act destined to bring her to reality.)⁴¹ At the very end of *The Piano Teacher*, the heroine, after stabbing herself, walks away (from the concert hall where she saw her young lover for the last time)—what if this self-inflicted wound is to be conceived as "traversing the fantasy"? What if, through striking at herself, she got rid of the masochistic fantasy's hold over her? In short, what if the ending is "optimistic": after being raped by her lover, after her fantasy has got back at her in reality, this traumatic experience enables her to leave it behind? Furthermore, what if the fantasy she puts in the letter she gives her lover is *his own* fantasy of what he would really like to do to her, so that he is disgusted precisely because he gets from her *directly* his own fantasy?

More generally, when I am passionately in love and, after not seeing my beloved for a long time, ask her for a photo to remind me what she looks like, the true aim of this request is not to check if the properties of my beloved still fit the criteria of my love, but, on the contrary, *to learn (again) what these criteria are*. I am in love absolutely, and the photo *a priori* cannot be a disappointment—I need it just so that it will tell me *what* I love. . . . This means that true love is performative in the sense that it changes its object—not in the sense of idealization, but in the sense of opening up a gap in it, a gap between the object's positive properties and the *agalma*, the mysterious core of the beloved (which is why I do not love you because of your properties which are worthy of love: on the contrary, it is only because of my love for you that your features appear to me as worthy of love). This is why finding oneself in the position of the beloved is so violent, even traumatic: being loved makes me tangibly aware of the gap between what I am as a determinate being and the unfathomable X in me which stimulates love. Everyone knows Lacan's definition of love ("Love is giving something one doesn't have . . ."); what we often forget is to add the other half which completes the sentence: ". . . to someone who doesn't want it." And is this not confirmed by our most elementary experience when somebody unexpectedly declares passionate love to us—is not our first reaction, preceding the possible positive reply, that something obscene, intrusive, is being forced upon us? In the middle of Alejandro Iñárritu's *21 Grams*, Paul, who is dying of a weakened heart, softly declares his love to Cristina, who is traumatized by the recent death of her husband and two young children, and then quickly withdraws; when they meet the next time, Cristina explodes into a complaint about the violent nature of declaring love:

> You know, you kept me thinking all day. I haven't spoken to anyone for months and I barely know you and I already need to talk to you. . . . And there's something the more I think about the less I understand: why the hell did you tell me you liked me? . . .

Answer me, because I didn't like you saying that at all. . . . You can't just walk up to a woman you barely know and tell her you like her. Y-o-u-c-a-n't. You don't know what she's going through, what she's feeling. . . . I'm not married, you know. I'm not anything in this world. I'm just not anything.[42]

After this, Cristina looks at Paul, raises her hands, and desperately starts kissing him on the mouth; so it is not that she did not like him and did not desire carnal relations with him—the problem for her was, on the contrary, that she *did* want him, that is to say, the point of her complaint was: what right does he have to stir up her desire?—In a kind of Hegelian twist, love does not simply open itself up for the unfathomable abyss in the beloved object; what is in the beloved "more than him- or herself," the presupposed excess of/in the beloved, is reflexively posited by love itself. This is why true love is by no means an openness to the "transcendent mystery of the beloved Other": true love is well aware that, as Hegel would have put it, the excess of the beloved, what, in the beloved, eludes my grasp, is the very place of the inscription of my own desire into the beloved object—transcendence is the form of appearance of immanence. As the melodramatic wisdom puts it: it is love itself, the fact of being loved, that ultimately makes the beloved beautiful.

Let us return to our fundamentalist: the obverse of his turning into a dupe of his fantasy is that he loses his sensitivity to the enigma of the Other's desire. In a recent case of analytic treatment in the UK, the patient, a woman who was a victim of rape, remained deeply disturbed by an unexpected gesture of the rapist: after brutally enforcing her surrender, and just prior to penetrating her, he withdrew a little bit, politely said "Just a minute, lady!", and put on a condom. This weird intrusion of politeness into a brutal situation perplexed the victim: what did it mean? Was it a strange care for her, or a simple egotistic protective measure on the part of the rapist (making sure that he would not get AIDS from her, not the other way round)? This gesture, much more than explosions of raw passion, stands for the encounter with the "enigmatic signifier," with the desire of the Other in all its impenetrability.

Does such an encounter with the Other's desire follow the logic of alienation or that of separation? It can be an experience of utter alienation (I am obsessed with the inaccessible obscure impenetrable divine Desire which plays games with me, as in the Jansenist *dieu obscur*); however, the key shift occurs when, in a Hegelian way, we gain insight into how "the secrets of the Egyptians were also secrets for the Egyptians themselves," that is to say, into how our alienation from the Other is already the alienation of the Other (from) itself—it is this redoubled alienation that generates what Lacan called separation as the overlapping of the two lacks.

And the link between the two features of the fundamentalist's position is clear: since fantasy is a scenario the subject builds in order to answer the enigma of the Other's desire—since fantasy provides an answer to "What does the Other want from me?"—the immediate identification with the fantasy, as it were, closes the gap: the enigma is solved, we know the whole answer.

On account of its very obvious imbecility, the American Christian fundamentalist imaginary is a much more paradoxical, properly postmodern, phenomenon than it may appear. The story of the rise of Scientology is relevant here: the founder, L. Ron Hubbard, started as a science-fiction writer, with a series of novels about events in another galaxy before humanity evolved on Earth; at a certain point, he got caught in his own game, as it were, and started to present his literary fiction as "serious" religious texts—so what began as fiction turns retroactively into religion, in a precise reversal of the story of modernity, where texts which were originally religious survive as artistic monuments to the greatness of the human spirit . . . A similar story lies behind the great literary bestseller of US Christian fundamentalism, Tim F. LaHaye's and Jerry B. Jenkins's *Left Behind* series of twelve novels about the forthcoming end of the world which, ignored by the mass media, have sold over sixty million copies. Their story begins when, all of a sudden, millions of people inexplicably disappear—the innocent ones whom God has directly called to himself in order to spare them the horrors of Armageddon. The Antichrist then appears: the slick, sleazy, charismatic young Romanian politician Nicolae Carpathia who, after being elected General Secretary of the UN, moves the seat of the UN to Babylon, and succeeds in imposing the UN as the anti-American world government that enforces the disarmament of all nation-states . . . and so on until, in the final battle, all non-Christians, the Jews included, are burned in a cataclysmic fire—imagine what an outcry a similar story, written from a Muslim standpoint and becoming a big bestseller in the Arab countries, would cause in the Western liberal media! It is not so much the breathtaking poverty and primitivism of these novels that is so incredible, but, rather, the strange overlapping of a "serious" religious message with the lowest popular culture commercial trash.

The credentials of those who, even prior to its release, virulently criticized Mel Gibson's *The Passion of the Christ* seem impeccable: are they not fully justified in their concern that the film, made by a fanatical Catholic traditionalist who has made occasional anti-Semitic outbursts, might ignite anti-Semitic sentiments? More generally, is not *Passion* a kind of manifesto of our own (Western, Christian) fundamentalists and anti-secularists? Is it not therefore the duty of every Western secularist to reject it? Is not such an unambiguous attack a *sine qua non* if we want to make it clear that we are not covert racists attacking only the fundamentalism of *other* (Muslim) cultures?

The late Pope John Paul II's ambivalent reaction to the film is well known: immediately after seeing it, deeply moved, he muttered: "It is as it was!"—and this statement was quickly withdrawn by official Vatican spokesmen. A glimpse into the Pope's spontaneous reaction was thus quickly replaced by the "official" neutral stance, adjusted in order not to offend anyone. This shift is the best illustration of what is wrong with liberal tolerance, with the Politically Correct fear that anyone's specific religious sensibility may be hurt: even if it says in the Bible that the Jewish mob demanded the death of Christ, one should not stage this scene directly, but play it down and contextualize it to make it clear that the Jews are not to be collectively blamed for the Crucifixion. . . . The problem with such a stance is that, in this way, the aggressive religious passion is merely repressed: it is still there, smoldering beneath the surface and, finding no release, getting stronger and stronger. (And, incidentally, is not this compromise stance the same as that of today's enlightened anti-Semite who, although he does not believe in Christ's divinity, nonetheless blames the Jews for killing our Lord Jesus? Or as that of the typical secular Jew who, although he does not believe in Jehovah and Moses as his prophet, nonetheless thinks that the Jews have a divine right to the land of Israel?)

Within this horizon, the only "passionate" response to fundamentalist passion is aggressive secularism of the kind displayed recently by the French state, where the government prohibited the wearing of conspicuous religious symbols and dress in schools (not only the Muslim hijab, but also the Jewish yarmulke and overlarge Christian crosses). It is not difficult to predict what the final result of this measure will be: excluded from the public space, the Muslims will be directly pushed to constitute themselves as nonintegrated fundamentalist communities. This is what Lacan meant when he emphasized the link between the rule of postrevolutionary *fraternité* and the logic of segregation.

This is why, ultimately, passion *as such* is "politically incorrect": although everything seems to be permitted, prohibitions are merely displaced. Take the deadlock of sexuality or art today: is there anything more dull, opportunistic, and sterile than succumbing to the superego injunction incessantly to invent new artistic transgressions and provocations (the performance artist masturbating on stage or masochistically cutting himself, the sculptor displaying decaying animal corpses or human excrement), or to the parallel injunction to engage in more and more "daring" forms of sexuality. . . . Does this mean that, against the false tolerance of liberal multiculturalism, we should return to religious fundamentalism? The very ridiculous situation surrounding Gibson's film makes the impossibility of such a solution clear. Gibson first wanted to shoot the film in Latin and Aramaic, and to show it without subtitles; under the pressure of distributors, he later decided to allow English (or other) subtitles. This compromise on his part, however, is not just a concession to commercial pressure; sticking to the original plan would, rather, directly reveal the self-refuting nature of Gibson's project. That is to say: let us imagine the film, without subtitles, being shown in a large American suburban mall: the intended fidelity to the original would turn it into its opposite, into an incomprehensible exotic spectacle.

Thus Gibson's *Passion* pays the ultimate dialectical price for its attempt to be a fundamentalist Christian film: what it loses its precisely the trace of any authentic Christian experience, so that, at the level of its cinematic texture, the film imitates its declared enemy, Hollywood entertainment. That is to say: what is *Passion* if not the ultimate sacrilege, the staging of Christ's suffering and death as the ultimate sado-maso gay spectacle? What remains of the film is that a naked young and beautiful male body is slowly tortured to death (and, ironically, the film cheats here on its own "realist" terms: in all probability, Christ was naked on the Cross . . .).

Totally absent from the film is any kind of inquiry into the meaning of the crucifixion: why did Christ have to die? There are three main versions: (1) a Gnostic-dualist one: Christ's death was a chapter in the struggle between Good and Evil, that is, Christ's death was the price to be paid by God to the Devil for the redemption of humanity; (2) the sacrificial one: Christ paid the price for our sins—not to the Devil, but just to satisfy the sense and balance of justice; (3) the exemplary one: by his example of the ultimate act of love, Christ inspires people to follow him, to be good. . . . There is, of course, something missing here: the fourth version, which is the truth of the first three: what if Christ's death was a way for God-the-Father to repay his own debt to humanity, to excuse himself for having done such a botched-up job, creating an imperfect world full of suffering and injustice?

But there is a third position, beyond religious fundamentalism and liberal tolerance. Instead of trying to redeem the pure ethical core of a religion against its political instrumentalizations, we should ruthlessly criticize this very core—in *all* religions. Today, when religions themselves (from New Age spirituality to the cheap spiritualist hedonism of the Dalai Lama) are more than ready to serve postmodern pleasure-seeking, it is paradoxically only a comprehensive materialism which is able to sustain a truly ascetic militant ethical stance—and to pass a proper judgment on religious-political fundamentalism, far from its facile liberal dismissal.

OVER THE RAINBOW COALITION!

The enigmatic spectacle of a large-scale mass suicide is always fascinating—recall hundreds of Jim Jones's cult followers who obediently took poison in their Guyana camp. At the level of economic life, the same thing is going on today in Kansas. Thomas Frank[43] has aptly summed up the paradox of today's US populist conservatism, whose basic premise is the gap between economic interests and "moral" questions. That is to say: economic class opposition (poor farmers, blue-collar workers, versus lawyers, bankers, large companies) is transposed/coded into the opposition of true honest hard-working Christian Americans versus decadent liberals who drink latte and drive foreign cars, advocate abortion and homosexuality, mock patriotic sacrifice and the simple "provincial" way of life, and so forth. Thus the enemy is perceived as the "liberal" who, through federal state interventions (from school-busing to ordering Darwinian evolution and perverse sexual practices to be taught), wants to undermine the authentic American way of life. The main economic interest is therefore to get rid of the strong state which taxes the hard-working population in order to finance its regulatory interventions—the minimal economic program is "lower taxes, fewer regulations."

From the normal perspective of the enlightened rational pursuit of self-interest, the inconsistency of this ideological stance is obvious: the populist conservatives are literally *voting themselves into economic ruin*. Less taxation and deregulation means more freedom for the big companies that are driving the impoverished farmers out of business; less state intervention means less federal help to small farmers; and so on. In the eyes of the US evangelical populists, the state stands for an alien power and, together with the UN, is an agent of the Antichrist: it takes away the liberty of the Christian believer, relieving him of the moral responsibility of stewardship, and thus undermines the individualistic morality that makes each of us the architect of our own salvation—how do we combine this with the unprecedented explosion of state apparatuses under Bush? No wonder large corporations are delighted to accept such evangelical attacks on the state, when the state tries to regulate media mergers, to put strictures on energy companies, to strengthen air pollution regulations, to protect wildlife and limit logging in national parks, and so forth. It is the ultimate irony of history that radical individualism serves as the ideological justification of the unfettered power of what the large majority of individuals experience as a vast anonymous entity which, without any democratic public control, regulates their lives.[44]

As for the ideological aspect of their struggle, it is more than obvious that the populists are fighting a war that simply *cannot be won*: if the Republicans put a total ban on abortion, if they prohibited the teaching of evolution, if they imposed federal regulation on Hollywood and mass culture, this would mean not only their immediate ideological defeat, but also a large-scale economic depression in the USA. Thus the outcome is a debilitating symbiosis: although the "ruling class" disagrees with the populist moral agenda, it tolerates their "moral war" as a means of keeping the lower classes in check, that is, enabling them to articulate their fury without disturbing their economic interests. This means that *culture war is class war* in a displaced mode—so much for those who claim that we leave in a post-class society. . . .

This, however, only makes the enigma more impenetrable: how is this displacement *possible?* "Stupidity" and "ideological manipulation" are not an answer; that is to say, it is clearly not enough to say that that the primitive lower classes are brainwashed by the ideological apparatuses so that they are unable to identify their true interests. If nothing else, we should recall how, decades ago, this same Kansas was the hotbed of *progressive* populism in the USA—and people certainly have not become more stupid over the past decades. But a direct "psychoanalytic" explanation in the old Wilhelm Reich style (people's libidinal investments compel them to act against their rational interests) would not do either: it confronts libidinal economy and economy proper too directly, failing to grasp their mediation. Neither is it enough to propose the Ernesto Laclau solution: there is no "natural" link between a given socioeconomic position and the ideology attached to it, so that it is meaningless to talk about "deception" and "false consciousness," as if there were a standard of "appropriate" ideological awareness inscribed into the very "objective" socioeconomic situation; every ideological edifice is the outcome of a hegemonic fight to establish/impose a chain of equivalences, a fight whose outcome is thoroughly contingent, not guaranteed by any external reference like "objective socioeconomic position.". . . In such a general answer, the enigma simply disappears.

The first thing to note here is that it takes two to fight a culture war: culture is also the dominant ideological topic of "enlightened" liberals whose politics is focused on the fight against sexism, racism, and fundamentalism, and for multicultural tolerance.

The key question, therefore, is: why is "culture" emerging as our central life-world category? Where religion is concerned, we no longer "really believe," we just follow (some of the) religious rituals and mores as part of our respect for the "lifestyle" of the community to which we belong (nonbelieving Jews obeying kosher rules "out of respect for tradition," and so on). "I don't really believe in it, it's just part of my culture" seems in effect to be the predominant mode of the disavowed/displaced belief characteristic of our times. What is a cultural lifestyle, if not the fact that, although we do not believe in Santa Claus, there is a Christmas tree in every house, and even in public places, every December? Perhaps, then, the "nonfundamentalist" notion of "culture" as distinguished from "real" religion, art, and so on, is at its very core the name for the field of disowned/impersonal beliefs—"culture" is the name for all those things we practice without really believing in them, without "taking them seriously."

The second thing to note is how, while professing their solidarity with the poor, liberals encode culture war with an opposed class message: more often than not, their fight for multicultural tolerance and women's rights marks the counterposition to the alleged intolerance, fundamentalism, and patriarchal sexism of the "lower classes." The way to unravel this confusion is to focus on the mediating terms whose function is to obfuscate the true lines of division. The way the term "modernization" has been used in the recent ideological offensive is exemplary here: first, an abstract opposition is constructed between "modernizers" (those who endorse global capitalism in all its aspects, from economic to cultural) and "traditionalists" (those who resist globalization). Into this category of those-who-resist is then thrown everybody, from traditional conservatives and the populist Right to the "Old Left" (those who continue to advocate the welfare state, trade unions . . .). This categorization obviously does contain an element of social reality—recall the coalition of Church and trade unions which, in Germany in early 2003, prevented the legalization of stores being open on Sundays. It is not enough, however, to say that this "cultural difference" traverses the entire social field, cutting across different strata and classes; it is not enough to say that this opposition can be combined in different ways with other oppositions (so that we can have conservative "traditional-values" resistance to global capitalist "modernization," or moral conservatives who fully endorse capitalist globalization); in short, it is not enough to say that this "cultural difference" is one in the series of antagonisms which are operative in today's social processes.

The fact that this opposition fails to function as the key to social totality does not mean only that it should be articulated with other differences. It means that it is "abstract," and the wager of Marxism is that there is one antagonism ("class struggle") which overdetermines all others and is, as such, the "concrete universal" of the entire field. The term "overdetermines" is used here in its precise Althusserian sense: it does not mean that class struggle is the ultimate referent and horizon of meaning of all other struggles; it means that class struggle is the structuring principle which allows us to account for the very "inconsistent" plurality of ways in which other antagonisms can be articulated into "chains of equivalences." The feminist struggle, for example, can be articulated into a chain with the progressive struggle for emancipation, or it can (and certainly does) function as an ideological tool used by the upper middle classes to assert their superiority over the "patriarchal and intolerant" lower classes. And the point here is not only that the feminist struggle can be articulated in different ways with class antagonism, but that class antagonism is, as it were, doubly inscribed here: it is the specific constellation of the class struggle itself which explains why the feminist struggle was appropriated by the upper classes. (The same goes for racism: it is the dynamics of class struggle itself which explains why outright racism is strong among the lowest-class white workers.) Here class struggle is the "concrete universal" in the strict Hegelian sense: in relating to its otherness (other antagonisms), it relates to itself, that is to say, it (over)determines the way it relates to other struggles.

The third thing to note is the fundamental difference between feminist/antiracist/antisexist, etc., struggle and class struggle: in the first case, the goal is to translate antagonism into difference ("peaceful" coexistence of sexes, religions, ethnic groups), while the goal of the class struggle is precisely the opposite: to "aggravate" class difference into class antagonism. The point of subtraction is to reduce the overall complex structure to its "antagonistic" minimal difference. So what the series race–gender–class obfuscates is the different logic of the political space in the case of class: while the antiracist and antisexist struggles are guided by a striving for the full recognition of the other, the class struggle aims at overcoming and subduing, even annihilating, the other—even if this not mean direct physical annihilation, class struggle aims at the annihilation of the other's sociopolitical role and function. In other words, while it is logical to say that antiracism wants all races to be allowed freely to assert and further their cultural, political, and economic strivings, it is obviously meaningless to say that the aim of the proletarian class struggle is to allow the bourgeoisie fully to assert its identity and strivings. . . . In the one case, we have a "horizontal" logic of the recognition of different identities; in the other, we have the logic of the struggle with an antagonist.[45] The paradox here is that it is populist fundamentalism which retains this logic of antagonism, while the liberal Left follows the logic of the recognition of differences, of "defusing" antagonisms into coexisting differences: in their very form, the conservative-populist grass-roots campaigns took over the old Leftist-radical stance of the popular mobilization and struggle against upper-class exploitation. Insofar as, in the present US two-party system, red designates Republicans and blue Democrats, and insofar as populist fundamentalists, of course, vote Republican, the old anti-Communist slogan "Better dead than red!" now acquires a new ironic meaning—the irony residing in the unexpected continuity of the "red" attitude from the old Leftist grass-roots mobilization to the new Christian fundamentalist grass-roots mobilization.

This unexpected reversal is just one in a long series. In today's USA, the traditional roles of Democrats and Republicans are almost reversed: the Republicans spend government money, thus generating a record budget deficit, de facto build a strong federal state, and pursue a policy of global interventionism, while the Democrats pursue a tough fiscal policy that, under Clinton, abolished the budget deficit. Even in the touchy sphere of socioeconomic politics, the Democrats (like Blair in the UK) as a rule accomplish the neoliberal agenda of abolishing the welfare state, lowering taxes, privatization, and so on, while Bush proposed the radical measure of legalizing the status of the millions of illegal Mexican workers, and made healthcare much more accessible to the retired. The extreme case here is that of the survivalist groups in the West of the USA: although their ideological message is one of religious racism, their entire mode of organization (small illegal groups fighting the FBI and other federal agencies) makes them an uncanny double of the 1960s Black Panthers.

According to an old Marxist insight, every rise of Fascism is a sign of a failed revolution—no wonder, then, that Kansas is also the state of John Brown, the key political figure in the history of the USA, the fervently Christian "radical abolitionist" who came closest to introducing the radical emancipatory-egalitarian logic into the US political landscape: "John Brown considered himself a complete egalitarian. And it was very important for him to practice egalitarianism on every level."[46] His consistent egalitarianism led him to become involved in the armed struggle against slavery: in 1859, Brown and twenty-one other men seized the federal armory at Harper's Ferry, hoping to arm slaves and thus create a violent rebellion against the South. After thirty-six hours, however, the revolt was suppressed and Brown was taken to jail by a federal force led by none other than Robert E. Lee. After being found guilty of murder, treason, and inciting a slave insurrection, Brown was hanged on December 2, 1859. And even today, long after slavery was abolished, Brown is a divisive figure in the American collective memory—this point was made most succinctly by Russell Banks, whose magnificent novel *Cloud-splitter* retells Brown's story:

> The reason white people think he was mad is because he was a white man and he was willing to sacrifice his life in order to liberate Black Americans. . . . Black people don't think he's crazy, generally—very few African Americans regard Brown as insane. If you go out onto the street today, whether you are speaking to a school kid or an elderly woman or a college professor, if it's an African American person you're talking to about John Brown, they are going start right out with the assumption that he was a hero because he was willing to sacrifice his life—a white man—in order to liberate Black Americans. If you speak to a white American, probably the same proportion of them will say he was a madman. And it's for the same reason, because he was a white man who was willing to sacrifice his life to liberate Black Americans. The very thing that makes him seem mad to white Americans is what makes him seem heroic to Black Americans.[47]

For this reason, those whites who support Brown are all the more precious—among them, surprisingly, Henry David Thoreau, the great opponent of violence: against the conventional dismissal of Brown as bloodthirsty, foolish, and insane, Thoreau[48] painted a portrait of a peerless man whose embrace of a cause was unparalleled; he even goes so far as to liken Brown's execution (he states that he regards Brown as dead before his actual death) to that of Christ. Thoreau vents his wrath on the scores of those who have voiced their displeasure and scorn for John Brown: these same people can't relate to

Brown because of their inflexible stance and "dead" existence; they are truly not living, only a handful of men have lived.

And, when we talk about the Kansas populists, we should bear in mind that they also celebrate John Brown as their saint.[49] We should thus not only refuse the easy liberal contempt for the populist fundamentalists (or, even worse, the patronizing regret at how "manipulated" they are); we should reject the very terms of the culture war. Although, of course, where the positive content of most of the issues debated is concerned, a radical Leftist should support the liberal stance (for abortion, against racism and homophobia, and so on), we should never forget that it is the populist fundamentalist, not the liberal, who is, in the long run, our ally. In all their anger, they are not radical enough to perceive the link between capitalism and the moral decay they deplore. Remember how Robert Bork's infamous lament about our "slouching towards Gomorrah" ends up in a deadlock typical of ideology:

> The entertainment industry is not forcing depravity on an unwilling American public. The demand for decadence is there. That fact does not excuse those who sell such degraded material any more than the demand for crack excuses the crack dealer. But we must be reminded that the fault is in ourselves, in human nature not constrained by external forces.[50]

In what, exactly, is this demand grounded? Here Bork performs his ideological short circuit: instead of invoking the inherent logic of capitalism itself which, in order to sustain its expanding reproduction, has to create newer and newer demands, and thus admitting that, in fighting consumerist "decadence," he is fighting a tendency which lies at the very core of capitalism, he directly refers to "human nature" which, left to itself, ends up wanting depravity, and is thus in need of constant control and censorship: "The idea that men are naturally rational, moral creatures without the need for strong external restraints has been exploded by experience. There is an eager and growing market for depravity, and profitable industries devoted to supplying it."[51]

What moral conservatives fail to perceive, then, is how—to put it in Hegelese—in fighting the dissolute liberal permissive culture, they are fighting the necessary ideological consequence of the unbridled capitalist economy that they themselves fully and passionately support: their struggle against the external enemy is the struggle against the obverse of their own position. (Long ago, intelligent liberals like Daniel Bell formulated this paradox under the title of the "cultural contradictions of capitalism.") This throws an unexpected light onto the Cold Warriors' "moral" crusade against Communist regimes: the embarrassing fact is that the Eastern European Communist regimes were overthrown by forces which "represented the three great antagonists of conservatism: the youth culture, the intellectuals of the '60s generation, and the laboring classes that still favored Solidarity over individualism."[52] This fact returns to haunt Bork: at a conference, he "referred, not approvingly, to Michael Jackson's crotch-clutching performance at the Super Bowl. Another panelist tartly informed me that it was precisely the desire to enjoy such manifestations of American culture that had brought down the Berlin wall. That seems as good an argument as any for putting the wall back up again."[53] Although Bork is aware of the irony of the situation, he obviously misses its deeper aspect.

Recall Lacan's definition of successful communication: in it, I get back from the other my own message in its inverted—that is, true—form. Is this not what is happening to today's liberals? Are they not getting back from the conservative populists their own message in its inverted/true form? In other words, are not conservative populists the symptom of tolerant enlightened liberals? Is the scary and ridiculous Kansas redneck exploding in fury against liberal corruption not the very figure in the guise of which the liberal encounters the truth of his own hypocrisy? We should thus—to refer to the most popular song about Kansas, from *The Wizard of Oz*—definitely reach *over the rainbow*: over the "rainbow coalition" of single-issue struggles, favored by radical liberals, and dare to look for an ally in what often looks like the ultimate enemy of multi-culti liberalism: today's crucial "sites of resistance" against global capitalism are often deeply marked by religious fundamentalism.

ROBERT SCHUMANN AS A THEORIST OF IDEOLOGY

This means that, apropos of the "official" ideologico-political opposition between liberal democracy and religious fundamentalism, we should also perform the Hegelian gesture of displacing the external antinomy between the hegemonic liberal democracy and its fundamentalist opponent into a tension inherent to the hegemonic ideologico-political edifice itself: the true Other of liberal democracy is not its fundamentalist enemy, but *its own disavowed underside, its own obscene supplement.*

"Humoresque," arguably Schumann's piano masterpiece, is to be read against the background of the gradual loss of the voice in his songs: it is not a simple piano piece, but a song without the vocal line, with the vocal line reduced to silence, so that all we actually hear is the piano accompaniment. This is how one should read the famous "inner voice/*innere Stimme*" added by Schumann (in the written score) as a third line between the two piano lines, higher and lower: as the vocal melodic line which remains a nonvocalized "inner voice," a kind of musical equivalent to the Heidegger-Derrida "crossed-out" Being. What we actually hear is thus a "variation, but not on a theme," a series of variations without a theme, accompaniment without the main melodic line (which exists only as *Augenmusik*, music for the eyes, in the guise of written notes). (No wonder Schumann composed a "concert without orchestra," a kind of counterpoint to Bartók's "concert for orchestra.") This absent melody is to be reconstructed on the basis of the fact that the first and third levels (the right- and left-hand piano lines) do not relate to each other directly, that is to say, their relationship is not that of an immediate mirroring: in order to account for their interconnection, we are thus compelled to (re)construct a third, "virtual" intermediate level (melodic line) which, for structural reasons, cannot be played. Its status is that of an impossible-real which can exist only in the guise of a writing: its physical presence would annihilate the two melodic lines we hear in reality (as in Freud's "A Child is Being Beaten," in which the middle fantasy scene was never conscious, and has to be reconstructed as the missing link between the first scene and the last). Schumann brings this procedure of absent melody to an apparently absurd self-reference when, later in the same fragment of "Humoresque," he repeats the same two actually played melodic lines, yet this time the score contains no third absent melodic line, no inner voice—what is absent here is the absent melody, that is, absence itself. How are we to play these notes when, at the level of what is actually to be played, they exactly repeat the previous notes? The actually played notes are deprived only of what is not there, of their constitutive lack— or, to echo the Bible, they lose even that which they never had.

The true pianist should thus have the *savoir-faire* to play the existing, positive, notes in such a way that we are able to discern the echo of the accompanying unplayed "silent" virtual notes, or their absence . . . and is this not how ideology works? The explicit ideological text (or practice) is sustained by the "unplayed" series of obscene superego supplements. In Really Existing Socialism, the explicit ideology of socialist democracy was sustained by a set of implicit (unspoken) obscene injunctions and prohibitions, teaching the subject how not to take some explicit norms seriously, and how to implement a set of publicly unacknowledged prohibitions. One of the strategies of dissidence in the last years of Socialism was therefore precisely to take the ruling ideology more seriously/literally than it took itself by ignoring its virtual unwritten shadow: "You want us to practice socialist democracy? OK, you have it!" And when one got back from the Party apparatchiks desperate hints of how this was not the way things functioned, one simply had to ignore these hints.[54]

This is what happens with the proclamation of the Decalogue: its revolutionary novelty lies not in its content, but in the absence of the accompanying virtual texture of the Law's obscene supplement. This is what "acheronta movebo" (moving the underground) as a practice of the critique of ideology means: not directly changing the explicit text of the Law but, rather, intervening in its obscene virtual supplement.[55] Think of the relationship toward homosexuality in a soldiers' community, which operates at two clearly distinct levels: explicit homosexuality is brutally attacked, those identified as gays are ostracized, beaten up every night, and so on; this explicit homophobia, however, is accompanied by an excessive implicit web of homosexual innuendos, inside jokes, obscene practices, and so on. The truly radical intervention in military homophobia should therefore not focus primarily on the explicit repression of homosexuality; rather, it should "move the underground," disturb the implicit homosexual practices which *sustain* the explicit homophobia. The real choice is not between sticking to the universality of the symbolic Law, trying to purify it of its obscene supplements (a vaguely Habermasian option) and dismissing this very universal dimension as a theater of shadows dominated by the Real of obscene fantasies. *The true act is to intervene in this obscene underground domain, transforming it.*

In his reaction to the photos showing Iraqi prisoners tortured and humiliated by US soldiers, made public at the end of April 2004, George Bush, as expected, emphasized how these soldiers' deeds were isolated crimes which do not reflect what America stands and fights for: the values of democracy, freedom, and personal dignity. And, in effect, the very fact that the case turned into a public scandal which put the US administration on the defensive was in itself a positive sign—in a really "totalitarian" regime, the case would simply have been hushed up.[56] A number of disturbing features, however, complicate this simple picture. In the months before the outbreak of the Abu Ghraib scandal, the International Red Cross was regularly bombarding the US Army authorities in Iraq with reports about abuses in military prisons there, and these reports were systematically ignored; so it was not that the US authorities were getting no hint of what was going on—they simply admitted the crime only when (and because) they were faced with its disclosure in the media. No wonder one of the preventive measures was the prohibition for the US military guards to have digital cameras and cellular phones with video display—to prevent not the acts, but their public circulation. . . . Second, the immediate reaction of US Army command was surprising, to say the least: the explanation was that the soldiers had not been properly taught the Geneva Convention rules about how to treat war prisoners—as if one has to be taught not to humiliate and torture prisoners!

The main feature of the story, however, is the contrast between the "standard" way prisoners were tortured under Saddam's regime and the US Army tortures: under Saddam's regime the emphasis was on the direct brutal infliction of pain, while the US soldiers focused on psychological humiliation. Furthermore, *recording* the humiliation with a camera, with the perpetrators *included* in the picture, their faces stupidly smiling alongside the naked twisted bodies of the prisoners, is an integral part of the process, in stark contrast with the secrecy of Saddam's tortures. When I saw the well-known photo of a naked prisoner with a black hood over his head, electric cables attached to his limbs, standing on a chair in a ridiculous theatrical pose, my first reaction was that this was a shot of the latest performance art show in Lower Manhattan. The very positions and costumes of the prisoners suggest a theatrical staging, a kind of *tableau vivant*, which cannot fail to bring to mind the whole scope of American performance art and "theater of cruelty"—Robert Mapplethorpe's photographs, the weird scenes in David Lynch's films. . . .

And it is this feature that brings us to the crux of the matter: to anyone acquainted with the reality of the US way of life, the photos immediately brought to mind the obscene underside of US popular culture—for example, the initiatic rituals of torture and humiliation one has to undergo in order to be accepted into a closed community. Do we not see similar photos in regular intervals in the US press, when some scandal explodes in an army unit or on a high-school campus, where the initiatic ritual went too far and soldiers or students got hurt beyond a level considered tolerable, forced to assume a humiliating pose, to perform debasing gestures (like penetrating their anus with a beer bottle in front of their peers), to be pierced by needles, and so on. (And, incidentally, since Bush himself is a member of "Skull and Bones," the most exclusive secret society of the Yale campus, it would be interesting to learn which rituals he had to undergo to be accepted. . . .)

Of course, the obvious difference is that, in the case of such *initiatic* rituals—as their very name implies—one undergoes them of one's own free will, fully aware of what one has to expect, and with the clear aim of one's ultimate reward (being accepted into the inner circle, and—last but not least—allowed to perform the same rituals on new members . . .), while in Abu Ghraib, the rituals were not the price the prisoners had to pay in order to be accepted as "one of us," but, on the contrary, the very mark of their *exclusion*. Is not the "free choice" of those undergoing humiliating initiation rituals, however, an exemplary case of a *false* free choice, along the lines of the worker's freedom to sell his labor-power? Even worse, we should recall here one of the most disgusting rituals of anti-black violence in the old US South: a black guy is cornered by white thugs, then compelled to perform an aggressive gesture ("Spit into my face, boy!"; "Say I am a shit!". . .), which is supposed to justify the ensuing beating or lynching. Furthermore, there is the ultimate cynical message in applying to Arab prisoners the properly American initiatic ritual: you want to be one of us? OK, here you have a taste of the very core of our way of life. . . .

The Abu Ghraib tortures are thus to be located in the series of obscene underground practices that sustain an ideological edifice. Along the same lines, the true dark enigma of the behavior of the Vatican toward the Nazis was not the one which gets the most media attention, the Pope's silence on the subject of the Holocaust—this lack of response could be understood, if not condoned, by the specific circumstances. Much more sinister was, in the years after the Second World War, the full engagement of the Catholic Church in co-organizing the escape of the Nazi criminals to South America: the normal escape route led to Northern Italy, where they were hidden for some time in remote monasteries (or, in some cases, even in Vatican City itself); from there, they were smuggled to Spain or to a ship (usually in Genoa) which took them to Argentina.[57] Why this urge to save—not ex-functionaries of "soft" Fascist regimes like the one in Italy itself, but—Nazis themselves, whose ideology was explicitly anti-Christian, "pagan"? What deeper solidarity motivated the Vatican to engage in such a vast and well-organized effort? If, in the late 1940s, the Catholic Church was able to build such an impressive underground network to save the Nazis, why did it not build a similar network in the early 1940s to save Jews—for instance, in Rome, at least? And the same ambiguity persists today: it is true that Pope John Paul II apologized for all the injustices the Church has committed against the Jews in its long history—but the same Pope canonized the founder of Opus Dei, well-known for his anti-Semitic statements and his pro-Fascist sympathies.

More generally, today's Catholic Church itself relies on (at least) two levels of obscene unwritten rules. First, there is, of course, the infamous Opus Dei, the Church's own "white mafia," the (half-)secret organization which somehow embodies the pure Law beyond any positive legality: its supreme rule is unconditional obedience to the Pope and a ruthless determination to work for the Church, with all other rules being (potentially) suspended. As a rule, its members, whose task is to penetrate the top political and financial circles, keep their Opus Dei identity secret. As such, they are in effect "opus dei"—the "work of God"; that is to say, they adopt the perverse position of a direct instrument of the big Other's will. Then there is the abundance of cases of sexual abuse of children by priests—these cases are so widespread, from Austria and Italy to Ireland and the USA, that we can in fact talk about a separate "counterculture" within the Church, with its own set of hidden rules. And there is an interconnection between the two levels, since Opus Dei regularly intervenes to hush up sexual scandals involving priests. Incidentally, the Church's reaction to sexual scandals also shows how it actually perceives its role: the Church insists that these cases, deplorable as they are, are its own internal problem, and displays great reluctance to collaborate with the police in their investigations. And indeed, in a way, it is right: child abuse is the Church's internal problem, that is to say, an inherent product of its very institutional symbolic organization, not just a series of particular criminal cases concerning individuals who happen to be priests. Consequently, the answer to this reluctance should be not only that we are dealing with criminal cases and that, if the Church does not fully participate in their investigation, it is an accessory after the fact; moreover, the Church *as such*, as an institution, should be investigated with regard to the way it systematically creates the conditions for such crimes. This is also why we cannot explain the sexual scandals in which priests are involved as a strategy of the opponents of celibacy, who want to make their point that, if priests' sexual urges do not find a legitimate outlet, they have to explode in a pathological way: allowing Catholic priests to marry would not solve anything; we would not get priests doing their job without harassing young boys, since pedophilia is generated by the Catholic institution of priesthood as its "inherent transgression," as its obscene secret supplement.

Remember Rob Reiner's *A Few Good Men*, a court-martial drama about two US marines accused of murdering one of their fellow-soldiers; the military prosecutor claims that the act was a deliberate murder, whereas the defense (Tom Cruise teamed with Demi Moore—how could they fail?) succeeds in proving that the defendants followed the so-called "Code Red," the unwritten rule of a military community which authorizes the clandestine night-time beating of a fellow-soldier who has betrayed the Marines' ethical standards. Such a code condones an act of transgression, it is "illegal," yet at the same time it reaffirms the cohesion of the group. It has to remain under cover of night, unacknowledged, unutterable—in public, everyone pretends to know nothing about it, or even actively denies its existence (and the climax of the film is, predictably, the outburst of rage from Jack Nicholson, the officer who ordered the night-time beating: his public explosion is, of course, the moment of his fall). While it violates the explicit rules of community, such a code represents the "spirit of community" at its purest, exerting the strongest pressure on individuals to enact group identification. In Derridean terms, in contrast to the *written* explicit Law, such a superego obscene code is essentially *spoken*. While the explicit Law is sustained by the dead father *qua* symbolic authority (the "Name of the Father"), the unwritten code is sustained by the spectral supplement of the Name-of-the-Father, the obscene specter of the Freudian "primordial father."[58]

That is the lesson of Coppola's *Apocalypse Now*: in the figure of Kurtz, the Freudian "primordial father"—the obscene father-enjoyment subordinated to no symbolic Law, the total Master who dares to confront the Real of terrifying enjoyment face to face— is presented not as a remainder of some barbaric past, but as the necessary outcome of modern Western power itself. Kurtz was the perfect soldier—as such, through his overidentification with the military power system, he turned into the excess which the system has to eliminate. The ultimate horizon of *Apocalypse Now* is this insight into how Power generates its own excess, which it has to annihilate in an operation which has to imitate what it fights (Willard's mission to kill Kurtz is nonexistent for the offi- cial record—"It never happened," as the general who briefs Willard points out.) We thereby enter the domain of secret operations, of what the Power does without ever admitting it. This is where Christopher Hitchens missed the point when he wrote, apropos of Abu Ghraib:

> One of two things must necessarily be true. Either these goons were acting on some- one's authority, in which case there is a layer of mid- to high-level people who think that they are not bound by the laws and codes and standing orders. Or they were acting on their own authority, in which case they are the equivalent of mutineers, deserters, or traitors in the field. This is why one asks wistfully if there is no provision in the pro- cedures of military justice for them to be taken out and shot.[59]

The problem is that the Abu Ghraib tortures were *neither* of these two options: while they cannot be reduced to simple evil acts by individual soldiers, they were of course also not directly ordered—they were legitimized by a specific version of the obscene "Code Red" rules. This is why the assurance from US Army command that no "direct orders" were issued to humiliate and torture the prisoners is ridiculous: of course they were not, since, as everyone who knows army life is aware, this is not how such things are done. There are no formal orders, nothing is written, there is just unofficial pres- sure, hints and directives are delivered in private, the way one shares a dirty secret. . . . To claim that they were the acts of "mutineers, deserters, or traitors in the field" is the same nonsense as the claim that the Ku Klux Klan lynchings were the acts of traitors to Western Christian civilization, not the outburst of its own obscene underside; or that abuses of children by Catholic priests are acts of "traitors" to Catholicism. . . . Abu Ghraib was not simply a case of American arrogance toward a Third World people: in being submitted to humiliating tortures, the Iraqi prisoners were in effect *initiated into American culture*, they got the taste of its obscene underside which forms the necessary supplement to the public values of personal dignity, democracy, and freedom. No wonder, then, that it is gradually becoming clear how the ritualistic humiliation of Iraqi prisoners was not a limited case, but part of a widespread practice: on May 6,

2004, Donald Rumsfeld had to admit that the published photos are only the "tip of the iceberg," and that there are much stronger things to come, including videos of rape and murder.

In a recent debate about the fate of Guantánamo prisoners on NBC, one of the arguments for the ethico-legal acceptability of their status was that "they are those who were missed by the bombs": since they were the target of the US bombing, and accidentally survived it, and since this bombing was part of a legitimate military operation, one cannot condemn their fate when they were taken prisoner after the combat—whatever their situation, it is better, less terrible, than being dead. . . . This reasoning says more than it intends to say: it puts the prisoners almost literally into the position of living dead, those who are in a way already dead (their right to live forfeited by being legitimate targets of murderous bombings), so that they are now cases of Agamben's Homo sacer, the one who can be killed with impunity since, in the eyes of the law, his life no longer counts.[60] If the Guantánamo prisoners are located in the space "between the two deaths," occupying the position of Homo sacer, legally dead (deprived of an official legal status) while biologically still alive, the US authorities which treat them in this way are also in a kind of in-between legal status which forms the counterpart to Homo sacer: as a legal power, their acts are no longer covered and restricted by the law—they operate in an empty space that is still within the domain of the law. And the recent disclosures about Abu Ghraib only display the full consequences of locating prisoners in this place "between the two deaths."

The exemplary economic strategy of today's capitalism is outsourcing—giving over the "dirty" process of material production (but also publicity, design, accountancy . . .) to another company via subcontracting. In this way, one can easily avoid ecological and health regulations: production is done in, say, Indonesia, where the ecological and health regulations are much less stringent than they are in the West, and the Western global company which owns the logo can claim that it is not responsible for the violations of another company. Are we not getting something analogous with regard to torture? Is not torture also being "outsourced," left to the Third World allies of the USA, which can do it without worrying about legal problems or public protest? Was such outsourcing not explicitly advocated by Jonathan Alter in Newsweek immediately after 9/11? After stating: "we can't legalize torture; it's contrary to American values," he nonetheless concludes: "we'll have to think about transferring some suspects to our less squeamish allies, even if that's hypocritical. Nobody said this was going to be pretty."[61] This is how, today, First World democracy increasingly functions: by "outsourcing" its dirty underside to other countries. . . . We can see how this debate about the need to apply torture was by no means academic: today, Americans do not even trust their allies to do the job properly; the "less squeamish" partner is the disavowed part of the US government itself—an eminently logical result, once we recall how the CIA taught America's Latin American and Third World military allies the practice of torture for decades. And, insofar as the predominant skeptical liberal attitude can also be characterized as one of "outsourced beliefs" (we let the primitive others, "fundamentalists," do their believing for us), does not the rise of new religious fundamentalisms in our own societies indicate the same distrust toward Third World countries: not only are they incapable of doing our torturing for us, they can't even do our believing for us any longer. . . .[62]

In March 2005, the USA was in the grip of the Terri Schiavo case: she suffered brain damage in 1990 when her heart stopped briefly as a result of a chemical imbalance believed to have been brought on by an eating disorder; court-appointed doctors claimed that she was in a persistent vegetative state with no hope of recovery. While her husband wanted her disconnected so that she could die in peace, her parents argued that she could get better, and that she would never have wanted to be deprived of food and water. The case reached the highest level of the US government and judicial bodies, with the Supreme Court and the President involved, Congress passing fast-track resolutions, and so on. The absurdity of this situation, in the wider context, is breathtaking: with tens of millions dying of AIDS and hunger all around the world, US public opinion focused on a single case of prolonging the run of *naked life*, of a persistent vegetative state bereft of all specifically human characteristics. This is the truth of what the Catholic Church means when its representatives talk about the "culture of life" as opposed to the "culture of death" of contemporary nihilistic hedonism. What we encounter here is, in effect, a kind of Hegelian infinite judgment which asserts the speculative identity of the highest and the lowest: the Life of the Spirit, the divine spiritual dimension, and the life reduced to inert vegetation. . . . These are the two extremes we find ourselves today with regard to human rights: on the one hand those "missed by the bombs" (mentally and physically full human beings, but deprived of rights), on the other a human being reduced to bare vegetative life, but this bare life being protected by the entire state apparatus.

So Bush was wrong: what we are getting when we see the photos of the humiliated Iraqi prisoners on our screens and front pages is precisely a direct insight into "American values," into the very core of the obscene enjoyment that sustains the US way of life. These photos therefore put into an appropriate perspective Samuel Huntington's well-known thesis on the ongoing "clash of civilizations": the clash between the Arab civilization and the American civilization is not a clash between barbarism and respect for human dignity, but a clash between anonymous brutal torture and torture as a mediatic spectacle in which the victims' bodies serve as the anonymous background for the stupidly smiling "innocent American" faces of the torturers themselves. At the same time, we have here a proof of how—to paraphrase Walter Benjamin—every clash of civilizations is the clash of the underlying barbarisms.

This obscene virtual dimension is inscribed into an ideological text in the guise of the fantasmatic background that sustains the emptiness of the Master-Signifier. The Master-Signifier is the signifier of potentiality, of potential threat, of a threat which, in order to function as such, has to remain potential (just as it is also the signifier of potential meaning whose actuality is the void of meaning: "our Nation," for instance, is the thing itself, the supreme Cause worth dying for, the highest density of meaning—and, as such, it means nothing in particular, it has no determinate meaning, it can be articulated only in the guise a tautology—"The Nation is the Thing itself").[63] This emptiness of the threat is clearly discernible in everyday phrases like "Just wait! You'll see what will happen to you!"—the very lack of the specification of *what* exactly will befall you is what makes the threat so threatening, since it invites the power of my fantasy to fill it in with imagined horrors.[64] As such, the Master-Signifier is the privileged site at which fantasy intervenes, since the function of fantasy is precisely to fill in the void of the signifier-without-signified: that is to say, *fantasy is ultimately, at its most elementary, the stuff which fills in the void of the Master-Signifier*: again, in the case of a Nation, all the mythic obscure narratives which tell us what the Nation is.[65] In other words, sovereignty always (in its very concept, as Hegel would have put it) involves the logic of the universal and its constitutive exception: the universal and unconditional rule of Law can be sustained only by a sovereign power which reserves for itself the right to proclaim a state of exception, that is, to suspend the rule of law(s) on behalf of the Law itself—if we deprive the Law of its excess that sustains it, we lose the (rule of) Law itself.

In the twentieth and twenty-first centuries, this link between power and invisible threat gets in a way redoubled or reflected-into-itself: it is no longer merely the existing power structure which, in order to maintain its efficiency, its hold over its subjects, has to rely on the fantasmatic dimension of the potential/invisible threat; the place of the threat is, rather, externalized, displaced into the Outside, the Enemy of the Power—it is the invisible (and for that very reason all-powerful and omnipresent) threat of the Enemy that legitimizes the permanent state of emergency of the existing Power (Fascists invoked the threat of the Jewish conspiracy, Stalinists the threat of the class enemy—right up to today's "war on terror," of course). This invisible threat of the Enemy legitimizes the logic of the preemptive strike: precisely because the threat is virtual, it is too late to wait for its actualization, we have to strike in advance, before it is too late. . . . In other words, the omnipresent invisible threat of Terror legitimizes the all-too-visible protective measures of defense (which pose the only *true* threat to democracy and human rights, of course). If the classic Power functioned as the threat which was operative precisely by never actualizing itself, by remaining a threatening gesture (and this functioning reached its climax in the Cold War, with the threat of mutual nuclear destruction which *had* to remain a threat), with the war on terror, the invisible threat causes the incessant actualization—not of itself, but—of measures against itself. The nuclear strike had to remain the threat of a strike, while the threat of the terrorist strike triggers the endless series of strikes against potential terrorists. The power which presents itself as being under threat all the time, living in mortal danger, and thus merely defending itself, is the most dangerous kind of power, the very model of Nietzschean *ressentiment* and moralistic hypocrisy—and, in fact, was it not Nietzsche himself who, more than a century ago, provided the best analysis of the false moral premises of today's "war on terror"?

No government admits any longer that it keeps an army to satisfy occasionally the desire for conquest. Rather, the army is supposed to serve for defense, and one invokes the morality that approves of self-defense. But this implies one's own morality and the neighbor's immorality; for the neighbor must be thought of as eager to attack and conquer if our state must think of means of self-defense. Moreover, the reasons we give for requiring an army imply that our neighbor, who denies the desire for conquest just as much as our own state does, and who, for his part, also keeps an army only for reasons of self-defense, is a hypocrite and a cunning criminal who would like nothing better than to overpower a harmless and awkward victim without any fight. Thus all states are now ranged against each other: they presuppose their neighbor's bad disposition and their own good disposition. This presupposition, however, is inhumane, as bad as war and worse. Fundamentally, indeed, it is itself the challenge and the cause of wars, because, as I have said, it attributes immorality to the neighbor, and thus provokes a hostile disposition and hostile acts. We must abjure the doctrine of the army as a means of self-defense just as completely as the desire for conquests.[66]

In Laclau's terms, then, is not the ongoing "War on Terror" a proof that Terror is the "constitutive outside" of democracy, its antagonistic Other, the point at which the democratic agonism of plural options turns into antagonism which relies on the logic of equivalence ("in the face of the terrorist threat, we are all together, forgetting our petty differences . . .")? More pointedly even, is not the relationship between the Empire and the threat of Terror analogous to the one between Enlightenment and its "superstitious" religious Other as described by Hegel in the chapter on "The Struggle of Enlightenment with Superstition" in *Phenomenology of Spirit*? That is to say: is not the inherent notional structure of the fundamentalist Terror the same as that of the enlightened Empire? Are they both not based on an insight with a claim to universality? In other words, the difference between the War on Terror and worldwide twentieth-century struggles like the Cold War is that while, in the earlier cases, the enemy—despite its spectrality—was clearly identified with the really existing Communist empire, the terrorist threat is inherently spectral, without a visible center. It is a bit like the characterization of the figure of Linda Fiorentino in *The Last Seduction*: "Most people have a dark side . . . she had nothing else." Most regimes have a dark oppressive spectral side . . . the terrorist threat has nothing else.[67] The paradoxical result of this spectralization of the enemy is an unexpected reflexive reversal: in this world without a clearly identified Enemy, it is the USA itself, the protector against the threat, which is emerging as the main enemy . . . as in Agatha Christie's *Murder on the Orient Express*, where, since the whole group of suspects committed the murder, the victim himself (an evil millionaire) should turn out to be the criminal.

What then, if *Heidegger was right* in his notorious doubt about democracy: "How can any political system be coordinated to the technological age, and which political system would that be? I know of no answer to this question. I am not convinced that it is democracy."[68] What Heidegger had in mind as a more adequate political response to the technological age was probably a kind of "totalitarian" sociopolitical mobilization in the Nazi or Soviet style; he could not see how liberal-democratic "tolerance" mobilizes individuals much more effectively, turning them into workaholics—Beistegui puts forward this obvious counterargument:

> One can wonder as to whether Heidegger was right to suggest, as he did in the *Der Spiegel* interview, that democracy is perhaps not the most adequate response to technology. With the collapse of fascism and of soviet communism, the liberal model has proven to be the most effective and powerful vehicle of the global spread of technology, which has become increasingly indistinguishable from the forces of Capital.[69]

Does not the ongoing "silent revolution," limitation of democracy, however, make the self-evident character of this argument problematic? Does not the dynamic of today's global capitalism enable us to discern inherent limits to the liberal-democratic model?

OF EGGS, OMELETS, AND BARTLEBY'S SMILE

This "speculative identity" of opposites in the ongoing "War on Terror" compels us to draw a series of crucial politico-theoretical consequences, the first being about conspiracy theories. We all know the cliché about conspiracy theories as the poor man's ideology: when individuals lack the elementary cognitive mapping capabilities and resources that would enable them to locate their place within a social totality, they invent conspiracy theories which provide an ersatz mapping, explaining all the complexities of social life as the result of a hidden conspiracy. As Fredric Jameson (the author of the term "cognitive mapping") himself pointed out, however, this ideologico-critical dismissal is not enough: in today's global capitalism, we *are* all too often dealing with actual "conspiracies" (the destruction of Los Angeles's public transport network in the early 1950s was not an expression of some "objective logic of capital," but the result of an explicit "conspiracy" between car companies, road construction companies, and public agencies—and the same goes for many "tendencies" in today's urban developments).

The dismissal of the "paranoiac" ideological dimension of conspiracy theories (the supposition of a mysterious all-powerful Master, and so on) should alert us to *actual* "conspiracies" going on all the time: today, the ultimate ideology is the self-complacent critico-ideological dismissal of conspiracies as mere fantasies. In other words, if, in the old days of traditional capitalism, the appearance of Order, of a central controlling agency, masked the underlying chaos, the uncontrolled, "natural-historical," character of social processes, today, the appearance of "chaos" (in all its dimensions, up to the celebration of "postmodern" capitalism which relies on chaotic autopoietic processes, decentralized decisions, and so on) is the ideological mask of the unprecedented growth of state apparatuses and other forms of social and economic control and regulation. The neocolonialist enslavement of Third World countries, for example, is not a "blind" natural process, obeying the anonymous "logic of capital," but a well-organized and coordinated process. Or—to put it in Foucauldian terms—it is not that power, which in effect functions as a chaotic complex network of localized micro-practices, wants to be seen as emanating from a central point of decision, the supreme Subject of Power; it is, rather, that today's power follows the strategy of denying itself, presenting its organized apparatuses as elements of a chaotic network.[70]

The second consequence, linked to the first, is our awareness of how, in accusations about "fundamentalism," the Evil often resides in the very gaze which perceives the fundamentalist Evil (to paraphrase Hegel)—this holds especially in the case of Muslim fundamentalism. The great eighth-century Muslim intellectual Abu Hanita wrote: "Difference of opinion in the community is a token of Divine mercy."[71] That this attitude was actually a guiding principle of Muslim communities until their encounter with European modernity is aptly demonstrated when we ask a simple question: when did the Balkans (a geographical region of southeastern Europe) become "Balkan" (what this term designates in the European ideological imaginary)? The answer is: in the middle of the nineteenth century, that is to say, at the very moment when the Balkans were fully exposed to the (political, economic, military, ideological) effects of European modernization.[72] The gap between earlier Western European perception of the Balkans and the image of "Balkan" over the last 150 years is absolutely breathtaking: in the sixteenth century, Pierre Belon, a French natural scientist, noted how "the Turks force nobody to live according to the Turkish way"[73]—no wonder that, after Ferdinand and Isabella expelled the Jews from Spain in 1492, most of them were given asylum (and the freedom to practice their religion) in Muslim countries, so that, in a supreme twist of irony, many Western travelers were disturbed by the public presence of Jews in big Turkish cities. From a long series of examples, here is a report from N. Bisani, an Italian who visited Istanbul in 1788:

> A stranger, who has beheld the intolerance of London and Paris, must be much surprised to see a church here between a mosque and a synagogue, and a dervish by the side of a capuchin friar. I know not how this government can have admitted into its bosom religions so opposite to its own. It must be from degeneracy of Mahommedanism, that this happy contrast can be produced. What is still more astonishing, is to find that this spirit of toleration is generally prevalent among the people; for here you see Turks, Jews, Catholics, Armenians, Greeks, and Protestants conversing together, on subjects of business or pleasure, with as much harmony and good will as if they were of the same country and religion.[74]

Note how the very feature which Europeans celebrate today as the sign of their cultural superiority—the spirit and practice of multiculturalist tolerance—is dismissed as an effect of the "degeneracy of Mahommedanism"! A case in point here is the strange fate of the "Star Mary," a large French Trappist monastery: after being expelled from France by the Napoleonic regime, the monks first found refuge in Germany; when, in 1868, they were driven out of Germany too, no Christian state was willing to take them in, so they asked (and received!) the sultan's permission to purchase land in the neighborhood of Banja Luka (in the Serb part of today's Bosnia), where they lived happily

thereafter . . . until they got caught up in the Balkan conflicts among *Christians*.[75]
The irony of a Christian monastery allowed to thrive only in the Muslim-dominated
part of Europe is unbeatable. Where, then, do the features which we, Westerners, usually associate with the word "Balkan" (the spirit of intolerance, ethnic violence, obsession with historical traumas, and so on) come from? There is only one answer: from
Western Europe itself. In a nice case of what Hegel called "reflexive determination,"
what Western Europeans observe and condescendingly deplore in the Balkans is what
they themselves introduced there: what they fight in the Balkans is their own historical legacy run amok. Let us not forget that the two great ethnic crimes imputed to the
Turks in the twentieth century, the Armenian genocide and the oppression of the
Kurds, were not executed by the traditionalist Muslim political forces, but precisely by
the military modernizers who wanted to liberate Turkey from its traditional ballast and
change it into a European nation-state. Mladen Dolar's old quip, based on a detailed
reading of Freud's references to the Balkan area, on how European unconscious is
structured like the Balkans, is thus literally true: in the guise of the Otherness of
"Balkan," Europe takes cognizance of the "stranger in itself," of its own repressed.

This, however, does not in any way entail that one can simply oppose a "true" identity of a culture to its falsification by a foreign gaze—the next consequence is that this
"true" identity itself, as a rule, forms itself through the identification with a foreign gaze
which plays the role of the culture's Ego-Ideal. Argentinian identity, for example, formed
itself in the mid-nineteenth century, when its main mythical themes were established
(gaucho melancholy, and so on); all these themes, however, had already appeared in the
memoirs of European travelers a couple of decades earlier—this means that, from the
very beginning, Argentinian ideological self-identity relied on an alienating identification with the Other's gaze. The same holds even more for modern Greece: in 1800
Athens was a provincial peasant village with 10,000 inhabitants; it was not even the first
capital of independent Greece. It was under pressure from Western powers (mostly Germany and England) that the capital was moved to Athens, where a series of neoclassical
government buildings were constructed by Western architects; it was also the Westerners, fascinated by antiquity, who instilled in the Greeks a sense of continuity with
ancient Greece. Modern Greece thus literally arose as the materialization of the Other's
fantasy, and, since the right of fantasy is the fundamental right, should we not draw
from this the extremely non-PC conclusion not only that Germany and England should
not return to Greece the ancient monuments they plundered, which are now displayed
in the Pergamon Museum and the British Museum—the Greeks should even voluntarily offer to Germany and England whatever ancient monuments they still possess,
since these monuments have value only for the Western ideological fantasy?

The general methodological guideline that imposes itself from these observations
can be best exemplified by the old story about a worker suspected of stealing: every
evening, when he left the factory, the wheelbarrow he rolled in front of him was carefully inspected, but the guards did not find anything inside, it was always empty—
until, finally, they got the point: what the worker was stealing were the wheelbarrows

themselves. . . . This is the trick that those who claim today "But the world is nonethe-less better off without Saddam!" try to pull on us: they forget to include in their ac-count the effects of the very military intervention against Saddam. Yes, the world is better off without Saddam—but it is not better off with the military occupation of Iraq, with the new rise of Islamic fundamentalism provoked by this occupation.[76]

And we should not be afraid to draw the same consequence apropos of democracy itself: to look for the wheelbarrow which is stolen from the people when they are bombarded by claims that "things are nonetheless better in a democracy.". . . The first thing to note here is that the certainty that democracy is "inessential," that it makes the destiny of a nation dependent on a whim of a minority which can shift the vote, and the corresponding conviction of a political agent that its mission is grounded in an insight into the true state of things, and so on, are not false "naturalizations" which disavow authentic democratic openness, claiming a privileged position for them-selves, and thus posing a potential threat to democracy; they are, rather, the necessary outcome and ingredient of the democratic logic itself. That is to say: such claim to a privileged insight, dismissive of the democratic rules of the game, is possible only within the democratic space—it is the content which necessarily supplements the dem-ocratic form, the "stuff" of democratic procedure.

This is why the notion of *evaluation* is crucial for the functioning of democratic so-ciety: if, at the level of their symbolic identity, all subjects are equal; if, here, un *sujet vaut* l'autre; if they can be indefinitely substituted for one another, since each of them is re-duced to an empty punctual place (*$*), to a "man without qualities-properties" (to recall the title of Robert Musil's *magnum opus*)—if, consequently, every reference to their properly symbolic mandate is prohibited—how, then, are they to be distributed within the social edifice, how can their occupation be legitimized? The answer is, of course, *evaluation*: one has to evaluate—as objectively as possible, and through all pos-sible means, from quantified testing of their abilities to more "personalized" in-depth interviews—their potential. The underlying ideal notion is to produce their charac-terization deprived of all traces of symbolic identities. Furthermore, egalitarianism itself should never be accepted at face value: the notion (and practice) of egalitarian justice, insofar as it is sustained by envy, relies on the inversion of the standard renun-ciation accomplished to benefit others: "I am ready to renounce it, so that others will (also) *not* (be able to) have it!"

It is fashionable to complain how, today, when one's intimate personal details, right down to details of one's sex life, can be exposed in the media, private life is threatened, even disappearing. . . . [77] This is true, on condition that we turn things around: what is in fact disappearing in the public display of intimate details is *public life itself*, the public sphere proper in which one operates as a symbolic agent who cannot be reduced to a private individual, to a bundle of intimate properties, desires, traumas, idiosyncrasies.[78] This means that the "deconstructionist"/"risk-society" commonplace according to which the contemporary individual experiences himself as thoroughly denaturalized, that he experiences even his most "natural" features (from his ethnic identity to his sexual preferences) as something chosen, historically contingent, to be learned, is profoundly deceptive: what we are actually witnessing today is the opposite process of an unprecedented *renaturalization*: all big "public issues" are (re)translated into questions about the regulation of and stances toward intimate "natural"/"personal" idiosyncrasies. This is also why, at a more general level, pseudo-naturalized ethnic-religious conflicts are the form of struggle which fits global capitalism: in our age of "post-politics," when politics proper is progressively replaced by expert social administration, the only remaining legitimate sources of conflict are cultural (religious) or natural (ethnic) tensions.[79] And "evaluation" is precisely the regulation of social promotion that fits this massive renaturalization. So, perhaps, the time has come to reassert, as the truth of evaluation, the perverted logic to which Marx refers ironically in his description of commodity fetishism, when he quotes Dogberry's advice to Seacoal from Shakespeare's *Much Ado About Nothing* (Act III, Scene 3) which concludes Chapter 1 of *Capital*: "To be a well-favoured man is the gift of fortune; but reading and writing comes by nature." Today, in our times of evaluation, to be a computer expert or a successful manager is a gift of nature, while to have beautiful lips or eyes is a fact of culture. . . .

Democracy presupposes a minimum of alienation: those who exert power can be held responsible to the people only if there is a minimal distance of representation between them and the people. In "totalitarianism," this distance is cancelled, the Leader is supposed to represent the will of the people directly—and the result is, of course, that the (empirical) people are even more radically alienated in their Leader: he directly *is* what they "really are," their true identity, their true wishes and interests, as opposed to their confused "empirical" wishes and interests. In contrast to the authoritarian Power alienated from its subjects, the people, here the "empirical" people are alienated *from themselves*.[80]

In his (unpublished manuscript) *La logique des mondes*, Alain Badiou elaborates the eternal Idea of the politics of revolutionary justice at work, from the ancient Chinese "legalists" through the Jacobins to Lenin and Mao, which consists of four moments: *voluntarism* (the belief that one can "move mountains," ignoring "objective" laws and obstacles); *terror* (a ruthless will to crush the enemy of the people); *egalitarian justice* (its immediate brutal imposition, with no understanding of the "complex circumstances" which allegedly compel us to proceed gradually); and, last but not least, *trust in the people*—the catch, of course, lies in the ambiguity of this supplementary term, "trust in the people": are the people who are trusted "empirical" individuals or the People, on behalf of whom one can turn terror on behalf of the people against the people's enemies into terror against the people themselves?

This, of course, does not in any way imply a simple plea for democracy and a rejection of "totalitarianism": on the contrary, there is a moment of truth in "totalitarianism." Hegel pointed out how political representation does not mean that people already know in advance what they want, then charge their representatives with advocating their interests—they know it only "in itself," it is their representative who formulates their interests and goals for them, making them "for-itself." The "totalitarian" logic thus makes explicit, posits "as such," a split which always-already cuts from within the represented "people."The line of separation between the "totalitarian" leader and the analyst is thus thin, almost imperceptible: both are *objets petit a*, objects of transferential love; the difference between them is the difference between the perverse social link (in which the pervert *knows* what the other really wants) and the discourse of the analyst who, while occupying this place of supposed knowledge, keeps it *empty*.

Here we should not be afraid to come to a radical conclusion concerning the figure of the leader: as a rule, democracy cannot reach beyond pragmatic utilitarian inertia, it cannot suspend the logic of "servicing goods"; consequently, just as there is no self-analysis, since the analytic change can occur only through the transferential relationship to the external figure of the analyst, a leader is necessary to trigger enthusiasm for a Cause, to bring about radical change in the subjective position of his followers, to "transubstantiate" their identity.[81]

There is a precise line of separation between a nonrevolutionary and a revolutionary situation. In a nonrevolutionary situation, one can solve the pressing immediate problems while postponing the big key problem ("people are dying now in Rwanda, so forget about anti-imperialist struggle, let us just prevent the slaughter"; or: "we have to fight poverty and racism here and now, and not wait for the collapse of the global capitalist order"); in a revolutionary situation, this strategy no longer works, and one has to tackle the Big Problem in order even to solve the "small" pressing ones. The procedure of prescription is therefore, in a strictly formal sense, the one whose presence indicates the proximity of a "revolutionary situation": instead of pragmatically solving local problems, the political agents, confronted with a local problem or deadlock, as it were overtake themselves and escape into the future, that is, they directly posit the fundamental Axiom as the starting point for solving *present* local problems.

This, however, does not mean that the notion of a proper revolutionary situation concerns only the difference between short-term and long-term goal—in every authentic revolutionary explosion, there is an element of "pure" violence; that is to say, an authentic political revolution cannot be measured by the standard of servicing goods (to what extent "life got better for the majority" afterward)—it is a goal in itself, an act which changes the very concept of what a "good life" is, and a different (higher, eventually) standard of living is a by-product of a revolutionary process, not its goal. Usually, revolutionary violence is defended by evoking proverbial platitudes like "You can't make an omelet without breaking eggs"—a "wisdom" which, of course, can easily be rendered problematic through boring "ethical" considerations about how even the noblest goals cannot justify murderous means to achieve them. Against such compromising attitudes, we should directly admit revolutionary violence as a liberating end in itself, so that the proverb should, rather, be turned around: "You can't break eggs (and what is revolutionary politics if not an activity in the course of which many eggs are broken?), especially if you're doing it in great heat (of a revolutionary passion), without making omelets!" This excess of violence is what even the most "tolerant" liberal stance is unable to come to terms with—witness the uneasiness of "radical" postcolonialist Afro-American studies apropos of Frantz Fanon's fundamental insight into the unavoidability of violence in the process of effective decolonization. Here we should recall Fredric Jameson's idea that violence plays in a revolutionary process the same role as worldly wealth plays in the Calvinist logic of predestination: although it has no intrinsic value, it is a sign of the authenticity of the revolutionary process, of the fact that this process is actually disturbing the existing power relations—the dream of a revolution without violence is precisely the dream of a "revolution without revolution" (Robespierre).

And, to add a final twist, this violent breaking of eggs should also not be immediately identified with outbursts of violence. When we are caught in the vicious cycle of the imperative of *jouissance*, the temptation is great to opt for what appears to be its "natural" opposite, the violent renunciation of *jouissance*. Is this not the fundamental underlying theme of all so-called "fundamentalisms"? Do they not all endeavor to contain (what they perceive as) the excessive "narcissistic hedonism" of contemporary secular culture with the call to reintroduce the spirit of sacrifice? However, a psychoanalytic perspective immediately enables us to see why such an endeavor goes wrong: the very gesture of renouncing enjoyment ("Enough of decadent pleasures! Renounce and sacrifice!") generates a surplus-enjoyment of its own. Do not all "totalitarian" universes which demand of their subjects violent (self-)sacrifice to the Cause exude the bad smell of fascination with a lethal obscene *jouissance*? (And vice versa: a life oriented toward pleasures cannot but end up in the utmost discipline needed to guarantee the maximum of pleasures: a "healthy lifestyle," from jogging to dieting and mental relaxation, respect for others.) The superego injunction to enjoy is immanently intertwined with the logic of sacrifice: the two form a vicious cycle, each extreme supporting the other.

This, of course, does not in any way imply that we should rule out violence as such. Violence is needed—but *what* violence? There is violence and violence: there are violent *passages à l'acte* which merely bear witness to the agent's impotence; there is a violence the true aim of which is to make sure that nothing actually changes—in a Fascist display of violence, something spectacular should happen all the time so that, precisely, nothing will really happen; and there is the violent act of actually changing the basic coordinates of a constellation. In order for the last kind of violence to take place, *this very place should be opened up* through a gesture which is thoroughly violent in its impassive refusal, through a gesture of pure withdrawal in which—to quote Mallarmé—*rien n'aura eu lieu que le lieu*, nothing will have taken place but the place itself.

And this brings us back to Melville's Bartleby. His "I would prefer not to" is to be taken literally: it says "I would prefer not to," *not* "I don't prefer (or care) to"—so we are back at Kant's distinction between negative and infinite judgment. In his refusal of the Master's order, Bartleby does not negate the predicate; rather, he affirms a nonpredicate: he does not say that he *doesn't want to do it*; he says that *he prefers (wants) not to do it*.[82] This is how we pass from the politics of "resistance" or "protestation," which parasitizes upon what it negates, to a politics which opens up a new space outside the hegemonic position *and* its negation. We can imagine the varieties of such a gesture in today's public space: not only the obvious "There are great chances of a new career here! Join us!"—"I would prefer not to"; but also "Discover the depths of your true self, find inner peace!"—"I would prefer not to"; or "Are you aware how our environment is endangered? Do something for ecology!"—"I would prefer not to"; or "What about all the racial and sexual injustices that we witness all around us? Isn't it time to do more?"—"I would prefer not to." This is the gesture of subtraction at its purest, the reduction of all qualitative differences to a purely formal minimal difference.

Are we not making the same point here as Hardt and Negri in *Empire*, who also refer to Bartleby as the figure of resistance, of saying No! to the existing universe of social machinery?[83] The difference is double. First, for HN, Bartleby's "I would prefer not to" is interpreted as merely the first move of, as it were, clearing the table, of acquiring a distance toward the existing social universe; what is then needed is a move toward the painstaking work of constructing a new community—if we remain stuck at the Bartleby stage, we end up in a suicidal marginal position with no consequences. . . . From our point of view, however, this, precisely, is the conclusion to be avoided: in its political mode, Bartleby's "I would prefer not to" is *not* the starting point of "abstract negation" which should then be overcome in the patient positive work of the "determinate negation" of the existing social universe,[84] but a kind of *arche*, the underlying principle that sustains the entire movement: far from "overcoming" it, the subsequent work of construction, rather, gives body to it.

This brings us back to the central theme of this book: the parallax shift. Bartleby's attitude is not merely the first, preparatory, stage for the second, more "constructive," work of forming a new alternative order; it is the very source and background of this order, its permanent foundation. The difference between Bartleby's gesture of withdrawal and the formation of a new order is—again, and for the last time—that of parallax: the very frantic and engaged activity of constructing a new order is sustained by an underlying "I would prefer not to" which forever reverberates in it—or, as Hegel might have put it, the new postrevolutionary order does not negate its founding gesture, the explosion of the destructive fury that wipes away the Old; it merely *gives body* to this negativity. The difficulty of imagining the New is the difficulty of imagining Bartleby in power. Thus the logic of the move from the superego-parallax to the Bartleby-parallax is very precise: it is the move from something to nothing, from the gap between two "somethings" to the gap that separates a something from nothing, from the void of its own place. That is to say: in a "revolutionary situation," what, exactly, happens to the gap between the public Law and its obscene superego supplement? It is not that, in a kind of metaphysical unity, the gap is simply abolished, that we obtain only a public regulation of social life, deprived of any hidden obscene supplement. *The gap remains*, but reduced to a structural minimum: to the "pure" difference between the set of social regulations and the void of their absence. In other words, Bartleby's gesture is what remains of the supplement to the Law when its place it emptied of all its obscene superego content.

We should draw the same conclusions at the most general level of ontological difference itself: it brings to an extreme the traditional philosophical difference between the physical level and the metaphysical level, between the empirical and the transcendental, by reducing it to the "minimal" difference between what is, something, and—not another, "higher," reality, but—*nothing*. Overcoming metaphysics does not mean reducing the metaphysical dimension to ordinary physical reality (or, in a more "Marxist" way, showing how all metaphysical specters arise from the antagonisms of real life), but reducing the difference between material reality and another, "higher" reality to the immanent difference, gap, between this reality and its own void; that is, to discern the void that separates material reality *from itself*, that makes it "non-all."[85] And the same goes for the ultimate parallax of political economy, the gap between the reality of everyday material social life (people interacting among themselves and with nature, suffering, consuming, and so on) and the Real of the speculative dance of Capital, its self-propelling movement which seems to be disconnected from ordinary reality. We can experience this gap very tangibly when we visit a country where life is obviously in a shambles, we see a lot of ecological decay and human misery; the economist's report we read afterward however, informs us that the country's economic situation is "financially sane.". . . Marx's point here is not primarily to reduce the second dimension to the first (to demonstrate how the supranatural mad dance of commodities arises out of the antagonisms of "real life"); his point is, rather, that *we cannot properly grasp the first (the social reality of material production and social interaction) without the second*: it is the self-propelling metaphysical dance of Capital that runs the show, that provides the key to real-life developments and catastrophes.

Second (and more important, perhaps), the withdrawal expressed by "I would prefer not to" is not to be reduced to the attitude of "saying no to the Empire" but, first and foremost, to all the wealth of what I have called the *rumspringa* of resistance, all the forms of resisting which help the system to reproduce itself by ensuring our participation in it—today, "I would prefer not to" is not primarily "I would prefer not to participate in the market economy, in capitalist competition and profiteering," but—much more problematically for some—"I would prefer not to give to charity to support a Black orphan in Africa, engage in the struggle to prevent oil-drilling in a wildlife swamp, send books to educate our liberal-feminist-spirited women in Afghanistan. . . ." A distance toward the direct hegemonic interpellation—"Involve yourself in market competition, be active and productive!"—is the very mode of operation of today's ideology: today's ideal subject says to himself: "I am well aware that the whole business of social competition and material success is just an empty game, that my true Self is elsewhere!" If anything, "I would prefer not to" expresses, rather, a refusal to play the "Western Buddhist" game of "social reality is just an illusory game."

A wonderfully ambiguous indicator of our present ideological predicament is *Sandcastles: Buddhism and Global Finance*, a documentary by Alexander Oey (2005) with commentaries from the economist Arnoud Boot, the sociologist Saskia Sassen, and the Tibetan Buddhist teacher Dzongzar Khyentse Rinpoche. Sassen and Boot discuss the gigantic scope, power, and social and economic effects of global finance: capital markets, now valued at an estimated $83 trillion, exist within a system based purely on self-interest, in which herd behavior, often based on rumor, can inflate or destroy the value of companies—or whole economies—in a matter of hours. Khyentse Rinpoche counters them with ruminations about the nature of human perception, illusion, and enlightenment; his philosophico-ethical statement "Release your attachment to something that is not there in reality, but is a perception," is supposed to throw a new light on the mad dance of billion-dollar speculations. Echoing the Buddhist notion that there is no Self, only a stream of continuous perceptions, Sassen comments about global capital: "It's not that there are $83 trillion. It is essentially a continuous set of movements. It disappears and it reappears." . . .

The problem here, of course, is: how are we to read this parallel between Buddhist ontology and the structure of virtual capitalism's universe? The film tends toward the humanist reading: seen through a Buddhist lens, the exuberance of global financial wealth is illusory, divorced from objective reality—the very real human suffering created by deals made on trading floors and in boardrooms invisible to most of us. If, however, we accept the premise that the value of material wealth, and one's experience of reality, is subjective, and that desire plays a decisive role in both daily life and neoliberal economics, is it not possible to draw precisely the opposite conclusion? Is it not that our traditional life-world was based on naive-realist substantialist notions of external reality composed of fixed objects, while the unprecedented dynamic of "virtual capitalism" confronts us with the illusory nature of reality? What better proof of the nonsubstantial character of reality could there be than a gigantic fortune which can dissolve into nothing in a couple of hours, just because of a sudden false rumor? Consequently, why complain that financial futures speculations are "divorced from objective reality," when the basic premise of Buddhist ontology is that there is no "objective reality"?

Thus the only "critical" lesson to be drawn from the Buddhist perspective about today's virtual capitalism is that we should be aware that we are dealing with a mere theater of shadows, with insubstantial virtual entities, and, as a result, that we should not fully engage ourselves in the capitalist game, that we should play the game with an inner distance. Virtual capitalism could thus act as a first step toward liberation: it confronts us with the fact that the cause of our suffering and enslavement is not objective reality itself (there is no such thing) but our Desire, our craving for material things, our excessive attachment to them; all we have to do, after we rid ourselves of the false notion of substantialist reality, is thus to renounce our desire itself, to adopt an attitude of inner peace and distance . . . no wonder such Buddhism can function as the perfect ideological supplement of today's virtual capitalism: it allows us to participate in it with an inner distance—with our fingers crossed, as it were.

It is against such a disengagement that Bartleby repeats his "I would prefer not to"—not "not to do it": his refusal is not so much the refusal of a determinate content as, rather, the formal gesture of refusal as such. It is therefore strictly analogous to

Sygne's No!: it is an act of *Versagung*, not a symbolic act. There is a clear holophrastic quality to "I would prefer not to": it is a signifier-turned-object, a signifier reduced to an inert stain that stands for the collapse of the symbolic order.

There are two cinema versions of *Bartleby*: a TV film from 1970, directed by Anthony Friedman, and a 2001 version set in today's Los Angeles, directed by Jonathan Parker; however, a persistent, albeit unverified, rumor is haunting the Internet underground of a third version in which Bartleby is played by Anthony Perkins. Even if this rumor turns out to be false, *se non è vero, è ben trovato* holds here more than ever: Perkins, in his Norman Bates mode, would have been the Bartleby. We can imagine Bartleby's smile, as he delivers his "I would prefer not to," being that of Norman Bates in the very last shot of *Psycho*, when he looks into the camera, his (mother's) voice saying: "I couldn't even hurt a fly." There is no violent quality in it; the violence pertains to its very immobile, inert, insistent, impassive being.

Bartleby couldn't even hurt a fly—that's what makes his presence so unbearable.

Introduction: Dialectical Materialism at the Gates

1. See Giles Tremlett, "Anarchists and the Fine Art of Torture," *The Guardian*, January 27, 2003.

2. See Stuart Jeffries, "Did Stalin's Killers Liquidate Walter Benjamin?," *The Observer*, July 8, 2001.

3. Perhaps the most succinct definition of revolutionary utopia is a social order in which this duality, this parallax gap, would no longer be operative—a space in which Lenin *could* in fact meet and debate with the Dadaists.

4. If we take a closer look, it becomes clear that the very relationship between these two stories is that of a parallax: their symmetry is not pure, since the Laurenčič anecdote is clearly about politics (political terror and torture), using modernist art as a comical counterpoint; while the Benjamin anecdote is about "high theory," using, on the contrary, Stalin as its comical counterpoint.

5. I share with Alain Badiou the conviction that the time has come openly to assume this problematic term (in his forthcoming *La logique des mondes*, Badiou designates as today's principal politico-philosophical opposition that of "democratic materialism" and "materialist dialectics").

6. V. I. Lenin, *Collected Works*, vol. 33 (Moscow: Progress Publishers, 1966), p. 282.

7. The same holds for truth: it is crucial to move from *true* propositions to the *truth itself which speaks.*

8. Who, today, must remain unnamed, like the dwarf hidden within the puppet of historical materialism.

9. Here I should acknowledge my debt to Kojin Karatani's *Transcritique: On Kant and Marx* (Cambridge, MA: MIT Press, 2003).

10. Thus drive emerges as a strategy to profit from the very failure to reach the goal of desire.

11. Quoted from Anne Norton, *Leo Strauss and the Politics of American Empire* (New Haven: Yale University Press, 2004), p. 217.

12. René Descartes, *Discourse on Method* (South Bend: University of Notre Dame Press, 1994), p. 33.

13. Karatani, *Transcritique*, p. 134.

14. Is the Hegelian totality, however, such an "organic" totality relying on the Particular as mediating between the Universal and the Individual? On the contrary, is not the (in)famous "contradiction" which propels the dialectical movement the very contradiction between the "organic"Whole (the structure of U-P-I) and the singularity which directly—without mediation—stands for the Universal?

15. However, we should not forget that a (fake) version of the Kantian "world-civil-society" already exists—in the guise of the so-called new "symbolic class" of executives, journalists, scientists, cultural workers, and so on, who directly participate in a worldwide cultural or professional network, and are thus much closer to members of the same class in the remotest part of the world than to members of other classes in their own society. The problem with this universal "symbolic class" is that its very universality is based on a radical division within each particular society: in an emblematic Hegelian way, universality is inscribed into every particular situation as its inner split.

16. Do these three moments, then, embody the triad of the Absolute (Being)–the Object (Science)–the Subject (Politics)? It is, rather, the opposite order of succession that holds, the properly Hegelian one: Subject-Object-Absolute. The One which differs from itself is the Absolute *qua* Subject; sciences endeavor to grasp it as object; politics is the Absolute "as such," a contingent, fragile process in which the very fate of the Absolute is at stake.

17. Along the same lines, we can imagine how Heidegger's newly discovered notes on sexuality would have looked. The essence of woman is *sich anzustellen*, to ex-pose oneself, *sich anzubieten*, to propose/offer oneself: here I am, pick me up, catch me, take me. In contrast to this stance of provocative exposure, *Herausforderung*, a man is boastfully putting himself up, parading before the woman's eyes: his stance is that of *sich aufstellen*, in the sense of *sich aufspielen, sich brüsten*. A man *stellt sich auf*; a woman *stellt sich an*. From here, we can imagine a Heideggerian erotic of disclosure/withdrawal: Being provokes us in its very disclosure, it provokes us through the withdrawal at the heart of its disclosure: the essence of *Sich-Anzustellen* is the *Sich-Anzustellen* of the essence itself, and the destiny of man is to screw things up, to fail in his attempt to respond properly to this provocative exposure. . . . So why not take the risk of enacting Heidegger's rhetorics of reversal ("the essence of truth is the truth of the essence itself," etc.) also apropos of the notion of *Abort* (toilet): the essence of abort is the *Ab-Ort* (dis-placing) of the essence itself. . . . Along the same lines, the *Er-Örterung* (explaining, literally: locating in its proper place) of a poem is simultaneously its *Ab-Örterung* (flushing it down the toilet). And what about abortion itself? What if the essence of abortion (*Ab-Treibung, Fehl-Geburt*) is nothing ontic, but the abortiveness of the essence itself?

1 THE SUBJECT, THIS "INWARDLY CIRCUMCISED JEW"

1. Furthermore, the very term "subject" has three main meanings: subject as an autonomous agent; subject as this same agent submitted ("subjected") to some power; topic, "subject matter." It is not difficult to recognize in these three meanings the triad of the Real, the Symbolic, and the Imaginary: pure subject as the "answer of the Real"; a subject of the signifier, submitted to—caught in—the symbolic order; the imaginary stuff that provides the matter, the "content," of the subject.

2. Jacques Lacan, *The Four Fundamental Concepts of Psycho-Analysis* (New York: Norton, 1979), p. 63.

3. For a condensed overview of the problem of the two versions of *Tender Is the Night*, see Malcolm Cowley's "Introduction" to the Penguin edition (Harmondsworth: Penguin, 1948).

4. Even the "complete" narrative of the second edition is structured around a black hole: it jumps directly from the events that led to marriage to the couple living on the Riviera, with their marriage already starting to disintegrate: the first few "happy years" are left out.

5. For this reason, I am tempted to suggest that the only feasible solution would have been to do something similar to what Luis Buñuel did in his Mexican adaptation of *Wuthering Heights* from the early 1950s (there, the story begins with Heathcliff's return—past events are evoked only as something mysterious that happened years ago between Heathcliff and Cathy, never directly shown or even narrated): to leave out the past completely, and merely to evoke it as a dark stain, as something indescribable, the "absent Cause" of the story.

6. See Jean Laplanche, *New Foundations for Psychoanalysis* (Oxford: Basil Blackwell, 1989).

7. See Kojin Karatani, *Transcritique: On Kant and Marx* (Cambridge, MA: MIT Press, 2003).

8. Ibid., p. 3.

9. And, as René Girard has pointed out, is not the first full assertion of the ethical parallax the book of Job, in which the two perspectives are confronted (the divine order of the world and Job's complaint), and neither is the "truthful" one—the truth lies in their very gap, in the shift of perspective. See René Girard, *Job: The Victim and His People* (Stanford: Stanford University Press, 1987).

10. Karatani, *Transcritique*, p. 6.

11. See chapter 1 of Slavoj Žižek, *Tarrying with the Negative* (Durham: Duke University Press, 1993).

12. Along these lines, the paradox of Kant's *Ding an sich* is that it is at the same time the excess of receptivity over intellect (the unknowable external source of our passive sensible perceptions) *and* the purely intelligible content-less construct of an X without any support in our senses.

13. So why does Kant call judgments like "The soul is non-mortal" infinite? Because, in contrast to "The soul isn't mortal," it covers an infinite set—not only the limited set of "immortal souls" as one of the species of the genus "souls," the other species being "mortal souls," but the open-ended, limitless set of souls which belong to the third domain, neither mortal nor immortal. For a closer elaboration of this distinction, see chapter 3 of Žižek, *Tarrying with the Negative*.

14. Perhaps the satisfaction obtained by cutters ("self-harmers") does not pertain so much to the way the feeling of intense bodily pain brings us back to reality, but, rather, to the fact that cutting oneself is a form of *making a mark*: when I cut into my arm, the "zero" of the subject's existential confusion, of my blurred virtual existence, is transformed into the "one" of a signifying inscription.

15. When Lacan defines himself as an anti-philosopher, as rebelling against philosophy, this is again to be conceived as a Kantian indefinite judgment: not "I am not a philosopher," but "I am a not-philosopher," that is, I stand for the excessive core of philosophy itself, for what is in philosophy more than philosophy (which is why his main references are philosophical—in the index of *Écrits*, Hegel outnumbers Freud!).

16. Immanuel Kant, *Critique of Practical Reason* (New York: Macmillan, 1956), pp. 152–153.

17. See *On Feminine Sexuality, the Limits of Love and Knowledge: The Seminar of Jacques Lacan*, Book 20, *Encore* (New York: Norton, 1999).

18. Cannot "multitude," in its opposition to crowd, also be conceived along the lines of the Lacanian non-All? Is multitude non-all, while there is nothing outside it, nothing that is not its part, and is crowd multitude under the sign of One, the "common denominator" of identification?

19. The same goes, say, for the fact that, in the Kantian dialectic of the Sublime, there is no positive Beyond whose phenomenal representation fails: there is nothing "beyond," the

"Beyond" is only the void of the impossibility/failure of its own representation—or, as Hegel put it at the end of the chapter on consciousness in his *Phenomenology of Spirit*, beyond the veil of phenomena, the consciousness finds only what it itself has put there. Again, Kant "knew it" without being able to formulate it consistently.

20. Claude Lévi-Strauss, "Do Dual Organizations Exist?," in *Structural Anthropology* (New York: Basic Books, 1963), pp. 131–163; the drawings are on pages 133–134. For a more detailed analysis of this example, see chapter 3 of Slavoj Žižek, *The Puppet and the Dwarf* (Cambridge, MA: MIT Press, 2003).

21. Lacan's thought moves from the "internal externality"—the famous "ex-timacy"—of the Real qua Thing to the Symbolic (the Real as the inaccessible traumatic core around which symbolic formations circulate like flies around the light which burns them if they approach it too closely) to the absolute inherence of Real to Symbolic (the Real has no subsistence, no ontological consistency of its own, it is *nothing but* the inherent inconsistency, gap, of the Symbolic). This, however, does not solve the key *materialist* question: if the Real has not subsistence of its own, if it is inherent to the Symbolic, how, then, are we to think the emergence-explosion of the Symbolic out of the presymbolic X? Is the only alternative to naive realism really a kind of "methodological idealism" according to which "the limits of our language are the limits of our world," so that what is beyond the Symbolic is strictly unthinkable?

22. *Kieślowski on Kieślowski*, ed. Danusia Stok (London: Faber & Faber, 1993), pp. 54–55.

23. Ibid., p. 86.

24. For a more detailed account of this passage, see chapter 1 of Slavoj Žižek, *The Fright of Real Tears* (London: BFI, 2001).

25. The problem with "abstract" universal terms like hybridity and nomadic subjectivity is that they tend to iron out, to render invisible, the antagonism that cuts across their content: when hybridity covers the globetrotting academic as well as the refugee from a war-torn country, it does something similar to obfuscating the gap that separates starving from dieting.

26. Rebecca Comay, "Dead Right: Hegel and the Terror," *South Atlantic Quarterly* 103: 2/3 (Spring/Summer 2004), p. 393.

27. Ibid., p. 392.

28. Fredric Jameson, *A Singular Modernity* (London and New York: Verso, 2002), p. 12.

29. See Ernesto Laclau and Chantal Mouffe, *Hegemony and Socialist Strategy* (London and New York: Verso, 1985).

30. Similarly, with regard to sexual difference, woman is not the polar opposite of man: *there are women because man is not fully itself.*

31. See F. W. J. Schelling, "Philosophical Investigations into the Essence of Human Freedom," in *Philosophy of German Idealism*, ed. Ernst Behler (New York: Continuum, 1987).

32. For a closer elaboration of this reflexive structure, see chapter 3 of Žižek, *The Puppet and the Dwarf.*

33. Gérard Wajcman, "The Birth of the Intimate (II)," *lacanian ink* 24–25 (New York, 2005), p. 44.

34. Jacques Derrida, *Acts of Literature* (New York: Routledge 1992), p. 201. In one of the supreme cases of the signifier's irony, the (real!) name of the big-breasted sex symbol of Slovene pop music today is Natalija *Verboten*—the German word for "prohibited": the Thing is not

simply prohibited, it is immediately the very emblem of prohibition, its agent. Therein resides the reflexivity of prohibition: *what is ultimately prohibited is the very agent of prohibition*, not the Thing access to which is prevented by this agent.

35. Jacques Derrida, *Acts of Religion* (New York: Routledge, 2002), p. 270.

36. Let us take an unexpected example: why does *Visions de l'amen*, Olivier Messiaen's masterpiece for two pianos (1943), consist of seven movements? He himself mentions four main versions of Amen: the Amen of creation ("So be it!"), the Amen of acceptance (of the divine will by his creatures), the Amen of desire, the Amen of paradisiacal bliss—are these four not Lacan's four elements of discourse $(S_1, S_2, \mathcal{S}, a)$? So why the other three? First, the Amen of acceptance is split into the Amen of creatures which pronounce their acceptance of their existence to their Creator ("Here we are, as you interpellated us!") and the Amen of Christ's acceptance of his suffering by means of which he will redeem the creatures. Secondly, the Amen of desire is inherently split into two aspects/sides of desiring: pure and peaceful spiritual longing, and the frantic torment of passion; these two are then externalized in two further movements: the Amen of the song of angels, saints, and birds (who exert pure spiritual desire) and the Amen of the Day of Judgment (on which ordinary humans will pay the price for their sinful passions). The whole is thus structured in a perfectly symmetrical way: in the middle, the Amen of desire, by far the longest movement, marked by an inherent split and surrounded by two triads, God-Creatures-Christ (Master and the split of the Servant's acceptance) and Angels-Judgment-Paradise (the division of the subject between pure and "pathological" desire, and the reconciliation of paradisiacal bliss). We begin with the One of the Master, followed by the triple split (of the serving creatures; of desire; of subjectivity), and conclude with the Sameness of paradisiacal bliss. Although this is a deeply Christian work, the structure of *Visions de l'amen* thus simultaneously renders the most elementary signifying structure.

37. See Ernesto Laclau, "Populist Reason," *Umbr(a)*, 2004.

38. See Karl Marx and Friedrich Engels, *Selected Works*, vol. 1 (Moscow: Progress Publishers, 1969), p. 95.

39. In a social link, affects (collective hatred, love of a Leader, panic, and other "passions") thus also cheat—except anxiety, which (as Freud put it in his essay on "Fetishism"—see Sigmund Freud, *Studienausgabe*, vol. 3 [Frankfurt: Fischer Verlag, 2000], p. 384) arises when we experience the fact that "the throne is empty." Is enthusiasm, then, the opposite of anxiety? Is it simply that the relationship between anxiety and enthusiasm is that of a proper distance: in enthusiasm, the object remains at a proper distance, while anxiety arises when it gets too close?

40. Blinded as we all are by the "French" Spinoza in all his different guises, from Althusser through Deleuze to Negri, we should not forget other readings of Spinoza which played a crucial role in theoretical orientations the very mention of which makes "postmodern" Leftists shudder. First, Spinoza was a crucial reference in the work of Georgi Plekhanov, the key theoretical figure of Russian Social Democracy, who, a century ago, was the first to elevate Marxism into an all-encompassing world-view (incidentally, he also coined the term "dialectical materialism")—against Hegel, he designated Marxism as "modern Spinozism.". . . Then, the reference to Spinoza is central to the work of Leo Strauss, the father figure of today's US neoconservatives: for Strauss, Spinoza provides a model for the split between popular ideology, appropriate for ordinary people, and true knowledge, which should remain accessible only to the few. Last but not least, Spinoza's anti-Cartesian teaching on the human soul is considered an authority by some of today's most influential cognitivists and brain scientists—Antonio Damasio even wrote a popular book, *Looking for Spinoza*. It is thus as if every postmodern "French" figure of Spinoza is accompanied by an obscene disavowed double or precursor: Althusser's proto-Marxist Spinoza—"with

Plekhanov"; Negri's anti-Empire Spinoza of the multitude—"with Leo Strauss"; Deleuze's Spinoza of affects—"with Damasio.". . .

41. Apropos of Kant, Dieter Henrich deployed this same difference as the difference between person and subject—see Dieter Henrich, *Bewusste Leben* (Stuttgart: Reclam, 1999), p. 199.

42. Friedrich Nietzsche, *The Anti-Christ* (Harmondsworth: Penguin, 1978), p. 173.

43. Friedrich Nietzsche, *The Genealogy of Morals* (New York: Anchor Books, 1956), p. 255.

44. Friedrich Nietzsche, *The Will to Power* (New York: Random House, 1968), p. 288.

45. See Alenka Zupančič, *The Shortest Shadow* (Cambridge, MA: MIT Press, 2003).

46. Comay, "Dead Right: Hegel and the Terror," p. 386.

47. G. W. F. Hegel, "Jenaer Realphilosophie," in *Frühe politische Systeme* (Frankfurt: Ullstein, 1974), p. 204.

48. In more general terms, the spectral Real appears in three versions: the shadow of the spectral entities which accompanies fully constituted reality; the inscription of the gaze itself into perceived reality; the multiplication of realities themselves—that is, the idea that what we perceive as reality is just one in the multitude of alternatives. The link between these three versions is easy to establish: the gap which separates reality from its proto-ontological spectral shadow is not simply "ontological" (in the naive sense of the inherent properties of the objects themselves); it concerns the way the subject relates to reality—in short, this gap marks the inscription of the subject's gaze into perceived reality. To put it in standard Kantian terms, reality is accompanied by its spectral shadows only insofar as it is already in itself transcendentally constituted through the subject. And the moment gaze is included in the picture, we no longer have one fully constituted reality accompanied by its multiple shadows, but a multitude of realities which emerge against the background of the indistinct preontological Real. The inscription of the gaze itself into perceived reality is thus the "vanishing mediator" between the two extremes: the one reality accompanied by proto-ontological spectral shadows, and multiple realities emerging out of the abyssal plasticity of the Real.

49. See Giorgio Agamben, *L'ouvert* (Paris: Payot & Rivages, 2002), p. 57.

50. See Darian Leader, *Stealing Mona Lisa* (London: Faber & Faber, 2002), p. 89.

51. Lacan, *The Four Fundamental Concepts of Psycho-Analysis*, p. 221.

52. G. W. F. Hegel, *Hegels Philosophie des subjektiven Geistes / Hegel's Philosophy of Subjective Spirit* (Dordrecht: Riedel, 1978), pp. 6–7.

53. Ibid.

54. Ibid.

55. *Hegel's Science of Logic* (Atlantic Highlands: Humanities Press International, 1989), p. 402. Various nationalist movements, with their striving for a "return to origins," are exemplary here: it is the very return to the "lost origins" which literally constitutes what was lost, and in this sense the Nation/notion—as a spiritual substance—is the "product of itself."

56. See Theodor W. Adorno, *Nachgelassene Schriften*, vol. 10, *Probleme der Moralphilosophie* (Frankfurt: Suhrkamp, 1996).

57. See Bernard Williams, *Moral Luck* (Cambridge: Cambridge University Press, 1981).

58. Ibid., p. 45.

59. Ibid., p. 34.

60. Ibid., p. 35.

61. "Soave sia il vento, / Tranquilla sia l'onda / Ed ogni elemento / Benigno responda / Ai nostri desir."—The trap we must avoid here is that of reading this trio as a proof that Mozart was the last of the premodern (pre-Romantic) composers who still believed in the preestablished harmony between the turmoils of our inner lives and the ways of the world. On the contrary, Mozart was the first post-classicist, truly modern, composer: his appeal to the elements to respond gently to our desires already implies the Romantic gap between subjectivity and the ways of the world.

62. Williams, Moral Luck, p. 125.

63. Ibid., p. 126.

64. Ibid., p. 130.

65. More closely, with regard to morals, Kant rejects both the rationalist notion of a transcendent (metaphysical or communal) substantial Good and the individualist-utilitarian notion of ethics grounded in the calculus of pleasures, profits, and emotions—they are all "heteronomous." If we are to arrive at autonomous ethics, one should bracket both communal substantial notions of Good and individual "pathological" pleasures and emotions.

66. Karl Marx, "A Contribution to the Critique of Political Economy," in Collected Works, vol. 29 (New York: International Publishers, 1976), p. 390.

67. With this accent on the salto mortale of capitalist circulation, on how capitalism lives and thrives on future credit, on the wager that the cycle of circulation will be accomplished, I am almost tempted to put it in Heideggerian terms: the essence of credit is the being-credited of the essence itself. . . .

68. See, among others, Helmut Reichelt, Zur logischen Struktur des Kapitalbegriffs (Frankfurt: Europäische Verlagsanstalt, 1970); Hiroshi Uchida, Marx's Grundrisse and Hegel's Logic (New York: Routledge, 1988).

69. Karatani, Transcritique, p. 9.

70. See Brian Rotman, Signifying Nothing (London: Macmillan, 1975).

71. The same logic of living off credit borrowed from the future also goes for Stalinism. The standard evolutionary version is that, while Stalinist socialism did play a certain role in enabling the rapid industrialization of Russia, starting in the mid-1960s, the system obviously exhausted its potential; what this judgment fails to take into account, however, is the fact that the entire epoch of Soviet Communism from 1917 (or, more precisely, from Stalin's proclamation of the goal of "building socialism in one country" in 1924) lived on borrowed time, was "indebted to its own future," so that the final failure retroactively disqualified the earlier epochs themselves.

72. Karl Marx, Grundrisse (Harmondsworth: Penguin, 1993), pp. 420–421.

73. Karatani, Transcritique, p. 20.

74. Ibid., p. 290.

75. Is not a nice linguistic example of the parallax between production and consumption that of the different use of "pork" and "pig" in modern English? "Pig" refers to animals with whom farmers deal, while "pork" is the meat we consume—and the class dimension is clear here: "pig" is the old Saxon word, since the Saxons were the underprivileged farmers, while "pork" comes from French "porque," used by the privileged Norman conquerors who mostly consumed the pigs raised by farmers.

76. When post-Marxist Leftists talk about the "consumtariat" as the new form of proletariat (see Alexander Bard and Jan Soderqvist, *Netrocracy: The New Power Elite and Life After Capitalism* [London: Reuters, 2002]), what they indicate is the ultimate identity of worker and consumer—it is for this reason that, in capitalism, a worker has to be formally free.

77. Karatani, *Transcritique*, p. 241.

78. I first developed this argument in chapter 1 of *The Sublime Object of Ideology* (London: Verso, 1989). And, against Karatani's anti-Hegelianism, we should remember that this notion of form is more Hegelian than Kantian: "Thus in the movement of consciousness there occurs a moment of *being-in-itself* or *being-for-us* which is not present to the consciousness comprehended in the experience itself. The *content*, however, of what presents itself to us does exist *for it*; we comprehend only the formal aspect [*das Formelle*] of that content, or its pure origination. For it, what has thus arisen exists only as an object; *for us*, it appears at the same time as movement and a process of becoming." (G. W. F. Hegel, *Phenomenology of Spirit* [Oxford: Oxford University Press, 1977], p. 56.)

79. Karl Marx, *Capital*, Volume 1 (New York: International Publishers, 1967), p. 166.

80. Ibid., p. 167.

81. Ibid., pp. 163–164.

82. Sigmund Freud, *The Interpretation of Dreams* (Harmondsworth: Penguin., 1977), p. 650.

83. Karatani, *Transcritique*, p. 239.

84. What cannot fail to strike anyone who is well versed in the history of Marxism is the conspicuous absence of any reference to Alfred Sohn-Rethel in Karatani's book: Sohn-Rethel directly deployed the parallel between Kant's transcendental critique and Marx's critique of political economy, but in the opposite critical direction (the structure of the commodity universe is that of the Kantian transcendental space).

85. Karatani, *Transcritique*, p. 183. Here Karatani evokes the example of ancient Athenian democracy; but is not the ultimate combination of ballots and lots advocated by him the unique procedure for electing the Doge in Venice, established in 1268, after a Doge tried to obtain hereditary monarchic powers? Thirty members would first be balloted for, then a ballot held to select nine of them. These nine then nominated 40 provisional electors who, in turn, chose twelve by lot, who then elected 25. These were reduced to nine, who then each nominated five. The 45 so nominated were reduced to eleven by casting lots; nine of the eleven votes were needed to choose the final 41 who, meeting in conclave, would elect the Doge. . . . The aim of this procedure was, of course, to prevent any group or family exercising undue influence. Furthermore, in order to prevent the Doge himself from getting too much power, there was a list of duties he could not undertake (his sons or daughters could not marry outside the Republic, he was allowed to open official letters only in the presence of others, etc.).

86. Ibid.

87. Marx, *Capital*, Volume 1, p. 253.

88. Ibid., p. 254. It is with this shift to the universal form of circulation as an end in itself that we pass from premodern ethics, grounded in a reference to some substantial supreme Good, to the paradigmatically modern Kantian ethics in which it is ultimately only the form of duty that matters—in which duty is to be accomplished for the sake of duty. This means that Lacan's emphasis on how Kant's ethics is the ethics inherent to the Galilean-Newtonian universe of modern science has to be supplemented by the insight into how Kant's ethics is also the ethics inherent to the capitalist logic of circulation as an end in itself.

89. Ibid., pp. 254–255.

90. Ibid., pp. 236–237.

91. This paradox is structurally analogous to that of Casanova who, in order to seduce a naive peasant girl, draw a circle on the grass and claimed that staying within it protected you from all dangers, such as being hit by lightning; when, however, immediately afterward, an actual violent storm broke out, Casanova, in a moment of panic, stepped into this circle himself, acting as if he believed in its power, although he knew very well that it was just part of his deception. . . .

92. Marx, *Capital*, Volume 1, p. 171.

93. Ibid., pp. 171–173.

94. See Jacques-Alain Miller, "Le nom-du-père, s'en passer, s'en servir," available on <www.lacan.com>.

95. Ibid.

96. See Eric Santner, *On the Psychotheology of Everyday Life* (Chicago: University of Chicago Press, 2001).

97. F. W. J. von Schelling, *Ages of the World* (Ann Arbor: University of Michigan Press, 1997), pp. 181–182. For a more detailed reading of this notion, see chapter 1 of Slavoj Žižek, *The Indivisible Remainder* (London and New York: Verso, 1997).

98. G. W. F. Hegel, *Lectures on the Philosophy of Religion*, vol. 3 (Berkeley: University of California Press, 1985), p. 233.

99. G. W. F. Hegel, *Philosophy of Mind* (Oxford: Clarendon Press, 1971), p. 263.

100. Ermanno Bencivenga, *Hegel's Dialectical Logic* (Oxford: Oxford University Press, 2000), p. 64.

101. G. W. F. Hegel, *Elements of the Philosophy of Right* (Cambridge: Cambridge University Press, 1991), pp. 204–205.

102. Ibid., pp. 322–323.

103. Hannah Arendt, *Eichmann in Jerusalem: A Report on the Banality of Evil* (Harmondsworth: Penguin, 1963), p. 98.

104. Stalinism was not far behind Nazism in inventing "ethical" justifications of evil measures. In the early 1930s, Western humanist fellow-travelers were shocked to learn that the Soviet Union had extended the death penalty to children from the age of twelve—since Bukharin and some other main candidates for show-trials had children of that age, the measure was meant to put additional pressure on them, and thus to ensure their participation in the trials. One of the explanations was that in the Soviet Union, the most highly developed country in the history of humanity, children matured faster than they did in the West; they were already adults at the age of twelve, so they should also assume full adult responsibility.

2   Building Blocks for a Materialist Theology

1. Martin Heidegger, "Language in the Poem," in *On the Way to Language* (New York: Harper & Row, 1982), pp. 170–171 (translation modified).

2. Ibid., p. 191.

3. The reason for the ultimate failure of Bergman's *Persona* is as follows: the film's modernist reflexivity in its multitude of levels (up to us seeing the film reel burning) does not work: for it to work, it is not enough for the "inner" narrative diegetic action to be encompassed

by the frame of its "actual" production process; this process itself also has to fit the diegetic story, it has to emerge out of diegesis's own tensions—for instance, as a materialization of the narrative's inner tensions and intensities.

4. The implicit reference to Otto Weininger's notion of femininity is crucial to the work of Kafka: the uncanny proximity of Kafka, the Jewish writer, to Weininger, the anti-Semite. In effect, according to the standard of the great anti-Semites like Wagner and Weininger for whom the greatest victim of the Jewish curse are the Jews themselves, haunted as they are by the curse of their predicament, condemned to wander around with no prospect of redemption, Hitler can no longer be perceived as the disgraceful figure of extreme anti-Semitism but, rather, as a disgrace to anti-Semitism.

5. Heidegger, "Language in the Poem," p. 174.

6. Ibid., p. 179.

7. Is not this notion of "creatureliness" as the excess-of-life, life in its undeadness, to be linked to the notion of "Animal" in the Bible, this mythic monster which personifies the primitive chaos of negative forces (Daniel 7)?

8. Stephen Farber and Estelle Changas, in their perceptive essay on *The Graduate*, available on-line at <http://web.infoave.net/~dennmac/review3.html>.

9. Ibid.

10. Søren Kierkegaard, *Journals and Papers* (Bloomington: Indiana University Press, 1970), entry 2509.

11. Ibid., entry 6818.

12. Søren Kierkegaard, *Concluding Unscientific Postscript* (Princeton: Princeton University Press, 1968) (hereafter CUP), p. 279.

13. CUP, p. 279.

14. Ibid., p. 272.

15. Ibid., p. 108.

16. See Jacques-Alain Miller, "Introduction to the Erotics of Time," *lacanian ink* 24/25 (New York, 2005).

17. See Walter Benjamin, "Theses on the Philosophy of History," in *Illuminations* (New York: Schocken Books, 1969).

18. See F. W. J. Schelling, "Philosophical Investigations into the Essence of Human Freedom," in *Philosophy of German Idealism*, ed. Ernst Behler (New York: Continuum, 1987).

19. CUP, p. 281.

20. Ibid., p. 79.

21. Ibid., p. 80.

22. Kierkegaard, *Journals and Papers*, entry 1405.

23. Søren Kierkegaard, *Works of Love* (London: Harper Books, 1962), p. 355.

24. Søren Kierkegaard, *Training in Christianity* (Princeton: Princeton University Press, 1972), p. 121.

25. Kierkegaard, *Journals and Papers*, entry 1608.

26. Michael Weston, *Kierkegaard and Modern Continental Philosophy* (London: Routledge, 1994), pp. 85–86.

27. Quoted in ibid., p. 89.

28. Lacan provided a detailed interpretation of Claudel's *L'otage* in his Seminar VIII on transference (*Le séminaire, livre VIII: Le transfert* [Paris: Éditions du Seuil, 1982]; see also my reading of *Versagung* in chapter 2 of *The Indivisible Remainder* [London and New York: Verso, 1997]).

29. Regina Barecca, "Introduction" to Henry James, *The Portrait of a Lady* (New York: Signet Classics, 1995), p. xiii.

30. The first to accomplish an analogous gesture was Medea as anti-Antigone: she first kills her brother (her closest family relative), thus cutting off her roots radically, rendering any return impossible, putting all her bets on the marriage with Jason; after betraying everyone close to her for Jason and then being betrayed by Jason himself, there is nothing left for her, she finds herself in the Void—the Void of self-relating negativity, of the "negation of negation," that is subjectivity itself. So it is time to reassert Medea against Antigone: Medea or Antigone, that is the ultimate choice today. In other words, how are we to fight Power? Through fidelity to the old organic Mores threatened by Power, or by out-violencing Power itself? Two versions of femininity: Antigone can still be read as standing for particular family roots against the universality of the public space of State Power; Medea, on the contrary, out-universalizes universal Power itself.

31. How are we to read Lars von Trier's "feminine" trilogy: *Breaking the Waves*, *Dancer in the Dark*, and *Dogville*? In all three films, the heroine (Emily Watson, Bjork, Nicole Kidman) is exposed to terrifying, if not outrageously melodramatic, suffering and humiliation; however, while in the first two films her ordeal culminates in a painfully desperate death, in *Dogville* she mercilessly strikes back and exacts full revenge for the despicable way the residents of the small town where she has taken refuge have treated her, personally killing her ex-lover. This dénouement cannot fail to give rise, in the spectator, to a deep, if ethically problematic, satisfaction—all the wrongdoers certainly get their comeuppance, with interest. Should we also give it a feminist twist: after spectacles of masochistic feminine suffering dragging on at an unbearable length, the victim finally summons up the strength to strike back with a vengeance, asserting herself as a subject regaining full control over her predicament? In this way we seem to get the best of both worlds: our thirst for vengeance is not only satisfied, it is even legitimized in feminist terms . . . what spoils this easy solution is not the predictable (but false) "feminist" counterargument that her victory is won by her adopting the "masculine" violent attitude. There is another feature which should be given its full weight: the heroine of *Dogville* is able to enact her ruthless revenge the moment her father (a Mafia boss) comes to the city in search of her—in short, her active role indicates her renewed submission to paternal authority. On the contrary, it is the apparently "masochistic" acceptance of suffering in the first two films which is much closer to the feminine *Versagung*.

32. Dominick Hoens and Ed Pluth, "The *sinthome*: A New Way of Writing an Old Problem?", in Luke Thurston, ed., *Re-Inventing the Symptom* (New York: Other Press, 2002), pp. 8–9.

33. Ibid., p. 9.

34. See Jacques Lacan, *Le séminaire, livre X: L'angoisse* (Paris: Éditions du Seuil, 2004).

35. See Jacques Lacan, "La subversion du sujet et la dialectique du désir," in *Écrits* (Paris: Éditions du Seuil, 1966).

36. Jacques-Alain Miller, "Introduction à la lecture du Séminaire de *L'angoisse* de Jacques Lacan," *La Cause freudienne* 58 (Paris, 2004), p. 99.

37. Weston, *Kierkegaard and Modern Continental Philosophy*, pp. 154–155.

38. For a more detailed analysis of Tarkovsky's films, see Slavoj Žižek, "The Thing from Inner Space," in *Sexuation* (SIC, vol. 3) (Durham: Duke University Press, 2001).

39. See Patricia Huntington, "Heidegger's Reading of Kierkegaard Revisited: From Ontological Abstraction to Ethical Concretion," in *Kierkegaard in Post/Modernity*, ed. Martin Matustik and Merold Westphal (Bloomington: Indiana University Press, 1995).

40. Søren Kierkegaard, *The Concept of Anxiety* (Princeton: Princeton University Press, 1982), p. 41.

41. Ibid.

42. Ibid., p. 45.

43. Ibid., p. 61.

44. As for God beyond Being, this topic is part of the metaphysical tradition from Plato (the highest good as *epekeina tes ousias*) and the tradition of negative theology, up to the unsurpassable formulations of the late Schelling about God who is a Freedom beyond Being in the precise sense that he can freely decide not only if he is to create the universe or not, but also if he himself is to exist or not—*he freely chooses his being*. See Schelling, "Philosophical Investigations into the Essence of Human Freedom."

45. Kierkegaard, *The Concept of Anxiety*, p. 59.

46. And is it not possible to analyze the notion of anxiety in Lacan along the axis of the ISR triad? In Lacan's early work, anxiety is located at the imaginary level, as the ego's reaction to the threat of the *corps morcelé*, the dismembered body; later, anxiety is located in the (symbolic) subject, signalling the moment the overproximity of the Other's desire threatens to cover up the distance, the lack, which sustains the symbolic order; finally, anxiety concerns the overproximity of *jouissance*.

47. G. K. Chesterton, *Orthodoxy* (San Francisco: Ignatius Press, 1995), p. 45.

48. See Bernard Williams, *Moral Luck* (Cambridge: Cambridge University Press, 1981), p. 125. See also Chapter 1 above.

49. Lorenzo Chiesa, "Imaginary, Symbolic and Real Otherness: The Lacanian Subject and His Vicissitudes," thesis, University of Warwick, Department of Philosophy, 2004, pp. 223–224. (The numbers attached to E refer to the page in Lacan, *Écrits*.)

50. Monique David-Menard, *Les constructions de l'universel* (Paris: PUF, 1997), p. 64.

51. Another aspect of this same ambiguity is de Sade's oscillation between the solipsism of pleasure and the intersubjective logic of blasphemy: is the point merely that I must ignore the Other's dignity, reducing him to an instrument to satisfy my whims, so that the Other is not subjectivized but reduced to an impersonal tool, a kind of masturbatory resource for my solitary pleasure, or is it that I derive pleasure from the very awareness that I am humiliating the Other and causing him unbearable pain?

52. In his "Badiou without Žižek" (to appear in *Polygraph* 17 [2005]), Bruno Boostels proposes a critical analysis of the "antiphilosophical" series opened up by Lacan's "Kant avec Sade," in which the second term, an anti-philosopher, is supposed to bring to light the obscene "truth" of the philosopher's ethical position: Lacan's "Kant avec Sade" "directly posits the Sadeian universe of morbid perversion as the 'truth' of the most radical assertion of the moral weight of the symbolic Law in human history (Kantian ethics). . . . Sade, for all his fantasies about nature's complicity in the omnipotence of perversion, proves to be both more honest and more radical than Kant. The libertine, like the psychoanalyst who finds inspiration in his bedroom, is one who gives us the painful 'truth' that is otherwise hid-

den, disguised, or disavowed by the philosopher. The interpretive scheme behind Lacan's text reveals the secret double bind that ties even the most sublime moral law to the dark continent of morbid desires and obscene superego injunctions—a continent first conquered by Freud more than a century after parts of it had been discovered by Sade." We can clearly see here how Boostels misses the central point of Lacan's "Kant avec Sade."

Furthermore, far from being restricted to Lacan, this procedure of reading "X with Y" has a long Marxist lineage strangely unmentioned by Boostels: is not the main point of Marx's critique of Hegel's speculative idealism precisely to read "Hegel with political economy," that is, to discern in the speculative circular movement of Capital the "obscene secret" of the circular movement of the Hegelian Notion?

53. Michel Surya, *Georges Bataille* (London and New York: Verso, 2002), p. 479.

54. Georges Bataille, *Visions of Excess* (Manchester: Manchester University Press, 1985), p. 154.

55. Surya, *Georges Bataille*, p. 176.

56. Georges Bataille, *Oeuvres complètes* (Paris: Gallimard, 1971–1988), vol. 3, p. 512.

57. Ibid., 12: 296.

58. Ibid., 12: 232.

59. And it is surprising to see how even Jacques-Alain Miller reduces the identity of Law and desire to this transgressive model, thereby missing Lacan's properly Kantian emphasis: "'Desire is law' stands for a compressed formula of Oedipus. It means: desire and law have the same object, because law is the word which prohibits the object of desire and, through this prohibition, directs desire towards this object. This therefore means that the principle of desire is the same as the principle of the law." (Miller, "Introduction à la lecture du Séminaire de *L'angoisse* de Jacques Lacan," p. 93.)

60. See Chiesa, "Imaginary, Symbolic and Real Otherness," p. 242.

61. See Peter Sloterdijk, *Nicht gerettet. Versuche nach Heidegger* (Frankfurt: Suhrkamp, 2001), p. 98.

62. We should note an ironic overlapping here: the standard advice to Jews from "noble" anti-Semites like Wagner is that their only salvation lies in willful self-annihilation—but was Jesus Christ not the Jew who *did precisely that*, to redeem us all?

63. Bertolt Brecht, *Prosa 3* (Frankfurt: Suhrkamp, 1995), p. 18.

64. With regard to the standard complaint about the violence of monotheism, it is instructive to note the violent message of many a New Age ideologist. According to José Argüelles, leader of PAN and New Age Transformation, Pan was the first son of Mother Earth, and used to live close to his mother in the primeval forest with his brothers and sisters, who went out and founded the temple-building societies (Aztecs, Egyptians, etc.). When Pan refused to join his siblings in the cities, they called him evil and Satan. They invented their own selfish religion, Christianity, which must be removed because it includes a vision of an Apocalypse. Right now Mother Earth is bringing Pan back to save us and lead us into the New Age. We can help by surrendering to him, tuning into the crystal matrix frequencies and carrying out the directions received while tuned in; this might include the physical removal of Christians, because they are the biggest obstacle to transformation.

65. Jean-Yves Leloup, "Judas, le révélateur," *Le Monde des Religions*, March-April 2005, p. 42.

66. F. W. J. Schelling, *Die Weltalter. Fragmente. In den Urfassungen von 1811 und 1813*, ed. Manfred Schröter (Munich: Biederstein, reprint 1979), p. 13.

67. George Lucas, quoted in "Dark Victory," *Time*, April 22, 2002.

68. What if, then, politically, Zhang Yimou's *The Hero*, the People's Republic of China's answer to Hollywood, is the true alternative to *StarWars*? A nameless warrior (Jet Li) is involved in a complex plot to kill the King of Qin, whose obsession is to become the first Emperor of China by unifying its seven warring states; in the course of the plot, however, the nameless warrior becomes aware that the Emperor, although he is a ruthless despot, is pursuing a grand patriotic dream of a unified China, so he decides to sabotage his own plot, sacrificing himself and his closest friends for the unity of all China "under one heaven." Can we imagine the *StarWars* saga rewritten in this way, with the Emperor as the great galactic Unifier, and Anakin sacrificing his friends for global peace and unity "under one heaven"?

69. Martin Heidegger, *Identity and Difference* (London: Harper & Row, 1974), p. 72.

70. See Jacques Derrida, *Acts of Religion* (New York: Routledge, 2002).

71. What this suspension puts in question is what I am tempted to call—turning around Arendt's famous formula—the *banality of the Good*. Recall the much-celebrated heroism of the New York firefighters on 9/11: in their heroism, they did nothing exceptional, they "just did their job.". . .This banality is not the same as the "banality" of the normal democratic process: it designates the "banality" of extraordinary *heroism*, not the peaceful flow of ordinary (political) life.

72. Søren Kierkegaard, *Either/Or* (New York: Anchor Books, 1959), vol. 1, pp. 137–162.

73. It was Hegel who intuited that the modern stance of desublimation undermines the tragic perception of life. In his *Phenomenology*, he supplements the famous French proverb "There are no heroes for a room-servant" with "Not because the hero is not a hero, but because the room-servant is just a room-servant," that is, the one who perceives in the hero just his "human, all too human" features, minor weaknesses, petty passions, etc., and is blind to the historic dimension of the hero's deed—in modernity, this servant's perspective is universalized; all dignified higher stances are reduced to lower motivations.

74. It is crucial to note that Abraham is otherwise in no way a timid yes-sayer but a man who is not afraid to confront God openly: he boldly opposes God's plan to destroy the Sodomites, he tries to convince God to spare the righteous ones who might be killed along with the sinners—so why does he comply when his own son's life is at stake? Following the recent fashion for alternate history ("What if?") narratives, it would be interesting to entertain the hypothesis of what would have happened if Abraham had said "No" to God's demand.

75. See *The Humor of Kierkegaard: An Anthology*, edited and introduced by Thomas C. Oden (Princeton: Princeton University Press, 2004).

76. Two scenes from Hitchcock clearly echo each other: in *Rebecca*, when the nameless new Mrs. de Winter, in order to impress her husband, dresses up for the big party in an exact copy of the deceased Rebecca's dress; and in *Vertigo*, when Midge, in order to provoke Scottie, paints a reproduction of the portrait of Carlotta Valdes, replacing Carlotta's face with her own ordinary bespectacled face. In both cases, the ordinary feminine face find itself occupying the wrong place. A Slovene punk group, Strelnikoff, caused a local scandal (an outcry in the Catholic Church) when, in a similar way, it reproduced a well-known classic painting of Mary holding the infant Christ on her lap, just replacing Christ's head with the head of a rat—instead of being shocked by this blasphemy, we should see in it a properly Christian comic reversal.

77. However, the repressed comedy aspect of the religious always returns—if nowhere else, then in comical details like the one concerning the Dalai Lama's flight to India in 1959. When the Dalai Lama considered the difficult option to emigrate from Tibet, he made the final decision upon the advice of the official prophet who, induced into a mystic trance, professes confused words which give a hint about what choice to make—what a surprise,

then, to learn that this prophet was on the payroll of the CIA and that, in his advice, he followed the CIA's guidelines, since the Dalai Lama's escape perfectly suited the CIA's purposes in its struggle against the Chinese Communists.

78. Consequently, although we should agree with Nietzsche that the entire history of Christianity is based on the forgetting, even repression, of its original (comic) gesture, we should nonetheless locate this gesture differently: not at the very beginning, at its origins, but a little later. It is not, as Nietzsche claimed, that "the only true Christian was Christ himself"; it is, rather, the much-maligned Saint Paul, the one who allegedly "institutionalized" Christianity and thus betrayed its anti-institutional subversive core, who, in his radical rereading of the meaning of Christ's death, clearly formulated its comic aspect. That is to say: for the "original (pre-Pauline) Christians," Christ's death was a traumatic shock which totally disoriented them, a tragic event if ever there was one; only with Paul is this tragedy reinterpreted as comedy; and it is this comic aspect which again gets lost with the later transformation of Christianity into a state religion, when Christ's incarnation and death are interpreted as part of the divine exchange-bargain with humanity, leaving humanity with the superego burden of an ineffable debt ("Christ loved you so much that he freely gave his life for you, so you are forever indebted to him . . .").

79. This is the phallic aspect of comedy: in the phallus as signifier, opposite features coincide. The phallus is simultaneously the *"pure" signifier*, the signifier without a signified, the signifier of the lack of signifier, a signifier which, deprived of any determinate meaning, stands for the pure virtuality of meaning "as such," and, as Lacan never ceases to repeat, the exemplary *imaginary* signifier, the most "impure" one, irreducibly rooted in the physical image of an excessive organ which, on account of its erectile shape, sticks out, stands up, defying the earthbound inertia of the body. The ultimate couple of opposites that coincide in the concept of the phallus is, of course, that of phallic potency and castration. One consequence of the fact that the phallus is itself the signifier of castration is that we should give an unexpected turn to the infamous Freudian concept of "penis envy": "penis envy is most profoundly felt precisely by those who have a penis" (Richard Boothby, *Freud as a Philosopher* [New York: Routledge, 2002], p. 292).

80. This is why "What is the difference between . . ." jokes are most efficient when difference is denied, as in: "What is the difference between toy trains and women's breasts? None: both are meant for children, and with both it is mostly adult men that play."

81. On whose "'Concrete Universal' and What Comedy Can Tell Us about It" (to appear in *Lacan: The Silent Partners*, ed. Slavoj Žižek (London and New York: Verso, 2005) I rely here extensively.

82. Significantly, the only joke—or, if not joke, then at least moment of irony—in Heidegger occurs in his rather bad-taste quip about Lacan as "that psychiatrist who is himself in need of a psychiatrist" (in a letter to Medard Boss).

83. See Theodor W. Adorno, *Nachgelassene Schriften*, vol. 10, *Probleme der Moralphilosophie* (Frankfurt: Suhrkamp, 1996).

84. See Max Horkheimer and Theodor W. Adorno, *Dialektik der Aufklärung* (Frankfurt: Fischer Verlag, 1971).

85. For a more detailed account of this status, see Chapter 1 above.

86. See Emmanuel Levinas, *Ethics and Infinity: Conversations with Philippe Nemo* (Pittsburgh: Duquesne University Press, 1985).

87. At a different level, the same goes for Stalinist Communism. In the classic Stalinist narrative, even the concentration camps were a site of the fight against Fascism where imprisoned Communists were organizing networks of heroic resistance—in such a universe, of course, there is no place for the limit-experience of the *Muselmann*, of the living dead deprived

of the capacity for human engagement—no wonder Stalinist Communists were so eager to "normalize" the camps into just another site of the anti-Fascist struggle, dismissing *Muselmannen* simply as those who were to weak to endure the struggle.

88. See Giorgio Agamben, *What Remains of Auschwitz: The Witness and the Archive* (Stanford: Stanford University Press, 2002).

89. See the last chapter of *The Seminar of Jacques Lacan, Book II: The Ego in Freud's Theory and in the Technique of Psychoanalysis* (1954–1955) (New York: Norton, 1991).

90. See Primo Levi, *If This Is a Man/The Truce* (London: Abacus, 1987).

91. I owe this reference to Eric Santner.

92. Franz Kafka, "The Cares of a Family Man," in *The Complete Stories* (New York: Schocken Books, 1989).

93. Isabel Allende, "The End of All Roads," *Financial Times*, November 15, 2003, W 12.

94. Jean-Claude Milner, "Odradek, la bobine de scandale," in *Élucidation* 10 (Paris: Printemps, 2004), pp. 93–96.

95. How can we not recall, apropos of the fact that Odradek is a spool-like creature, the spool in the Freudian *Fort-Da* game from his *Beyond the Pleasure Principle* (New York: Norton, 1990).

96. Stephen Mulhall, *On Film* (London: Routledge, 2001), p. 19.

97. Ibid., p. 132.

98. See Walter Benjamin, "Capitalism as Religion," in *Selected Writings*, Volume 1 (Cambridge, MA: Harvard University Press, 1996), pp. 288–291.

99. See Emmanuel Levinas, *On Escape* (Stanford: Stanford University Press, 2003), p. 65.

100. I rely here on Joan Copjec's path-breaking work on the notion of shame, "May '68, the Emotional Month," in Žižek, ed., *Lacan: The Silent Partners*.

101. I rely here on Lilja Kaganovska's excellent "Stalin's Men: Gender, Sexuality, and the Body in Nikolai Ostrovsky's *How the Steel Was Tempered*" (manuscript, courtesy of the author).

102. Nikolai Ostrovsky, *How the Steel Was Tempered* (Moscow: Progress Publishers, 1979), pp. 195–196.

103. No wonder we find another Kafkaesque feature in the climactic scene in Vsevolod Pudovkin's film *Deserter* (1933), which stages a weird displacement of the Stalinist show-trials: when the hero, a German proletarian working in a gigantic Soviet metallurgical plant, is praised in front of the entire collective for his outstanding labor, he replies with a surprising public confession: no, he does not deserve this praise; he came to the Soviet Union to work only to escape his cowardice and betrayal in Germany itself (when the police attacked the striking workers, he stayed at home, because he believed Social Democratic treacherous propaganda)! The public (simple workers) listen to him with perplexity, laughing and clapping—a properly uncanny scene reminding us of the scene in Kafka's *The Trial* when Josef K. confronts the courts—here also, the public laughs and claps at the most unexpected and inappropriate moments. . . . The worker then returns to Germany to fight the battle in his proper place. This scene is so striking because it stages the secret fantasy of the Stalinist trial: the traitor publicly confesses his crime of his own free will and guilt feelings, without any pressure from the secret police.

104. There is a minor, but rather unpleasant, chirurgical intervention in which, under conditions of only local anesthesia, the eye is taken out of its socket and (partially, at least) turned around outside the body, so that the patient can see himself from the outside, with an "objective" gaze—this experience is that of our eye as an organ without a body, separated from

the body. We could characterize this experience as that of a disembodied divine gaze—or as the ultimate nightmare.

105. See Jacques Lacan, "La position de l'inconscient," in Écrits.

106. Walter Benjamin, *Illuminations* (New York: Schocken Books, 1989), p. 128.

107. And does the uterus not function in the same way in the old notion of "hysteria" as a disease of the traveling womb? Is hysteria not the illness in which the partial object within the subject runs amok, and starts to move around?

108. See Gilles Deleuze, *The Logic of Sense* (New York: Columbia University Press, 1990), pp. 119–120.

109. See Eric Santner, *On the Psychotheology of Everyday Life* (Chicago: University of Chicago Press, 2001).

INTERLUDE 1: KATE'S CHOICE, OR, THE MATERIALISM OF HENRY JAMES

1. I rely here on Seymour Chatman, *The Later Style of Henry James* (Oxford: Basil Blackwell, 1972). (The numbers in brackets after the quotes that follow in the text refer to this volume.)

2. Robert Pippin, *Henry James and Modern Moral Life* (Cambridge: Cambridge University Press, 2000), pp. 10–11.

3. And perhaps this is where James was not radical enough: despite his sympathetic portrayal of the powerless poor in the slums, he was unable fully to confront the *ethical claim* on society that sustains revolutionary radicalism. (Hegel, on the contrary, was fully aware of this problem: his scornful statements on the "rabble / Pöbel" should not blind us to the fact that he admits that their aggressive stance and unconditional demands on society are fully justified—since they are not recognized by society as ethical subjects, they do not owe it anything.)

4. The edition used is Henry James, *The Princess Casamassima* (Harmondsworth: Penguin, 1987).

5. Irving Howe, "The Political Vocation," in *Henry James*, ed. Leon Edel (Englewood Cliffs: Prentice-Hall, 1963), p. 157.

6. Ibid., p. 166.

7. James, *The Princess Casmassima*, Derek Brewer's "Introduction," p. 17.

8. Ibid., p. 21.

9. And perhaps, starting from this point, we could deploy an entire theory of the Aesthetic (like Lévi-Strauss who, in the famous passage from *Tristes Tropiques*, conceived of face-drawings as attempts to resolve social deadlocks).

10. Fredric Jameson, *The Seeds of Time* (New York: Columbia University Press, 1994), p. 89.

11. Sigi Jöttkandt, "Metaphor, Hysteria and the Ethics of Desire in *The Wings of the Dove*," paper presented at the International Henry James Conference (Paris, 2002).

12. The Jamesian "MacGuffin" is, rather, the lost manuscript (or pack of letters) around which the narrative circulates, like the "Aspern papers" from the story of the same title, or the notorious secret from "The Figure in the Carpet." The supreme example of the circulating Hitchcockian object-stain in James is arguably the row of pearls in "Paste" (a minor story from 1899): they pass from the narrator's dead stepmother to his cousin, then back to him, then to a third lady, and their very suspect authenticity poses a threat to the family honor (if they are authentic, then the stepmother must have had a secret lover who bought them).

And, as expected, we find in James also the third Hitchcockian object, the traumatic-impossible Thing which threatens to swallow the subject, like the "beast in the jungle" from the story of the same title; the Lacanian triad of objects (*a*, S of the barred A, the big Phi [the overwhelming phallic presence]) is thus completed. For this triad, see the Introduction to *Everything You Ever Wanted to Know about Hitchcock, but Were Afraid to Ask Lacan*, ed. Slavoj Žižek (London and New York: Verso, 1993).

13. In more political terms, Densher is a model "honest" bourgeois intellectual who masks his compromising attitude by "ethical" doubts and restraints—types like him "sympathize" with the revolutionary cause, but refuse to "dirty their hands." They are usually (and deservedly) shot in the middle stages of a revolution (it is all the Millies of this world—those who like to stage their own death as a sacrificial spectacle—whose wishes are met in the early stages of a revolution).

14. Guillermo Arriaga, *21 Grams* (London: Faber & Faber, 2003), pp. xiii–xiv.

15. This, of course, is why the interpretation that follows is merely an improvised first approach, with no pretense to completeness.

16. This is one of the great failures of the Merchant-Ivory cinema version of *The Golden Bowl*: the film goes out of its way to make the "robber baron" as sympathetic as possible. As befits our Politically Correct times, obsessed with "hurting the Other," considerate behavior counts for more than brutal capitalist exploitation.

17. For this story, see Gloria C. Erlich, *The Sexual Education of Edith Wharton* (Berkeley: University of California Press, 1992).

18. Pippin, *Henry James and Modern Moral Life*, p. 77.

3 THE UNBEARABLE HEAVINESS OF BEING DIVINE SHIT

1. Is postmodern art, then, a return to pleasure?

2. Ronald Woodley, accompanying text to the recording by Martha Argerich and Gideon Kremer (Deutsche Grammophon 431 803-2).

3. Here Shostakovich is more traditional than Prokofiev; the exemplary "explosion of the Thing" in his work is undoubtedly the second movement of his Tenth Symphony, a short but violently energetic Scherzo with slashing chords that is usually referred to as the "Stalin portrait" (although we must wonder why—why not simply an explosion of excessive vitality?). It is interesting to note how this shortest movement of them all (a little over four minutes, compared with twenty-three minutes for the first and twelve for the third and fourth) nonetheless functions as the energetic focus of the entire symphony, its wild theme echoed and reverberating in other movements, its excessive energy spilling over into others—as if it is here, in the second movement, that we court the danger of getting "burned by the sun.". . .

4. Do not the three emblematic figures of musical genius, Bach-Mozart-Beethoven (vaguely corresponding to the painter's triad of Leonardo-Raphael-Michelangelo), stand for the three modes of coping with the traumatic-excessive Thing in me which is my genius? One can either practice one's genius as an artisan, unburdened with any divine mission, just doing one's hard work (Bach); or one can be lucky enough to be able to deploy one's genius into an unencumbered flow of creativity, with an almost childlike spontaneity (Mozart); or one's genius is a kind of inner demon which compels the artist to create his work in the process of painful Titanic struggle (Beethoven), enforcing its will against and onto the resisting stuff.

5. Bertolt Brecht, *Gedichte in einem Band* (Frankfurt: Suhrkamp, 1982), pp. 1009–1010.

6.   Reference to Alain Badiou's notion of truth is crucial here, of course.

7.   Alan Gardiner, *The Poetry of William Wordsworth* (Harmondsworth: Penguin 1990), p. 84.

8.   See also: ". . . the midnight storm / Grew darker in the presence of my eye."

9.   We encounter a similar problem in the work of Malevich. During his visit to Berlin in 1927, Malevich left all his remaining paintings (about 70) there. After his return to the USSR, there was a "regression" in his work—he started once more to paint in earlier styles, from impressionism almost up to Socialist Realism in his portrait (1932) of the model worker (*Red Army Member Scharnowsky*), and also his impressive late self-portrait, when he was already dying of cancer. What does this "regression" mean? Is it a Stravinsky-like gesture of freely practicing all styles? The enigma is: was this "regression" really just a regression, irrelevant to the Event of his breakthrough, or was it the working-out of this breakthrough, that is, *stricto sensu*, a post-evental fidelity?

10. Alejandra Pizarnik and Susan Bassnett, *Exchanging Lives* (Leeds: Peepal Tree, 2002), p. 20.

11. Ibid., p. 25.

12. Ibid., p. 26.

13. Ibid., p. 32.

14. Georg Lukács, "Hölderlin's Hyperion," in *Goethe and His Age* (London: Allen & Unwin, 1968), p. 137.

15. See Eric Santner, *Friedrich Hölderlin: Narrative Vigilance and the Poetic Imagination* (Piscataway: Rutgers University Press, 1986).

16. What must look like the most radical opposite of Heidegger's reading, the Oedipal reading of Hölderlin's breakdown (elaborated in the 1960s by Jean Laplanche), is thoroughly convincing: as Hölderlin himself clearly noted, he was unable to *locate the lack*, that is, he was living in a permanent state of ontic-ontological short circuit in which every experience of (even a minor) ontic failure or imperfection threatened to explode into an ontological catastrophe, into a disintegration of the entire world. Instead of dismissing this reading as psychologically reductionist, ontic, missing the ontologico-historical level, we should, rather, elevate the unfortunate "Oedipus complex" to the dignity of ontology.

17. Why does Heidegger focus almost exclusively on Hölderlin's poems? Why does he practically ignore his philosophical fragments and the novel *Hyperion*? There is a good reason: his late poems signal the breakdown of the solution Hölderlin tried to articulate in *Hyperion* and his philosophical fragments from the last years of 1790s.

18. Halldor Laxness, *World Light* (New York: Vintage, 2002).

19. The same tension between a Communist political commitment and the fascination of the incestuous Thing characterizes the unique cinematic work of Luchino Visconti; his incestuous Thing has its own political weight, as the decadent *jouissance* of the old ruling classes in decay. The two supreme examples of this deadly fascination are the obvious *Death in Venice* and the lesser known but much better earlier black-and-white masterpiece *Vaghe stelle dell'Orsa*, a chamber cinema gem. What both films share is not only the prohibited "private" passion which ends in death (the composer's passion for the beautiful boy in *Venice*, the incestuous passion of brother and sister in *Vaghe stelle*); both films are also built around and sustained by a musical piece which represents late Romanticism at its most passionate: in *Venice*, it is the Adagietto from Mahler's Fifth Symphony; in *Vaghe stelle* it is César Franck's B minor *Prélude, choral et fugue*. In contrast to Laxness, however, the duality of the artist's Leftist political commitment (until his death, Visconti was a member of the Italian Communist Party) and his fascination with the decadent *jouissance*, pleasure-in-pain, of the

ruling class in decay, functions here as a simple split between enunciated and enunciation, as if Visconti, in the highest mode of prudish puritanical revolutionaries, publicly condemns what he personally enjoys and is fascinated by, so that the very public endorsement of the necessity of abolishing the reign of the old ruling class is "trans-functionalized" into an instrument of providing decadent pleasure-in-pain, in the spectacle of one's own decay.

20. Susan Sontag, "Journey to the Centre of the Novel," *The Guardian*, March 5, 2005.

21. Ibid.

22. See Thomas Metzinger, *Being No One: The Self-Model Theory of Subjectivity* (Cambridge, MA: MIT Press, 2004).

23. Paul Broks, *Into the Silent Land: Travels in Neuropsychology* (London: Atlantic Books, 2003), p. 17.

24. Jeremy Campbell, *The Liar's Tale* (New York: Norton, 2001), p. 27.

25. Here Sloterdijk is right, although we may disagree with his specific version of the account: Heidegger has to be supplemented with an account of how Clearance itself is generated. See Peter Sloterdijk, *Nicht gerettet. Versuche nach Heidegger* (Frankfurt: Suhrkamp, 2001).

26. See John Caputo, *Demythologizing Heidegger* (Bloomington: Indiana University Press, 1993).

27. This is how we should locate the shift from the biological instinct to drive: instinct is just part of the physics of animal *life*, while drive (*death* drive) introduces a metaphysical dimension. In Marx, we find the analogous implicit distinction between working class and proletariat: "working class" is the empirical social category, accessible to sociological knowledge; while "proletariat" is the subject-agent of revolutionary Truth. Along the same lines, Lacan claims that drive is an *ethical* category.

28. See Alain Badiou, *L'être et l'événement* (Paris: Éditions du Seuil, 1989). Badiou identifies four possible domains in which a Truth-Event can occur, four domains in which subjects emerge as the "operators" of a truth-procedure: science, art, politics, and love. Do not the first three truth-procedures (science, art, and politics) follow the classic logic of the triad True-Beautiful-Good—the science of truth, the art of beauty, the politics of the good? So, what about the fourth procedure, love? Does it not stick out from the series, being somehow more fundamental and universal? Thus there are not simply four truth-procedures, but *three plus one*—a fact that is perhaps not emphasized enough by Badiou (although, regarding sexual difference, he does observe that women tend to color all other truth-procedures through love). What is encompassed by this fourth procedure is not just the miracle of love, but also psychoanalysis, theology, and philosophy itself (the *love* of wisdom). Is not love, then, Badiou's "Asiatic model of production"—the category into which he throws all truth-procedures which do not fit the other three modes? This fourth procedure also serves as a kind of underlying formal principle or matrix of all procedures (which accounts for the fact that, although Badiou denies religion the status of truth-procedure, he nonetheless claims that Saint Paul was the first to deploy the very formal matrix of the Truth-Event). Furthermore, is there not another key difference between love and other truth-procedures in that, in contrast to others which try to force the unnameable, in "true love" one endorses/accepts the loved Other *because of the very unnameable X in him or her.* In other words, "love" designates the lover's respect for what should remain unnameable in the beloved—"whereof one cannot speak, thereof one should remain silent" is perhaps the fundamental prescription of love.

29. Alain Badiou, *Theoretical Writings* (London: Continuum, forthcoming).

30. This is why we should ask the key question: is there a Being without an Event, simply external to it, or is *every* order of Being the disavowal-obliteration of a founding Event, a "perverse" *je sais bien, mais quand même . . .*, a reduction-reinscription of the Event into the causal order of Being?

31. Badiou's counterargument against Lacan (formulated, among others, by Bruno Boostels) is that what really matters is not the Event as such, the encounter with the Real, but its consequences, its inscription, the consistency of the new discourse which emerges from the Event. I am tempted to turn this counterargument against Badiou himself. That is to say: against his "oppositional" stance of advocating the impossible goal of pure presence without the state of representation, I am tempted to claim that we should summon up the strength to "take over" and assume power, no longer just to persist in the safety of the oppositional stance. If we are not ready to do this, then we continue to rely on state power as that against which we define our own position.

32. See David Chalmers, *The Conscious Mind* (Oxford: Oxford University Press, 1996).

33. Ibid., p. 101.

34. Along the same lines, what makes Saul Kripke's argument against the classic identity theory (see Saul Kripke, "Identity and Necessity," in *Identity and Individuation*, ed. Milton K. Munitz [New York: New York University Press, 1971]) so interesting and provocative is the strong claim that, in order to refute the identity between subjective experience and objective brain processes, it is enough for us to be able to *imagine* the possibility of a subjective experience (say, of pain) without its material neuronal correlative.

   More generally, it is crucial to note how the entire anti-identity argumentation follows Descartes in resorting to hyperbolic imagination: it is possible to *imagine* that my mind exists without my body (or, in more modern versions: to imagine that, even if I were to know everything about the processes in a person's brain, I would still not know what his subjective experience is).

35. In quantum physics, things get complicated further, since its central notion of the "collapse" of quantum oscillations deploys a strange process which is an almost symmetrical opposite of the birth of appearance out of reality: the birth of our common reality itself—the univocal reality of material objects—out of the pure processionality of quantum oscillations.

36. Jacques Lacan, *Encore* (New York: Norton, 1998), p. 95.

37. Sigmund Freud, *Dora: An Analysis of a Case of Hysteria* (New York: Macmillan, 1963), p. 101.

38. Jean Laplanche, *Vie et mort en psychanalyse* (Paris: Flammarion, 1989), p. 58.

39. Karl Marx, *Capital*, Volume 1 (New York: International Publishers, 1967), p. 163.

40. See Kojin Karatani, *Transcritique: On Kant and Marx* (Cambridge, MA: MIT Press, 2003).

41. Karl Marx, "A Contribution to the Critique of Hegel's Philosophy of Law: Introduction," in *Collected Works*, vol. 3 (New York: International Publishers, 1970), p. 175.

42. This point—about the theological core of capitalism, which has nothing to do with Weber's thesis on Protestant ethic and the rise of capitalism, since it designates a "theological" character of the very capitalist mechanism—was emphasized by Walter Benjamin in "Capitalism as Religion," *Selected Writings*, vol. 1 (Cambridge, MA: Harvard University Press, 1996), pp. 288–291.

43. See Chalmers, *The Conscious Mind*, p. 231.

44. I owe this observation to Adrian Johnston.

45. Martin Heidegger, *Basic Writings* (New York: Routledge, 1978), p. 376.

46. The paradox of the Dieter Henrich–Manfred Frank school is of a different kind: although they tried to save the Kantian transcendental legacy and criticize cognitivism, their mode of argumentation is already "analytic"—pure abstract reasoning (best exemplified by the

argument that self-reflection, the recognition of the subject in its other, presupposes self-acquaintance, or by Henrich's classic analysis of the ambiguity of Hegel's notion of immediacy) without any reference to the historical dimension of the problem. (No wonder their status is already in-between: some overviews of the analytic philosophy of mind contain a chapter on them, usually under the heading "New Conceptions of Self-consciousness.") And that is the exact location of the Hegelian legacy which disappears here: what Hegel claims is that the historical aspect of a notion—in all senses and dimensions of this term (how we argue about it, how it emerged, its past) is part of this notion itself.

47. Of course, confronted with the practical consequences of their epistemic claims ("Does this mean that Hitler was not responsible for his crimes, and that he should not have been punished?"), most of them (with honorable exceptions like the Churchlands) repeat their own version of the neo-Kantian retreat, claiming that, in our daily lives, we should respect our self-experience as free responsible agents, and continue to punish criminals.

48. See Chapter 4 below for a more detailed analysis.

49. And what about cloning for the production of organs, that is, "growing" a person just for the use of some of his organs? The ethical monstrosity of this procedure is self-evident: a person is reduced to the bearer of his or her organs. Moreover, the juxtaposition of the "natural" original and his clone inexorably confronts us with the following alternative: either we do not recognize the clone as a fully human person, just a soulless living machine (since he was not "naturally conceived," as they say in Christianity); or, if he is fully human, then there is ultimately no fundamental difference between the original and its clone (and there is none), so why not also use the original for organs?

50. George Glider, quoted in John L. Casti, *Would-Be Worlds* (New York: John Wiley & Sons, 1997), p. 215.

51. See Peter Sloterdijk, *Regeln für den Menschenpark* (Frankfurt: Suhrkamp, 1999).

52. Sloterdijk, *Nicht gerettet*, p. 365.

53. "A Conversation with Alain Badiou," *lacanian ink* 23 (New York, 2004), pp. 100–101.

54. Jacques-Alain Miller, "Religion, Psychoanalysis," *lacanian ink* 23 (New York, 2004), pp. 18–19.

55. Furthermore, should we not bear in mind here also the key difference between truth and knowledge? Is not "truth," from a certain standard perspective, the very name for a conjunction of knowledge and meaning, so that the real materialist task is not primarily to dissociate knowledge from meaning but, rather, to articulate the possibility of asserting a dimension of truth outside meaning?

56. See Sloterdijk, *Nicht gerettet*, p. 99.

57. For a concise description of these three positions, see Franklin Sherman, "Speaking of God after Auschwitz," in *A Holocaust Reader*, ed. Michael L. Morgan (Oxford: Oxford University Press, 2001).

58. F. W. J. Schelling, "Philosophical Investigations into the Essence of Human Freedom," in *Philosophy of German Idealism*, ed. Ernst Behler (New York: Continuum, 1988), p. 274.

59. Quoted in Morgan, ed., *A Holocaust Reader*, p. 237.

60. See Martin Heidegger, "Only a God Can Save Us," in *The Heidegger Controversy*, ed. Richard Wolin (Cambridge, MA: MIT Press, 1993).

61. David Tracy, "Religious Values after the Holocaust," in Morgan, ed., *A Holocaust Reader*, p. 237.

62. Jürgen Habermas, *The Future of Human Nature* (Cambridge: Polity Press, 2003), p. 110.

63. In Walter Benjamin, *Illuminations* (New York: Schocken Books, 1969), p. 254.

64. These three Christian attitudes also involve three different modes of God's presence in the world. We start with the created universe directly reflecting the glory of its Creator: all the wealth and beauty of our world bears witness to the divine creative power, and creatures, when they are not corrupted, naturally turn their eyes toward Him. . . . Catholicism shifts to a more delicate logic of the "figure in the carpet": the Creator is not directly present in the world; His traces are, rather, to be discerned in details which escape the first superficial glance—God is like a Hitchcockian film-maker or a painter who withdraws from his finished product, signaling his authorship merely by a barely discernible signature at the edge of the picture. Finally, Protestantism asserts God's radical absence from the created universe, from this gray world which runs like a blind mechanism and where God's presence becomes discernible only in direct interventions of his Grace which disturb the normal course of things.

65. For those who know Hegel, it is easy to locate this excessive element: at the very end of his *Science of Logic*, Hegel addresses the naive question of how many moments we should count in a dialectical process, three or four? His reply is that they can be counted as either three or four: the middle moment, negativity, is redoubled into direct negation and the self-relating absolute negativity which directly passes into the return to positive synthesis.

66. Incidentally, there is a traumatic occurrence in Exodus 4: 24–26 in which precisely "the man comes around": God himself comes to Moses' tent in the guise of a dark stranger, and attacks him ("the Lord met him, and sought to kill him"); Moses is then saved by his wife Ziporrah, who appeases God by offering him the foreskin of their son.

67. Jacques Lacan, *The Ethics of Psychoanalysis* (London: Routledge, 1992), p. 70.

68. In the Koran, there is a well-known passage about how Satan confused the Prophet's mind: "We sent not ever any Messenger or Prophet before thee, but that Satan cast into his fancy, when he was fancying; but God annuls what Satan casts, then God confirms His verses" (q22: 52) The idea is that Satan often confuses the minds of the prophets, making them utter a heresy, like the famous "Satanic verses": while Mohammed was reciting Sura 53, Satan took advantage of his state of mind to cast onto his tongue the two verses which celebrate three pagan goddesses as legitimate intermediaries between man and God: "These are the exalted cranes, and their intercession is to be hoped for." This concession to polytheism, of course, greatly pleased the pagans to whom this Sura was recited; subsequently, Gabriel upbraided Mohammed for his lapse, but God reassured him. . . . What, however, if—under the hypothesis of the identity of God and Satan—God himself was engaged here in a little bit of manipulation? What if he first confused the Prophet and made him resort to polytheism in order to seduce the pagans, and then, once the task was accomplished, cancelled this concession?

69. Luther was obsessed with anal bodily functions, suffering from (psychologically conditioned) constipation—no wonder he defined man as something that fell out of God's anus, as divine shit.

70. The paradox of today's public space is that the way to become a public person is to make one's private life (hobbies, love affairs, idiosyncratic tastes) public—the TV talk show is the model here.

71. So what should we say to the couple of paternal authority and the woman as image displayed to its gaze? In this relationship, it is the man who is castrated—his castration being the positive condition/price for his authority; while the woman is precisely non-castrated and, for that very reason, impotent, reduced to an object.

72. In the first months after the independence of Slovenia in 1991, the old Yugoslav money was no longer valid and the new Slovene currency not yet in circulation; so, in order to bridge this gap, the authorities issued temporary currency, units from 1 to 5,000, but without a name—this paper money had the signature of the Slovene national bank, the number designating its value, but no name, no "dinars" or whatever. We thus had pure units, without any schematization (in the Kantian sense), without the specification of what they were the units of: the price of a book, for example, was 350—350 what? Nothing, just 350 units. . . . The strange thing was that no one even remarked on this absence.

73. See Keith Bradsher, "Sad, Lonely? For a Good Time, Call Vivienne," New York Times, February 24, 2005. Thanks to Jeff Martinek for drawing my attention to this item.

74. See Carl Zimmer's report, "The Ultimate Remote Control," in Newsweek, June 14, 2004, p. 73.

75. Lacan, The Ethics of Psychoanalysis, p. 207.

76. Ibid., p. 231.

77. Lorenzo Chiesa, "Imaginary, Symbolic and Real Otherness: The Lacanian Subject and His Vicissitudes," thesis, University of Warwick, Department of Philosophy, 2004, p. 233.

78. One of the most boring Leftist mantras apropos of the digitalization of our daily life is: "In our fascination with digitalization, cyberspace, and so on, we should bear in mind that all this concerns only the developed minority—more than half of humanity has never even made a phone call, their problem is not digitalization but food, health, and other matters of simple survival. . . ." What makes this argument suspect is that it was put forward by, among others, Bill Gates himself. Against this humanist platitude, we should bear in mind the lesson of cyberpunk: how digitalization, virtual reality, biogenetics, and so on, can fully coexist with slum poverty.

79. Vernor Vinge, quoted in Bill McKibben, Enough: Staying Human in an Engineered Age (New York: Henry Holt, 2004), p. 102.

80. J. Storrs Hall, quoted in Enough, p. 102.

81. Quoted in Enough, pp. 102–103.

82. Robert Ettinger, quoted in Enough, p. 110.

83. Ibid.

84. McKibben, Enough, p. 127.

85. In the near future, digital technology will probably make possible the fabrication of perfect fakes of sexual scenes: actual video shots of a real person will be changed so that the same person will be seen performing sexual acts indistinguishable from "real" hardcore shots. The proper deception, however, would have been for this person to put into circulation shots of his or her actual sexual acts, counting on the fact that everyone will assume that they are dealing with digital fakes—truth is still the most effective form of lying.

86. Nicholas Humphrey, A History of the Mind (New York: Simon & Schuster, 1992), p. 171.

87. Ian Taterstall, Becoming Human (New York: Harvest Press, 1998), p. 170.

88. Humphrey, A History of the Mind, p. 268.

89. Francisco Varela, "Le cerveau n'est pas un ordinateur," interview with H. Kempf, La Recherche 308 (Paris, 1998), p. 112.

1. Quentin Tarantino's *Kill Bill 2* brings this temporal structure to its extreme point, that of death itself: in the final confrontation between the Uma Thurman character and her father ("Bill"), she kills him by dealing him a series of special blows targeted around the heart area. These blows do not finish him off immediately—for a minute or so, Bill can walk around and feel as normal; after this delay, however, he will suddenly collapse. The poignancy of the scene, of course, lies in the fact that Bill is aware of his predicament of a living dead, of one who is in a way already dead, although he continues to walk around normally, finishing his last drink. . . .

2. See Benjamin Libet, "Do We Have Free Will?," *Journal of Consciousness Studies* 1 (1999): 47–57.

3. Based on the Philip K. Dick short story of the same title.

4. It would be interesting to link *Minority Report* to Spielberg's previous (failed) *AI*, in which the hero is also confronted with the loss of his son. Furthermore, is not Agatha, the "prescient" cognitive medium, submerged in water, immersed in the pure medium of drive, reduced to a kind of *Muselmann*, living dead? Is not her escape from water her awakening to subjectivity?

5. Daniel Wegner, *The Illusion of Conscious Will* (Cambridge, MA: MIT Press, 2002).

6. Henri Bergson, *Oeuvres* (Paris: PUF, 1991), pp. 1110–1111.

7. Ibid.

8. Ibid., p. 1340.

9. For a closer analysis of this predicament, see "Appendix," in Slavoj Žižek, *The Puppet and the Dwarf* (Cambridge, MA: MIT Press, 2003).

10. I owe this reference to *Minority Report* to Juan Jorge Michel Farina (Buenos Aires).

11. Daniel C. Dennett, *Freedom Evolves* (Harmondsworth: Penguin, 2003).

12. Quoted from Elaine Feinstein, *Ted Hughes* (London: Weidenfeld & Nicolson, 2001), p. 166.

13. Quoted in ibid., p. 234.

14. Perhaps we should risk the following short circuit in order to produce the enlightening jolt effect: to record Sylvia Plath's most celebrated poems, starting with "Daddy," as popular-music songs in the pre-rock style of her times (Connie Francis, etc.), including the "rich" kitschy orchestration.

15. Francisco Varela, "The Emergent Self," in John Brockman, ed., *The Third Culture* (New York: Simon & Schuster, 1996), p. 212.

16. Is the mutual entanglement of impotence (disturbed sexual life) and social-symbolic problems in a failed marriage not a perfect example of the Hegelian entanglement of positing and presuppositions? We can say that growing conflicts and tensions reflect the underlying fact of the partners' sexual inadequacy ("they fight because they are not satisfied sexually"), but we can also say that sexual inadequacy is a result and symptom of socio-symbolic tensions between the partners, that these tensions "posit their presupposition" (the failed sexual life which they express).

17. Varela, "The Emergent Self," pp. 215–216.

18. Philip K. Dick, *Minority Report* (London: Gollancz, 2002), p. 20.

19. Ibid., pp. 23–24.

20. Ibid., p. 42.

21. Ibid.

22. Here we should take into account the radical ambiguity of the Lacanian "big Other": it simultaneously designates the symbolic "substance" (the determining order which "pulls the strings" in the mode of the "cunning of Reason," the subject supposed to know) and the pure appearance (the big Other, which "should not know it," for whom appearances should be maintained, so that his blessed ignorance is not disturbed, the subject supposed not to know).

23. Catherine Malabou, *Que faire de notre cerveau?* (Paris: Bayard, 2004).

24. Such parallels have a long history: it is a well-known fact that Darwin himself arrived at his notion of evolutionary selection by transposing onto nature the Malthusian economic view.

25. Malabou, *Que faire de notre cerveau?*, p. 88.

26. See chapters V and VI of Antonio Damasio, *The Feeling of What Happens: Body, Emotion and the Making of Consciousness* (London: Vintage, 2000).

27. Damasio, *The Feeling of What Happens*, p. 147.

28. Taylor can serve as an example of a "non-bestselling" neural science, a patient work more interested in precise formulations of new cognitions than in big provocative world-view statements.

29. John G. Taylor, *The Race for Consciousness* (Cambridge, MA: MIT Press, 2001), p. 37. (The numbers in brackets after the quotes that follow in the text refer to this volume.)

30. Thomas Metzinger, *Being No One: The Self-Model Theory of Subjectivity* (Cambridge, MA: MIT Press, 2004), p. 331. (The numbers in brackets after the quotes that follow in the text refer to this volume.)

31. On a closer analysis, of course, we should introduce a further distinction between "Self" as the image of the I, and "Me" as its unrepresentable substance.

32. See Colin McGinn, *The Mysterious Flame* (New York: Basic Books, 1999).

33. Jacques Lacan, *Le séminaire, livre III: Les psychoses* (Paris: Éditions du Seuil, 1981), p. 48.

34. There is a personal idiosyncrasy of Metzinger's writing which cannot fail to strike us: in order to specify or quantify a statement, he compulsively (practically on every page) starts a sentence with "Please note how . . ." or "Please note that . . .". And, incidentally, this idiosyncrasy is far more agreeable than the more pretentious one of Damasio, who, in order to package a "gray" thesis about the functioning of our brain more attractively, likes to evoke examples from high culture and art—for instance, he introduces an explanation of the mechanism of hearing thus: "A couple of days ago, a top Portuguese pianist visited me in my apartment and played some wonderful pieces by Bach. . . ."

35. Todd Feinberg, quoted in Metzinger, *Being No One*, p. 177.

36. See John L. Casti, *Would-Be Worlds* (New York: John Wiley & Sons, 1997), pp. 183–187.

37. This parallax shift from "inside" to "outside" is not symmetrical to the opposite one, where we undergo a shattering experience of an object which suddenly, unexpectedly, displays signs of the presence of a subject, and starts to talk (*Frankenstein, When a Stranger Calls . . .*). In the first case, we shift from subjective empathy to desubjectivized object ("Look, there's no Self behind the face, just the flesh and blood of the pulsating brain"); while in the second case, comparable to the well-known science-fiction scene in which a dead object turns

out to be alive ("Look, it's alive! This piece of meat is thinking!"), we do not simply traverse the same road backwards—it is rather that the object remains an object, a foreign body resisting subjectivization or subjective empathy, and it is as such, as impossible-inhuman object, that it "humanizes" itself, and starts to talk. The object that talks remains a monstrosity—something that should not talk starts to talk.

38. Damasio, The Feeling of What Happens. (The numbers in brackets after the quotes that follow in the text refer to this volume.)

39. What explodes with "thick consciousness" is a certain gap which becomes tangible in agnosia, where the sufferer physiologically perceives all forms, colors, and so on, but does not "see" anything, that is to say, he is unable to recognize known objects in perceptions. At the level of the Real, his perceptive mechanisms function normally, but he is unable to subjectivize their perceptive input—paradoxically, his perceptions (or, rather, sensations) remain objective. We should thus posit a radical discontinuity between "objective" sensations and "subjective" perceptions: there is an ontological gap separating them; sensations are not basic elements out of which perceptions of objects are composed.

40. For a more detailed account of this paradox, see Chapter 1 above: "The Kantian Parallax."

41. And, since I am discussing Hegel here, I am immediately tempted to conceive this joke as the first term of a triad. Thus, since the basic twist of this joke resides in the inclusion in the series of the apparent exception (the complaining patient is himself dying), its "negation" would have been a joke whose final twist would, on the contrary, involve exclusion from the series, that is to say, the extraction of the One, its positing as an exception to the series, as in a recent Bosnian joke in which Fata (the proverbial ordinary Bosnian wife) complains to a doctor that Muyo, her husband, makes love to her for hours every evening, so that, even in the darkness of their bedroom, she cannot get enough sleep—again and again, he jumps on her. The good doctor advises her to apply shock therapy: she should keep a bright lamp on her side of the bed, so that when she gets really tired of sex, she can suddenly illuminate Muyo's face; this shock is sure to cool his excessive passion. . . . The same evening, after hours of sex, Fata does exactly as advised—and recognizes the face of Haso, one of Muyo's colleagues. Surprised, she asks him: "But what are you doing here? Where is Muyo, my husband?" The embarrassed Haso answers: "Well, last time I saw him he was there at the door, collecting money from those waiting in line. . . ."

The third term here would be a kind of joke-correlative of "infinite judgment," tautology as supreme contradiction, as in the anecdote about a man who complains to his doctor that he often hears the voices of people who are not present with him in the room. The doctor replies: "Really? In order to enable me to discover the meaning of this hallucination, could you describe to me in what precise circumstances you usually hear the voices of people who are not with you?" "Well, it mostly happens when I talk on the phone. . . ."

42. Affects are usually conceived as obstacles to our access to reality, as something that blurs, distorts, our perception of reality—in clear contrast to this, Lacan determines anxiety as the (only) affect that indicates our approach to the Real, guarantees our access to the Real. Is anxiety, however, the only affect of this kind? What about enthusiasm? Perhaps the entire struggle of Badiou against Lacan can be encapsulated in this feature—that, for Badiou, enthusiasm (of the fidelity to the Event) is also a signal of our access to the Real.

43. Joseph LeDoux, Synaptic Self (London: Macmillan, 2002), p. 320.

44. Ibid., p. 323.

45. See Antonio Damasio, Descartes' Error: Emotion, Reason, and the Human Brain (New York: Quill, 1995).

46. Gary Tomlinson, Metaphysical Song (Princeton: Princeton University Press, 1999), p. 94.

47. Here I accept the reading of *Tristan* according to which Isolde's arrival and death are hallucinations of the dying Tristan. See Mladen Dolar and Slavoj Žižek, *Opera's Second Death* (New York: Routledge, 2001).

48. Antonio Damasio, *Looking for Spinoza* (London: Heinemann, 2003), p. 30.

49. Dennett, *Freedom Evolves*, p. 173.

50. Richard Dawkins, "Viruses of the Mind," in *Dennett and His Critics*, ed. Bo Dahlbom (Oxford: Blackwell, 1993), p. 26.

51. Daniel C. Dennett, "Back from the Drawing Board," in *Dennett and His Critics*, pp. 204–205.

52. Questions remain here, of course: is the illusion of qualia a constitutive illusion, or can it be "unlearned"? Plus, what about the role of fantasy in the Freudian sense of the "objective" appearance?

53. See Friedrich Engels, *The Origin of the Family, Private Property, and the State, in the Light of the Researches of Lewis H. Morgan* (Moscow: International Publishers, 1972).

54. Daniel C. Dennett, *Consciousness Explained* (Boston: Little, Brown, 1991), p. 244.

55. Karl Marx, *Capital*, Volume 1 (Harmondsworth: Penguin, 1990), p. 1026.

56. Ibid., p. 1035.

57. G. W. F. Hegel, *Phenomenology of Spirit* (Oxford: Oxford University Press, 1977), p. 332.

58. Ibid.

59. Dennett, *Freedom Evolves*, pp. 109–122. (The numbers in brackets after the quotes that follow in the text refer to this volume.)

60. Dennett detects the need for "conversation-stoppers" in the endless pursuit of argumentation which, because of the finitude and limitation of our situation, never comes to an end: there are always other aspects to take into account, and so on (506). Is not this need the need for what Lacan called the Master-Signifier (Dennett himself refers to the "magic word," or to a fake dogma): for something that will sever the Gordian knot of endless pros and cons with an act of (ultimately arbitrary and imperfect) decision?

61. Damasio, *Looking for Spinoza*, p. 30.

62. In philosophy, the term "intentional stance" is used in two different meanings: (1) doing something with intention, that is, a purposeful activity; (2) the attitude of our mind's activity being directed to some objective content (Husserl, Meinong). How are these two meanings related?

63. For a more detailed reading of Dennett's critique of the "Cartesian theater," see Slavoj Žižek, "The Cartesian Theater versus the Cartesian *cogito*," in *Cogito and the Unconscious* (SIC, vol. 2), Durham: Duke University Press, 1999.

64. See Benjamin Libet, "Unconscious Cerebral Initiative and the Role of Conscious Will in Voluntary Action," *The Behavioral and Brain Sciences* 8 (1985): 529–539; Libet, "Do We Have Free Will?", *Journal of Consciousness Studies* 1 (1999): 47–57.

65. What characterizes human perceptive apparatus is the immense gap between the infinite flux of subliminal data it can register (millions of bytes per second) and the very limited amount of data consciousness can register (7 bytes per second): consciousness is fundamentally a filtering apparatus which reduces the complexity of the raw Real to a very limited series of features. The role of language is crucial here: language is in itself a machine of "abstraction," transposing the complexity of the perceived real entity into a single fea-

ture designated by its symbol. So, instead of dismissing language as a limited medium which necessarily misses the overwhelming complexity of the Real, we should celebrate this infinite power of abstraction, of violently reducing the complexity of the Real, which is the precondition of thought. (An exemplary case of "less is more" is provided by the way color-blind people proved useful in the Second World War: they were able almost immediately to see through the camouflage and identify a tank or a gun behind the protective cover—proof that this cover worked at the level of color, by reproducing colors which blended smoothly into its surroundings, not at the level of shapes.)

66. See Nicholas Humphrey, "The Thick Moment," in John Brockman, ed., *The Third Culture* (New York: Touchstone, 1996).

67. See Robert Kane, *Free Will* (Oxford: Blackwell, 2001).

68. Quoted in Dennett, *Freedom Evolves*, p. 127.

69. Ibid., p. 135.

70. For a closer development of this notion, see the end of Chapter 1 above.

71. Jacques Derrida, *Adieu à Emmanuel Lévinas* (Paris: Galilée, 1997), p. 87.

72. For a detailed explanation of this notion of the atemporal choice of one's character, see chapter 1 of Slavoj Žižek, *The Indivisible Remainder* (London and New York: Verso, 1996).

73. It was Fichte who was compelled to assume this paradox and to acknowledge that Self-Consciousness's primordial, absolute act of self-positing is never accessible to human consciousness.

74. See Geoffrey Miller, *The Mating Mind: How Sexual Choice Shaped the Evolution of Human Nature* (London: Vintage, 2001). (The numbers in brackets after the quotes that follow in the text refer to this volume.)

75. Steven Pinker, *How the Mind Works* (Harmondsworth: Penguin, 1998), p. 524.

76. Ibid.

77. Ibid.

INTERLUDE 2: *OBJET PETIT A* IN SOCIAL LINKS, OR, THE IMPASSES OF ANTI-ANTI-SEMITISM

1. See Jean-Claude Milner, *Les penchants criminels de l'Europe démocratique* (Paris: Éditions Verdier, 2003).

2. Ibid., p. 42.

3. Ibid., p. 141.

4. Milner cited the post-Yugoslav war of the early 1990s as a "particularly revelatory example" (ibid., p. 66) of this erasure: in order to account for this conflict, we have to return to historical moments which, as Milner puts it acerbically, come "earlier than the Treaties of Rome": to the Second World War, to the Treaty of Versailles, to the Congress of Vienna, and so on—perplexed by this intrusion of history, Europe raised its hands and had to appeal to the USA. . . . What we have here is a "particularly revelatory example" of the ignorance of Milner himself: the reference to history, to "ancient passions and unsettled accounts exploding again," was one of the commonplaces of the Western European perception of the post-Yugoslav crisis—all the media and politicians endlessly repeated the cliché that, in order to understand what was going on in ex-Yugoslavia, one had to know about hundreds of years of history. Far from Western Europe refusing to confront the "weight of history"

in the Balkans, these specters of the past served, rather, as an ideological screen recreated in order to enable Europe to avoid confronting the actual political stakes of the post-Yugoslav crisis.

5. Ibid., p. 97.

6. Ibid., p. 119.

7. Ibid., p. 126.

8. See François Regnault, *Notre objet a* (Lagrasse: Verdier, 2003).

9. Milner, *Les penchants criminals de l'Europe démocratique*, p. 74.

10. See Heinz Höhne, *The Order of the Death's Head: The Story of Hitler's SS* (Harmondsworth: Penguin, 2000), pp. 336–337.

11. This is why both the Jewish neocons and old-style anti-Semites display animosity toward the Frankfurt School.

12. So while the French public is appalled to learn that 9 percent of Frenchmen display anti-Semitic attitudes, no one is particularly shocked by the fact that twice as many Frenchmen display anti-Muslim attitudes.

13. Jacques-Alain Miller and Jean-Claude Miller, *Voulez-vous être évalué?* (Paris: Grasset, 2004), p. 9.

14. I draw here on the report by Maria Cristina Aguirre, available online at <www.amp-nls.org/lacaniancompass.1.pdf>.

15. Transcription of the J. P. Elkabbach broadcast with Jacque-Alain Miller and Bernard Accoyer on the phone on Europe 1, October 31, 2003, available on <www.lacan.com>. For a more detailed reading of this intervention, see Appendix I in Slavoj Žižek, *Iraq: The Borrowed Kettle* (London and New York: Verso, 2004).

16. Jacques-Alain Miller, *Letter to Bernard Accoyer and to Enlightened Opinion* (Paris: Atelier de psychanalyse appliquée, 2003), p. 23.

17. Michael Hardt and Antonio Negri, *Multitude* (New York: Penguin Press, 2004), p. xvi. The numbers in brackets after the quotes that follow in the text refer to this edition.

18. I address them in Chapter 3 of Part II of *Organs without Bodies* (New York: Routledge, 2003).

19. This is also why HN's reference to Bakhtin's notion of carnival as the model for the protest movement of the multitude—they are carnivalesque not only in their form and atmosphere (theatrical performances, chants, humorous songs) but also in their non-centralized organization (208–211)—is deeply problematic: is not late-capitalist social reality itself already carnivalesque? Furthermore, is not "carnival" also the name for the obscene underside of power—from gang rapes to mass lynchings? Let us not forget that Bakhtin developed the notion of carnival in his book on Rabelais written in the 1930s, as a direct reply to the carnival of the Stalinist purges.

20. Giorgio Agamben, *The Coming Community* (Minneapolis: University of Minnesota Press, 1993), pp. 5–6.

21. Ibid., pp. 6–7.

22. See Ernesto Laclau and Chantal Mouffe, *Hegemony and Socialist Strategy* (London and New York: Verso, 1985).

23. For a more detailed analysis of this failure of Marx, see chapters 3 and 4 of Slavoj Žižek, *The Fragile Absolute* (London and New York: Verso, 1999).

24. See chapters 6 and 8 in Albert-László Barabási, *Linked* (New York: Plume, 2003).

25. See Mike Davis's excellent report, "Planet of Slums: Urban Revolution and the Informal Proletariat," *New Left Review* 26 (March/April 2004).

26. Should not slum-dwellers, then, be classified as what Marx, with barely concealed contempt, dismissed as the "lumpenproletariat," the degenerate "refuse" of all classes which, when politicized, as a rule serves as the support of proto-Fascist and Fascist regimes (in Marx's case, of Napoleon III)? A closer analysis should focus on the changed structural role of these "lumpen" elements in the conditions of global capitalism (especially large-scale migrations).

27. The precise Marxian definition of the proletarian position is: substanceless subjectivity which emerges when a certain structural short circuit occurs—not only do producers exchange their products on the market, but there are producers who are forced to sell on the market not the product of their labor, but directly their labor-power as such. It is here, through this redoubled/reflected alienation, that the surplus-object emerges: surplus-value is literally correlative to the emptied subject, it is the objectal counterpart of $. This redoubled alienation means not only that "social relations appear as relations between things," as in every market economy, but that the very core of subjectivity itself is posited as equivalent to a thing. We should look closely here at the paradox of universalization: the market economy can become universal only when labor-power itself is also sold on the market as a commodity; that is to say, there can be no universal market economy with the majority of producers selling their products.

5 FROM SURPLUS-VALUE TO SURPLUS-POWER

1. Why do two people as different as Bertolt Brecht and Martin Heidegger, both key figures of German art and thought in the twentieth century, share the feature of being extremely unpleasant? Is this a mere idiosyncratic coincidence, or does it indicate some kind of necessity?

2. René Descartes, *Discourse on Method* (South Bend: University of Notre Dame Press, 1994), pp. 38–39.

3. Peter Sloterdijk, *Nicht gerettet.Versuche nach Heidegger* (Frankfurt: Suhrkamp, 2001), p. 41.

4. Martin Heidegger, *Schelling's Treatise on the Essence of Human Freedom* (Athens: Ohio University Press, 1985), pp. 40–41.

5. See Étienne Balibar, "La violence: idéalité et cruauté," in *La crainte des masses* (Paris: Éditions Galilée, 1997).

6. What makes it so easy to parody Heidegger? Is it not because there is something faked in his rhetoric of the difficult struggle of the thought with its object, of the impossibility of directly designating the matter of thought, of the necessity of relying on poetic hints, of passively exposing oneself to the Word of Being, and discerning its obscure message? It is as if Heidegger knows very well what he has to say, and could put it in the form of direct explicit propositions, but, out of pure rhetoric, he envelops it in obscure sayings which cannot but appear comical. And, incidentally, for this very reason, it is often Heidegger himself who sounds like a parody of himself, as in the comment on the Stalingrad defeat quoted above ("the essence of victory has nothing to do with an ontic military victory; the essence of victory is the victory of the essence itself"). Or—an even more ridiculous example (reported to me by a witness): when, in 1962, Heidegger visited René Char's cottage in Provence, with its rustic furniture, he commented: "Poetically dwells a man. . . ."

7. Martin Heidegger, *Being and Time* (New York: Harper & Row, 1962), p. 436.

8. Miguel de Beistegui, *Heidegger and the Political* (London: Routledge, 1998), pp. 17–19.

9. Martin Heidegger, *Gesamtausgabe*, vol. 39, *Hölderlins Hymnem, Germanien und "Der Rhein"* (Frankfurt: Klosterman, 1980), pp. 72–73.

10. Martin Heidegger, *Gesamtausgabe*, vol. 45, *Grundprobleme der Philosophie* (Frankfurt: Klostermann, 1980), p. 41.

11. Heidegger, *Being and Time*, p. 383.

12. Theodor Kiesel, "Heidegger's Philosophical Geopolitics," in *A Companion to Heidegger's Introduction to Metaphysics*, ed. Richard Polt and Gregory Fried (New Haven: Yale University Press, 2003), p. 231.

13. Martin Heidegger, *Introduction to Metaphysics* (New Haven: Yale University Press, 2000), p. 16.

14. See Jacques Derrida, *Of Spirit: Heidegger and the Question* (Chicago: University of Chicago Press, 1991).

15. See See Brian A. Victoria, *Zen at War* (New York: Weatherhilt, 1998).

16. When, in his *Introduction to Metaphysics*, Heidegger conceives the essence of man as the violent confrontation with the All of beings, doomed to failure yet displaying heroic greatness in its very failure, is he not aiming at something like Ahab in *Moby Dick*, for whom also the whale stands for the overpowering violence of the All of beings?

17. Heidegger, *Introduction to Metaphysics*, p. 125.

18. For such a reading, see Clare Pearson Geiman, "Heidegger's *Antigones*," in *A Companion to Heidegger's Introduction to Metaphysics*.

19. When Peter Sloterdijk opposes the drive to infinite mobility that characterizes our subjective attitude to the "Euro-Taoist" *Gelassenheit*, abandoning of control, letting-it-go, the acceptance of our irreducible finitude and being-thrown into the world, he seems to miss the fundamental paradox: the spontaneous ideology of today's capitalist mobilization is *already* that of "Euro-Taoism," of playing the game with an inner distance, being aware that it is just a game of ultimately insignificant appearances. What is more and more unthinkable today, in our constant mobility, is the concept of radical *engagement* itself.

20. Martin Heidegger, *Sein und Wahrheit* (1933/34), *Gesamtausgabe*, vols. 36/37 (Frankfurt: Klostermann, 2001), pp. 90–91. Here we should also establish a link with Laclau's couple of agonism/antagonism: Heidegger was against democracy, since its basic premise is the transposition of antagonism into agonism. In fact there is no room in Heidegger for the politics of the compromise of interests, dialogue, negotiation, agreement, which mark the "normal" run of things: "The one who looks in Heidegger for a theory of the political will only find a poetic of emergency state" (Sloterdijk, *Nicht gerettet*, p. 58).

21. See Martin Heidegger, "Language in the Poem," in *On the Way to Language* (New York: Harper & Row, 1982), pp. 170–171.

22. Friedrich Nietzsche, *Sämtliche Werke: Kristische Studienausgabe*, vol. 2 (Berlin: Walter de Gruyter, 1980), p. 679.

23. Ibid., 1: 529.

24. Here I draw on Alenka Zupančič, *The Shortest Shadow* (Cambridge, MA: MIT Press, 2004).

25. Quoted in Victoria, *Zen at War*, p. 110.

26. Quoted from Jon Lee Anderson, *Che Guevara: A Revolutionary Life* (New York: Grove, 1997), pp. 636–637.

27. Quoted in Peter McLaren, *Che Guevara, Paulo Freire, and the Pedagogy of Revolution* (Oxford: Rowman & Littlefield, 2000), p. 27.

28. Heidegger, *Introduction to Metaphysics*, p. 102.

29. When, enumerating modern heroes, Heidegger puts Leo Schlageter (the German nationalist killed by the French occupying army in Rhineland for terrorist acts) in the same series with Hölderlin, Nietzsche, and Van Gogh, is this not something like Marx's famous "freedom, equality *and Bentham*"? The ridiculous addition of Schlageter makes the entire series problematic.

30. Heidegger, *Gesamtausgabe*, vol. 48, p. 333.

31. Ibid., pp. 94–95. Here we encounter a case of Heidegger's "hermeneutics of everyday life": he often quotes a political statement, a conversational turn of phrase, a technological breakthrough, reading them as indexes of our historico-metaphysical predicament. He quotes Lenin's "Socialism = electrification + the power of soviets" as articulating the metaphysical truth of Soviet Communism; he mentions the colloquial use, among German students, of "Uni" for "university" as bearing witness to the technological instrumentalization of language; he quotes man's landing on the Moon as the proof that man's dwelling in his historical world on Earth is threatened.

32. See Hubert L. Dreyfus, "Highway Bridges and Feasts," available online at <http://www.focusing.org/apm_papers/dreyfus.html>.

33. Heidegger's *silence* about Nazism after the Second World War is to be conceived as the very form of his *fidelity* to the pseudo-Event "the Nazi revolution." It is interesting to note that the only time Heidegger came close to an open political engagement after the War was in 1949, when he was invited to attend the Congreso Nacional de Filosofía in Mendoza, Argentina, from March 30 to April 9, with the participation of—among others—Hans-Georg Gadamer, Ludwig Landgrebe, Karl Löwith, Eugen Fink, and Nicola Abbagnano (not to mention readings of papers by Karl Jaspers, Benedetto Croce, Jean Hyppolite, Ludwig Klages, Nicolai Hartmann, and Gabriel Marcel). This big event was organized by Juan Perón himself in order to provide a philosophical underpinning for his "neither-capitalism-nor-Communism" vision of what he called "organized community." Perón was so eager to get Heidegger that the Argentinian state offered him a special plane to fly him directly from Schwarzwald to Argentina; furthermore, since, in 1949, Heidegger was still forbidden by the French occupying forces to practice any public academic activity, Argentinian diplomats intervened with top French state functionaries (Foreign Minister Robert Schumann) to clear this obstacle. Although, in the end, Heidegger declined (for totally unrelated reasons: he feared that the visit to Argentina, a country which was known to be a safe haven for refugee Nazis, would conclusively discredit him as a Nazi sympathizer), he sent warm greetings to the congress. Until the 1960s, Heidegger remained interested in what Peronism stood for, asking occasional visitors from Latin America about the news from Argentina. See a report in Guillermo David, *Astrada. La filosofía argentina* (Buenos Aires: Ediciones El cielo por asalto, 2004).

34. Martin Heidegger, *Hölderlin's Hymn "The Ister"* (Bloomington: Indiana University Press, 1992), p. 98.

35. See Beistegui, *Heidegger and the Political*, pp. 154–156.

36. It started a year ago when the Croat ski champion Ivica Kostelić, asked the evening before the big race if he was well prepared, snapped back: "Like the German army on the evening of June 21, 1941, warming up their tanks to attack Russia!"

37. See Alain Badiou, *L'éthique* (Paris: Hatier, 1993).

38. See J. Arch Getty's and Oleg V. Naumov's outstanding *The Road to Terror: Stalin and the Self-Destruction of the Bolsheviks, 1932–39* (New Haven: Yale University Press, 1999).

39. Sheila Fitzpatrick, *The Russian Revolution* (Oxford: Oxford University Press, 1994), p. 148.

40. I owe this reference to Božidar Jezernik, Philosophical Faculty, University of Ljubljana.

41. This means that, precisely on account of the unbearable horror of Stalinism, any direct moralistic portrayal of Stalinism as evil misses its target—only through what Kierkegaard called "indirect communication," by practicing a kind of irony, can one communicate its horror.

42. Here again we find the theme of *Versagung* developed in chapter 1 above: "The Kantian Parallax."

43. I owe this point to Boris Buden, Zagreb/London/Berlin.

44. Another sign of the Enlightenment legacy: if there is one proposition which condenses Stalinist politics, it is the "anti-essentialist" theme, repeated endlessly in his work: "Everything depends on circumstances."

45. There is, of course, a fundamental lie in the all-too-slick pseudo-Marxist point that modern anti-Semitism is just a by-product of capitalism, so that the Jews should not be in any way privileged as victims—we should focus on how to fight capitalism. However, although *shoah* is a unique excess, it could have occurred only against the background of this shift in the anti-Semitic figure of the Jew.

46. Friedrich Nietzsche, *Beyond Good and Evil* (Oxford: Oxford University Press, 1998), para. 251.

47. Jean-Claude Milner, *Le périple structural* (Paris: Éditions du Seuil, 2002), p. 214.

48. The mutual fascination between Stalin and the Russian writers who are today perceived as "dissidents" reveals not only Stalin's belief in the secret wisdom of poets but, even more, the weird conviction of the writers themselves that Stalin, this total Master, a kind of Freudian primordial father (*Ur-Vater*), possessed a mysterious insight into the ultimate secrets of life and death. In April 1930, Stalin unexpectedly phoned Bulgakov to persuade him not to emigrate; after assuring him that he would get a job at the Art Theater, he added: "We should meet, to talk together." Bulgakov immediately replied: "Yes, yes! Iosif Vissarionovich, I really need to talk to you." After this, Stalin unexpectedly cut the conversation short (quoted from Solomon Volkov, *Shostakovich and Stalin* [New York: Little, Brown, 2004], p. 90). A similar thing happened to Pasternak in June 1934, when he got a phone call from Stalin, asking him about Mandelstam, who was at that time out of favor and in exile: "This is Stalin. Are you interceding on behalf of your friend Mandelstam?" Fearing a trap, the confused Pasternak replied: "We were never actually friends. Rather the reverse. I found it difficult dealing with him. But I've always dreamed about talking to you. About life and death." Here Stalin cut the conversation short, reprimanding Pasternak for not standing up for his friend: "We old Bolsheviks never deny our friends. And I have no reason to talk to you about other things" (ibid., p. 106). The same ambivalent fascination is clearly discernible in Shostakovich and Meyerhold, and even in Mandelstam.

49. I owe this anecdote to Adam Chmielewski, who was present when it occurred.

50. Ernst Nolte, *Martin Heidegger—Politik und Geschichte im Leben und Denken* (Berlin: Propyläen Verlag, 1992).

51. Isaac Deutscher, *The Prophet Outcast* (London and New York: 2003), p. 88.

52. Milner, *Le périple structural*, p. 213.

53. I draw here on "La passe. Conférence de Jacques-Alain Miller," IV Congrès de l'AMP—2004, Comandatuba—Bahia, Brazil.

54. For a more detailed analysis of the University discourse, see Appendix II in Slavoj Žižek, *Iraq: The Borrowed Kettle* (London and New York: Verso, 2004).

55. For a more detailed analysis of this excess constitutive of capitalism, see chapters 8 and 9 of Slavoj Žižek, *Revolution at the Gates* (London and New York: 2001).

56. Lacan deploys the matrix of the four discourses in *Le séminaire, Livre XVII: L'envers de la psychanalyse* (Paris: Éditions du Seuil, 1973), pp. 92–95.

57. See Eric Santner, *My Own Private Germany* (Princeton: Princeton University Press, 1996).

58. See "La passe. Conférence de Jacques-Alain Miller."

59. One cannot help noticing a strange fact about Miller's latest excursions into the cultural-political domain: they come dangerously close to the quick pop-psychological journalism practiced by American writers who love to dwell on topics like "the anxieties of modern man," and so on. There is a kind of poetic justice at work here: it is as if Miller, prone to outbursts against the primitivism of US intellectual life, himself becomes affected by the worst aspects of American pop-theorizing.

60. See Giorgio Agamben, *The State of Exception* (Stanford: Stanford University Press, 2004).

61. Kevin B. MacDonald, *The Culture of Critique: An Evolutionary Analysis of Jewish Involvement in Twentieth-Century Intellectual and Political Movements* (Westport: Praeger, 1998). All non-attributed quotes that follow are from this book.

62. To bring this line of thought to its ridiculous climax: a well-known Slovene Catholic intellectual, ex-Minister of Culture and ex-Slovenian ambassador to France, recently wrote, apropos of Derrida: "the only weapon is rebellion and destruction, as the recently deceased apostle Jacques Derrida taught us. Wherever you see a window, throw a brick into it. Where there is a building, there must be a mine. Where there is a high-rise building, bin Laden should come. Where there is any kind of institution, law, or link, one should find a falsification, a 'law' of the street or of the underground" (Andrej Capuder, "Vino in most," *Demokracija* 9, no. 50 [Ljubljana, December 9, 2004], p. 9; translation mine). Incidentally, does not "Where there is a high-rise building, bin Laden should come" sound like a new politicized version of Freud's *wo es war soll ich werden?*

63. See Jacques Lacan, *The Four Fundamental Concepts of Psycho-Analysis* (New York: Norton, 1979).

64. Perversion occurs when the "pound of flesh," the partial object which stands for what is "in me more than myself," is taken literally, as in a short story by Patricia Highsmith in which a father, when his daughter's suitor asks him for her hand, cuts off the daughter's hand with a knife, and sends it in a package to the suitor. His reply to the surprised suitor is: "Oh, you wanted all of her, not only her hand? Why didn't you *say* so, then?" It is like when we read the emotional statement "My heart belongs to you!" as the statement of a potential heart donor. . . .

65. Women frequently complain how difficult it is for them to reconcile two orders or levels of their activity (home and work, lover and mother . . .), while men have to take care of only one thing—what if this complaint does not only refer to a sociological fact, but also bears witness to a more radical "ontological" division of the feminine subjective position between what Lacan called the phallic order and the signifier of the lack of the Other?

66. The crucial point not to be missed here is how Lacan's late identification of the subjective position of the analyst as that of *objet petit a* presents an act of radical self-criticism: earlier, in the 1950s, Lacan conceived the analyst not as the small other (*a*), but, on the contrary, as a kind of stand-in for the big Other (A, the anonymous symbolic order). At this level, the function of the analyst was to frustrate the subject's imaginary misrecognitions, and to make him or her accept their proper place within the circuit of symbolic exchange, the

place which effectively (and unbeknownst to them) determines their symbolic identity. Later, however, the analyst stands precisely for the ultimate inconsistency and failure of the big Other: for the symbolic order's inability to guarantee the subject's symbolic identity.

67. Jacques Lacan: *Le séminaire, livre XX: Encore* (Paris: Éditions du Seuil, 1973), pp. 92–95.

68. As Jacqueline Rose put it succinctly: "Right at the heart of group adherence, [Freud] places killing. . . . To be a member of a group is to be a partner in crime" (Jacqueline Rose, "In Our Present-Day White Christian Culture," *London Review of Books*, July 8, 2004, p. 17). So the question is: is this partnership in crime the only way to form a collective?

69. See Lorenzo Chiesa, "Imaginary, Symbolic and Real Otherness: The Lacanian Subject and His Vicissitudes," thesis, University of Warwick, Department of Philosophy, 2004.

70. See Esteban Echeverría, *El matadero* (*The Slaughterhouse*), bilingual edition, edited and translated by Angel Flores (New York: Las Americas Publishing Co., 1959).

71. The ironic twist of this stance in the case of the anti-Israeli attitude cannot be missed: on the one hand, one of the major arguments against the State of Israel in the popular Arab press, the final "proof" of its perverted nature, is that women also serve in the army; on the other, remember the publicly praised role of women suicide bombers (although two decades ago, the role of women in the PLO was much more visible—an indication of the de-secularization of the PLO).

72. This duality is reflected in the ambiguous status of the "undead": undeadness is simultaneously the name for the excess of drive *and* the name for the vampyric pseudo-excess covering up the fact that "we are not really alive."

73. See Alain Badiou, "The Caesura of Nihilism," lecture delivered at the University of Essex, September 10, 2003.

74. Alain Badiou, "L'entretien de Bruxelles," *Les Temps Modernes* 526 (1990): 6.

75. What if the greatest courage is not that of fidelity to the Event, but that of assuming the thankless role of undoing the catastrophe/disaster of the Event gone awry (the role of Jaruzelski in Poland, etc.)? There is no fame in it, just the role of "vanishing mediator" whose very success is measured in terms of how much he himself will be maligned or erased as the last remainder of the old oppressive regime.

76. Alberto Toscano, "From the State to the World? Badiou and Anti-Capitalism," *Communication & Cognition* 36 (2003): 1–2.

77. Alain Badiou, "Prefazione all'edizione italiana," in *Metapolitica* (Naples: Cronopio, 2002), p. 14.

78. Toscano, "From the State to the World?," p. 3.

79. See Michael Hardt and Antonio Negri, *Multitude* (New York: The Penguin Press, 2004). Is the cyberspace World Wide Web, then, inherently "communist," the materialization of social(ized) intellect, a direct embodiment of the collective mind? Could one put it in the standard Marxist sense that WWW is already communist "in itself" (just as, for Marx, big factory industry was already in itself collectivized, in contradiction with individual ownership of the means of production), so that all is needed is a passage from In-itself to For-itself?

80. Although, in order to make this point clear, Hallward cannot resist the temptation to attribute the "bad" version of one's own principle to others—which, in this case, is more a sign of his own guilt feeling: "Each in their own way, Negri, Agamben, Derrida and Žižek all accept this absolutisation as the condition of an effectively *desperate* politics, a condition

that solicits the equally absolute affirmation of an un-mediated creativity (Negri), of a potentiality that subsists in the annulment of actuality (Agamben), of a decision withdrawn from activity (Derrida), of a radical act uncontaminated by reflection (Žižek)." Badiou himself could easily be added to this series!

81. Margaret Washington, on <http://www.pbs.org/wgbh/amex/brown/filmmore/reference/interview/washington05.html>.

82. At a conference for the European Graduate School in Saas Fee, August 2002.

83. It also seems problematic to conceive of "Stalinism" as a too-radical "forcing" of the Order of Being (existing society): the paradox of the 1928 "Stalinist revolution" was rather that, in all its brutal radicality, it *was not radical enough* in effectively transforming the social substance. Its brutal destructiveness has to be read as an impotent *passage à l'acte*. Far from simply standing for a total forcing of the unnameable Real on behalf of the Truth, Stalinist "totalitarianism" designates, rather, the attitude of absolutely ruthless "pragmatism," of manipulating and sacrificing all "principles" for the sake of retaining power.

84. See Alain Badiou, "L'Un se divise en Deux," intervention at the symposium *The Retrieval of Lenin*, Essen, February 2–4, 2001.

85. See Sylvain Lazarus, "La forme Parti," intervention at the symposium *The Retrieval of Lenin*.

86. Wendy Brown, *States of Injury* (Princeton: Princeton University Press, 1995), p. 14.

87. A conference from 2002 translated by Boostels himself.

6   THE OBSCENE KNOT OF IDEOLOGY, AND HOW TO UNTIE IT

1. We should, of course, resist the stupid temptation to use this fact as a reason for the retroactive legitimization of Stalin's brutal suppression of Trotskyism ("So Stalin was right when he pointed out how Trotskyism ends up directly serving imperialism—he was half a century ahead of his time!"); such a reasoning can only end up in a cheap paraphrase of De Quincey: "How many an honest man started with a modest Leftist critique of Stalinism and ended up as a servant of imperialism. . . ."

2. Available online at <http://www.politicaltheory.info/essays/critchley.htm>.

3. Alain Badiou, "Fifteen Theses on Contemporary Art," available online at <http://www.lacan.com/frameXXIII7.htm>.

4. See Bernard Williams, *Moral Luck* (Cambridge: Cambridge University Press, 1981), p. 125.

5. Karl Marx and Friedrich Engels, *Selected Works*, Volume 1 (Moscow: Progress Publishers, 1969), p. 83.

6. Karl Marx and Friedrich Engels, *Collected Works*, Volume 2 (Moscow: Progress Publishers, 1975), p. 148.

7. Ibid., 193.

8. Ibid., p. 188.

9. Étienne Balibar, "Gewalt" (entry for *Historisch-Kritisches Wörterbuch des Marxismus*, forthcoming from Das Argument Verlag, Berlin).

10. See Hannah Arendt, *On Violence* (New York: Harvest Books, 1970).

11. Rony Bauman, "From Philanthropy to Humanitarianism," *South Atlantic Quarterly* 103: 2/3 (Spring/Summer 2004), pp. 398–399, 416.

12. Wendy Brown, "Human Rights as the Politics of Fatalism," *South Atlantic Quarterly* 103: 2/3, p. 453.

13. Ibid., p. 454

14. Étienne Balibar, "Is a Philosophy of Human Civic Rights Possible?", *South Atlantic Quarterly* 103: 2/3, pp. 320–321.

15. Hannah Arendt, *The Origins of Totalitarianism* (New York: Meridian, 1958), p. 297.

16. See Giorgio Agamben, *Homo sacer* (Stanford: Stanford University Press, 1998).

17. See Jacques Rancière, "Who Is the Subject of the Rights of Man?", *South Atlantic Quarterly* 103: 2/3, pp. 297–310.

18. Ibid., p. 305.

19. Ibid., pp. 307–309.

20. Ibid., p. 309.

21. Ibid., p. 301.

22. In what follows, I draw on ideas developed by Rob Rushing (University of Illinois, Champaign-Urbana).

23. All three marriages in the movie are portrayed as fundamentally flawed: Sean is traumatized because his wife has left him; Dave's wife does not trust him and betrays him, causing his death; Jimmy's wife displays excessive trust, and provides false security.

24. For Ethiopian Christians, the lion is a sacred animal and, as such, observes the Sabbath, that is, does not "work" (hunt for food) on it; however, while they *believe* in this sacredness of the lion, they *know* he will nonetheless pose a threat to their sheep, and thus do not take them out to pasture on the Sabbath. . . . This may appear to be a case of fetishist disavowal, but in fact it effectively turns it around: the standard *je sais bien, mais quand même* . . . ("I know, but even so . . . [I believe . . .]") is inverted into "I believe you, but even so I know very well. . . ."

25. In the glamorous 1960s, being an air stewardess was considered an exciting career for a woman—of course, more a male fantasy of such a career, since part of the glamour of the figure of the stewardess was her assumed sexual availability, the dream that when we are offered a drink on a flight, the offer had to be read as including an implicit supplement: "Coffee or tea . . . *or me?*"

26. From my own youth, in the old Yugoslavia of the late 1960s and early 1970s, I remember a similar constellation on the Slovene philosophical scene dominated by the opposition between (official) Frankfurt School Marxists and (dissident) Heideggerians: the moment "French structuralism" appeared, these "mortal enemies" both started to speak the same language against it. . . .

27. There is also, of course, an observe side to it: the utopian potential present in the universe of cartoons, with its lack of realistic depth, plasticity of "undead" bodies, and so on. And, as Leslie points out (see Esther Leslie, *Hollywood Flatlands* [London and New York: Verso, 2002]), the crucial shift occurs in the mid-1930s, when cartoons develop from their early anarchic plasticity, lack of depth, gags, and so on, to the more "realistic" and emotional universe of Disney's long feature cartoons—a domestication strictly correlative to that of the Marx Brothers who, after the financial failure of *Duck Soup*, were reinvented by Irving Thalberg at MGM: their uncontrollable aggressiveness and anarchic spirit of subversive gags was made into an element of the main narrative of a love-couple, with numerous bor-

ing musical numbers—in short, they were reduced to the role of benevolent helpers to the couple in distress, organizing their final unification.

28. That would be a certain pseudo-psychoanalytic reading of the famous last sentence of Wittgenstein's *Tractatus*: whereof one cannot speak, thereof one should utter a cry—when articulate words fail, one should supplement them with a wild cry.

29. See Jacques Derrida, "Faith and Knowledge," in *Religion*, ed. Jacques Derrida and Gianni Vattimo (Stanford: Stanford University Press, 1998).

30. A newspaper column attacking George Bush's plans for privatizing social security provides an additional twist to such reliance on the Other's belief: "Privatization, in other words, requires Americans to accept a theory (stocks are better than bonds) that *can be true only as long as lots of people believe that it is false*. And the White House is campaigning hard to convince everyone that the theory is true. If the campaign succeeds, the theory fails." (Michael Kinsey, "Privatization's Empty Hype," *LA Times*, December 26, 2004. Thanks to Jeff Martinek for drawing my attention to this text.)

31. Karl Marx, *Capital*, vol. 1 (Harmondsworth: Penguin, 1990), p. 163.

32. Ibid., pp. 176–177.

33. Alenka Zupančič, "'Concrete Universal' and What Comedy Can Tell Us About It" (to appear in *Lacan: The Silent Partners*, ed. Slavoj Žižek [London and New York: Verso, 2005]).

34. G. K. Chesterton, *Orthodoxy* (San Francisco: Ignatius Press, 1995), p. 145.

35. Zupančič, "'Concrete Universal' and What Comedy Can Tell Us About It."

36. It is still fashionable today to mock the Freudian notion of the phallus by ironically discerning "phallic symbols" everywhere—for example, when a story mentions a strong, forward-thrusting movement, this is supposed to stand for "phallic penetration"; or, when the building is a high tower, it is obviously "phallic," and so on. One cannot help noticing that those who make such comments never fully identify with them—either they impute such a believe in "phallic symbols everywhere" to some mythical orthodox Freudian, or they themselves endorse the phallic meaning, but as something to be criticized, to be overcome. The irony of the situation is that the naive orthodox Freudian who sees "phallic symbols everywhere" does not exist, that he is a fiction of the critic himself, his "subject supposed to believe." The only believer in phallic symbols in both cases is the critic himself, who believes through the other—who "projects" (or, rather, transposes) his belief onto the fictive other.

37. Why are cinema-lovers so obsessed with gaffes, small mistakes, like the legendary child covering his eyes in *North by Northwest*? We derive immense pleasure from discovering them, and far from destroying the diegetic illusion, they, if anything, reinforce it in a kind of fetishist denial. Is not the entire ambiguity of belief encompassed in this paradox? Is not our pleasure in discovering gaffes a kind of revenge of the ego against our unconscious beliefs?

38. The reason why the First World War had a traumatic impact which surpassed even that of the Second World War was that, as Freud put it in his "Thoughts for the Times on War and Death" (1915), in 1914, "the war in which we had refused to believe broke out": the unthinkable took place.

39. Again, in his (unpublished manuscript) *La logique des mondes*.

40. When Robert Pfaller (in *Illusionen der Anderen*, Frankfurt: Suhrkamp 2002) praises the ancient or Oriental cultures, with their circulation of beliefs without a subject, against the Western Christian and modern obsession with beliefs to be fully assumed by a subject, does he not thereby fall into the trap of Barthes (apropos of Japan), Vernant, and Foucault's late work

(apropos of ancient Greece), and others, who all proposed a vision of a civilization without the ascetic Subject, a civilization in which codes and beliefs circulate freely, enabling us to indulge in pleasures without traumatic guilt and responsibility? Are such visions not *stricto sensu* Europe's fantasmatic projection onto the Other of its own ideological fantasy of a space freed from the traumatic cut of the Real?

41. I owe this point to Geneviève Morel, Paris.

42. Guillermo Arriaga, *21 Grams* (London: Faber & Faber, 2003), p. 107.

43. See Thomas Frank, *What's the Matter with Kansas? How Conservatives Won the Heart of America* (New York: Metropolitan Books, 2004).

44. How come conservative evangelicals who, against Darwinism, like to insist on the literal truth of the Bible, are never tempted to read literally Christ's "Sell all that you have, and give to the poor" (Mark 10: 21)?

45. The pure difference of antagonism, however, has nothing to do with the difference between two positive social groups one of which is to be annihilated, that is, the universalism that sustains antagonistic struggle is not exclusive of anyone—that is why the greatest triumph of antagonistic struggle is not the destruction of the enemy, but an explosion of "universal brotherhood" in which agents of the opposite camp change sides and join us (recall the proverbial scenes of police or military units joining demonstrators). It is in such an explosion of enthusiastic all-encompassing brotherhood, from which no one is in principle excluded, that the difference between "us" and "the enemy" as positive agents is reduced to a *pure* formal difference.

46. Margaret Washington, on <http://www.pbs.org/wgbh/amex/brown/filmmore/reference/interview/washington05.html>.

47. Russell Banks, on <http://www.pbs.org/wgbh/amex/brown/filmmore/reference/interview/banks01.html>.

48. See Henry David Thoreau, *Civil Disobedience and Other Essays* (New York: Dover Publications, 1993).

49. Some anti-abortionists draw a parallel between Brown's fight and their own: Brown acknowledged as fully human Blacks—that is to say, people who, for the majority, were less-than-human and, as such, denied basic human rights; in the same way, anti-abortionists acknowledge the unborn child as fully human. . . .

50. Robert H. Bork, *Slouching towards Gomorrah* (New York: ReganBooks, 1997), p. 132.

51. Ibid., p. 139.

52. Quoted from <www.prospect.org>.

53. Bork, *Slouching Towards Gomorrah*, p. 134.

54. Crucial for the Communist regimes is the difference between the official History and the secret archives: the official History is the public version, it contains reports on the enthusiastic construction of Socialism, presented in the media, museums, and so on; the secret police archives contain the (ideologically censored, but factually mostly accurate) truth about discontent, unrest, strikes, economic failures, and so forth. Access to the secret archives was strictly controlled—it was the sign of belonging to the *nomenklatura*. Although everyone knew about their existence, their status was that of a fascinating secret, as if learning what was in my archive would tell me what I really was for the big Other. Secret archives were neither public (the official history) nor private, but the secret/private supplement to the public/official discourse itself. They were simultaneously both utterly alienated, writ-

ten in a cold impersonal style, *and* touching on the most intimate topics, right up to the observed people's sex lives.

55. For this reason, the proclamation of the Decalogue is not a normal case of ideological interpellation: the Decalogue is precisely a law *deprived* of the obscene fantasmatic support.

56. In the same way, let us not forget that the very fact that the US forces did not find weapons of mass destruction is a positive sign: a truly "totalitarian" power would have done what cops usually do—plant drugs and then "discover" evidence of a crime. . . .

57. See the ample documentation in Uki Goñi, *La auténtica Odessa. La fuga nazi a la Argentina de Perón* (Buenos Aires: Paidos, 2004).

58. For a more detailed elaboration of this topic, see Chapter 3 of Slavoj Žižek, *The Metastases of Enjoyment* (London and New York: Verso, 1995).

59. Christopher Hitchens, "Prison Mutiny," available online (posted on May 4, 2004).

60. There is a vague similarity between their situation and the—legally problematic—premise of the movie *Double Jeopardy*: if you were convicted of killing A and you later, after serving your sentence and being released, discover that A is still alive, you can now kill him with impunity, since you cannot be tried twice for the same offense. In psychoanalytic terms, this killing would clearly display the temporal structure of masochist perversion: the order is inverted—you are punished first, and thus gain the right to commit the crime.

61. Jonathan Alter, "Time to Think about Torture," *Newsweek*, November 5, 2001, p. 45.

62. Although the two procedures seem to coexist: according to Bob Herbert (see "Outsourcing Torture," *International Herald Tribune*, February 12–13, 2005, p. 4), US government agencies running the "War on Terror" follow a secret program known as "extraordinary rendition": a policy of seizing suspicious individuals without even the semblance of due process, and sending them off to be interrogated by allied regimes known to practice torture.

63. Is not the Master's speech act *par excellence* that of uttering proverbs or "deep thoughts," with their ominous aura which stands for the invisible threat? You can generate them one after another: "A wise man doesn't run after luck; he lets luck run after him." "It's not life which is deferred death; it's death itself which is endlessly protracted life." "Don't worry about lost opportunities: they all remain registered in the harmony of the universe." "Was the first Word not the scream of a stupid giant whose testicles were being squeezed by the Devil?". . .

64. I draw here on Mladen Dolar, "Moč nevidnega / The Power of the Invisible," *Problemi* 1–2 (Ljubljana, 2004).

65. It is the same with anti-Semitism: the Jew is the Master-Signifier, the ultimate empty point of reference which accounts for the (inconsistent) series of phenomena that bother people (corruption, moral and cultural decadence, sexual depravity, commercialization, the class struggle and other social antagonisms . . .); as such, the figure of the Jew has to be sustained/encircled by the swarm of fantasies about their mysterious rituals and properties. On the other hand, a closer examination makes it clear how the structure of the Freudian threat *par excellence*, the threat of castration, is much more complex than it may appear: far from signaling the threat of the loss of a specific object (the penis), its true threat resides in the fact that, no matter how much I lose, I will never really get rid of it—namely, of the disturbing excess/remainder of surplus-enjoyment. Why? Precisely because the threat of castration involves the loss of the phallus as in itself the signifier of symbolic castration: so, paradoxically, what we lose in castration is (symbolic) castration itself.

66. Friedrich Nietzsche, *Sämtliche Werke: Kritische Studienausgabe*, vol. 2 (Berlin: Walter de Gruyter, 1980), p. 678.

67. This, perhaps, is why books like the last two by Oriana Fallacci, which directly delineate the source of the terrorist threat (Islam), are marginalized and perceived as unacceptable: the true cause is not today's Politically Correct sensitivity, but the necessity for the "enemy" to retain its spectral status. This is why, after every big call to rally against the fundamentalist threat, Bush (or Blair, or Sharon, or . . .) goes out of his way to emphasize that Islam is a great religion of peace and tolerance which is merely misused by the fundamentalists. See Oriana Fallacci, *The Rage and the Pride* (New York/Milan: Rizzoli, 2002); as well as her "reply to critics," *La forza della ragione* (Milan: Rizzoli, 2004).

68. "Only a God Can Save Us: *Der Spiegel*'s interview with Martin Heidegger," in *The Heidegger Controversy*, ed. Richard Wolin (Cambridge, MA: MIT Press, 1993), p. 55.

69. Miguel de Beistegui, *Heidegger and the Political* (London: Routledge, 1998), p. 116.

70. Another aspect of this is that the global market model has to rely on exceptions. Take the price of agricultural products: while the developed countries put pressure on undeveloped ones to privatize and open themselves up to foreign competition, they ruthlessly protect their own agriculture by high import tariffs and state support—how can Mali, which produces cotton for half the price of the USA, compete with US farmers, whose state subsidies are greater than the entire GNP of Mali? How can Third World cattle production compete with the European Union, where every single cow gets a subsidy of over 400 euros a year, which is more than the per capita product of most Third World countries? The key point here is that these imbalances cannot be dismissed as simple cases of "unfair trade practices" to be superseded through "fair" international trade regulations—these imbalances are *structural*.

71. Quoted from Ziauddin Sardar and Merryl Wyn Davies, *The No-Nonsense Guide to Islam* (London: New Internationalist and Verso, 2004), p. 77.

72. I draw here on Božidar Jezernik, *Wild Europe: The Balkans in the Gaze of Western Travellers* (London: Saqi Press, 2004).

73. Quoted in ibid., p. 231.

74. Quoted in ibid., p. 233.

75. See ibid., p. 232.

76. Back in 1979, in her essay "Dictators and Double Standards," published in *Commentary*, Jeanne Kirkpatrick elaborated the distinction between "authoritarian" and "totalitarian" regimes, which served as the justification for the US policy of collaborating with Rightist dictators, while treating Communist regimes much more harshly: authoritarian dictators are pragmatic rulers who care about their power and wealth, and are indifferent to ideological issues, even if they pay lip service to some big cause; in contrast, totalitarian leaders are selfless fanatics who believe in their ideology, and are ready to stake everything for their ideals. So while one can deal with authoritarian rulers who react rationally and predictably to material and military threats, totalitarian leaders are much more dangerous, and have to be directly confronted. . . . The irony is that this distinction encapsulates perfectly what went wrong with the US occupation of Iraq: Saddam was a corrupt authoritarian dictator striving for power and guided by brutal pragmatic considerations (which led him to collaborate with the USA throughout the 1980s), and the main outcome of the US intervention is that it has generated a much more uncompromising "fundamentalist" opposition which precludes any pragmatic compromise.

77. This mediatization-of-privacy and/or privatization-of-the-public also explains how can one lose what one does not have. A couple of years ago, Britney Spears complained (in widely publicized interviews, of course) how her media exposure robs her of her true per-

sonality: did she ever really possess the thing whose loss she bemoans, something that would deserve to be called "personality"?

78. And although psychoanalysis, with its "interpretation" of public stances as expressions of private traumatic conflicts, can be seen as the fundamental tool of this tendency, the truth is, rather, the opposite one: the lesson of Lacan is that our symbolic identity, precisely, *cannot* be reduced to an expression of intimate psychic idiosyncrasies.

79. I draw here on Alenka Zupančič's masterpiece *Poetika: Druga knjiga / Poetics: Book Two* (Ljubljana: Analecta, 2005).

80. Derrida's precise expression "democracy-to-come" is accurate here: democracy is this "to-come," that is, if our horizon is that of "to-come," of the irreducible opening toward the unfathomable future, then democracy is our destiny.

81. The ultimate stupid argument against the political radicalization of an intellectual is: "Are you aware that, if the revolution you are advocating were to happen, you would be the first to be shot?" The answer should *not* be "That's not true!," but "So what!". . . This stupidity bears witness to the limit of the reference to the subjective position of enunciation as the ultimate measure of the truth of a proposition.

82. This observation was made by Alenka Zupančič in "Bartleby: In beseda je mesto postala/Bartleby: And the Word Was Made Flesh," in *Bartleby* (Ljubljana: Analecta, 2004).

83. See Michael Hardt and Antonio Negri, *Empire* (Cambridge, MA: Harvard University Press, 2001).

84. The pun of this Hegelian formulation is intentional: HN, the two great anti-Hegelians, make apropos of Bartleby the most classic (pseudo-)Hegelian critical point—indeed, neglect of Hegel takes its revenge in the guise of the return of the most common vulgar-Hegelian themes.

85. We should therefore resist the temptation to propose a kind of direct "ontic" genesis of ontological difference, as Peter Sloterdijk does, trying to discern the roots of what Heidegger calls "opening of the world" in primitive man's use of tools to interact with objects—the world is open to me within the constraints of my material engagement with things in it (see Peter Sloterdijk, *Nicht gerettet. Versuche nach Heidegger* [Frankfurt: Suhrkamp, 2001]).